TEACHING HAFTARAH

BACKGROUND, INSIGHTS, & STRATEGIES

LAINIE BLUM COGAN AND JUDY WEISS

A.R.E. Publishing, Inc.
Denver, Colorado

ACKNOWLEDGEMENTS

We would like to thank the following people for their helpful feedback, creative ideas, encouragement, and support:

Rabbi Steven Bayar, Naomi and Bob Blum, Kopel Burke, Miriam Cogan, Samuel Cogan, Sandy and Barry Cogan, Seth Cogan, Treasure Cohen, Rabbi Allen Darnov, Joan Bronspiegel Dickman, Madeline P. Dreifus, Rabbi Adam Feldman, Rabbi Robert Freedman, Beth Garfinkle, Henry and Marjorie Goldhirsch, Rabbi Maralee Gordon, Rabbi David Greenstein, Bruce Helft, Ora Horn Prouser, Janice and Alan Shotkin, Alan Weiss, Ben Weiss, David Weiss, Karen Weiss, and Jodi Zeichner.

Finally, we would like to thank Rabbi Raymond A. Zwerin and Audrey Friedman Marcus of A.R.E. Publishing, Inc. for selecting us to write this book, for being available to us at each stage of the project, and for contributing their valuable insights to our manuscript.

Published by:
A.R.E. Publishing, Inc.
Denver, Colorado

Library of Congress Control Number 2002101244
ISBN 0-86705-054-3

© A.R.E. Publishing, Inc. 2002
Printed in the United States of America
10 9 8 7 6 5 4 3 2 1

DEDICATION

This book is dedicated to the two greatest families in the world.

CONTENTS

HAFTAROT IN ORDER OF THE BOOKS OF THE PROPHETS

Note: Where Ashkenazim and Sephardim read entirely different Haftarot for a particular Sedra or Holiday, each one is indicated separately. However, in those cases where they read the same Haftarah but read slightly different verses, we note those variations with an asterisk here and provide the detailed information with the specific Haftarah. Note also that some of the asterisks may represent differences between traditional readings and Reform Movement readings.

HAFTAROT BY SHABBAT SEDRA AND SPECIAL OCCASION

Shabbatot

Beresheet	Isaiah 42:5-43:10*	275
Noah	Isaiah 54:1-55:5*	314
Lech Lecha	Isaiah 40:27-41:16	263
Vayera	II Kings 4:1-37*	183
Chayay Sarah	I Kings 1:1-31	102
Toledot	Malachi 1:1-2:7	602
Vayaytzay	Hosea 12:13-14:10 (Ashkenazim)	525
Vayaytzay	Hosea 11:7-12:12 (Sephardim)	519
Vayishlach	Hosea 11:7-12:12 (Some Ashkenazim)	519
Vayishlach	Obadiah 1:1-21 (Sephardim and Some Ashkenazim)	560
Vayayshev	Amos 2:6-3:8	545
Mikaytz	I Kings 3:15-4:1	118
Vayigash	Ezekiel 37:15-28	470
Vayechi	I Kings 2:1-12	110
Shemot	Isaiah 27:6-28:13; 29:22-23 (Ashkenazim)	244
Shemot	Jeremiah 1:1-2:3 (Sephardim)	364
Vaera	Ezekiel 28:25-29:21	451
Bo	Jeremiah 46:13-28	422
Beshalach	Judges 4:4-5:31*	21
Yitro	Isaiah 6:1-7:6; 9:5-6*	230
Mishpatim	Jeremiah 34:8-22; 33:25-26	413
Terumah	I Kings 5:26-6:13	127
Tetzaveh	Ezekiel 43:10-27	481
Ki Tisa	I Kings 18:1-39*	164
Vayakhel	I Kings 7:40-50 (Ashkenazim)	145
Vayakhel	I Kings 7:13-26 (Sephardim)	138
Pikuday	I Kings 7:51-8:21 (Ashkenazim)	152
Pikuday	I Kings 7:40-50 (Sephardim)	145
Vayikra	Isaiah 43:21-44:23	286
Tzav	Jeremiah 7:21-8:3; 9:22-23	382

Special Shabbatot
(on which we read the regular Sedra,
but a special Haftarah)

Holidays
(on which we read a special Torah reading
and a special Haftarah)

Introduction

WHAT IS A HAFTARAH?

A Haftarah is a selection from the prophetic books of the Bible chosen to accompany and complement the Torah portion on Shabbat, holidays, and fast days. The connections between a Haftarah and its Sedra or holiday can be clear and obvious or subtle and complex.

It is not known for certain when or why the practice of chanting a Haftarah after the Torah reading started. There are many theories about the origin of Haftarot, although there is little hard evidence in support of any of them. Some scholars suggest that Haftarot were introduced in ancient Palestine in the second century B.C.E. when the Syrians had forbidden the reading of the Torah. Others argue that the Syrians would have also prevented the reading of prophets. Others maintain that Rabbi Akiba in 132 C.E. created the Haftarah reading in response to the Roman Emperor Hadrian's ban on Torah reading. In lieu of the theory that the Haftarah developed during a period of persecution, a more widely accepted view today is that a custom developed to conclude a Torah reading with a special message for that week (the word Haftarah is based on a Hebrew verb which has several meanings, including "to conclude"). The reading of a Haftarah on Festivals and some Special Shabbatot seems to have been initiated first; these concluding prophetic readings provided special messages for the season. The custom of concluding the Torah reading with a portion from prophets eventually spread to include all Shabbatot and other special days.

The prophetic books comprise the second section of Tanach (the Jewish Bible), called *Nevi'im* in Hebrew. The first books of that section (Joshua, Judges, I and II Samuel, and I and II Kings) are known collectively as the Former Prophets. These works are primarily historical in nature and narrative in style. They record the stories of Israel from the conquest of the Promised Land to the destruction of Jerusalem and the exile of the Israelites by the Babylonians. Some of the prophets featured in these books include Joshua, Deborah, Samuel, Nathan, Elijah, and Elisha. Haftarot are taken from all of these books.

The 15 Latter Prophets are also known as the literary prophets, for each is credited with contributing a book of his own to the biblical canon. They preached in Israel, Judea, or Babylonia from the eighth century through the fifth century B.C.E. — from a time of prosperity in Israel and Judah, through the annihilation of Israel and the destruction of Judah, to the return of the Judean exiles to Jerusalem and the building of the Second Holy Temple. Haftarot are taken from all of these Latter Prophets except Nahum, Zephaniah, and Haggai.

WHO CAN USE THIS BOOK

Teaching Haftarah provides texts and resources about Israel's prophets, their times, their works, and their ageless wisdom. With its broad interdisciplinary approach, *Teaching Haftarah* also uses the Prophets — and Haftarot in particular — as a launching point from which to teach such topics as Jewish ethics, law, customs, rituals, holidays, *midrash*, and Zionism. The Haftarot also provide an insightful lens through which to view and gain new understanding of the weekly Torah readings. As such, *Teaching Haftarah* is an indispensable resource for all teachers and students of Judaism.

- This is a guidebook to help educators teach middle school or high school students in formal instructional courses and to teach all students about the prophets in an informal setting, such as in youth group or camp.

- The book can serve as the basis of a curriculum for Rabbis and educators who teach adult students about any or all of the prophets, prophetic books, and Haftarot.

- Rabbis and educators will find new ideas and directions for sermons and discussions that open up subject matter previously overlooked in favor of Sedra study. Any of the (more than 30) entries in each chapter can be a springboard for a *D'var Torah* about the Haftarah.

- *Teaching Haftarah* is ideal in a home setting for families who wish to educate themselves about and involve themselves with the Haftarot assigned to their own children for school study and/or for their Bar/Bat Mitzvah ceremony.

- Teachers seeking to further their own Jewish education, in seminars or individually, will benefit from the material in this book.

- For people interested in educating themselves about the history and literature of the prophetic period in Israel, *Teaching Haftarah* is essential.

- *Teaching Haftarah* is a companion to *Teaching Torah: A Treasury of Insights and Activities* by Sorel Goldberg Loeb and Barbara Binder Kadden (Denver, CO: A.R.E. Publishing, Inc., revised 1997). The two books may be used in tandem when training Bar/Bat Mitzvah students, preparing *Divray Torah*, designing holiday curricula, or studying the weekly Sedra.

CONTENT AND ORGANIZATION
Arrangement of the Book

The Haftarot in this book are presented in the order in which they appear in the biblical text, as indicated in the Contents on page *v*. For easy reference, the Haftarot are also listed according to Shabbat Sedra and Special Occasions in a second Contents on page *ix*.

Throughout this book, Haftarot that were selected for holidays and Special Shabbatot are designated with the following special icons which appear on the first page of those selections:

Holidays
Fast Days

Special
Shabbatot

Overview of Each Prophetic Book

At the beginning of each prophetic book, an Overview highlights the main historical and thematic elements of the Haftarot contained within that book. Because the historical, social, and religious context is so crucial to understanding any individual Haftarah, each Overview is essential reading for anyone using *Teaching Haftarah*.

Each Haftarah within each prophetic book contains the following sections:

Synopsis

Each Synopsis places a Haftarah into its historical context and goes on to provide a clear and concise summary of the content of the Haftarah. Because prophetic texts can be difficult to understand, the Synopsis offers a clear road map for reading the original text. The Synopsis provides the framework for all the Insights and Strategies that follow.

Insights from the Tradition

This section follows the Synopsis and presents a collection of Rabbinic interpretations and explanations (*Midrash*). Rabbinic insights were selected to illustrate and emphasize the timelessness of the text. Each Insight is followed by pertinent questions that enable the student to understand how the ancient and medieval words still teach us important lessons today.

Strategies

The Strategies provide numerous opportunities for the teacher and student to interact with the Haftarah and to gain a broader, deeper, and more personal understanding of the many meanings and messages of the text. Strategies employ modalities ranging from literary analysis to art projects to games and puzzles, which are designed to accommodate all types of teaching and learning styles. (Please note that the Holiday Haftarot do not contain all the strategy sections.)

Following is a description of each category of Strategy.

Analyzing the Text

Haftarot are rich in metaphor, allusion, and poetic language, which require quite a bit of decoding. This section provides ancient and modern literary and historical analysis to help open the text to greater understanding. Each item is followed by questions, activities, or debates that help students to master the language and ideas of the text and to make the text relevant to their daily lives.

Connecting the Text To the Sedra

The connections between a Sedra and its Haftarah can be obvious or obscure. This section explores many possible connections — big and small, liturgical and literary, ancient and modern, contextual and thematic — between the two texts. This section elucidates the many ways in which Haftarot augment or emphasize or otherwise comment on ideas in the Torah portion. In the case of Holiday Haftarot, the section is called "Connecting the Text To the Holiday," and it investigates the way the Haftarah ties into and sheds light on the holiday on which it is read. For Special Shabbatot, the section is called "Connecting the Text To the Special Shabbat."

Extending the Text

Herein is an exploration of Jewish ideas, ideals, *mitzvot*, history, liturgy, songs, stories, and customs that relate in some way to the Haftarah text.

This section also broadens the perspective of the lessons in each Haftarah to the larger world. Each item is presented through creative activities and multimedia modalities to appeal to all kinds of teachers and learners. Internet web sites are provided for further study and investigation of subjects.

Personalizing the Text

Students really become a part of the text through this section. Creative activities have been designed to help the student relate in a personal way to the ideas and characters in the Haftarah. Through writing, singing, art, games, interviews, theme parties, and debate, students will solidify their knowledge of the material, form their own opinions, and clarify for themselves values that have been raised in the text.

Other Resources

In this section educators are provided with ample avenues through which to expand their lessons from *Teaching Haftarah*. Stories, songs, books, popular films, Jewish and general curricula, Internet web sites, and other materials are suggested for further exploration into the themes presented in the Haftarah.

Involving the Family

Because Jewish learning at its best is a family affair, activities are provided that encourage the whole family to become involved in the study and life lessons of the Haftarah. From *mitzvah* projects to family discussions, these activities enable families to share in the joy of Jewish learning and living. These activities also lend themselves to Havurot sessions or to family retreats. Many of the Strategies in other subsections can also be adapted for use by families.

Bar/Bat Mitzvah Project(s)

An ever growing number of congregations are encouraging or requiring their B'nai Mitzvah students to engage in a *mitzvah* project. Becoming a Jewish adult means becoming an active member of one's community. This section provides ideas and resources for creative long-term and short-term *mitzvah* projects related to the theme of the Haftarah. Students are encouraged to consider the *mitzvah* projects listed for all the Haftarot from their particular prophetic book, because these Haftarot are often thematically related and can be interchanged.

USING THIS BOOK

Because Haftarot and prophets tend to be unfamiliar if not mysterious to teachers and students alike, *Teaching Haftarah* endeavors to provide any necessary background information. Each Overview provides the historical, religious, and social context, whether one is teaching a single Haftarah or multiple prophetic books. The Synopses further that contextual understanding, and give specific information pertaining to a particular Haftarah.

Each prophetic book contains characteristic themes and messages. While each Haftarah stands firmly on its own, the Haftarot from any one book inevitably shed light on each other. Many Insights and Strategies can be generally applied to all the Haftarot within a particular prophetic book, and may give the educator additional instructional options and the student additional ideas for writing a *D'var Torah*. Therefore, it is strongly recommended that in order to gain a deeper meaning of the important themes of any particular Haftarah, the reader should skim through all the Haftarot of that prophet. This is especially the case with the Latter Prophets because of their non-narrative nature.

Please note that whereas the Haftarot in *Teaching Haftarah* are arranged in sequential order and provide a solid representation of the prophetic books, the entire text of any of these books is not included in this volume. Anyone wishing to teach a course in the Book of Samuel, for example, can use *Teaching Haftarah* as a basis, but ought to consult the original text for material that was not selected by the Rabbis as Haftarot. That having been said, *Teaching Haftarah* does provide quite enough material and textual selections for any type of overview class on the middle school, high school, or adult level — a sort of "Prophets' Greatest Hits."

Internet resources are cited throughout the book, and teachers are encouraged to use the Internet whenever possible to engage the students.

Every effort has been taken to make the material in *Teaching Haftarah* as inclusive as possible. Traditions and viewpoints from the various branches of Judaism have been included. Wherever possible, gender neutral language has been used. Still, it is always important to be sensitive to the individual background of each student. Topics such as marriage, divorce, conversion, death, and suffering should be approached with great care so as not to alienate any student.

All English translations of biblical verses quoted in *Teaching Haftarah* are based on the new translation of the 1985 edition of the Jewish Publication Society — *Tanakh: A New Translation of the Holy Scriptures According To the Traditional Hebrew Text.*

The style of transliteration used in this book was chosen to parallel that of other books in the A.R.E. Teaching Series. Please note that occasionally the word "Parashah" is spelled "Parashat" in order to indicate the name of a particular Parashah, such as *Parashat Lech Lecha.* The word "Sedra" should undergo a similar grammatical transformation when it appears as the name of a particular Sedra. We chose, however, not to alter the form of the word because we felt that the altered form, which is rarely heard in common usage, would be confusing to readers.

APPENDIXES

There are three Appendixes at the back of the book:

Appendix A: Commentators/Commentaries

This Appendix (see pp. 617-621) contains brief biographies of the traditional and modern commentators, as well as information about the significant commentaries and resources used in *Teaching Haftarah.*

Appendix B: Blessings

The blessings recited before and after the Haftarah vary among the Jewish movements. Translations of the Traditional, Reform, and Reconstructionist versions of the blessings are included in this Appendix (see pp. 622-623).

Appendix C: Maps

Five reproducible maps have been included in Appendix C for reference purposes and for use in projects (see pp. 624-628): The Twelve Tribes, The Kingdom of David and Solomon, The Kingdom of Israel and Judah in Elijah's Time, The Kingdom of Judah in Isaiah's Time (after the Destruction of the Northern Kingdom c. 700 B.C.E.), and The Province of Judah in the Time of Zechariah, Haggai, and Malachi.

BIBLIOGRAPHY

The concluding Bibliography (see p. 629-636) contains a selected, annotated listing of the books used most frequently in the text. These useful and important books are recommended for further study.

HAFTAROT IN THE LITURGY

There are variations in the Haftarot used on any particular occasion between Ashkenazim and Sephardim and among the various Jewish movements. Some of the differences are minor, such as adding or deleting a verse or two. Some of the differences are major, involving entirely different prophetical selections for a particular Sedra or holiday. This book attempts to cover all the options, and multiple texts are listed where required.

This study guide should not be used as an authoritative reference for which Haftarah should be read on which occasion, as customs vary greatly from movement to movement and from congregation to congregation. Always consult your Rabbi or Cantor to find out the practice of your particular congregation.

OVERVIEW

The Book of Joshua, the sixth book of the Bible, is part of the Deuteronomic history of Israel. This history begins with the Book of Deuteronomy (the fifth book of the Torah) and continues through Joshua, Judges, Samuel I and II, and Kings I and II, a collection known as the Former Prophets. The Book of Joshua describes the entry of the children of Israel into the land promised them by God as the culmination of the Exodus from Egypt and the wanderings in the desert.

Moses dies at the end of the Book of Deuteronomy. As Joshua becomes the leader of the people in the beginning of his book, he faces three challenges: taking the land (chapters 1-12), establishing a community (chapters 13-22), and maintaining loyalty to God in future generations (chapters 23-24). All three of these challenges involve questions of identity.

In the first section of this book, as the children of Israel are victorious in various battles, they are also reminded they are God's people. The Jordan River parts for the Israelites to enter Canaan, reminding them of the parting of the Reed Sea and their birth as a nation. The Israelites undergo a communal circumcision ceremony (chapter 5), which also links them to those who left Egypt and reaffirms their identity as God's people. They engage in a series of battles to conquer the land and eliminate the original inhabitants who could potentially undermine Israelite identity (chapters 9-12).

In the second section of the book, the Israelites establish their community and apportion the land. The text states that many non-Israelite peoples continue to dwell in the land in their midst (chapters 13, 15-17), posing a constant threat to Israelite separatism. Several events show us that all Israelites are not in complete agreement about what constitutes Israelite identity. For example, some choose to live east of the Jordan River, even though others think that Israelites must live to the west (chapter 13). Some tribes decide to allow women to inherit land (chapter 17), but others believe women's inheritance poses a problem to the continued identity of the tribes (Numbers 36). In religious matters, some Israelites believe an altar to God may be built outside the central sacrificial location, while others insist an altar may only be at the central designated location. This conflict nearly leads to civil war (chapter 22).

Before his death, Joshua exhorts the Israelites to fulfill all the commandments in order that they retain their identity and remain separate from other nations (chapters 23 and 24). Israel responds by asserting its commitment to God, the covenant, and identity, after which Joshua dies in peace. The Haftarot selected from the Book of Joshua highlight this central issue of identity.

JOSHUA 1:1-18 Ashkenazim
JOSHUA 1:1-9 Sephardim
V'ZOT HABRACHAH; SIMCHAT TORAH

 This Haftarah has been paired with the holiday Simchat Torah, on which we read Deuteronomy 33:1-34:12. See "Connecting the Text To the Holiday," pp. 4-5, for an exploration of the many ways the two texts and the holiday shed light on each other.

SYNOPSIS

On Simchat Torah, we complete the annual cycle of synagogue Torah readings, with the conclusion of the Book of Deuteronomy and the death of Moses. It is appropriate, then, that the Rabbis chose as the Simchat Torah Haftarah the first chapter of the Book of Joshua and the appointment of Joshua as Moses' successor.

The parallels between the first chapter of the Book of Joshua and the Five Books of Moses are strong indeed. God speaks to Joshua in words that echo those spoken to Moses throughout his career as the Israelite leader. God assures Joshua son of Nun that as the new leader, he will continue in Moses' footsteps, finally bringing to fruition God's promise of a homeland for the Israelite people. God also promises Joshua the same divine protection and support that had been pledged (Exodus 3:12) and delivered to Moses. Finally, God urges Joshua to "be strong and courageous (resolute)" four times in this Haftarah, just as Moses encouraged his successor with the same words three times in Deuteronomy (3:28, 31:7, 31:23). Of course, God explicitly reminds the new leader of Israel to observe the teachings of God, which will ensure his success and prosperity.

In the second half of the Haftarah, Joshua does the talking. He instructs his officers to go through the camp and tell the fighting men to prepare to go across the Jordan River to conquer the land. Joshua reminds the tribes that have chosen to remain east of the Jordan River of their promise to assist the rest of the Israelites in the conquest of the Land of Israel. Reuben, Gad, and the half-tribe of Manasseh quickly respond that they are ready and willing to help their kinfolk. The Israelites confirm that just as they listened to Moses, so, too, will they continue to obey Joshua. Anyone who rebels against Joshua, they agree, will be put to death. The Haftarah concludes with the Israelites echoing the words of Moses and of God, encouraging Joshua son of Nun to "be strong and courageous." They will be behind him.

INSIGHTS FROM THE TRADITION

A Joshua's name was originally Hosea, but Moses changed it to Joshua. According to Rashbam, it was the custom of kings to give their favorite servant a new name. Pharaoh renamed Joseph, and God renamed Abraham, Sarah, and Jacob.

◆ What is the significance of "pet names" or terms of endearment?

◆ What are the pet names by which your parents and/or sibling(s) call you?

◆ Do your parents have pet names for each other?

◆ Is there anyone for whom you have a special pet name?

B The meaning of "strength" in verse 1:7, according to *Berachot* 32b, is to be vigorous and strong in the study of all the Torah.

◆ Does the phrase (1:7) "do not deviate from it to the right or left" mean our vigorous study must make us perfect?

◆ What does it mean, as the United States Army says, to "be all that you can be"?

◆ What wisdom about human behavior can we gain from the knowledge that only God is perfect?

C Rashi explains that being strong and courageous in verse 1:7 means to do and observe all of the *mitzvot* in the Torah.

◆ Why might it take courage to be different from others and observe such *mitzvot* as *kashrut* or Shabbat?

◆ How does observance of *mitzvot* reflect someone's inner strength and moral courage?

◆ List three *mitzvot* and explain how it takes courage and strength to fulfill them.

D Joshua tells the people in verse 1:11 to prepare provisions for themselves. *Yalkut Shimoni* (Sec. 7) explains that these were to be spiritual provisions before entering the Promised Land.

◆ Refer to *Israel: A Spiritual Travel Guide: A Companion for the Modern Jewish Pilgrim* by Lawrence A. Hoffman for spiritual preparation for visiting various sites in Israel.

◆ What does it mean to be spiritually prepared for an event? How is "getting psyched" similar to becoming spiritually prepared?

◆ How do you "get psyched" for such events as a major test in school, a championship game, or a school dance?

◆ How do you think the Israelites might have gotten themselves spiritually prepared for entering the Promised Land?

STRATEGIES
Analyzing the Text

1 In verse 1:10 Joshua commands the people on the day when the 30-day mourning period for Moses is completed.

It is customary for Jewish mourners to observe a period of grief for 30 days following the death of a loved one. This period is called *shloshim*, which means 30. During *shloshim* (which is a less intense period of mourning than *shivah*) mourners return to school or work, but avoid festive occasions, parties, and dancing. Some mourners also refrain from shaving and enjoying music, theater, films, or television during this period.

◆ How do you think *shloshim* helps a mourner to ease his or her way back into regular life, following the loss of a loved one?

◆ Explain why the people may have waited 30 days after Moses' death before proceeding with plans to enter the Promised Land.

2 Joshua is told to be strong four different times (see verses 6, 7, 9, and 18).

◆ Strength is clearly an important enough quality to be emphasized four times. There are many ways to be strong: physically, in courage, and in the study and observance of Torah. List and/or act out four different ways to show strength.

3 In verse 1:12 Joshua reminds the tribes of Reuben and Gad and the half-tribe of Manasseh of their obligation to help the other tribes settle in the Promised Land. This is a reference to a negotiation that took place in Numbers 32. The two and one-half tribes decided that they wanted to settle east of the Jordan River because it seemed better for raising cattle. They asked permission to settle permanently there. Moses gave them permission, provided they first helped the other tribes settle in the Promised Land before returning to their own land on the other side of the Jordan.

◆ Explain how the obligation of these two and one-half tribes to their community (helping the other nine and one-half tribes settle west of the Jordan) took precedence over their personal plans (settling on the east side of the Jordan).

4 Joshua's name means "God is salvation."

◆ How does Joshua's name suit his vocation?

◆ How can his name serve as a motto for the Israelites, as they go about their business of possessing the Land of Israel?

Connecting the Text To the Holiday

5 On Simchat Torah, we end and begin again the annual cycle of reading from the Torah. The Haftarah emphasizes this sense of continuity, as described in the Synopsis, p. 2.

In verses 1:7-8 of the Haftarah, God's instructions to Joshua quote phrases from the Book of Deuteronomy. God says, "be very strong and resolute to observe faithfully all the Teaching that My servant Moses enjoined upon you." Quoting Deuteronomy, God reminds Joshua to be strong and courageous, not to deviate to the right or the left, and to recite the Teaching day and night.

◆ By quoting words said to Moses, how does God help to make Joshua become a leader of the people?

6 Moses dies in the Torah reading, but life for Israel continues after his death in the Haftarah. His work and message live even today, whenever Jews rewind the Torah and study it again and live by its teachings.

Pirke Avot 5:22 teaches regarding the study of Torah:

"Ben Bag Bag used to say, 'Turn it and turn it, for everything is in it. Reflect on it and grow old and gray with it. Don't turn from it, for nothing is better than it.'"

◆ Explain how Ben Bag Bag is saying that unlike other texts, Torah needs to be read again and again, slowly, always looking for new meanings.

◆ How does this statement from *Pirke Avot* reflect the ritual of turning the Torah back to the beginning of Genesis on Simchat Torah?

7 Moses gave us the commandments of the Torah in Deuteronomy 33:4.

The Haftarah reminds us that Torah was given to us by Moses in verses 1:7-8.

◆ Learn and sing the song *"Torah Tzivah Lanu Moshe,"* which means "Torah was commanded to us by Moses." (Find it on the CD *Celebrate with Cindy* by Cindy Paley.)

8 Moses is called the servant of *Adonai* in Deuteronomy 34:5 and in Joshua 1:1. Abraham, Isaac, and Jacob are all called servants of *Adonai*.

◆ What do you think it means to be a servant of *Adonai*?

◆ Rabbi Zabara once said, "The servant is moulded of his master's clay." What do you think he meant?

◆ In what ways can it be empowering to be God's servant?

◆ What responsibilities does such a role entail?

9 The period of mourning for Moses ends in Deuteronomy 34:8. In the very next verse, Joshua is recognized by the people as the leader of Israel. They promise to do what Joshua tells them. According to *Baba Bathra* 75a, the face of Moses was like the sun, and the face of Joshua was like the moon.

◆ How does this metaphor depict continuity of leadership?

◆ Do you imagine that Jewish history might have turned out differently had Moses (and God) not appointed a successor?

◆ How is the circle of life (Moses sets, Joshua rises) echoed in the annual cycle of Torah reading, which is celebrated on Simchat Torah?

10 Moses sees the Promised Land, but dies without entering it. In the Haftarah the people prepare at last to enter the Land.

You might say that on Simchat Torah, as we complete the reading of the Torah, we can see the Promised Land. But instead of entering it, we go right back to the beginning and start again.

◆ What is the symbolic message of going back to the beginning as soon as we are finished reading the Torah?

◆ Will we ever be sufficiently prepared to stop studying Torah? Explain your answer.

◆ How does Simchat Torah emphasize that Jewish learning is not a one-way road, but an endless cycle?

11 As we finish reading the last book of the Torah on Simchat Torah, we stand for the last verse and recite the phrase, "Be strong, be strong, and let us strengthen one another." Joshua is told by God to be strong in the Haftarah.

◆ Learn to say this Hebrew phrase: *"Chazak, chazak, v'nitchazek."*

◆ Why do you think we end the reading of each book of the Torah with this phrase?

◆ What does it mean to be strong and strengthen one another?

JOSHUA 2:1–24
SHELACH LECHA שלח לך

This Haftarah has been paired with *Parashat Shelach Lecha*, Numbers 13:1-15:41. See "Connecting the Text To the Sedra," pp. 8-11, for an exploration of the many ways the two texts shed light on each other.

SYNOPSIS

As the children of Israel get ready to enter the Land, Joshua makes preparations for their first battle and quietly sends two spies to collect information about the city of Jericho, a major entry point into the Land.

The spies go to Jericho and enter the establishment of Rahab, a harlot. Unfortunately, Jericho's leaders realize that spies have entered the city and immediately begin a search for them. Rahab hides the spies and when the authorities ask her about them, she lies and suggests that they already fled the city gates. She then advises the two spies on the state of mind of her people, which is valuable pre-war information. Furthermore, she gives them detailed instructions on where to continue hiding until the manhunt has ended and on how to return safely to Joshua.

In a moving speech, Rahab expresses her desire to join the Israelites and faithfully serve their God, Whose power has impressed her. In return for her kindness, the spies promise to spare her life and that of her parents and siblings in the upcoming battle, provided she marks her house with a red cord hung from the window.

The Haftarah concludes with the spies' successful return to Joshua and their private report back to him.

INSIGHTS FROM THE TRADITION

A Joshua became the leader of the Israelites immediately following the death of Moses. According to the Gaon of Vilna, Joshua waited until the 30-day mourning period for Moses had ended before sending spies to investigate Jericho. Alternatively, Rashi says that Joshua sent the spies during the 30-day mourning period for Moses.

◆ Why might Joshua have waited for the mourning period to end?

◆ Why might Joshua have decided not to wait for the mourning period to end?

◆ Our traditional interpretations sometimes present opposite opinions. Do you think that this represents a strength or a weakness in our tradition?

B Joshua sent two men to spy secretly. The Hebrew word חרש, which is translated as "secretly," is ambiguous: from whom was the secret kept? According to Radak, it may mean that the secret was kept from the children of Israel in order to prevent the type of pre-battle anxiety that troubled the people during Moses' time. This precaution may have been taken because when Moses sent 12 spies in *Parashat Shelach Lecha* (Numbers 13), the people knew spies were sent and waited anxiously for the report. When the spies returned they did not report privately to Moses, but publicly to all the people, causing a general panic. Joshua may have wanted to prevent the Israelites from knowing about the spy mission in order to prevent a similar panic.

◆ Can you identify other occasions when something is done for someone's welfare, but should be kept secret from them?

C Rashi explains that the secrecy, חרש, means that the spies hid their identity from the Canaanites. Rashi suggests that the spies may have pretended to be deaf (חרש also means "deaf"). Townspeople would then speak freely in front of the spies without concealing any vital information, thinking they were deaf. Alternatively, the spies may have outfitted themselves to look like potters (it happens that the Hebrew word חרש may also sometimes mean "pottery"), in order to scope out the city without drawing attention to themselves.

◆ It seems that the spies lied about themselves in order to collect information. Consider other times when deceptive behavior seems morally justified.

D In verse 2:14 the spies assure Rahab that they would save her and her family. However, they add a stipulation that they will not be held accountable for the promise to save her unless she and her family follow specific instructions: they may not discuss the agreement with the spies with anyone, they may not leave Rahab's house, and they must hang a red cord out her window to identify her house.

◆ List the three requirements the spies made of Rahab.

◆ Explain why the spies may have chosen these three things to stipulate.

◆ *Yalkut Me'am Lo'ez* comments that we learn from the spies' conditional promise that one should never promise definitely to do something because the future is not truly in our hands. Explain the lesson taught by this commentator. How is it the same as the traditional expression: "God willing, I will do it"?

◆ Describe events that might prevent a person from keeping a promise.

STRATEGIES
Analyzing the Text

1 Rahab helped the spies hide when townspeople heard that strangers were present in their city. The verb used in the text (verse 2:4) for "to hide" is the root צפן. Curiously, this verb is used only one time in the entire Five Books of Moses: when Moses' mother hides him from the Egyptian authorities to protect him from the law that would have had him killed (see Exodus 2:3).

When the biblical text uses a rare word in a story, it sometimes intends for us to compare the stories in which the word appears.

◆ What similarities might you find between the story of Moses' mother hiding him and Rahab hiding the spies? (Note how both women resist the law, engage in hiding, enable escape, and ultimately aid the Jewish people.)

2 In verse 2:3 the king orders Rahab to turn over the two spies who came to her house. She admits that they had been in her house, but adds: "but I didn't know where they were from."

◆ Why do you think it is important for Rahab to add this information when responding to the king?

3 In verse 2:10 Rahab recounts some of the miracles God performed on behalf of the Israelites. She mentions that God dried up the Sea of Reeds when the Israelites were fleeing from the Egyptians (Exodus 14:26-31). She also refers to the Israelites' victory over two Amorite kings, Sihon and Og (Numbers 21:21-35, Deuteronomy 2:24-3:8).

◆ Why did the inhabitants of Jericho "lose heart" when they heard about these events?

4 In verse 2:12 Rahab says that she has shown loyalty to the spies. She uses the Hebrew word *chesed* to describe the loyalty she has shown them. Scholars agree that there is no exact equivalent of the word *chesed* in the English language, though they suggest it is somewhat similar to "mercy," "loyalty," "grace," or "kindness."

◆ Which meaning do you like best, and why?

Connecting the Text to the Sedra

5 In *Parashat Shelach Lecha*, (see *Teaching Torah* by Sorel Goldberg Loeb and Barbara Binder Kadden, p. 248), Moses' effort at sending spies to Canaan failed. According to tradition, he was wrong to send spies because the Israelites should have had proper faith that God would help them with the battle. They wanted spies to reassure them the battle could be won.

In contrast, Joshua's decision to send spies to Jericho succeeded. Therefore, according to tradition, when Joshua sent spies, he had no doubts about carrying out God's order to enter the land and destroy Jericho. Joshua simply wanted to scope out the city and find the best entry point to help the battle go as well as possible *(Yalkut Me'am Lo'ez 2:1)*.

According to this interpretation, Joshua had faith and yet also, took action to help the battle succeed.

◆ Do you think "having faith" means passively waiting for what you want to happen?

◆ How would you define "faith"?

◆ How do you know when to act (like Joshua acted) and when not to act (like Moses should have refrained from acting)?

6 In both the Sedra and Haftarah, spies are sent to investigate the Promised Land. According to a *midrash* (see Connecting the Text To the Sedra #5, p. 8), Moses' spy mission was unsuccessful because it had a bad motive. However, Joshua's spy mission was successful because it had a good motive.

◆ Explain why one mission had a good motive and the other a bad motive.

◆ Give other examples of actions that can be good if associated with a positive motive, but bad if associated with a negative motive.

◆ Make a list of all the possible good motivations for preparing to become a Bar/Bat Mitzvah.

7 According to the Sedra, of the generation in the desert, only Joshua and Caleb will enter the Promised Land because only they truly trusted God (Numbers 14:30). The Haftarah shows us how the Sedra's prediction comes true by highlighting Joshua's role as leader in the conquest of the Promised Land.

◆ When reading the Sedra, is it important to you to know that this promise to Joshua and Caleb comes true? How would you feel if the promise and the punishment of Numbers 14:30 had not been fulfilled?

◆ And what about Caleb, about whom the Haftarah is silent? *Numbers Rabbah* 16:1 suggests that Caleb was one of the unnamed spies whom Joshua sent to spy on Jericho.

◆ Imagine that Joshua holds a testimonial dinner for his longtime friend and comrade Caleb. Plan and hold such a celebration with each class member writing a brief toast in honor of Caleb. (For more information on Caleb, see the following texts: Numbers 13-14; Joshua 15:13-19, Judges 1:12-15, 3:9, and I Chronicles 4:15.)

8 In verse 2:11 Rahab quotes Deuteronomy 4:39 ("for *Adonai* your God is the only God in heaven above and on earth below"), which we say in the *"Alaynu"* prayer.

◆ Read the *"Alaynu"* prayer and identify the phrase that resembles Rahab's statement. (Hint: See the second paragraph.)

◆ Explain what Rahab's statement means.

◆ The sentiment is also echoed in the Sedra (Numbers 14:21) when God says: "as *Adonai's* Presence fills the world." What does it mean to you that God's presence fills the whole world?

◆ Create a banner for your classroom that expresses this idea.

9 Rahab chooses to join the Israelite community. In the Sedra (Numbers 15:16), we learn that "the same rule shall apply to you and to the stranger who resides among you." This is an indication that, in Bible times, converts were welcome. Judaism also welcomes converts today.

◆ Study Judaism's position on conversion in *Jewish Literacy*, pp. 624-626 and *Jewish Wisdom*, pp. 374-381, both by Joseph Telushkin, or by using the Conversion To Judaism Resource Center web site: www.convert.org.

◆ Interview your Rabbi about your synagogue's attitude toward converts.

10 In the Sedra (Numbers 14:1), when the spies reported back, "the whole community broke into loud cries, and the people wept that night" out of fear of impending death in war. Similarly, in the Haftarah, the spies inform Joshua that "all the inhabitants of the land are quaking before us."

◆ Explain some of the ways in which an impending war might cause panic.

◆ List other types of events that are scary to anticipate.

◆ War is terrifying for both sides. Invite a veteran of either your country or Israel to come and speak to your class about their experiences.

11 In the Sedra (Numbers 14:3-4), the Israelites worry that they are unable to fight against the superior forces in the Promised Land. Likewise, in the Book of Joshua, the Israelites are often the weaker party in their conflicts. Without the benefit of military advantage, the Israelites resort to using clever strategies, such as espionage and hiding, in order to defeat their stronger opponents.

◆ Why might weaker parties in a conflict resort to clever strategies? What other strategic tricks might they use?

◆ Tricks are used not only in battles between nations. During an election, weaker candidates often resort to bold strategies to undermine their opponents. Examine the advertisements in a current local or national election, and identify the tricks the candidates use.

◆ Even in our own lives, when people feel weaker in interpersonal relationships, they may use tricks to try to get their way with stronger people. Can you describe some of the strategies weaker people may use to gain the advantage? Are they effective? Are they justifiable?

12 The Sedra mentions both the sending of spies by Moses and the laws of Israelites regarding the wearing of *tzitzit* or *tallit* (see Numbers 15:37-41). The *tzitzit* is supposed to have a thread of blue in it to remind us of the heavens so as to observe all God's commandments. Traditionally, *tzitzit* is also considered to protect us by keeping us from impulsively pursuing every silly idea that comes into our head or going after every inappropriate thing we see.

◆ In the Haftarah Rahab is told to suspend a red cord from her window. What will the cord do?

◆ What similarities or differences can you define between the blue thread of the *tzitzit* and the red cord on Rahab's window? (For example, both serve as reminders, both serve as protectors, both require users to take action.)

◆ What do the colors red and blue symbolize to you, and why might one be blue and the other red? (For example, blue is cool and red is hot, blue symbolizes the heavens, and red warns of danger.)

13 In the Sedra we are warned to wear *tzitzit* so that we always observe God's laws and follow God's ways and not follow after our hearts and eyes and lustful urges (see Numbers 15:37-41). The expression in Hebrew for straying from God's ways is *zonim*. The verb *zonim* means to commit adultery, prostitution, and the worship of other gods instead of being faithful to God. *Zonim* clearly has negative meanings in the Sedra.

In the Haftarah Rahab is described as a *zonah*, typically translated as either a prostitute or an innkeeper. Rahab decides not to follow the practices of her people, but to worship God instead. She is considered a good, positive role model in the Haftarah.

◆ Compare the use of the word *zonah/zonim* in the two texts. Why is it positive in one text and negative in the other? (For example, its negative use in the Sedra and its positive use in the Haftarah may be telling us that, in life, we are not limited by our present status; even though Rahab was a lowly, frowned upon *zonah*, she could turn things around for herself and realize the dream that had been promised to the children of Israel — i.e., to live as a

free person in the Promised Land, worshiping God.)

◆ Alternatively, it may be warning us to look for other differences between the two texts. Can you suggest other explanations for the difference?

14 The Haftarah goes into great detail about the spies' mission while they were in Jericho and gives us a small picture of their report to Joshua. In contrast, the Sedra does not tell us much detail about the spies' mission to Canaan, but focuses in detail on the way in which they give their report to Moses. It seems the spies never really interacted with the local residents. In contrast, in the Haftarah, the spies interact with a local woman and even trust her with their lives.

◆ Explain how the Haftarah may be suggesting that it is important not to stereotype your enemies. To get to know them as people may help you make some of them stop being your enemies. To think of them as people helps resolve disputes rationally and peacefully without panic. By knowing them better, if war does occur, you will have more information about them. Can you suggest other explanations?

15 In the Sedra the spies lied about the dangers involved with going into the land and taking possession of it (Numbers 13:32). Similarly, Rahab lied to her authorities about the whereabouts of the Israelite spies.

Rahab's lie led to the defeat and extermination of everyone in her city except for her and her family. The spies' lie led to the decree that the generation that left Egypt would wander in the desert until they died and would not be allowed to enter the Promised Land (except for Joshua and Caleb).

◆ Why do you think the text applauds Rahab's lie, but the spies are punished for their lie? Is there a difference between a "good" lie and a "bad" lie?

Extending the Text

16 Rahab hid people who were in danger from the authorities and, in reward, she and her whole family were saved. During the Holocaust, righteous gentiles hid Jews who were in danger from local authorities cooperating with the Nazis. The righteous gentiles endangered their own families by providing shelter to Jews.

◆ To research the subject of righteous gentiles, go to the Yad Vashem web site at www. yadvashem.org and see their page on "The Righteous Among the Nations." Alternatively, go the United States Holocaust Memorial Museum web site at www.ushmm.org. Also see *Rescue: The Story of How Gentiles Saved Jews in the Holocaust* by Milton Meltzer and *The Courage to Care: Rescuers of Jews During the Holocaust* by Carol Rittner and Sondra Myers.

◆ As a class prepare an exhibit on righteous gentiles for the rest of the school to view. Include statistics by country and information and pictures on some of the following: Oskar Schindler, Raoul Wallenberg, The Village of Nieuwlande, The Danish Boat, Chiune (Sempo) Sugihara, and the town of Le Chambon in France.

17 Rahab chooses to join the Israelite community and apparently converts. In the Tanach there are no specific requirements of a foreign woman who wished to join the Israelite community. However, Judaism later developed requirements for conversion. Traditionally, a convert to Judaism studies Jewish law and customs, meets with a *Bet Din* (a group of Rabbis who question the convert), immerses in a *mikvah,* and

if male has a circumcision. However, the modern requirements for conversion vary from community to community.

◆ Interview a convert to learn about the process he/she went through before converting and his or her reasons for choosing Judaism.

◆ For more information on the requirements of a convert see *A Guide To Jewish Religious Practice* by Isaac Klein, pp. 440-448.

18 The spies made their promise to save Rahab conditional (see Insights from the Tradition #D, p. 7). Some Bar/Bat Mitzvah or wedding invitations are printed with Hebrew letters in the upper right-hand corner: ב"ה or בס"ד. These letters stand for "with God's help."

◆ Why do you think we might put these letters on invitations? Discuss whether or not you would want to include them on your invitations.

◆ Many cultures acknowledge that, plan as we might, the future is not in our hands. A Yiddish folk saying, for example, says: "Man plans and God laughs." The eighteenth century Scottish poet Robert Burns wrote, "The best laid plans o' mice an' men often go astray." Explain both quotations. Do they reflect the same idea as "with God's help"?

◆ Can you find another folk saying or write your own aphorism about this phenomenon?

19 The story of Joshua's battle against Jericho continues in Joshua 6.

◆ Read chapter 6 to discover what happens to Rahab and her family in the conquest of Jericho.

◆ Make a diorama of Jericho during the siege. Be sure to feature Rahab's house and the red string.

20 According to some archaeologists and historians, Jericho was destroyed and in ruins by approximately 1400 B.C.E. But the entry of the children of Israel into Canaan is dated to roughly 1220 B.C.E. This would mean that Jericho and its walls were indeed destroyed, but not by Joshua and the children of Israel. One possible explanation is that Joshua 2 and 6 comprise not a historical account, but rather an etiological story that attempts to explain the pile of rubble that the children of Israel saw at Jericho's location when they entered Canaan.

◆ For more information on etiological stories see *Teaching Torah* by Sorel Goldberg Loeb and Barbara Binder Kadden, Strategy #8, p. 7. See also other etiological stories such as Rudyard Kipling's *Just So Stories* or *Aesop's Fables*.

◆ Try writing your own etiological story explaining the origin of a physical phenomenon (e.g., why the sun sets in the west, why your town has a particular mountain or river nearby).

21 In Judges 1:22-26 the tribe of Joseph plans war against the city of Bethel and sends spies to check out the city. The person who helps them in this story is a man.

◆ Compare the two stories. In what ways are they the same and in what ways are they different?

◆ Was the hero/heroine of one story braver than the other? more righteous?

◆ Professor Tikva Frymer-Kensky argues in her book *In the Wake of the Goddesses*, that the Bible does not stereotype behavior as "masculine" or "feminine." Men and women in the Bible engage in similar actions and behaviors. How do these two stories support her contention?

22 Rahab initially helps the spies with no expectation of receiving anything in return. She then spells out for them how they could do an act of *chesed* for her that would pay her back for the *chesed* she had done them (see Analyzing the Text #4, p. 8).

In the book *The Hesed Boomerang*, Jack Doueck discusses how our doing acts of *chesed* can change the world and, in turn, offer us opportunities to benefit from other acts of *chesed*. He suggests a list of acts of *chesed* that we might consider doing regularly. For example: give your seat on a train to someone carrying packages or to an elderly person, drop off flowers at a hospital to be delivered to a lonely patient, help someone cross the street, put your shopping cart away at the grocery store, pick up trash from the sidewalk, give a waiter an extra big tip, smile or say good day to everyone you meet, put your neighbor's newspaper on their doorstep so they don't have to go out to get it, talk to strangers.

◆ Why might any of these acts be considered an act of *chesed*?

◆ How might your doing any of these acts boomerang and help you in return? How might your doing any of these acts of *chesed* serve to model behavior for someone else?

Personalizing the Text

23 Rahab hid people who were in danger from her government, as did Righteous Gentiles who, at great risk to themselves, hid Jews during the Holocaust.

◆ Under what circumstances would you endanger your own family for the benefit of somebody else?

24 Rahab chooses to become a member of the Israelite community (see Connecting the Text to the Sedra #9, p. 9).

◆ Write a diary entry by Rahab that explains her reasons for adopting Israelite beliefs and practices.

◆ Make a party for Rahab following her conversion. Prepare for the party by making decorations symbolizing Judaism and Jewish events (e.g., stars of David, signs saying "Mazel Tov!," a poster of the *Alef-Bet*). Cook and serve Jewish foods, such as potato *latkes*, bagels and lox, and *sufganiyot*. Have grape juice on hand to make a special *Kiddush* for the occasion. At the party, everyone can bring a Jewish ritual object to "give" to Rahab for her new Jewish life (a *tallit*, *Kiddush* cup, or *mezuzah*, for example). Be sure to have Jewish or Israeli music playing at your party, and consider doing some Israeli folk dancing as well.

25 *The Five Books of Miriam* by Ellen Frankel (pp. 216-217) contains a *midrash* about Rahab based on her name and three anagrams of it. This *midrash* suggests that Rahab's name (רחב) teaches us about her by being related to the following words:

• חבר *haver* (she is a "friend" to Israel),

• חרב *herev* ("sword" because Israel will fight her people),

• רחב *rahav* ("wide" because she opens her door wide in hospitality to strangers),

• בחר *bahar* (she "chooses" to join the Israelites).

◆ Consider possible anagrams for your own Hebrew name. List all the possible word combinations of the consonants in your name and consult a dictionary or Hebrew teacher to find the various meanings. Write about how these different anagrams give clues to your personality, your roles in your family, your goals in life.

◆ Alternatively, make an acrostic of your name that uses each letter of your English or Hebrew name to give clues to your personality, your roles in your family, your goals in life.

26 The Book of Joshua is, in part, concerned with issues of Israelite identity.

◆ Review the discussion of these issues in the Overview. What are the components of your Jewish identity?

◆ Play a game from *Jewish Identity* by Richard Israel to explore aspects of your group's ideas about Jewish identity.

27 There are similarities between Rahab's story and acts of *chesed* discussed in Extending the Text #22, p. 12.

◆ Consider these similarities. Then identify one act of *chesed* you might commit to doing on a regular basis. Keep a log of what you did, when and how, the reactions of the people who saw you doing the act of *chesed* and the reactions of the people you affected. Also, include your reactions.

28 Perhaps Joshua, the spies, or Rahab would have wanted to wear a *tallit* (see Connecting the Text To the Sedra #12, p. 9).

◆ Design a *tallit* for Joshua, the spies, or Rahab. What would the *atarah* (neck band) say? Would you quote a particular verse from the text? What colors would the *tallit* and fringes be? Would there be a design? How would it reflect living in their Promised Land?

◆ For ideas, see the cover of the Summer 2000 issue of *Women's League Outlook* magazine, which features an artist's rendition of the *tallitot* that would have been worn by the five daughters of Zelophehad (Joshua 17).

Other Resources

29 The first *Star Wars* film (1977, rated PG, 121 minutes) contains many similarities to the story of Joshua's invasion of the Promised Land. The similarities extend to Rahab, who, according to some *midrashim*, owned a tavern in which she served food and drinks, and helped the spies. View and discuss the film, considering especially the commonalities between the film and the Haftarah. Consider why people involved in illegal activity might meet at inns, taverns, or restaurants. Consider what types of subterfuge the "weaker" people in the film employed in order to defeat the "stronger" people.

30 View and discuss the film *The Long Walk Home* (1990, rated PG, 97 minutes). Set in 1955 Montgomery, Alabama, it tells the story of two women, one black and one white, who must decide what they are going to do in response to the famous bus boycott led by Martin Luther King. Their friendship itself transcended the laws of their community and through it they helped to change our nation. (See Analyzing the Text #1, p. 7, which discusses this Haftarah and the story of Moses' birth. The film and both biblical stories involve women resisting and undermining authority.)

31 The Disney film *Mulan* (1998, rated G, 88 minutes) features some clever battle strategies, not unlike those used by Joshua. View and discuss the film, examining how the underdog manages to defeat the superior power.

32 Read, act out, and discuss the skit involving Rahab and the spies, in *Bible Scenes: Joshua To Solomon* by Stan J. Beiner, p. 5.

33 Discuss the illustration of this Haftarah in *The Illustrated Torah* by Michal Meron, p. 158. What characteristics are attributed to Rahab based on this illustration?

34 For a story about the importance of doing acts of kindness for one another, read "The Ghetto Rebbe and His 'Kingdom of Children'" by Shlomo Carlebach in the book *Chosen Tales,* edited by Peninnah Schram, pp. 70-75.

35 Read portions of the book *Rescuers: Portraits of Moral Courage in the Holocaust* by Gay Block and Malka Drucker for a collection of true stories of righteous gentiles who, like Rahab, hid people in danger.

36 Read *Harry Potter: Chamber of Secrets* (volume 2 in the series) by J. K. Rowling, in which Harry learns the valuable lesson that the most important thing in life is not the talents with which we were born or the family into which we were born, but the choices we make in living our lives. Compare this lesson to Rahab and her choice to join the Jewish people.

37 For a film on righteous gentiles, view *The Righteous Enemy* (1987, not rated, 84 minutes), a documentary that reveals one of the most remarkable rescue operations of the Holocaust: the active protection given by Italian military and government officials to 40,000 Jews in Italian-occupied France, Greece, and Yugoslavia. (Available from The National Center for Jewish Film.)

38 Complete page 1 in *Prophets Copy Pak™* by Marji Gold-Vukson.

Involving the Family

39 Add a discussion topic to your Friday night dinner conversation. Every Friday night, go around the table and ask each person (family member and guest): what act of *chesed* was done for you this week and what act of *chesed* did you do this week? (See Extending the Text #22, p. 12.)

Bar/Bat Mitzvah Projects

40 Rahab and her family were saved by a red cord hanging from her window which reminded the Israelites of their promise to save her. Distribute pink ribbons for breast cancer awareness. Raising public consciousness regarding this disease may one day help to save the lives of many women.

41 Design (and create) your own *tallit* to represent your own particular Jewish identity (see Connecting the Text To the Sedra #12, p. 9).

JOSHUA 3:5-7, 5:2-6:1, 6:27 Ashkenazim
JOSHUA 5:2-6:1, 6:27 Sephardim
FIRST DAY PASSOVER

 This Haftarah has been paired with the first day of Passover on which we read Exodus 12:21-51. See "Connecting the Text To the Holiday," pp. 18-19, for an exploration of the many ways the two texts and the holiday shed light on each other.

SYNOPSIS

The first celebration in the Promised Land of the Passover Festival is recorded in this Haftarah (5:10-11), making it an obvious choice for the first day of Pesach. Under the leadership of Joshua, the children of Israel have crossed the Jordan River and arrived safely in the Promised Land. Joshua's spies have returned with good reports from Jericho, but before they can begin the business of conquering the land, they must attend to some religious matters. God commands Joshua to make knives of flint and circumcise the Israelites. The text explains to us that all the people who escaped from Egypt, who had been circumcised, had died in the wilderness. Those who were born in the wilderness, on the other hand, had never been circumcised. Joshua, therefore, sees to it that all males are circumcised at a place called Gilgal, where they rest until they heal.

While camping at Gilgal, the Israelites celebrate Passover on the fourteenth day of the month of Nisan, as prescribed in Exodus 12:6. On that day, the manna ceases to fall from the sky, and the Israelites must eat the produce of the land and unleavened cakes they bake themselves. Hence-

forth, the Israelites provide food for themselves from the crops of the land.

On the eve of the invasion of Jericho, an angel of God appears to Joshua (recalling for us Moses' encounter years before with the Burning Bush in Exodus 3:5). "Remove your sandals from your feet, for the place where you stand is holy," the angel says, and Joshua obeys.

The actual battle of Jericho is omitted from the Haftarah. Only the verses immediately preceding and following it are included. We are reminded in the final verse that God is with Joshua, whose name is known throughout the Land.

INSIGHTS FROM THE TRADITION

A Verse 5:12 says that the manna stopped falling and the children of Israel began to eat the produce of the land. According to Rashi, if the manna had continued, they would not have bothered to eat the local produce because the manna was more pleasing. Their situation is compared to a child who will not eat barley bread (which doesn't taste so good) as long as wheat bread (which does taste good) exists.

◆ Why do you think it was important for the children of Israel to stop eating manna and begin eating the local food?

◆ What does this parable and Rashi's insight say about human nature?

B Concerning the end of the manna, Saadiah Gaon commented that the exact precision and reliability with which the manna fell every day (except Shabbat) for 40 years was a miracle worthy of commemoration. God can be counted on to fulfill an obligation.

◆ Identify obligations that human beings may take on for a long period of time. What happens if the person fails to fulfill the obligation?

◆ When human beings become parents, they take on the obligation to feed, clothe, and care for their children for at least 18 years. How is this like God providing the daily manna in the desert for 40 years? In what ways do some parents fail to fulfill their obligations? How might the successful fulfillment of this obligation to children be commemorated?

◆ Debate: Before people are allowed to become parents, government psychologists should evaluate them and make sure they can fulfill the obligations of parenthood. As with driving, parenting should require a license.

C Why did the angel come to Joshua before the invasion of Jericho? *Megillah* 3a explains that it was to remind Joshua of the neglect of intensive study of Torah, which is a continual obligation.

You might think the angel was out of line in reminding Joshua to study Torah on the night before a big military invasion. But the message here is that it is always time to study Torah.

◆ Shammai taught in *Pirke Avot* 1:15, "Make the study of the Law a fixed duty." What does this mean?

◆ Do you know anyone who studies Torah regularly?

◆ What do you consider to be your own fixed responsibilities that you never fail to do? Can

you envision Torah study becoming one of them?

D God's angel tells Joshua to remove his sandals from his feet in verse 5:15. Malbim explains that this meant Joshua should strip his soul of material encumbrances.

◆ What kinds of things might encumber our souls?

◆ Does an excessive amount of material possessions encumber our souls?

◆ Do bad habits encumber our souls?

◆ Do guilt, stress, or anxiety encumber our souls?

◆ How might we resolve to free ourselves of what encumbers us?

STRATEGIES
Analyzing the Text

1 When they had circumcised themselves, God proclaimed, "Today I have rolled away from you the disgrace of Egypt."

It is unclear what is meant by "the disgrace of Egypt." Some commentators suggest that the Israelites had been uncircumcised like the idolatrous Egyptians, and were thus disgraceful until they corrected the situation.

Other commentators suggest that when the Israelites arrived in the Land of Canaan, they adopted the custom of circumcision, which was practiced by the inhabitants of the land.

◆ Which interpretation makes sense to you, and why?

2 For the 40 years that the children of Israel wandered in the desert, they were sustained by manna from God. As soon as they entered the

Land, circumcised themselves, and celebrated the first Passover, they stopped receiving manna and began eating of the produce of the land.

◆ Explain how the end of the manna indicates that their wandering is truly over and that the children of Isreal have finally come home.

3 Joshua is told in verse 5:15 to remove his sandals.

◆ Compare this scene to that in Exodus 3, in which Moses is given the same instruction. How are these two scenes similar and different?

◆ How are Moses and Joshua similar and different?

◆ Explain how Joshua is not being presented as another Moses, and why.

Connecting the Text To the Holiday

4 In verse 5:10 the Israelites offer the Passover sacrifice on the fourteenth day of Nisan. This was done in accordance with the law set out in Exodus 12:6.

◆ What do we do on the evening of the fourteenth day of Nisan to observe the Passover holiday? How are we reminded of the Passover offering?

5 While wandering 40 years in the wilderness, the Israelites did not observe the ritual of circumcision. Therefore, Joshua instructed them to be circumcised immediately upon entering the Land of Israel.

◆ Why did all the boys and men have to be circumcised immediately on entering the Promised Land? (There may have been more than one reason: They entered the Promised Land immediately before Passover; all partici-

pants in the paschal sacrifice had to have been circumcised (see Exodus 12:44, 48); they entered the Promised Land in fulfillment of God's covenant with Abraham to give Abraham and his descendants this land. The sign of this covenant with Abraham was circumcision (see Genesis 17:7-10); they were preparing to begin a war as instructed by God, and circumcision was an initiation rite.)

◆ Explain how these answers involve affirmation of the covenant with God.

◆ Before Passover, we spend a lot of time preparing our houses and kitchens for Passover, but we rarely spend time preparing ourselves for the holiday. Consider the following ways to prepare oneself for Passover: visit a *mikvah* for personal purification, go on a long strenuous hike for identification with those journeying in the desert, reaffirm the covenant by studying a relevant text, prepare a family *Haggadah*. Suggest other preparatory acts. How might these acts help you be in the right frame of mind for the Passover *Seder*?

6 In verse 5:11 Joshua and the Israelites ate unleavened cakes, as required by Exodus 12:39.

◆ Why did they, and why do we, eat *matzah* on Passover? One answer can be found in Exodus 12:39. Consider a variety of other answers as well, such as the following:

Passover was originally a holiday of shepherds, and shepherds traditionally ate flat, pita-type bread (this is possibly what *matzah* was meant to be).

Chag HaMatzot, originally a separate holiday from Passover, was a holiday for farmers who would refrain from eating leavened bread in anticipation of a new crop. They hoped that by giving up bread for a week they would have a better crop.

Matzah is the bread of slaves who do not have enough time to let their dough rise and so must bake it quickly.

◆ Learn to make *matzah*.

7 The Holiday Torah reading (Exodus 12:25) provides that the Passover service should take place once the Israelites come to the Land *Adonai* will give them. The Haftarah marks that moment and the first celebration of Passover.

◆ Imagine what it must have been like to anticipate this moment for so many years. Has there ever been an occasion that you have anticipated for a long time? Did it meet your expectations? Did it turn out as you had anticipated? How did you feel when the big moment finally arrived?

◆ Write a journal entry or a letter to a friend describing how the Israelites felt when they arrived in the Land and were able to observe their first Passover there.

8 The Haftarah also contains a surprise meeting between Joshua and an angel or messenger from God. The angel approaches Joshua with his sword drawn.

◆ Compare this scene to a similar one involving David in I Chronicles 21:16. In that scene, David threw himself on the ground as soon as he saw the angel. In contrast, Joshua approached this angel and asked whose side he was on. Only when the angel told Joshua that he was part of God's hosts did Joshua understand that this was a Divine being. Then Joshua fell on his face.

◆ Explain how both David and Joshua reacted with fear or awe when they realized they had seen a Divine being.

◆ In the Holiday Torah reading, there is an angel (the Destroyer) who will go through the land of Egypt and kill all the firstborn. In popular culture, angels are generally considered friendly, beneficent helpers. How are these biblical angels viewed?

9 The Haftarah says (verse 6:1) that Jericho was "closed" (shut up tight).

Similarly, after the children of Israel left Egypt, Pharaoh changed his mind about freeing them. He thought that his troops would be able to catch up with the Israelites because he thought that the wilderness had "closed" in on them.

◆ Explain how in both stories, it seems that the Israelites will be stymied in their objectives because all avenues are closed before them. Yet in both situations, with God's guidance and help, they are successful.

◆ Have you ever felt stymied, but then met with success? What got you through?

10 Most congregations conclude the Haftarah with verse 6:27, which says that God was with Joshua whose fame spread throughout the Land. Similarly, after God took the Israelites out of Egypt with signs and wonders, they were known far and wide. Some Ashkenazic communities omit verse 6:27 and conclude with verse 6:1.

◆ Compare verse 6:27 to verse 6:1. Which ending do you like better, and why?

Judges

OVERVIEW

The seventh book of the Bible, the Book of Judges, continues the Deuteronomic History of Israel. "Judges" is perhaps a misleading title, since the featured characters are neither legal nor religious authorities, as one might expect. Rather, these judges are charismatic individuals who "pass judgment" on the enemies of Israel by defeating them in battle, continuing the process of Israel's conquest of the Promised Land, and fulfilling God's promise that Israel alone would inhabit the Land of Israel.

There is a recurring pattern in the Book of Judges, which is outlined in the second chapter. Without a strong leader like Moses or Joshua to guide the people, the Israelites repeatedly fail to honor the Covenant with God. They worship idols, break commandments, and abandon belief in God. Consequently, God delivers them into the hands of their enemies. The Israelites then plead with God to save them, and God mercifully responds by providing a judge to redeem them from their oppressors. The people then repent of their evil ways and turn again toward God. Unfortunately, when the current judge dies, the Israelites yield once again to temptation and revert to their sinful behavior, and the cycle begins again.

The judges are a diverse group of individuals who have in common only their God given ability to lead Israel from crisis to freedom. The Book of Judges records the exploits of a variety of avenging heroes, often adding intriguing stories about their lives. We read about likely saviors — a strong man named Samson who can kill a lion with his bare hands, as well as unlikely heroes — an unarmed woman named Yael, who kills an army general by hammering a tent pin through his brain. The period of the Judges of Israel is from about 1200-1020 B.C.E. The formidable enemies the Israelites defeat include the Moabites, Philistines, Canaanites, Midianites, and Ammonites.

The final chapters of the book (Judges 17-21) include stories of the unraveling of the Israelite tribal society, as the people make and worship idols, engage in depraved behavior and religious anarchy, and fight deadly battles among themselves. The concluding verse (21:25) sums up: "In those days there was no king in Israel; everyone did as he pleased."

The Haftarot from the Book of Judges reflect in historical account, narrative tale, and poetic verse the turmoil of these turbulent years in Israelite history. At the same time, they highlight for us the power of courageous leaders to bring redemption to the people. In doing so, the Book of Judges begins to make a good case in favor of establishing a king to unite and rule over Israel.

JUDGES 4:4–5:31 Ashkenazim
JUDGES 5:1–5:31 Sephardim
BESHALACH בשלח

This Haftarah has been paired with *Parashat Beshalach*, Exodus 13:17-17:16. See "Connecting the Text To the Sedra," pp. 24-26, for an exploration of the many ways the two texts shed light on each other.

SYNOPSIS

Deborah is unique among the judges in that she is both the only woman judge and the only one referred to as a prophet. In the first part of the Haftarah (Judges 4:4-24), she calls upon the warrior Barak to lead the tribes of Naphtali and Zebulun in battle against the Canaanites who, under King Jabin, have been oppressing the Israelites. Barak agrees to fight only if Deborah accompanies him, which she does. They lead 10,000 troops into battle, during which the Israelites annihilate the enemy, despite the Canaanites' superior weaponry.

The Canaanite General, Sisera, manages to escape during the chaotic battle and seeks shelter in the tent of Heber the Kenite. Heber's wife, Yael, invites Sisera to rest and gives him some milk to drink. When he dozes off, Yael takes a tent pin and hammers it through his temple, killing him. When Barak arrives at her tent in pursuit of Sisera, Yael presents him with the murdered general. With Sisera dead, the Israelites continue to defeat the Canaanites and destroy King Jabin.

The second part of the Haftarah (Judges 5) comprises the Song of Deborah, a literary masterpiece retelling in poetic verse the triumphant saga of Israel's oppression by and subsequent victory over King Jabin and the Canaanites.

INSIGHTS FROM THE TRADITION

A Verse 4:5 says that Deborah sat under the Palm of Deborah. *Midrash* suggests that the palm tree is called by her name because she was wealthy enough to own land. As a wealthy woman, she was, therefore, free from external influences and able to judge fairly and respond to God's demands (see *Nedarim* 38a).

◆ According to tradition, Abraham was also wealthy and Moses was raised in wealth in Pharaoh's court. Why might wealth free these people to follow God?

◆ How might factors other than wealth contribute to a person's spiritual, religious, and ethical development? Consider the role of education, free time, parents, etc.

◆ As residents of a wealthy nation, do we have an extra obligation not to pollute the earth? not to buy products made by slave labor? What other ethical standards might we be wealthy enough to insist upon?

B In verse 4:8 Barak tells Deborah, "If you go with me, I will go." It seems as if Barak is too cowardly to carry out God's order to go to war. According to Malbim, however, Barak accepted God's command to carry out the battle, but was worried that the people would refuse to follow him. How might Deborah's presence have been a source of inspiration to the people and a guarantee of Divine aid in battle?

♦ On the battlefield, Deborah may have been both an advisor and a sort of team mascot and good luck charm. What role do you think Deborah played? Do you think mascots and good luck charms help us today? Bring in your favorite good luck charm for show-and-tell.

C Deuteronomy 22:5 has been interpreted as prohibiting a woman from using weapons, and Rabbinic *midrash* praises Yael for having killed Sisera with household objects instead of military weapons (see *Targum Jonathan* 5:26).

♦ There remains today ambivalence about women serving in modern armies. Debate: Women should be allowed to take an active role in military combat.

D In verse 5:21 the River Kishon is called a "raging torrent." However, the term "raging torrent" has also been translated as an "ancient brook." Radak suggests that God created the Kishon in the beginning of the world expressly for the role it would play in the future battle between Israel and Canaan.

Other commentaries, such as *Metsudat David*, add that God caused the small brook to swell at a critical moment in the battle, sweeping away the enemy.

It is interesting that although Radak believes that God did nothing miraculous other than create the River, *Metsudat David* suggests that God acted at a specific moment to create the miraculous swelling.

♦ Do you think God intervenes in the world to create a miracle when natural phenomena bring about a desired result?

♦ Or, do you think God does not intervene in the world even when a fortunate coincidence occurs?

E Radak's explanation of the translation "ancient brook" (see Insights from the Tradition #D, p. 22) suggests that from the beginning of time, the river had a special purpose for its existence. In some sense, the happiest people in life are those who discover the one thing they were born to do.

♦ Explain why Radak's explanation could be extended to say that all of us have a specific purpose.

♦ Do you think everyone (indeed, everything) has a specific job to do on earth?

♦ How would a person discover his or her gift or purpose?

F Verse 5:23 contains a curse of all those who dwell in Meroz, apparently for failing to capture Sisera. From this verse, Talmud *Mo'ed Katan* 16a derives laws of excommunication. These have been used since Talmudic times to eliminate dangerous influences in the community by isolating Jews who hold controversial views.

For example, just as verse 5:23 is a public statement of the curse against Meroz, excommunication requires that a public announcement be made, stating the reason and the authority behind the action. Among the most famous Jews excommunicated are such intellectual giants as Maimonides (in the twelfth century), Spinoza (in the seventeenth), and Rabbi Mordecai Kaplan, the founder of Reconstructionism (in the twentieth century).

♦ For more information on excommunication, see *The Second Jewish Book of Why* by Alfred J. Kolatch, pp. 55-56.

◆ Excommunication is extremely rare in today's Jewish world. Do you think it is a good means of protecting our communities?

◆ Do you think the Jewish community needs protection against individuals perceived to hold dangerous views?

STRATEGIES
Analyzing the Text

1 Look up the meaning of Deborah's name in a Hebrew/English or name dictionary. There are several possible meanings, but many scholars think that "bee" is the most likely, drawing comparisons between a bee and a military leader.

◆ What traits do you think a bee and a good military leader share?

2 Yael's name means "mountain goat."

◆ What aspects of this animal seem to apply to her?

◆ How does thinking about Yael as a mountain goat (quick reflexes, agile, feisty) help you interpret her story?

◆ What animal do you think you are most like, and why? Draw the animal you are most like, and explain the similarities to the class.

3 Words can be very symbolic. In verse 4:15 Sisera gets down from his chariot.

◆ How does this act foretell his fate?

◆ Contrast the symbolism of Sisera descending from his chariot and Yael descending from the dead Sisera.

4 The narrative in chapter 4 includes only the tribes of Naphtali and Zebulun in the fight against Sisera's army. The poetic version in chapter 5 adds Ephraim, Benjamin, Issachar, and Machir (Manasseh).

◆ Can you find other examples in which Deborah's Song differs from, or elaborates on, the narrative account? (For example, in the prose version, Yael kills Sisera when he is lying under a blanket asleep. In the song version, he seems to be awake and standing, and falls to the ground when she kills him.)

◆ Why might there be differences between the two versions? In *The Haftarah Commentary*, Plaut suggests (p. 162) that the two versions were written at different times, the song version being much older than the prose version. It may be that when an editor put the two texts together in the Bible, the editor noticed the differences, but did not want to change one to conform to the other or leave one version out due to respect for the traditions.

◆ Make up your own reason(s) for the differences between the song version of the events and the prose version.

5 In verse 5:7 Deborah is called a "Mother in Israel." According to *Yalkut Me'am Lo'ez*, this means that she prayed and worried about her people. According to *Metsudat David*, Deborah reproved her people. According to Abrabanel, she pitied them.

◆ What evidence in the story do you find to support any of these interpretations?

◆ Aside from worrying, pitying, and reprimanding, what else would the image of "mother" convey for you?

6 In verse 5:27 the words "sank" and "lay" are repeated several times. From a literary perspective, the repetition may serve a variety of purposes.

◆ Explain how repetition might: emphasize Sisera's death, slow down the narrative after Yael rushed to kill him, serve other purposes?

◆ In verse 5:28 Sisera's mother looks out the window and twice repeats her concern over his delayed return. Does this repetition signify to you anxiety, tension, irony, Deborah mocking her, or other implications?

7 It is Sisera's mother, not his wife, whose worry and grief are highlighted. Plaut deduces that this suggests that Sisera was a young man.

◆ Do you agree or disagree with this interpretation?

◆ What could be another explanation for the focus on his grieving mother? (For example, does a mother create more sympathy than a wife, does Sisera's mother parallel Deborah being called a mother of Israel?)

Connecting the Text To the Sedra

8 With other Haftarot, the Rabbis edited biblical stories to suit their liturgical needs. Yet in this case, they chose to include not just one rendition of the story of Deborah, but two complete versions, making this the longest Haftarah of the annual cycle.

Both Haftarah and Sedra first tell the story of a military victory and redemption in prose form and then retell the same story in poetic form.

◆ Identify the verses of the prose form of each story.

◆ Identify the poetic retelling of each story.

◆ Does the mood of one version differ from the mood of the other?

9 The first three verses of Judges 4 are excluded from the Haftarah. By starting with verse 4:4, the Haftarah seems to focus attention on Deborah, who appears in that verse. In addition to Deborah, the Haftarah also tells the story of Yael, a strong and courageous woman.

◆ Explain why Deborah and Yael may be considered brave and strong.

◆ The Sedra concludes the story of the Exodus from Egypt. The Exodus could not have happened without the efforts of several strong, brave women (e.g., Miriam, Moses' mother, Pharaoh's daughter, the midwives). Review Exodus 1-3 to see how these women were courageous and essential to the Exodus.

◆ Hold a press conference. Select three students to play the parts of Deborah, Yael, and Miriam. Have the class prepare questions for these women to understand their accomplishments and how they helped their people.

10 There are many striking similarities between the Sedra and this Haftarah. Compare the following:

• Chariots of the Canaanites with chariots of Pharaoh

• Military battle resulting in Israel's liberation from oppression

• The River Kishon with the Sea of Reeds

• God's role as warrior

◆ Can you identify other similarities between the Sedra and the Haftarah?

◆ Chose one item that is common to the two stories and depict it artistically.

◆ For more information on the Sedra, see *Teaching Torah* by Sorel Goldberg Loeb and Barbara Binder Kadden, p. 107.

11 In the Haftarah Deborah is sitting under a palm tree (4:5). Similarly, an oasis with palm trees is mentioned in the Sedra (Exodus 15:27).

◆ In *The Illustrated Torah* by Michal Meron, p. 75, Deborah is depicted sitting under a palm tree. Discuss this illustration as a representation of the Haftarah. What does it convey about Deborah as a leader? Is her palm tree a type of oasis?

◆ Make a micrographic picture of Deborah's palm tree. Such a picture uses the words of a text, written very small, to outline an image. Choose a portion of this Haftarah in either Hebrew or English for your micrographic art. For more on Jewish micrographic art, see an online exhibit at www.jtsa.edu/library/exhib/microg.

◆ Eat dates, which grow on palm trees.

12 In the Haftarah Barak refused to go into battle if the prophet Deborah did not go with him. In the Sedra the Israelites fought a battle against Amalek. Moses, the prophet, helped them win their battle by holding his arms up high. When his arms were up, Israel prevailed. When his arms tired, Israel lost their focus. Moses had to have help holding his arms up until Israel won the war. Mishnah *Rosh HaShanah* 3:8 explains how Moses helped the children of Israel win the war: when Moses held up his hands, Israel prevailed. Now, did the hands of Moses wage war or crush the enemy? No. The text only teaches that as long as Israel turned their thoughts above and subjected their wishes to that of God, they prevailed. Otherwise they failed.

◆ Explain how this Mishnah rules out the possibility that Moses' hands magically won the war.

◆ How does the Mishnah interpret Moses' help (i.e., did it help the people focus on one united goal)?

◆ How might we understand the role Deborah the prophet played in Barak's battle?

◆ Did Moses have to focus in order to keep his arms raised? Hold a contest in class. Everyone should hold both hands up high throughout the class while studying a subject. See who is able to last the longest.

13 The Haftarah begins with Barak telling Deborah that he would go into battle only if she came along.

◆ Do you think Barak was afraid of the war? Why else might he have wanted Deborah to accompany him into battle?

In the Sedra (Exodus 13:17-18), the Israelites were just freed from slavery and God leads them away from Egypt and toward the Land of Israel. God did not lead them on the most direct route, however, because on that route there was a possibility of war, and the Israelites might fear a war and want to return to slavery in Egypt.

Both Barak and God recognized potential fears and found ways to deal with fear (i.e., taking Deborah along to give him confidence, finding a less risky route). There are many ways to deal with fear so that it doesn't stop us from doing what we want or need to do.

◆ Make a list of things that scare young kids.

◆ Make a "Do and Don't List" to teach young kids strategies for how to deal with being afraid.

14 The Haftarah says in verse 4:16 that no one remained of the enemy army. An unusual phrase is used to say no one remained: עד אחד *(ahd echad)*.

Similarly, in the Sedra, Pharaoh's army is destroyed when the Reed Sea closes up on them. No one survives and the text uses the same phrase: עד אחד (Exodus 14:28).

◆ Explain how the phrase עד אחד indicates the victory was total. Would you expect a partial victory if God supported the war?

◆ Play musical chairs until no one remains except the victor.

15 In the Sedra God provides the children of Israel with manna to sustain them in the desert. According to Exodus 16:33, some manna was put in a jar and saved as evidence for future generations about this miraculous act of God.

There are many important ordinary objects in the Haftarah which could be considered evidence of God working a miracle for the Israelites. For example, Yael used a hammer, blanket, and milk.

◆ Explain how each of these items contributed to the miraculous victory over Sisera.

◆ What object from the Haftarah might you want to take and save to remember the story?

◆ The Bar/Bat Mitzvah year is a milestone time for the student and his/her family. Identify five ordinary items from your thirteenth year that helped make this an extraordinary year, then assemble a Memory Jar for yourself.

Extending the Text

16 If you review verses 4:11 and 4:17-22, you will notice that the text is unclear about who Heber the Kenite and Yael are and to whom their loyalties belong. We, therefore, cannot know why Yael acted the way she did. Scholars disagree on her motives.

One scholar, Danna Nolan Fewell, writes in *The Women's Bible Commentary*, edited by Carol Newsome and Sharon Ringe (p. 69), that Yael had no choice; the Israelites had won the battle and would have suspected her of giving refuge to the enemy if they had found the enemy general hiding in her tent.

Other scholars suggest that Yael acted out of loyalty to God (not unlike Rahab in the Haftarah for *Shelach Lecha*, p. 6). This may also explain why the narrator mentions in verse 4:11 that Yael's husband was related to Moses' father-in-law.

◆ Do you see evidence in the text for any of these explanations for Yael's motives?

◆ Using information you find in the text, write your own *midrash* explaining why Yael killed Sisera.

17 There are many indications in this story of the Israelites (and Yael) using creative battle strategies to try to defeat their stronger, better equipped enemy. For example, the foot soldiers trapped the enemy's iron chariots in a muddy riverbed, and the Israelites attacked from above so they could have an advantage.

◆ See if you can find more instances of creating battle strategies.

In addition, in the Sedra the Israelites may have used strategy to escape from the better equipped Egyptians. The Egyptians were dependent on their chariots that could not operate in the wetlands around a sea; the Israelites headed for the Reed Sea (see Exodus 14:25), in which the chariot wheels were locked and moved with difficulty.

◆ Review the history of the contested Golan Heights: usually military advantage goes to the nation that possesses the high position over the Hula Valley. Discuss or debate whether Israel should release control of the Golan to Syria.

◆ For more information on the modern battle to control the Golan, see *The Course of Modern Jewish History* by Howard Sachar, pp. 771-778.

18 "Women in a Window" is a common theme within artwork of the Ancient Near East (see verse 5:28). One example, an ivory carving from Nimrud, can be found in *The Ancient Near East in Pictures* by James Pritchard, p. 39, item #131.

◆ Research modern paintings that use the theme of a woman in a window. One painting by Yossl Bergner, "Woman at the Window," can be found in *The Museums of Israel*, edited by L. Y. Rahmani, p. 133, and another painting, "Weeping Woman," can be found in *Art in Israel*, edited by B. Tammuz, #27).

◆ For an art project, find an old window frame (often available at garage sales). Clean and paint the frame. Then put picture(s) in the window facing out. Will your pictures be of men, women, children, animals, or inanimate objects, and why?

19 The last verse of the Haftarah became a popular Israeli song: "So may all Your enemies, perish, O Lord! But may Your friends be as the sun rising in its might!"

◆ Why might these words be meaningful for modern Israelis?

◆ Read and analyze the words to some traditional American battle songs, such as "The Battle Hymn of the Republic" or the French national anthem, *"La Marseillaise."* Compare the words of one of these songs with the Song of Deborah and identify similarities between them.

20 This Haftarah is part of the Book of Judges. The first verse of the Book of

Ruth seems to indicate that Ruth's story also took place during the period when Judges ruled Israel: "In the days when the chieftains/judges ruled, there was a famine in the land."

When the Bible was canonized, there was a difference of opinion about whether the Book of Ruth should be placed between Judges and Samuel (the Christian Bible's order) or with the other writings (the Jewish Bible's order).

◆ Why do you think the order differs in these two traditions?

◆ Learn the order of the Jewish Bible. Compare it to the order (and contents) of the Christian Bible. For more information on the formation of the Bible, see the *Encyclopaedia Judaica* article "Bible: Canon," vol. 4, pp. 816-830.

21 Since Deborah's song was chosen to parallel the Song at the Sea in the Sedra (Exodus 15), this Shabbat has been named *Shabbat Shirah* (Shabbat of Song). And since the Sedra and Haftarah both involve strong, take-action women, Jewish women's organizations, such as the Women's League of United Synagogue, sponsor women-led Sisterhood Shabbat services each year on *Shabbat Shirah*.

◆ Find out if there is such a service at your synagogue or in your community. If so, attend as a class.

◆ The Song at the Sea is traditionally sung with a special melody. Learn this melody and volunteer to chant Torah at *Shabbat Shirah* services.

22 Consider the obligation that wealth brings to its owner in the following story and review Insights from the Tradition #A, p. 21.

A Rebbe tried to collect charitable donations for the poor and hungry from a very wealthy man.

The wealthy man would give the Rebbe only a few pennies, nothing that could be enough to feed someone hungry.

One day, the Rebbe asked this rich man to describe what he usually ate. The rich man explained that he needed very little; he ate only bread and water. The Rebbe argued with the rich man until he promised to change his eating habits. The wealthy man had to promise the Rebbe that he would start eating like other rich people: meats, fruits, vegetables, and delicacies. The Rebbe's students were surprised to hear their teacher encourage a person to spend money on luxuries for himself when he had refused to give adequate *tzedakah*. The Rebbe explained that as long as the rich man would eat only bread, he would think the poor can live on practically nothing; when he would start eating well, he would realize the poor needed decent food. (One version of this story is told in *Everyday Miracles: The Healing Wisdom of Hasidic Stories*, edited by Howard Polsky and Yaella Wozner, pp. 161-162.)

◆ Explain how the wealthy man did not know how to use his wealth properly.

◆ Do you agree that the rich man had an obligation to eat well and also to help feed others well?

Personalizing the Text

23 Deborah is called in verse 4:4 "wife of Lapidoth." Alternatively, others have translated this phrase as "woman of Lapidoth," while others have interpreted it to mean "woman of torches" for the Temple in Jerusalem (see *Megillah* 14a). Rashi says that this indicates that she made torches for the Temple, while Hirsch suggests that the appellation reflects her "fiery enthusiasm." *Yalkut Shemoni*, Sec. 42, also explains that Deborah was chosen as a prophet

and judge because she made candles for the sanctuary with very thick wicks that would burn brighter and longer.

◆ Design and make your own candles to light up your synagogue sanctuary.

24 Deborah is "a wife of Lapidoth." The heir to the throne in England is "Charles, Prince of Wales," and Elvis Presley was called the "King of Rock and Roll."

◆ Write a word description for yourself, following the same model: your name, then a (noun) of (noun). Explain why this description reflects your relationships, personality, and hopes about your life and career.

25 We learned above that Deborah means "bee" and Yael means "mountain goat."

◆ Use a Hebrew dictionary to find the meaning(s) of Barak.

◆ Write a *midrash* using the symbolic names of these characters.

26 The Haftarah contains a narrative account of the story of Deborah and a poetic version of the same important events.

◆ Write or find in the newspaper a narrative account of a real event. Then write a poetic version, which may also express thanks for that same event. Alternatively, you can draw a picture, do a dance interpretation, or write a song about the event. Compare the impact and emphasis of each mode of expression.

◆ In a classroom setting, form groups. One student in each group writes a narrative account of an event, one writes a poetic version, one orchestrates or writes music, one prepares a pictorial version, etc. The group can then present their multimedia version of the event.

27 Perhaps the Song of Deborah was sung in her time.

◆ Choose a portion (or the entirety) of the Song of Deborah and set it to music. The music can be a tune you already know or an original composition.

Other Resources

28 Read, act out, and discuss the skit in *Bible Scenes: Joshua To Solomon* by Stan J. Beiner, pp. 38-42.

29 The Haftarah ends with Deborah's enemy Sisera dead, and Sisera's mother waiting for him to return from his ill-fated battle.

◆ See the poem about Deborah and the poem about Sisera's mother found in *Modern Poems on the Bible: An Anthology*, edited by David Curzon, pp. 185-186. Also see "For the Day of Atonement" a poem by Ruth Brin in her collection *A Time to Search*, pp. 21-24.

30 For a story about a wise bee *(devorah)*, read "The Wisdom of Solomon," told by Merna Ann Hecht in *Chosen Tales*, edited by Peninnah Schram, pp. 155-160.

31 On the CD *Bible Women* by Elizabeth Swados, there is a song called "Deborah Lead Me To the Rock." On this same CD, there is also an adaptation of the Song of Deborah from Judges 5. Listen to both songs.

Listen also to a song based on Judges 5:12 called "Arise My Love" on the CD *Debbie Friedman at Carnegie Hall*.

32 Complete page 4 in *Prophets Copy Pak™* by Marji Gold-Vukson.

Involving the Family

33 Using a Hebrew/English dictionary or name dictionary, discover the meaning behind your family's last name and each family member's first and middle names. In addition, research your family's last name to discover where you're from, what your ancestors did for a living and more.

34 Choose an important event or time in your family's history. Together, write a narrative and a poem about the event.

Bar/Bat Mitzvah Project

35 Remember, living in a wealthy nation gives one the freedom of choice that others may not have (see Insights from the Tradition #A, p. 21). Become involved in an environmental cause. Or, identify a popular consumer item or brand that utilizes child or slave labor in its production, and resolve to abstain from purchasing that product and to write to the company in protest.

JUDGES 11:1-33
CHUKAT חקת

This Haftarah has been paired with *Parashat Chukat*, Numbers 19:1-22:1. See "Connecting the Text to the Sedra," p. 33, for an exploration of the many ways the two texts shed light on each other.

SYNOPSIS

Jephthah (pronounced *yeef-tach* in Hebrew) the Gileadite, who will rise as a great hero in Israel, endures a difficult childhood. He is ostracized by his stepbrothers because he is the son of another woman. Later, Jephthah is thrown out of his father's house by his stepbrothers, who want to exclude him from their father's inheritance. Exiled in the land of Tob, Jephthah joins a crowd of outlaws and earns himself a reputation as a ruthless fighter.

After some time, the Ammonites declare war on Israel. The elders of Gilead want to bring Jephthah back from Tob to lead the Israelites in battle. Jephthah is not anxious to return to the land from which he had been cruelly exiled. The elders bargain with Jephthah, promising him that if he returns, he will be made the leader of all Gilead. Convinced and vindicated, Jephthah agrees.

Once confirmed as the commander-in-chief of Gilead, Jephthah first attempts to negotiate peace with the enemy through diplomacy. Though the Ammonite king complains that Israel had stolen Ammonite land, Jephthah explains that at the time the Israelites won that land in battle, it was owned by the Amorites, who had conquered the Ammonites. Furthermore, Jephthah argues, the land was given to Israel by God. How could the Ammonites risk offending Israel's God? Despite

Jephthah's best diplomatic efforts, the Ammonite king was not convinced and resolved to go to war with Israel.

As with the other judges, the spirit of *Adonai* comes over Jephthah and ensures his military victory. Just to make sure, however, Jephthah swears an oath to *Adonai* that if God will lead him to victory, he, Jephthah will sacrifice to God the first thing that comes out of his door to greet him when he gets home. The Haftarah concludes with the military victory of the Israelites over the Ammonites. (Sadly, we discover in the text that follows the Haftarah that Jephthah's beloved daughter is first to greet him when he returns home.)

INSIGHTS FROM THE TRADITION

A Although he was an "able warrior," a powerful man who could have forced himself on his family as their ruler, Jephthah flees from his stepbrothers (verse 11:3). According to *Yalkut Me'am Lo'ez*, Jephthah set aside his anger and avoided conflict in anticipation that God would restore him to his family and his possessions.

◆ How can we understand patience and restraint as the virtues of an able, mighty warrior?

◆ How does this understanding of power or might differ from the usual definition?

◆ Do you feel powerful when you exercise restraint or when you are patient?

B In verse 11:5 we learn it was the elders of the town, and not his brothers, who approach Jephthah for help. Jephthah accuses the elders in verse 11:7 of having hated him and driven him away, although we know from the text that it was his brothers who forced him out. According to Abrabanel, Jephthah's accusation of the elders indicates that because the elders never protested the actions of the brothers or intervened on Jephthah's behalf, it was as if they themselves were responsible for his cruel exile.

◆ Do bystanders have a moral (or legal) responsibility to intervene to prevent an injustice? Explain your answer.

◆ Do you agree that bystanders are to blame as if they had done the cruel deed themselves?

C In many ways, the exile and return of Jephthah is a microcosm of the repeating cycle of sin and repentance throughout the Book of Judges. *Yalkut Me'am Lo'ez* explains: Just as the Israelites repeatedly reject God, but plead for God's help when they are in need, so, too, do the Gileadites reject Jephthah, only to call upon him when they are in trouble.

◆ God and Jephthah respond to the call for help. What do their responses tell us about them?

◆ Alexander Pope wrote, "To err is human, to forgive Divine." Do you agree that forgiveness is a Godly act?

◆ Have you ever been asked to help someone who had wronged you in the past? What did you do?

D Although the text is clear in verse 11:29 that the spirit of *Adonai* was on Jephthah before he went into battle, Jephthah feels compelled to make a vow in verse 11:30 to assure his victory.

◆ Jephthah felt he had to take the extra step. Would you have done the same? What else might you have done to assure victory?

◆ According to *Midrash Tanhuma*, God was angered by Jephthah's vow (and, in anger,

God determined that Jephthah would first see his only daughter upon his arrival home). Why was God angry? Do you think God's response was appropriate?

◆ How do you feel when you promise something to someone, but they don't believe you will follow through on your promise?

E Vows are taken extremely seriously in Jewish tradition. According to *midrash*, Jephthah's vow would have been valid if the first thing to come out of his house was an animal that would make an appropriate burnt offering to God. However, *Genesis Rabbah* 60:3 says the vow was invalidated as soon as Jephthah's daughter emerged from his house, since human sacrifices are unacceptable to God.

◆ Explain the argument in the *midrash*. (The *midrash's* logic indicates that a vow becomes void if circumstances change, making the fulfillment of the vow illegal.)

STRATEGIES
Analyzing the Text

1 Jephthah is a resident of a place called Gilead. We are also told his father's name is Gilead. Scholars disagree on the significance of this coincidence.

According to Telushkin (*Biblical Literacy*, p. 178), Jephthah is called a son of Gilead because any man in town could have been his father. In contrast, Plaut says Gilead is both the name of his ancestor and the region.

◆ Which explanation do you prefer, and why?

◆ How might you explain the symbolic significance of Jephthah's being literally a son of his city?

◆ Where were you born? Has your birthplace been, in any way, an influence on your life?

2 In verse 11:7 Jephthah asks the elders of Gilead, "How can you come to me now when you are in trouble?" Jephthah points out to the elders that if they truly repented for the wrong done him, they could have come at any earlier time and not waited until they needed his services.

◆ Help Jephthah make his decision whether or not to help the Gileadites. Hold a debate on the question, outlining reasons why he should or should not help them.

◆ Which argument is more convincing?

3 Words play an extremely important role in Jephthah's story.

◆ Review the first 11 verses of the Haftarah. How convincing are his words to the elders?

◆ Review Jephthah's negotiations with Ammon. Are his words equally convincing to you? to Ammon?

◆ Finally, consider Jephthah's vow in verses 11:30-31. Do you think the words of his vow are well chosen?

4 Jephthah's name means "he will open."

◆ What does his name signify to you?

The Rabbis ended the Haftarah in verse 11:33, but in verse 11:36 we find out why Jephthah bears his name. As he mourns the rashness of his vow and his daughter's impending death, Jephthah's doomed daughter says, "Father, you have uttered a vow to *Adonai*; do to me as you have vowed." However, this is not a literal translation; literally she says: "My father, you opened your mouth to *Adonai*, do to me according to that which has proceeded out of your mouth."

◆ Explain Jephthah's name.

◆ What is ironic about Jephthah's name?

◆ Jephthah's daughter has no name in the biblical text. *Midrash* ascribes to her the name Sheilah, "the one who is demanded." Do you think this name is appropriate? What other symbolic name might you suggest for her?

◆ Make an illustration of both Jephthah and Sheilah, showing the symbolic importance of their names.

5 See the discussion on Jephthah's rash vow in *Teaching Torah* by Sorel Goldberg Loeb and Barbara Binder Kadden, p. 281.

◆ Compare the story of Jephthah's daughter to I Samuel 14:24-45, in which Saul makes a rash vow. According to his vow, Saul's son Jonathan was to be put to death. But the people protested Saul's vow and saved Jonathan's life.

◆ Why, do you speculate, did no one intervene on Jephthah's daughter's behalf?

◆ If you could rewrite the story of Jephthah and his daughter, what changes would you make?

◆ Compare your rewrite with the medieval *midrash* (Radak and Abrabanel) that teaches that Jephthah did not sacrifice his daughter, but rather isolated and dedicated her to God's service.

6 For advanced study, compare the story of Jephthah's daughter to the binding of Isaac in Genesis 22. Some scholars suggest that the story of Jephthah's daughter is a *midrash* on Isaac's ordeal. From it, we learn that God was once willing to intervene in the world and, therefore, stop the sacrifice of Isaac in Genesis. By Jephthah's time, however, God no longer intervened in the world and could not, therefore, stop such a horrible act.

◆ What are the implications of this *midrash*, especially as it relates to evil in the world?

Connecting the Text To the Sedra

7 Verses 11:19-22 in the Haftarah repeat Numbers 21:21-25. They summarize the events that transpired between the Israelites and the Amorites, resulting in the conquest of the Amorite land by Israel.

◆ Are these two accounts identical, or can you identify any differences between them?

◆ In what context are they used in each case, and how are they connected?

8 David Marcus points out in *Jephthah's Vow* that typically the promise one makes in a vow is directly related to the condition requested. For example, in the Sedra (Numbers 21:2), Israel requests God's help in destroying their enemy. They promise, in return, to destroy utterly the enemy's city.

◆ Explain how what they asked for and what they promise in return are directly connected.

◆ In the Haftarah Jephthah forces the elders of Gilead to vow that if he helps them win the battle as their leader, he may remain their leader after the battle is over (see verse 11:9-10). Explain how the promise of this vow by the elders connects to the condition requested by the elders.

◆ However, in the Haftarah, Jephthah goes on to make his own vow in Judges 11:30-31. Explain how offering to sacrifice something that comes out of his house is not connected to his request to win the battle.

◆ What could Jephthah have promised that would be more directly related to victory in battle?

◆ Could the vow itself be a literary sign that his vow would backfire?

9 In the Sedra Miriam dies. The Haftarah leads to the death of Jephthah's daughter. Ellen Frankel tells the story of Jephthah's daughter in *The Five Books of Miriam*. She suggests (page 328) that the story of Jephthah and his daughter is the Haftarah for this Sedra in order to parallel the death of Miriam.

◆ Can you suggest connections between the lives and deaths of these two women?

◆ Write an obituary for Miriam and one for Jephthah's daughter (don't forget to name her!).

10 The Haftarah does not include the most controversial part of Jephthah's story, the sacrifice of his daughter. We can guess that the Rabbis excluded the saga from the Haftarah because it is so troubling and difficult. Alternatively, they may have simply wanted to end the Haftarah on a good note.

◆ Is it fair to omit texts that trouble us?

◆ The Rabbis didn't always choose to exclude troubling texts from the liturgy. See, for example, the Haftarah for *Bamidbar* or the Yom Kippur Minchah Torah reading. Can you suggest reasons to include problematic texts in our liturgy?

◆ Many congregations today read Leviticus 19 instead of Leviticus 18 on Yom Kippur afternoon. If a particular text is troubling for us today, should we change it or use an alternative?

Extending the Text

11 Throughout the Book of Judges, Israel repeatedly abandons God, but returns when threatened by enemies.

◆ Is Israel truly repenting?

◆ In his book *Rosh Hashanah Yom Kippur Survival Kit*, pp. 78-79, Shimon Apisdorf outlines the four steps to true repentance *(teshuvah)*:

a. Regret – feel a sense of loss for what you have done.

b. Abandonment – identify the excuse you have been making for your bad behavior and stop using it as an excuse.

c. Confession – say you're sorry.

d. Resolve – promise (and mean) it will never happen again.

Do you agree that all four steps are essential for true repentance?

12 In the story of Jephthah, the town elders do not object when Jephthah's brothers banish him from town. As we see in Insights from the Tradition #B, p. 30-31, Jephthah holds them responsible for their silence and inaction.

Regarding the culpability of bystanders, a story is told in *Gittin* 55b-56a. A certain man had a friend, Kamza, and an enemy, Bar Kamza. This man once gave a party and asked his servant to invite his friend Kamza. The servant mistakenly invited Bar Kamza.

When Bar Kamza arrived at the party, the host told him to leave.

However, Bar Kamza suggested that since he was already there, the host should let him stay and eat and Bar Kamza should pay for whatever he ate. The host refused.

Bar Kamza even offered to pay for half the cost of the party. Again, the host refused.

When Bar Kamza offered to pay for the whole party, the host threw him out of the house.

Bar Kamza decided that since learned Rabbis were at the party and they watched without stopping the host, he would go to the Roman government and tell them that the Rabbis and all the Jews were rebelling.

Bar Kamza's act of revenge led, according to the Talmud, to the destruction of Jerusalem and the exile of the Jews.

◆ Discuss the story.

◆ Was it fair for Bar Kamza to blame the bystander Rabbis?

◆ Was Bar Kamza right to exact revenge? such revenge?

◆ Compare the response of Bar Kamza to that of Jephthah.

13 Jephthah is able to give the Ammonites a detailed historical account of the possession of the land.

◆ Does a national leader need to know his/her country's history?

◆ Jephthah had other skills that made him a good leader, such as being able to communicate effectively. List other important leadership skills and assess whether or not Jephthah had them.

14 According to verse 11:20, Sichon did not trust Israel, and we can infer from 11:28 that the Ammonites did not trust the Israelites either. In both cases, lack of trust leads to war.

◆ What is required to build trust between nations or even individuals?

◆ Consider how the erosion of trust is a significant obstacle in the attempts at making peace between peoples who have been at war with one another for generations: the Israelis and the Arabs, Protestants and Catholics in Northern Ireland, the Hutus and Tutsis, the Serbs and the Croatians.

◆ Search for newspapers or online news articles on well-known conflicts and peace processes. Identify references to problematic history between the two sides and the resulting historical lack of trust that stands between them, and analyze the effects of these on present-day situations.

15 Some scholars say Jephthah sacrificed his daughter; others say he sent her to live in solitude, dedicated to God.

◆ Tell the story "The Court Jester's Last Wish" in the book *While Standing on One Foot* by Nina Jaffe and Steve Zeitlin. The story involves a court jester who gets into trouble one day by telling a joke that offends the head of the king's army. The commander demands the court jester be put to death, and the king, although he enjoys his court jester's humor, must consent to the commander's demand. The king, however, allows his court jester to choose his own manner of death. The court jester responds: old age.

◆ Discuss how this story similarly contains a death sentence which was not exactly carried out.

16 In verse 11:35 Jephthah sees his daughter come first out of the house. Understanding that he would have to sacrifice her according to his vow, he tears his clothes in mourning.

◆ Why do you think Jephthah rips his clothes?

The Talmud teaches us that any person present at the death of any other human being must tear his or her clothes, as a sign of sorrow. Today, the practice of tearing *(keriah)* is done only by those who are in mourning for the deceased (parent, child, sibling, spouse). Before tearing their garment, or cutting a necktie or black ribbon pinned to their clothing, mourners recite, "Blessed are You, *Adonai* our God, Sovereign of the universe, the true Judge" (*ArtScroll Siddur*, p. 796).

The tearing, which is usually performed at the funeral, is done on the left side (over the heart) when one is mourning the loss of a parent. For other relatives, the tearing is done on the right side. (See *A Guide To Jewish Religious Practice* by Isaac Klein, pp. 278-279.)

◆ What emotions are we helping to express by this mournful act and what message are we giving others by wearing torn clothing?

◆ Why might a mourner wish to be identified by others as someone who has recently lost a loved one?

◆ Does the tearing of his clothes affect your opinion about whether or not Jephthah actually sacrifices his daughter?

17 In the Haftarah Jephthah made a vow that was painful to keep. Often in life we may find we have made vows we cannot keep. We begin our observance of Yom Kippur, the Day of Atonement, with the *"Kol Nidre"* prayer, which nullifies our vows from the previous year. The text is translated in *The New Maḥzor* as follows:

"All vows, oaths and promises which we made to God from last Yom Kippur to this Yom Kippur and were not able to fulfill — may all such vows between ourselves and God be annulled. May they be void and of no effect. May we be absolved of them and released from them. May these vows not be considered vows, these oaths not considered oaths, and these promises not be considered promises."

♦ Explain the *"Kol Nidre"* prayer in your own words.

♦ Some Rabbis opposed introducing the *"Kol Nidre"* prayer because they were concerned about teaching the public that vows can be annulled. Why do you think this concerned the Rabbis?

♦ Do you think people are less likely to take vows seriously if they know that vows can be nullified?

In addition, there was a concern that the vows a person made to another person would not be kept. The Rabbis taught, however, that Yom Kippur atoned only for sins committed by a person against God, not against another person. As it says in Mishnah *Yoma* 8:9:

"For transgressions between a human being and God, repentance on Yom Kippur brings atonement. For transgressions between one human being and another, Yom Kippur brings no atonement until the injured party is reconciled."

♦ The *"Kol Nidre"* prayer did not develop until more than 1500 years after the setting of Jephthah's story. Ignore this fact and consider this: if Jephthah had not kept his vow to sacrifice the first thing to come out of his door, do you think *"Kol Nidre"* would have helped Jephthah?

Personalizing the Text

18 Jephthah has trouble getting along with his stepbrothers.

♦ Draw a comic strip illustrating a conflict between you and your sibling(s). Be sure to include a resolution in the last frame.

19 If Jephthah had consulted with the High Priest of his time, the religious authority would have explained the illegality of Jephthah's vow and prevented the sacrifice of his daughter. However, *Genesis Rabbah* 60:3 says that Jephthah was too proud to go to the High Priest and ask for help to find a way out of this predicament.

♦ Consider the strengths and weaknesses of pride.

♦ Why is it sometimes so difficult to admit we don't know the answer and to ask for help?

♦ Interview your family for stories about times when they let their pride stop them from asking for help.

20 Jephthah tries to achieve peace through diplomacy with Israel's enemy.

♦ Learn and sing the song *"Shalom al Yisrael"* (Peace for Israel), which expresses Israel's ageless desire for peace with its neighbors. (See the songbook *B'kol Echad*, edited by Jeffrey Shiovitz, p. 109, and the accompanying audiocassettes, *Shirei B'Kol Echad*, both of which may be ordered from the web site of United Synagogue for Conservative Judaism, www.uscj.org/booksvc.)

21 Trust is considered an essential element of a successful relationship.

♦ Why is this so?

♦ If someone breaks your trust (see Extending the Text #14, p. 34-35), what does it take for you to regain that trust?

♦ Imagine that you are an advice columnist and someone has written a letter asking how he/she can learn to trust someone who has betrayed him or her. Write your response.

22 Jephthah's vow was spoken rashly and led to great regret.

♦ Design signs reminding people to speak carefully and recognize the power of words to do both good and harm. Hang the signs in various locations (classroom, lunchroom, your family dining room, synagogue social hall) where people might need such a reminder.

23 According to Rabbinic tradition, Jephthah intended that his vow would involve a special sacrifice, despite the prohibition against human sacrifice. These *midrashim* argue that because Jephthah was making a vow to save his people from destruction, he felt he had to offer something very special (see *The Legends of the Jews* by Louis Ginzberg, vol. 4, pp. 43-44).

♦ If you and your family were in danger, what special thing would you vow to give up in exchange for safety?

24 The Supreme Court is the highest court in the United States and in Canada.

♦ Form three groups. One group writes and presents an appeal to the Supreme Court asking it to nullify Jephthah's vow, providing precedent from Torah. For more information, see arguments presented in *The Haftarot* by Hirsch, pp. 341-344, and in the book *Biblical Literacy* by Joseph Telushkin, pp. 176-178. A second group argues to uphold Jephthah's vow and human sacrifice, also providing proof from the Torah. For references, see Genesis 22, II Kings 16:3, and Ezekiel 20:25-26. A third group prepares questions to ask as they sit as Supreme Court Justices. (You might ask your Rabbi or Cantor for black robes for the judges to wear.)

25 Jephthah's daughter received a two-month reprieve before her death.

♦ Write journal entries from Jephthah's daughter's diary during these two months of reprieve.

♦ Alternatively, write journal entries for Jephthah immediately after the battle and then later when he arrives at home and sees his daughter come out of the door first.

Other Resources

26 For a good exercise on the power of words, complete the Torah Aura Instant Lesson *Wounding with Words* by Steven Bayar.

27 For a story relating the importance and power of words, read "Feathers," as told by Heather Forest in the book *Chosen Tales*, edited by Penninah Schram, pp. 93-96.

28 There are many parallel stories in other traditions to Jephthah's daughter. Read some of them in *Myth, Legend and Custom in the Old Testament* by Theodor Gaster, pp. 430-432.

29 Adults might consider viewing the film *The End of the Affair* (1999, rated R, 109 minutes). Compare the vow made by the woman in the film to the vow made by Jephthah. Did her vow work? Should she have kept the promise she offered in her vow?

30 See the Old English Ballad, "Jephthah, Judge of Israel," quoted in *The Haftarah Commentary* by W. Gunther Plaut, p. 384, and referred to by Shakespeare in Hamlet, Act II, Scene 2, lines 440ff., "One fair daughter." What did Shakespeare mean by citing this ballad and the reference to Jephthah?

31 Read the short story "Sunbeams" by Dvora Baron found in *The Oxford Book of Hebrew Short Stories*, edited by Glenda Abramson. Consider the similarities and differences between the story's main character Haya-Fruma and Jephthah. Would Haya-Fruma ever use words carelessly? Would her cow ever be sacrificed?

32 Read, act out, and discuss the skit about Jephthah and his daughter found in *Bible Scenes: Joshua To Solomon* by Stan J. Beiner, p. 56.

33 Discuss the illustrations of this Haftarah in *The Illustrated Torah* by Michal Meron, p. 166.

34 See the book *Texts of Terror* by Phyllis Trible. In her analysis is a poetic lament of Jephthah's daughter written by Trible in biblical style (pp. 108-109). Write your own such lament.

35 See *Encyclopaedia Judaica*, vol. 9, pp. 1343-1345, for a listing of art and musical works inspired by the story of Jephthah and his daughter. Find one of these works and look at it/listen to it.

36 Read selections from *Words That Hurt, Words That Heal* by Joseph Telushkin.

37 See the discussion on vows in *Parashat Matot* in *Teaching Torah* by Sorel Goldberg Loeb and Barbara Binder Kadden, p. 278.

Involving the Family

38 Remember the power of words! Family members may criticize one another more than they compliment one another. At Shabbat dinner, or whenever your family eats a meal together, go around the table and have each family member say one positive thing about everyone else.

Bar/Bat Mitzvah Project

39 Jephthah was the kid everyone hated and ostracized. Every school has kids just like Jephthah; no one will talk to them. Make a point this year at school of talking to good kids everyone else avoids.

JUDGES 13:2-25
NASO נשא

This Haftarah has been paired with *Parashat Naso*, Numbers 4:21-7:89. See "Connecting the Text To the Sedra," pp. 41-43, for an exploration of the many ways the two texts shed light on each other.

SYNOPSIS

Samson, perhaps the most famous of the judges, is literally given to Israel by God. His barren mother is met by an angel of God, who informs her that she will have a son. He admonishes her to refrain from drinking wine or strong drink and from eating unclean food, for the son she will bear will be a Nazirite dedicated to God's service. The angel adds that the child's hair must never be cut.

The excited woman tells her husband Manoah of the strange messenger and his wonderful message, though neither of them recognizes that he is an angel. In response, Manoah prays to God to send the messenger again to teach them what they must do with their special expected child. The angel does return, although once again to the woman alone. She hurries to get her husband, who returns to meet the man. The angel repeats his message and advice for both husband and wife, but refuses to share either his name or a meal with the grateful couple.

Manoah sacrifices a burnt offering to God, as requested by the angel, and as the flames rise up to heaven, the angel ascends with them. Frightened, Manoah is convinced that he and his wife will die because they have seen God. His wife calmly reassures him that God would not send an angel to promise them a son if God

planned to kill them anyway. In time, the woman bears a son and calls him Samson. He grows and is blessed by *Adonai*.

INSIGHTS FROM THE TRADITION

A In verse 13:7 Samson's mother tells Manoah what the angel instructed her about their future child. However, she omitted some of the details. Alshich suggests that Samson's mother left out the rest of the information so as not to make Manoah feel bad that she was worthy to receive the exciting news, but he was not.

◆ Is it acceptable, in your opinion, to tell half-truths or leave out some information to avoid hurting someone's feelings? Can you think of a situation when you did this (or should have)?

B In verse 13:7 the angel dictates to Samson's mother laws prohibiting her child from ingesting alcohol and certain foods, even in the womb. According to *Numbers Rabbah* 10:5, these restrictions were designed to curb Samson's desires, thus helping him to control his behavior.

◆ Parents often set limits on their children in order to teach them self-control. Can you think of an example of these kinds of limits? Do you think such limits are effective? Based on the entire Samson story, would you consider him a man of restraint or curbed desires?

C *Metsudat David* explains that Manoah was unaware that the messenger was an angel because he offered him food (verse 13:15). Others say his offer of food was a test to see whether or not the messenger was an angel. In verse 13:17 Manoah asks the angel his name, again either evidence of the man's ignorance or a second test.

◆ If a stranger approached you with incredible news about your future, would you believe him/her?

◆ How would you test the stranger to see whether he/she was credible?

D Talmud *Bava Bathra* 91a tells the story of the judge Ibzan (Judges 12:8-9), who had not invited Manoah and his wife to any of the feasts in honor of the marriages of his 60 children. Short-sightedly, he assumed that the childless couple would never be in a position to repay his invitation. Of course, Manoah and his wife were eventually blessed with an extraordinary son, while the *midrash* tells us that Ibzan's 60 children all died during his lifetime.

◆ What lesson can we derive from Ibzan's behavior?

◆ Can you think of a time you were short-sighted and came to regret it?

◆ Is there a rule in your school about inviting everyone in the class to a Bar/Bat Mitzvah party? Do you agree with this kind of rule?

STRATEGIES
Analyzing the Text

1 Samson's father's name is Manoah, which means "rest." According to Plaut, his name foreshadows the period of rest which will be granted to Israel after Samson defeats the Philistines. According to *Numbers Rabbah* 10:5, Manoah was so named because he was the recipient of Divine prophecy, which is sometimes called *menuchah.* He concludes that Manoah was worthy of receiving Divine prophecy.

◆ Which explanation do you like better, and why?

◆ Which is better grounded in the text?

◆ Can you suggest another explanation for the name, based on the Haftarah?

2 Hirsch notes that Samson, truly a larger than life hero, hails from a modest family from the small tribe of Dan.

◆ Many Israelite leaders came from humble beginnings, including Moses, King Saul, King David, Joseph (who at one time was a house servant), Ruth, and Amos. Create a crossword puzzle with clues about these famous leaders. Use the *Encyclopaedia Judaica* to find out more about these figures and to discover additional facts to include in the puzzle.

3 Rabbinic tradition gives Samson's mother the name Tzlelponi (*Numbers Rabbah* 10:5), meaning "she saw the angel's face clearly."

◆ Explain why Samson's mother was given this name. Suggest other names you think might be appropriate for her.

◆ Biblical women are often unnamed. Can you think of other important women in Torah who have no names? Why do you think they are nameless?

◆ The fact that so many biblical women are nameless is often considered a sign that women were not considered important. For a discussion of nameless women in the Book of Judges, see *A Feminist Companion To Judges*, edited by Athalya Brenner, pp. 10-14.

4 The angel appears to the woman, who relays the information to her husband. The husband requests that the angel appear again, this time to him. Yet when the angel does reappear, it is once again to the woman, who must run to get Manoah. One would expect that the summoned angel would appear before the person who had summoned him.

Why didn't the angel appear the second time before Manoah? Many explanations have been suggested, such as: by visiting only her, the angel honored Samson's mother; by refusing to visit Manoah, the angel made fun of him.

◆ Which explanation do you prefer? Can you suggest other reasons?

5 In verse 13:18 the angel refuses to divulge his name to Manoah, saying "it is unknowable." However, a similar expression used in 13:19 is, מפלא לעשות (mafli la'asot), translated literally as "does wondrously."

◆ Consider the meaning of this phrase as a name for the angel who announces Samson's future birth, given that Samson's mother had previously had no children, and Israel was downtrodden by the Philistines.

6 According to Abrabanel, Samson's name, שמשון (Shimshon) may mean that he devoted his life to being a servant, שמש (shamash) of God.

Yalkut Me'am Lo'ez suggests he was named after the sun שמש (shemesh) because he was radiant and powerful.

Plaut tells us he was named for the sun because a heavenly being announced his birth.

Modern biblical scholar Edward Greenstein suggests that Samson's name is related to the word שם (name), as if the author wants to leave Samson as an unnamed entity.

According to *The Legends of the Jews* by Louis Ginzberg, vol. 6, p. 205, Samson's name is related to שמן (shemen) — oil, which indicates that he was God's anointed leader.

◆ Which explanation for Samson's name do you prefer, and why?

◆ If Samson is a symbol for all of Israel, which explanation of his name works best?

◆ Make business cards for Samson, including a logo that incorporates your favorite explanation for his name.

Connecting the Text To the Sedra

7 The Sedra contains the laws of the Nazirite (Numbers 6) and, in the Haftarah, Samson was a Nazirite from birth.

◆ Compare the laws of the Nazirite in the Sedra to the explanation of Samson's status as a Nazirite as explained by the angel to his mother.

◆ List three things in the Sedra that a Nazirite is not allowed to do. A Nazirite gives up these things for a limited time period as a symbol of his dedication to God.

◆ In your Bar/Bat Mitzvah year, what might you give up in order to be more dedicated to your studies?

8 In the Sedra when a person makes a special vow to be a Nazirite, an unusual word for making the vow is used in Numbers 6:2: יפלא (yafli). This word, when used with the making of a vow, indicates that the vow is special, extraordinary, or difficult. This is the same word used in the Haftarah when the angel says his name is פלאי — wondrous (see Analyzing the Text #5, above).

◆ Why do you think a Nazirite's vow is considered special, hard, or wondrous?

◆ Why do you think the angel is named special, extraordinary, difficult, or wondrous?

◆ List modern day deeds that you consider to be holy acts serving God. In what way are the people who do those deeds doing something special, extraordinary, or difficult?

9 In the Sedra a census is taken of Levitical families who were required, based on their birth into this tribe, to serve God under the direction of the priest (Numbers 4:21-49).

In the Haftarah Samson was chosen to serve God as a Nazirite from before he was born.

◆ Explain how in both texts, the Levites and Samson were born into their roles (professions) in life.

◆ We tend to take it for granted in the modern era that people are free to chose their professions and life paths. What do you think it must have been like for those who were not free to chose?

◆ Write a diary entry for either Samson or a Levite about the positive and negative aspects of being born into a certain role.

10 The Sedra (Numbers 5:11-31) contains the troubling account of the bitter waters ordeal that a jealous man can order his wife to go through. The ordeal is particularly unjust because if a woman is found to be innocent of infidelity, her husband who had accused her is not held accountable for his accusation; he is forgiven. (See the discussion of this ordeal in *Lifecycles* by Debra Orenstein and Jane Litman, vol. 2, p. 384.)

◆ Do you think the Haftarah comments in any way on this aspect of the Sedra? If so, how? (For example, according to ancient *midrash*, told by Josephus, Manoah was jealous because his wife had a male visitor. This is why he insisted the visitor appear to him, and even after he met the angel face-to-face, he was still jealous.)

◆ Manoah seems to be portrayed in the Haftarah as someone who does not understand anything that is going on. Could the Rabbis have chosen this Haftarah in order to say that jealous husbands are confused and do not understand anything?

◆ Jealousy is a powerful, often destructive emotion. Interview family members for stories about when they were jealous or were affected by someone else's jealousy.

11 In the Sedra (Numbers 6:22-27), Aaron and his sons bless the children of Israel with the priestly blessing:

May *Adonai* bless you and protect you.
May *Adonai* deal kindly and graciously with you.
May *Adonai* bestow favor upon you and grant you peace.

◆ Traditionally, this blessing is recited by parents over their children on Friday nights and for a Bar/Bat Mitzvah on the *bimah*. Paraphrase Aaron's wishes for the children of Israel. In what ways is this blessing wishing for appropriate things for a Bar/Bat Mitzvah celebrant?

◆ Similarly, Samson was blessed, according to the last verse of the Haftarah. Explain in what ways you think that Samson was blessed.

◆ How have you been blessed?

12 Recently, a women's group has begun selecting alternative Haftarot. They consider some of the issues in a Sedra, then find another text that addresses these issues which the traditional Haftarah ignores.

◆ For more information, see the article by Lori Lefkovitz in *Kerem: Creative Explorations in Judaism*, vol. 5, 1997, pp. 101-105.

◆ Could you suggest another text, biblical or non-biblical, which might be a suitable alternative Haftarah for this Sedra, and which would address the unfairness of the accused innocent woman in the Sedra? (See Ellen

Frankel's discussion of the accused adulteress in *The Five Books of Miriam*, pp. 200-205, or "A Woman of Valor, Who Can Find?" by Renee Alfandary in *Sarah's Daughters Sing*, edited by Henny Wenkart, pp. 126-127.)

Extending the Text

13 Samson's parents had been childless. The text does not tell us what this meant to them, but we know from other biblical texts that children were highly desired. In biblical times, an infertile couple needed a divine miracle to have a baby. Infertile couples today have other options, including (but not limited to) fertility drugs, in vitro fertilization, surrogate mothers, and adoption.

◆ Choose one of these options and research Judaism's views on it. Possible resources include: *Encyclopaedia Judaica*, vol. 2, pp. 298-302, or the web site of the Conservative movement: www.uscj.org/publicaffairs/review/egg/htm.

14 In the Haftarah Samson's mother is warned not to drink alcohol while she is pregnant because Samson will be a Nazirite. Today, there are warning labels on cigarette packages for pregnant women, and in bars there are warning signs reminding pregnant patrons that alcohol poses a danger to the unborn.

◆ Debate the appropriateness of such warnings. Those on the pro-warning side should present why the signs should be printed and posted. They should explore the issues involved in posting warning signs to diabetics in bakeries and candy stores or in other places for other people with dietary restrictions.

15 Samson's mother was told by an angel that she would have a son who would be a Nazirite (see the Synopsis, p. 39).

◆ Read about the Bible's other famous Nazirite, Samuel, in I Samuel 1:1-28, and compare his birth and life to that of Samson (see the Haftarah for the First Day of Rosh HaShanah, p. 48).

16 Compare Analyzing the Text #5, p. 41, with the following blessing from the morning prayers. In this blessing, we thank God for making our organs function properly. The blessing ends: "Blessed are you, *Adonai*, Who gives health to all flesh and does wondrously (מפלא לעשות)."

◆ Explain what you think the blessing means. (Rabbi Moses Isserles wrote an explanation for this blessing, saying that it seems that 'who does wondrously' refers to the soul which God put in people. It is not possible for a person's soul to function intelligently when the person is ill or in physical pain because the physical discomfort distracts him/her from performing properly.)

17 Samson's mother spared Manoah's feelings by omitting some of the angel's information (see Insights from the Tradition #A, p. 39). The Rabbis use this story to teach the principles of *sh'lom bayit* (maintaining peace in the home by avoiding the creation of bad feelings between spouses and other family members). Similarly, there is the following Talmudic story of Rabbi Meir promoting *sh'lom bayit* (*Deuteronomy Rabbah* 5:15, also found in *Voices of Wisdom*, by Francine Klagsbrun, p. 154).

Rabbi Meir taught adult education classes. A woman who enjoyed his lectures attended regularly. One evening, when she went home, she was greeted by her angry, jealous husband who wanted to know where she had been. When she responded that she had been at the Rabbi's lecture, her husband vowed that she would not be allowed back in their home until she had spat in the Rabbi's eye. The upset woman went to stay with a neighbor. Eventually Rabbi Meir heard about the incident and sent for the woman. He pretended to have a painful illness in his eyes and asked her to help cure the illness. She agreed, and he instructed her that the cure was for her to spit in his eyes seven times. The woman was confused, but followed the Rabbi's instructions. The Rabbi then told her to go home and tell her husband that he might have wanted her to spit in his eye once, but she did it seven times! When the Rabbi's students heard of this, they were outraged at the humiliation caused to their teacher. Rabbi Meir responded that no act is disgraceful if it promotes peace and happiness between husband and wife.

◆ How did Rabbi Meir help restore peace between husband and wife?

◆ Was the husband right or wrong for being jealous? Did it matter to Rabbi Meir? What was most important to Rabbi Meir? In the story of the Haftarah, when Manoah demanded that the angel return to see him, what would Rabbi Meir have told the angel to do, and why?

◆ For more on *sh'lom bayit*, see *Jewish Literacy* by Joseph Telushkin, p. 538.

18 We read in verse 13:10 that the woman "ran in haste" to bring her husband back to the messenger. From this, *Numbers Rabbah* 10:5 teaches us that the righteous always hurry enthusiastically to perform appointed tasks and *mitzvot*. It is customary, then, to perform *mitzvot* as soon as one is able. For example, *Brit Milah* ceremonies are traditionally held early in the morning of the eighth day.

◆ Prepare a public service announcement or poster reminding people to rush to do their *mitzvot*.

19 Delilah is generally considered the villainess of the Samson story.

◆ Read the Samson and Delilah story in chapter 16 to learn her role in his life. Then discuss feminist commentaries that may see it somewhat differently. Discuss the commentary in *Listen To Her Voice: Women of the Hebrew Bible* by Miki Raver, pp 103-105.

◆ Write your own analysis of blame and responsibility.

20 Samson ends his life with the ultimate sacrifice of martyrdom for the Israelites.

◆ Read the story of Samson's final act in Judges 16:25-30.

◆ What do you think of martyrs and martyrdom?

◆ Read and discuss Hannah Senesh's poem, "Blessed Is the Match." You can access it, along with a brief biography, at http://holocaust.hklaw.com/essays/1996/962.htm.

◆ Read and discuss *Blessed Is the Match* by Marie Syrkin, a biography of Hannah Senesh. While this Jewish Publication Society book is out of print, it is available in many libraries and resource centers and can be obtained secondhand through www.amazon.com.

21 This Haftarah only tells the story of Samson's birth. Read the Haftarah again and write your first impressions about Samson based solely on the Haftarah.

◆ For advanced study: Read the rest of the story of Samson (Judges 14-16). Then write a character profile describing Samson. How does this characterization of Samson compare to your first impressions?

Personalizing the Text

22 There are humorous aspects to the appearance of the angel in the Haftarah text.

◆ Write a comical skit or story about the angel reporting back to God and the other angels about his encounter with Samson's parents.

◆ For another comical story of a magical creature meeting humans, see "Djinni in the Bottle" by Lenny Bruce in *Because God Loves Stories*, edited by Steve Zeitlin, p. 37.

23 Samson's mother is unnamed (see Analyzing the Text #3, p. 40). It is a custom to have a tomb to remember the unknown soldiers who died in a war.

◆ Make a plaque to honor the unnamed women of the Bible.

24 As we learned in Analyzing the Text #3, p. 40, names are important. Learning people's names when you meet them is a vital skill; when you remember a person's name, it indicates that the person is important.

◆ Practice learning names by repeating the name when you are introduced to someone.

◆ Play a name game with your class, using middle names instead of already familiar first names. Sit in a circle. Go around the circle with each person saying his/her middle name and something he/she likes that starts with the same letter as the middle name. The next person then must repeat the name and favorite item of everyone who came before, then add his/her own name and favorite item to the list.

25 Samson's mother, having wanted a child so intensely, may very well have spoiled Samson when he was small.

◆ Imagine that Samson's mother made him a beautiful baby quilt. Design such a quilt for the baby Samson. Alternatively, design a baby book and write prenatal and newborn entries for Samson. Remember his superhuman strength.

26 Samson's father panicked and concluded that they would die because they encountered an angel of God. Samson's mother stayed calm by pointing out that his fear was illogical.

◆ What types of situations make you panic? What do you do to stay calm (for example, making plans, taking one day at a time, asking for help, reviewing the situation rationally, etc.)?

27 Samson's mother did not completely relate to her husband what the angel told her about their soon-to-be-born son. It is difficult to remember detailed information and accurately transmit it.

◆ Play a game (such as *Telephone*) that demonstrates how hard it is to hear and repeat detailed information.

Other Resources

28 See Samson-related activities in *Teaching Torah* by Sorel Goldberg Loeb and Barbara Binder Kadden, pp. 238-239.

29 Read, act out, and discuss the skits in *Bible Scenes: Joshua To Solomon* by Stan J. Beiner, pp. 60-68. These skits involve information from the rest of Samson's life as well as the introductory information in this Haftarah.

30 Discuss the illustration of this Haftarah in *The Illustrated Torah* by Michal Meron, p. 150.

31 Samson has been compared to Hercules of ancient Greek mythology. Hercules's birth was under special circumstances, too. Read about Hercules and compare the events surrounding his birth and his feats (see www.perseus. tufts.edu/Hercules) to those of Samson's. Two books about Hercules are: *The Twelve Labors of*

Hercules by James Riordan (Grades 4-6) and *Hercules: The Mythic Journey Retold* by Bob Svihovec (Young Adult). There is also a full-length Disney cartoon with music called *Hercules* (1997, rated G, 92 minutes).

32 See films involving angels, such as *It's a Wonderful Life* (1946, not rated, 90 minutes) and *Angels in the Outfield* (1994, rated PG, 102 minutes).

33 Although they are not often discussed, angels play a significant role in Jewish tradition. For example, angels are mentioned at least twice a day, every time we say the *"Kedushah"* in the *"Amidah."* Read more about angels in the Bible in the *Encyclopaedia Judaica* article "Angels," and about angels in Jewish tradition in *The Jewish Bible Almanac* by Ronald H. Isaacs, pp. 9-12.

34 For a story dedicated to nameless biblical women, read "Noah's Wife" by Judith Black in *Chosen Tales*, edited by Peninnah Schram.

35 Read "Nettie Blumenthal," a short story about angels, as told by Gerald Fierst in *Chosen Tales*, edited by Peninnah Schram, pp. 89-92.

36 Read "The Warning" by Henry Wadsworth Longfellow in *Poems of Slavery*, which compares the slave in America to the blind and bound Samson (an excerpt is in *The Haftarah Commentary* by W. Gunther Plaut).

37 Listen to the Debbie Friedman song, *"Mi Kamocha"* on the cassette *And the Youth Shall See Visions*. In this daily prayer, God is described, like the angel, as one who does wondrous things.

38 Concerning marriages troubled by fertility problems, see "The Most Precious Thing" in *While Standing on One Foot* by Nina Jaffe and Steve Zeitlin.

39 Rembrandt painted Manoah's Sacrifice (see *Rembrandt and the Jews and the Bible* by F. Landsberger, p. 156, item #58). He also painted "The Blinding of Samson," which depicts events at the end of Samson's life. It is available on-line at: www.artchive.com. Also look at this same web site for Michelangelo's bronze statue of Samson and two Philistines and a 1912 painting of Samson by Corinth. Study Samson's story and these artistic interpretations, then paint or draw your own interpretation.

40 Complete page 5 in *Prophets Copy Pak*™ by Marji Gold-Vukson.

Involving the Family

41 Review the topic of *sh'lom bayit* in Extending the Text #17, pp. 43-44. Consider three things your family can do to improve and maintain peace in your household (e.g., don't raise your voice, don't borrow something from someone without permission). List the three items on a poster where everyone will be reminded regularly.

Bar/Bat Mitzvah Project

42 Donate a percentage of your Bar/Bat Mitzvah gifts to the March of Dimes or other charity involved in promoting prenatal health.

שמואל א

I Samuel

OVERVIEW

Originally one unified book, the two books of Samuel were first divided in the Greek translation of the Bible called the *Septuagint* because the book was too long to fit on the standard sized scroll. The Hebrew versions began to follow the convention of the *Septuagint* in the sixteenth century, and the Book of Samuel has remained divided ever since.

The First Book of Samuel begins with the story of the birth of the prophet for whom the book is named. Grateful for the gift of a child, Samuel's mother, Hannah, dedicates her son to the service of God. The young Samuel serves Eli the Priest and is chosen by God to be a prophet over Israel.

Samuel ascends to power in an age when Israel is engaged in constant wars against enemy nations. Samuel pleads with the Israelites to remain loyal to God, and when they are, the Israelites defeat their enemies under Samuel's leadership. Nonetheless, the Israelites clamor for a king so as to be like the other nations. Samuel warns them not to reject God as their only king, but Israel persists, and God ultimately grants their request. Saul, a tall, handsome man from the tribe of Benjamin, is chosen by God and anointed by Samuel as king of Israel.

Saul proves himself to be a good king and leads Israel in victorious battles against the Ammonites and Amalekites. However, when Saul disregards God's instructions regarding the conquest of the Amalekites, Samuel informs Saul that God has rejected him and will choose another to reign in his place. A disheartened Saul continues to lead Israel in battle, but is increasingly troubled by emotional distress.

Samuel follows God's commandment and anoints David to be the next king of Israel after Saul. A gifted musician, David is called upon to play the harp so as to soothe the agitated King Saul. David also volunteers to fight the Philistine giant, Goliath, whom he kills with ease. David goes on to join Saul's army, where he wins great favor in Israel for his bravery.

Saul becomes consumed with jealousy toward David, and spends more and more of his time pursuing David to kill him. Saved by Saul's son, Jonathan, David goes into hiding, where he builds his strength and reputation as a valiant warrior, staying clear of Saul's murderous designs.

The book concludes with the tragic deaths of Saul and Jonathan at the hands of the Philistines.

I Samuel, from which four Haftarot are taken, is an historical account of the coming of age of the Israelite nation, in the years just before 1000 B.C.E. The earthly leadership role is passed from God's prophets to the kings of Israel, both of whom remain ultimately accountable to God.

I SAMUEL 1:1-2:10
FIRST DAY ROSH HASHANAH

 This Haftarah has been paired with the first day of Rosh HaShanah on which we read Genesis 21. See "Connecting the Text To the Holiday," pp. 50-52, for an exploration of the many ways the two texts shed light on each other.

SYNOPSIS

This Haftarah introduces us to the namesake of the Books of Samuel. The last of the prophet-judges, Samuel ushers the 12 tribes of Israel into an era of united monarchy. This is the story of his miraculous birth.

Elkanah, from the tribe of Ephraim, has two wives. Peninnah has children, but Hannah, his favorite wife, has none. Every year, Elkanah would go up to worship and sacrifice to God at Shiloh. And every year, Peninnah would tease Hannah because she had no children.

One year at Shiloh, Hannah fervently prays to God, vowing that if she had a son, she would dedicate him to God for his entire life. He would be a Nazirite, dedicated to God from birth, forbidden to drink wine or to shave.

The priest Eli watches Hannah praying, and scolds her because he thinks she is merely a drunken woman talking to herself. When Hannah explains her silent prayer to Eli, the priest wishes that God will grant her request. Sure enough, Hannah conceives and gives birth to a son, whom she names Samuel, which means, "I asked him of God (and was heard)."

During Samuel's early childhood, Hannah and her son stay home while the rest of the family goes on the annual trip to Shiloh. But when Samuel is weaned, Hannah brings him, along with a bull, some meal, and wine, directly to Eli the priest. She identifies herself as the woman who prayed in fervent silence for a son and turns Samuel over to Eli and God's service, according to her vow.

The last ten verses of the Haftarah comprise Hannah's prayer of thanksgiving to God, praising God for feeding the hungry, raising up the poor, and enabling childless women to have offspring.

INSIGHTS FROM THE TRADITION

A We learn in verse 1:3 that Elkanah goes every year to offer a sacrifice at Shiloh. Rashi explains the *midrashic* tradition that every year Elkanah followed a different route from his home to Shiloh. This way, Elkanah made sure that each year a new set of people would see him and would learn from his example to do likewise.

◆ How would you act if you thought everything you did was being watched by someone else?

◆ Ask your parent(s) if they changed their behavior in any way once they became parents and, if so, why?

B Verse 1:5 says that Elkanah gave Hannah one portion. The Hebrew for "one portion" אַפָּיִם (*apa'yim*) is difficult to translate and, according to *midrash*, seems related to the word "face." From this, Rashi explains that Elkanah gave Hannah an excellent portion that was fit to be accepted with a friendly face.

◆ We are all taught as children to accept gifts with grace and gratitude, whether we like the gift or not. Why is this a valuable lesson? What does it help children to understand?

◆ We can take this childhood lesson a step further by learning to accept all that life gives us with grace — even the bad things that come our way. Why is this an important lesson?

◆ How do you go about accepting life's lumps graciously?

C In verse 1:13 Hannah is praying, speaking in her heart. No words are heard coming from her, but her lips are moving. Although she is at first misunderstood by Eli, Hannah has become a role model for how we are supposed to pray. Radak says she gave deep thought to her prayer. From Hannah we learn that we are supposed to pray without a sound, but moving our lips with great attention to the words.

◆ Why do you think we should move our lips when we recite our prayers?

◆ What else might we do to increase our concentration during prayer?

D *Berachot* 31a-b teaches that when Eli chastised Hannah for drinking excessively in verse 1:14, he was serving as a role model for us. Eli taught us that if we see someone engaging in unfitting behavior, we are obligated to reprimand that person.

◆ Do you agree with the lesson taught by Eli?

◆ Debate: If one sees someone doing wrong and does nothing about it, one shares the blame if the person repeats the wrongdoing.

E Rashi teaches concerning verse 2:2 that there is no painter or artist like God. A human being can paint a picture or sculpt a statue, but it is just art. Only God can create a creature that lives and breathes. (Note: Rashi's interpretation is based on the fact that the words for "rock" and "artist" are the same in Hebrew.)

◆ Use disposable cameras to take pictures of God's artwork. Since you are only human, do your pictures adequately capture the beauty of God's creation?

STRATEGIES
Analyzing the Text

1 Shiloh is where Joshua set up the Tabernacle (Joshua 18:1). During the period of the judges, Shiloh was Israel's central sanctuary.

◆ See the tribal map on p. 624 in Appendix C to find out where the hill country of Ephraim is.

2 Elkanah had two wives, Peninnah and Hannah. Polygamy was permitted by Jewish law until a tenth century ruling by Rabbi Gershom of Germany made it illegal and immoral. In fact, polygamy had not been widely practiced among Jews for about 1,000 years before Rabbi Gershom's time.

◆ Why do you think polygamy is wrong?

◆ Can you think of any reason polygamy might have been permitted in the ancient world? (Hint: remember the emphasis on becoming a numerous nation.)

3 This Haftarah is filled with symbolic and meaningful names: Hannah means "grace," Peninnah means "pearl," Samuel means "I asked him of God (and was heard)," Eli means "My God," and Elkanah might mean "jealous God."

◆ Explain how each of these meanings might fit the characters in the story.

◆ Find out the meaning of your Hebrew name. Does its meaning fit you? Explain.

4 In verses 1:6 and 7, Peninnah tormented Hannah.

◆ About what did Peninnah torment Hannah?

◆ How did Hannah react?

5 In verse 1:8 Elkanah tried to comfort Hannah and make her feel better.

◆ What did he say to reassure her? Did it work?

◆ Do you think Elkanah was sensitive to Hannah's problems and feelings?

6 In verse 1:11 Hannah calls God, "*Adonai* of Hosts." This is the first time this name for God appears in the Bible, and it has made its way into many of our prayers. The meaning of the name "*Adonai* of Hosts" is unclear, but two possible explanations are: "God of the Armies of Israel" and "God of the Hosts of the Heavens" (angels, stars).

◆ Which meaning do you prefer, and why?

◆ Do you have another explanation?

7 Samuel was to be a Nazirite dedicated to God's service. Read about the Bible's other famous Nazirite, Samson, in the Haftarah for *Naso*, p. 39. Read the biblical laws concerning the Nazirite in Numbers 6. For more discussion and activities concerning Nazirites, see the Haftarah for *Naso*, Connecting the Text To the Sedra #7, p. 41; and Extending the Text #14 and #15, p. 43.

8 Reread Hannah's song of thanksgiving in verses 2:1-10. She repeatedly talks about how God can reverse fortunes, like her own.

◆ Identify four metaphors Hannah uses to make her point.

9 Complete page 6 in *Prophets Copy Pak*™ by Marji Gold-Vukson.

Connecting the Text To the Holiday

10 According to *midrash*, Elkanah took Peninnah as his second wife only because Hannah could not have children. Similarly, in the Torah reading, Abraham had a child with Hagar because Sarah could not conceive. In both stories, a bitter rivalry existed between the childless woman and the woman with children.

◆ Rosh HaShanah begins the period of repentance during which we examine our past behavior, make amends for any wrongs we have done, and resolve to try harder in the future. How might we avoid feelings of jealousy and rivalry in the year to come?

11 The Haftarah says in verse 1:10 that Hannah prayed to God and wept. According to *Berachot* 32b, "Even if the gates of prayer are shut, the gates of tears are not." That is, heartfelt prayers are always accepted.

◆ How is this an appropriate message for Rosh HaShanah?

12 Hannah calls herself God's maidservant in verse 1:11 in the Haftarah.

◆ What does it mean to be God's servant, especially on Rosh HaShanah? For more discussion on this topic, see the Haftarah for Simchat Torah, Connecting the Text To the Holiday #8, pp. 4-5.

13 Rashi avoids understanding verse 1:12 to mean that Eli watched Hannah pray, as we should not watch someone engaged in prayer. Instead, Rashi suggests that by watching her mouth, Eli waited for Hannah to stop praying so he could speak to her.

In many synagogues on Rosh HaShanah, the Cantor prostrates himself or herself during a special recitation of the *"Alaynu"* prayer. We are not supposed to watch as the Cantor is humbled before God.

◆ Why might it be somehow an invasion of privacy to watch someone pray?

◆ Can you think of other reasons it is improper to watch someone pray?

◆ Do you tend to be more self-conscious if you think you are being watched?

◆ How might private (unobserved) prayer be more sincere?

14 Eli fails to give Hannah the benefit of the doubt in verse 1:13. An important part of the repentance and forgiveness of the High Holy Days is giving others (and indeed yourself) the benefit of the doubt.

◆ For more discussion on the importance of giving someone the benefit of the doubt, see *Teaching Jewish Virtues* by Susan Freeman, pp. 26-38.

15 The Haftarah relates the story of the birth of a son to a previously barren couple. Similarly, the Torah reading for Rosh HaShanah concerns the birth of Isaac to a previously childless mother. Rosh HaShanah is also known as Yom Harat HaOlam, the Birthday of the World.

◆ Review how each text and even the day involve newborns.

◆ Newborn babies start life with a clean slate. We hope on Rosh HaShanah to have our sins forgiven and to have our slate wiped clean. How is this like being a newborn?

16 Another name for Rosh HaShanah is *Yom HaZikaron*, Day of Remembrance. In the Haftarah God remembers Hannah in verse 1:19 by giving her a child. In the Torah reading, God remembers Sarah (Genesis 21:1) by giving her a child.

The liturgy for Rosh HaShanah often mentions God remembering. For example, the *"Amidah"* recited during the Musaf service of Rosh HaShanah includes a section called, *"Zichronot,"* or "Remembrances."

◆ In a Machzor, read the *"Zichronot,"* which are biblical verses about God remembering.

◆ On Rosh HaShanah, we want God to remember a wide variety of things. We want God to remember our ancestors who were meritorious, and we want to look good as their descendants. We want God to remember our good deeds and, therefore, judge us with mercy. However, we also want God to remember our bad deeds. Explain how if God did not remember our bad deeds, we would never have to atone and try harder. How we behave would not matter at all.

◆ In what way do you want God to remember you and your family this year?

17 In the last verse of the Haftarah, Hannah says that *"Adonai* will judge the ends of the earth." Rosh HaShanah is called by the name Yom HaDin, Day of Judgment, because on it God judges our deeds of the past year.

◆ Read the prayer *"Unetaneh Tokef,"* which describes the Day of Judgment as envisioned by our ancestors. Does this prayer reflect your own ideas about Rosh HaShanah?

◆ Write your own additional verse for this prayer.

18 In both Sedra and Haftarah, a party is made when the child is weaned.

We learn on Rosh HaShanah that life is fragile: we do not know who will live through the coming year and who will die (see *"Unetaneh Tokef"* in the Musaf *"Amidah"* for Rosh HaShanah and Yom Kippur). We pray that God will bless us with another year of days filled with happiness, fulfillment, and many *simchahs*. Perhaps the message of Rosh HaShanah — like that of the Sedra and Haftarah — is that all life's big and small milestones should be celebrated.

◆ What developmental milestones does your family celebrate (birthdays, weaning, starting school, graduation, driving)? Consider adding more celebrations to your life. What might these be? Write a short prayer thanking God for allowing you to celebrate any one of these special occasions.

19 Hannah warns against arrogant speech in verse 2:3.

According to Rashi, this is directed at people who become haughty because of the good fortune they have enjoyed. (Rashi also says it may refer to Peninnah, who was haughty about having children.)

Targum Jonathan says Hannah is referring to King Nebuchadnezzar of Babylon, who was haughty about his victory over Israel because he did not understand that he will be paid back with divine punishment in the future. (Note that Babylonia will not invade Israel for several hundred years after the time of Hannah.)

According to Hertz (quoting Driver), Hannah meant that we should watch our words because God has full knowledge of what we say and do.

◆ In your view, which interpretation of verse 2:3 best relates to the message of Rosh HaShanah?

I SAMUEL 11:14-12:22
KORACH קרח

This Haftarah has been paired with *Parashat Korach*, Numbers 16:1-18:32. See "Connecting the Text To the Sedra," pp. 56-57, for an exploration of the many ways the two texts shed light on each other.

SYNOPSIS

The Haftarah opens with the last two verses of chapter 11, in which the people confirm Saul as their king with ceremony, sacrifices, and great rejoicing before God at Gilgal.

Chapter 12 comprises Samuel's farewell address to the people, his last moment in the spotlight before he recedes into the background of the newly established monarchy. In the first five verses, Samuel defends his term as Israel's leader, asking God and the Israelites to bear witness to his unassailable integrity.

In the following seven verses, Samuel delivers a brief history of God's loyalty to Israel and Israel's continual cycle of rejection of and return to God from the time of Jacob in Egypt through the days of the Judges. Samuel next reminds the Israelites that although God ultimately consented to set a human king over them, God alone remains their true leader. Samuel urges the people to fear and serve God and follow the commandments, emphasizing that the king is subject to the same statutes. Therefore, the king may not rule at will but only according to God's laws. Samuel assures them that Divine punishment will be meted out to those who transgress.

In verses 12:16-18 Samuel sets out to demonstrate that only God is the true king, with power unparalleled by any human. He announces that God will send miraculous summer thunder and rain, which God immediately does. In fear and awe, the people beg Samuel to pray for them and save them from God's wrath (verse 12:19). Samuel reassures the people in the remaining verses. He promises them that even though they have sinned by requesting a king, God will nevertheless continue to reward them if they follow God's ways. After assuring them that he will pray for them and will instruct them, Samuel concludes his address with a reminder of God's graciousness and a stern warning that if the Israelites pursue evil, then both they and their king will be destroyed.

INSIGHTS FROM THE TRADITION

A The text in verse 11:15, which records the crowning of Saul as king, repeats the phrase "before God." According to Hirsch, the reason for the repetition is to show that the king's main purpose is to serve God, keeping God's laws and encouraging the people to do the same. The phrase "before God" also reinforces that king or no king, God is Israel's true leader and savior.

- Do you think God's superior leadership position makes the human king's job more difficult or easier? Explain your answer.

- In the U.S. Pledge of Allegiance, it says that we are "one nation under God." Does this mean that God is our true leader (not our government)? Find out if there is a Canadian equivalent of the Pledge of Allegiance and, if so, whether or not God is mentioned in it.

- What does it mean to you to be a citizen of a country whose creed is "one nation under God"?

◆ In your opinion, does the Pledge of Allegiance affect the way our leaders lead?

◆ Interview a local mayor or member of Congress to see how his or her ideas about leadership are affected by the words, "one nation under God."

B Abrabanel wonders why Samuel feels compelled to offer a defense of his administration as leader. He suggests that it was the custom to have the incoming magistrate review and judge the deeds of the outgoing judge. Samuel, therefore, was judged by Saul for any misdeeds he may have committed while he served over Israel.

◆ What would be the benefits and handicaps of a system in which judges review each other's work?

◆ Does our government have such a system?

◆ Do any of your schools have a system by which teachers observe each other and review each other's work? Debate the pros and cons of such a system of peer evaluation at the schools you attend.

C Samuel recounts a portion of Israelite history in verses 12:6-11. He mentions by name the great leaders Moses and Aaron, two minor judges, Jerubbaal (a.k.a. Gideon) and Bedan, and one judge of questionable behavior, Jephthah. In verse 12:11 he also names himself.

According to Talmud (*Rosh HaShanah* 25b), the three minor judges are mentioned in the same context as the three major leaders (Moses, Aaron, and Samuel) to show that all leaders, exceptional or not, are to be respected and followed.

◆ What makes someone a good leader? What makes someone an exceptional leader?

◆ Why do you think Talmud avers that all legitimate leaders are to be respected and followed?

◆ Can you think of any examples of good leaders and outstanding leaders? What makes them so?

D There are three enemies listed in Samuel's brief history: Sisera, the Philistines, and Moab. There are also three judges listed: Jerubbaal, Bedan, and Jephthah. The three enemies were selected because they were the most powerful, and the three judges because they were the least significant. The lesson to be drawn is that it was God, in fact, and not the judges, who delivered the Israelites from the hands of superior enemies. It did not matter how strong and influential the judge was personally, as he/she was only God's instrument.

◆ Do you agree that the judges were God's instruments?

◆ How are you an instrument of God? How are your parents or teachers instruments of God?

◆ What job or career might you choose that would enable you to do God's work?

◆ In what ways were Moses, Martin Luther King, Jr., and Gandhi instruments of God who had important personal influence on the world?

◆ For more on this subject, see *Being God's Partner* by Jeffrey K. Salkin.

E According to Hirsch, Samuel requested miraculous summer rain in verses 12:16-18 in order to demonstrate to the Israelites that the mortal king was powerless compared with God, who could do anything.

◆ How might this have made the people feel about their request for a king?

◆ Some people might argue that it was not in Israel's best interest to have a mortal king, but they wanted one anyway. Why do people sometimes want things that are not good for them?

◆ Why is it so difficult to demonstrate to someone that what they want is not in their best interests?

STRATEGIES
Analyzing the Text

1 Samuel reminds the Israelites in verse 12:1 that he installed a king over them as they had requested. According to Abrabanel, this reminder is also a reproof, because the Israelite's request for a king to rule them was a rejection of God's sole rule over them.

In choosing a human king, Israel was in many ways choosing to have an inferior leader rule over them. In school, local, and national elections, it sometimes seems that the people choose the inferior leader.

◆ Why might people choose an inferior leader?

In 1970, President Richard Nixon appointed Harold Carswell to the Supreme Court. During Senate hearings to confirm his appointment, legal scholars told the Senate that Carswell's legal abilities were at best "mediocre." In response, a Republican Senator defended Carswell, saying, "Even if he is mediocre, there are a lot of mediocre judges and people and lawyers, and they are entitled to a little representation, aren't they? We can't all be Brandeises and Cardozos and Frankfurters and stuff like that." Carswell was rejected by the Senate.

◆ In your opinion, what is wrong with the Senator's view?

◆ How might the Senator's speech also have applied to the Israelites' demand for a human king?

2 There are similarities and differences in Samuel's speeches in chapter 12 and I Samuel 8:10-18.

◆ Compare the content and tone of these two speeches. How are they similar? how different?

◆ In which speech does Samuel appear more indignant? more resigned? Why?

◆ Compare also the Israelites' reactions in verses 12:19 and 8:19-20. How has their attitude changed, and why?

3 In verse 12:2 Samuel says he is old and has gray hair. He also comments that his sons are with the Israelites.

◆ To discover the significance of these comments, read I Samuel 8:5.

◆ Why does Samuel begin his farewell address by mentioning his advanced age and his sons? (According to Robert Alter in his book *The David Story*, p. 65, the reference to Samuel's sons is an allusion to the dynasty Samuel failed to establish. Samuel's sons were dishonest and unfit to serve in his stead. Samuel wishes that his sons, who wanted a king like the rest of the people, wanted instead to follow their father.)

4 In verse 12:11 Samuel oddly refers to himself in the third person. Some scholars explain that because Samuel was transmitting a divine prophecy, he calls himself "Samuel" to make the prophecy sound more authoritative and objective. There are many other possible interpretations. For example, other scholars believe the text originally said "Samson," not "Samuel."

◆ Does this last explanation seem to fit the context?

◆ Why do you think Samuel might refer to himself in the third person?

◆ Do you ever refer to yourself in the third person?

5 There is no judge by the name of Bedan mentioned in the Book of Judges. However, Rabbinic tradition reads "Bedan" in verse 12:11 as "Ben Dan," thereby identifying the mystery judge as "the son of Dan."

◆ Which judge from the tribe of Dan could this be?

◆ Do you think this is a good explanation of who Bedan is?

◆ Can you think of another explanation?

6 In verse 12:14 Samuel outlines a lot of "if" statements: if you fear *Adonai*, if you serve God, if you listen to God's voice, if you don't rebel, if you and your king follow God. But, oddly, there is no apodosis, or corresponding "then" clause, and we are left to assume the rest.

◆ Why do you think the implied conclusion is left unsaid? What is the implied conclusion?

◆ In the verse that follows, however, there is a fully expressed "if" and "then" statement. What is it, and why do you think this time the text spells it out for us?

7 Commentators have had trouble explaining the end of verse 12:15, which literally says " . . . the hand of *Adonai* will strike you and your fathers."

◆ Explain how the phrase "your fathers," which means ancestors, doesn't make sense.

◆ Can you explain a way in which the verse might make sense?

◆ The Greek translation of the Bible (*Septuagint*) translates the end of the verse as "and your king." How does this alternative translation resolve the problem in the text?

8 In verse 12:22 Samuel assures the Israelites that God will never abandon them. The phrase he uses, "כי לא יטש" *(kee lo yitosh)*, appears only one other time in the Bible, in Psalm 94:14. It means "God will not abandon God's people."

◆ Compare the context of Psalm 94:14 with that of I Samuel 12:22.

◆ What is ironic about Samuel's usage of the verse in his farewell address? (Hint: the people have abandoned God.)

Connecting the Text To the Sedra

9 Michael Fishbane teaches in the *Etz Hayim Chumash* (p. 876) that the attributes of Moses and Samuel have been linked since biblical times. The ancient Rabbis considered them to be "paragons of the righteous judge, completely just and beyond reproach." Fishbane notes that the Sedra and Haftarah "underscore their ideal common denominator: selfless service on behalf of justice and a commitment to righteousness in societal affairs."

◆ Prepare a research presentation on some other exceptional judges, such as the following Jewish members of the United States Supreme Court: Ruth Bader Ginsburg, Felix Frankfurter, Benjamin Cardozo, and Louis Brandeis. Make a presentation to your class on these (or other) judges' "selfless service on behalf of justice and commitment to righteousness in societal affairs."

10 Korach tries to take Moses' place as leader of the Israelites in the Sedra (See *Teaching Torah* by Sorel Goldberg Loeb and Barbara Binder Kadden, p. 254). In the Haftarah the Israelites want a king to replace God as their ruler.

◆ Write and perform a skit in which Moses and God commiserate and complain about the problems they are having with their people.

11 Samuel defends himself by asserting he never took anything from the people. Similarly, Moses states in the Sedra (Numbers 16:15) that he never took anything not belonging to him. Notice, however, that Moses appeals to God, whereas Samuel defends himself to the people.

◆ Why is this so?

◆ Can you think of a time when you might need to defend your actions to your parents? Can you think of a time when you might need to defend your actions only to yourself (and God)?

12 To prove his point, Samuel calls upon God to send miraculous summer rain to ruin the wheat harvest (I Samuel 12:17-18). Similarly, Moses asks God to prove his point by enabling the earth to open up miraculously and swallow Korach and his followers (Numbers 16:30).

◆ How are the predicaments of Samuel and Moses similar? How do the outcomes differ?

◆ What are their respective points, and how do their miracles prove them?

13 Samuel is a descendant of the same tribe as Korach (see I Chronicles 6).

◆ Make a family tree showing the link between Samuel and Korach. Explain how Samuel's leadership success redeems his family's history. How do the failings of Samuel's sons reinforce Korach's legacy?

14 Korach was driven by base jealousy for Moses' job.

◆ What role did jealousy play in Israel's demand for a king?

◆ How do Samuel and Moses demonstrate their lack of jealousy by always putting God first as the true leader of the nation?

◆ Everyone feels jealousy sometimes. Is jealousy ever a productive emotion?

◆ Write about a time you have been jealous of someone or something.

15 In the Sedra Moses deals with a difficult situation by asserting his power.

◆ Explain the situation and show how Moses asserted his power.

◆ In the Haftarah Samuel deals with a difficult situation by relinquishing his power. Explain the situation and show how Samuel relinquishes his power.

◆ When should a leader assert power and when yield?

◆ How do you know when to pick your battles?

16 God makes it clear in the Sedra that God chose Moses and Aaron as leaders. In the Haftarah the people choose to have a human king as the leader.

◆ List criteria important for a leader of the Jewish people.

◆ List criteria important for a peer leader of a Jewish youth group.

◆ Compare the lists.

◆ Play the game "An Election" in the book *Jewish Identity Games* by Richard Israel, p 68.

Extending the Text

17 Typically, in the Bible, being old and gray is a sign of wisdom and experience. As we read in Proverbs 16:31: "The hoary head is a crown of glory."

Samuel emphasizes his age at the beginning of his speech in the Haftarah.

◆ Why might people want to call attention to their advanced age?

◆ Why might people want to hide their age?

◆ How does our modern society view being old and gray?

◆ Why do people dye their gray hair? Would you do so? Why or why not?

18 Samuel gives a bit of Israelite history (see Insight #C, p. 54) to bolster his arguments in his farewell address.

◆ Read the Gettysburg Address (available at http://eserver.org/history/gettysburg-address.txt), and consider Abraham Lincoln's brief reference to the history of the United States. How did the historical events Lincoln cited support his contentions in the Gettysburg Address? How did Samuel's (verse 12:6-11)?

◆ Why must a national leader be familiar with the country's history?

◆ What assets other than historical knowledge must one possess to be a good political leader?

19 In verse 12:17 Samuel asks, "Is it not wheat harvest today?" In Israel, the wheat is harvested during May and June, in the middle of the country's dry season (April through October).

◆ Learn about Israel's geography and climate, and their effect on agriculture. How is the climate and agriculture in Israel different from where you live? (For information, go to the Internet, tourist guide books, or *Encyclopaedia Judaica*, vol. 9, pp. 181-194.)

20 Samuel caused it to rain during the summer when it never rains in the Land of Israel. From Shemini Atzeret until Pesach each year (i.e., during the winter), Jews insert a prayer for rain in Israel into the *"Amidah."*

◆ Why do we pray for rain during this period?

◆ Why do we not pray for rain during the summer?

◆ The Rabbis teach us that we should not pray for what is already determined, such as the gender of a fetus or for an A on a test we have already taken. Why should we pray only for things that are possible? Do you agree or disagree with this teaching?

◆ Find the prayer for rain at the beginning of the *"Amidah"* and memorize it. When do you think you will use this prayer?

21 Samuel insisted that he had never stolen from anyone. Is it possible to go through life without ever stealing anything?

◆ Does stealing always involve a concrete object? What actions may be subtle forms of stealing?

◆ Read and discuss the following story, "The Pomegranate Seed," from *A Portion in Paradise and Other Jewish Folktales*, edited by H. M. Nahmad, pp 139-140.

A poor man once stole a piece of food and was ordered by the king to be hanged. On his way to the gallows, the condemned thief told one of the king's guards that he had a secret which he would like to share with the king. The thief was taken to the king and told the king that he was able to put a pomegranate seed in the ground, and make it grow and – miraculously — bear fruit overnight. The king was impressed, and demanded that the thief demonstrate this miracle. While the king and all his men and guards watched, the thief dug a hole and said, "This seed can be planted in the ground only by a man who never in his life has stolen or taken anything which did not belong to him. Being a thief, I cannot, of course, do it."

The king turned to his men, but they all refused to plant the seed. One remembered keeping something that wasn't his. Another worried that he may have made a little mistake in the king's accounting records. A guard thought of how he took a condemned prisoner's belongings. The king himself remembered that he once took and kept something belonging to his father.

When no one, not the king nor any of his men or guards, would plant the seed that had to be planted by a person who had never stolen anything, the thief chastised them all, saying, "You are all mighty and powerful persons. You are not in want of anything, yet you cannot plant the seed; while I, who stole a little food to keep myself from starvation, am to be hanged."

The king, pleased with the man's cleverness, laughed and pardoned him, and sent him away with a present.

22 Samuel's children failed to honor him.

◆ Act out and discuss the following contrasting story of Abimi and his elderly father, found in *Kiddushin* 31b:

Rabbi Abbahu said, "My son Abimi has fulfilled the precept of honor." Abimi had five sons who became Rabbis in his father's lifetime, yet when Rabbi Abbahu came and called at the door, Abimi himself speedily went and opened it for him, crying "yes, yes" until he reached it. One day, Abbahu asked Abimi for a drink of water. By the time he brought it, Abbahu had fallen asleep. So Abimi bent and stood over him, waiting, until he awoke.

◆ In what ways did Abimi honor his father?

◆ In what ways do you honor your parents?

23 Contrast the above story with this one based on "The Old Grandfather and the Grandson" by Leo Tolstoy. It can be found in *The Moral Development of Children* by Robert Cole, pp. 10-11:

A grandfather, who lived with his son, daughter-in-law, and grandson, had become very old. His legs couldn't walk, his eyes didn't see, his ears didn't hear, he had no teeth. And when he ate, food dripped from his mouth.

The son and daughter-in-law stopped letting him eat at the table and gave him his meals in the cellar. Once they brought dinner down to him in a cup. The old man wanted to move the cup, but dropped and broke it. The daughter-in-law began to complain that the grandfather spoiled and broke everything. They decided to give him his meals in an unbreakable dog's dish on the floor. The grandfather could say nothing.

Then, one day the husband and wife were watching their small son playing on the floor with some wooden toys; he was building something. The father asked his son what he was doing. The son replied that he was building a cellar with dog food bowls so that he could feed his parents one day when they were old.

The husband and wife looked at each other and began to cry. They became ashamed of how they had treated the grandfather, and from then on seated him at the table and waited on him.

◆ What lessons did the son teach his parents?

Personalizing the Text

24 One possible explanation for verse 12:15 cited in Analyzing the Text #7 (p. 56) is that parents can be held accountable for the sins of their children, or that a king or leader can be responsible for their people's wrongdoings.

◆ Is this fair?

◆ Are there any circumstances under which an authority (parent or leader or teacher) should be held accountable for the behavior of a subordinate (child or citizen or student)?

◆ Do you believe that a parent should have to spend time in jail for crimes committed by his or her minor child? Why or why not?

25 Samuel's speech indicates that he thinks that he is old. He summarizes his life's work and personal experiences.

◆ Choose an age at which you think you will consider yourself "old." Write a description of yourself at that age and be sure to include: what you do during the day, where you live and with whom, what you look like, some of your regrets, some of your successes, what makes you happy and what makes you sad.

26 The prayer *"Ayn Kelohaynu"* proclaims God as our only king. The CD *With Every Breath: The Music of Shabbat at BJ,* produced by B'nai Jeshurun Congregation in New York, contains two different melodies for *"Ayn Kelohaynu."*

◆ Listen to the two cuts and learn one or both of the melodies.

27 In our time, many elderly people live in a home for the aged.

◆ Plan a class or youth group trip to a Jewish home for the aged. Conduct a discussion with residents in which they share how they spend their days and describe their earliest Jewish memories.

28 Samuel's sons were unsuccessful in their father's line of work. Aaron's sons had varying degrees of success as priests.

◆ You will notice that many local businesses are family run operations, in which parents and children work together. Interview the family members of such a business and learn some of the benefits and difficulties involved.

29 Samuel expresses much sadness about the course of events that has led to his farewell.

◆ What do you think is the most regrettable part of Samuel's life as revealed in this speech?

◆ What do we learn from the fact that even great leaders like Samuel have disappointments and regrets throughout their lives and careers?

◆ How can we apply this lesson to our own lives?

30 At the end of this Haftarah, Samuel states that he is "old and gray." Samuel gives the people his last message, and declares that Saul is now leader of the people.

◆ Complete your studies of this Haftarah by planning and holding a retirement party for Samuel. Prepare food, music, decorations, and speeches suitable for a retiring judge and prophet of Israel.

31 Samuel embodied many admirable qualities. Reward your own family members for their admirable qualities by holding a family "Awards Night." To prepare for the Awards Night, each family member draws the name of another family member from a hat. Then each prepares an award for an outstanding achievement or admired quality of that person. The awards can be funny or serious (e.g., homemade trophies, plaques, certificates, or tributes). All awards can be presented, along with a festive meal and perhaps some complimentary testimonials, on Awards Night.

Other Resources

32 For a portrayal of abuse of power by a king, view and discuss any film version of Robin Hood. Two good ones are: *Robin Hood* (1973, unrated Disney cartoon, 83 minutes) and *Robin Hood: Prince of Thieves* (1991, rated PG-13, 144 minutes).

33 Samuel predicted that the king would abuse his power. View and discuss the film *All the President's Men* (1976, rated PG, 138 minutes), for an account of President Richard Nixon's abuse of power.

34 The books *The Chosen* and *My Name Is Asher Lev* by Chaim Potok are good stories about sons, some of whom do and some of whom do not, follow in their father's footsteps. *The Chosen* was also made into a film (1981, rated PG, 108 minutes).

35 Read, act out, and discuss "Samuel's Inauguration Address" in *Bible Scenes: Joshua To Solomon* by Stan J. Beiner, pp. 98-100.

36 For a short tale on being the best you can be (without trying to be someone else), read "The Storyteller" by Reuven Gold in *Chosen Tales*, edited by Peninnah Schram, p. 110.

37 See the film *Defending Your Life* (1991, rated PG, 112 minutes), which is about accounting for your deeds before a panel of judges in the afterlife.

38 Discuss the illustrations of this Haftarah in *The Illustrated Torah* by Michal Meron, p. 162. How do the illustrations differ?

39 Complete p. 8 in *Prophets Copy Pak*™ by Marji Gold-Vukson.

Involving the Family

40 Samuel may have needed an acknowledgement of appreciation at the end of his career, such as the applause at the end of a performance. We all would benefit from some positive feedback from time to time. For one month, try expressing appreciation at Shabbat dinner for everyone at the table.

Bar/Bat Mitzvah Projects

41 Serve on the student council for your school, as an officer on the board of your Jewish youth group, or in another leadership capacity. See if the experience of serving your community makes you "turn gray."

42 One teenager devoted one afternoon a week for the entire year before her Bat Mitzvah to visiting the residents of a local Jewish nursing home. She became so attached to the people she met there that she ultimately decided to hold her Bat Mitzvah service and party at the nursing home. You can read about her in the Winter 2000 issue of *Lilith* magazine, pp. 28-30.

Consider making regular visits to a local nursing home or having an extra Bar or Bat Mitzvah party at the home to share the joy of your *simchah* with the elderly in your community.

I SAMUEL 15:2-34 Ashkenazim
I SAMUEL 15:1-34 Sephardim
SHABBAT ZACHOR

This Haftarah has been paired with *Shabbat Zachor*, on which we read a special Maftir Torah reading, Deuteronomy 25:17-19 . See "Connecting the Text To the Special Shabbat," pp. 65-67, for an exploration of the many ways the two texts and this special Shabbat shed light on each other.

SYNOPSIS

In the beginning of this dramatic Haftarah, Samuel delivers to King Saul a message from God. In one of the Bible's most troubling passages, God commands Saul utterly to destroy the nation of Amalek, including its men, women, children, and animals. Amalek earned its brutal punishment years before as the first nation to attack the Israelites on their way out of Egypt.

Saul gathers 210,000 soldiers to attack the main settlement of Amalek. Living here among the Amalekites are the Kenites, who were kind to the Israelites when they left Egypt. Saul sends word to the Kenites to separate themselves from Amalek and save themselves from destruction. Once the Kenites have departed, Saul and his army utterly massacre Amalek. However, Saul disregards God's commandment to destroy all Amalekites and takes King Agag as his prisoner. In addition, the Israelites spare the best sheep and oxen, also in violation of God's instructions.

God is greatly vexed by Saul's breach, and complains bitterly to Samuel about having made Saul king in the first place. After a sleepless night, Samuel seeks out Saul. Saul greets the prophet and proudly reports that he has performed God's bidding. When Samuel asks Saul about the sheep and oxen he hears, Saul responds that the best animals have been saved to sacrifice to God. When pressed further, Saul admits that he has also spared Agag.

Enraged, Samuel accuses Saul of rebellion and stubbornness. In a scathing indictment, Samuel sentences Saul in verse 15:23: "Because you rejected the command of *Adonai*, God has rejected you as king." Saul pleads guilty to the charge and explains that he yielded to the desires of the people instead of holding firm to God's commandment. He prays for forgiveness, and when Samuel denies his request and turns to leave, Saul grabs Samuel's robe, which rips. Samuel points out that just as his robe has ripped, so has God ripped the kingdom of Israel from Saul and given it to someone better than he. Samuel assures Saul that God will not reconsider.

A bereft Saul begs Samuel to pray with him, which the prophet does. Then Samuel sends for King Agag, who is brought to him in chains. After pronouncing Agag's death sentence, Samuel himself kills the Amalekite.

The Haftarah concludes poignantly with Samuel and Saul going their separate ways.

INSIGHTS FROM THE TRADITION

A Saul summons, enrolls, and counts the soldiers at Telaim in verse 15:4. According to *Yoma* 22b, Telaim is not a place, but means "lambs." Rabbinic tradition teaches that Saul gave each person to be counted a lamb, then counted the lambs, because it was not acceptable to number people directly. For example, see Exodus 30:11-12, in which it is considered dangerous to count people directly. Moses is, therefore, directed to take a census of the people by collecting a half-shekel from each person and then counting the coins.

◆ Can you think of any reasons why it is forbidden to count people?

◆ Since Jewish tradition forbids the counting of people, how do we know we have the ten people required for a *minyan*? (It is customary to use a verse from the Book of Psalms (28:9), or to use the second verse of the *"Mah Tovu,"* which in Hebrew has ten words. Each person is assigned a word, to determine how many are present. An alternative custom is to "not count," saying "not one, not two, etc.")

◆ Can you think of any other way to count without actually counting?

B Saul either "lay in wait in the wadi" or "fought in the wadi" in verse 15:5; the meaning of the Hebrew is uncertain. Furthermore, since the battle with Amalek is not described until verse 15:7, if he "fought in the wadi" in verse 15:5, with whom did he fight? According to *Yoma* 22b, Saul fought there not with the enemy, but with his conscience.

◆ What does it mean to fight with your conscience?

◆ With what moral issue could Saul have been dealing before going to battle against Amalek? (Perhaps he was uncomfortable with the order to commit genocide, perhaps he worried that the Amalekite children and animals were innocent.)

C The command to eliminate Amalek did not bother just Saul; commentators over the generations have been troubled with this apparent command to commit genocide. One interpretation by Hirsch suggests that the command to blot out Amalek is a command to eliminate the worship of power, force, and violence. This nineteenth century European Rabbi taught that we should neither sing songs of glorious battles nor teach about military heroes.

◆ Debate Hirsch's points.

◆ What do you think Hirsch would say about the words of "Star Spangled Banner"?

◆ Many people think that "America the Beautiful" should be the national anthem of the United States. Compare the words and moods of both songs. Which do you think makes a better national anthem, and why?

◆ Find the words of "O Canada," the Canadian national anthem. Does it speak of battles or military heroes?

D Apparently because of Saul's failure to kill Agag, the monarchy was removed from his house (i.e., Saul would be the last king in his family).

◆ Do you think this is an appropriate punishment?

◆ *Yoma* 22b suggests that it was not Saul's failure to kill Agag, per se, that was being punished. Rather, it was Saul's tendency to be excessively righteous that prevented him from killing Agag that made him an inadequate leader for Israel. What do you think "excessive righteousness" means?

◆ Can you find another example in the Haftarah of Saul behaving excessively righteously?

◆ Do you think excessive righteousness is a fault in a leader or in anyone?

◆ What personality traits do you think a leader should exhibit?

STRATEGIES
Analyzing the Text

1 Saul gathers 200,000 soldiers, plus another 10,000 from the tribe of Judah in verse 15:4. According to Plaut (*The Haftarah Commentary*, p. 547), this translation is based on a misunderstanding of the Hebrew word *elef*, which in modern Hebrew means "a thousand." Plaut contends that the word originally meant "contingent," which comprised about 10 people. Therefore, Saul's army consisted of fewer than 2,000 men, with about 100 additions from Judah.

◆ How does this alternative translation affect your view of Israel's battle against Amalek?

◆ Translation is a tricky business. Why is it important to consider all possible translations?

◆ What should be the criteria for choosing the best translation?

2 Samuel angrily asks Saul (verse 15:14) about the sound of sheep that he is hearing, since the sheep of Amalek should have all been slaughtered in the battle. The word in Hebrew for "what" is typically pronounced "mah," but in this verse it is vocalized as "meh."

◆ Explain how this pronunciation might be both onomatopoeia and irony.

◆ Make a political cartoon-style drawing of this scene.

3 While speaking to Samuel in verses 15 and 30, Saul calls God "your God."

◆ Why do you think Saul distances himself from God by not saying "our God," or simply "God"?

◆ What does it mean when one parent says to their child's other parent, "Do you know what *your* child did today?"

4 Samuel says to Saul in verse 17, "You may look small to yourself."

◆ What does this comment imply about Saul's self-confidence and leadership abilities?

◆ When Saul was chosen to be king, we were told that he was very tall (I Samuel 9:2). Discuss the irony of Samuel now saying that Saul is small in his own eyes. (See also I Samuel 9:21, in which Saul humbly says he is from the smallest of the tribes and, therefore, undeserving of Samuel's attention.)

◆ What is the difference between humility and low self-esteem?

◆ How did Saul's self-image change, and why?

◆ Is humility an asset or handicap for a leader?

◆ How about good self-esteem?

5 Saul sins by not killing all of Amalek's animals and reserving the best of them to sacrifice to God. In verse 15:22 Samuel asks Saul, "Does *Adonai* delight in burnt offerings and sacrifices as much as in obedience to God's command? Surely, obedience is better than sacrifice, compliance than the fat of rams."

◆ Do you think this verse means that God does not want sacrifices?

◆ What do you think God wants?

◆ This is a familiar theme; many of the prophets preach that it is essential to lead ethical lives in obedience with God's laws and not to rely solely on the making of sacrifices. For examples of this theme in other prophets, see the Haftarah for *Devarim*, Analyzing the Text #6, p. 223.

◆ Do you agree or disagree with the prophets?

◆ Can a religion be sustained on rituals without morals? Explain your answer.

◆ Can a religion be sustained on morals without rituals? Explain your answer.

6 Saul offers two excuses in his defense (verse 15:21). He says that it was the army, not he, who spared the animals; and he says the animals were not taken for selfish reasons, but to be sacrificed to God.

◆ Find indications in the text that contradict Saul's excuses.

◆ Should a leader make excuses or take ultimate responsibility when things go wrong?

7 Samuel was known for his distinctive robe, his prophetic garb. When in verse 15:27 Saul grabs Samuel's robe to try to stop the prophet from leaving, the robe rips.

◆ See verse 15:28 to find out what reality is symbolized in the tearing of this special garment.

◆ Tearing one's clothing is an act of mourning (see Extending the Text #16 in *Chukat*, p. 35). At the conclusion of chapter 15, what is being mourned, and who is doing the mourning? Try to find reasons that Saul, Samuel, and God are all mourning.

8 In verse 15:29 Samuel uses a name for God which does not appear any other time in the Bible. He refers to God as literally "Eternal of Israel."

◆ What does this name for God imply?

◆ Why is this name particularly fitting for this verse?

9 Samuel calls for Agag to be brought to him. In verse 15:32 the Hebrew word מעדנת

(*ma'adanot*) is used to describe how Agag approaches Samuel. There are many possible translations for this difficult and obscure Hebrew word: Radak suggests it means that Agag was wearing leg fetters; Plaut (*The Haftarah Commentary*, p. 552) translates it as "confidently" because Agag assumes Samuel wants to spare his life and have a diplomatic meeting. In contrast, Gaster proposes in *Myth, Legend and Custom in the Old Testament* that Agag limps purposely to express mourning over his impending death. The JPS translation says Agag approached "with faltering steps."

◆ How does the translation you are using in class treat this word?

◆ Which explanation do you think fits the story best?

◆ Can you suggest any other explanations?

10 At the end of the Haftarah, Saul and Samuel go their separate ways — the king to Gibeah and the prophet to Ramah.

◆ What does this physical parting symbolize?

Connecting the Text
To the Special Shabbat

11 The Shabbat before Purim is specially named *Shabbat Zachor*, the Shabbat of Remembrance. On it we read a special Maftir reading, Deuteronomy 25:17-19, which begins with the phrase, "Remember what Amalek did." Notice that in the (Ashkenazic) Haftarah, the first verse of chapter 15 is omitted. The Haftarah begins at 15:2, with God remembering and exacting the penalty for what Amalek did to Israel.

◆ What did Amalek do to Israel, and when?

◆ Why was what Amalek did so reprehensible?

◆ For a brief discussion of the sins of Amalek, see *Teaching Torah* by Sorel Goldberg Loeb and Barbara Binder Kadden, p. 109.

◆ Do you prefer the Sephardic version of the Haftarah, which includes verse 15:1, or the Ashkenazic version, which excludes it? Explain the reasons for your choice.

12 Agag, the King of Amalek, appears in the Haftarah and is an ancestor of Haman, the villain of Purim. *Midrash* tells us that the child of Agag who would become Haman's ancestor was conceived while Agag was Saul's prisoner of war (see *The Legends of the Jews* by Louis Ginzberg, vol. 4, p. 68).

Interestingly, both Saul and Mordecai (of the Purim story) were members of the tribe of Benjamin.

◆ Explain how the story of Esther seems to be a rematch of these same enemies.

◆ Write a fanciful *Purimshpiel* in which Agag, Haman, Saul, and Mordecai all have roles in the story of Esther.

13 The Sedra and Haftarah both begin with the command to remember Amalek. The Torah reading adds, "Don't forget what Amalek did."

Maimonides describes these two separate *mitzvot* in his Book of Commandments. Negative Commandment #59 instructs us never to forget what Amalek did to us. Rambam explains, "that is to say, we are not to relax our hatred of Amalek, nor are we to remove it from our hearts." Positive Commandment #189 instructs us to remember by speaking about what Amalek did to us in attacking us unprovoked, "to the end that this matter be not forgotten and that hatred of him be not weakened or lessened with the passage of time."

◆ What is the difference between the command to remember and the command not to forget?

◆ Why are some events never forgotten, even if they are unpleasant ones?

◆ Write your own positive or negative commandment regarding remembering Hitler and the Shoah. A positive commandment is something you must do. A negative commandment is something you must not do.

14 Grappling with the moral difficulty of genocide, commentators have suggested different ways to understand the command to annihilate Amalek. One interpretation is to understand Amalek not as a nation, but as the representation of the evil inclination within each of us. Consequently, when we refrain from doing wrong and instead commit ourselves to doing *mitzvot*, we are wiping out Amalek.

◆ Accordingly, hold a "Caylim Costume Contest" before Purim. *Caylim* is Hebrew for persons or things that may be used as tools in any holy *mitzvah* endeavor. A *tzedakah* box, *chanukiah*, and *Kiddush* cup are examples of *caylim*. A Rabbi, Cantor, teacher, or doctor, or any of their implements, may also be *caylim* because the work they do may be holy. (Do you think someone could dress up as a *sukkah*?)

◆ Design creative *caylim* costumes to fight Amalek and other threats to Judaism.

◆ For more information on how anyone or anything can be *caylim*, see *Gym Shoes and Irises* by Danny Siegel, p. 88.

15 God commands the genocide of Amalek in verse 15:3. Genocide is, of course, repugnant to our modern sensibilities.

Commentators have struggled with the commanded genocide of Amalek and have tried to explain why genocide in this case was not morally wrong. One suggestion is that Amalek's attack on Israel immediately after the Exodus from Egypt was really an attack on God, to show the world that God was not really all that powerful. Because Amalek effectively attacked God, the mass killing of Amalek is warranted.

Another understanding of this commandment involves a figurative interpretation of Amalek as the evil inclination within ourselves. As such, we are not being asked to commit genocide at all (see Extending the Text #14, p. 66). Since wiping out the evil inclination is not murder, it is unequivocally morally justified.

A third interpretation of this commandment is that we are not to wipe out people, but rather we are to eliminate a certain type of human behavior which encourages violence (see Insights from the Tradition #C, p. 63). Preventing future violence is a morally correct act.

◆ Review these interpretations of the command to wipe out Amalek. Do you think they justify the morality of the commandment?

◆ Can an act be right (or wrong) just because God says to do it?

◆ In the story of Esther which we read on Purim, Haman plans the genocide of all the Jews. His plan fails, and the king gives the Jews permission to massacre any people who attack them. Compare this situation to that of Amalek and the Israelites. Does this situation not seem morally questionable because the Jews would only exterminate their enemies in self-defense? Or does this aspect of the story of Esther bother you?

16 Samuel executes Agag. In the story of Esther, King Ahasuerus sentences Haman to death.

In 1960, Israel captured Adolf Eichmann, one of the leaders of the Nazi plan to exterminate all European Jews, and brought him to Israel for trial. He was tried and convicted in Israel. Under Israeli

law, there is no death penalty, except in the case of Holocaust crimes. When Eichmann was convicted and sentenced to death, there was vigorous debate in Israel about whether or not to execute him. The Prime Minister met with the cabinet to discuss the death penalty in Eichmann's case. When the President of Israel announced that Eichmann would be executed, he began his announcement citing I Samuel 15:33: "As your sword has made women childless, so shall your mother be childless among women."

◆ Do you believe in the death penalty? Why or Why not?

◆ Conduct a class debate on the subject.

◆ Do you agree that Eichmann's case was sufficiently different from a standard murder case that Israel was justified in executing the former Nazi? Explain your answer.

◆ Explain why you think the president of Israel cited I Samuel 15:33.

◆ Do you believe that Agag and Haman and Eichmann deserved the death penalty? Why or why not?

◆ For more information on the Eichmann trial, see *Jewish Literacy* by Joseph Telushkin, pp. 374-6.

17 Maimonides teaches (see Connecting the Text to the Special Shabbat #13, p. 66) that the command to remember is to be completed using one's mouth (by reading the Torah portion and speaking of the evil that Amalek did), and that the command not to forget is to be fulfilled with the heart (by allowing our hatred of Amalek to burn forever in our hearts).

◆ Hold a Purim debate about which is mightier: the mouth or the heart. Don't be too serious. A Purim debate is supposed to be silly.

Extending the Text

18 Saul puts up a monument to himself (verse 15:12). According to Robert Alter in *The David Story*, p. 89, this may have been a war memorial, an upright stone with an inscribed surface.

◆ Visit a war memorial near you or the Vietnam War Memorial online at www.thevirtualwall. org. What lessons or sentiments is the memorial trying to convey?

◆ Do you agree with the sentiments of the memorial? Explain your answer.

◆ What would you memorialize if you could?

◆ Design and make (if possible) a memorial.

19 Notice in the Synopsis that Saul disregards God's commandment to kill all Amalekites and spares Agag.

◆ Saul didn't think he was disregarding the commandment, just reinterpreting it (see Insights from the Tradition #B, p. 63). Thus, is it fair to use the word "disregard"?

◆ How do the different movements in American Judaism view the commandments and who may interpret them? When one movement reinterprets a commandment or chooses not to follow a commandment, is it "disregarding" the commandment?

◆ Organize a panel discussion of Rabbis representing the various movements, and explore these issues.

20 Saul asks Samuel twice for forgiveness before forgiveness is granted. According to Jewish tradition, one must ask for forgiveness only three times. If the aggrieved refuses to grant forgiveness on the third request, the penitent is automatically forgiven and the aggrieved becomes guilty of wrongdoing.

◆ Do you think this is a fair rule? Explain your answer.

◆ Why might someone not want to accept an apology?

◆ Do you think it is always better to forgive, or is it sometimes better to hold a grudge? Explain the reasons for your choice.

◆ Which is more difficult — to ask for forgiveness or to grant forgiveness? How so?

◆ Why do you think it is considered a sin to refuse forgiveness?

21 We analyzed the symbolism of the tearing of Saul's cloak in Analyzing the Text #7 (p. 65). The tearing or cutting of a cloak is very powerful. In fact, it occurs twice more in the Former Prophets: in I Samuel 24:5 and I Kings 11:30.

◆ Find these incidents and compare them with the episode in this Haftarah.

◆ The following exercise might help students understand the consequences of war. Each student tears up and destroys a clean piece of white paper as thoroughly as possible. Use glue, tape, paper clips, staples, and other tools to repair the sheets of paper. Try to put the papers back together again. No matter how hard the students try, they will ultimately fail to restore their papers to their original condition. The lesson? Once a nation is ravaged by war (the torn paper), it is impossible to return to a pristine peace. The damage is already done. Discuss this lesson with regard to the State of Israel and peace and war in the Middle East and also to the war against terrorism.

22 In 15:29, Samuel uses an unusual name for God — literally, the "Eternal of Israel." There are many names for God in the

Bible (see a list in *The Jewish Bible Almanac* by Ronald H. Isaacs, p. 121) and in Jewish tradition (see an even longer list in the source book *Higher and Higher* by Steven M. Brown, p. 62).

◆ Play a game with a group. The teacher provides everyone with a list of names for God. Each person takes a turn explaining in 30 seconds why he/she thinks one particular name is the best name for God. Make sure that one group member times each person, and that another member verifies that no names are repeated.

Personalizing the Text

23 When God is angry with Saul, God complains to Samuel.

◆ Why doesn't God address Saul directly?

◆ Why is it sometimes easier to complain to a third party? Explain your answer.

◆ How would you feel if you did something wrong and your parents complained about you to your siblings instead of addressing you directly?

◆ Is it always better to address your complaint directly to the person who offended you? Why or why not?

24 United States President Harry S. Truman had a sign on his desk that read, "The Buck Stops Here."

◆ What does Truman's sign mean?

◆ How did King Saul attempt to "pass the buck" (see verse 15:21)?

◆ Why should "the buck stop" with the leader?

◆ Why is it sometimes difficult to accept responsibility for a wrongdoing?

25 We cope with evil leaders in a variety of ways, such as using *graggers* to drown out the name of Haman at the *Megillah* reading on Purim.

◆ Make your own unusual *gragger* to use on Purim.

Other Resources

26 On the complicated issues surrounding Amalek, see the essay for Shabbat Zachor in *The Haftarah Commentary* by W. Gunther Plaut, pp. 553-554.

27 Read, act out, and discuss the skit in *Bible Scenes: Joshua To Solomon* by Stan J. Beiner, p. 105.

28 The feature film *King David* (1985, rated PG-13, 114 minutes), has a surprisingly accurate portrayal of this Haftarah. Because there is some material that might not be appropriate for classroom viewing, the teacher should preview and cue the film to the appropriate scene.

29 In some Holocaust literature, Hitler is portrayed as Amalek. Read "4580," a memoir by Yehoshua Perle in *The Literature of Destruction*, edited by David Roskies, pp. 450-454. Compare the elimination of the author's name in the memoir with the command to obliterate Amalek's name.

30 "Connecting the Text To the Special Shabbat" #16, p. 67, features a discussion of Adolf Eichmann vis-à-vis capital punishment. For an interesting account of the capture of Eichmann, read *The House on Garibaldi Street* by Isser Harel.

31 Discuss the portrayal of this Haftarah in *The Illustrated Torah* by Michal Meron, p. 227.

Involving the Family

32 Collect and record your parents' and grandparents' memories of the Holocaust, oppression, and/or anti-Semitism. Find out if they have been able to forgive what they cannot forget, and why or why not.

Bar/Bat Mitzvah Projects

33 Participate in an interfaith or interracial social action group. How can your participation help break the cycle of hate and distrust which leads communities to see each other as enemies?

34 Rituals are an important part of being Jewish. They enrich our lives and reinforce morals. For example, saying a blessing before eating reminds us not to steal from God (or anyone). Explore the possibility of adding a new ritual to your life, such as reciting the *"Shema"* at bedtime or saying the *Motzi* before eating. Consider what moral lesson your new ritual will teach.

I SAMUEL 20:18-42
SHABBAT MACHAR CHODESH

This Haftarah has been paired with *Shabbat Machar Chodesh*. See "Connecting the Text To the Special Shabbat," pp. 74-75, for an exploration of the many ways the text and the Special Shabbat before the holiday shed light on each other.

SYNOPSIS

This story of friendship and loyalty introduces us to one of the Hebrew Bible's most endearing and admirable characters: Jonathan, son of King Saul. In the chapters preceding the Haftarah, David, a valiant war hero, wins the favor of both King Saul and his son Jonathan. While a lasting friendship develops between the two young men, King Saul becomes increasingly jealous of the very popular David. Ultimately consumed with an insane jealousy, Saul attempts several times to kill David, after which David goes into hiding for safety.

The Haftarah begins with a meeting between David and Jonathan on the day before the New moon. It was customary for King Saul to hold a feast on Rosh Chodesh, and both Jonathan and David knew that if David attended, as was expected of a military leader, his life would again be in grave danger. As such, the friends agree that David remain in hiding. Jonathan would determine if David's life is still at risk. On the third day after the feast, Jonathan would send David a secret message regarding the King's intentions toward him.

At the festive meal, King Saul privately notes David's absence, but figures he has a good reason for missing the occasion. However, when David is again missing from the King's table the next day,

Saul asks Jonathan about his friend's absence. Jonathan offers an excuse for David, and Saul becomes enraged with his son for protecting the enemy. When Jonathan defends David against Saul's tirade, the King's anger gets the best of him, and he throws his spear at his own son.

Worried about David and shamed by his father's violent actions against himself, Jonathan fasts the second day, and on the third, sets out to deliver his secret message to David, warning him that he is still very much in danger. According to their plan, Jonathan goes out to the field with a boy to shoot arrows. He and David had agreed that Jonathan would shoot three arrows, and David would know if it was safe to return based on where Jonathan shot the arrows. To deliver the message of danger, Jonathan shoots the arrows far and shouts to the boy that the arrows are past him. To emphasize his point to David, Jonathan adds that he should hurry up and get them. The boy thinks Jonathan is talking to him, of course, but David understands the message loud and clear.

When the boy leaves to take Jonathan's bow and arrows back to town, Jonathan and David meet. David bows to his friend three times, and then they kiss each other and cry. Before separating, Jonathan tells his friend to go in peace and to remember forever the oath between them and their descendants.

INSIGHTS FROM THE TRADITION

A Rashi explains that Jonathan devised a signal for David that means "God is sending you away." We understand that Jonathan does not want to speak ill of his father.

- What words about his father, King Saul, was Jonathan trying to avoid having to say, and why?

- Throughout the conflict between Saul and David, Jonathan struggles to remain faithful to both, doing his best to uphold the fifth commandment to honor one's parents.

- How is Jonathan following the fifth commandment by avoiding negative words about his father?

B Saul couldn't fathom that his own flesh and blood would defend the King's enemy, David. In verse 20:30 Saul angrily insults Jonathan by calling him a "son of a perverse, rebellious woman." Radak explains that Saul worried that because of Jonathan's lack of loyalty to the King, people would think Jonathan was not Saul's real son (i.e., people would think that Jonathan's mother conceived him through an adulterous relationship with another man, which is why Saul called her a perverse woman). After all, how could someone's real son defend his father's enemy?

- Was Jonathan wrong to disagree publicly with his father on the subject of David? Why or why not?

- Why did Saul feel the need to distance himself from Jonathan emotionally?

- Does loyalty to your parents require you to have the same views as they have? Explain your answer.

- Is it fair for parents to expect that their children will share their views on politics, religion, etc.? Why or why not?

C According to Radak in Insights from the Tradition #B, p. 72, Saul was worried about what people would think if his son disagreed with him.

- Why did Saul care what other people thought?

- Should parents care about what others think of their children?

- In general, how much do you think other people's opinions about us should affect our behavior or our decisions?

D Saul asks about David's absence and refers to David not by name but as "the son of Jesse." *Pesikta Rabbatai* 32:2 explains that this term derides David by suggesting that David has no name, no merits of his own.

- Why would Saul use a derogatory term for David?

- Saul called David by his "last name" — son of Jesse — which in this instance is used in a negative way. We often address our friends by their last names. How can the same name be used in both friendly and unfriendly ways?

- It seems that there is a fine line between an acceptable and affectionate nickname and an insulting one. Discuss the different ways nicknames are used.

- Who determines whether or not a name is acceptable?

E When David fled from Saul at the end of the Haftarah, Jonathan did not give David provisions for the trip. Consequently, a *midrash* teaches that his intense hunger drove David illegally to eat bread reserved for the Priests at the town of Nob.

From this the Rabbis teach that one should always send a guest with enough provisions for the trip (*Sanhedrin* 104a).

Travel in biblical times was quite a different affair from what it is now. It was dangerous and arduous, and travelers needed to bring their own provisions with them, as there was no place to buy them en route.

Nevertheless, even today, travelers bring with them things that make them feel safe and secure on their trips, whether on a brief commute to work or a long journey.

◆ What are some things today's travelers need to have with them? (Hint: safety items we should keep in our cars, and so on.)

◆ What are some things you like to bring with you when you travel?

◆ Create a word-find puzzle, including items necessary for today's travel.

STRATEGIES
Analyzing the Text

1 In verse 20:25 Saul assumes that David's absence is due to ritual impurity. He says, "he is unclean; surely he is not clean."

◆ Why do you think Saul repeats his thought twice? (Some commentators point out that Saul appears to be convincing himself by repeating the reason over and over.)

◆ Why does Saul seem to ignore the obvious reason for David's absence: because he is afraid that Saul will once again try to kill him?

◆ What might we learn about Saul and his state of mind regarding David from this episode?

2 When Jonathan tries to protect David, Saul reacts very angrily (verses 20:30-33). In part, Saul is angry because he (correctly) fears that David will take the kingship away from Saul's family in general and from Jonathan in particular. In a fit of fury, Saul throws a spear at Jonathan, threatening to kill the son whose future kingship Saul is actually trying to protect.

◆ What is ironic about Saul's reaction?

◆ Have you ever said or done something in a fit of anger that you later regretted? What happened?

3 When in verse 20:34 Saul insults his son and throws his spear at him, Jonathan storms away from the table and refuses to eat the whole day because "his father shamed him."

◆ What do you think shamed Jonathan most: Saul calling him a bad name, Saul throwing his spear at him, or Saul threatening David's life?

◆ Did Jonathan do the right thing to storm away from the dinner table?

◆ Have you ever stormed away from the dinner table? What happened?

◆ Why do you think Jonathan refused to eat the rest of the day?

◆ It is possible that Jonathan lost his appetite. It is also possible that he went on a short hunger strike to protest his father's actions and words. How might a hunger strike by Jonathan have affected his father?

4 David came out of hiding (verse 20:41) and bowed down to the ground three times before his friend Jonathan.

◆ Why do people bow and on what occasions?

◆ What do you think David's bowing meant to him and to Jonathan?

5 The number 3 plays an important role in this story.

◆ Identify, list, and discuss where the number 3 appears in this story.

◆ For more information on the symbolic importance of numbers in the Bible, see *Encyclopaedia Judaica,* pp. 1254-60 and p. 1256, for the number 3 specifically, or *The Encyclopedia of Jewish Symbols* by Ellen Frankel and Betsy Platkin Teutsch.

6 The Hebrew text for verse 20:42 reads: "*Adonai* shall be between me and you . . . " While this verse may appear just fine the way it is, the Greek *Septuagint* and some other ancient translations have a slightly different version of the verse: "*Adonai* shall be witness between me and you . . . "

Commentators disagree as to whether or not "witness" should be included. Without "witness," the verse suggests that God stands intrusively between the two friends because Jonathan understands that God has chosen David, instead of him, to be the next King of Israel. However, by adding "witness," the verse means that God is between the two friends in a positive way because God is involved in the covenant between Jonathan and David.

◆ Which translation do you prefer, and why?

◆ Why might you want to write something that has an ambiguous meaning?

◆ Why might you want to write something that is very clear and leaves no room for interpretation?

Connecting the Text To the Special Shabbat

7 The first verse of the Haftarah (which is the middle of chapter 20) says that "tomorrow will be Rosh Chodesh, the new month." We read this Haftarah only on those Shabbatot which immediately precede a Sunday Rosh Chodesh.

◆ Why might we recite special Haftarot before or after a special occasion?

◆ There are special Haftarot for many occasions in the Jewish calendar. To learn more about the special Haftarot, see *The Comprehensive Hebrew Calendar* by Arthur Spier, p. 9.

8 Plaut explains in *The Haftarah Commentary*, p. 596, that the Haftarah deals with the harmony one finds in a loving friendship, while the new moon represents the harmony of the heavens.

◆ Read and discuss the following story about the rivalry between the sun and the moon from *Hullin* 60b:

During the six days of Creation, on the fourth day, God made the two great luminaries (Genesis 1:16). However, the same verse continues by saying that God created one great light and one smaller light. Did God create two large lights or did God create one large and one small light? This *aggadah* explains that the two stars were originally the same large size, but then the moon asked God: "Can two kings share one crown?" God answered the moon, "Go and make yourself smaller." The moon protested to God, saying, "Because I raised a proper claim, why must I make myself smaller?" God realized the justice in the moon's protest and promised the moon that, in exchange for her making herself smaller, Israel would base its calendar on her.

◆ Discuss the rivalry between the sun and moon when they were both the same size and both vying to be "king."

◆ Contrast the relationship between the sun and the moon with that between David and Jonathan. How was Jonathan willing to make himself smaller?

◆ Saul and David had a rivalry similar to that of the sun and moon in our story. For advanced study about the tumultuous relationship between the current and future King of Israel, see the following passages and compare Saul and David's saga to that of the sun and moon: I Samuel 16:11-20:17; 22:6-10; 24; and 26.

9 On the Shabbat preceding a New Moon, a prayer for the new month is recited. We pray to God for a month filled with life, health and peace, gladness and joy, salvation and comfort, abundance and honor, love of Torah, reverence for God and dread of sin, and freedom from shame and reproach. In the prayer we also declare that all Israel are friends (*chaverim kol yisrael*).

◆ This Haftarah reflects in so many ways the major themes of this prayer. Outline and discuss the parallels.

◆ If you were writing a prayer for the new month, for what would you ask?

◆ As a class or individually, write your own prayer for the new month. For an example of a prayer for the new month of Elul, see *Four Centuries of Jewish Women's Spirituality*, edited by Ellen M. Umansky and Dianne Ashton, pp. 318-320.

10 King Saul hosted a celebration meal for Rosh Chodesh.

◆ As a class, organize and hold your own festive meal for the New Moon. Be sure to include special foods, special prayers or speeches, decorations, and so on.

◆ For more information on planning a Rosh Chodesh meal see the article, "This Month Is for You" by Arlene Agus in *The Jewish Woman*, edited by Elizabeth Koltun, pp. 84-93.

Extending the Text

11 In verse 20:19 Jonathan reminds David of the place where he once hid. The verb "to

hide" in Hebrew is based on the root סתר, which corresponds to the English letters STR. According to some, STR is the origin of the English word "mySTeRy."

◆ There are many English words with biblical Hebrew origins. Can you list any?

◆ See *The Jewish Bible Almanac* by Ronald H. Isaacs, p. 107, for a list of such words.

12 Verse 20:26 indicates that Saul did not say anything when he noticed that David was not present on the first day of the New Moon. Saul assumed David was missing due to some ritual impurity, which would make it inappropriate for him to join the feast. Saul thus gave David the benefit of the doubt by thinking of a reason for his absence instead of getting angry.

◆ Why is it good to avoid jumping to conclusions and to give people the benefit of the doubt?

◆ How does giving other people the benefit of the doubt help keep you calm and happy?

◆ Try to find other examples in this Haftarah of people giving each other the benefit of the doubt.

◆ See *The Other Side of the Story* by Y. Samet for stories that reinforce this important lesson.

13 Saul assumed that David was absent from his table the first day due to some ritual uncleanness that would preclude David from attending a sanctified feast.

Ritual purity is a complicated biblical concept that has few practical applications in the modern world, the most common of which is the ritual washing of hands before meals. In order to sanctify the meal and make the everyday activity of eating into something holy, it is a Jewish custom to wash hands in a specially prescribed manner before eating. Water is poured from a cup first twice over the right hand and then twice over the left hand. The hand washing also includes a blessing: "Blessed are You, *Adonai* our God, Sovereign of the Universe, who has sanctified us with Your commandments and has commanded us concerning the washing of the hands."

◆ Why might it be important to transform the regular act of eating into a holy activity?

◆ Why might we want to make our lives more holy?

◆ Learn the hand washing ritual and blessing and perform this *mitzvah* before meals.

◆ Design and make a special hand washing cup out of clay that can be glazed and fired in a kiln or, if this is not possible, decorate in a special way any cup or mug.

◆ For more information on the subject of ritual hand washing, read *The Jewish Religion: A Companion* by Louis Jacobs, p. 216.

14 In verse 20:30 Saul harshly rebukes Jonathan for defending David. Rambam teaches in the *Mishneh Torah, Ethical Ideas*: 6:7-8: "If you notice that a person has committed a sin or behaved badly, you must point out what the person did wrong. You should speak gently and nicely, informing him or her that your reproach is for their own good."

◆ In your view, did Saul reprimand Jonathan in a proper way? Defend your answer.

◆ How might Saul have let Jonathan know he was upset without flying off the handle?

◆ Rambam adds, "We have learned that whoever shames someone in public has committed a great sin. One must never call someone else a bad name, or embarrass him in public." How did Saul violate this rule?

◆ Would Rambam agree that "sticks and stones may break my bones, but words will never hurt me?" Why or why not?

◆ Role-play this scene between Saul and his son Jonathan. But instead of acting out what is written in the text (verses 20:30-34), portray how the situation could have been handled differently and better.

15 According to Jewish law, parents are obligated to discipline their children, but they should never use means that teach that physical assault is a right of those in authority. Striking a child with a fist or instrument is strictly forbidden.

◆ How did Saul violate Jewish law?

◆ Do you agree or disagree that corporal punishment is an inappropriate means of discipline?

◆ What are some nonviolent methods of discipline for parents and children, for schools and students, for the state and criminals?

16 David and Jonathan are the two most famous friends in the Bible.

◆ Look at the following biblical quotations concerning friendship. Then form three groups, with each group representing one of the quotations. Hold a debate over which quotation best represents the friendship between David and Jonathan. Each group can make a poster with its quotation on it that can be used to support their arguments in the debate and later as classroom decoration.

"There are men who pretend friendship; and there is a true friend who sticks closer than a brother" (Proverbs 18:24).

"Make no friendship with an angry man; and with a furious man you shall not go" (Proverbs 22:24).

"Two are better than one; because they have a good reward for their labor. For if they fall, the one will lift up his fellow; but woe to him that is alone when he falls; for he has not another to help him up" (Ecclesiastes 4:9-10).

17 David bows to Jonathan in verse 20:41. Bowing plays an important role in the choreography of Jewish prayer.

◆ Why do you think we bow when we pray?

◆ Identify five times we bow in prayer and discuss why each time it is an appropriate action.

◆ Ask your Cantor to teach you when and how to bow during the *"Amidah"* prayer.

◆ For information on bowing in prayer, see *Higher and Higher: Making Jewish Prayer Part of Us* by Steven M. Brown, pp. 55-57.

18 David has to hide to save his life.

◆ During the Holocaust, many Jews had to hide from the Nazis. If you had to leave your home and hide for an extended period of time, what five (portable) items would you take with you, and why?

◆ For a remarkable account of life in hiding, read and discuss *The Diary of Anne Frank*.

19 Jonathan and David reiterate their vow of loyalty to one another in verse 20:42: *"Adonai* shall be between me and you, and between my seed and your seed, for ever." In II Samuel, after Jonathan's death, David does indeed honor the oath by caring for Jonathan's disabled son, Mephibosheth. (For more information, read II Samuel 4:4 and II Samuel chapter 9.)

◆ Interview your parents about the provision in their will for a caregiver for you in the event of their death. Find out who are your custodians and why your parents chose them.

◆ As a class discuss the factors that went into your own family's choice.

◆ Decide whom you might appoint as the caregiver for your pet if you became unable to care for it.

20 Jonathan understood that David would be king instead of him, yet he was able to overcome any jealousy and maintain his close friendship with David. We learn from the Ten Commandments that it is a sin to covet, so Jonathan must be doing a *mitzvah* by not coveting David's position.

◆ Why is it sometimes so difficult not to be jealous of someone or of what someone has?

◆ We are taught in *Pirke Avot* 4:21 that "envy, craving, and the drive for acclaim take a person out of the world." Many scholars even think that every sin stems from coveting. Do you think this is so, and why or why not?

◆ As a class, test this theory. Form groups. Each group chooses a newspaper article that covers a crime. Each group then studies their assigned crime, imagining the circumstances that might have lead someone to commit the crime, and mapping out a flow chart of factors that led to the crime. See if any or all of the flow charts trace the crime back to some kind of coveting by the wrongdoers involved.

◆ For more information and exercises on not coveting, see *Teaching Mitzvot* by Barbara Binder Kadden and Bruce Kadden, pp. 71-74.

21 When David learns of Jonathan's death, he composes a poem in his honor.

◆ Read and discuss this poignant poem in II Samuel 1:19-27. See if you recognize any lines, many of which are still quoted today.

◆ Write a poem or song in honor of your best friend.

Personalizing the Text

22 Jonathan and David devised a secret code involving archery.

◆ As a class or individually, list and rank your own Jewish values (education, *tzedakah*, belonging to a synagogue, etc.). When completed, create a Jewish values target, with your most important value as the bull's-eye.

23 Jonathan and David arranged a code between them.

◆ Work with a partner or in a group to develop your own secret code. Each group can develop a code, send messages within their group, and then attempt to decipher the other students' codes. Ideas include using letter equivalents, like a=z, using number equivalents, like a=1, or inventing signals to transmit messages.

24 Like David, Jonathan was a warrior.

◆ Knowing how important family and friends were to him, design and create a battle shield that depicts Jonathan's values.

Other Resources

25 Read, act out, and discuss the skit in the book *Bible Scenes: Joshua To Solomon* by Stan J. Beiner, pp. 120-125.

26 Discuss the portrayal of this Haftarah in *The Illustrated Torah* by Michal Meron, p. 225.

27 Jonathan does his best to honor his father, despite his friendship with David. For more exploration into Judaism's view of parents' obligations toward their children and children's obligations toward their parents, have stu-dents complete the Torah Aura Instant Lesson *What Must Parents Do? — What Must Children Do?*

28 For more texts and exercises on the topic of giving other people the benefit of the doubt, see *Teaching Jewish Virtues* by Susan Freeman, pp. 26-38.

29 View and discuss the film *Julia* (1977, rated PG, 118 minutes), which is based on the book *Pentimento* by Lillian Hellman. This story about a Jewish writer highlights her lifelong friendship with Julia, a political activist devoted to fighting Nazi fascism. Compare the friendship of the two women in this film with that of Jonathan and David. Do you think one of the women makes herself and her concerns secondary to that of her friend as does Jonathan?

30 For more information and exercises on the *mitzvah* to sanctify the New Moon, see *Teaching Mitzvot* by Barbara Binder Kadden and Bruce Kadden, pp. 27-31.

31 View and discuss the popular film about boys' friendships, *Stand by Me* (1986, rated R, 87 minutes).

32 See the painting by Rembrandt entitled, "David's Farewell To Jonathan" which may be found at: http://www.lyons.co.uk/rem/albumb/Farewell.htm.

Discuss the different clothing, poses, and emo-tions of the two characters. Identify verses in the biblical text that support the artist's portrayal of the two characters.

33 For a Rosh Chodesh study guide, see *Moonbeams: A Hadassah Rosh Hodesh Guide*, edited by Carol Diament, which contains a history of Rosh Chodesh observances as well as monthly study topics suited to each month of the Jewish calendar.

34 Read and discuss the article, "This Month Is for You: Observing Rosh Chodesh as a Women's Holiday" by Arlene Agus in the book *The Jewish Woman*, edited by Elizabeth Koltun, pp. 84-93.

35 Complete page 11 in *Prophets Copy Pak*™ by Marji Gold-Vukson.

Involving the Family

36 Jonathan had a dilemma: Should he obey his father, who wanted to kill his best friend, or protect innocent David from Saul's wrath. Family members often face dilemmas about loyalty and other matters. Play the "Dilemma Game" in *The Jewish Experiential Book* by Bernard Reisman, pp. 303-305, which allows the players to learn from each other's perspectives. To play the game, the leader (or the class) prepares in advance a pack of Dilemma cards (like the Chance cards in *Monopoly*). On each card is written a moral or ethical dilemma. Participants take turns picking cards and discussing how they would handle the situation. After each participant gives his/her own response, the other players can offer their responses to the dilemma. Consider using these sample dilemmas:

- Your restaurant check is about $10 less than it should be. What do you do?

- You inherit $10,000. What do you do with the money?

- You see your friend cheating on a test. What do you do?

- Your friends are picking on someone at school. What do you do?

37 Having his family and friends together at his table was very important to King Saul. Make a point to share a family dinner at least once a week, and see if it becomes important to you, too, and why.

Bar/Bat Mitzvah Projects

38 According to Rambam in *Hilchot Rotzeach Ushmirat Nefesh* 1:14, all Jews are commanded to take lifesaving action. Jonathan was doing such a *mitzvah* by saving David's life from Saul. There are countless big and small ways in which we can save lives daily, from wearing seatbelts in the car and helmets when riding our bicycles, to learning CPR, to giving blood, registering in a bone marrow registry, and carrying an organ donor card in our wallets. Choose a lifesaving action to do alone or with your family. You may not be old enough to do some of these suggested activities, but you are still doing a *mitzvah* if you encourage your adult family members to do them.

39 Take archery lessons.

שמואל ב

II Samuel

OVERVIEW

The Second Book of Samuel tells the tales of David, King of Israel, who rose to power following the death of Saul around the year 1000 B.C.E. David assumed the throne at age 30 and reigned over Israel until his death (recorded in I Kings) 40 years later. Although the book bears Samuel's name, that prophet does not appear anywhere in the narrative, as he had died years before (in the First Book of Samuel). The book is called II Samuel because, as explained in the Overview for I Samuel, the two books were originally one work, later divided for convenience.

As Saul's rightful successor, King David consolidates power as the leader of the unified kingdom of Israel. He defeats his opponents, both within and without the kingdom. II Samuel chronicles David's successful battles against the Philistines, Moabites, Arameans, Edomites, and Ammonites. Although he defeats his enemies among the followers of Saul, David nevertheless honors his oath to Saul's son Jonathan, and cares for Jonathan's surviving son.

In addition to managing political and military matters, David tends to his religious duties as King of Israel. David brings up the Ark of the Covenant into Jerusalem, establishing that city once and forever as the capital of Israel. He also expresses his plans to build a Temple for Adonai in Jerusalem, which are thwarted by the prophet Nathan who tells David that God does not desire a House. God does promise that the dynastic house of David will endure forever.

King David's marriages, children, and family affairs are recorded in the second half of the book. In particular, his relationship with and marriage to Bathsheba, who becomes the mother of Solomon, is described in great detail. It is during the course of that relationship that David temporarily forgets that even kings are subject to the laws of God. David's sinful abuses of power exact a price of punishment on the remainder of his life. The end of David's life, as chronicled in II Samuel, is overshadowed by family traumas, including the rape of one daughter (Tamar), the political rebellion of one son (Absalom), and the deaths of three sons (an unnamed infant, Amnon, and Absalom). Although David was an excellent and righteous king anointed by God, his authority always remained second to that of God.

II SAMUEL 6:1-7:17 Ashkenazim
II SAMUEL 6:1-19 Sephardim
SHEMINI שמיני

This Haftarah has been paired with *Parashat Shemini*, Leviticus 9:1-11:47. See "Connecting the Text To the Sedra," pp. 85-86, for an exploration of the many ways the two texts shed light on each other.

SYNOPSIS

The Haftarah begins as David, now King of Israel, gathers 30,000 men to bring the Ark of God from the house of Abinadab in Baale-Judah up to Jerusalem. It is a time of great celebration for Israel, until tragedy strikes when the oxen, on whose back the Ark is carried, stumble. To secure the falling Ark, a man by the name of Uzzah grabs hold of it. God responds angrily to Uzzah's action and kills him on the spot. God's brutal treatment of Uzzah, who was only trying to help, disturbs David, who decides to abandon his plan to move the Ark and leaves it at the house of Obed-Edom the Gittite.

When David learns that God has rewarded Obed-Edom for hosting the Ark, he is reassured and decides to resume carrying the Ark up to Jerusalem. David and his men offer a sacrifice of thanksgiving and bring the Ark into Jerusalem with great rejoicing. After the sacrifices are made, David blesses the people and gives out bread and cake.

Meanwhile, as David is dancing in celebration, his wife Michal, the daughter of the late King Saul, looks down with contempt on his behavior. When David returns home to her, Michal criticizes her husband for behaving in a manner unbecoming a king. David harshly rebukes Michal,

and the text suggests in verse 6:23 that because of this altercation, Michal and David never have children together.

The beginning of chapter 7 informs us that Israel enjoys a period of peace, during which David decides to build a Temple to God in Jerusalem. David expresses this desire to the Prophet Nathan, who initially gives David permission to build it. Later, however, Nathan learns that God does not need or want a House for worship and passes the message to David. Nathan adds that God will grant David and Israel more years of peace. Finally, Nathan tells David that God will establish the House of David as the royal family of Israel forever.

INSIGHTS FROM THE TRADITION

A In verse 6:2 the word שם *(shaym)*, name, appears twice concerning the Ark, even though the context seems to suggest it is only needed once. *Baba Batra* 14b explains that the duplication of "name" refers to the two sets of tablets kept in the Ark. The first set was broken, but still kept in the Ark. The second set was whole. We learn from this that even when a scholar becomes ill, like the broken tablets, we still treat him or her with respect (*Menahot* 99a).

◆ What does this lesson reveal to us about Judaism's opinion of scholars?

◆ Can you think of other applications for this lesson, with regard to humans or objects?

TEACHING HAFTARAH

B Uzzah's death is very difficult to explain. *Metsudat David* 6:7 suggests that Uzzah's action demonstrated his lack of faith in God. Uzzah doubted God when he thought God would let the Ark fall.

◆ How do you feel about this interpretation?

◆ Does having faith in God mean that we are to do nothing to help ourselves and the world?

◆ Does *tikkun olam*, repairing the world, show faith in God or a lack thereof? Explain your answer.

C Another explanation for Uzzah's death, offered by *Numbers Rabbah* 4:20, suggests that Uzzah's death was David's fault. The Ark is supposed to be carried only by Levites, on poles, on their shoulders. David was therefore wrong to have the Ark loaded onto a cart and escorted by non-Levites.

◆ How do you feel about this interpretation?

◆ Do you think it was David's lack of attention to details (using the wagon) that led to Uzzah's death?

◆ How can our own carelessness or lack of attention to details hurt us or others? Give examples.

D Plaut offers an interesting explanation for Uzzah's death in *The Haftarah Commentary*, p. 263. "The celebration was in full swing, the joy was immense — and suddenly the man who guided the cart fell down dead. Death is all too often inexplicable, and sudden death especially so. The storyteller believed that everything that happens is God's will; thus, what happened to Uzzah must have been deserved — even though the reason was not at all clear."

Some commentators suggest that Uzzah slipped and fell by accident, but because people couldn't believe it was an accident, they blamed it on a transgression and God's resulting anger.

◆ Do you believe that some events happen randomly and without explanation? Why or why not?

◆ Do you believe that everything that happens is God's will? Explain your view.

◆ In your opinion, does this mean that every bad thing that happens is a Divine punishment of some kind? Why or why not?

◆ What may be problematic about this view?

E When Uzzah dies, David becomes angry. According to *Metsudat David*, David became angry at himself, in self-admonition.

◆ Why might David have been angry with himself?

◆ Which interpretation(s) (Insights from the Tradition #B, #C, or #D) above does this commentary support, and why?

◆ How might self-admonition be constructive? How might self-admonition be destructive?

◆ View and discuss the film *Ordinary People* (1980, rated R, 124 minutes). The film portrays the ways that one son's guilt over his brother's death affects his entire family.

F Obed-Edom provided hospitality for the Ark, which contained the laws from God. According to *Berachot* 63b, Obed-Edom simply dusted and swept around the Ark. Nonetheless, he was blessed and rewarded by God for his hospitality.

The Talmud goes on to suggest that an even greater reward is in store for anyone who hosts a scholar in his/her house because, unlike the Ark, which requires only a little cleaning, scholars (who also "contain" the laws from God) require food, drink, and the use of their host's possessions.

◆ Why do you think our tradition encourages such hospitality?

◆ Do you like having overnight guests?

◆ Do your parents like having overnight guests?

◆ Why can hosting guests be difficult? Why can hosting guests be rewarding?

◆ The next time you host overnight guests at your home, keep a journal. Record what you must do to keep your guests comfortable, the fun you have together, whatever might be difficult about the visit, etc.

◆ Hospitality is an important Jewish virtue. For Jewish texts on hospitality, see *Voices of Wisdom* by Francine Klagsbrun, pp. 58-61, and for texts and exercises, see *Teaching Jewish Virtues* by Susan Freeman, pp. 102-108.

G Michal had ill feelings toward David, according to verse 6:16. Alshich suggests that such bad feelings can be sensed even before they are verbally expressed.

◆ How can we portray our feelings without expressing them in words?

◆ It is said that "actions speak louder than words." How? Do you agree or disagree?

H David admits to Michal in verses 6:21-22 that he was behaving foolishly with joy before God. According to Rambam (*Laws of Lulav* 8:15), an act that would be debasing if done for a secular purpose would not be debasing if done in fulfillment of God's commandments.

◆ Why is the intention of an act so important? (See Insights from the Tradition #D for the Haftarah for *Machar Chodesh* on p. 72.)

◆ Can you think of any examples of an act that would be humiliating for a secular purpose but not for a holy purpose?

◆ On Rosh HaShanah and Yom Kippur, the Cantor sings *"Alaynu"* and bows low to the ground. Is this an example of a "debasing act" which, when done for a *mitzvah*, is not debasing?

◆ On Purim, adults are commanded to get so drunk that they can't tell the difference between Mordecai and Haman. How is this an example of a "debasing" act done for a *mitzvah*?

STRATEGIES
Analyzing the Text

1 After the Ark stayed a while with Obed-Edom, David saw the signs were right to move the Ark to Jerusalem.

◆ Compare the beginning of this second attempt to move the Ark with the first attempt at the beginning of the Haftarah.

◆ In which attempt does David seem more hurried?

◆ In which attempt does David offer a ritual sacrifice to God?

◆ In which attempt is the Ark accompanied by frivolity — משחקים (*mesachakim*)?

◆ In which attempt is the Ark accompanied by joyous celebration — שמחה (*simchah*)?

◆ What is the difference between frivolity and joyous celebration? We learn from this that we are to celebrate our holidays with true *simchah* and not frivolity.

2 The Ark was stored temporarily on the property of Obed-Edom the Gittite. The meaning of the term "Gittite" is unclear. *Berachot* 63b-64a understands Obed-Edom to be an Edomite, a descendant of Esau and brother of the Israelites. According to Robert Alter, his name indicates that

Obed-Edom was a foreigner. Furthermore, the term Gittite can also refer to a musical instrument (see the title of Psalm 8); perhaps, therefore, Obed-Edom was one of the musicians playing as the Ark was carried to Jerusalem.

It is also possible that during biblical times people understood the significance of "Gittite," but over the years the meaning has been lost.

◆ Which explanation about Obed-Edom do you prefer, and why?

◆ Does it matter if Obed-Edom was an Israelite or a foreigner? Why or why not?

◆ Why might the text have been purposely unclear on this point?

3 The second time David and his troops transport the Ark, they cautiously take six steps, and then sacrifice a bull to God. Some translations suggest that this sacrifice took place once, after the first six steps. Other translations say that a sacrifice was made every six steps over the whole trip.

◆ Explain why David and his men, when transporting the Ark, might have done it in each of the above different ways.

4 Psalm 132 appears to be telling the same story as II Samuel 6.

◆ Compare Psalm 132 to II Samuel 6. Which account do you like better, and why?

◆ Identify some of the main differences between the two. For example, the Psalm mentions a vow made by David and a resting place. Are these mentioned in II Samuel 6? In addition, does the Psalm mention Obed-Edom, Uzzah, or Michal? Some scholars believe that the Psalm omitted these details because they were not part of the main story. If so, what was the Psalmist's main concern?

5 Michal angrily watches from a window the joyous celebration by David of the arrival of the Ark in Jerusalem.

◆ Draw your interpretation of this scene. Compare your drawing to the illustration of this Haftarah in *The Illustrated Torah* by Michal Meron, p. 116.

◆ For advanced study, compare Michal's looking through a window with Sisera's mother anxiously watching through the window for her son after he had lost his battle in Judges 5:28-30 (see the Haftarah for *Beshalach*, Analyzing the Text #7, p. 24). Compare also Michal's inaction at what she sees to Jephthah's daughter joyously bounding from her house in Judges 11:34.

6 Michal is described in verse 6:20 as Saul's daughter, but not as David's wife, even though Saul is dead and she has been married to David for some time.

◆ How might this phrase reflect Michal's changed attitude toward David or the current state of their marriage, following the spectacle he made of himself with the Ark in Jerusalem?

7 Nathan first tells David in verse 7:3 to go ahead and build the Temple with God's approval. However, later that night Nathan receives a message from God that David is *not* to build the Temple.

◆ If a prophet is supposed to know God's will, how can we explain Nathan's error?

◆ What is the danger of assuming we know an answer we might really not know?

8 In verses 7:1-17, the word בית (*bayit*), house, appears numerous times. First David wants to build a "house" for God's Ark, then God promises to establish a "house" for David.

◆ How do the usages of the word "house" differ?

◆ List as many synonyms for "Temple" as you can.

◆ List as many synonyms for "dynasty" as you can.

◆ List as many synonyms for "house" as you can.

9 Michal, the daughter of King Saul and the wife of King David, remains childless until her death.

◆ Why is this point important? For a clue, see I Samuel 15:28, when God removes the kingship from the House of Saul.

Connecting the Text To the Sedra

10 In the Haftarah God draws a distinction between David and Solomon: David may not build the Temple; Solomon may. In the Torah reading, many distinctions are also drawn. The people of Israel are allowed to mourn the deaths of Aaron's sons, but Aaron and his two remaining sons are not allowed to engage in mourning rituals because they have been anointed as Priests. The Parashah also tells us that some animals are fit to be eaten, while others are not.

◆ Do you see other distinctions drawn in the Haftarah and Sedra?

◆ As a religion, Judaism draws many distinctions — between holy and profane, between Shabbat and weekday, between kosher and non-kosher. Discuss why distinctions may be important to any religion.

◆ Why might it be an important life skill to be able to assess, distinguish, and categorize people or actions?

11 In the Haftarah the Holy Ark has the power both to bless and to kill. In the Sedra the Tabernacle has the same seemingly opposite powers. Michael Fishbane explains in the *Etz Hayim Chumash* (p. 644) that in both the Haftarah and the Sedra, "holy objects are presented as bivalent entities, affecting human life by the manner in which they are approached and used." From this we can learn that indeed all objects can be used for holy purposes or for evil ones. Consider that in the fall of 2001 we discovered that: airplanes can be used to destroy buildings and kill masses of people, or to deliver food to starving refugees; religion can be used as an excuse to murder innocent people, or as a source of life and strength for those in need; and technology can be used to make chemical or biological weapons, or to make medicines that cure deadly diseases.

◆ Choose an ordinary object and, on one half of a poster, draw ways in which this object can be used for holy purposes. On the other half, draw ways in which it can be used for evil.

12 In both the Torah reading and Haftarah, the subject is a moment of great celebration. The Sedra describes the first use of the Tabernacle after the Israelites completed its construction in the desert. Building the Tabernacle was a huge feat. The Haftarah describes the moving of the holy Ark of God, which had been lost for a time to the Philistines, to the capital city of Jerusalem. This was an act of great joy and relief.

◆ What does your family or your community do to celebrate moments of great joy (completing an enormous task) and great relief?

◆ Form two groups. One will compose a rap or poem describing the joy and relief at having completed the Tabernacle in the desert. The other group will write a rap or poem describing the joy and relief at having recaptured the

Ark from the Philistines and bringing it safely to Jerusalem. The groups can read or perform their compositions for each other.

13 In the Sedra Aaron's sons Nadab and Abihu are killed in the middle of offering an improper sacrifice in the Tabernacle. In the Haftarah Uzzah dies after helping to secure the Ark. In each case, the celebration is interrupted by a tragedy involving the symbol of God's presence.

◆ Do you usually think of encounters with God as being potentially dangerous and scary?

◆ Write a eulogy for one or more of these men, including a summary of the circumstances of their deaths.

14 In both the case of Nadab and Abihu and of Uzzah, we are left wondering why the tragedy happened. Both seem inexplicable.

◆ Discuss other tragedies that seem inexplicable.

◆ Create memorial monuments (using clay, popsicle sticks, dioramas, pictures, etc.) to Nadab and Abihu and to Uzzah, describing or depicting the circumstances of their mysterious deaths.

15 God's anger accompanies both tragedies. Review II Samuel 6-7 and Leviticus 10:1-2.

◆ In your opinion, is God's anger justified in either case? Why or why not?

◆ Do you usually associate anger with God as God is portrayed in the Bible? Do you usually associate anger with God as God is portrayed in our prayers? Do you usually associate anger with God as you define God for yourself?

16 David becomes angry at the death of Uzzah.

◆ Does the text seem to indicate David expressing his anger? With whom is he angry?

◆ Similarly, in the Sedra, God kills Aaron's two eldest sons. One might expect Aaron to respond with anger toward God. However, the text says that "Aaron was silent" (Leviticus 10:3). Commentators suggest that Aaron's silence indicates he was resigned to God's action and not angry. Would you have expected David or Aaron to have been more angry with God than they were? Why or why not?

◆ Write and perform a skit about what David or Aaron might have said in anger to God and God's reply to David or Aaron.

◆ For more material about being angry with God, see *Teaching Jewish Virtues* by Susan Freeman, p. 96, #5.

◆ Rabbi Levi Isaac of Berditchev was famous for expressing his anger toward God and holding God accountable. Read and discuss his *"Kaddish"* or the short story "A Lenient Illiterate" in *The Yom Kippur Anthology*, edited by Philip Goodman, p. 118.

17 The sons of Aaron who die in the Sedra are named Nadab and Abihu. In the Haftarah we are told that the Ark had been housed in the home of Abinadab (6:3), which seems to be a combination of the names of the two sons of Aaron. Nadab means "he volunteered," and Abihu means "he is my father."

True to the meaning of his name ("my father volunteered"), Abinadab may have volunteered to house the Ark. He also may have volunteered his two sons to help move it. Find out your parents' or grandparents' Hebrew names and what they mean. Write a story about a fictional child whose parents have these names, and how the names affect events in the child's life.

Extending the Text

18 We learn in Insights from the Tradition #A, p. 81, that damaged sacred texts are to be treated with utmost respect. In fact, badly damaged Torah scrolls and sacred texts, like prayer books, are buried in a Jewish cemetery with the same dignity as a deceased person. Consequently, such items are not thrown away before burial, but carefully kept in storage in a *genizah*.

◆ Ask your Rabbi what your congregation does with discarded sacred texts. If the texts are taken to a cemetery for burial, see if your class can go along. If possible, your class can dig a "grave" on your synagogue's property and bury discarded sacred texts yourselves. Compose and conduct an appropriate burial ceremony.

19 As with carrying the Ark and offering sacrifices, certain synagogue rituals must be done in a precise way.

◆ Ask your Rabbi or Cantor to present the proper way to have an *aliyah* to the Torah to your class. Then, practice the procedure in the sanctuary.

20 Uzzah's death is blamed on a sin he committed (see Insights from the Tradition #B, p. 82 Michal's barrenness is blamed on her altercation with David (see Analyzing the Text #9, p. 85).

◆ How might both explanations be seen as "blaming the victim?"

◆ In what cases is it ever fair to blame the victim?

◆ Are there always good explanations for why bad things happen to people?

◆ For more on this subject, read and discuss *When Bad Things Happen To Good People* by Harold Kushner.

21 At the end of David's celebration in Jerusalem, he gives all the people bread and two kinds of cake (verse 6:19). Food plays an important role in all Jewish holidays and celebrations.

◆ As a class, compile a list of your favorite dishes for each Jewish holiday. Each student can then get family recipes for some of the dishes. Include the recipes in a class cookbook you can copy for everyone to take home. If facilities are available, you may also wish to create some of the recipes for a classroom feast.

22 Michal and David were very angry at each other.

◆ Although our tradition teaches that it is always important to give one another the benefit of the doubt, (see *Teaching Jewish Virtues* by Susan Freeman, pp. 26-38), does it appear that Michal and David did?

◆ What might this failure to give each other the benefit of the doubt indicate about the state of their relationship, even prior to David's return with the Ark to Jerusalem?

◆ Why might we fail to give someone the benefit of the doubt?

◆ Write a journal entry for Michal the day before the event, the day of the event, and the day after the event, describing her feelings toward her husband.

23 In verses 7:8-16 God offers an unconditional promise to establish forever the dynasty of the house of David. It turns out in the following chapters that David commits sins far more grievous than those of his predecessor, Saul, who loses the kingship because of his failure to exterminate his enemy completely. Still, the kingship is never wrested from David's family. Our tradition even teaches that the Messiah will be a descendant of David.

- What is an unconditional promise?

- Why do you think God made an unconditional promise to David?

- A U.S. Supreme Court Justice is appointed for life. Invite a lawyer to come to your class and discuss what it means to be a Supreme Court Justice. Be sure to find out whether or not the lifetime appointment is unconditional.

Personalizing the Text

24 Despite many explanations, the reason for Uzzah's death remains a mystery.

- With Uzzah as the plaintiff and God as the defendant, conduct a classroom trial of the event. Were God's actions justified? Be sure to have attorneys and witnesses and a jury to decide the case. The teacher could be the judge and keep "order in the court."

25 Judaism often draws distinctions (see Connecting the Text To the Sedra #10, p. 85). One important distinction Judaism makes is between pre-Bar Mitzvah age and post-Bar Mitzvah age.

- List and explain some of the Jewish legal distinctions between these two age groups.

- When one is old enough to drive, one obtains a driver's license, which is a kind of adult identification card. Design and create your own post-Bar Mitzvah Jewish adult identification cards. The cards should contain words and/or images that identify the bearer as a Jewish adult, with all the privileges and responsibilities that such status brings.

26 The Ark was stationed at the home of Obed-Edom. In return for his hospitality, we are told that Obed-Edom is blessed by God.

- How do you think Obed-Edom was blessed?

- Write a list of ten blessings in your own life.

- Do you always recognize the good things in your life as blessings? How does viewing them as blessings change the way you feel about your life and your relationship with God?

27 David brought the Ark into Jerusalem with a joyful procession.

- Choose any occasion to celebrate with your own similar procession in your school building or yard or at a local park. Use costumes, musical instruments, songs, and dance.

- Of what modern day event does this procession remind you?

- Alternatively, participate as a class in a local parade, especially an Israeli Day Parade.

28 We learn in Insights from the Tradition #G, p. 83, that actions often speak louder than words and that attitudes can be portrayed nonverbally. In *Pirke Avot* 1:15, Shammai says, "Say little and do much, and receive everyone with a cheerful countenance." Commentators explain that this means we must conduct all of our daily interactions in a friendly manner.

- A public service announcement is a 30-second message on television or radio that is meant to convey some message of importance to the public. In groups, write 30-second public service announcements on the importance of being cheerful. Include in your announcement how the world would be a better place if everyone were cheerful. After the announcements are written and rehearsed, the teacher can videotape each group's message. View the video-tapes together.

29 Messages can be delivered verbally or nonverbally.

◆ Play a game of *Charades*, paying attention to the ways we deliver messages without using words. Or try a more difficult version by playing *Fifteen Seconds Charades*. In this version, the person acting out the charade has only 15 seconds to act. After 15 seconds, he/she must give the charade card to anyone of his/her choice in the class who must then continue acting out the same charade within 15 more seconds (but the first actor may not guess). The game keeps going until the charade is correctly guessed or until there are no more players to guess.

30 In Insights from the Tradition #G, p. 83, we learned that Michal communicated her ill feelings to David even before she spoke. Body language is one type of nonverbal communication.

◆ Make a body language poster. Cut out pictures from magazines of facial expressions and body gestures. Paste them on poster board and write below each picture the emotion being portrayed.

31 Michal's face may have expressed her feelings even before she spoke.

◆ Listen to the Billy Joel song "The Stranger" on the album of the same name. Identify the different faces in the song and what emotions might go along with each face. The song says that we hide some of these faces. Discuss why we do that.

◆ Make masks to represent each face and sing along with Billy Joel while wearing the masks.

32 Nathan first tells David that he can build a Temple to God, but has to retract the permission once he checks with God.

◆ Can you think of any examples when one of your parents gave you permission to do something, but reneged after checking with your other parent?

◆ How did you feel when this occurred?

◆ Can you put yourself into your parents' positions to see how they felt?

◆ Role-play a situation that you can remember, or invent one, in which someone gives permission and then takes it away.

Other Resources

33 The film *King David* (1985, rated PG-13, 114 minutes), starring Richard Gere, features a controversial portrayal of David bringing the Ark into Jerusalem. (This film contains brief nudity. Please preview and cue before viewing. The recommended scene is appropriate for all audiences.) View the scene and discuss why it engendered so much bad publicity. Write your own review of the scene. Do you think the scene is accurately portrayed, according to the text?

34 Read and discuss the poem "Michal" by the Israeli poet Rachel in *Modern Poems on the Bible*, edited by Dan Curzon, p. 205.

35 Complete the Torah Aura Instant Lesson *Think Prophets: Nathan* by Joel Lurie Grishaver.

36 View and discuss the Disney film *The Little Mermaid* (1978, rated G, 82 minutes), in which Ariel gives away her voice and must rely on nonverbal communication to win the man of her dreams. How does she do it? Do you think you could communicate effectively without using words?

37 View and discuss the film *Raiders of the Lost Ark* (1981, rated PG, 115 minutes), in which the dangerous power of the Ark is very evident.

Involving the Family

38 The next time your synagogue hosts a scholar in residence or a visiting Rabbi or Cantor, volunteer to host the visitor at your home (see Insights from the Tradition #F, pp. 82-83).

39 David made thanksgiving sacrifices after every six steps while carrying the Ark to Jerusalem. For six days (or six weeks or six months), each member of your family should offer thanks by giving *tzedakah* every time something good happens. Collect the *tzedakah* and decide as a family where it will go.

Bar/Bat Mitzvah Projects

40 Teach your parents and other family members the proper way to have an *aliyah* to the Torah for your Bar or Bat Mitzvah. Be sure to ask your Rabbi or Cantor for help if you are uncertain how to do this. (See Extending the Text #19, p. 87.)

41 We learn in the Haftarah that David feeds bread and cake to the people. Since the Sedra *Shemini* is always read just before or just after Passover, organize a food drive for *matzah* and Passover cake to distribute to the needy members of your community.

42 In recognition of sacred objects, volunteer to polish the silver crowns and breastplates adorning your synagogue's Torah scrolls.

43 For the entire month before your Bar or Bat Mitzvah, follow the Rabbis' advice and greet everyone with a cheerful face (see Personalizing the Text #28, pp. 88-89).

II SAMUEL 22:1-51
HA'AZINU האזינו
SEVENTH DAY PASSOVER

 This Haftarah was paired with *Parashat Ha'azinu*, Deuteronomy 32:1-32:52, and the seventh day of Passover on which we read Exodus 13:17-15:26. See "Connecting the Text To the Sedra," pp. 93-95, for an exploration of the ways the texts and the holiday shed light on each other.

SYNOPSIS

A poet and musician, King David sings a Song of Thanksgiving in this Haftarah. Although it is found near the end of II Samuel, 22 chapters after the death of King Saul, the introduction to David's hymn indicates that it was composed shortly after David was saved from the hand of Saul.

In poetic and vividly symbolic language, the King of Israel expresses his faith in God, whom David calls his "rock" and "shield," his "tower" and "refuge" (verses 2-4). David then recalls the danger from which he has been saved by Divine intervention (verses 5-21).

The next four verses (22-25) declare God's love for the King. David asserts that it is his own righteousness that makes him worthy of Divine love and protection. Based on his own experience, King David teaches us that God is always merciful toward people who are merciful, that God saves the afflicted, and that God humbles the arrogant (verses 26-28).

In verse replete with graphic and sometimes brutal military imagery, David continues to praise God and acknowledges that his successes were all due to God's grace (verses 30-46). The Haftarah con-

cludes (verses 47-51) with emphatic praise for God and a final expression of David's gratitude to God, his "tower of salvation."

INSIGHTS FROM THE TRADITION

A David calls to God with praise in verse 22:4. Ralbag teaches from this that all our prayers should begin with praise for God.

◆ Why do you think it is a good idea to begin a prayer with praise?

◆ When you ask your parents for something, what praise might you offer them first?

B Describing his times of trouble in verses 22:12-13, David says that although God hid behind darkness, there was still a brightness surrounding God. Hirsch understands this to mean that even in the darkest most tragic periods of history, the light of God is visible if we choose to recognize it.

David also refers in verse 22:12 to thick storm clouds gathering water. Hirsch explains that just as dark clouds collect water, which is needed for life, so, too, can dark and difficult times in our lives lead to growth and happiness.

◆ In what ways do Hirsch's interpretations remind you of the aphorism, "When life hands you lemons, make lemonade"?

◆ Do you agree that "every cloud has a silver lining"? Explain your answer.

◆ Why is it sometimes so difficult to look on the bright side?

C We learn in verse 22:26 that what you do in your life comes right back at you. Radak teaches that if you do *chesed* (kindness), God does *chesed* for you, too.

◆ How would you know if God was merciful and kind toward you?

◆ There is a popular bumper sticker that says, "Engage in random acts of kindness." Design a bumper sticker slogan conveying the message that if you do *chesed, chesed* comes back to you.

D In verse 22:35, Hirsch understands "bending the bow" as "lowering the bow." This means that while it is important to know how to fight wars, it is equally important to know how to lower the bow and prevent wars.

◆ Is war and/or hatred ever justified and right? (For example, was the United States right to retaliate for the September 11, 2001 terrorist attacks?) Justify your answer.

◆ What might be some ways that nations can prevent wars from occurring?

◆ In the Book of Ecclesiastes we are taught that there is a time for everything, including a "time for loving and a time for hating; a time for war and a time for peace" (verse 3:8). Do you agree with the Ecclesiastes statement?

◆ Does the Ecclesiastes statement support or contradict Hirsch's point of view?

E Hirsch understands verse 22:37 to mean that with God's help and support, David accomplished more than he could have alone.

◆ Do you ever feel that God is helping and supporting you? Describe such a time.

◆ How does having your parents' support help you in a particular endeavor or activity?

◆ How do fans actually help athletic teams?

STRATEGIES
Analyzing the Text

1 You might have noticed that even though there are two books bearing Samuel's name, the prophet appears only in I Samuel. This is explained by the fact that the two books were originally one single book, but the books were divided in two for convenience by the Greek translation of the Hebrew Bible, the *Septuagint*.

◆ Interestingly, the first book of Samuel begins with the song of Hannah and the second book of Samuel ends with a song. How does this poetic "frame" help to support the idea that the two Samuels were once one?

◆ Why do you think we continue to treat the two books separately, even though we know the books were once one?

2 The Haftarah's introduction makes it sound as if David was just recently saved from Saul, but scholars agree the rest of the poem seems to have been written much later in David's life, long after he was made king.

◆ Why might the memory of Saul's pursuit have been so fresh in David's mind after so many years?

◆ Write about or draw a vivid memory of something that happened to you a long time ago.

3 Some translations of verse 22:1 say that David is grateful for being saved "from the grasp of [King] Saul," while other versions say "from the grasp of the netherworld." The netherworld is a biblical euphemism for death. The two interpretations stem from the Hebrew word שאול, which can be read as either *Sha'ul* (Hebrew for "Saul") or *She'ol* (Hebrew for "netherworld"), depending on the vowels.

◆ Which interpretation do you like better, and why?

◆ Which interpretation resolves the conflict mentioned above (Analyzing the Text #2, p. 92) regarding when David wrote the poem?

◆ For David, what did Saul and death have in common?

4 David uses several different expressions in verse 22:2 to describe how God protects him. Hirsch explains how these expressions are metaphors:

God is a rock upon which David can stand to raise himself and strengthen himself against his enemies.

God is a fortress that surrounds David in protection.

◆ Identify five other metaphors for God that David uses in the Haftarah, and explain their symbolic significance.

5 Biblical poetry often utilizes the literary devices called parallelism and repetition. In this Haftarah there are many examples of parallelism, in which consecutive verses express the same idea in different ways. See, for example, verse 22:3:

"O God, the rock wherein I take shelter:

My shield, my mighty champion, my fortress and refuge!

My savior, You who rescue me from violence!"

◆ What is the thought expressed in verse 22:3?

Verses 22:38-39 employ the device of repetition:

"I pursued my enemies and wiped them out,

I did not turn back till I destroyed them.

I destroyed them, I struck them down;

They rose no more, they lay at my feet."

◆ What idea is expressed here?

◆ Find one other example of parallelism or repetition in the Haftarah.

6 The relationship between God and human beings is portrayed in parallel form in verses 22:26-27. The poet says that God acts with loyalty toward those who are loyal, that God is blameless with those who are blameless, and that God is pure with those who are pure. In each of these phrases, God's action uses the same exact word as the description of the good people.

◆ Contrast this with a comment in verse 22:27 about evil people and God's actions toward them: "With the perverse — עִקֵּשׁ *(eekaysh)*, You are wily — תִּתְפָּל *(tetapal)*." Here, God's action is not described with the same word and the description of the people, breaking the pattern of repetition. This break in the repetition calls the reader's attention to the verse.

◆ Why might the poet have not wanted to use the same exact word to describe God and evil people?

◆ What is the difference between "perverse" and "wily"?

7 For more advanced study, compare the Haftarah, which is David's prayer of thanksgiving to God after his victory over his enemies, with Psalm 18, which is a very similar song of thanksgiving.

◆ To learn more about these texts, see the discussion in *The David Story* by Robert Alter, p. 336.

Connecting the Text To the Sedra

8 The Sedra contains a song acknowledging the role of God in the history of Israel. Moses explains (Deuteronomy 32:3) that it is his intent to proclaim God's greatness in his song. Similarly, the Haftarah is a song of David in which the king praises God for helping him all his life (II Samuel 22:4).

◆ In our own prayers, we have devised many different words to express praise for God. List all the words you can think of that are in some way synonymous with "praise."

◆ Now read the English translation of the *"Yishtabach"* prayer: "Praised be Your name forever, O our Sovereign, great and holy, in heaven and on earth. For to You, *Adonai* our God and God of our ancestors, it is fitting to render song and praise, hymn and psalm, ascribing to You power and dominion, victory and glory, holiness and sovereignty. To You we offer blessing and thanksgiving from this time forth and forevermore. Blessed are You, *Adonai*, exalted in praises, God of thanksgiving, *Adonai* of wonders, who takes delight in songs and psalms, You are God and Sovereign, the life of the universe."

◆ Identify at least a dozen words in this prayer that we use to praise God.

9 You may notice that in the Sedra Moses expresses thanks to God on behalf of the entire nation, while in the Haftarah David's gratitude to God is for his own personal success. Michael Fishbane observes in the *Etz Hayim Chumash* (p. 1197) that "through the liturgical juxtaposition of this Haftarah and this Parashah the reader is faced with two religious paths: a God-centered way of remembrance and humility and a self-centered way of forgetfulness and pride. The one gives life; the other destroys." Indeed, King David's life goes precipitously downhill once he forgets that it is God — and not David — who is in charge (see II Samuel 11 through the end of the book).

◆ Find in the Sedra where Moses expresses thanks from a communal perspective. Why

do you think this expression of gratitude is considered God-centered?

◆ Find in the Haftarah where David expresses thanks. Do you think that it is self-centered?

◆ What is the difference between living a God-centered life and a self-centered one?

◆ Discuss how the following Jewish rituals encourage remembrance and humility and a God-centered life: communal prayer, reciting *Kiddush* (recalling the Exodus from Egypt), wearing *tzitzit*, hanging *mezuzot* (containing the words of the *"Shema"*).

◆ Make a list of ten ways one can live a God-centered life filled with gratitude for life's blessing.

10 The Sedra contains many references to God as a "Rock" (see Deuteronomy 32: 4, 15, 18, 30, and 31). Similarly, the Haftarah contains several descriptions of God as a "Rock" (see II Samuel 22:3, 32, and 47).

◆ What do you think it means that God is a "Rock?"

◆ Imagine a kite blowing in the wind. If it is not controlled from the ground, it may go too far one way into the trees or too far another way into electric wires. If, however, the kite is tied to a rock on the ground, will it be able to stray far? What does the rock do for the kite?

◆ Can you think of other examples, besides rocks, of things or people that keep other things or people steady? (Examples include a captain for a basketball team or cleats for a soccer player or an anchor for a boat.)

◆ Who is a rock for you, and why?

◆ For whom are you a rock, and why?

◆ The metaphor of God as "our Rock" can express the idea that God helps us avoid dangerous extremes in life and helps keep us anchored. Explain how each of the following can keep us anchored and on the right path: our religion, traditions, values, prayers, and community.

◆ Many years ago, "pet rocks" were very popular. Make your own pet rock by decorating a rock any way you wish. Keep your rock on your desk at home to remind you to stay steady on the right path.

11 Two very unusual words appear in the Sedra and also in the Haftarah. Moses says in Deuteronomy 32:5 that the children of Israel are perverse (עקש) and wily (פתלתל). This is the only time the word "perverse" appears in the Pentateuch, and the word "wily" appears only here and questionably in Genesis 30:8. These two words, therefore, stand out as being quite unusual.

Interestingly, these same two roots also appear in the Haftarah in verse 22:27 (see Analyzing the Text #6, p. 93). The word "perverse" appears only five times in the prophetic books, and "wily" appears only here. Thus, the words are also unusual in the books of prophets.

◆ Look these two words up in an English dictionary. Decide which definitions seem most appropriate to the use of the words in the Sedra and in the Haftarah.

◆ Write a story or skit about someone who is either wily or perverse.

12 In the Haftarah David makes it clear that God deals out to people what they deserve (see II Samuel 22:26-28). Similarly, in the Parashah Moses explains that God's punishment of Israel was provoked by Israel's bad behavior (Deuteronomy 32:15-21).

◆ Do you believe that everything that happens to us in life is divine reward or retribution?

◆ Do you believe that our actions have consequences, that "what goes around comes around"?

◆ Think of examples from your life or from current events that demonstrate either the principle that "what goes around comes around" or that things just happen.

13 The Torah reading, *Ha'azinu*, is read on *Shabbat Shuvah* (the Shabbat of Repentance between Rosh HaShanah and Yom Kippur) or on the next Shabbat, which immediately follows Yom Kippur. The Haftarah for *Ha'azinu* is read only when the Sedra follows Yom Kippur. When *Ha'azinu* is read on *Shabbat Shuvah*, the Haftarah for *Shabbat Shuvah* is read instead.

◆ On Yom Kippur, we are held accountable for how we have behaved. What verses in the Haftarah for *Ha'azinu* reflect this concept of accountability?

14 According to Hirsch, a few congregations do not read this Haftarah for *Ha'azinu*. Instead, they have the custom of reading Ezekiel 17:22-24, 18:1-32.

◆ For an advanced lesson, look at that passage to see why it is a tradition among some congregations to read Ezekiel instead.

◆ Explain how this choice of text also sheds light on the theme in this Haftarah that people get what they deserve.

Extending the Text

15 David offers this prayer of thanksgiving to God. We are given the opportunity to thank God every morning in the prayer *"Modeh Ani,"* which is to be said immediately upon waking. In words reminiscent of David's, the prayer says: "I gratefully thank You, O living and eternal Sovereign, for You have returned my soul within me with compassion — abundant is Your faithfulness."

◆ Why should we thank God every morning?

◆ What does it mean that God "returns our soul" to us every day?

◆ The commentary in one *Siddur* explains that we must recognize that each day God restores our faculties to us in the hope that we will serve God in return (*The Complete Artscroll Siddur*, p. 3). Do you think God expects anything from us in return for the gift of life?

16 David opens his hymn with praise for God, teaching us that all our prayers should begin with praise for God (see Insights from the Tradition #A, p. 91).

The weekday *"Amidah"* is a lengthy prayer comprising 19 blessings in three sections: praise, petition, thanksgiving.

◆ Analyze the 19 blessings in the *"Amidah"* and put them into their proper categories. To make this more of a hands-on lesson, the teacher can photocopy the blessings and cut them into individual strips which the students can physically arrange in categories.

◆ Is it always clear which blessing should go into which category?

◆ Why do you think we begin with praise?

◆ For what kinds of things do we ask, and why does this section go in the middle section of the *"Amidah"*?

◆ Why do you think we conclude with thanksgiving?

17 Many of the metaphors David used for God in this Haftarah are also found in our

prayer books. The following prayers all use metaphors found in verse 3 of the Haftarah:

At the end of the first blessing of the *"Amidah,"* God is called the Shield of Abraham.

The blessing we recite just before the morning *"Amidah"* refers to God as Rock of Israel.

At the end of the Shabbat morning service, just before *"Alaynu,"* we recite *"Ayn Kelohaynu,"* in which we say God is our Savior.

In *"Adon Olam"* we call God both a Rock and a Refuge.

◆ Find three more examples of similar metaphors for God in our prayers.

◆ What do these metaphors mean to you? Are they relevant images for your life and your relationship to God?

18 Samuel 22:51 is included toward the end of the Grace after Meals.

You will notice that in the Grace after Meals there are two versions of the verse, one to be said on weekdays and one to be said on special occasions. The weekday version vocalizes the word *"magdil,"* while the special version vocalizes *"migdol."* The first version is taken from Psalm 18:51, and the second from this Haftarah.

Actually, the pronunciation found in II Samuel 22:51 *(migdol)* was originally supposed to be used for all occasions. However, a reference to II Samuel was inserted next to the verse in the prayer so that people would know that this is where the verse came from. The reference for II Samuel was abbreviated with the Hebrew שׁב *(Shmuel Bet)*, which was later misunderstood as שׁבת (Shabbat). Based on this misunderstanding, a custom derived to use this pronunciation only on Shabbat and holidays and to use the pronunciation from Psalm 18 for weekdays.

◆ For advanced study, find this passage.

◆ Many synagogues have booklets containing the "Grace after Meals" to be used for communal meals. Design a cover for such a booklet using images from II Samuel 22:51.

◆ Alternatively, design place mats that will remind someone sitting down to eat that we have food because God is our "tower" and "deals graciously" with us.

19 Malbim suggests that in verse 22:21 "righteousness" means doing positive commandments and "cleanness" means passively not breaking negative commandments. The positive commandments in our tradition tell us what to do, and the negative commandments tell us what sins not to do (see Malbim on Psalms 18:21).

◆ Review the Ten Commandments and divide them into positive and negative.

◆ Why do we need both types of commandments? Which, as a whole, are harder to follow?

◆ Think of three examples in your country of positive and negative laws.

◆ Play the game *Democrazy*, in which players make up and pass or defeat positive and negative laws (4 to 10 players, ages 12+, 30-45 minutes, available from Descartes, agdusa@aol.com).

20 In verses 22:22-25 David seems to be declaring that the laws serve as guidelines for living a better life. Many people today think, on the other hand, that the restrictions imposed on us by Jewish law only cheat us out of life's many joys.

◆ Hold a class debate over whether social laws (not stealing, not giving false testimony, not coveting) add to or take away from life's enjoyment.

◆ Hold a class debate over whether private ritual laws (*tallit, tefillin, kashrut*) add to or take away from life's enjoyment.

21 God is given so many names and descriptions in the Haftarah and in our *tefilah* (prayers).

◆ Decide which image of God is most meaningful to you. Explain to your classmates why you chose it.

◆ We are taught by Rambam in his Thirteen Principles of Faith that God has no physical body or appearance. If this is so, how can we use all these descriptions of God?

◆ Do visual images help us to relate to God? Explain your answer.

◆ Is it difficult to relate to something you cannot see or hear or smell or touch? Why or why not?

◆ Can you see, hear, smell, or touch love? How can you tell when it is there?

◆ How is sensing love similar to sensing God?

22 David thanks God for saving him from danger in this Haftarah. There is a blessing traditionally recited by someone who has survived a life threatening situation. It says, "Blessed are You God, Sovereign of the Universe, Who bestows good things upon the guilty, Who has bestowed every goodness upon me."

◆ What might be a life threatening situation?

◆ What do you think "Who bestows good things upon the guilty" means?

◆ Write your own version of this blessing.

◆ The blessing requires a congregational response, which says, "May God Who has bestowed goodness upon you continue to bestow every goodness upon you forever." Is this an appropriate response to someone who has just survived disaster? Why or why not?

Personalizing the Text

23 David offers, in this Haftarah, a prayer of thanksgiving to God (see Extending the Text #15, p. 95).

◆ Learn to recite our daily prayer of thanksgiving, *"Modeh Ani,"* in Hebrew. Make a plaque on wood or poster board with the words of the prayer in Hebrew and English to hang in your bedroom.

24 David thanks God for saving him from trouble. The fourth paragraph of the hymn, *"Adon Olam,"* contains imagery that echoes David's, and the last line says, *"Adonai* is with me, I have no fear."

◆ Learn a new melody from the Cantor for *"Adon Olam."*

◆ Alternatively, learn to sing all the verses of the Chanukah hymn, "Rock of Ages."

25 David believed that he was worthy of God's attention and kindness.

◆ What is the difference between having a good opinion of yourself and being conceited?

◆ Everyone deserves God's love and attention. Tell your classmates how they are worthy: Each student takes off one shoe and labels it with his/her name. Place the shoes in a straight line. On small slips of paper, each student writes one nice thing about each of his/her classmates, including himself or herself. (If there are 20 students in the class, each student should be given 20 slips of paper.) After students write their anonymous compliments, the teacher should review each comment for appropriateness, then place the comment in the appropriate shoe. At the end of the

exercise, each student may retrieve his/her own shoe and take a few minutes to read the comments. You might choose to conclude with a group discussion about the exercise.

26 David trusts God unconditionally, and willingly accepts God's help.

◆ It is not always easy to know who to trust or when to accept assistance. Play a trust game by dividing the class into partners. One partner is blindfolded, while the other leads him/her around the classroom or even outside in a safe place, if possible. After several minutes, the partners may switch roles.

◆ After the exercise, have a group discussion about their experience of trusting and being trusted.

◆ To explore the issues of trust and helping, do and discuss the three "Helping Relationship" exercises in *Jewish Identity Games* by Richard Israel, pp. 58-67.

27 The Synopsis of this Haftarah divides David's hymn into several sections.

◆ Make a pictorial version of David's poem. First, write in a single sentence the theme of each section of the hymn. Write each theme on the top of one sheet of poster board. Then, paste onto the poster board pictures cut out from magazines that help to illustrate each theme. Hang the completed posters in your classroom.

28 David vividly remembers being saved from Saul in his younger days.

◆ Interview an elderly family member on audio or videotape. Ask that person to recall a distant memory that seems fresh in his/her mind, as if it occurred just yesterday. Be sure to get as much vivid detail as possible about the remembered event. Ask why that particular recollection is so prominent in his/her memory.

◆ Share and discuss your recording with the other members of the class.

29 The images and words in David's Song of Thanksgiving make war seem exciting and almost glamorous.

◆ View the first horrific scene of the film *Saving Private Ryan* (1998, rated R, 170 minutes), directed by Steven Spielberg. (This scene is appropriate for older students only.) Compare the visual images in this scene with the verbal images in the Haftarah.

◆ How is your own personal view of war affected by both the film and the Haftarah?

◆ Alternatively, invite a war veteran to come to the class and describe his or her memories of battle. Compare the images the veteran uses with those in the Haftarah.

30 In his Song of Thanksgiving, David praises God for helping him.

◆ Write your own song or poem or note thanking someone who has helped you out of a jam in your life.

Other Resources

31 *Higher and Higher: Making Jewish Prayer a Part of Us* by Steven M. Brown includes a comprehensive list of the names of God found in the Jewish tradition (pp. 61-64). Review the list using Brown's discussion questions on p. 62. You may also choose to expand the topic and do Exercises 3 and 4, which deal with faith and "Godbeliefs" (pp. 65-66).

32 For a story on accepting help and support from others, read and discuss "The Mountain and the Cliff," told by David Holtz in *Chosen Tales*, edited by Peninnah Schram, pp. 161-165.

33 Discuss the illustration of this Haftarah in *The Illustrated Torah* by Michal Meron, p. 220.

Involving the Family

34 Learning how to recognize the potential for good even in the worst situations is a valuable life skill. Discuss events in your family's history that may have been difficult, but eventually led to something good.

35 Whenever one family member asks another family member to do something, be sure to include some words of praise first and some words of gratitude last. See how this changes the way you respond to one another's requests.

Bar/Bat Mitzvah Projects

36 Recite the *"Modeh Ani"* every morning during the month of your Bar/Bat Mitzvah.

37 We learned in Insights from the Tradition #C, p. 91, that when you do *chesed*, *chesed* comes back to you. Put that theory to the test during the month of your Bar/Bat Mitzvah by doing as many random acts of kindness as you can. Some examples include: carrying your friend's schoolbooks, helping your brother with his chores, putting money in a parking meter that is about to run out, and so on. How do your acts of kindness make you feel about yourself and the world?

OVERVIEW

As the First Book of Kings begins, King David has grown old. His eldest son, Adonijah, attempts to assume the throne as his father lay dying, but David proclaims the younger Solomon as the next king of Israel.

Around 961 B.C.E., after reigning over Israel for 40 years, David dies and is buried in the City of David. King Solomon ascends the throne and firmly establishes his reign by disposing of his enemies, according to David's dying wishes. Solomon proves to be a remarkable king, renowned for his great wisdom and wealth. People from many lands, like the famous Queen of Sheba, come to avail themselves of Solomon's great wisdom.

Solomon's greatest accomplishment is the building of the Temple in Jerusalem, the construction of which is documented in painstaking detail in the first half of this book. The Temple is dedicated on the festival of Sukkot, when the Ark of the Covenant is brought into it with great celebration.

Solomon's downfall is brought about by his marriages to hundreds of foreign women, many of whom bring with them idolatrous practices, which they pass on to the people of Israel. As punishment for Solomon's sinfulness, God proclaims that the kingdom of Israel will be divided after Solomon's death between Solomon's son and his adversary, forever ending the days of a united kingdom of Israel. As in the books of Judges and Samuel before it and the remaining prophetic books after it, the First Book of Kings repeatedly demonstrates that obedience to God results in national success, while rebellion leads to disaster.

When Solomon dies in 922 B.C.E., his son Rehoboam rules over the Southern Kingdom of Judah, while the rebel leader, Jeroboam, claims dominion over the Northern Kingdom of Israel. The second half of the book chronicles the tumultuous events during the reigns of successive kings in each kingdom.

After Solomon, the second bright star of the First Book of Kings is Elijah the Prophet, who lived during the reign of King Ahab in the Northern Kingdom of Israel (869-850 B.C.E.). King Ahab and his wife Jezebel lead the people to idol worship, and Elijah punishes the sinning Israelites with a three-year drought. At Mount Carmel Elijah dramatically demonstrates that Adonai is the only true God, hoping to convince the Israelites to abandon their evil ways and follow God's commandments. Subsequently, Elijah follows God's instructions and appoints Elisha as his successor.

The concluding chapters record the constant battles between Israel and her enemies and the evil escapades of King Ahab and Jezebel, for which they are condemned by Elijah. At the end of the book, King Jehoram reigns over Judah and King Ahaziah reigns over Israel.

Like the two books of Samuel, First Kings and Second Kings were originally one complete book that was later divided by the translators of the Greek version of the Bible, the *Septuagint*. The division was finally accepted by the Jewish community with Daniel Bomberg's printing of the Bible in Venice (1516-1517).

I KINGS 1:1-31
CHAYAY SARAH   חיי שרה

This Haftarah has been paired with *Parashat Chayay Sarah*, Genesis 23:1-25:18. See "Connecting the Text To the Sedra," pp. 104-106, for an exploration of the many ways the two texts shed light on each other.

SYNOPSIS

In this Haftarah we meet King David in his old age. No longer able to care for himself, he is provided with a nursemaid, Abishag the Shunammite, to attend to his needs.

As it is clear that David is approaching death, his son Adonijah (by wife Haggith) prepares to succeed his father on the throne of Israel. He confers with David's general, Joab, and with the Priest Abiathar, who help him in his preparations. However, the Priest Zadok, as well as Nathan the Prophet and the warriors Shimei and Rei, do not support Adonijah's accession to the throne.

While Adonijah arranges a feast to proclaim himself as his father's successor, Nathan the Prophet visits David's wife Bathsheba, the mother of Solomon. He advises her of Adonijah's plot and asks her to go with him and remind David of his promise to her that her son Solomon would be the next king.

According to Nathan's instructions, Bathsheba goes in to David first. She bows before her frail husband and humbly reminds him that he swore that Solomon would be his successor. She informs him of Adonijah's preparations to announce his plans to reign, and pleads with the aging King David to proclaim publicly that Solomon will be his successor.

While she is talking to David, Nathan enters the room, according to their plan. He bows to the King and informs him that Adonijah is preparing to proclaim himself king. He asks David if it is his wish for Adonijah to succeed him.

In response, King David swears before Bathsheba and Nathan the Prophet that Solomon will reign in his place. Bathsheba bows with her face to the ground and praises David, saying in verse 1:31, "May my lord King David live forever!"

INSIGHTS FROM THE TRADITION

A In verse 1:5 we learn that Adonijah assumes that he will be the next king. Verse 1:6 informs us that his father, David, never scolded Adonijah. Rashi explains that David's failure to discipline his child ultimately leads to Adonijah's downfall and death.

- How, according to Rashi, might David be partially responsible for Adonijah's death?

- Why is it a parent's obligation to discipline his/her child?

- Discuss: A child who is never disciplined by his/her parents will grow up to be unrestrained and irresponsible.

B Alternatively (Rosenberg, *I Kings*, Judaic Press, p. 5), although Adonijah was the oldest living son of David, he was not entitled to be king because his father was not yet king when Adonijah was born. Solomon was the first child born to David after he had attained the status of king. All his previous children were, therefore, mere commoners.

◆ Hold a class debate: One side argues that Adonijah should be king because he is the oldest surviving brother and, therefore, next in line to the throne. The other side argues that Solomon, who is the first son born to David as King of Israel, is next in line.

C The text tells us in verse 1:6 that Adonijah is very handsome. Why does the text mention this? According to *Metsudat David*, good looks make one fit to be a public leader. We are also told that David (I Samuel 16:12) and Saul before him (I Samuel 9:2) were very handsome.

◆ Do you agree that good looks are an asset for a public leader? Why?

◆ Do you think people vote for national leaders, at least in part, based on looks? Is this equally true in school elections and local elections? If so, what could be done to avoid this stress on good looks?

◆ List five characteristics of an electable leader.

D Bathsheba bows before David in verse 1:16. Malbim says it was unusual for a wife to bow before her husband. It was therefore evident that she had a special request of David.

◆ Do you act differently when you ask your parents for something? In what way, and why?

◆ Notice how your parents act when they make requests of one another or of you. Do they act differently than usual? Do their actions signal that they are about to ask for something?

STRATEGIES
Analyzing the Text

1 Nathan says in verse 1:12 that Bathsheba must save her own life and that of Solomon. *Metsudat David* explains that it was customary for a usurper (like Adonijah) to remove all his rivals and their supporters. This was true not only of usurpers, but of heirs to the throne, as well. In I Kings 2:5-8 David instructs Solomon to dispose of his enemies.

◆ Why would a king resort to murder in order to consolidate his power?

◆ Contrast this system to the process of electing leaders in a democracy. How do new presidents or prime ministers assert their power?

2 When talking to David, Bathsheba refers to Solomon as "your servant" instead of "my son" or even "our son."

◆ Explain Bathsheba's choice of terms.

3 Nathan and Bathsheba approach King David with basically the same information in two different ways. Bathsheba tells the King what Adonijah was doing behind the King's back. She carefully informs David of the problem without accusing him or putting him on the defensive.

◆ Why might you want to avoid putting someone on the defensive?

◆ Can you think of a situation in which you would want to put someone on the defensive?

◆ Rewrite Bathsheba's speech in verses 1:17-21, attacking David and putting him on the defensive. Then, act out both the original scene and your revised version. Which approach is more effective, yours or the original?

4 Nathan arrives after Bathsheba. He asks King David if he had in fact approved Adonijah's actions, but simply neglected to inform Nathan about the change in future leadership.

◆ How does Nathan's approach give David the benefit of the doubt?

♦ Rewrite Nathan's speech (verses 1:24-27) in a more accusatory tone. Then, act out both the original scene and your revised version. Which approach is more effective, yours or the original?

5 Nathan wants Bathsheba to approach King David on her own; he then follows independently of Bathsheba.

♦ Suggest reasons why Nathan might have wanted both of them to appeal individually to David. Do you think the strategy was effective?

6 David announces (verse 1:30) that not only will he uphold his vow that Solomon would sit on his throne after him (i.e., succeed him), but he now adds that Solomon will sit on David's throne in his place (i.e., in his stead).

♦ What is the difference between "succeed me as King" and "sit upon my throne in my stead"?

♦ Why do you think David decided to anoint Solomon immediately as king?

Connecting the Text To the Sedra

7 In the Sedra Abraham is old and dying. In the Haftarah David is old and dying. The once mighty and agile David is unable to keep himself warm or care for himself. Similarly, the once well traveled Abraham must send a servant to find a wife for Isaac; he can no longer travel. The comparison between the two is underscored further because the same expression for "old, advanced in years" is used in both Genesis 24:1 and I Kings 1:1.

♦ We often fail to see frail, elderly people as the individuals they really are and have been. Create a pictorial history book of one of your great grandparents or grandparents, using pho-

tographs of them from their childhood to the present. If possible, interview your grandparent about each photo and write a descriptive caption for each. Present the books in class.

8 In the Sedra Abraham is concerned about which child will succeed him as leader of his family and inherit his fortune. By planning before his death for Isaac to rule after him, Abraham hopes for the orderly transfer of assets and leadership. Accordingly, he gives gifts to all his children (except Isaac) and sends them away (Genesis 25:6).

David likewise hopes for the orderly transfer of assets and authority to Solomon and arranges for Solomon to be anointed prior to David's death.

♦ Why do you think people are concerned about what happens to their family and their possessions after their death?

♦ Create a family tree for Abraham and for David. Include all their wives and children. For more information, see these verses: Genesis 25:1-15, II Samuel 3:2-5, 12:15-25, 13:1, and 6:23.

9 In the Sedra the servant has a difficult mission to fulfill for Abraham and Abraham's God — finding a wife for Isaac who can carry on Sarah's matriarchal role. The servant is unsure how to go about carrying out his mission and whether or not he will be successful. Notice, however, that the servant does not passively wait for a sign from God. Instead, he tells God what he wants to have happen (Genesis 24:12-14). This does happen, and he completes his task.

In the Haftarah there is a risky Divine mission (determining the next king of Israel) for Nathan and Bathsheba to undertake and they don't know if they will succeed. They formulate a plan and carry it out without waiting for Divine intervention.

◆ Explain how Abraham's servant and Nathan and Bathsheba recognize when action must be taken, then respond immediately without waiting for divine intervention. In so doing, they help accomplish divine goals.

◆ Imagine and discuss how biblical history might have been different had Abraham's servant not found a wife for Isaac or had Solomon not become king after David.

10 Hirsch points out that Abraham's story takes place in the family's tent, while David's story occurs in the King's palace. The head family of the Israelites has come a long way — from tents to palaces. However, in David's fancy palace, there was an attempt at usurping the throne and undermining David's plans by his other children and his servants. In Abraham's simple tent, there was no rebellion against his plans by his servant or by other children.

In addition, in Abraham's tent there is heartfelt mourning over the death of his wife; they had a special relationship. But, in David's palace, Bathsheba seems to have been replaced by Abishag. Moreover, Bathsheba seems to visit her husband only when she has a critical situation to handle; she bows in homage before him and formally calls David, "my lord."

◆ Make a living tableau of both "deathbed" scenes. Create scenery and props and costumes for the characters to wear, emphasizing the differences between life in Abraham's tent and life in David's royal palace. Set the scenes, but instead of acting them out, simply pose as wax museum figures. The teacher can photograph the scenes.

11 According to *Sanhedrin* 21b, Adonijah tries to become king and wear David's crown, but the crown does not fit him. Rashi adds to this a legend that David's crown had a special gold rod that ran through it and would only fit people who had a dent in their skulls to accommodate the rod, and Solomon had such a dent.

◆ How does the test described in this legend make it seem that Solomon was destined to be king?

◆ Do you think the test helped to convince the people that Solomon was the right son of David to succeed him as king?

◆ How does this legend resemble the story of Cinderella and the glass slipper? As a class, make a Cinderella-like video of this Talmudic story.

◆ Similarly, in the Sedra, Abraham's servant sets up a test (Genesis 24:12-14) to be certain that Rebecca is destined to marry Isaac. What is this test?

◆ How do you think this test helped to prove the right person had been selected?

◆ Which test do you think was a better indicator (the servant's test or the dent in Solomon's skull)?

◆ As a class, design a test (real or fanciful) that can be used to determine who is best suited to be president or prime minister.

12 Both texts provide examples of the failure of the law of primogeniture (the right of the eldest child to inherit the leadership role in the family) in Bible times. Solomon assumes the kingship even though he is not David's oldest living child. Similarly, Isaac takes over his father's position even though Ishmael is Abraham's oldest living child.

◆ Make a list of other eldest children in the Bible who do not become their families' leaders.

◆ The car rental company, Avis, has an ad campaign featuring the slogan: "We're #2. We try harder." Write an ad campaign for the younger children of Israel in the Bible who end up #1.

◆ Ancient Israel was one of the smallest, weakest, and youngest nations of the world. Why might the ancient Israelites have enjoyed all the biblical stories in which the youngest wins?

13 When telling to David the story of Adonijah's party, Nathan adds something not mentioned previously by either the narrator (verse 1:5-10) or Bathsheba (verse 1:17-20). He says in verse 1:25 that the celebrants with Adonijah have been proclaiming "Long live King Adonijah!"

◆ Why might Nathan have added or emphasized this fact?

◆ How does David seem to react to this new fact?

◆ Does this additional information from Nathan improve or hurt Adonijah's chances of being king? Why?

◆ Similarly, in the Sedra, Abraham's servant adds details to his story to convince Laban to allow Rebecca to marry Isaac. Compare the events as they happen (Genesis 24:15-27) versus the way the servant retells them to Laban (Genesis 24:45-49).

◆ In the retelling, what points does the servant emphasize, and why?

◆ For advanced study, see *New Studies in Genesis* by Nehama Leibowitz, pp. 231-234, wherein she highlights the differences line by line.

14 In the Sedra a young woman is sought to be Isaac's bride and bring life back into the tents of Sarah. In the Haftarah a young woman is sought to comfort and tend the dying king.

◆ Write a classified help wanted ad for each of these positions, including job responsibilities, qualifications, and any other pertinent information.

15 The Haftarah deals with the impending death of King David, and the Sedra deals with the deaths of both Sarah and Abraham.

◆ Write obituaries or eulogies for all three great Israelite leaders.

Extending the Text

16 Adonijah couldn't become king because David wasn't yet king when Adonijah was born, making Adonijah a mere commoner (see Insights from the Tradition #B, p. 102). Yet Solomon, who was born after David had become king, was an acceptable heir. According to the tradition of matrilineal descent, the children of a female convert born before her conversion are not considered Jewish unless they themselves convert to Judaism. However, children born to the woman after she has converted are automatically Jewish.

◆ Explain the possible rationale for this.

◆ Hold a class debate on this topic.

17 David needed Abishag to take care of him in his old age. Today, many elderly people needing care move into nursing homes where a staff of nurses, doctors, aides, physical therapists, and other professionals can assist them with the tasks of daily life.

◆ Try one of the following exercises to learn why it might be hard for an elderly or infirm person to live on his/her own:

• Put on a garment that zips up the back. Zip it yourself.

- Tie your shoe or button your shirt with only one hand or with masking tape around your knuckles.

- Develop a system to identify three different medicine bottles of the same shape and size, so that they are distinguishable to a blind person who must take each medicine at different times and in different amounts during the day.

18 Nursing homes (also known as care centers) assist elderly individuals who cannot live independently. Some of these centers provide simply "assisted living"; others provide a higher level of care, in some cases even hospital care on the premises.

- Interview a social worker from a local nursing home. Ask about all the ways in which care centers help those who cannot live on their own. If the social worker is from a non-Jewish nursing home, find out what they do to help their Jewish residents continue to observe their religious traditions. Ask what you could do to help with Jewish observances. Organize a class trip to help with a Jewish celebration at the home.

19 Bathsheba is acting in the tradition of an impressive line of biblical mothers who go to great lengths to secure leadership roles for their sons. Sarah advocates for Isaac, and Rebecca ensures Jacob's future.

- Review these stories in Genesis 21:1-11 and 27:1-28:5.

- Choose three students to play Sarah, Rebecca, and Bathsheba. The other students are news reporters. Hold a press conference with the three mothers, probing them about their roles in their sons' success. Be sure to address issues of moral concern about their behavior.

Which of the three mothers comes out looking the best to the reporters, and why?

20 The Haftarah ends with Bathsheba saying, "May my lord King David live forever." Since King David was certainly on his deathbed, one early commentator found it impossible that Bathsheba was reciting a prayer for his recovery, suggesting instead that she prayed for the eternal life of David's soul.

- We say a *"Mi Shebayrach"* for the recovery of someone who is ill. In it, we ask God to heal, strengthen, and deliver a complete recovery to the ailing person. Would you advise one to make a *"Mi Shebayrach"* prayer if there is no hope for recovery?

- Is the *"Mi Shebayrach"* prayer only for the sick, or can the prayer also somehow provide support for the loved ones of the sick individual?

- Is a prayer for wellness limited to physical health?

- Conduct a class debate on the subject of whether a *"Mi Shebayrach"* prayer may be said for the terminally ill.

- Ask your Rabbi to discuss his/her views on the *"Mi Shebayrach"* prayer in general, and in terminal cases in particular.

Personalizing the Text

21 Adonijah's good looks made him overly proud and caused him to rebel against his father. Our society emphasizes good looks above almost everything else.

- What does this say about society's values?

- List five traits (other than good looks) that are necessary qualities in a good person.

22 Adonijah and his brother Solomon were rivals for the throne.

◆ Sibling relationships can be very complicated and, at times, difficult. Think of a recent rivalry you had with a sibling. Draw a comic strip depicting the problem you had and its (real or hoped for) resolution.

23 It took courage for Bathsheba to approach the King with her special request.

◆ Write a letter from Bathsheba to Dear Abby, seeking advice on how to talk to David about Solomon. Write a response from Dear Abby to Bathsheba.

◆ For advanced study, compare Bathsheba's courageous request of King David with Esther's careful approach to and request of her king (Esther 4:10-11, 7:1-4).

24 David lived to 70, which was the expected length of life then (*Yevamot* 64b). There is a Jewish custom that once you live to 70, you have lived one life span and you start counting over. Consequently, some people celebrate their second Bar/Bat Mitzvah at age 83.

◆ Plan your own future second Bar/Bat Mitzvah. Who will attend? Will you recite the same Haftarah, or choose another one? Where will you be living? Where will you hold the Bar/Bat Mitzvah, and what kind of celebration will you have? Write a speech. How might your feelings about your second Bar/Bat Mitzvah differ from your feelings about your first?

25 David was old and dying, but he still had not publicly announced his successor. He didn't "get his affairs in order." When he is pressed by Nathan and Bathsheba, David not only announces his successor, but decides to anoint Solomon as the next King without delay.

◆ Rabbi Eliezer taught in *Pirke Avot* 2:10 that each person should repent for all sins committed on the day before his/her death. Since no one can know for certain which will be the day of death, we learn to behave righteously and repent for our wrongdoings each and every day. A famous saying goes, "Live every day as if it were your last." Imagine you have one week (or one year) to live. List all the things you would be sure to do in your remaining days.

◆ Are any of the listed items things you could do right now?

26 According to legend, God told David he would die on a Shabbat. Therefore, every Saturday night after Havdalah, David would celebrate his survival with a meal and party. Today, the custom of having a meal and celebration on Saturday night is called *Melaveh Malkah*, which means "accompanying the [Sabbath] queen."

◆ Plan and host your own *Melaveh Malkah*, with food and music and games.

◆ How is your Bar or Bat Mitzvah celebration a sort of *Melaveh Malkah*?

Other Resources

27 Read, act out, and discuss the skit in *Bible Scenes* by Stan J. Beiner, pp. 206-211.

28 Review and discuss both pictures illustrating this Haftarah in *The Illustrated Torah* by Michal Meron, p. 30.

29 Read and compare five poems about Abishag in *Modern Poems on the Bible*, edited by Dan Curzon, pp. 209-214.

30 It is a *mitzvah* to visit the sick (see *Teaching Mitzvot* by Barbara Binder

Kadden and Bruce Kadden, pp. 115-118). Study the texts provided in this book, and engage in at least one exercise.

31 The British national anthem, "God Save the Queen/King" finds its origin in verse 1:25. Discuss the application of the lyrics, which you can find at: www.copcity.com/anthems/uk.html.

32 For an outstanding film about the importance of siblings, sibling rivalry, and visiting the sick, view and discuss the film *The Straight Story* (1999, rated G, 111 minutes), which is about a man who makes a long trip on his lawnmower to visit his sick, older brother and mend their relationship.

33 View and discuss the film *The Man in the Iron Mask* (1998, rated PG-13, 132 minutes), which retells the legendary story of the royal rivalry between King Louis XIV and his twin brother Philippe. Compare this story with that of Solomon and Adonijah. (It is necessary for the teacher to preview this film, as it contains some sexuality and may not be appropriate for all audiences.)

34 Read and discuss excerpts from the poem, "Crabbit Woman" by Phyllis McCormack. The poem may be found on the web site www.phon.ucl.ac.uk/home/dave/TOC_H/Poetry/Crabby.html.

35 The Fuchsberg Center for Conservative Judaism in Jerusalem offers a commentary on this Haftarah at www.uscj.org.il/haftarah/haya-sarah5762.html.

36 The Reform Movement's web page, Family Shabbat Table Talk, offers commentary, discussion questions, and a project at http://uahc.org/shabbat/stt/3chayesarah.shtml.

Involving the Family

37 Use a computer program to map your family tree. Mail a copy to all your living relatives to confirm the information and get more details. Examine your family tree, and just before each relative's birthday, send him or her a birthday card with a piece of candy.

38 Plan and celebrate a second Bar/Bat Mitzvah for a grandparent or great grandparent.

Bar/Bat Mitzvah Projects

39 Visit a nursing home regularly, especially to help out with Jewish programming.

40 Don't procrastinate: do your Bar/Bat Mitzvah preparation, and after your *simchah*, promptly write your thank-you notes.

I KINGS 2:1–12
VAYECHI ויחי

This Haftarah has been paired with *Parashat Vayechi*, Genesis 47:28-50:26. See "Connecting the Text To the Sedra," pp. 112-114, for an exploration of the many ways the two texts shed light on each other.

SYNOPSIS

In this Haftarah David delivers his dying words to his son and heir to the throne of Israel, Solomon. In a speech that addresses religious matters first and practical issues second, David exhorts Solomon to be strong in the aftermath of his father's impending death. David urges his son always to follow God's laws, commandments, rules, and admonitions, in order that he will succeed. He reminds Solomon of God's promise that David's dynasty will continue forever if his descendants obey God scrupulously.

That having been said, David turns to practical matters, advising Solomon on the importance of eliminating his enemies and rewarding his allies. He instructs Solomon to execute General Joab in retribution for Joab's past sins. He asks Solomon to reward the sons of Barzillai the Gileadite, who had been loyal friends of the King. Shimei son of Gera, who insulted David, must also be executed by Solomon.

With these words, David dies in 961 B.C.E. and is buried in the City of David. We are reminded that David had reigned over Israel for 40 years, seven in Hebron and 33 in Jerusalem. Finally, King Solomon ascends the throne and firmly establishes his reign.

INSIGHTS FROM THE TRADITION

A The Hebrew in verse 2:1 uses an idiom to say that David was near death. It says "the days of David drew near to die." According to *Midrash Yalkut Shimoni* (Sec. 169), this expression indicates that righteous people don't really die — their days on earth end, while their souls continue to live.

◆ It is said that when living people remember those who have died, it is as if the dead person continues to live. How is this so?

B David says to Solomon in verse 2:2, "Be strong and show yourself a man." Radak said this means to be disciplined.

◆ What does it mean to be "disciplined"?

◆ Why might a king or leader need discipline?

◆ For what in your life do you need to have discipline? Who helps you develop discipline skills, and in what ways?

C Alternatively, *Metsudat David* interprets "show yourself a man" to mean, "Even though you are but a lad, strengthen yourself to function like a grown man, as I will not be here to guide you." Commentators disagree as to Solomon's age at the time of David's death, but estimates range from 12 to 20.

◆ We often say to someone, "Grow up!" What do we mean by this?

◆ Are grownups necessarily more courageous than children? In what ways do you see children being courageous?

◆ List the ways in which Solomon's life will change after the death of his father, King David.

D In verse 2:5, David says that Joab, his army general, had sinned by shedding the "blood of war in peacetime." Malbim understands from this phrase that Joab killed two men he considered threats to David's throne, even though peace reigned in the land.

As a soldier accustomed to killing his enemies, Joab was probably in the habit of not trusting the enemy and reacting violently. When people get used to acting a certain way, it becomes a habit they cannot easily break.

◆ Even though peace had been negotiated with Saul's officers, why may it have been hard for Joab to trust his former enemies and refrain from disposing of them?

◆ List some habits that people have.

◆ Divide the list into good habits and bad habits.

◆ Why are bad habits so hard to break?

◆ Joab's inclination to kill his enemies was a good habit in times of war, but became a bad habit in peacetime. Can you think of an example from your own life of a good habit that might become a bad habit you have to break?

E David mentions to Solomon in verse 2:8 that Shimei is with him, despite the fact that Shimei had cursed David. According to *Berachot* 8a, Shimei is Solomon's teacher, who lived near Solomon in Jerusalem for many years until the teacher's death. According to his father's wishes, Solomon has Shimei killed at the end of chapter 2. In the first verse of chapter 3, we are told that Solomon marries Pharaoh's daughter.

The Rabbis figure that Solomon probably delayed marrying Pharaoh's daughter (a particularly problematic intermarriage, considering the history of the Israelites and Egypt) out of respect for his nearby teacher. From this they teach that a person would benefit from always living near his/her teacher.

◆ Is there anyone in your life whose presence causes you to behave better than you otherwise might? Why does this person have this effect on you?

F Hirsch suggests that David's commands to kill his enemies were not borne of vengeance. Rather, David's instructions were of a practical nature. David commanded Solomon to kill these men in order to prevent the rebellions he was sure they would cause following his death.

◆ Do you think David's motivation affects the justness of the murderous acts he requested?

◆ Some political thinkers believe that the ends justify the means, which is to say that it is the end result, not the way in which it is achieved, that really matters. Hold a class debate on the following statement: A ruler is allowed to do whatever is necessary to maintain control. How is this an example of the ends justifying the means?

G We learn in verse 2:10 that David slept with his fathers. According to *Shabbat* 30b, the Angel of Death came to take David, but could not because David spent the entire day studying Torah, which protected him. Only when David was distracted into taking a break from his studies was the Angel of Death able to take him.

◆ This is a fanciful story, but with a real message. In what real ways can Torah study and Judaism in general add to the quality (if not length) of your life?

◆ We all know the saying, "An apple a day keeps the doctor away." Write your own saying about how Torah study and Judaism help to improve the quality of your life. Design posters illustrating your saying.

STRATEGIES
Analyzing the Text

1 David orders Solomon to kill Joab, David's army commander. No doubt, David wants Joab killed to avenge the death of Absalom, David's favorite son whom Joab killed in cold blood and against David's wishes.

Though it occurred many years before, David never forgot this wrong done to him. The Bible never tries to paint our leaders as saints, and always tells us their weaknesses and failings.

◆ How is the need for vengeance a human weakness?

◆ What might be a better route to conflict resolution than revenge?

2 Compare David's farewell speech here with the farewell speech he makes in I Chronicles 28-29. Compare subjects mentioned in each speech.

◆ Which speech is more noble?

◆ Compare David's farewell speech to George Washington's farewell speech when he completed his term as President of the United States. You can find this speech at: www.virginia.edu/gwpapers/farewell/transcript.html.

3 In verse 2:4, David repeats to Solomon God's promise that a member of David's house would always sit on the throne of Israel. The promise, originally stated by God in II Samuel 7:12-16, was unconditional. However, here David indicates that there is a condition: In order to retain the throne, the king must remain faithful to God and all God's ways.

◆ Explain the condition.

◆ Is the condition fair?

◆ Modern scholars believe that the Book of Kings was not assembled and edited until many years after the reign of Solomon and David, after the destruction of the kingdom and Solomon's Temple. If this was the case, why might the author have decided in hindsight to include this condition?

Connecting the Text To the Sedra

4 The Haftarah and Sedra use similar expressions to refer to death. For example, I Kings 2:1 says, "The days of David drew near that he die." Similarly Genesis 47:29 states, "The days of Israel drew near that he die."

The Haftarah contains several additional expressions that allude to death. In verse 2:2 David says, "I am going the way of all the earth . . . " Twice David says that his enemies should not "go down to Sheol" in peace (verses 2:6 and 2:9). In verse 10 the text says, "David slept with his fathers . . ."

The expressions above are all euphemisms for death and dying. We are all a little uncomfortable talking about death, and so we make up different ways to refer to death.

◆ Why does calling something by a different name make it easier to talk about?

◆ List as many euphemisms for death or dying as you can.

◆ Did the previous exercise make people laugh? If so, why?

◆ View and discuss the clip of the Monty Python film *And Now for Something Completely Different* (1972, rated PG, 89 minutes), which is a skit about a dead parrot.

5 In both the Sedra and Haftarah, the dying father "commands" his offspring about how to act after his death (Genesis 49:33, I Kings 2:1).

In the Sedra the instructions are given to all Jacob's children as they gather around his deathbed. However, in the Haftarah David addresses only Solomon. In the *Etz Hayim Chumash* (p. 313), Michael Fishbane observes the sharp contrast between the final requests of Jacob and David: Jacob seeks to foster reconciliation among his children, while David offers Solomon advice on how to consolidate the king's power and dispose of his enemies. This, in turn, causes great conflict among David's children.

◆ Imagine you can right the wrong David commits in causing trouble among his children. Do some research in the Second Book of Samuel and list all of David's children. As a class, have a testimonial ceremony for Solomon at which all his siblings (living and dead) deliver a speech in honor of the new king.

6 I Kings 2:9 contains an interesting expression that is also used by Jacob in the Sedra. Here David says in anger that Solomon must punish Joab and "send his gray hair down to Sheol in blood." Similarly, when Joseph's brothers tell Jacob that Benjamin has to go with them to Egypt to get food, Jacob insists he will die if Benjamin were lost. Jacob echoes David's words, saying, "you will send my white head down to Sheol in grief."

◆ What do the expressions "gray hair" and "white head" convey?

◆ In Proverbs 16:31, we learn, "Gray hair is a crown of glory; It is attained by the way of righteousness." What does this proverb mean?

◆ Today, many people hide their age by dyeing their gray hair. What might this say about our society's view of old age and youth?

◆ Do you plan to dye your hair when it goes gray?

7 Hertz suggests that as David reminds Solomon to keep all God's laws, David realizes that he has failed to keep the law of guarding justice by neglecting to bring Joab to justice himself. Now David wants Solomon to enforce the law against Joab and put him to death.

Similarly, Jacob never punished Levi and Simeon for murdering all the people in the town of Shechem (see Genesis 34). But on his deathbed, he chastised them and proclaimed they would be punished.

◆ Is it ever too late to right a wrong? Why or why not?

8 In the Haftarah the eldest son is not elevated, which is also the case in the Sedra. Ephraim, the younger, is elevated over his younger brother Manasseh (Genesis 48:14-19), while Reuben, Simeon, and Levi are all replaced by the younger Judah in Genesis 49:10.

◆ Why is birth order not necessarily the best sign of leadership?

◆ What are good signs of leadership?

◆ Design a leadership course for the head of a large family, the head of a school, the head of a city, the head of a nation.

9 As a sojourner in a foreign land, Joseph had to get permission from Pharaoh to bury his father in Canaan. Solomon, on the other hand, is king in Canaan and needs permission from no one to bury his father.

◆ In what way is the Haftarah commenting on the Sedra? How is the Haftarah emphasizing for us that no matter how successful we are in someone else's land, we still are not free until we have our own land?

◆ Throughout time, Jews have sought sovereignty in our own homeland. Based on the above information, why is it so important for a people to have their own country?

◆ Why is the modern State of Israel so important to Jews all over the world?

◆ In what ways is your room your own land? Do you have sole sovereignty over it?

10 The Sedra ends with the promise that God will rescue the Israelites from exile in Egypt. In the Haftarah Solomon is promised an everlasting dynasty, as long as the people follow God's laws.

◆ What is the difference between a conditional promise and an unconditional promise? Are the promises in the Haftarah and Torah reading conditional or unconditional, and why?

Extending the Text

11 David twice tells Solomon to act in accordance with his wisdom. We often say things like, "Think before you act," or "Look before you leap."

◆ What do these expressions mean?

◆ To discover the difference between thinking before acting and just acting without thinking, do the following exercise: Play a game of chess or checkers or *Scrabble* (your choice), taking your time to decide your next move. Then, play the same game against the same partner in a speed round. Have a third person keep the time and give each player five seconds to make each move. Compare your performance and state of mind in the two rounds.

12 We learned in Insights from the Tradition #A, p. 110, that when living people remember those who have died, it is as if the deceased person continues to live.

It is a custom among Ashkenazic Jews to name their children after someone who has died in order to remember and honor the deceased and with the hope that the child grow up to emulate the best characteristics of the deceased loved one.

Sephardic Jews customarily name their children for parents and grandparents who are still alive as a way to honor the parent.

◆ Which custom do you like better, and why?

◆ For whom were you named?

◆ Write a short biography of your namesake, including photographs if possible. At the conclusion, write how you hope to be like him or her.

13 David tells Solomon in verse 2:2 to be a man. The Rabbis wrote in *Pirke Avot* 2:5: "In a place where there are no men, strive to be a man."

◆ What do you think this means?

◆ Rewrite the Rabbis' saying in gender neutral, all-inclusive language.

14 David spells out to Solomon how he wanted him to behave and treat people after David's death. Today, this is known as an ethical will.

◆ Why is it important for parents to let their children know their expectations of them for the future?

◆ What do you think your parents expect of you, today and when you are an adult?

◆ Read examples of ethical wills in *So That Your Values Live On: Ethical Wills and How to Prepare Them* by Jack Riemer and Nathaniel Stampfer, or in *Four Centuries of Jewish Women's Spirituality*, edited by Ellen M. Umansky and Dianne Ashton.

15 David is buried in the City of David in Jerusalem.

◆ Invite someone into your class to do a slide presentation about the neighborhoods and important sites in the old and new city of Jerusalem, including what is thought to be David's burial site.

16 The following story about parental expectations for children is told in *The Memoirs of Gluckel of Hameln* by Gluckel, p. 2.

A father bird set out to cross a windy sea with his three baby birds. He had to carry the babies across one at a time. When he was half way across with the first, the wind grew too strong, and he said to the baby bird, "My child, look how I am struggling and risking my life for you. When you are grown, will you do as much for me and take care of me in my old age?" The baby bird answered that, if brought to safety on the other side of the sea, the baby bird would do everything the father ever asked. The father bird called the baby bird a liar and dropped him into the sea.

The father bird returned to shore to pick up the second of his babies. In the middle of his trip over the sea, he asked the second baby the same question, received the same answer and dropped the second baby into the sea. Finally, flying over the sea with the third baby, he asked the third baby the same question, but received a different answer. The third baby responded: "It is true you are struggling and risking your life for me right now. I would be wrong not to repay you when you are old, but I just can't commit myself. I can, however, promise you that when I am grown and have children of my own, I will do as much for them as you have done for me." This answer pleased the father bird, and he carried the baby bird to safety on the shore.

◆ Read and discuss this story.

◆ What is the meaning of the story? How is it connected to parents' expectations of their children?

17 David asks Solomon to show kindness to the family of Barzillai for the kindness he did years before for David (see II Samuel 17:27-28). Barzillai provides food to David when David flees from Absalom; Barzillai knows that David and his troops are hungry and thirsty after traveling in the desert. Similarly, on several other occasions, people feed David when he is in need. In II Samuel 16:1-4, Ziba knows David is approaching and in need of food. He brings David food, wine, and animals for transportation. Abigail also feeds David in I Samuel, and the priest Ahimelect at Nob gives David bread (I Samuel 21).

◆ Compare these different stories in which people provide food to David and his men. Contrast the rewards and consequences for each provider of food.

◆ Cook, bake, and taste, some of the many foods that were offered to David in these stories.

◆ We hear little about Abigail in the Bible even though she went on to become David's wife. For an exercise on Abigail, complete p. 12 in *Prophets Copy Pak*™ by Marji Gold-Vukson.

◆ For more information on and classic paintings of Abigail, see pp. 112-177 in *Listen To Her Voice: Women of the Hebrew Bible* by Miki Raver.

Personalizing the Text

18 Solomon is known in legends by several different names: Jedidiah, "the friend of God"; Ben, because he built the Temple; Jakeh, because he ruled the whole world; Ithiel, because God was with him; Koheleth, the author of the book of Ecclesiastes, which means "collector of wisdom"; and, of course, Solomon, which means "peace," because his reign as king was peaceful.

♦ Design and curate a museum exhibit on Solomon, featuring an installation for each of his nicknames.

19 Solomon was known by many different names (see #18, immediately above).

♦ If nicknames can be seen as a measure of affection, how well loved was Solomon?

♦ Why do you think some people don't like nicknames?

♦ Write a *D'var Torah* that identifies and explains the meanings of all your own names and nicknames. What do your nicknames (or lack thereof) convey about you?

20 In verse 2:3 David instructs Solomon to keep God's laws, commandments, rules, and admonitions. Hirsch notes that the Hebrew for "admonitions" – עדותיו *(aydotav)* is related to the word "adornment" – עדי *(adi)*. He explains that those commandments called "admonitions" are an "adornment" for those who observe them.

♦ Make a poster of a life-size outline of a person. Choose *mitzvot* that you think are adornments, and write and draw them next to the body part they adorn. Some examples include: *tallit, tefillin, tzedakah*, visiting the sick, obeying your parents, and reciting the *"Shema."*

21 David gives Solomon a quick lesson in leadership.

♦ To explore the qualities your class deems important in a Jewish leader, play this game. Students individually rank the following Jewish leadership qualities from 1 to 10, with

1 being the most important and 10 being the least important. (Each student should have his/her own ranking sheet.)

Maturity
Jewish knowledge
Religious commitment
Prestige in the non-Jewish community
Organizational know-how
Personal assertiveness
Wealth
Youth
Political connections
Intelligence
Prominence in Jewish organizational life

When students have completed their rankings, form discussion groups of three to four students to compare and discuss results. (Source: *The Jewish Experiential Book* by Bernard Reisman, pp. 358-359.)

22 The artist Salvador Dali is perhaps most famous for his creative renderings of a simple clock.

♦ To view his famous interpretation of time, visit the Dali web site at: www.dali-gallery. com/html/dali.php.

♦ Design your own clock that conveys the message that it is never too late to do the right thing.

23 Upon David's death, Solomon entered his adulthood. With your Bar or Bat Mitzvah, you will be entering your Jewish adulthood.

♦ Write down what kind of Jewish adult you want to be and how you can achieve your goals.

Other Resources

24 Read, act out, and discuss the skit in *Bible Scenes* by Stan J. Beiner, pp. 212-215.

25 Discuss the illustration of this Haftarah in *The Illustrated Torah* by Michal Meron, p.60. Explain why you think the artist included certain details.

26 Joab couldn't appropriately adjust his behavior from wartime to peace. View and discuss the film *Alan and Naomi* (1992, rated PG, 96 minutes) about a young survivor of the Holocaust who must relearn how to trust and interact with people in her new home in Brooklyn.

27 Jewish law prevents us from taking revenge. For more texts and exercises on the subject of vengeance, see *Teaching Mitzvot* by Barbara Binder Kadden and Bruce Kadden, pp. 131-135.

28 The film *Groundhog Day* (1993, rated PG, 101 minutes), brilliantly portrays the principle that it is never too late to do the right thing. View and discuss this entertaining and thought provoking film.

29 Solomon follows David's instructions to dispose of his enemies and reward his friends, fulfilling the *mitzvah* to honor one's parents. See more on this subject in *Teaching Mitzvot* by Barbara Binder Kadden and Bruce Kadden, pp. 167-170.

30 Read and discuss stories about King Solomon in *Stories of King Solomon* by Lillian S. Freehof, or in *The Legends of the Jews* by Louis Ginzberg, vol. 4, pp. 130-176.

Involving the Family

31 Research the *yahrzeit* dates of your family ancestors. Light a memorial candle to remember them on those dates.

32 Encourage your parents to write an ethical will, describing to you and your siblings what kind of adults they want you to be and what values they want you to have.

Bar/Bat Mitzvah Project

33 Based on Insights from the Tradition #D, p. 111, identify three bad habits that you would like to break. Work at conquering those bad habits during the year of your Bar/Bat Mitzvah. Keep a log of your efforts.

I KINGS 3:15-4:1
MIKAYTZ מקץ

This Haftarah has been paired with *Parashat Mikaytz*, Genesis 41:1-44:17. See "Connecting the Text To the Sedra," pp. 120-122, for an exploration of the many ways the two texts shed light on each other.

SYNOPSIS

In the first verse of the Haftarah, Solomon wakes from a dream in which God grants him many blessings, including great wisdom. A grateful Solomon then goes to Jerusalem to offer burnt offerings and peace offerings and to hold a celebratory feast.

In the next verse, Solomon is immediately given an opportunity to demonstrate his God given wisdom and good judgment. Two women — prostitutes — come before Solomon to settle a dispute. The first woman reports that she recently delivered a baby in the house in which the two women live together. She continues that three days after her child was born, the second woman also delivered a baby, which died in the night because the mother accidentally smothered it. The first woman claims that the second woman rose at midnight, took the first woman's son from her bedside and laid the dead infant in its place. When the first woman arose the next morning to nurse her baby, she realized that the dead child beside her was not her son. At the conclusion of the first woman's story, the second woman denies any wrongdoing and insists that the live child is *her* son.

King Solomon reviews the situation: both women claim to be the living child's mother. He asks for a sword and declares that the living baby must be divided, giving one half to each mother. At this suggestion, one of the women pleads with Solomon to refrain from committing this horrible act of splitting the baby in two. She says in verse 3:26, "Please, my lord, give her the live child; only don't kill it!" The other woman insists, "It shall be neither yours nor mine; cut it in two!" Based on the two responses, Solomon determines that the woman who wants to save the baby's life is the real mother.

When the Israelites hear this story, they stand in awe of the king, whose wisdom and good judgment are truly gifts from God. The final verse (4:1) of the Haftarah declares triumphantly that Solomon is king over all Israel.

INSIGHTS FROM THE TRADITION

A In I Kings 3:1-14, just before the Haftarah begins, God asks Solomon in a dream what he wants most from God. Solomon responds that he wants a wise and understanding heart. Radak teaches that a wise heart uses what it learned, and an understanding heart knows how to reach the right conclusions based on what it knows. The Haftarah demonstrates how Solomon is able to reach a right conclusion in the case of the two women and the baby.

◆ Radak's interpretation suggests that being able to apply what one has learned is better than learning alone. In your opinion, does all learning have to have a practical goal to be worthwhile?

◆ Do you think there is value in learning just for the sake of learning?

◆ Some students go to college to become better educated and plan to learn a profession after they graduate, while others go to college intending to learn a profession there (such as nursing, education, or engineering). Which approach to college did your parents take, and which do you think might be right for you?

B Why does Solomon restate the testimony of the women in verse 3:23? *Radak* says that a judge must repeat the claims of both sides in order to be sure he/she understood them correctly.

◆ Why is this a good idea?

◆ Does this listening and communication skill have applications outside a courtroom?

C Did Solomon's strategy for finding the real mother truly work? Rashi says that a "heavenly voice" whispered to Solomon who the true mother was.

We'll never know whether or not Solomon intended to cut the baby in two. However, threats alone are often useful in getting people to do what we want.

◆ Why do you think threats are effective?

◆ Effective or not, do you think it is a good idea to make threats? Why or why not?

◆ How do parents and teachers use threats to get you to do what they want?

◆ Do you ever use threats to get what you want? Describe such a time.

D *Kohelet Rabbah* 10:17 says, "Woe to you, O Land, whose king is a boy" (and obviously makes decisions in childish ways). The *midrash* explains that Solomon deserved his own death sentence because it wasn't enough for him that one child was dead, he showed no mercy for the second.

◆ Which of these words would you use to describe Solomon's strategy: wise, foolish, impetuous, arrogant, superficial, and/or childish? Explain your answer.

E We learn in verse 3:28 that all Israel feared King Solomon and his great wisdom. Radak explains that the people feared a king who could display such acute wisdom and shrewd judgment because they knew that they could not get away with their crimes (even those done secretly) when judged by a king with such keen powers of detection.

◆ Is fear of getting caught an effective deterrent to crime? Explain your answer.

◆ List other deterrents to crime.

STRATEGIES
Analyzing the Text

1 The first verse of the Haftarah says Solomon awoke from his dream, offered sacrifices and made a feast, apparently to celebrate receiving wisdom from God. The next verse immediately says, "Later two women came to the king and stood before him." We might wonder why the dream story and the baby story were placed back to back by the editor of the Book of Kings. Scholars have offered the following suggestions:

The women came to the feast seeking the king to hear their case.

The women came to test Solomon's wisdom after his dream about wisdom.

There were no witnesses in the house with the women because everyone was at the feast the king made for the people.

◆ Which of the explanations makes the most sense to you, and why?

2 King Solomon is not mentioned by name even once throughout the story of the two women and the baby. Review 3:16-28 to verify that this is true.

Some commentators suggest that the story was a popular legend which originally had nothing to do with Solomon. By including verse 3:15, which mentions Solomon by name, with the next story which does not mention him, the editor implies that Solomon was in fact the king before whom the two women present their case.

◆ In what ways is this story a good illustration of Solomon's great wisdom?

3 In verse 3:18 the woman states three times that the two women were alone in the house, with no stranger present. *Metsudat David* points out that the lack of strangers in the house means that there were no witnesses to corroborate either woman's story.

◆ How does this information make King Solomon's job of adjudicating more difficult?

4 The other woman tells the king in verse 3:26: "It shall be neither yours nor mine; cut it in two!"

◆ Imagine what would have happened if, like the first woman, she, too, had said, "Give her the live child; only don't kill it!"

◆ Alternatively, what would have happened if she had accepted the child, grateful that "her" child was being returned to her.

◆ Think of alternative scenarios and role-play them.

Connecting the Text To the Sedra

5 The Haftarah opens in I Kings 3:15 with Solomon waking from his dream. The word for waking in Hebrew is וייקץ (*vayikatz*). The Sedra opens in Genesis 41:1 with a similar Hebrew word, מקץ (*mikaytz*). Later in the Sedra (41:7), Pharaoh wakes, וייקץ (*vayikatz*), from his dreams.

Dreams play a very important role in both Sedra and Haftarah, in part because dreams are considered a source of revelation from God.

◆ Review the messages that God was sending by dreams both to Solomon and Pharaoh.

◆ Contrast Solomon's ability to understand his dream by himself and Pharaoh's need for an interpreter.

◆ What do you think your dreams tell you?

◆ Describe a recent dream of yours to the class, and ask for possible interpretations.

6 Solomon makes a celebratory banquet for his people in I Kings 3:15. Joseph makes a feast for his brothers in Genesis 43:16. Compare Solomon's and Joseph's motivations for making their dinners.

◆ List five occasions for which your family holds celebration feasts. Describe the feasts.

7 Both stories feature very hard, mean tests set up by the leader for those who come before him. Solomon wants to determine which woman is the baby's real mother, and so tests their reactions to a horrifying suggestion. In the Sedra Joseph sets up a difficult test to see if his brothers have changed since their wicked childhood.

◆ In your opinion, were these leaders justified in setting up difficult tests?

◆ Does setting up such tests make these leaders seem like cruel people?

◆ Each of us is faced with many tests of our own character every day. Consider these possible tests and discuss your responses to them:

• A friend offers you a cigarette and pressures you to smoke.

- Classmates get a copy of the answers to an upcoming test and offer to share them with you.

- You forget to do your homework or a household responsibility. Do you tell the truth or make up an excuse?

◆ Can you think of other tests we may face in our everyday lives?

8 In the Sedra Judah offers himself up to his father as a pledge for Benjamin's life. Willing to make this self-sacrifice, Judah stands out as the new leader of the family. In the Haftarah the true mother makes the self-sacrifice of giving up her rights as mother of the child to save the baby's life. In doing so, she is rewarded with custody of the child.

In both cases, self-sacrifice leads to ultimate personal reward. Yet self-sacrifice need not be so extreme to be worthwhile. Volunteerism, for example, is a form of self-sacrifice.

◆ In his inauguration address in 1960, President John F. Kennedy said to all Americans, "Ask not what your country can do for you, but what you can do for your country." What is the meaning of Kennedy's message?

◆ How can the self-sacrifice of volunteerism give direct benefit to the volunteer?

◆ Design a media campaign to convince people to become volunteers.

9 In the Haftarah Solomon recognizes that his wisdom is a gift from God. In the Sedra Joseph attributes his ability to interpret dreams to God (Genesis 41:16).

◆ Do you consider your intelligence or wisdom to be a gift from God?

It is truly amazing when our brains come up with new, creative ideas. It's possible that each idea,

and even the ability to think of them, are gifts from God. If we were to recite a blessing every time we think of something new and creative, we would learn to marvel over and appreciate creativity.

There are many blessings in our liturgy which may apply to having a new, creative thought. Consider this one from the morning blessings: "Blessed are You, *Adonai*, Sovereign of the universe, Who has given the mind understanding to distinguish between day and night." Or this one from the *"Amidah"* prayer: "Blessed are You, *Adonai*, Who bestows knowledge upon humans." Or even this one from the morning service: "Blessed are You, *Adonai*, Who makes sources of light" (like the good idea light bulb!).

◆ Which of these do you think best applies to having a new, creative thought?

◆ Write your own blessing, expressing awe and offering thanks to God for new and creative ideas.

10 In the Sedra Pharaoh wants to find a man with wisdom (Genesis 41:33) to rule the country and prepare for the famine. In the Haftarah Solomon wants wisdom to help him rule and judge fairly.

The Greek philosopher Plato thought the best possible leader was a "philosopher king."

◆ Is wisdom and intelligence an important characteristic in a leader? Is it the most important characteristic? What are other characteristics you think are important in a good leader?

11 The Haftarah concludes in I Kings 4:1 with the statement that "King Solomon was now king over all Israel." That phrase is echoed three times in the Sedra, describing Joseph as the leader over all the land of Egypt (Genesis 41:41-45).

◆ In your opinion, which is a greater achievement: Solomon ruling over all his own people or Joseph ruling, second to Pharaoh, over a foreign nation? Hold a class debate on the subject, with one side claiming Solomon's as the greater achievement and the other side claiming Joseph's as the greater.

Extending the Text

12 Solomon celebrates his acquisition of wisdom with a grand feast. A *Seudat Mitzvah* is a festive meal that accompanies a Jewish ritual ceremony, such as a Bar/Bat Mitzvah, wedding, *Brit Milah*, or *Simchat Bat*. Similarly, when a scholar has finished the study of a major text, a meal called a *Siyyum* is held. It is considered a *mitzvah* to attend a *Seudat Mitzvah* or *Siyyum*.

◆ Why do Jews celebrate important events and holidays with festive meals?

◆ How else might important events be celebrated?

13 According to The Rama (*Laws of Lulav* 669:1), we have a custom to make a feast on Simchat Torah. This feast is based on Solomon's feast in the Haftarah (*Song of Songs Rabbah* 1:9).

◆ Interview the Rabbi of your synagogue to learn how your community celebrates Simchat Torah. Explore reinstituting the feast and discuss different ways in which your class can help (publicity, setup, shopping, serving).

14 Being wise is an important attribute for a leader. This may be one reason that Albert Einstein was asked to be the second president of the State of Israel in 1952. However, he declined in the following speech:

"I am deeply moved by the offer from our State of Israel, and at once saddened and ashamed that I cannot accept it. All my life I have dealt with objective matters, hence I lack both the natural aptitude and the experience to deal properly with people and to exercise official functions. For these reasons alone I would be unsuited to fulfill the duties of that high office, even if advancing age was not making increasing demands on my strength. I am more distressed over these circumstances because my relationship to the Jewish people has become my strongest human bond, ever since I became fully aware of our precarious situation among the nations of the world."

◆ Einstein was probably recognized as the smartest man in the world at the time (if not of all time). Do you think he was asked to be Israel's president because of his renowned intelligence? Explain your answer.

◆ Why did Einstein decline?

◆ What qualities did Einstein believe were important for a leader to have?

15 In the Haftarah one baby died when its sleeping mother lay on it. Throughout the ages, Jewish mothers offered a prayer upon going to bed that they would not accidentally smother their babies in their sleep (see *Out of the Depths I Call To You* by Nina Beth Cardin, pp. 110).

◆ Ask your parents if they worried about this, too. What else did they worry about or pray for when you were a new baby?

16 Solomon didn't invent the solution of dividing disputed property in half in cases when there is no other evidence to substantiate ownership. Such action is in fact required by Jewish law, as outlined in Exodus 21:35 and II Samuel 19:30.

◆ Is it fair to divide property in half when there is no evidence as to ownership?

On the subject, Mishnah *Bava Metzia* 1:1 says, "If two people are holding a garment and one says, 'I found it,' and the other says, 'I found it,' or if one says, 'It is all mine,' and the other says, 'It is all mine,' the one must swear to owning no less than one-half of it, and the other must swear to owning no less than one-half of it, and they must divide it."

Since a garment cannot be practically divided, Jewish law requires that the monetary value of the item be determined, and that monetary value be divided between the two parties claiming ownership.

◆ Does the logic of this system make sense to you?

◆ Here is an interesting — and somewhat related — court case from November 2001. The baseball hit by major leaguer Barry Bonds for his record setting home run #73 was originally caught in the stands by fan Alex Popov. Popov claims that after he caught the ball, he was mobbed by other fans and was robbed of the ball by Patrick Hayashi. Hayashi says he found the ball loose in the crowd of fans. According to experts, the ball could be worth more than one million dollars. California Court Judge David Garcia ruled that the ball should remain locked up until a trial determines the proper owner of the ball. Pretend you are King Solomon the Wise and resolve this case for Judge Garcia.

17 The Book of Proverbs, containing wise words and life lessons, is traditionally attributed to King Solomon. Study these statements about Wisdom:

Wisdom is better than rubies . . . (Proverbs 8:11)

Happy is the person who finds wisdom and the person who gets understanding. (Proverbs 3:13)

Get wisdom, acquire understanding; forget it not . . . (Proverbs 4:5)

Get wisdom, therefore use all your means to acquire understanding. (Proverbs 4:7)

◆ Which of these sayings do you like best, and why?

◆ Find other sayings about wisdom in a book of quotations (see, for example, *Familiar Quotations* by John Bartlett; *Two Jews, Three Opinions*, edited by Sandee Brawarsky and Deborah Mark; or *Jewish Wisdom* by Joseph Telushkin).

18 Legend has it that the Queen of Sheba once came to test the renowned wisdom of King Solomon. After offering many riddles, which Solomon easily solved, she presented one last test. She set before the king two vases: one contained fresh flowers and the other held flowers made of enamel by skilled artisans. She challenged Solomon to decide which was real (of course, he wasn't permitted to touch or smell them). Solomon took a long time to examine the flowers carefully. They were strikingly similar. Suddenly, a bee entered the room, and headed toward to the two vases of flowers. Solomon pointed to the flowers on which the bee landed. The Queen of Sheba bowed respectfully before Solomon, because both of them understood that the wise know when to learn from even the humblest of teachers.

◆ What do you think is the lesson of this story?

◆ The Rabbis taught in *Pirke Avot* 4:1 that a wise person learns from everyone. How does this story demonstrate the Rabbis' lesson? Do you agree that we can learn something from everyone and everything?

◆ For a more complete account of the Queen of Sheba's tests of Solomon's wisdom, read "The Wisdom of Solomon," as told by Merna Ann Hecht in *Chosen Tales*, edited by Peninnah Schram, pp. 155-160.

19 Solomon judged in his court by himself. Today some communities have a Rabbinic *Bet Din*, made up of three Rabbis, and they rule on certain issues, such as divorce, conversion, or business disputes within the Jewish community.

◆ Ask your Rabbi what he/she does when in need of a *Bet Din*.

◆ See if you can interview someone who has served on a *Bet Din* about what a *Bet Din* does.

Personalizing the Text

20 Solomon wishes for wisdom from God.

◆ If you could make one wish, what would it be?

◆ Assess how your one wish might change your life.

◆ Would your wish help humanity?

21 Solomon throws a celebration feast when he gets his wish.

◆ Plan the party you would throw to celebrate getting your wish. Whom would you invite? Where would it be? Write the speech you, the guest of honor, would give to explain the occasion of the celebration, to give thanks, and to describe how you intend to use your wish.

22 Rashi explains that Solomon awoke from his dream and immediately understood he had been granted wisdom because he could understand the language of dogs barking and birds chirping.

◆ In what ways do we measure our own intellectual achievement?

◆ Is academic achievement always the same as wisdom?

◆ How do you know when you have acted wisely?

◆ Report cards measure our academic achievement. Design a report card that can measure wisdom and good sense.

23 According to tradition, Solomon wrote the Book of Proverbs.

◆ Design and play the following game, which teaches some wise sayings from the Book of Proverbs. Each participant receives an index card with half of a proverb written on it. Each student can hold their index card or tape it to his/her shirt. Each player must find the person who has the other half of his or her proverb. To make the game more challenging, players may not talk. Alternatively, the index cards can be taped to the players' foreheads, where they cannot see what their own cards say. In this case, classmates will have to help match people up with their pairs.

24 Solomon practiced "active listening" when he repeated what he heard from the two women.

◆ Participate in an active listening exercise. Form pairs. The first partner has one minute to talk about the subject of his or her choice. The second partner must listen carefully, because in the next minute, he/she must repeat in his or her own words what the first partner has just said. Repeat the exercise, reversing roles.

◆ Discuss as a class why active listening is important and how it can improve relationships between people.

25 Solomon could have given the two women shared custody of the child.

◆ Be a lawyer and draft a joint custody agreement, outlining all the specifics of the shared arrangement.

26 Solomon tested the women to determine who was the real mother, but he did not hold a formal legal hearing.

◆ Hold a mock arbitration before a judge. Have each mother with her attorney present her case — call witnesses, and offer testimony proving she is the real mother of the baby. The judge should weigh the evidence and determine who is the real mother. Was the judge right?

Other Resources

27 Read, act out, and discuss the skit in *Bible Scenes* by Stan J. Beiner, pp. 216-220.

28 Discuss the illustration of this Haftarah in *The Illustrated Torah* by Michal Meron, p.53. How is King Solomon portrayed in this illustration?

29 For an excellent contemporary exercise teaching the lessons of *Bava Metzia*, Chapter 1, Mishnah 1, see *The Jewish Law Review*, vol. II, by Hillel Gamoran.

30 See *Myth, Legend and Custom in the Old Testament* by Theodor Gaster, pp. 491-4, which provides many examples of this same story in the folktales of other cultures.

31 Discuss the poem "O to Be a Dragon" by Marianne Moore in *Modern Poems on the Bible*, edited by D. Curzon, p. 217, in which the poet imagines having one wish come true.

32 Look at the paintings of King Solomon in *The Illustrated Hebrew Bible* by Ellen Frankel, pp. 182 and 184.

33 Obviously one of the women in this Haftarah gives false testimony. One of the Ten Commandments prohibits the bearing of false witness. Read the lesson on this *mitzvah* in *Teaching Mitzvot* by Barbara Kadden and Bruce Kadden, pp. 79-82.

34 A story involving Solomon's wisdom can be found in *While Standing on One Foot*, edited by N. Jaffe and S. Zeitlin, pp. 18-22.

35 Read Sherlock Holmes stories to compare his clever deductions to that of King Solomon. Who seems smarter?

36 Read and discuss stories about King Solomon in *Stories of King Solomon* by Lillian S. Freehof, or in *The Legends of the Jews* by Louis Ginzberg, vol. 4, pp. 130-176.

37 Discuss the following political cartoon and its use of our Haftarah.

Reprinted with permission of dePIXion Studies, Inc., Denver, Colorado.

38 Complete pp. 16 and 18 in *Prophets Copy Pak™* by Marji Gold-Vukson.

Involving the Family

39 Have a family discussion in which you will decide together the one thing you would wish for as a family if you were all collectively granted one wish. This is a great opportunity to discuss family values, goals, etc.

40 Learn to be an active listener. During a family dispute, take time to listen to and repeat one another's complaints or differing positions. Be sure each of the disputants understands the other's point of view and makes them feel they are being taken seriously.

Bar/Bat Mitzvah Projects

41 Organize a fundraiser or get otherwise involved in the Make a Wish Foundation, which grants wishes to terminally ill children. Visit their web site at www.wish.org.

42 Make your Bar or Bat Mitzvah party a *Seudat Mitzvah*. To learn how and why, read the chapter entitled "Rites and Wrongs of Passage" in *Putting God on the Guest List* by Jeffrey Salkin. While you're at it, read the whole book!

I KINGS 5:26-6:13
TERUMAH תרומה

This Haftarah has been paired with *Parashat Terumah*, Exodus 25:1-27:19. See "Connecting the Text To the Sedra," pp. 131-132, for an exploration of the many ways the two texts shed light on each other.

SYNOPSIS

This Haftarah opens with the familiar refrain: God gives Solomon wisdom. Because of the peaceful alliance Solomon has struck with King Hiram of Tyre, Solomon can turn the nation's full attention to the long anticipated construction of the Holy Temple in Jerusalem.

King Solomon levies a human tax by conscripting a labor force of 30,000 men to work in month-long shifts to gather the timber and stones in Lebanon. Solomon also has 70,000 porters, 80,000 quarriers in the hills, and 3,300 officials in charge of the work. The Israelite stoneworkers toil along with Hiram's masons and Gebalite masons from Phoenicia.

The actual construction of the *Bet HaMikdash* begins, we are told in verse 6:1, in the 480th year after the Exodus from Egypt, in the fourth year of Solomon's reign over Israel, in the second month of the year. The Temple is to be 60 cubits long, 20 cubits wide and 30 cubits high. The Haftarah includes such construction details as the size of the porch, the shape of the windows, the dimensions of the side structures, the doors and stairs, the beams and supports, and the cedar planks in the roof.

In the last three verses of the Haftarah, God addresses Solomon, reminding him to follow God's laws and statutes. If he does so, God's presence will dwell in the Temple among the children of Israel, and God will never forsake the people Israel.

INSIGHTS FROM THE TRADITION

A Why does this Haftarah about the building of the Temple commence with a reminder that God gave Solomon wisdom? Ralbag explains that it was Solomon's great wisdom that was the main factor in his long-term peaceful relationship with Hiram of Tyre; because of his wisdom, Hiram wanted a peace with him.

◆ How is achieving peace with Solomon a wise thing for Hiram to do?

Solomon enjoys a peaceful tenure as King of Israel. He has successfully negotiated treaties with neighboring nations, like Tyre. In I Kings 3:1, he allies himself with Pharaoh, ruler of Egypt, by marrying Pharaoh's daughter. He ultimately acquires 700 royal wives from at least six different nations (I Kings 11:1-3), many of whom, we can guess, were chosen for political purposes. Throughout world history, members of royal families of varying nations would marry each other to strike political alliances.

◆ How do national leaders achieve peace with one another today?

B Solomon waits until the fourth year of his reign to build the Temple (verse 6:1). According to Abrabanel, he waited to gather his own resources to use for the Temple instead of depending on the wealth and material accumulation of his father, David.

According to this interpretation, Solomon wanted to establish independence from his father before attempting the massive undertaking of building the Temple.

◆ Why do you think Solomon wanted to wait?

◆ Do you agree with Solomon's decision to wait? Explain your answer.

◆ Is this what David might have wanted?

◆ At what age do you think children may become financially independent from their parents? Discuss this issue with your own parents and compare your view with theirs.

C According to *The Legends of the Jews* by Louis Ginzberg, 4:156, Solomon built the Temple using his own resources instead of his father's because David acquired most of his wealth as booty from battles against pagan nations. Solomon did not want anyone to think that the Temple was built with materials from pagan temples. He feared that if one day the Temple were destroyed, someone might think that a pagan god destroyed it to get his gold back.

Given that the writers of the *midrash* didn't actually think a pagan god could come and take back the gold, the Rabbis were probably worried that people might get the wrong impression if the pagan gold were used in construction of the Holy Temple.

◆ How might using pagan gold in the Holy Temple send the wrong message to the Israelites? (People might think they used secondhand materials to build the Temple, or that they used materials tainted by the blood of war.)

◆ We all get impressions — good and bad — from the actions of others. Is it your responsibility as older students to make a good impression and act as role models for younger children?

◆ Is it adults' responsibility to act as role models for children?

◆ Role-play five good adult behaviors and five irresponsible adult behaviors and discuss what lessons each teaches kids.

D The Temple's length and width were each double those of the Tabernacle. The height of the Temple was to be three times the height of the Tabernacle. According to Abrabanel, the Temple had to be twice as long and wide as the Tabernacle in order to support the increased height.

◆ All engineers and architects know that good, strong foundations enable builders to create soaring structures. What life lesson can we learn from the engineering principle of broad, strong foundations?

E We learn in verse 6:4 that the Temple's windows were wide inside and narrow outside. Obviously, this would let very little light into the building. *Midrash* suggests that the design was meant to demonstrate that God and God's Temple needed no light from outside because the light of God's presence in the Temple radiated out and lit up the world (*Menachot* 86b and *Leviticus Rabbah* 31:7).

◆ Explain the phrase, "you light up my life."

◆ If God is a role model for us, then it would be our responsibility to light up the lives of others. Whose life do you light up, and how?

F Solomon built the Temple using cedarwood and the wood of cypress (verses 5:24 and 6:10). These species were acceptable for use in the building of the Temple because neither gives fruit.

◆ Why would fruit-bearing trees be protected from use in building?

◆ Why, then, do we learn in verse 6:23-33 that olive wood was used for part of the Temple? Olive trees do give fruit. Radak teaches that they used wood only from very old olive trees that were no longer giving fruit.

◆ The Torah (Deuteronomy 20:19-20) teaches that even in times of war, fruit-bearing trees are to be spared, teaching us the concept of *Bal Taschit*, protecting the environment. List fruit-bearing trees that would be excluded as building materials.

G God says in verse 6:12 that God will dwell in the new Temple if the people keep God's laws. *Metsudat David* explains that God cannot be present where God's ways are ignored.

◆ If, as some believe, God is everywhere, how can God's presence ever be absent from the Temple or from anywhere? (Suggested answer: when people act wickedly or treat holy objects inappropriately, God is ignored and God's presence fades.)

◆ If God is the Creator of the world, what must we do for the environment that would make God's presence felt? (Suggested answer: take care of the environment and care for God's creatures.)

◆ If God cares for the poor, the orphan, and the widowed, what must we do for those in need that would suggest God's presence? (Suggested answers: Give *tzedakah*, volunteer at a shelter, collect clothing.)

◆ See *In God's Name* by Sandy Eisenberg Sasso for many other names for God, and for a story about how God got those names.

STRATEGIES
Analyzing the Text

1 In the verses preceding the Haftarah, we learn that King Hiram had been a friend of David, and was delighted when Solomon succeeded his father. Solomon writes to Hiram, asking for his help in building the Temple. The two arrange a contract wherein Hiram provides Solomon with all the cypress and cedarwood he needs, and Solomon in return delivers wheat and oil as payment to Hiram.

Scholars suggest that a covenant or contract was a way to make an outsider feel like a member of the family. Today, business people enter into contracts with each other, and often business partners become like family to one another.

◆ Why might it be important to feel that someone with whom you are in business is like a family member? (you would trust him/her more, you would be more likely to treat him/her fairly and run an ethical business)

◆ Design a survey to send home to parents, asking them about their business relationships. Survey questions can include: Do you have a business partner? For how long have you been in business with your partner? Is your partner a family member? If not, do you feel as if your partner is a part of your family? On a scale of one to ten, how much do you trust your partner? Would you trust him/her more or less if your partner was a member of your family?

2 King Solomon in verse 5:27 imposes a levy (which is another word for tax) of 30,000 men on Israel.

◆ How can people be a tax?

◆ In *The Haftarah Commentary*, Plaut (p. 188) explains that Solomon's forced labor practices stirred resentment among the people, who ultimately revolt against the reign of Solomon's successor, bringing dire consequences to the kingdom. Does a nation ever have the right to require forced labor from its citizens?

◆ Since its inception in 1948, Israel has required military service of all its young men and women. Debate the pros and cons of mandatory military service.

3 We are told that it was 480 years after the Exodus from Egypt that Solomon began to build the Temple.

◆ Why do you think the editor of this story used the Exodus from Egypt as the measure of time?

◆ Do you think the Exodus was the most important event in Jewish history? Why or why not? If not, what was?

◆ Compare and contrast the time of the Israelites in Egypt (Exodus 1-6) with the time of Solomon's reign over an independent Israel. Consider the following: two powerful leaders, two building campaigns, two forced labor programs.

◆ How does the comparison make Solomon look?

4 Nahum Sarna points out in *Understanding Genesis* that if the Exodus really did occur 480 years before Solomon built his Temple, then the Exodus would have been in the year 1440 B.C.E. (Solomon reigned from 961-911 B.C.E.). This is far too early based on other evidence that suggests the Exodus was approximately 1275 B.C.E. (some say as late as 1215 B.C.E.).

Sarna explains that 480 is considered a symbolic number: 40 times 12. Forty represents the years of a generation, and 12 represents the tribes of Israel.

◆ Do you accept that information in the Bible is sometimes symbolic and not literal history? Why or why not?

◆ Sarna suggests that often the numbers used in the Bible are intended to create literary and historical harmony. Consider how the number 40 is used repeatedly: The Israelites wander 40 years in the desert, it rains 40 days and 40 nights in the Noah's Ark story; Moses was on Mount Sinai 40 days and 40 nights in Exodus 24:18, there are 40 years of peace after Deborah defeats Sisera in Judges 5:31, the Israelites are enslaved in Egypt for 40 times 10 years; the Temple is built 40 times 12 years after the Exodus. How does this repetition create a kind of harmony?

◆ Use the numbers in your birth date to develop a symbolic message about you. You can consider the numbers as they are, or add, subtract, multiply and/or divide them for hidden messages. For example, if your birth date is 4/18/77, you can say that 4 stands for your being the fourth person in your family, 18 means you will have a long life, and 77 indicates that you will always keep the seventh day, Shabbat.

5 The work on *Bet HaMikdash* (the Temple) begins in the month of *Ziv*, which is the biblical name for what we call Iyar. *Ziv* means "brightness." Find Iyar on a Jewish calendar and explain why it is also called "brightness."

◆ Why might this time of year have been particularly good (in both practical and symbolic terms) to begin the massive construction project?

◆ There is a *tzedakah* fund by the name of Ziv. The founder of the Ziv Tzedakah Fund, Danny Siegel, brings attention to and raises money for people he calls "*mitzvah* heroes," who light up the world by doing great works of *gemilut chasadim* and *tzedakah*. You can visit his web site at www.ziv.org to find out more about *mitzvah* heroes, what they do, and how you can help.

◆ How do these *mitzvah* heroes make the world a brighter place?

6 The stones for the Temple were fully prepared at the quarry, according to verse 6:7. Therefore, there was no need of hammer or ax or any iron tool in *Bet HaMikdash* itself.

◆ Iron tools are associated with war and destruction. Why would iron tools be prohibited at the site of the Holy Temple?

◆ When you were young, were you permitted to play with pretend guns and weapons at home? How about now? Do you think children should be allowed to play with pretend weapons? Why or why not? Does this apply to computer games as well?

7 The minutest details of Temple construction are given, but we are never told the precise location of *Bet HaMikdash* (the Temple).

◆ Why do you think this is so? Perhaps, according to our tradition, we are not to focus too much on places, but rather on practice.

Connecting the Text To the Sedra

8 The Tabernacle was a temporary dwelling, designed to be portable like a nomad's tent to meet the needs of a wandering people (see *JPS Torah Commentary: Exodus* by Nahum Sarna, p. 158). In contrast, the Temple was a massive, permanent house.

◆ How do the two different dwelling places for the Tablets of the Covenant reflect the vastly different lives of the two generations of Israelites who built them?

◆ Would you rather have lived during the time of Moses and the wandering in the wilderness, or in the time of Solomon and the established kingdom of Israel?

◆ Pretend you are a newspaper reporter. Write an article covering some aspect of building the Tabernacle and another article covering some aspect of building the Temple. Include some description of what life was like at the time.

9 The Temple was built with forced labor, while the Tabernacle was funded by freewill offerings.

◆ Do you feel differently about doing something (such as reading or practicing an instrument) that you are forced to do and doing something because you want to do it?

◆ Do you think the Israelites felt differently about the building of the Tabernacle and of the Temple?

◆ *Midrash HaGadol* on Exodus 25:2 says the Tabernacle, which was built with whole-hearted, voluntary donations, was impervious to the evil eye. On the other hand, the Temple, which was built with required donations that were given halfheartedly, was ultimately destroyed by the enemy's hand.

◆ Do you think the Israelites felt differently about the Tabernacle and the Temple after they were built?

10 In the Haftarah God promises to dwell in the Temple. The Hebrew word for "dwell," שכנתי (*shachanti*), is related to the Hebrew word for the Tabernacle built in the desert, משכן (*mishkan*). Nahum Sarna observed that the word implies temporary lodging (see *JPS Torah Commentary: Exodus* by Nahum Sarna, p. 158). Therefore, God's presence, even in the permanent dwelling, is a roving presence.

This can mean that the Temple is not God's permanent dwelling place, but rather a place toward which people can orient their prayer and a place in which God's presence is always felt.

◆ Why do you think people need to go to special place like a Tabernacle, Temple, or sanctuary and engage in special sacrifices or other rituals in order to feel God's presence? Explain how while this is a human requirement, God's presence may be experienced in any location while engaging in a wide variety of activities.

◆ Read and discuss the following story about the Baal Shem Tov:

It used to be that when the Baal Shem Tov wanted to feel God's presence, he would go to a special place in his favorite woods, he would light a fire in a special way, and sing a special melody. A generation after he died, people no longer remembered the special melody, but they would go to the special place and light the special fire. A generation later, they no longer remembered how to light the fire, so they would just go to the special place. Now, we no longer remember even where the place is, but we have something just as good — we have the story we can tell.

◆ Describe all the ways God's presence is felt in this story. How does telling the story replace all the other ways?

◆ Does the story mean to say that these are the only ways to experience God?

11 In the Sedra we learn that the Tabernacle is made from many different fabrics in a variety of colors. *Bet HaMikdash*, on the other hand, is built of wood and gold.

◆ Which of the two seems to be warmer and more inviting?

◆ Synagogues vary greatly in their decor and atmosphere. Some people prefer to pray in a small, homey *shtebl*, while others enjoy a large, fancy building. Do you prefer to pray in a formal or informal atmosphere? Explain your answer.

◆ Ask your parents and grandparents which they prefer, and why.

◆ Describe your ideal sanctuary, or even build a model of it using clay, popsicle sticks, colored paper, foil, fabric, etc.

12 In the Sedra Moses is told by God exactly how to make the Tabernacle. God repeatedly emphasizes to Moses that the Tabernacle is to be built exactly as Moses was shown.

◆ Review Exodus 25:9 and 40, 26:30, and 27:8. Explain how God emphasized to Moses that he was to do exactly as he was commanded.

◆ Why do you think these reminders were necessary?

◆ In the Haftarah Solomon is told by God that God will always dwell with the people, provided that God's laws and commandments are kept (6:12-13). Why do you think that Solomon needed to be reminded to keep God's laws?

◆ What connection can you draw between these two texts?

Extending the Text

13 Israel and Tyre both benefit from peaceful relations between their two leaders. In 1978, Israeli Prime Minister Menachem Begin and Egyptian President Anwar Sadat signed the Camp David Peace Accords with the help of American President Jimmy Carter. After years of enmity and warfare, Israel and Egypt decided it was time for peace.

Israel and Egypt have enjoyed peaceful relations since 1978, but not without a high price. Israel paid for peace with the Sinai peninsula, which it turned over to Egypt. Egypt paid for peace with the life of Sadat, who was assassinated because he signed a treaty with Israel.

◆ Study the Camp David Peace Accords, which you can find on the Internet at: www.israelmfa. gov.il/mfa/go.asp?MFAH00ie0.

14 Solomon required his citizens to donate their time in national service. In the United States, lawyers are supposed to do at least 50 hours annually of *pro bono* work, which is volunteer work for people who cannot afford a lawyer.

◆ How and why are lawyers required to pay this kind of tax?

◆ Find out if any other professionals are similarly required to donate their time for the common good.

◆ For more information, see the front page article in *The New York Times*, August 17, 2000.

◆ Interview a local lawyer about the type of *pro bono* work he/she has done.

15 The word "light" is used to symbolize many things.

◆ Make a list of all the symbolic meanings of "light." To get you started, think of the idea light bulb from cartoons, the torch in the Statue of Liberty, the phrase "sweetness and light." (See an exhaustive list of the symbols of light in *Encyclopedia of Jewish Symbols* by Ellen Frankel and Betsy Teutsch, pp. 96-98.)

◆ Have a "sing down" with your class. Divide into two or more teams, and list all the songs you know with the word "light" in the lyrics. Then, take turns singing some lines from the songs, with each team crossing out songs that

have already been sung. The team with the most songs wins.

16 We learned in Insights from the Tradition #C, p. 128, that it was important to the Rabbis that Solomon didn't make a bad impression by using gold won from pagans in the construction of the Temple.

There is a concept in Jewish law known as *marit ayin*, meaning "how things appear to the eye." A Jew should take care to avoid situations in which any observer might be led to misconstrue what he/she sees. For example, if a Jew who observes *kashrut* goes into a McDonald's for a Coke, someone may think he/she is going in for a non-kosher burger or that McDonald's burgers are kosher. Therefore, to avoid giving the wrong impression, some observant Jews refrain from going into a place like McDonald's even for a cold drink.

◆ Do you think we should be concerned about what others may think of our actions?

◆ Can you think of other examples of situations to avoid for the sake of *marit ayin*?

17 In 1967, the State of Israel recaptured sections of Jerusalem which had long been under foreign control and prohibited to all Jews, including the site of the long gone Temple. When the Israeli soldiers took control of Jerusalem and reached the Temple Mount, they were understandably quite emotional.

Mordechai Gur, commander of the parachute brigade that captured Jerusalem, radioed, "The Temple Mount is in our hands. Repeat. The Temple Mount is ours" (quoted in *Two Jews, Three Opinions*, edited by Sandee Brawarsky and Deborah Mark, p. 270).

◆ Imagine you are a newspaper reporter. Interview Commander Gur and his paratroopers about seeing and touching the Western

Wall for the first time. Consider videotaping the interview for class viewing.

18 There are many laws regarding the construction of a synagogue.

◆ Review these laws (e.g., a synagogue must be built on a hill or by a river, a synagogue must have at least one window in the sanctuary, and the sanctuary must be oriented toward Jerusalem).

◆ Ask your Rabbi about other regulations and the reasons behind them, or research the subject in the *Encyclopaedia Judaica*, vol. 15, pp. 591-592.

◆ Does your synagogue comply with all these rules?

◆ Can you think of other rules that should apply to synagogue construction (access for the disabled, for example)?

Personalizing the Text

19 Solomon waits four years until he has achieved enough independence to build the Temple.

◆ Your Bar/Bat Mitzvah signals a milestone in your own development. Decide three ways you will assert your independence as a Jewish adult.

20 According to *Metsudat David*, even though the foundation stones of the Temple were not visible to the eye, equal care was given to their preparation (verse 5:31).

Rabbi Dov Peretz Elkins writes, "Sometimes we think that because our mistakes and misdeeds are not known to others, we can 'get away with it.' Judaism teaches that the really honest person is honorable in public and in private . . . " (*Moments of Transcendence: Inspirational Readings for*

Rosh Hashanah, edited by Rabbi Dov Peretz Elkins, p. 78).

Rabbi Elkins continues by telling the story of a former hockey goalie, Jacques Plante, who once asked, "How would you like a job where, if you make a mistake, a big red light goes on and 18,000 people boo?"

◆ Why is it easier to sin when we think no one is watching?

◆ How does this lesson apply to the non-visible foundation stones of the Temple?

◆ Would it be easier to be honest all the time if a big red light went on every time we lied? Why or why not?

◆ Make a poster to hang in your classroom with the words of Jacques Plante, reminding people always to do the right thing.

21 We learned the importance of good foundations in Insights from the Tradition #D, p. 128. The Rabbis wrote in *Pirke Avot* 3:17:

"He whose wisdom exceeds his deeds, to what is he like? To a tree whose branches are many but whose roots are few, and the wind comes and uproots it and overturns it . . . But he whose works exceed his wisdom, to what is he like? To a tree whose branches are few, but whose roots are many, so that even though all the winds in the world come and blow against it, it can not be stirred from its place . . . "

◆ We might have guessed that the Rabbis thought that wisdom was the foundation of humanity, but according to this, what is the foundation?

◆ Do you agree or disagree with the Rabbis' opinion? Why or why not?

◆ Design a class tree: the branches represent what you are studying this year; the roots represent the Bar/Bat Mitzvah projects you are doing. Display the tree prominently in your school.

22 The month of Iyar is characterized by brightness.

◆ Design a calendar for the Jewish year, giving each month a descriptive name of your own choosing, such as "brightness" for Iyar. Note that in I Kings 8:2, Tishre is called "strength." Make an illustration or collage for each month based on its descriptive name.

23 Fruit trees are meant to be used for food production only (see Insights from the Tradition, #F, pp. 128-129).

◆ Find out what fruit trees grow locally, and enjoy them by picking their fruit in season.

24 Every synagogue has unique and beautiful features.

◆ Take a class trip through your synagogue and sanctuary and make a list of some of the most beautiful features (doors, windows, paintings).

◆ Research your favorite feature. Find out where and how and by whom it was created, and who decided to purchase it. If it was donated by a congregant, try to talk to that congregant or a descendant of that congregant to find out more about the item and its purchase.

◆ As a class, volunteer to clean the windows, polish the woodwork, or help in some other way to beautify your synagogue.

25 The nooks and crannies of the Western Wall of the Temple in Jerusalem are crammed with handwritten notes and prayers from worshipers from all over the world.

◆ Write a Bar/Bat Mitzvah wish or prayer to inserted in the *Kotel*. Give the note to someone you know who is going to Israel, or keep it in a safe place so that you can do it yourself some day.

◆ Alternatively, you can make a virtual visit to the *Kotel* via live video camera. You can also send a prayer, free of charge, to the Western Wall through e-mail. Visit www.Kotelkam.com.

◆ Learn the song *"HaKotel,"* found on the recording *The Songs We Sang* by the Zamir Chorale of Boston.

26 Tradition teaches that King Solomon was the author of the biblical Book of Proverbs.

◆ Study the following proverbs about peace and wisdom:

• [Wisdom's] ways are pleasant ways, and all her paths, peaceful (3:17).

• He who speaks contemptuously of his fellow man is devoid of sense; a prudent man keeps his peace (11:12).

• A gentle response allays wrath; harsh word provokes anger (15:1).

◆ Which of these sayings do you like best, and why?

◆ Write your own proverb about the connection between wisdom and peace.

◆ Solomon accomplished great things during times of peace with Israel's neighbors. Learn the Israeli song about yearning for peace in our time, *"Shir LaShalom."* Be sure to read a translation of the words. The song may be found in translation and transliteration at the web site www.radiohazak.com/shir/html. Guitar chords are also available at this site. The song may also be found, along with many other songs about peace, in *Songs of Peace* by Velvel Pasternak (Tara Books).

27 Some say the traditional song *"Lo Alecha Ham'la'cha Ligmor"* is about building the Temple again in our time. Others maintain that it refers to the life work of each human being.

◆ Learn and sing the song, which may be found in *B'Kol Echad*, edited by Jeffrey Shiovitz, p. 89, and on the accompanying audiocassettes, *Shirei B'Kol Echad*, both of which may be ordered from the web site of United Synagogue for Conservative Judaism, www.uscj.org/booksvc.

◆ Which interpretation do you prefer, and why?

28 A *midrash* in *Numbers Rabbah* 14:3 mentions that the Holy Temple actually built itself.

◆ Write your own story expanding on this idea. You may use the idea expressed in the first chapter of Genesis, wherein God creates the world just by saying so.

29 There is a model of the Second Temple at the Holy Land Hotel in Jerusalem.

◆ Try to find someone who has visited the Holy Land Hotel who can show you their photographs. You can visit it yourself online at www.inisrael.com/holyland/model.html.

◆ Do more research on the design of the Temple. Using clay, Lego, or other media, make a model of Solomon's *Bet HaMikdash* in Jerusalem.

Other Resources

30 Read and discuss the story of two brothers — one single and one married — whose farm was to be the site of the Holy Temple. You can find it in *The Legends of the Jews* by Louis Ginzberg, vol. 4, p. 154.

31 The play "A Holy Place," found in *The Magic Tanach* by Gabrielle Suzanne Kaplan, is a modern adaptation of the story of the two brothers for Grades 1-3. Read and/or perform this play.

32 For a touching Holocaust story on the subject of light and hope in the darkest of times, see "The Light in the Wall" by Renee Brachfeld in *Chosen Tales*, edited by Peninnah Schram, pp. 50-53.

33 For more on *Bal Tashchit* (don't be wasteful), see *Teaching Mitzvot* by Barbara Binder Kadden and Bruce Kadden, pp. 143-146.

34 Understanding the other side's point of view is crucial for negotiating treaties. For an exercise teaching this skill, do "Warring Camps" in *Jewish Identity Games* by Richard Israel, pp. 48-49.

35 Read and discuss stories about King Solomon *in Stories of King Solomon* by Lillian S. Freehof, or in *The Legends of the Jews* by Louis Ginzberg, vol. 4, pp. 130-176.

36 Discuss the illustration of this Haftarah in *The Illustrated Torah* by Michal Meron, p. 87. Would you have portrayed King Solomon differently? Why or why not?

Involving the Family

37 Solomon wanted to build the Temple independently of his father. Discuss independence issues in your family. Compare what you do for various issues (bedtimes, curfews, going out with friends, money) with what other families do. Make plans for building independence over the next year.

38 Mark special occasions and family milestones by planting fruit trees around your yard.

Bar/Bat Mitzvah Projects

39 Trees are a precious commodity in the Bible and today in Israel. Contact the Jewish National Fund at 42 East 69th Street, New York, NY 10021, 800-542-TREE, www.jnf.org, and inquire about their different donation opportunities. Choose a program in honor of your Bar/Bat Mitzvah and buy some trees to help "make the desert bloom."

40 Offer yourself as a "tax" to your synagogue or town. Volunteer to clean a park or garden, visit the elderly or infirm, do office work, give computer lessons, or tutor younger students in Hebrew.

I KINGS 7:13-26
VAYAKHEL ויקהל Sephardim

This Haftarah has been paired with *Parashat Vayakhel*, Exodus 35:1-38:20. See "Connecting the Text To the Sedra," pp. 140-141, for an exploration of the many ways the two texts shed light on each other.

SYNOPSIS

King Solomon enlists the help of Hiram, a skilled bronze artisan, to build some special features of the Temple. Hiram's deceased father was a coppersmith in Tyre, and his widowed mother was a member of the tribe of Naphtali. He fashions two pillars of bronze, each 18 cubits high and 12 cubits in circumference. He makes two capitals of molten bronze, each five cubits high, to set upon the bronze pillars. Finally, Hiram creates ornate nets and wreaths, bronze pomegranates, and lilies to adorn the capitals and pillars.

He sets the pillars on the portico of the Temple and names the one on the right "Yachin" and the one on the left "Boaz."

Hiram then creates a large, richly ornamented cast metal basin, called the molten sea, which was ten cubits in diameter and five cubits deep. The molten sea stood upon 12 bronze oxen, three looking north, three looking south, three looking east, and three looking west. The brim of the molten sea was shaped like lily petals, and it was encircled with gourds.

INSIGHTS FROM THE TRADITION

A Hiram makes two huge bronze pillars for the entrance to the sanctuary. He names the pillars "Yachin," which means "God will establish

or secure it [the Temple] forever," and "Boaz," which means "May Israel find strength through her service in the Temple" (*Metsudat David*).

We can understand the message here to be that through devotion to God's law, we will gain strength.

◆ Give examples of ways God's laws strengthen and make more securely established our Jewish identity, our family life, our Jewish community, and the world in general.

◆ Having a strong sense of right and wrong gives a person strength. Belonging to an active, caring community gives a person strength. Having a secure homeland in Israel gives strength to Jews around the world. Suggest your own examples of how Judaism makes all of us stronger.

B Hiram was from Tyre, outside of Israel. Yet Radak explains, he had been born in Israel and moved to Tyre, making Hiram an Israelite and not a foreigner.

◆ Why do you think it was important to demonstrate that Hiram was an Israelite?

◆ Do you think that an important national symbol should be crafted only by a citizen of that nation?

◆ The Statue of Liberty, which is probably the most abiding symbol of the United States, was in fact crafted in France by the French. Does its French origin make the Statue of Liberty any less of an American icon?

C In an alternative viewpoint, Rabbi Leo Honor explains that Solomon invited a foreign artist because Hiram was the best craftsman for the job.

◆ Should the best artist always be hired for the job, or should there be other considerations? Explain your answer.

STRATEGIES
Analyzing the Text

1 The Haftarah provides biographical information about Hiram in verse 7:13-14.

◆ Summarize this biographical information.

◆ Why do you think we are given this information about Hiram? (Note that *Metsudat David* and most commentators agree that this Hiram was not the same as King Hiram.)

◆ Imagine you are on a synagogue committee that must hire an architect to build a new synagogue building or an artist to redecorate your existing facility. Write a list of questions you might want to ask during an interview. Do you want to know anything about his or her personal life?

2 The Hebrew for the word "capital" on top of each pillar in verse 7:16 is כתרת (*koteret*), and is related to the word "crown" (*keter*).

Pillars and capitals, like those in the Temple, were important architectural elements in ancient Greece and Rome.

◆ For more information on the styles of ancient columns and capitals, see this web site: http://harpy.uccs.edu/greek/greek.html.

3 All the measurements in the Haftarah are given in cubits, which was the prevailing measurement at the time. A cubit is the distance from the elbow to the end of the middle finger. The standard cubit is somewhere between 18.9 inches and 22.7 inches.

◆ Make a height chart for everyone in your class. Measure and record everyone's height in cubits. Determine the length of the average cubit in your class by measuring everyone's personal cubit and averaging the length.

4 Pomegranates are featured prominently in the decoration of the columns. The pomegranate is a very important Jewish symbol, as it represents such ideas as fertility, prosperity, love, and kingship.

◆ Examine and eat a pomegranate to discover what it is about this fruit that lends itself to these representations.

◆ For a complete account of the symbolism of the pomegranate, see *The Encyclopedia of Jewish Symbols* by Ellen Frankel and Betsy Platkin Teutsch, p. 128, or the entry for "Pomegranate" in *Encyclopaedia Judaica*, vol. 13, pp. 841-842.

5 The "molten sea," a large brass container of water, was so-called because of its huge size. It is thought to have held between 11,000 and 12,000 gallons of water.

◆ It is difficult to conceptualize volume. Do you think the molten sea was approximately the size of a telephone booth, a school bus, or an Olympic swimming pool? (The closest answer is a school bus.)

◆ To give the students some fun practice estimating volume, the teacher can bring to class a large glass or clear plastic container (fish tank, plastic snack container, etc.). Fill the container with M&Ms or jelly beans and have the students guess how many fit inside the container. After all the guesses are written down and handed in, students can count (and eat!) the contents. A prize may be awarded to the best guesser. (Washing hands before counting is a good idea.)

Connecting the Text To the Sedra

6 In the Sedra (Exodus 35:30), it is God who calls Bezalel to work on the Tabernacle.

◆ Compare this with the Haftarah, in which Hiram is hired by Solomon to work on the Temple.

◆ Consider the differences between doing something as a calling from God and doing something because you are hired and paid to do it.

◆ It is often said that Rabbis, ministers, and priests are "called" to their professions. Interview your own Rabbi and a local minister and priest to learn about their decisions to become religious leaders.

◆ In what ways do artists follow their "calling" and also do the jobs they're paid to do? Can you think of other professions that can be both "callings" and jobs?

7 Pillars are a key feature of the architecture of both the Tabernacle and the Temple. Hiram's columns were absolutely massive, approximately 27 to 36 feet high. These free-standing pillars stood at the top of the stairs in front of the entrance to the Temple to welcome and inspire all visitors who passed between them.

◆ What qualities do pillars represent?

◆ In what ways is becoming a Bar/Bat Mitzvah like passing through a doorway into Jewish adulthood?

◆ What other Jewish life cycle events are like doorways from one reality to another?

◆ Draw or paint a picture or cartoon depicting the transformation that takes place in a particular Jewish life cycle event. Represent the life cycle event as a doorway, and portray someone entering it one way and emerging somehow changed.

◆ Alternatively, people who contribute to their communities are often called "pillars" of the community. Are they aptly named?

◆ In what ways do you (or do you plan to) serve as a pillar of your community?

8 Hiram in I Kings 7:13 is said to have been endowed with "skill, ability, and talent for executing all work." The artist Bezalel, who builds the Tabernacle, is described in the Sedra in Exodus 31:3-4 and 35:31, as "endowed with a Divine spirit of skill, ability, and talent in every kind of craft."

◆ What is the difference among these qualities: skill, ability, and talent (some translate them as: wisdom, understanding, and skill)?

◆ For a full discussion on this subject, see Extending the Text #7 in *Parashat Vayakhel* in *Teaching Torah* by Sorel Goldberg Loeb and Barbara Binder Kadden, p. 151.

9 Bezalel and Hiram were gifted artisans.

◆ Identify some of your many gifts. Are any of them artistic talents?

◆ Plan a class talent show, in which every student can showcase his or her talent(s). Those whose talents are not of the performing variety can create something to display instead.

10 Hiram and Bezalel are renowned biblical artisans. Match the following list of biblical people with their professions:

1. Oholiab, Exodus 38:23 (a)
2. Ezra, Ezra 7:6 (h)
3. Nehemiah, Nehemiah 1:11 (c)
4. Heman, I Chronicles 6:18 (e)
5. Jehoshaphat, I Kings 4:3 (b)
6. Ishmael, Genesis 21:20 (f)
7. Hiram's father, I Kings 7:14 (g)
8. Naboth the Jezreelite, I Kings 21:1 (i)

9. Tubal-cain, Genesis 4:22 (j)
10. Huldah, II Kings 22:14 (d)

a. embroiderer
b. recorder
c. cupbearer
d. prophetess
e. singer
f. archer
g. coppersmith
h. scribe
i. vintner
j. forger

11 The Sedra begins with the laws of keeping Shabbat and refraining from work — מלאכה (malachah). The Haftarah in verse 7:14 also uses the word מלאכה.

◆ For a discussion of "work" and Shabbat, see *Teaching Torah* by Sorel Goldberg Loeb and Barbara Binder Kadden, Analyzing the Text #1, p. 150.

12 In the Sedra Bezalel creates beautiful things to adorn the Tabernacle, while Hiram in the Haftarah crafts the magnificent pillars and basin for the Temple. There is a concept in Judaism of doing *mitzvot* in the nicest possible way; it is called *hiddur mitzvah*. A plain Tabernacle and Temple would have served the same purpose, but how wonderful to have a beautiful Tabernacle and Temple!

◆ Do you think it is better to do *mitzvot* in the nicest possible way? Explain your answer.

◆ Scan your home for beautiful Jewish ritual objects, such as *tefillin, tallitot, mezuzot, chanukiyot,* and so on. Bring in one of them for a *hiddur mitzvah* show-and-tell.

◆ Bezalel and Hiram create magnificent objects to adorn Jewish holy places. Create a beautiful ritual object, such as a *mezuzah* case, a *mizrach* sign, or a *chanukiah* for your home.

Extending the Text

13 In verse 7:14 we read that Hiram was endowed with skill, ability, and talent. Daily, in the weekday *"Amidah,"* we, too, ask God for wisdom and understanding.

◆ We pray for many things in the weekday *"Amidah,"* including: health, peace, forgiveness, prosperity, wisdom, and justice. Rank these requests in order of importance to you. Discuss and compare your ranking with your classmates.

◆ Are there any other blessings you think we should ask for in our daily prayers?

14 Rabbi Simon taught in *Pirke Avot* 4:13: "There are three crowns: the crown of Torah, the crown of priesthood, and the crown of royalty, but the crown of a good name excels them all."

◆ What is a good name, and why is it more important than knowledge (Torah), career (priesthood), heredity (royalty), or nationality?

◆ Despite their athletic prowess, exceptional baseball players such as Daryl Strawberry and Pete Rose engaged in behaviors that damaged their good names. How do you think their baseball legacies will be affected by their questionable reputations?

◆ Should these individuals be allowed into the Baseball Hall of Fame? Why or why not?

◆ Can you think of any other great athlete or politician whose good name has been damaged by questionable behavior?

◆ How do you go about getting a good name for yourself?

15 Two pillars stood at the entrance to the Holy Temple. The Rabbis taught in *Pirke Avot* 1:2 that the world stands on three things: Torah, *avodah*, and *gemilut chasadim*.

◆ What are these three things, and what does it mean that the world stands on them?

◆ In a variation on this theme, the Rabbis also taught in *Pirke Avot* 1:18 that the world stands on justice, trust, and peace. Which version do you prefer, and why?

◆ Learn and sing the song about these ideas, *"Al Shloshah D'varim,"* which may be found in *B'Kol Echad*, edited by Jeffrey Shiovitz, p. 77, and on the accompanying audiocasettes, *Shirei B'Kol Echad*, both of which may be ordered from the web site of United Synagogue for Conservative Judaism, www. uscj.org/booksvc.

16 Hiram was a talented artist who may or may not have been an Israelite. Jewish artists have created great works in every medium throughout history.

◆ Consult the *Encyclopaedia Judaica*, vol. 3, pp. 594-614 for an alphabetical listing of Jewish artists, including brief biographies. As you will see, the list is quite impressive! Choose an artist on whom and on whose works to prepare a presentation for your class. The artists with an asterisk next to their names have biographies under a separate entry in the *Encyclopaedia Judaica*.

◆ Hold an art show for your school, displaying either reproductions of famous artwork (post-cards are inexpensive and generally available, and many paintings can be downloaded) or your own renditions of the masterpieces.

17 Hiram's pillars were symbols of strength. Tradition teaches that King Solomon was the author of the biblical Book of Proverbs.

◆ Study the following proverbs about strength:

• The glory of youths is in their strength; The majesty of old men is their gray hair. (Proverbs 20:29)

• A wise man is strong; a knowledgeable man exerts power. (Proverbs 24:5)

• [A woman of valor] is clothed with strength and splendor; She looks to the future cheerfully. (Proverbs 31:25).

◆ Which one of these sayings do you like best, and why?

◆ Write your own proverb about strength.

18 Abrabanel teaches that Hiram lived in Naphtali to comfort his widowed mother. The loss of a mate is one of the most severe stresses many people face in life. A list published in the *Journal of Psychosomatic Research*, vol. II, 1967, p. 214, by Thomas Holmes and Richard Rahe rates many of the stresses we face in life in order of severity. You can find their research at: www.teachhealth.com.

◆ On the following partial list of stresses, rank them in order of severity. (The entries are in order. The teacher should mix the list before giving it to students.)

Death of a mate
Divorce
Serious personal illness or injury
Marriage
Fired from job
Retirement
Change (positive or negative) in financial state
Trouble with in-laws or children
Begin or end school
Move to new home

◆ What would you include in your own top ten list of stressful life events?

Personalizing the Text

19 Review all the details of the description of Hiram's pillars and capitals in verses 7:15-22.

♦ Do a charcoal, pencil, or chalk drawing of your understanding of what the pillars looked like.

♦ Compare your drawing to the illustration of this Haftarah in *The Illustrated Torah* by Michal Meron, p. 100.

20 Hiram and Solomon represent two nations working together to create something of beauty. The Anti-Defamation League has an advertising campaign that teaches "Hate Kills, Love Builds."

♦ Help to reduce hatred in your community by sponsoring a speaker from the ADL. Or, your class can join forces with a church group or other group to work together on a *mitzvah* project to make the world a better place.

21 Hiram names his two pillars.

♦ Why do people name inanimate objects?

♦ Have you ever named an inanimate object, such as a family car?

♦ Make a poster featuring an object you have named. Include a drawing or photograph of the object, its name, the reason for the name, and any other facts about the object you want to share.

22 Some suggest that Yachin and Boaz, the names of the two pillars, were the beginning of quotations written on the pillars. The quotations were never recorded. Yachin means "God will establish and secure it," and Boaz means "with strength."

♦ Write your own attempt at the completion of both quotations.

23 Congregational presidents are pillars of the Jewish community.

♦ Find out who your synagogue's past presidents are. Send each of them a certificate of your own design, declaring them pillars of the community and thanking them for their service. Also consider throwing a party to honor the past presidents.

24 Hiram and Solomon must have been proud of their accomplishments in building the Temple. Whenever Professor Samuel Lachs concluded one of his lectures, people would surround him in praise. A friend once said to him, "You must really enjoy how much they admire you." To this, Lachs replied, "It's not what people think of you that counts, but what *you* think of the quality of what you do" (from a eulogy in memory of the late Samuel Lachs by Professor Jeffrey Tigay, which can be found at: www.sas.upenn.edu/~jtigay/lachs.htm)

♦ Do you agree or disagree with the reply of Professor Lachs? Why or why not?

Other Resources

25 Read, act out, and discuss the skit in *Bible Scenes* by Stan J. Beiner, pp. 221-224.

26 Read *My Name Is Asher Lev* by Chaim Potok, which is about a religious Jewish boy who must make difficult decisions to follow his dream of becoming an artist.

27 The Temple Mount in Jerusalem continues to be considered holy 2,000 years after the destruction of the Second Temple. People are still drawn to it and want to be in the presence of holiness. View and discuss the film *Field of Dreams* (1989, rated PG, 107 minutes), in which a baseball field garners the same response from people. Consider the metaphor of the baseball field and all the things it represents.

28 See the painting of Solomon and Hiram planning the Temple by Jack Levine in *The Jewish Spirit* by Ellen Frankel, p. 211. Here also you will find a story by Hayyim Nachman Bialik called "The Mysterious Palace," which is about King Solomon.

29 Hiram lived with his mother to comfort her in her widowhood. For more on children's responsibilities to their parents, see Torah Aura Instant Lesson *What Must Parents Do? — What Must Children Do?*

30 Hiram and Bezalel are still recognized today as being among the world's greatest artisans. We can only imagine how proud they must have been of their accomplishments. Taking pride in one's work is a Jewish virtue. Read more about it in *Teaching Jewish Virtues* by Susan Freeman, p. 140.

31 Complete p. 17 in *Prophets Copy Pak™* by Marji Gold-Vukson.

Involving the Family

32 Make your Bar or Bat Mitzvah an occasion for *hiddur mitzvah*. Select beautiful *kipot* to give to the congregation and a special *tallit* to wear yourself.

33 Your family will be giving a lot of Bar/Bat Mitzvah gifts this year. Select a particular ritual object, such as a *mezuzah* case, Star of David pendant, or Torah pointer *(yad)* that you and your family can give to your friends in the name of *hiddur mitzvah*.

34 Read and discuss stories about King Solomon in *Stories of King Solomon* by Lillian S. Freehof, or *The Legends of the Jews* by Louis Ginzberg, vol. 4, pp. 130-176.

Bar/Bat Mitzvah Projects

35 Be a pillar of your community. Hiram was a foreigner who offered his talents and services to the Israelites. Hospitals, nursing homes, shelters, and soup kitchens are always understaffed on Christmas and Easter. Volunteer to offer your services so that your Christian neighbors can enjoy their holidays.

36 Start your own collection of some type of Jewish ritual object, for example, *mezuzah* cases, *chanukiyot*, *Kiddush* cups, or Havdalah spice boxes.

I KINGS 7:40-50
VAYAKHEL וקהל Ashkenazim
PIKUDAY פקודי Sephardim
SECOND SHABBAT CHANUKAH

 This Haftarah was paired with *Parashat Vayakhel* (Exodus 35:1-38:20), *Parashat Pikuday* (Exodus 38:21-40:38), and the second Shabbat of Chanukah. See "Connecting the Text To the Sedra," pp. 146-148, for an exploration of the ways the texts and the special Shabbat shed light on each other.

Note: There is a great deal of overlap and related material in the two Haftarot for *Vayakhel*, plus some overlap with *Terumah* and *Pikuday* as well. Therefore, the Insights from the Tradition and the Strategies for these Haftarot may be regarded as largely interchangeable.

SYNOPSIS

In this Haftarah we are given a complete inventory of the things Hiram created in burnished bronze for the Temple: two columns, two capitals atop the columns, two pieces of network to cover the capitals upon the columns, 400 pomegranates for the network covering the capitals upon the columns, ten stands and ten lavers upon the stands, one huge tank with 12 oxen beneath it, pails, scrapers, and sprinkling bowls.

Although Solomon had all the bronze cast in earthen molds, he did not weigh the items because of their vast quantity. Therefore, the total used weight of bronze remained undetermined.

Finally, all the Temple furnishings made of gold are listed: the altar, the table for the shewbread, the ten lampstands, the petals, the lamps, the tongs, the basins, the snuffers, the sprinkling bowls, the ladles, the fire pans, the hinge sockets for both the doors of the innermost chamber of the Temple and the doors of the Great Hall.

INSIGHTS FROM THE TRADITION

A Commentators teach that Solomon commissioned the creation of more Temple implements than he would actually need, and put the remainder away for future use (based on *Targum Jonathan* 7:47).

◆ What lessons can we learn from Solomon's foresight?

◆ In what ways do you or your parents prepare for the future?

B The Hebrew words *sippot* and *m'zamrot* in verse 50 are generally translated as "basins" and "snuffers." However, Rashi suggests that they were actually musical instruments.

◆ Does your synagogue use musical instruments in religious services? If so, which ones?

◆ Do you think musical instruments enhance or detract from services?

STRATEGIES

Analyzing the Text

1 In verse 7:48 Solomon makes a table for the bread of display לחם הפנים *(lechem hapanim). Lechem hapanim* is first mentioned in Exodus 25:30, and is further explained in Leviticus 24:5-9: "You shall take choice flour and bake of it 12 loaves, two-tenths of a measure for each loaf. Place them on the pure table before *Adonai* in two rows, six to a row . . . He shall arrange them before *Adonai* regularly every Sabbath day — it is a commitment for all time on the part of the Israelites. They shall belong to Aaron and his sons, who shall eat them in the sacred precinct . . . "

On Shabbat and holidays, we transform our dining room tables into holy altars. We place on our tables two *challot*, which are symbolic of the two rows of display bread in the Temple. We engage in ritual handwashing before the meal, recalling the ancient practice of the Temple priests. And the *Kiddush* wine we drink sanctifies the meal as a holy occasion.

◆ Hold a "model" Shabbat dinner, emphasizing all the ways we have replaced the priests as the only holy people performing holy acts.

2 Hiram was a foreign artist commissioned by Solomon to build the Holy Temple. Hiring foreign artists for large projects was apparently common practice in the ancient Middle East. Archaeologists have uncovered evidence that the Hittite king hired an Egyptian artist to build his palace. Other evidence indicates that when one king wanted to build a palace for himself, he often sought descriptions of the palaces of other kings.

◆ Do you seek the examples of others to help you make decisions? about what kinds of things?

3 This Haftarah records a long list of utensils used in Temple worship, including pails,

A small bronze incense shovel. Handle molded in the shape of a Corinthian capital. Leaves in the corners of the pan give it the appearance of an altar with horns. Dated to first century C.E., and thought to have originated in Jerusalem although found in a cave near the Dead Sea. As pictured in *Biblical Archaeology Review*, January/February 2001.

Reprinted with permission of Beth Saida Excavations Project, University of Nebraska at Omaha.

scrapers, sprinkling bowls, tongs, basins, snuffers, ladles, and fire pans (see photo of a small bronze incense shovel on this page).

◆ To learn how these implements were described, see Exodus 27:4, Exodus 38:3, and Numbers 4:13ff.

◆ There are utensils in the list above that are not specifically described in the Torah. Which are they, and how do you imagine they were used?

Connecting the Text To the Sedra

4 *Parashat Vayakhel* records an inventory list of what Bezalel was to build for the Tabernacle (Exodus 35:10-19), while the Haftarah contains a summary of all the items created by Hiram for the Temple.

- Retailers must always keep track of their inventory, as must manufacturers and real estate brokers. Why?

- We tend to forget how much we have accomplished throughout our lives. Take stock! Compile an inventory list of good things you have done or lessons you have learned this year. Why is it important for us to keep an inventory of our achievements?

5 The Tabernacle is completed in Exodus 39:32, just as Hiram and Solomon finish building the Temple in the Haftarah.

Midrash tells us that the Tabernacle was the finishing touch to the creation of the world (*The Legends of the Jews* by Louis Ginzberg, vol. 3, pp. 184-185). From the creation of the world to the revelation at Sinai, the world owed its existence to God's loving-kindness. From revelation to the building of the Tabernacle, the world stood on God's loving-kindness and Torah. Only when the Israelites could sacrifice to God at the Tabernacle did the world stand on all three pillars: loving-kindness, Torah, and service to God.

- Discuss why these three are the pillars of the world.

- Make a mural depicting the creation of the world, according to this *midrash*.

- The Rabbis outline the three things responsible for the world's existence. On what three things do you think our world or your own existence depends?

6 In *Parashat Pikuday*, Moses assembles the Tabernacle after Bezalel does all the work preparing the parts. In the Haftarah Solomon is given credit in verse 7:48 for making all the vessels that were actually made by Hiram. In Psalm 30, called "A Song on the Dedication of the Temple of David," King David is given credit for building the Temple, even though Solomon was the one who built it.

- Is it fair for Moses (instead of Bezalel), Solomon (instead of Hiram), and David (instead of Solomon) to get the credit for the building projects? Explain your answer.

- Why does the boss — and not the workers — generally get the credit for the work?

- Find out from your family and friends if this has been an issue in their professional lives. Ask bosses how they credit their employees, and ask employees how they are given credit by their bosses.

7 We learn in the Haftarah that pomegranates are an important decoration in the Temple. Pomegranates are also found on the robes of the priests (see *Parashat Pikuday* Exodus 39:24-26).

- For a complete account of the symbolism of the pomegranate, see *The Encyclopedia of Jewish Symbols* by Ellen Frankel and Betsy Platkin Teutsch, p. 128, or the entry for "Pomegranate" in *Encyclopaedia Judaica*, vol. 13, pp. 841-842.

- Look around your own synagogue for pomegranates as decoration on Torah crowns and covers, Ark curtains, stained glass windows, and elsewhere.

- Eat a pomegranate to see how good it tastes and to learn why it is symbolic of fertility and prosperity.

8 The Haftarah and Sedra are both about institutions that haven't existed for thousands of years. Yet several Haftarot are devoted to detailed discussion of the Temple, and multiple Parashiot deal with the intricacies of the Tabernacle, both of which seem irrelevant to our modern existence.

- One cannot help but ask why we still read these portions? Wouldn't it make more sense to skip them or find substitutes that seem more pertinent to our lives?

◆ List three reasons why we should continue to read about the Tabernacle and Temple, and three reasons why we should not continue to read about them.

◆ We also wonder why Jews continue to read other texts that are apparently irrelevant or troubling or even offensive to our modern sensibilities. Year after year, we read texts that are misogynistic or homophobic or about slavery. Discuss or debate why we might want to continue studying these difficult texts and why we might want to abandon them altogether.

◆ Find out from your Rabbi if your congregation has chosen to read any alternative Torah or Haftarah readings instead of troublesome traditional readings.

9 This Haftarah is traditionally also read on the Shabbat of Chanukah, the holiday that celebrates the rededication of the Second Temple.

◆ Why is this Haftarah an appropriate reading for Chanukah?

10 The Tabernacle had only one seven-branched *menorah*. According to the Haftarah, Solomon's Temple had many *menorot*. The Second Temple had one seven-branched *menorah*, which was taken by Roman Emperor Titus.

◆ The official emblem of Israel is a seven-branched *menorah* surrounded by olive branches. For more information about the *menorah*, pictures of *menorot,* and the official emblem of Israel, see "*Menorah*" in *Encyclopaedia Judaica*, vol. 11, pp. 1355-1371.

◆ What does the national emblem symbolize?

◆ A sculpted *menorah* stands outside the *Knesset* in Jerusalem. To view and learn about

the symbols that cover the *menorah*, visit the web site: www.knesset.gov.il/engframe.htm.

Extending the Text

11 It is possible that foreign architecture influenced the style of the Temple, as discussed in Analyzing the Text # 2, p. 146. Modern day Jewish religious services have also been influenced by other cultures.

◆ Consider these features that have been adapted from church worship: Rabbis wearing robes, congregants facing the *bimah* at the front of the sanctuary, mixed seating, responsive readings, and organ music. Does your synagogue have any of these features?

◆ Do these features make your service more or less enjoyable? Explain your answer.

12 According to *The Legends of the Jews* by Louis Ginzberg, 4:161, the population in the days of Solomon was divided into four groups, and each wore a designated color of clothing: the king, courtiers, sages, priests, and Levites wore blue; Israelites living in Jerusalem wore white; villagers wore red; other nations visiting the king wore green.

◆ Can you think of explanations for matching these colors with these particular groups?

◆ Another *midrash* explains that each of these colors also represents a season of the year: blue for Tishre-Tevet, months that sparkle; white for the snowy months of Tevet-Nisan; green for Nisan-Tammuz, when the sea is safe to travel; and red for the fruits of Tammuz-Tishre. Choose a color to represent each season where you live, and design a calendar featuring the colors and other seasonal symbols.

13 The Temple that Hiram built looms large in the collective memory of the Jewish people. For those who lived while it was still in existence, the Holy Temple was a treasure.

◆ Read Psalm 27:4 and 122:1 to see how jubilant the people felt about visiting the Temple in Jerusalem.

◆ Learn and sing the song *"Achat Sha'alti,"* taken from Psalm 27. Find it in *B'Kol Echad*, edited by Jeffrey Shiovitz, p. 89, and on the accompanying audiocassettes, *Shirei B'Kol Echad* (order from www.uscj.org/booksvc).

14 The Haftarah lists many kinds of holy vessels, כלים *(kayleem)*, that were used in the Temple to perform ritual *mitzvot*.

Danny Siegel teaches in *Gym Shoes and Irises* (p. 88) that almost any "thing" can be an instrument or tool for *mitzvot*. Computers, for example, can be used to organize volunteers for Passover food package deliveries, and cars can be used to deliver food to the hungry. Even people can be *kayleem* if they are used to perform *mitzvot*.

◆ List five items, normally used for ordinary purposes, which can also be used to perform *mitzvot*.

◆ List five ways in which you can be a holy instrument.

15 The Haftarah lists many kinds of holy vessels used in the Temple. *Pirke Avot* 5:15 teaches that four types of vessels represent the four types of students: a sponge, who soaks in everything; a funnel, who takes in everything on one side and lets out everything on the other; a strainer, who lets out the wine and keeps in the dregs; and a sifter, who lets out the regular flour but keeps in the finest flour.

◆ Which do you think is the best kind of student, and why?

◆ What kind of "vessel" are you? Explain your answer.

16 Every synagogue contains many ritual objects, such as candlesticks, *Kiddush* cups, *chanukiyot*, *shofarot*, *Sifray Torah*, *mezuzot*, *Ner Tamid*.

◆ Have a treasure hunt for ritual objects in your synagogue. The teacher should make the list of objects to find as extensive as desired. Students write down a fact about each object that can be discovered only by actually finding and seeing it.

17 Gourds, pomegranates, and lilies were motifs used in the Temple decor.

◆ Match the following fruits and vegetables with their uses in the Bible:

1. Cucumbers - Numbers 11:5 (b)
2. Palm tree branches - Leviticus 23:40 (c)
3. Wild grapes - Isaiah 5:1-7 (g)
4. Mandrakes - Genesis 30:14-16 (e)
5. Olive oil - Exodus 30:24-29 (a)
6. Lentils - Genesis 25:34 (f)
7. Fig leaves - Genesis 3:7 (d)

a. Used to anoint a priest or holy utensils
b. Eaten by the children of Israel in Egypt and missed by them in the desert
c. Used to rejoice before God
d. Used for loincloths
e. Used for fertility
f. Used to make a stew
g. Compared to the children of Israel

◆ Choose one of these biblical foods and use it in a recipe to cook and eat in class. Alternatively, have a feast using some ingredients in various recipes and others for decoration.

Personalizing the Text

18 Each Jewish ritual object has a particular function.

◆ Bring to class ten or more different ritual objects (e.g., *Kiddush* cup, spice box, *mezuzah*, *chanukiyah*, candlesticks, *yad*, *tefillin*, *tallit*, Havdalah candle, *lulav*, etc.). Place the objects on a table and review the function of each. Send one student out of the room and remove one ritual object from the display table. The student returns and must ask the others "yes or no" questions to discover which object is missing. You can repeat the process for every object, or for as many as you wish.

19 The song *"Yerushalayim Shel Zahav"* (Jerusalem of Gold) has a connection to this Haftarah.

◆ Read the translation to discover the connection. The song and translation may be found in *B'Kol Echad*, edited by Jeffrey Shiovitz, pp. 114-115.

◆ Learn and sing the song (also on the album *Best of Serenade* by Serenade).

20 According to this Haftarah, Hiram made the Temple building and its decorations out of burnished bronze, and Solomon made all the furnishings out of gold.

◆ To get the feel of what it's like to work with metal, make copper jewelry.

21 The two *challot* help to transform our Shabbat table into a holy altar reminiscent of the Temple.

◆ Make a *challah* cover for use on Shabbat and festivals.

22 Solomon was no doubt delighted with the artistic contributions of Hiram to the Temple. However, the Haftarah doesn't tell us how Solomon expressed his gratitude.

◆ Write a thank-you card from Solomon to Hiram, or design a plaque of recognition for all of Hiram's contributions to the Temple.

23 Preparing for your Bar or Bat Mitzvah can be seen as a monumental task, much like building the Temple or Tabernacle. In some ways, you have been preparing your whole life to become a Jewish adult.

◆ Make an inventory list of the skills you have mastered to become a Bar/Bat Mitzvah.

◆ Write a speech comparing your Bar/Bat Mitzvah preparations to building the Temple or Tabernacle. Be sure to mention and thank everyone who helped you (just as Hiram helped Solomon). Conclude your speech by describing how it feels to have accomplished your goal. (Read Psalm 30 to see how Israel felt upon the Dedication of the Temple.)

Other Resources

24 Read, act out, and discuss the skit in *Bible Scenes* by Stan J. Beiner, pp. 221-224.

25 Discuss the illustration of this Haftarah in *The Illustrated Torah* by Michal Meron, p. 100 (*Vayakhel* for Ashkenazim) or p. 104 (*Pikuday* for Sephardim). Compare the two illustrations.

26 Read and discuss the story "Challahs in the Ark" in *Because God Loves Stories*, edited by Steve Zeitlin, pp. 31-32.

27 The Haftarah mentions the gold hinges that were created for the Temple doors. Read to young children the story "Nicanor's Door" in *Lively Legends Jewish Values* by Miriam P. Feinberg and Rena Rotenberg, pp. 80-82. This is a beautiful tale of one of the miracles involved in building the Second Temple.

28 Read to young children the story "The Pomegranate Girl" in *The Jewish Spirit* by Ellen Frankel, pp. 126-130.

29 Read and discuss the short story "The Menorah" by Theodor Herzl in *The Jewish Spirit* by Ellen Frankel, pp. 31-33. This version of the story also contains three pictures of traditional and modern *chanukiyot*. Consider reasons why we often want something more when it is prohibited than when we are free to have it.

30 *The Illustrated Hebrew Bible* by Ellen Frankel, pp. 150-151, contains beautiful illustrations of ceremonial objects from the Temple. Look at and discuss these illustrations. Compare the objects from Temple times to present-day ritual objects.

31 Pillars and capitals, like those in the Temple, were important architectural elements in ancient Greece and Rome. For more information on the styles of ancient columns and capitals, see this web site: http://harpy.uccs.edu/greek/greek.html.

Involving the Family

32 If you do not do so already, place two *challot* on your table for holidays and Shabbat. Dress them with a beautiful *challah* cover. Try ritual handwashing, then recite the *Motzi* over the *challah* before enjoying it. How does having *challah* and reciting *Motzi* make your table a holy place? *The Shabbat Seder* by Ron Wolfson is an easy to use guide for these Shabbat rituals.

Bar/Bat Mitzvah Project

33 Be a holy instrument working to make the world a better place through *tikkun olam*. Organize a food drive or toiletry drive for a local shelter. How do the ordinary items you collect become holy? Alternatively, you can offer yourself for some holy purpose, such as visiting the sick or reading to the blind.

I KINGS 7:51-8:21
PIKUDAY פְּקוּדֵי Ashkenazim
I KINGS 8:2-21
SECOND DAY SUKKOT

(Note: On the second day of Sukkot, a subset of this Haftarah is read.)

This Haftarah has been paired with *Parashat Pikuday*, Exodus 38:21-40:38, and with the second day of Sukkot on which we read Leviticus 22:26-23:44. See "Connecting the Text To the Sedra," pp. 155-156, for an exploration of the ways the texts and holiday shed light on each other.

SYNOPSIS

This Haftarah picks up exactly where the last one leaves off: Solomon finishes all the work on the Temple around the year 952 B.C.E. Solomon also deposits in the Temple treasury all the silver, gold, and vessels that had been donated by his father, King David.

On the festival of Sukkot, Solomon assembles all the elders and tribal leaders of Israel to bring up into the Temple the Ark of the Covenant of *Adonai* from the City of David. First, the priests carry up the Ark, then the priests and Levites bring up the Tent of Meeting and all the holy vessels that were in it. Meanwhile, Solomon and the elders are sacrificing great numbers of sheep and oxen.

The priests carry the Ark of the Covenant into the Shrine, which is in the holiest place within the Temple. While the priests are in the Holy of Holies, the Presence of *Adonai* in the form of a cloud fills the Temple, forcing the priests out.

When they emerge, Solomon declares that God now has a House in which God can dwell forever. The whole congregation of Israel stands, and Solomon blesses them. He praises God for fulfilling the promise to David that Solomon would be permitted to build a Holy Temple.

INSIGHTS FROM THE TRADITION

A Solomon put into the completed Temple all the gold and silver objects of his father, David (verse 7:51). Solomon did not use these objects in the actual building of the Temple. David acquired these riches as spoils of war and dedicated them to God. Ralbag suggests that the Temple should not be built with anything that has been won through the shedding of blood (also see I Chronicles 28:3).

◆ It seems that the items somehow retain the "taint" of the way in which they were acquired or used. Why would war taint the gold and silver objects?

◆ Does this *midrash* support the idea that the ends never justify the means?

◆ Discuss any items you might have that are special because of who gave them to you or where they are from.

B Another *midrash* suggests Solomon did not use the gold and silver of David for the Temple because David held on to these valuables during a period of dire famine (II Samuel 21:1) instead of selling them to buy food for his people (see *The Legends of the Jews* by Louis Ginzberg, 6:296).

Solomon finds fault with the priorities of his father. Others may defend David's concern for the long-term rather than the short-term welfare of his nation.

◆ With which point of view do you agree?

◆ Leaders often need to weigh short-term concerns against the long-term concerns. Conduct a debate, with each side defending one the following statements:

• To reduce America's economic dependence on foreign oil, we should drill wherever we can to discover our own sources of fuel.

• We must not destroy our nation's natural treasures by drilling for oil, but we should develop new fuels and practice fuel conservation.

C When the Temple was complete, Solomon called together a congregation of leaders of the Israelite community to witness the arrival of the Ark at the Temple. According to *midrash*, God's presence (represented by the Ark) can only exist in the midst of community.

◆ Do you agree with the statement in the *midrash*?

◆ In what ways does a private ceremony feel different from a public ceremony (consider, for example, a small, intimate wedding versus a large affair)?

◆ Explain how all these statements can be simultaneously true:

God is everywhere.

God is only in a community.

God is anywhere we let God in.

D Solomon says the Temple is a place for God to dwell forever (verse 8:13). In *midrash,* "forever" means in the past as well as in the future. Therefore, we are taught in *Genesis Rabbah* 14:6 that Adam was formed on the spot that would be the Temple altar. (Also, Isaac was nearly sacrificed on this same spot, and here Jacob dreamt of the ladder reaching heaven.) Incidentally, Muslims believe that their prophet Mohammed ascended to heaven from the same spot, which is why the Dome of the Rock shrine was built upon the Temple Mount.

We learned above in Insights from the Tradition #A, p. 152, that it is possible that objects somehow retain the memory of how they were obtained. Is it also possible that places retain the memory of what happened there?

For centuries, Jews and Muslims have fought over control of the Temple Mount in Jerusalem.

◆ Can you think of any other places that have become hallowed because of events that happened there?

◆ Can you think of any places that will forever bear the burden of an unfortunate event that occurred there (the site of the World Trade Center, Chernobyl, Columbine High School in Colorado, or Nuremberg, for example)?

E In verse 8:18 Solomon recalls that God commended David for having the good intention of wanting to build a Temple for God. According to Hertz, "Our own cherished high aims may not be fulfilled, but we are better for striving for them."

◆ What do you think this statement means?

◆ The father of Zionism, Theodor Herzl, once said, "If you will it, it is no dream." This memorable Hebrew line has been set to music. Learn the song and the hand motions for *"Im Tirtzu,"* which may be found on the recording

Not by Might, Not by Power by Debbie Friedman.

STRATEGIES
Analyzing the Text

1 The dedication and celebration of the Temple takes place in Etanim, which is the seventh month of the year. We learned in I Kings 6:38 that the construction of the Temple was completed in Bul, the eighth month. Apparently, then, Solomon waited a full 11 months for the celebration.

◆ Why do you think Solomon waited so long?

◆ How does anticipation make an event more special?

2 In verse 8:9 we are told that in the Ark were the two tablets of stone which Moses received at Horeb. According to Rabbinic tradition, Horeb is another name for Sinai. Horeb means "parching heat," and Sinai can mean either "dirt or clay" or "bush," as in the burning bush.

◆ Create a word-find puzzle using words that are associated with Horeb/Sinai (e.g., commandments, Moses, golden calf, wilderness, lightning, etc.).

3 We know from the story in Exodus 19:16-18 that Sinai (Horeb) was covered in a cloud while Moses received the Torah from God. Verse 8:10 informs us that once again a cloud filled the Temple, forcing the priests out. In both cases the cloud is clearly associated with God's presence.

◆ Explain why a cloud is a good portrayal of God's presence.

◆ The following images are also commonly used as symbols of God's presence: light, Torah, love, burning bush, and birth. Choose one and explain why you think it is a good image

through which to portray God's presence. Then, paint your favorite symbol in watercolors.

4 The text says in verse 8:14 that Solomon blesses the people. But in the very next line Solomon begins his blessing of God, which continues to the end of the Haftarah. Scholars disagree as to the content of Solomon's blessing of the people. Some say that his blessing to God is his blessing of the people. Others point out that Solomon actually does bless the people, but not until verses 56-61 of chapter 8.

◆ How can Solomon's blessing of God in verses 8:15-21 also be read as a blessing of the people?

5 The concluding words of the Haftarah in verse 8:21 are a reference to the Exodus from Egypt.

◆ Why would the Exodus — in many ways, the birth of the free Israelite nation — be mentioned at a ceremony dedicating the Temple?

◆ Why do you think we talk so much about the Exodus — in our prayers, in the Torah, and even in the *Kiddush* for Shabbat evening?

◆ It is a *mitzvah* to recall the Exodus from Egypt. For more on the subject, read pp. 21-25 in *Teaching Mitzvot* by Barbara Binder Kadden and Bruce Kadden.

◆ Is there one event in your country's history that you think is so important it deserves to be mentioned at every national holiday and government function?

Connecting the Text To the Sedra

6 It may seem odd that instead of beginning with the first verse of chapter 8, the Haftarah opens with the last verse of chapter 7.

- To see why this verse may have been included, compare it to the discussion in Exodus 39:32 of the building of the Tabernacle.

- It is interesting to note that the Haftarot were selected before the chapters were officially divided. The Rabbis who did the selecting, therefore, were unencumbered by the chapter divisions as we have them. If you were in charge of placing the chapter divisions, would you have put the last verse of chapter 7 in chapter 7 or as the first verse of chapter 8? Why?

7 Exodus 40:20 mentions the tablets of the Ten Commandments. The Haftarah (verse 8:9) mentions the same tablets, and calls them the Covenant that God made with Israel.

- Why are the Ten Commandments at the center of both the Tabernacle and Temple?

- Do you think the Ten Commandments are similarly at the center of Judaism? Explain your answer.

- Locate the Ten Commandments in your synagogue prayer book. Do they play an important role in the liturgy of your services?

- Can you find the Ten Commandments or a depiction of the tablets anywhere in your synagogue building?

- Do any of the following exercises with the Ten Commandments: Students list as many of the Ten Commandments as they can. Whoever lists the most or completes the list first wins.

- Alternatively, the teacher can write the Ten Commandments on a sheet of paper, then photocopy the page for each student. Before class, he/she should cut the commandments into individual strips, giving each student all ten strips in no particular order. In class, students put the Commandments into their proper order, or in order of difficulty or importance.

They can also put the Commandments into one of two categories: *mitzvot* between people *(bayn adam l'chavero)* and *mitzvot* between people and God *(bayn adam l'makom)*. The possibilities are many and make for very interesting discussions.

8 In verses 8:10-11 of the Haftarah, the priests are forced from the Temple because of the presence of God. In *Parashat Pikuday* 40:34-35, Moses cannot go into Tabernacle because of God's presence there.

Once the Hasidic master Baal Shem Tov stopped before entering a synagogue. He insisted that he could not go in, complaining that the synagogue was too crowded with teachings and prayers extending from floor to ceiling and from wall to wall. There was no room for him to enter. He explained, "The words of teaching and prayer which do not come from the heart but only from the lips of the speaker are unable to rise up to heaven. They hang around and fill the synagogue" (see *Everyday Miracles* by Howard Polsky and Yaella Wozner, p. 134).

- What does the Baal Shem Tov mean when he says that the prayers had come only from the lips and not from the heart? When have you ever said a prayer from your heart?

- Do you think prayers always reach God? Explain your answer.

- Do you think God's presence would make you feel crowded out or welcomed? Why?

9 When the work on the Tabernacle was completed, Moses blessed all of the people (Exodus 39:43). When the Temple was completed, Solomon blessed all of the people (1 Kings 8:14).

- When you chant your Haftarah and lead services for your Bar/Bat Mitzvah, you will have accomplished a great goal. Some Rabbis bless a student at his/her Bar/Bat Mitzvah service. Does yours?

◆ Would you like to be blessed at your *simchah*?

◆ Why do you think people like to receive a blessing from their religious leader?

◆ Write a blessing you would like to be given upon the occasion of becoming a Bar or Bat Mitzvah. Alternatively, everyone in the class may work together to compose a blessing to be used at every Bar/Bat Mitzvah of the students in your grade. Clear the idea and review the blessing with your Rabbi.

10 In verse 8:2 of the Haftarah, we are told that The Holiday (*HehChag*) was celebrated in the seventh month. In the Bible "The Holiday" always refers to the festival of Sukkot. This Haftarah, beginning with verse 8:2, has therefore been chosen as the prophetic reading for the second day of Sukkot.

◆ Because of the name "The Holiday," it might seem that Sukkot is the most important festival in the Bible. Which is your favorite Jewish holiday? With a group of your classmates, write and perform a commercial for your favorite holiday. Videotape the commercials and show them to the entire class.

◆ Rank the following Jewish holidays in order of your most to least favorite, and discuss the reasons why: Rosh HaShanah, Yom Kippur, Sukkot, Simchat Torah, Chanukah, Purim, Pesach, Shavuot, and Shabbat.

11 We use a *Haggadah* to guide our celebration of Pesach, but we have no such guide for the festival of Sukkot (which is mentioned in the Haftarah).

◆ Design a *Haggadah* to use on Sukkot, including the following information: Preparation for the holiday, including building and decorating

your *sukkah*; how to light candles for *Yom Tov*; how to make *Kiddush* for *Yom Tov*; how and when to say *"Shehecheyanu,"* how to make the blessing for sitting in the *sukkah*; information about the tradition of *Ushpizin* (see Personalizing the Text #24, p. 159); information about *lulav* and *etrog*, including how to shake them; how to make the *Motzi*; and some Sukkot-related songs. Also include the story of the Exodus, wandering in the desert, and living in *sukkot*. Since the *sukkah* is outside, you may even want to suggest some outdoor activities for kids to play while the adults finish their meal and clean up after it. (To facilitate this project, the teacher can photocopy the required practices, laws, and blessings for each student to include, as well as copies of various songs, stories, recipes, and craft ideas from which the students can choose.)

◆ For ideas, stories, and information, consult *The Sukkot/Simhat Torah Anthology* by Philip Goodman.

Extending the Text

12 The name of the month Etanim (verse 8:2) may mean "strength," and refers to perpetual rivers that even contain water in the fall.

◆ See and do the calendar exercise in the Haftarah for *Terumah*, Personalizing the Text #22, p. 135.

13 Verse 8:9 says nothing was in the Ark except the stone tablets from Mount Sinai. By the same token, there was nothing in the Holy of Holies in the Temple except the Ark. Since the Ark was lost in the destruction of the First Temple, there was nothing at all placed in the Holy of Holies of the Second Temple.

◆ Imagine you could place five items of critical importance to the Jewish people in the Ark, along with the tablets of the Commandments. What would they be, and why would you put them there?

14 Solomon dedicated the Temple with great ceremony and celebration. It is a *mitzvah* today to dedicate a new home by affixing a *mezuzah* to the doorpost and saying the appropriate blessing: "Blessed are You, *Adonai*, Sovereign of the universe, Who has sanctified us with God's commandments, and has commanded us to affix a *mezuzah*."

◆ The *mezuzah* both identifies a house as a Jewish home and reminds those who live there about their own Jewish identity. The *"Shema"* is written on the *mezuzah* scroll. Read the *"Shema"* to understand why it has been chosen to be part of a *mezuzah*.

◆ For more information on the *mitzvah* of affixing a *mezuzah*, read *Teaching Mitzvot* by Barbara Binder Kadden and Bruce Kadden, pp. 53-56, or *The How-To Handbook for Jewish Living* by Kerry M. Olitzky and Ronald H. Isaacs, pp. 104-5.

15 Like the Temple in ancient times, our sanctuaries are special places to which we go to worship. Just as there were rules regarding conduct at the Temple, there are also rules about how to behave in the sanctuary. For example, according to Jewish law, we are not supposed to sit at the entrance to the synagogue. At least three reasons are given:

• If you sit at the entrance, you might be able to see the street and be distracted by what is going on outside;

• If you sit at the entrance, it will look as if you are not happy about being there and are just itching to get out;

• The time we spend walking all the way into the synagogue and taking a seat about six feet from the door was deemed to be the minimum amount of time needed to prepare ourselves for prayer.

◆ What do these rules and reasons reveal about optimum conduct in the sanctuary?

◆ Can you add other rules regarding appropriate sanctuary behavior for your congregation?

◆ Write a short guide to sanctuary conduct for your congregation.

16 We learned in Insights from the Tradition #C, p. 153, that God's presence can exist only in a community. The Talmud teaches in *Berachot* 7b that one should make every effort to pray in a *minyan*, or prayer community of ten adults. If one is unable to go to the synagogue for a *minyan*, one should arrange for the *minyan* to come to one's house, as is often done for a *shivah minyan*. If it is too difficult to arrange for the *minyan* to come to one's house, one is to find out from the Rabbi what time the congregation will be praying at the synagogue and pray at home at the same time.

◆ Why might it feel good for someone sick at home to pray at the same time as the *minyan* at the synagogue?

◆ May one pray or form a *minyan* over the Internet? See a Conservative Movement Responsa on this question at: www.jtsa.edu/news/jtsmag/11.1/hateshuvah.shtml.

◆ Do you think it is easier to pray in private or with a community?

◆ When you pray with a community, do you feel part of something bigger than yourself?

◆ Imagine your best friend is moving to another state. What can you arrange to do at the same time everyday in order still to feel close to each other?

◆ View and discuss the opening scene in the film *Mission To Mars* (2000, rated PG, 113 minutes). The father in the film is about to go away for two years and consoles his distraught young son by proposing they read the same book at the same time every evening, as if they were reading the story together. Compare this to praying at home at the same time as the *minyan* in synagogue.

17 Every synagogue has an *Aron Kodesh* — a holy ark.

◆ Do some research on your Temple's *Aron Kodesh*. Who designed it? When was it built, and of what materials? What are the symbols it incorporates? If it has a curtain, find out about that, too.

18 Solomon is considered to be the author of the biblical Book of Ecclesiastes, which is traditionally read on the Shabbat of Sukkot.

Ecclesiastes is a rich and complex book with many provocative messages. Since Sukkot is also known as *Z'man Simchataynu*, the Time of Our Happiness, here are some messages from Ecclesiastes on the subject of happiness:

" . . . whenever a man does eat and drink and get enjoyment out of all his wealth, it is a gift of God." (3:13)

"I saw that there is nothing better for man than to enjoy his possessions, since that is his portion." (3:22)

"Only this, I have found, is a real good: that one should eat and drink and get pleasure with all the gains he makes under the sun, during the numbered days of life that God has given him; that is his portion." (5:17)

"Go, eat your bread in gladness, and drink you wine in joy . . . " (9:7)

"O youth, enjoy yourself while you are young!" (11:9)

◆ Which saying do you like best, and why? Which do you like least, and why?

◆ Write your own proverb about happiness.

Personalizing the Text

19 Sidney Greenberg teaches in *Words to Live By*, p. 284, that although David did not build the Temple, he helped to pave the way for Solomon to build the Temple. Without his father's initiation and effort, Solomon might not have had such an opportunity.

◆ List ways you think David helped to pave the way for Solomon to build the Temple.

◆ Explain how the "seeds" that David planted gave "fruit" to the opportunity for Solomon.

◆ Tell and discuss the following famous story:

One day Honi was walking down the road and noticed a very old man planting a carob tree. He wondered aloud to the old man why someone so advanced in age would plant a tree whose fruit he would never live to enjoy. After all, carob trees take many, many years to bear their first fruit. To this question, the old man responded, "Just as those before me planted trees whose fruit I could enjoy, so, too, do I plant this tree for those who will come after me."

◆ What lesson did Honi learn? Compare this lesson to that of David and Solomon.

◆ Ask your parents how their parents and grandparents laid the groundwork for your parents' successes.

20 David and Solomon seemed to have different priorities (see Insights from the Tradition #B, p. 152-153).

◆ As a class, discover your own Jewish priorities by holding a Jewish Values Auction. Make signs, each with one Jewish value on it. Present and discuss all the values up for auction. Each student receives $1000 in play money with which to bid and some time to decide their own priorities and bidding strategies. Then start the auction. Each student will end up with at least one Jewish value. Suggested Jewish values include: Shabbat, *tzedakah*, *gemilut chasadim*, Bar or Bat Mitzvah, Jewish education, synagogue affiliation, Federation, Hebrew language, Jewish culture, Jewish food, Jewish marriage, holidays, *kashrut*, and Israel. Be creative!

21 Like the Tabernacle and Temple before them, synagogues continue to have central importance in the Jewish religion and culture. According to *Berachot* 8a, "Whoever has a synagogue in town and does not go there in order to pray is called an evil neighbor."

◆ Why is synagogue affiliation so important to the Rabbis of the Talmud? Why is it important today?

◆ Synagogue membership is a two-way relationship of give and take. Why must members of synagogues give as well as take? How can families give to the synagogue?

◆ Consider this statement from Rabbi Michael Goldberg: "Some synagogues are like religious 7-11's. When American Jews get a craving for something sweet and gooey — a Bar or Bat Mitzvah, a wedding, a baby naming — they drop in, plunk down their money, savor their choice, and then drive away, until the craving overcomes them again. The 'members' of such synagogues are essentially noth-

ing more than consumers" (from *Why Should Jews Survive? Looking Past the Holocaust toward a Jewish Future*, as quoted in the book *Two Jews, Three Opinions*, edited by S. Brawarsky and D. Mark, p. 504).

◆ Explain the analogy of a synagogue to a convenience store.

◆ Why is the "7-11" model for a synagogue not a model for success?

◆ Suggest your own model for a synagogue.

22 We learned above about the *mitzvah* of *mezuzah* and *Chanukat HaBayit* (Extending the Text #14, p. 157).

◆ Create your own *mezuzah* dedication ceremony that you can perform at the home of a classmate who has recently moved or does not currently have a *mezuzah* on his or her door.

◆ Alternatively, create your own *mezuzah* case of metal, ceramics, or other media.

23 Places can retain memories that make them special to us (see Insights from the Tradition #D, p. 153).

◆ Prepare a photo display or other artistic representation of your favorite place.

24 The Sukkot tradition of *Ushpizin* involves symbolically inviting Abraham, Isaac, Jacob, Joseph, Moses, Aaron, and David to share a day with us in our *sukkah*. In modern times, seven women have been added to the list, though there is no official agreement as to which seven. Commonly considered women include: Sarah, Miriam, Devorah, Hannah, Abigail, Hulda, Esther, Rebecca, Rachel, Leah, Asenat, and Tzipporah.

◆ Research these male and female *Ushpizin*, and decide which of them you would most like to have as your guests for dinner in the *sukkah*.

◆ Alternatively, make a list of any seven people (living or dead) whom you would like to have join you on Sukkot.

◆ Either way, have a class *Ushpizin* masquerade party at which every student dresses up as his or her favorite Jewish guest.

Other Resources

25 Read, act out, and discuss the skit in *Bible Scenes* by Stan J. Beiner, pp. 225-228.

26 Special memories turn ordinary objects and places into treasures. Play the "Jewish Memories Game" by Bernard Reisman in *Jewish Identity Games* by Richard Israel, p. 44.

27 Read and discuss "The Story of Bryan" by Tsvi Blanchard in *Chosen Tales*, edited by Peninnah Schram, pp. 47-49. This is a touching little story about how an ordinary pencil became a holy object because of the memory associated with it.

28 Learn about the *mitzvah* of dwelling in a *sukkah* in *Teaching Mitzvot* by Barbara Binder Kadden and Bruce Kadden, pp. 15-20.

29 Read and discuss the very interesting essay on the Ark by Plaut in *The Haftarah Commentary*, p. 228.

30 View and discuss the film *Hoosiers* (1986, rated PG, 114 minutes), which portrays the importance of individuals coming together as a community within the context of an Indiana high school basketball team.

31 Read and discuss stories about King Solomon in *Stories of King Solomon* by Lillian S. Freehof, or in *The Legends of the Jews* by Louis Ginzberg, vol. 4, pp. 130-176.

Involving the Family

32 Hang *mezuzot* in appropriate places that don't already have them in your house. Choose special *mezuzah* cases that have personal meaning to your family members.

33 Build a *sukkah* this year. If you have already built a *sukkah*, invite special guests or initiate the tradition of *Ushpizin*.

Bar/Bat Mitzvah Projects

34 Organize a "Sukkah Hop" for your community, which allows synagogue members to visit all or some of the *sukkot* built by fellow congregants.

35 Bar and Bat Mitzvah guests are not always familiar with the rules and rhythms of synagogue worship, which can be quite complicated. Compose a guidebook for your guests to explain the parts of the service, the behaviors that are permissible and forbidden, and any other information that will help to make visitors to your congregation more comfortable.

36 This Haftarah teaches us a great deal about dedicating houses. However, many Americans and people throughout the world do not have adequate housing. Remember these members of your community, and volunteer at a homeless shelter. Better yet, volunteer for an organization such as Habitat for Humanity, which uses volunteer labor to build affordable housing for families.

I KINGS 8:54-66
SHEMINI ATZERET

 This Haftarah has been paired with the holiday Shemini Atzeret on which we read Deuteronomy 14:22-16:17. See "Connecting the Text To the Holiday," pp. 162-163, for an exploration of the many ways the two texts and the holiday shed light on each other.

SYNOPSIS

Upon the occasion of the Dedication of the Temple, Solomon completes his prayer to God and stands to bless the whole congregation of Israel. The blessing begins with thanks to God for giving peace to Israel and fulfilling the promises God made to Moses. Solomon expresses his wish that God's presence will remain with Israel, as it had been with the nation's ancestors. He prays that the hearts of the Israelites will be turned toward God, in order that they will continue to walk wholeheartedly in God's path and follow God's laws. Solomon asks God to provide for his needs and those of Israel, so that all the nations of the earth will know that *Adonai* alone is God.

After Solomon concludes his blessing, he and the people offer sacrifices totaling 22,000 oxen and 120,000 sheep. Because the bronze altar could not accommodate the massive number of sacrifices, the burnt offerings, meal offerings, and fat parts of the well-being offerings were made in the Temple courtyard.

At the Temple, Solomon and Israelites from all over the country observe the Feast twice, for seven days and then for seven more days. On the eighth day following the second consecutive festival, called Shemini Atzeret, Solomon sends the people home, joyful and glad for the goodness

that *Adonai* had shown to David and to the people of Israel.

INSIGHTS FROM THE TRADITION

A Verse 8:58 says that we must walk in God's ways. Rashi understands "to walk in God's ways" to mean that just as God is merciful and does favors, so must we be merciful and do favors (Rashi on Deuteronomy 11:22).

◆ Explain in your own words how Rashi seems to be suggesting that God serve as a role model for us.

◆ In what other ways do we try to imitate God and lead better lives?

B In verse 8:58 we ask that God may incline our hearts to God. Malbim explains that there are two ways to get someone to incline his/her heart to you: one is by coercion and pressure, the other by kindness and protective acts.

◆ What does "incline our hearts" mean?

◆ Are you more likely to like and respect someone if they deserve it or if they force you to? How does someone go about deserving love and respect? Is it possible to "incline your heart" to someone who forces you to do so, such as a teacher or other authority figure?

C The Haftarah says in verse 8:62 that the king and all the people offered sacrifices before God.

According to *K'li Y'kar*, this is figurative; they did not actually offer real sacrifices. It means that they humbled themselves, as if they had sacrificed themselves.

◆ What does it mean to humble oneself before God?

◆ What does it mean to give of oneself?

◆ When you want to do an act of *tzedakah*, which is easier, giving money (like a sacrifice) or donating your time and yourself to do *mitzvah* work (like humbling yourself)?

D The Haftarah tells us in verse 8:66 that the Israelites blessed the king. Rashi explains that it became the custom to bless the king on Shemini Atzeret (*Rosh HaShanah* 4b).

◆ Interview the president of your synagogue to find out how leaders of your synagogue are treated by the community. Are they honored or blessed every year? Do you think they deserve to be?

STRATEGIES
Analyzing the Text

1 Solomon finished praying to God in verse 8:54.

◆ Describe Solomon's physical position for his prayer to God.

◆ Why might kneeling, being at God's altar, and having hands raised toward heaven be prayerful positions?

2 In verses 88:56-61 Solomon blessed the people.

◆ Compile a list of all the wishes contained within this blessing.

◆ Is there a logic to the order of items in the blessing? Make a flow chart to show the order.

◆ Could this blessing be included in your synagogue's service as a blessing of the congregation? Why or why not?

3 Reread the blessing contained in verses 8:56-61. The language of this blessing assumes that God is male, and that God's relationship with the Israelite people was only with the Israelite males.

◆ Did you notice this aspect of the language? What do you think about this?

◆ Rewrite these six verses using non-sexist language.

4 Solomon prays in verse 8:60 that all the peoples of the earth will know *Adonai* is the only God. This verse has a universalistic quality: *all* people will know.

◆ Do you usually think of God as the God of all peoples or just of the Jews?

Connecting the Text To the Holiday

5 The Haftarah says in verse 8:65 that on the eighth day King Solomon sent the people home. Yet we celebrate an eighth day of the holiday (Leviticus 23:34-38). *Numbers Rabbah* 21:24 explains:

This may be compared to the case of a king who made a banquet for seven days and invited all the people in the province during the seven days of the feast. When the seven days of the feast were over, he said to his friend: "We have already done our duty to all the people of the province, let us now make shift, you and I, with whatever you can find — a pound of meat, or of fish, or vegetables." So God said to Israel: "On the eighth day, you shall have a solemn assembly; make shift with whatever you can find; with one bull, one ram!"

◆ "Make shift" means to improvise or make do with what is left over. Explain how this means that God and Israel are like family who can hang out informally after everyone else has left.

6 Verse 8:65 seems to teach that the king and the people celebrate two sets of seven-day holidays back-to-back — 14 days in total. Based on the two distinct sets, we learn that on the first set of seven days, they held an inauguration festival for the Temple, and on the second set of seven days they celebrated the holiday of Sukkot.

The Rabbis observe from this that two different joyous events, the inauguration of the new Temple and the holiday of Sukkot, were not allowed to overlap. Similarly, we are taught that we may not intermingle one joyous event with another (*Mo'ed Katan* 9a). For example, one cannot get married on a joyous festival or on Shabbat.

◆ Why do you think the Rabbis did not want two special days to overlap?

◆ Do you know anyone whose birthday falls on a holiday? Do they celebrate the birthday on a different day? Find out if they feel cheated by the overlap.

7 Solomon blessed the people in verse 8:55 and then he blessed God in verse 8:56. In verse 8:66 the people blessed (translated as "bade") the king.

There is a lot of blessing going on in the holiday Torah reading, as well. Deuteronomy 14:29 promises that God will bless you in all the work of your hands. In addition, Deuteronomy 15:10 teaches that if you make loans to your brother (even at risk of it being cancelled in the sabbatical year) don't be upset about the loans and the sabbatical year because God will bless whatever you do. Deuteronomy 15:17-18 also instructs the Israelites to set free slaves in the seventh year, and God will bless the Israelites.

◆ How do holidays give us occasion to take stock of all the blessings in our lives?

◆ Make a list of the blessings in your life.

8 In the Haftarah all the people come to Jerusalem to celebrate the inauguration of the new Temple and the Sukkot holiday.

In the holiday Torah reading (Deuteronomy 14:22-16:17), making pilgrimage to Jerusalem is mentioned at least twice:

• Deuteronomy 14:25-26 says to take your money in your hand for your sacrifices and go to the place where God chooses (Jerusalem), and there you will rejoice.

• Deuteronomy 16:15 says to keep Sukkot seven days in the place where God chooses (Jerusalem).

◆ The Temple and Jerusalem were part of an effort to centralize worship in one fixed location. Explain how having centralized worship in one location might guarantee that the worship is done a certain way.

◆ Explain how having centralized worship in one location might distance the majority of the people from participating in the religious rituals. Would centralized worship seem feasible to you? Would centralized worship seem to make society outside the religious center more or less secular?

I KINGS 18:1-39 Ashkenazim
I KINGS 18:20-39 Sephardim
KI TISA כי תשא

This Haftarah has been paired with *Parashat Ki Tisa*, Exodus 30:11-34:35. See "Connecting the Text To the Sedra," pp. 167-169, for an exploration of the many ways the two texts shed light on each other.

SYNOPSIS

The Israelites are in the third year of a disastrous drought and famine when God decides to send rain and instructs the prophet Elijah to speak to Ahab, the king of Israel.

Meanwhile, Ahab calls his palace steward, Obadiah, to help him go through the land to find grass to feed the horses and mules. On his search for grass, Obadiah encounters Elijah. The steward immediately recognizes the great prophet and proclaims himself a devout follower of God. Elijah instructs Obadiah to summon Ahab. Based on Elijah's history of appearing and disappearing, Obadiah worries that Elijah will disappear before he returns with Ahab. However, once assured by Elijah, Obadiah leaves to find King Ahab.

When Obadiah returns to Elijah with Ahab, the king calls the prophet the "troubler" of Israel, blaming Elijah for the drought and famine. Elijah responds that it is Ahab who has brought suffering to Israel by forsaking God's commandments and worshiping *Baal*. Elijah directs Ahab to summon all Israel to join him at Mount Carmel, together with the 450 prophets of *Baal* and the 400 prophets of *Asherah*.

At Mount Carmel Elijah asks the Israelites to stop wavering and to choose between God and *Baal*.

Elijah proposes a test to prove once and for all which is the real God: the prophets of *Baal* should choose two bulls and decide which to keep for themselves and which to give to Elijah. Then, Elijah and the prophets of *Baal* will cut their bullocks into pieces and lay them on the wood, but put no fire under them. Whichever deity answers by sending fire for the sacrifice, will be the real God. The Israelites agree to the test.

After the prophets of *Baal* do their preparations, they proceed to call upon their god from morning until noon. When they receive no answer, Elijah mocks them. They respond by performing a hopping dance, shouting louder, gashing themselves with knives and spears until their blood pours over them. But still there is no response from *Baal*.

Elijah invites all the people to come close to him as he prepares his sacrificial altar. He takes 12 stones, according to the number of tribes of Israel, and with the stones builds an altar. He makes a trench around the altar, puts the wood in place, cuts his bull into pieces, and lays it on the wood. He asks three times for four jars of water to be poured over the bull and the wood, and then pours more water into the trench around the altar.

Finally, Elijah calls upon God to consume the offering with fire, and *Adonai's* fire falls and consumes the offering, the wood, the stones, the dust, and all the water in the trench. And when the people see what had happened, they proclaim, "*Adonai* alone is God, *Adonai* alone is God!"

INSIGHTS FROM THE TRADITION

A When he meets Elijah, Obadiah insists that he fears and obeys God. While most of the time it is unacceptable to praise oneself, according to *Nedarim* 62a, one may praise oneself in a place where one is unknown. Obadiah's statement was, therefore, not meant as self-glorification, but to introduce himself to Elijah as a loyal follower of God.

◆ There is a thin line between describing one's self positively and boasting. Can you explain the difference? Can you demonstrate the difference?

◆ Which is Obadiah doing?

B God tells Elijah at the beginning of the Haftarah in 18:1 that God wants to send rain. According to a *midrash* in the book *The Legends of the Jews* by Louis Ginzberg, vol. 6, p. 318, Elijah argues against this because Ahab had not yet repented of his grave sins. God reminds Elijah that God sent rain when Adam was the only human being, even though God could anticipate that Adam would sin in the future. God even continued to send rain after Adam did sin. God would, therefore, send rain now, even though Ahab and the people continued to sin, because human beings are still God's creatures, no matter how they behave.

◆ How is God's attitude in this story similar to the unconditional love of a parent for a child? What is unconditional love?

◆ We are taught that parents can emulate God by raising children with a blend of justice and mercy. For more on this topic, see *Teaching Jewish Virtues* by Susan Freeman, Language Arts Activity #4, p. 59.

C Ahab hopes to find grass to save the lives of the animals. Malbim suggests that animals cannot justly be punished by drought and famine directed at sinful people because animals were not given free will to make choices.

◆ Can we compare children with the animals in this Haftarah, in terms of their ability to choose between right and wrong? Does the ability of children to choose between right and wrong differ from that of adults?

◆ Debate this statement: Children who commit adult crimes deserve to be punished as adults.

D Elijah proposes a "test" sacrifice to prove which deity is real. To ensure accurate test results, one needs to have scientific controls. According to *Numbers Rabbah* 23:9, the bulls were identical twin bulls, so that no one could say one was not accepted because it was of inferior quality. In addition, the bulls were chosen by lot: Elijah's bull followed Elijah immediately, happy to be sacrificed to God. However, the other twin bull did not want to go to the prophets of *Baal*. Elijah explained to the twin bull that his sacrifice to *Baal* would not be consumed, which would sanctify God, too. Still, the reluctant bull refused to budge until Elijah delivered him into the hands of the *Baal* prophets.

◆ Why do you think the bull was reluctant to go to the prophets of *Baal*?

◆ If your parents or the leaders of your country asked you to do something you found pointless or even morally objectionable, would you do it?

◆ Thousands of young men dodged the draft to avoid fighting in Vietnam, a war they considered immoral. In your opinion, were they right or wrong?

◆ What would you do if your parents ask you to lie about your age in order to get a less expensive film ticket or restaurant meal?

E Upon offering his sacrifice, Elijah prays to God in verse 18:37, "Answer me, *Adonai*, answer me." According to *Berachot* 9b, the repetition indicates two separate requests: that God will send down the fire, and that the people understand it was truly an act of God, not magic by Elijah.

Elijah is apparently quite concerned that the people understand the successful sacrifice as an act of God and not as his own magic. *Metsudat David* teaches that Elijah tells the people to come near to him (verse 18:30) in order that they would see that Elijah is not a magician doing tricks.

◆ Some people confuse religion and magic. Why?

◆ Can you give examples?

◆ Can you think of examples of when we might want religion to work like magic?

F From Elijah's repetition, Radak teaches that when we pray, we must repeat our requests more than once.

◆ How does repeating our prayers remind us about what is important?

◆ When you request something from your friends, teachers, or parents, do you repeat your request more than once? Is the repetition effective?

G Finally realizing that only God has power, the Israelites declare twice, "*Adonai* alone is God." Radak says the declaration is repeated in order to fix it in their hearts.

◆ In what ways does repetition help us remember things?

◆ Repeat this declaration seven times in Hebrew: "*Adonai Hu HaEloheem.*" Determine how many students remembered it immediately. How many students remembered it in ten minutes? How many remembered it for the next class, or next month?

STRATEGIES
Analyzing the Text

1 Elijah tells Obadiah to get King Ahab. According to verse 18:9-14, of what is Obadiah afraid?

◆ Elijah apparently has a reputation for suddenly appearing and disappearing, but he assures Obadiah in 18:15 that he will be there when Obadiah returns with Ahab. How does this verse illustrate the importance of keeping one's word?

◆ Vows are taken extremely seriously in Jewish tradition. See the discussion on vows in *Parashat Matot* in *Teaching Torah* by Sorel Goldberg Loeb and Barbara Binder Kadden, p. 278.

2 King Ahab worried about finding food for his animals in verse 18:5, but Obadiah worried in verse 8:4 about feeding the prophets who were hiding from persecution by Ahab and his wife Jezebel.

◆ Do you think that Ahab is concerned about the animals or just about losing money if his animals die?

◆ Does Ahab seem equally concerned for his people and nation?

◆ If you were a national leader during a time of drought, would it be more important to you to feed the animals or the people, and why?

3 In the chapter preceding the Haftarah, Elijah announced that Israel's sins deserved a punishment — and a drought and famine ensued. In the Haftarah, King Ahab calls Elijah the "troubler" of Israel (verse 18:17). Elijah responds in the next verse that it is Ahab who brought trouble to Israel by sinning enough to warrant severe punishment.

◆ Stage a debate over who is the real "troubler" of Israel: Ahab, whose sins bring punishment, or Elijah, who exacts the punishment.

◆ Discuss whether or not it is fair for an entire people to be punished for the sins of their leader. Is it fair to place an embargo of food and medical supplies on an entire country because of the behavior of the leaders?

◆ Is it fair when a teacher punishes the entire class because of the misbehavior of a few students? Why do teachers sometimes do this?

4 Elijah's strategy to convince everyone to believe in God involves his mockery of *Baal*.

◆ Review verse 18:27. How does he make fun of *Baal*?

◆ Draw cartoons that make fun of *Baal* in the same or similar ways.

5 In verse 18:21 Elijah accuses Israel of literally "hopping on the two boughs." The expression implies that Israel is constantly vacillating between belief in God and belief in *Baal*.

◆ List other expressions for bouncing back and forth between beliefs or positions.

◆ Which expression do you think most accurately portrays ambivalence?

◆ Can you think of an issue about which your opinion has bounced back and forth?

6 Elijah douses his altar and wood with a lot of water before asking God to consume his offering with fire.

◆ How would a wet altar make the burning of the sacrifice appear more miraculous?

◆ Why would Elijah want to take this extra step?

7 The prophets of *Baal* try to get their god to send fire and consume their offering in verse 18:26. They dance and hop around the altar. According to *Myth, Legend and Custom in the Old Testament* by Theodor Gaster, vol. 2, pp. 506-508, there is evidence from other ancient literary sources that leaping or dancing with a limp was a ritual dance associated with mourning customs. The prophets of *Baal* also slash themselves with knives until they draw blood — another ancient mourning custom. Gaster suggests that these mourning rituals may have indicated that in times of drought people thought that *Baal* was dead.

◆ Why might the *Baal* prophets have thought their god was dead?

8 The story of Elijah and the prophets of *Baal* continues after the Haftarah ends.

◆ To find out the conclusion to the story, read I Kings 18:40-46. Why do you think the Rabbis omitted this conclusion from the Haftarah? Would you have made the same decision, and why or why not?

Connecting the Text To the Sedra

9 Obadiah's name means "servant of God," and yet he also serves King Ahab, who sins grievously against God by worshiping *Baal*.

◆ Review the story for evidence that Obadiah sometimes disobeys Ahab in order to serve God, but is sometimes not completely loyal to God in order to serve Ahab.

◆ How is Obadiah like Israel, "hopping on the two boughs"?

◆ How is the Obadiah in the Haftarah — Ahab's loyal steward and earnest servant of God — like Aaron when the Israelites enlist his help to build the golden calf in the Sedra?

◆ Can you think of a time in your life when you have bounced back and forth between religious beliefs or loyalties?

10 Both the Haftarah and Torah reading contain verses that are important elements of the Yom Kippur liturgy. The last verse of the Haftarah (18:39), "*Adonai* is God, *Adonai* is God," is repeated seven times immediately before the *shofar* is blown at the end of Yom Kippur. During the Yom Kippur Torah service, we sing the words of Moses, found in Exodus 34:6-7: "*Adonai! Adonai!* a God compassionate and gracious, slow to anger, abounding in kindness and faithfulness, extending kindness to the thousandth generation, forgiving iniquity, transgression, and sin."

In both the Torah and Haftarah readings, the statements of faith are offered after the people are apparently forgiven by God for sins.

◆ What messages do these passages, which we read on Yom Kippur, convey concerning: forgiveness, vacillation, and commitment? Discuss why these topics are relevant to Yom Kippur.

11 In the Sedra the people sin by making an idol while Moses is away. God sees the idol and tells Moses of God's intention to destroy the people, but Moses pleads on behalf of Israel for God to have mercy.

Conversely, in the Haftarah, Elijah has been unhappy with the sins of the people and proclaims a drought and famine as punishment. God wants to end the suffering caused by famine and drought, but Elijah has to be convinced.

◆ Compare the two stories and explain how the roles of God and prophet are interchanged in them.

◆ Write a letter from Moses to Elijah reminding him that part of a prophet's job is to defend the people to God, no matter how sinful they might be.

12 According to Jewish tradition, we rely on the merits of our ancestors to ensure that God will look favorably upon us, no matter how undeserving we may be.

In Exodus 32:13 Moses asks God to have mercy on the people and to remember the promise made to Abraham, Isaac, and Jacob.

Similarly, when in the Haftarah Elijah prays in verse 18:36 to God for fire to consume the sacrifice, he addresses the God of Abraham, Isaac, and Israel.

◆ What is the difference between Israel and Jacob?

◆ Why would both Moses and Elijah plead with God in the name of the Patriarchs?

◆ Have you ever been introduced as the child or grandchild of so-and-so? How did it make you feel? Did you benefit from their reputation or merit?

13 In the Sedra Moses and Joshua are on or near the mountain with God when they hear loud noises from the camp. Joshua thinks it is the sound of war, but Moses knows from the sound that the people have made an idol and tells Joshua, "אֵין קוֹל עֲנוֹת" (*Ayn kol anote* — it is not the sound). This phrase is repeated three times in Exodus 32:18.

◆ Sometimes it is hard to identify a sound without also being able to see what is going on. Can you give examples?

◆ Now compare the expression אֵין קוֹל עֲנוֹת with the expression in verses 18:26 and 18:29 of the Haftarah. The prophets of *Baal* called to their god to consume their sacrifice, but there was no sound, and none who responded or listened — אֵין קוֹל וְאֵין עֹנֶה (*Ayn kol, v'ayn anote)*. According to *Metsudat David*, there was no answer because there was no *Baal* god to listen (verse 18:29).

◆ Explain how this phrase was used to mock the idol worshipers.

14 God has mercy on the Israelites in the Haftarah, and Moses pleads for God's mercy in the Sedra. It is not always easy to know when to act with mercy and when with justice.

◆ If a classmate asks you immediately before class to have mercy and let him copy your homework, what should you do, and why?

◆ Think of other scenarios that require you to decide whether to act with mercy or justice, and role-play them in class.

15 Sephardim recite only verses 18:20-39 for the Haftarah. Compared with the Ashkenazic Haftarah, the Sephardic version omits the background information about Obadiah, Elijah, and Ahab before the Haftarah, and Elijah's offering and Israel's declaration of loyalty to God after the Haftarah.

◆ How do you think the message of the Haftarah is altered when it is limited to the central verses only? Consider how it focuses on the wavering of the Israelites and on who is responsible (Ahab, Elijah, Aaron, and/or the people).

Extending the Text

16 God wishes to act with mercy toward the Israelites by sending rain to relieve the drought and famine. Throughout the Bible, God has varying responses to sinners, ranging from very harsh to quite merciful.

◆ Match the following sinners with God's response to them:

1. Sodom and Gomorrah (b.)
2. The world before the flood (c.)
3. Adam and Eve (e.)
4. Cain (d.)
5. The people of Nineveh (a.)

a. God sends a messenger to ask the people to save themselves through repentance.

b. God bargains with Abraham over the conditions for saving the people.

c. God punishes the entire human race, except one family.

d. God spares the sinner's life but condemns him to a life of punishment.

e. God condemns the sinners and their descendants to a future of difficult labor.

◆ Why do you think each particular sinner(s) received his/her specific treatment from God?

◆ For advanced study, compare Jonah's response to his mission to Nineveh with Elijah's in the Haftarah and the chapters preceding it.

17 According to *The Haftarah Commentary* by W. Gunther Plaut, Obadiah hid the 100 Israelite prophets in the caves of Atlit, near Mount Carmel in verse 18:4. Currently Israel has a military center in Atlit, and during War War II there was a camp for immigrants there.

◆ Do more research on the history of this interesting Israeli site.

18 According to Jewish tradition, Elijah the Prophet will return to the world to announce the arrival of the Messiah.

◆ Do you believe in the Messiah?

◆ When do you think the Messiah will come?

◆ What do you think life will be like after the Messiah comes?

◆ For the Rabbis' views on life in the Messianic Age, read *Voices of Wisdom* by Francine Klagsbrun, pp. 442-5.

◆ There is a Hasidic tradition that we should treat all others as if they were the Messiah. What does this mean? How would you treat people differently if there was a possibility that anyone could be the Messiah?

◆ Write your own saying on the best way to treat people.

19 Self-mutilation, as practiced by the prophets of *Baal*, is expressly prohibited by the Torah (see Leviticus 19:28, Leviticus 21:5, and Deuteronomy 14:1). The Rabbis teach that God created the human body and, therefore, it must be treated in a holy manner. See also the discussion "Taking Care of Your Body" in *Teaching Jewish Virtues* by Susan Freeman, Text Study #B, p. 271.

◆ Consider this incident: in October 2000 a woman with over 100 body piercings died of massive infection. Debate whether this woman or any person has the right to treat his/her body in any way he/she wishes, or whether religion(s) can dictate guidelines for how we treat our bodies.

20 The prophets of *Baal* seemed worried that their god was dead. Similarly, after the Holocaust, many Jews suspected that God was dead. A story in *Because God Loves Stories*, edited by Steve Zeitlin (p. 264), considers the health and welfare of God. A 90-year-old woman was celebrating her birthday at a lovely family party. When her eldest child asked the woman to say a little something to the guests, she got up and said, "I'm very, very lucky. God has been very good to me. He should only live and be well."

◆ Is this woman's statement a declaration of gratitude, a blessing of God, a joke, or all of the above, and why?

◆ What did it mean to this woman that God is alive? What did it mean to survivors of the Holocaust that God might be dead? What do you think about God's existence?

21 Elijah is concerned that his miracle not look like a magic trick. The Torah prohibits magic (Deuteronomy 18:9-11). Specifically forbidden are divination, sorcery, casting spells, consulting mediums or wizards, and making inquiries of the dead.

◆ If magic tricks can convince people to change religions, why were Elijah and the Torah, in general, wary of magic and magicians?

◆ Write a Public Service Announcement warning Jews to be wary of magicians and their magic. The announcements can be rehearsed and then recorded on video, to be viewed at a later time.

22 The number 12 appears several times in our Haftarah. We are reminded of the 12 tribes of Israel and their special relationship to God, the 12 months of the year, and the 12 signs of the zodiac.

◆ What does the number 12 mean to you?

◆ For more information on the occurrences of the number 12 in the Bible and its symbolism, see *Encyclopaedia Judaica*, vol. 12, p. 1258.

Personalizing the Text

23 Obadiah chose to describe himself to Elijah in terms of his obedience to God's laws. How would you describe yourself to someone you just met?

TEACHING HAFTARAH

◆ Play the "I Am" game in *Jewish Identity Games* by Richard Israel, p. 42.

◆ To explore aspects of your Jewish identity, play "Ten Jewish Things" in *Jewish Identity Games* by Richard Israel, p. 42.

24 Obadiah walks a delicate line between describing himself and boasting to Elijah. There is a story (told in *A Treasury of Jewish Folklore*, edited by Nathan Ausubel, p. 144) about a rich man who was asked by his Rabbi if he gave charity. The rich man responded, "Rabbi, I give enough to charity, but I am modest and don't want to say much about it." The Rabbi responded, "Give more and say more about it!"

Many synagogues prominently display the names of generous donors, while other congregations object to the practice as ostentatious. Some believe that when big givers talk about giving, it helps to educate people about the benefits of generosity.

◆ What is your congregation's policy on publicizing the names of substantial donors? Interview your local Jewish Federation for its views on the subject. In your opinion, does publicity encourage bigger donations?

25 Two songs have a bearing on this Haftarah, *"Eliyahu HaNavee"* (Elijah the Prophet) and *Ani Ma'amin,"* (I Believe). The latter states the principle of belief by Maimonides in the coming of the Messiah.

◆ Learn and sing both songs. For music and lyrics, see *The Harvard Hillel Sabbath Songbook*, p. 34 and p. 164 respectively (David R. Godine). *"Ani Ma'amin"* may be found on the recording *The Jewish Soul* by Roslyn Barak.

◆ Discuss the meaning of the words of each song.

26 Elijah is able to perform a spectacular test to demonstrate God's existence and power.

◆ How would you endeavor to prove there is a God to a non-believer?

◆ Could an atheist design a test that would convince you there is no God?

◆ What are the problems inherent in trying to "prove" or "disprove" God's existence?

Other Resources

27 Complete the Torah Aura Instant Lesson, *Elijah.*

28 Ahab wishes to act with mercy toward his animals. According to the *mitzvah* of *tza'ar ba'alay chaim*, prevention of cruelty to animals, we are to feed our animals even before we eat. Debate the wisdom of this law. (As a reference, see *Teaching Mitzvot* by Barbara Binder Kadden and Bruce Kadden, pp. 99-104.)

29 See the painting of Elijah and the *Baal* priests as depicted in two scenes on the walls of the third-century C.E. synagogue at Dura-Europos, in modern Syria. Painted in tempera on dry plaster smeared over mud-brick walls, these scenes are among the earliest known biblical images. Go to the web site: www.bib-arch.org/bro00/jezebel-b.html.

30 Discuss the illustration of this Haftarah in *The Illustrated Torah* by Michal Meron, p. 96.

31 Read and discuss some of the stories in *Tales of Elijah the Prophet* by Peninnah Schram.

32 View and discuss the episode of the TV series "Seventh Heaven" entitled

KI TISA 171

"Cutters," which aired on October 5, 1998. This episode deals with the growing problem of young people performing acts of self-mutilation.

33 Read and discuss the chapter on "Elijah's War against Idolatry" in *Biblical Literacy* by Joseph Telushkin, pp. 254-258.

34 Read and discuss the story of "Elijah and the Poor Man's Wish," found in *Because God Loves Stories*, edited by Steve Zeitlin, pp. 34-36. Compare the characteristics of Elijah in the story and Haftarah. If you could make one wish, how difficult would it be to select just one thing? Who would you consult for advice on choosing?

35 Complete p. 19 in *Prophets Copy Pak™* by Marji Gold-Vukson.

Involving the Family

36 Subscribe to *Skeptical Inquirer Magazine* to learn how magicians try to fool people with all types of tricks and lies. See www.CSICOP.org.

37 Ahab was concerned for the animals during a drought. If your parents are supportive of the idea, adopt an abandoned pet from a local animal shelter.

Bar/Bat Mitzvah Projects

38 Ahab and Obadiah searched for food for their dying cattle and herds. Become involved in a cause supporting the humane treatment of animals, such as the ASPCA or PETA.

39 Growing numbers of young people today engage in self-destructive behaviors, such as self-mutilation, eating disorders, and substance abuse. Inquire if your school has a peer counseling and/or support group for teens in trouble. If not, talk to your guidance department about starting such a program. If so, consider volunteering to become a peer counselor.

I KINGS 18:46-19:21
PINCHAS פינחס

This Haftarah has been paired with *Parashat Pinchas*, Numbers 25:10-30:1. See "Connecting the Text To the Sedra," pp. 176-178, for an exploration of the many ways the two texts shed light on each other.

SYNOPSIS

After demonstrating God's power at Mount Carmel, the prophet Elijah runs to Ahab's palace at Jezreel. Ahab had already told his wife Jezebel about the miracle Elijah had done at Mount Carmel and how Elijah had then slain all the prophets of *Baal*. Jezebel, who was a worshiper of *Baal* and had previously killed many of God's prophets, sent a messenger to Elijah, threatening that she will have him killed.

A frightened Elijah runs for his life. In the wilderness, the prophet prays that he might die. Elijah falls asleep under a broom bush, and an angel touches him and gives him food and water. Elijah eats and drinks and then goes back to sleep. Again, the angel touches him and gives him food and water, which Elijah eats and drinks. This time, Elijah arises and walks for 40 days and 40 nights to Mount Horeb, where he spends the night in a cave.

When God asks Elijah why he is there, Elijah responds that he is the only one left who holds to the Covenant with God and so fears for his life. God tells Elijah to stand on the mountain before God. A great and mighty wind passes, splitting mountains and shattering rocks. After the wind, an earthquake occurs, and then fire. But God is not in the wind, the earthquake, or the fire. Finally, Elijah hears a soft murmuring sound, and in it the voice of God.

Again, God asks Elijah why he is there, and Elijah responds that he is the only one left who holds to the Covenant with God and so fears for his life. God tells Elijah to anoint Hazael as king of Aram, to anoint Jehu king of Israel, and to anoint Elisha as his own successor. God explains that whoever escapes the sword of Hazael shall be slain by Jehu, and whoever escapes the sword of Jehu shall be slain by Elisha. God proclaims that only 7,000 will be left in Israel — those who have not worshiped *Baal*.

At the end of the Haftarah, Elijah finds Elisha plowing in his family's field. Elisha bids his father and mother good-bye and follows the prophet Elijah.

INSIGHTS FROM THE TRADITION

A Elijah runs for his life from Jezebel's threats. Why he did not just wait and let God save his life by a miracle? Ralbag said Elijah did not want to depend on a miracle, while *Zohar* says that the righteous never burden God with requests for personal miracles.

◆ Does doing something to help yourself indicate a lack of faith in God?

There is a story about a man whose home is flooded in a storm. As the water begins to rise, a fire truck arrives to save the man. But he declines the help, saying, "God will save me." The water continues to rise, and the man is forced onto his roof. A boat comes by to bring him to safety, but again the man refuses, saying "God will save me." Finally, with the water almost up to the roof, a helicopter flies overhead, but again the man denies help, saying "God will save me." When the man drowns and goes to heaven, he asks God, "Why didn't You save me?" God responds, "I tried three times to save you, but each time you refused."

◆ How is this story the same or different from the idea that Elijah did not want to burden God with performing a personal miracle for him?

B God asks Elijah in verse 19:9 why he was in the cave at Mount Horeb. According to Malbim, this question means that Elijah's place was out preaching to the people and not hiding in seclusion.

Other religious traditions espouse periods of isolation and silence to enhance one's spiritual development. Judaism, as shown in Malbim's commentary, promotes enhancing one's spiritual development through involvement in the world.

◆ Does worship of God end when you exit a synagogue?

◆ We can transform ourselves by doing holy work through ordinary acts. Explain how buying and delivering groceries to a shut-in is a holy act. Can you think of other ordinary activities that can make us holy when we perform them as *mitzvot*? How do such acts contribute to our spiritual development?

C Elijah explains to God that he is hiding on Mount Horeb because he is too zealous about prophesying on behalf of God. His zeal prevents him from getting along with and living with the people, according to Malbim.

◆ Do you know people who are so committed to a cause that they are unable to get along with others who have a different view?

◆ Is it ever good to be so devoted to a cause that it makes it difficult for others to get along with us?

◆ Sometimes activists take radical action for their cause that can alienate others. Do you think it is appropriate for an animal rights activist to throw fake blood on a fur coat that someone is wearing?

◆ Discuss the benefits and shortcomings of other extremist methods used by activists to make their point.

D God was not in the wind, earthquake, or fire, all of which are violent and destructive phenomena. Ralbag teaches from this that God does not wish to destroy or punish unless there is hope that the victims will respond and learn from the experience. After three years of drought preceding the period of this Haftarah, it was clear to God that Israel was not learning from the punishment, so God was ready to call off the lesson.

◆ Experts have disagreed for years about the efficacy of punishment. Do you think punishment is an effective way to change behavior?

◆ What do you think children learn from being punished?

◆ How were you punished when you were young? How about now?

◆ What methods of behavior modification other than punishment can be useful and effective?

E God responds to Elijah that he should have learned from Moses' example of being patient and compassionate, instead of angry and zealous (*The Rabbis' Bible* by Solomon Simon and Morrison David Bial, vol. 2, p. 185).

◆ Which are better qualities in a leader — patience and compassion or anger and zeal? Why do you think so?

◆ Which are better qualities in a teacher/in a parent? In what ways are teachers and parents leaders?

STRATEGIES
Analyzing the Text

1 Elijah flees from Jezebel's henchmen to Beersheba in the south. Since Solomon's death, the Israelite nation has been split into two: Judah in the South and Israel in the North.

◆ For more on the events leading to the division, read I Kings chapters 11-13.

◆ Why was the kingdom divided after Solomon's reign?

2 Why do you think Elijah asks to die? According to Radak, he was tired of living in danger every day. *Metsudat David* suggests that Elijah would rather die by the hands of God than by the hands of the evil Jezebel. Hertz adds that Elijah states in verse 19:4 that he is no better than his fathers because, like the leaders before him, he has been unable to turn the Israelites from their sinful ways.

◆ Which explanation do you like best, and why?

3 Does the story of Elijah on Mount Horeb remind you of another story? This story about Elijah has many striking similarities to the story of Moses on Mount Sinai.

◆ Refer to Exodus 19:16-19, 24:18, 33:13-23, and 34:28. Look for the following elements the two stories have in common, then see if you can find others: 40 days and 40 nights, no food, cave/cleft of rock, God's presence, fire, wind, and earthquake.

◆ Which of the two accounts do you prefer, and why?

◆ Form two groups. One group makes a mural of Elijah on the mountain, and the other makes one of Moses on the mountain.

4 In the wilderness Elijah sits under a lonely broom bush.

◆ How does the shrub reflect Elijah's situation?

◆ Compare Elijah and his bush with the prophet Jonah and his plant in the Haftarah for Yom Kippur afternoon, p. 569. Do Jonah and Elijah seem equally alone, angry, frustrated, or unhappy?

◆ What else do these two prophets have in common? (For example, both seem to have run away and both want to die.)

5 Compare Elijah's plea for death to that of Moses in Numbers 11:14-15.

◆ Why do you think both prophets want to die?

◆ Can their desire for death be seen as a plea for help?

◆ Can their request to die be seen as a sign that they realize, but don't want to admit, that they were wrong about their own zealousness?

6 Elijah wants to die.

◆ If this is so, why does Elijah run away from Jezebel who wants to kill him?

◆ What else might Elijah have meant when he asks God to "take my life"?

◆ We often use the expressions, "I could have died," or "I wanted to die." List other expressions that mention dying. Discuss what the statements really mean.

7 The voice of God heard by Elijah in verse 19:12, which JPS translates as "a soft murmuring sound," is generally translated as "a still, small voice." A more literal translation of the Hebrew would be, "sound of fine silence."

◆ What is an oxymoron? How is the phrase "sound of silence" an oxymoron? Can you list any others? For an exhaustive and often humorous list of oxymorons in the English language, see www.oxymorons.com.

◆ Write a short story using as many oxymorons as you can.

◆ Alternatively, play a game. Write various oxymorons on index cards. Have groups of three students choose a card and improvise a skit based on the oxymoron on their card.

8 The interchange between God and Elijah is repeated verbatim before the epiphany in verses 18:9-10 and again after the epiphany in verses 18:13-14.

◆ Why do you think Elijah responds to God's second question with the same words he uses the first time? Do you think Elijah was dumbfounded by the experience? Do you think Elijah was unmoved by the experience?

◆ Role-play the scene and try to figure out what Elijah could have been thinking.

9 According to God's instructions, Elijah "threw his mantle" over Elisha in verse 18:19.

◆ What does this action symbolize?

◆ Can you think of any other action or expression (such as passing the torch) that symbolizes the same role transfer from one to another?

Connecting the Text To the Sedra

10 In his time, Pinchas responded zealously to disloyalty to God (Numbers 25:10), and Elijah responded zealously to idol worship in

his time. The Rabbis, however, were conflicted about zealous behavior. For example, when the Rabbis divided the Torah into separate weekly readings, they did not include the story of what Pinchas did (Numbers 25:7-8) in the same weekly Sedra as God's praise for Pinchas's act and Pinchas's reward.

◆ See where the break in the weekly Torah readings occur. Does this seem like a natural break place to you?

◆ In Numbers 25:7-8 Pinchas suddenly takes the law into his own hands, executing two people. Explain how the break between weekly readings reflects discomfort with rewarding someone who takes the law into his own hands.

◆ Why does fanatical commitment to a cause sometimes lead to criminal behavior?

◆ In the Haftarah Elijah is zealous in his commitment to God and God's covenant. His fanaticism, however, did not lead him to break the law. Where did it lead him? Could he still function successfully as a prophet?

◆ Give examples from current events of modern causes that sometimes attract zealous supporters. Are these causes worthwhile?

◆ Is the zealousness of the supporters necessarily bad?

◆ Give examples from current events of zealots who go overboard by breaking the law (for example, anti-abortion advocates who murder doctors or mail letters tainted with anthrax to clinics).

11 According to legend, Pinchas and Elijah were the same person, even though one lived during the desert wanderings and one lived during the period of the Northern Kingdom.

◆ Read both their stories and learn why the two are so closely related.

◆ Organize a pretend *This Is Your Life* TV program for Pinchas, and then for Elijah. Choose one student to be Pinchas and one to be Elijah, while the others play important people in their lives. First Pinchas and then Elijah must guess who the other characters are, based on the stories they share, information they give about how they know them, etc. Pinchas and Elijah can also ask questions.

◆ For more information, consult the *Encyclopaedia Judaica*, vol. 6, pp. 632-642 (Elijah), and vol. 13, pp. 465-467 (Phinehas a.k.a. Pinchas).

◆ For advanced study, read I Kings 16, in which an officer named Zimri committed treason against the King of Israel in the city of Tirzah. Compare these names and events to those in the Sedra (Numbers 25:14 and 27:1).

12 Both the Sedra and Haftarah feature great leaders at the ends of their careers. They both appoint successors who are first chosen by God. Moses appoints Joshua to lead the Israelites into the Promised Land in Numbers 27:16-23, while Elijah designates Elisha in 19:19-21.

◆ What advice would Moses and Elijah have offered their successors on how to lead the people? Write a speech that Moses or Elijah might have given at their retirement party, reflecting on their careers and addressing the future of the Israelite people.

13 In the Sedra God instructs Moses to "ascend the heights of Abarim and view that land that I have given to the Israelite people" (Numbers 27:12). In the Haftarah Elijah meets God on Mount Horeb.

◆ Why do you think both prophets speak to God on a mountain? If you were to have a close encounter with God, where would you want it

to take place? Draw or bring in a photograph of the perfect spot for meeting God.

14 In the Haftarah God promises that no one will survive in Israel unless he/she was completely loyal to God (verse 19:18); all who were disloyal would be killed. In the Sedra we are reminded that all who lacked faith that God was taking them to a wonderful land flowing with milk and honey, died in the desert; only Joshua and Caleb survived (Numbers 26:65).

◆ Why do you think the Israelites had trouble being loyal to God?

◆ To whom do you feel loyal? Is it ever difficult for you to remain loyal?

15 In the Sedra the daughters of Zelophehad went to Moses and requested land to keep their father's name and memory alive amongst his people (Numbers 27:1-5). According to some commentators, their request was meant solely to honor their father.

◆ Review the account of the daughters of Zelophehad. Do you agree that their request for land was meant solely to honor their father? Alternatively, do you think they really wanted land and phrased their request as they did so that it would appeal to Moses?

◆ In the Haftarah Elijah threw his mantle over Elisha, a sign that Elisha was to come with him and serve him. Elisha responded by requesting permission to say good-bye to his parents. Was Elisha's request intended to honor his parents?

◆ Do you agree that simply saying good-bye when leaving the house (i.e., not even asking permission to go) is a way in which one honors one's parents?

◆ In what other ways can one honor one's parents?

16 In the Sedra the daughters of Zelophehad demand land inheritance rights usually reserved for men. They are mentioned again in the book of Joshua, chapter 17, a perfectly reasonable alternative text for a Haftarah.

◆ Read Joshua 17, then write a case that this would have been a better Haftarah for *Parashat Pinchas*.

◆ Why do you think the Rabbis chose the Elijah story instead?

◆ Debate which would have made a better Haftarah for *Parashat Pinchas*.

Extending the Text

17 According to *Midrash* (see *The Legends of the Jews,* by Louis Ginzberg, 6:338), Elijah continued to disparage the people for not keeping the Covenant, and God decreed that for eternity Elijah would be present at every circumcision, the symbol of the continuation of the covenant with God. Some synagogues have a permanent Elijah's Chair, which is reserved for the prophet's presence at *Brit Milah* ceremonies.

◆ Why do you think Elijah was chosen for this particular honor and task?

◆ Design a Chair of Elijah. For ideas, see *Encyclopaedia Judaica*, vol. VI, pp. 643-645.

18 Elijah's presence is also invoked at the Havdalah service that ends every Shabbat. Learn to chant the Havdalah service and make it part of your Bar/Bat Mitzvah celebration.

19 Tradition teaches us that Elijah will one day come to make peace in the world, for according to the biblical prophet Malachi (verse 3:23-24), Elijah "shall turn the heart of the fathers to the children and the heart of the children to their fathers."

◆ Make a mural depicting this beautiful prophetic image of peace in the world.

20 Elijah the Prophet is mentioned in the blessing after the Haftarah (see Appendix B, p. 622).

◆ Read this blessing to see why Elijah is mentioned by name.

The Reconstructionist version of the blessing after the Haftarah (see Appendix B, p. 623) uses Elijah as he is described by Malachi (see Extending the Text #19).

◆ Identify which part of the traditional blessing the Reconstructionists omit. In your opinion, is the quotation from Malachi an appropriate replacement?

◆ Which version of the blessing do you like better, and why?

21 Elijah was zealous in his belief in God. However, he preferred to die on his own terms rather than be killed by the *Baal* worshipers. Perhaps the most famous zealots in Jewish history were the Jews of Masada, who collectively committed suicide rather than be killed by the Romans.

◆ Research the events at Masada. Decide for yourself if the zealots acted appropriately and for the glorification of God's name.

22 Elijah wanders in the wilderness for 40 days and 40 nights. The number 40 is a recurring theme in the Hebrew Bible.

◆ Can you think of other times the number 40 appears? Do any of these instances have similar themes to Elijah's wandering?

◆ For more information on the Bible's use of symbolic numbers, see the Haftarah for *Terumah*, Analyzing the Text #4, p. 130.

23 God is revealed to Elijah, not in loud thunder but in near silence. President Theodore Roosevelt was fond of quoting the West African proverb, "Speak softly and carry a big stick. You will go far."

◆ What is President Roosevelt's lesson? Do you agree or disagree with the lesson?

24 In verse 19:18 God mentions with great disdain that the Israelites have kissed the idols of *Baal*. The act of kissing as a sign of religious devotion continues to thrive today, as pious Jews kiss *mezuzot, tzitzit*, the Torah, and holy books.

◆ Why do we kiss religious objects?

◆ Every time you pass a *mezuzah* this week, remember to kiss it. Does this action make you self-conscious?

◆ Does kissing the *mezuzah* affect your sense of Jewish identity or connection with God? What other reactions do you have to this custom?

Personalizing the Text

25 The angel gives Elijah two meals before his 40-day trek through the wilderness.

◆ Plan the menu of a meal you would like to eat before going on such an arduous journey.

26 Elijah does much of his prophesying with a lot of yelling and drama. Yet he despairs that his work has been in vain because the people continue to worship *Baal*.

◆ It is said that you can catch more flies with honey than with vinegar. What does this mean, and do you agree or disagree?

◆ Is Elijah's approach to prophesying bitter or sweet?

27 Elijah heard "a soft murmuring sound" (verses 19:12-13).

◆ People have always enjoyed the soothing sounds of the surf, a babbling brook, or a forest. Today, you can even buy a machine that plays an assortment of quiet, relaxing sounds. What is your favorite quiet sound?

◆ Borrow a machine that plays soothing sounds. Play the various sounds and draw whatever comes to mind.

◆ Alternatively, record your favorite quiet sound. Compile a relaxing audiotape with all the students' selections.

◆ Hospitals sometimes collect relaxing audiotapes for their patients. Find out from the chaplain at your local hospital if your class could collect or make, then donate, such tapes.

28 Elijah the Prophet demonstrated many unusual qualities during his life.

◆ Pretend that Elijah wants to retire. Write a help wanted ad from the nation of Israel in search of a new prophet. What qualities might you want in a prophet? What qualifications? Don't forget to include a detailed job description and compensation package.

◆ Imagine all the things Elijah might do in his golden years, following his retirement from the prophecy business. Will he be a volunteer? Will he look for another job? Put together a resume for Elijah. Use this Haftarah and the Haftarah for *Ki Tisa* to discover his job experience and skills.

29 Elijah passes his mantle to Elisha.

◆ What do you imagine Elijah's mantle looked like?

◆ Design a mantle fit for a prophet.

◆ As a class, choose one of the designs and actually make the mantle out of fabric, felt, or even paper.

Other Resources

30 Read and discuss the stories about Elijah in *A Portion in Paradise* by H.M. Nahmad, pp. 21-35.

31 Read and discuss the stories in *Tales of Elijah the Prophet* by Peninnah Schram.

32 Elijah was a popular subject of the classical painters. Rubens painted Elijah being fed by an angel, Escalante painted Elijah being awakened by an angel. View these paintings at: http://cedar.evansville.edu/~ecoleweb/imagesE.html.

33 Discuss the illustration of this Haftarah in *The Illustrated Torah* by Michal Meron, p. 174.

34 Listen to and discuss the song, "Sounds of Silence" by popular Jewish musicians Paul Simon and Art Garfunkel, which may be found on their recording *Sounds of Silence*. How does the song relate to the concept of God's "still, small voice"?

35 For more stories on Elijah, see *The Legends of the Jews* by Louis Ginzberg, vol. 4, pp. 195-235.

36 Read a summary of Elijah's life in *Messengers of God* by Ronald H. Isaacs, pp. 70-71.

37 Elijah's job as prophet made him so miserable as to yearn for death. View and discuss the film *Oh, God!* (1977, rated PG, 98 minutes), starring George Burns and John Denver, in which Denver's character becomes a reluctant modern day prophet of God. Compare Denver's character with Elijah. Do you think it was easy to be a prophet in biblical times or at any time?

Involving the Family

38 This year at your Pesach *Seder* when you open the door for Elijah, play the following game: Invite one guest to dress up as Elijah and enter the door, delighting all the children at the table. Then, interview the prophet about his travels that night, with every person at the table asking him a question about the best food he's eaten, the best wine, the most exciting *Seder* he's attended, the largest gathering he's joined, etc. This fun experience is sure to add life and humor to your *Seder*.

39 Elijah is invoked as part of the Havdalah ceremony. Begin doing the Havdalah ceremony as a family at the end of Shabbat. Purchase or make a special candle, candle holder, spice box, and *Kiddush* cup for the ceremony.

Bar/Bat Mitzvah Projects

40 God speaks in a voice that is almost silent. Learn American sign language or volunteer to assist the hearing impaired in your community. Encourage your congregation to install a headset sound system for hearing-impaired congregants.

41 Wear the *tallit* of one of your parents, grandparents, or ancestors on the day of your Bar/Bat Mitzvah. How is this like Elijah's passing his mantle to Elisha? How do you feel wearing this *tallit*?

מלכים ב

II Kings

OVERVIEW

Like the two books of Samuel, First Kings and Second Kings were originally one complete book that was later divided by the translators of the Greek version of the Bible, the *Septuagint*. The division was finally accepted by the Jewish community with the printing of Daniel Bomberg's Bible in 1516-1517 in Venice.

Scholars agree that the Books of Kings were written or compiled some years after the destruction of Jerusalem by the Babylonians in 586 B.C.E.

II Kings delivers an historical account of the unraveling of the Israelite monarchy, which had been divided into two kingdoms since Solomon's death in 922 B.C.E. The book traces the histories of both kingdoms. In Israel, the Northern Kingdom, are the reigns of the kings from Ahaziah (850-849 B.C.E.) to the destruction of the Northern Kingdom of Israel in 722-721 B.C.E. In Judah, the Southern Kingdom, are the reigns of kings from Jehoshaphat (873-849 B.C.E.) to the reign of Zedekiah (597-586 B.C.E.) and the devastation of the Southern Kingdom of Judah by Babylonia. In both cases, historical events are portrayed as a cycle of divine reward and punishment for good and bad behavior, respectively. When the king and his people are loyal and true to the Temple, prophecy, and *Adonai*, the nation is

rewarded with national prosperity and military security. When the king and his people stray into idolatry and depravity, the nation is punished with military disaster.

While the Northern and Southern Kingdoms strive for survival against enemy nations, they are riddled from within by all sorts of usurpations, assassinations, coups d'état, vendettas, conspiracies, corrupt dynasties, and ends of dynasties. Religiously, they endure cycles of backsliding and repentance, the spoiling and restoration of the Temple.

The end of the Kingdom of Israel at the hands of the Assyrians in 722-721 B.C.E. is portrayed as punishment for neglect of God and the commandments and the adoption of idolatrous and depraved practices. The Israelite people are taken away into captivity, and their land is colonized by foreign settlers.

The Kingdom of Judah is also portrayed as subject to the same vicious cycle of sin, punishment, repentance, and reward. Kings Joash (837-800 B.C.E.), Hezekiah (715-687 B.C.E.), and Josiah (640-609 B.C.E.) are described as particularly righteous leaders. But in Judea, too, sin is blamed for their ultimate destruction at the hands of the Babylonians in 586 B.C.E.

The time period of II Kings was also the era of many important biblical prophets, including Elisha, Isaiah, Hosea, Jeremiah, Ezekiel, Amos, Micah, and Habakkuk, who urged the people toward repentance. Elisha, who is featured in two Haftarot, is perhaps best known for the amazing miracles he performed (increasing an oil supply, reviving a dead boy, feeding hungry people, and curing leprosy).

Hulda, who is not included in any Haftarah, was one of Israel's seven women prophetesses. The keeper of King Josiah's royal wardrobe, she told Josiah that his sincere repentance had saved him from the punishment that had been decreed by God. Other women, such as the disciple's widow, the Shunammite woman, and an Israelite slave, figure prominently in the Haftarot from II Kings.

II KINGS 4:1-37 Ashkenazim
II KINGS 4:1-23 Sephardim
VAYERA וירא

This Haftarah has been paired with *Parashat Vayera*, Genesis 18:1-22:24. See "Connecting the Text To the Sedra," pp. 186-187, for an exploration of the many ways the two texts shed light on each other.

SYNOPSIS

This Haftarah features two stories about miracles performed by the Prophet Elisha. In the first story, the widow of one of the prophet's disciples has come upon hard times. Her creditors, in fact, want to take her two children as slaves. She cries to Elisha for help because the only thing of any value she has in her house is a single jar of oil. Elisha tells her to borrow empty vessels from all her neighbors and to fill them all with the oil from her single jar. The oil miraculously increases to fill all the borrowed vessels. Elisha advises the widow to sell enough oil to pay off her debts and to keep the rest to support her and her children.

In the second story, Elisha visits Shunem, where he meets a wealthy woman who offers him a meal. Elisha visits Shunem frequently, and the woman and her husband always feed him and give him a room in which to stay. After some time, Elisha wonders how he can repay their kindness. His servant, Gehazi, tells him that the woman and her husband have no children. Elisha announces that next year she will embrace a son.

As promised, the Shunammite woman has a son. One day, the boy goes out to join his father in the fields, and suddenly collapses and dies. His mother leaves his body in the room reserved for Elisha and sets off to find the prophet. She arrives at Mount Carmel and entreats Elisha to come with her.

According to Elisha's instructions, Gehazi goes ahead and places Elisha's staff on the boy's face, but the boy does not stir. Then Elisha arrives and lays his own body over the child — mouth over mouth, eyes over eyes, hands over hands — and the body of the child begins to warm. Elisha steps off, walks around, then bends over the boy again, at which point the boy sneezes seven times and opens his eyes.

The Shunammite woman falls at Elisha's feet in gratitude and picks up her revived child.

INSIGHTS FROM THE TRADITION

As each vessel of oil is filled in the first story, it is taken away and a new one brought to the jug of oil. Rashi teaches that God made the jug of oil like a spring, which does not move from place to place. Containers had to be brought to the spring to be filled.

A lesson we may derive from this is that we have to go to seek help instead of waiting for help to come to us. In school, for example, you might have to take the initiative and seek extra help in math instead of waiting for your teacher to notice that you are having trouble.

◆ Do you consider asking for help a sign of strength or weakness?

◆ Can you think of another real-life example of when someone might need to take the initiative to look for help?

B Radak teaches that a miracle continues only in the place where it started.

◆ Do you believe in miracles? Why or why not?

◆ How do you define a miracle?

◆ Describe a miracle you have witnessed.

C Before the woman sells the oil that Elisha provided, she goes back to him and reports the situation. He instructs her to sell whatever is necessary to pay off her debts and to keep the rest to support her family. According to *midrash*, this teaches that if you receive something from someone or someone does you a favor, you have an obligation to keep the giver informed about what you have been able to do with the gift or favor.

◆ Why do you think the *midrash* teaches that you keep your benefactor informed?

◆ Have you ever had a coach or teacher who did something special for you? Take this opportunity to get in touch with these individuals, and let them know what you have been able to do because of their kindness.

D The Shunammite woman announces in verse 4:9 that she now knows that Elisha is a holy man of God. According to Rashi, Elisha kept his table so clean that a fly never appeared on it.

According to *The Legends of the Jews* by Louis Ginzberg, vol. 6, p. 346, a special fragrance came from pious people that repelled flies.

◆ Do you agree that cleanliness is next to godliness? List other virtues you think are as important or more important than cleanliness.

◆ For more insights and activities on cleanliness, see *Teaching Jewish Virtues* by Susan Freeman, pp. 271-272.

E Elisha asks the Shunammite woman in verse 4:13, "What is there to do for you?" Kara proposes an alternative reading of this verse: "What did you need me to do for you that made you go to this bother for me?"

◆ How is Kara's reading a cynical interpretation?

◆ Do you agree with his interpretation that the woman was hospitable toward Elisha only so that he would be indebted to her?

◆ Did you ever do something for someone just so that they would owe you, and you could get them to do something for you? Describe the situation.

F When Elisha offers in verse 4:13 to speak to the king for the Shunammite woman, she responds that because she lives among her own family, she does not need his intercession. Rashi explains that she lives with her family and no person causes her harm, so she needs no help from the king or the army.

◆ Imagine what it must be like to be a complete stranger in a city or country (i.e., with no family nearby). In what ways might you be vulnerable? How might you suffer harm?

◆ In what ways does your community (your congregation, town, state, country) help the stranger who lives in your midst?

◆ List ways in which our extended families can help and support us.

◆ In what ways have your own parents or grandparents helped members of your extended family?

STRATEGIES
Analyzing the Text

1 The Haftarah tells two different stories about Elisha.

◆ Compare the two stories and identify places that contain the following parallels:

- Elijah helps a woman by performing a miracle.

- Elijah says to a woman, "What can I do for you?"

- There are closed doors.

- There are children in jeopardy.

- The women update the prophet with developments after his initial help.

◆ Can you identify any other parallels?

2 Elisha helps the first woman by using something she already owns.

◆ What does Elisha use?

◆ Even though she is very poor, this woman nevertheless has one food staple. List some consumer items that you consider to be staples in any modern home, no matter how poor.

◆ Why do you think Elisha uses the oil rather than give the woman, say, a large gemstone or some magic beans as in the fairytale "Jack and the Beanstalk"?

3 Elisha instructs the woman in verse 4:4 to close the doors before pouring the oil into the borrowed vessels.

◆ Suggest ideas for what might have happened if the pouring had been done in public. What might the neighbors have thought?

◆ Write a newspaper article or evening television newscast story about this miraculous event.

4 We learn in verse 4:8 that a woman from the area of Shunem helped Elisha in his time of need. Another Shunammite woman helped King David in his time of need (see the beginning of the Haftarah for *Chayay Sarah*, p. 102).

◆ *Pirke de Rabbi Eliezer* (33) suggests that these two women were sisters. Why is this idea a bit far-fetched?

◆ Why do you think the Rabbis wanted to connect the two women in some way?

5 When Elisha tells the Shunammite woman that she will have a child, she tells him not to lie to her.

◆ Based on her reaction, what emotion(s) do you think the woman was feeling?

6 When the woman seeks Elisha's help after her son's collapse, she reports in verse 4:26 to Gehazi, the servant, that her family is doing well. When she encounters Elisha himself, she still does not report her bad news, but only collapses at his feet in distress.

◆ Why do you think the woman is reluctant to tell Elisha her bad tidings?

◆ How does Elisha figure out what is wrong?

7 Elisha sends his assistant to revive the boy, but the grieving mother insists that Elisha go himself. In fact, Gehazi fails in his attempts to save the child, and Elisha ultimately revives the boy himself.

◆ Do you agree that when you have something important to do, you must do it yourself?

◆ How do you know when tasks can be delegated or when you must do them yourself?

◆ Can you find another example in the second story of the Haftarah of someone insisting on doing an important job herself?

Connecting the Text To the Sedra

8 The woman in the first story of the Haftarah refers to her late husband as a God-fearing man (verse 4:1). Similarly, Abraham was called a God-fearing man in Genesis 22:12 after the binding of Isaac.

◆ What do you think it means to fear God?

◆ Do you think there is a difference between following the commandments out of fear of God or out of love for God? If so, describe the difference. If not, why not?

◆ List three secular and three religious rules you follow out of fear of consequences. List three secular and three religious rules you follow out of love and respect. Compare the lists.

9 In both the Sedra and Haftarah, a barren woman with an old husband is promised a child. Sarah responds to the news by laughing, and the Shunammite woman responds by telling Elisha not to lie to her.

◆ Why do you think each woman had the reaction she did?

◆ How would you react if someone, especially a stranger, told you something unbelievably good was going to happen to you?

◆ On the other hand, how would you react if someone told you something terrible was going to happen to you?

10 Children are in danger in both the Haftarah and Sedra. In the Haftarah the first set of sons is nearly taken away from their mother to be slaves to a creditor. In the second story, the son dies and is revived by the prophet Elisha. Isaac is almost sacrificed in the Sedra, and Ishmael almost dies of thirst in the desert.

◆ How do these stories, all of which involve children at risk, make you (and the audience) feel?

◆ Invite to your class a guest speaker who works locally with children at risk (from the Division of Youth and Family Services, for example). Find out what he/she does and what you can do to help.

11 Both Haftarah and Torah reading address how much parents value their children.

A story is told in *Midrash Proverbs* 31:3 about the children of Rabbi Meir. One Shabbat afternoon, while Rabbi Meir was in the house of study, his two sons, who were at home with their mother, died. Their mother laid them on the bed and covered them with a cloth. After Shabbat was over, Rabbi Meir came home and asked where the children were. His wife replied that they were somewhere else, and then asked her husband a question: "Earlier today, a man came here and gave me something to keep for him; now he has come back to ask for it again. Shall we return it to him or not?"

Rabbi Meir answered that when one accepts something in temporary trust, one must return it promptly when the owner asks for it back

Then his wife led him by the hand to the bed and took away the cloth. He saw his sons lying dead upon the bed. He began to weep, but his wife reminded him that they must return a possession taken in trust to its owner. As the saying goes: *Adonai* gave, *Adonai* took, blessed be the name of *Adonai*.

◆ According to the parable offered by Rabbi Meir's wife, what are children?

◆ If children are gifts on loan from God, how should they be treated?

◆ Ask your parents if they think of children as temporary gifts in trust from God.

◆ Discuss whether or not you think the parents in the Sedra and Haftarah viewed and treated their children as gifts from God. Consider Abraham and Ishmael, Abraham and Isaac, Sarah and Isaac, Hagar and Ishmael, the woman in the oil story and her sons, the Shunammite woman and her son.

12 Both Torah portion and Haftarah extol the virtues of hospitality. Abraham shows hospitality to the three men who come to visit him. The Shunammite woman is gracious and hospitable to Elisha. Both Abraham and the Shunammite woman involve their spouses in their good efforts.

◆ How are Abraham and Sarah and the Shunammite couple rewarded for their acts of hospitality?

◆ Hospitality is a Jewish virtue. For more insights and activities on the subject, see *Teaching Jewish Virtues* by Susan Freeman, pp. 102-118.

13 Hagar cries in the Sedra because she thinks she and her son have run out of water and will die of thirst in the hot desert. God hears her cries and opens her eyes to enable her to see there is a well of water right in front of her.

In the Haftarah the widow cries to Elisha because she and her sons have run out of food, and all she has left is a bit of oil in one bottle. Elisha shows her that she has an unending supply of oil with which to ensure her family's well-being.

◆ How is the supply of oil like the supply of water? We learn from this that often the keys to our success, and even our salvation, are right in front of us if only we know where — and how — to look.

◆ View and discuss the film *The Wizard of Oz* (1939, no rating, 101 minutes), especially the last several minutes. How does Dorothy come to realize that all she could ever want or need is right there in her own backyard?

◆ Do you feel the same way as Dorothy? Explain your answer.

14 God decides in the Sedra to destroy Sodom and Gomorrah without discussing the matter with Abraham, but then reconsiders if it is right to hide the plan from Abraham (Genesis 18:17). In the second story in the Haftarah, Elisha doesn't know that the child became sick and died. He sees that the woman is bitter and angry in verse 4:27, but says that God has hidden the information from him.

◆ Why do you think God wanted to hide the information from both Abraham and Elisha?

The prophets — Abraham and Elisha among them — were people who always spoke honestly with God, even criticizing God's decisions and actions when necessary. When Abraham discovers God's plans to destroy Sodom and Gomorrah, he protests on behalf of the innocent. Elisha, too, is outraged by God's decision to have the young boy die and intervenes to return him to life.

◆ Is there one person you trust to give you an honest opinion at all times?

◆ Why is such a person valuable?

◆ Do you fill this role for anyone? Describe the situation.

Extending the Text

15 Elisha helps the widow get money to pay off her debts. For hundreds of years, Jewish communities have had Free Loan Societies that offer interest free or low interest loans to help keep community members out of financial trouble.

- Does your synagogue or greater Jewish community have a Free Loan Society? If so, interview the director to find out what they do, whom they help, and where they get their funding.

- Visit the web site of the International Association of Hebrew Free Loans at www.freeloan.org, where you can read their mission statement and newsletter and also find your local affiliate.

16 According to *Shabbat* 63a, the greatest charity is to enable the poor to earn a living.

Rambam (*Mishneh Torah*, Laws of Charity 10:7) also teaches that there are various ways to give charity, but "the highest level . . . is that of the person who assists a poor Jew by providing him with a gift or loan, or by entering into a partnership with him, or helping him find work — in other words, by putting him where he can do without other people's aid."

There is also a folk saying that goes, "Give a man a fish, and you feed him for a day. Teach a man to fish, and you feed him for a lifetime."

- Explain these teachings.

- Explain how Elisha is performing this *mitzvah* in the first story of the Haftarah.

- Do you agree that teaching someone a skill is the highest form of *tzedakah*? Why or why not?

- There are a number of Jewish organizations in your country, in Israel, and abroad (such as ORT, Jewish Family Services, B'nai B'rith, and Hadassah) that are dedicated to teaching work skills to adults. Ask your Rabbi or call your Federation to find out about local organizations that help people find and train for new jobs.

- After the collapse of the Soviet Union, thousands of Russian Jews emigrated to North America. Local Jewish agencies helped to find homes and jobs for these people. Interview Russian émigrés in your community to find out what profession they had in the Former Soviet Union, what they do now, and how they were trained for their new job and life.

17 Olive oil was a very important staple in the ancient world.

- Make a list of all the ways olive oil can be used today. Compare your list to the ways it was used in biblical times: cooking ingredient, cosmetic, fuel for lamps, medicine, export in foreign trade, applied to leather shields before war, used in sacrifices, used to anoint kings, and sunscreen. (Source: *Encyclopaedia Judaica*, vol. 12, pp. 1347-1351.)

- It would appear that every ancient Israelite home, no matter how poor, had some olive oil. As a class, make a list of staples for today's households and collect them to donate to a local food bank or homeless shelter.

18 According to verse 4:23, it was customary to visit a prophet only on the New Moon and Shabbat.

- What is a New Moon?

- The Jewish calendar is a lunar calendar, based on the phases of the moon. Each month lasts as long as the moon's cycle, 29-30 days. To know what day of the month it is in the Jewish calendar, you simply have to look into the sky. A thin crescent moon in the shape of a backwards "C" marks the beginning of the month, with a full moon in the middle, and the opposite thin crescent (a "C" shape) at the end. At the beginning of the month, the moon is

19 According to *midrash*, Elisha's actions prove the duty of gratitude in return for hospitality.

◆ Discuss the following lesson from *Berachot* 58a:

What does a good guest say? He/she says: "How much trouble my host has taken for me! How much meat he has prepared for me! How much wine he has served me! How many cakes he has offered me! And all the trouble he has gone to only for my sake!"

What does a bad guest say? "How much did my host really put himself out? I ate only one piece of bread, I have had only one slice of meat, and I drank only one cup of wine! All the trouble my host went to was really for the sake only of himself and his family."

◆ Compare the two types of guests in this Talmudic lesson.

◆ How might the duty to feel gratitude change how one feels about an experience?

20 The Shunammite woman joins a long list of biblical women who are childless until God intervenes to make them mothers. Match the list of women below with their children, and list the biblical book in which their story is found:

1. Sarah (c., Genesis)
2. Rebecca (f., Genesis)
3. Rachel (d., Genesis)
4. Hannah (a., I Samuel)
5. Ruth (b., Ruth)
6. Manoah's wife (e., Judges)

a. Samuel
b. Obed
c. Isaac
d. Joseph
e. Samson
f. Jacob and Esau

Personalizing the Text

21 This Haftarah contains two stories of miracles performed by the Prophet Elisha.

◆ Form two groups. Each group performs a paper bag dramatics skit of one of the stories in the Haftarah. To do paper bag dramatics, every student must bring to class several items from home to use as clothing or props. Place the items into large paper bags from which the groups will randomly pick props for their skits.

22 We are not told why the first woman is in financial trouble.

◆ Write a story explaining why the woman has come upon hard times. You might want to consider that *midrash* tells us that her late husband was Obadiah, the steward of King Ahab (see the Haftarah for *Ki Tisa*, pp. 164-172). You might also find it interesting to know that in biblical times, the women were largely responsible for the economic viability of the family. (Source: Claudia V. Camp in her article in *Women's Bible Commentary*, edited by Carol Newsom and Sharon Ringe, p. 103.

23 The woman sells the oil and pays her debts, and with the remainder she supports her family. This teaches that if you come upon a sum of money, the best course of action is first to pay off your debts and then to use the remainder for your living expenses.

◆ If suddenly you received a huge sum of money, list the first five things you would do with it. Ask your parents to do the same, and compare and discuss lists. What observations about priorities can you make based on the comparison between your list and that of your parents?

24 Miraculously, the woman in the first story is able to fill many jars with the oil from her one jar.

◆ Using clay, create an oil pot that can be fired in a kiln, decorated, and used. (Note: Many communities have paint-your-own pottery studios, which would make a great field trip for this project.)

25 When the bereft Shunammite mother seeks Elisha, she tells him she would have rather remained childless than to have a son and lose him (verse 4:28). *Pirke de Rabbi Eliezer* (32) compares this to the statement, "I would rather have an empty vessel than one that was filled and then spilled out."

◆ Why might the woman have felt this way?

◆ The poet Alfred Lord Tennyson once wrote, " 'Tis better to have loved and lost than never to have loved at all." Compare this with the Shunammite's statement.

◆ Debate Tennyson's claim.

26 The stories in this Haftarah and the Sedra involve children at risk.

◆ Have a fund-raiser or collect necessary items, such as linens or toiletries, for a local shelter or other organization that supports women and/or children at risk.

27 Shunammite women are known in the Bible for their kindness and hospitality (see Analyzing the Text #4, p. 185, as well as the

beginning of the Haftarah for *Chayay Sarah*, p. 102).

◆ For what are people in your community known? Write a story about this.

◆ For what are you known?

Other Resources

28 Read the many folktales involving scant food multiplying and never running out in *Myth, Legend and Custom in the Old Testament* by Theodor Gaster, pp. 518-9.

29 Discuss the illustration of this Haftarah depicted in *The Illustrated Torah* by Michal Meron, p. 26.

30 In the Harry Potter stories by J.K. Rowling and in the movie version (2001, rated PG, 153 minutes), Harry's life has been threatened from the time he was a baby. Harry's continued survival in the face of adversity fascinates readers and makes Harry almost a celebrity. The characters in our Haftarah are survivors, too, despite great adversity.

◆ Why are we so fascinated by survivors, and especially by children who overcome difficult odds?

31 For a modern take on the miraculous quality of oil, view and discuss the film *Lorenzo's Oil* (1992, rated PG-13, 135 minutes). In this true story, parents save their young boy's life with a combination of olive oil and rapeseed oil. Through their tenacious efforts, Lorenzo's parents discover a treatment for the previously untreatable and fatal disease, Adrenoleukodistrophy (ALD).

32 For a story about a mother who guides her children through life's perils, read and discuss the story "The Path" by Nancy R. Ginsberg, in *Chosen Tales*, edited by Peninnah Schram, pp. 104-106.

33 View and discuss the film *It Could Happen To You*, (1994, rated PG, 101 minutes). This film is about a man who wins the lottery and must decide what to do with the money. Important moral issues are addressed.

34 Elisha was a true miracle worker. View and discuss the entertaining film *Leap of Faith* (1992, rated PG-13, 108 minutes), about a con man miracle worker who eventually performs an actual miracle that changes his life.

35 Rembrandt painted the Shunammite woman in "The Departure of the Shunammite Woman." You can find this painting in *The Illustrated Hebrew Bible* by Ellen Frankel, p. 207.

36 For information on prophecy in general, and on Elisha in particular, read *Messengers of God: A Jewish Prophets Who's Who* by Ronald H. Isaacs.

Involving the Family

37 Resolve as a family to make your home more hospitable to visitors. Some suggestions on how to do this include redecorating your guest room, planning a Passover *Seder* and inviting guests who may not have anywhere else to go, or inviting elderly congregants who live alone to share Shabbat or holiday dinners.

38 As we learned above in Connecting the Text To the Sedra #11, p. 186, children are precious gifts to parents. Let's not forget, also, that parents are precious gifts to their children. Use family birthdays (or the Friday night closest to them) as occasions for appreciation dinners for one another, featuring the birthday person's favorite foods. At each birthday appreciation dinner, the family can present a testimonial of some sort. The testimonial can be a kind speech, a poster on which all family members write something complimentary about the birthday person, or a special scrapbook recording favorite moments from the past year.

Bar/Bat Mitzvah Projects

39 The Rabbis taught that Elisha kept his room and table extraordinarily clean. For the year of your Bar/Bat Mitzvah, keep your room unusually clean and neat, and also take on the chore of clearing the table after family dinners.

40 Some people posit that Elisha saved the boy by using cardiopulmonary resuscitation (CPR) and artificial respiration. Whether or not this was the case here, it remains true that these skills can save lives. Take a Red Cross certification course in CPR and artificial respiration. Alternatively, organize a fund-raiser to purchase a lifesaving defibrillator for your school.

II KINGS 4:42-5:19
TAZRIA תזריע

This Haftarah has been paired with *Parashat Tazria*, Leviticus 12:1-13:59. See "Connecting the Text To the Sedra," pp. 194-195, for an exploration of the many ways the two texts shed light on each other.

SYNOPSIS

This Haftarah continues the telling of miracles performed by the prophet Elisha, begun in the previous Haftarah for *Vayera*. The first three verses relate the story of a man who brings Elisha 20 loaves of barley bread from the first reaping during a time of grave famine in the land. Elisha instructs him to give the bread to the people, but the man is concerned that the bread could not possibly feed 100 people. Nevertheless, he does as Elisha instructs him, and not only is there enough to feed all the people, but there are leftovers as well.

The next miracle story features Naaman, the commander of the Aramean army, who happens to suffer from leprosy (*tzara'at*). Naaman had once captured a young Israelite girl, who was now his wife's attendant. This Israelite girl suggested that Naaman should visit Elisha, the prophet in Samaria, who could cure his skin disease. Naaman is granted permission from the Aramean king to visit Elisha, which he does, taking with him a letter from his king to the king of Israel, plus silver, gold, and clothing.

When the king of Israel reads the letter, he worries that if Naaman isn't cured of his *tzara'at*, then the Aramean king will have a grievance against him. When Elisha hears that the Israelite king is upset, he sends for Naaman to prove that there is "a prophet in Israel."

Naaman arrives at Elisha's house, where Elisha instructs him to bathe seven times in the Jordan River. Naaman is insulted by this simple solution, but his servants urge him to try it. Naaman bathes and emerges from the Jordan with healthy flesh.

Moved by his experience, Naaman proclaims to Elisha that there is no God in the world except the God of Israel and offers the prophet a gift of gratitude. Elisha refuses the gift, but accepts Naaman's renunciation of all foreign gods. Naaman asks permission to take home Israelite soil to use in his personal altar. Elisha grants permission, blesses the Aramean commander, and sends him on his way.

Note: *Tazria* is often read as a double portion with *Metzora*, which follows it. The two Haftarot contain similar material. See *Metzora* for more Insights and Strategies that apply to *Tazria*.

INSIGHTS FROM THE TRADITION

A As a commander of the Aramean army, Naaman is credited by *Midrash Rabbah Psalms* (78:11) with killing the wicked Israelite, King Ahab. It seems that Naaman is a tool of God used by God to eliminate Ahab.

◆ A tool can be considered like a partner who helps get important work done. List three occupations that can be considered tools for God's work. For more on the subject, read *Being God's Partner* by Jeffrey Salkin.

B When he reads the Aramean king's request to heal Naaman, the Israelite king tears his clothes in mourning and cries in verse 5:7, "Am I God, to deal death or give life . . ." He seems to take the responsibility on himself, even though he must know that Elisha has the power to call on God for healing.

According to Radak, the Israelite king was ashamed to ask Elisha for a miracle because he had not heeded Elisha's demands to cease worshiping idols.

◆ Have you ever been trapped, like the Israelite king, by a guilty conscience?

◆ What do you think is Radak's lesson here?

C Radak points out that at the end of the Haftarah, Naaman could have taken the soil without asking permission. However, since he wanted to use it in his altar, he wanted to make sure the soil was untainted by theft or any dishonesty.

◆ Do you think charities have an obligation to check to make sure the money they receive from donors has been acquired honestly? Explain your answer.

◆ Hold a debate on this question.

D Naaman indicates in verse 5:18 that although he will continue to believe only in the one true God, he will nonetheless have to continue worshiping with his master to the Aramean god Rimmon. Elisha tells him to go in peace.

According to Hertz, Elisha is not indicating approval or disapproval of Naaman's plan. Perhaps because of Naaman's new devotion, it would be too much strain if Elisha judged his behavior.

◆ Do you think it is ever right or appropriate for us to judge others' beliefs or behaviors?

◆ How does it hurt us to be judgmental of others?

◆ How does it help us to judge ourselves fairly?

◆ For more insights and activities on the subject of judgment, see *Teaching Jewish Virtues* by Susan Freeman, p. 30, texts #A and #B.

STRATEGIES
Analyzing the Text

1 The Haftarah relates two stories, both involving miracles performed by Elisha: providing food for the Israelites and curing an Aramean army commander of his leprosy.

Midrash explains that the Haftarah begins with the miracle of Elisha generously providing food for the Israelites to demonstrate that Elisha acts selflessly.

◆ Discuss the qualities of Elisha that each story exemplifies.

2 We learned in Insights from the Tradition #B, p. 193, that the Israelite king might not want to contact Elisha to perform the healing because of a guilty conscience.

◆ Can you think of any other reasons the Israelite king might have reacted the way he does in verse 5:7? Consider the following suggestions:

• He thinks he is expected to heal the illness himself.

• He does not know of Elisha and his healing powers.

• He does not believe that Naaman can be healed.

• He thinks the request is a pretext for war.

Defend each possibility with evidence from the story.

3 Elisha requires Naaman to dunk in the Jordan River seven times.

◆ The number 7 has magical qualities in Jewish tradition. Try to list seven associations with the number 7 (e.g., Shabbat, a bride circles her groom seven times, many holidays are celebrated for seven days).

◆ For more information on the symbolic significance of the number 7, see *The Encyclopedia of Jewish Symbols* by Ellen Frankel and Betsy Platkin Teutsch, pp. 149-150.

4 Naaman's speech to Elisha in verse 5:18 contains a lot of repetitious language.

◆ Identify unnecessary, repetitious language in Naaman's speech.

◆ What might Naaman have been feeling that caused him to speak in such a repetitious manner?

◆ Think of times when you might tend to be repetitious.

5 Some *midrashim* explain that Naaman suffered from *tzara'at* as punishment for haughtiness.

◆ What is haughtiness?

◆ Would a haughty person take advice, as Naaman does, from a lowly servant girl captured from the enemy?

◆ Find other examples in the story that support or disprove the theory of Naaman's haughtiness.

6 The Haftarah ends before the completion of the story of Naaman.

◆ Read the rest of the story (II Kings 5:19-27). Then contrast the behavior and attitude of the Israelite servant girl who saves Naaman's life in the beginning of the Haftarah with that of Elisha's servant, Gehazi.

◆ Do you think Elisha's retribution for Gehazi's actions is appropriate?

Connecting the Text To the Sedra

7 The Sedra goes over the rules for diagnosing, treating, and purifying the healed victim of the skin disease *tzara'at*. In the Haftarah Naaman is cured of the disease by Elisha.

The skin disease is *midrashically* connected with moral wrongdoing. Torah commentaries teach that the *tzara'at* in the Sedra is punishment for gossip, slander, bloodshed, false oaths, immorality, pride, robbery, and selfishness, among other sins. Similarly, we learn in Analyzing the Text #5, p. 194, that Naaman was stricken because of his haughtiness (see *Numbers Rabbah* 7:5).

◆ Most of us do not believe today that illness is a punishment for sin. What do you think? Explain your answer.

◆ Invite a dermatologist to speak about the myths and facts about leprosy, which is known today as Hansen's Disease.

8 The Sedra requires that if someone is diagnosed with leprosy or certain other skin diseases, he/she is quarantined seven days and then examined again (Leviticus 13:4, 5, 11, 21, 26, 31, 33, 45-46, 50, 54).

In the Haftarah the King of Aram instructs the King of Israel to cure Naaman of his skin disease (verse 5:6). The verse literally says, "gather him from his skin disease." Rashi teaches that a person with *tzara'at* is quarantined, separated from his/her community. The Aramean king, then, is asking the Israelite king to cure Naaman so that he can be gathered back into his community.

◆ Do you know of any diseases today that are subject to strict quarantine?

◆ How can certain diseases impose a stigma, or social quarantine, on those who suffer from them?

There are other ways, other than illness, that we judge and stigmatize people. When we stigmatize them, we often make them feel like quarantined social outcasts. What are some of the ways we look at people and treat them like outcasts? (for example, size, age, "coolness," race, etc.)

◆ What can you do to stop someone from feeling like an outcast?

9 The Sedra teaches that after childbirth, a woman is to take two offerings to the Temple so as to return to a purified state. One is a burnt offering, symbolizing her rededication to God after an absence from the Temple. The other is a sin offering. In *Leviticus: The Traditional Hebrew Text with the New JPS Translation*, p. 74, Baruch Levine explains it is not for a sin — no sin had been committed — but rather it is a part of the cleansing process.

In the Haftarah Naaman asks to take soil from Israel with him to his land so that he can build an altar to God and make burnt offerings and other sacrifices only to God.

◆ Explain how Naaman is planning to dedicate himself to God with his future burnt offerings.

10 The Haftarah, which is mostly about Naaman being cured, nonetheless begins with a seemingly unrelated story. There has been a great famine and terrible hunger. A man brings a gift of food from the first crops, and Elisha tells his servant to distribute food to everyone. Even though there was just a modest quantity of food, the food miraculously lasts until everyone has been satisfied.

◆ Explain how this story teaches that God provides food and saves the people from death.

◆ In the story of Naaman, Naaman is angry that Elisha does not come out, wave his hands, and pronounce some type of magical healing formula. Explain how Naaman learned that God, and not Elisha, was responsible for his healing (verse 5:15).

◆ Similarly, in the Sedra, the priest checks the leper to see if he/she is healed, but does nothing to cure the leprosy. The priest only announces that healing has occurred. Explain how the healing of a leper is also from God, and not from a person.

◆ In contrast, however, a woman gives birth to a child in the Sedra. Do you see an indication in the Sedra that giving life to the child was due to God (as healing is)? (The ability of women to give life makes women seem to share this ability with God. Perhaps the Haftarah is meant to explain why a woman would bring a sin offering after giving birth — to atone for possibly having the arrogant thought that she was like God.)

◆ If someone (fireman, police, doctor) saves another person's life, should the rescuer make a charitable donation to humble him/herself and prevent arrogant ideas that he/she is like God (able to rescue, save, heal, give life)?

◆ Write a personal prayer to God, asking for humility and acknowledging that God is the source of all human power.

Extending the Text

11 Elisha provides food for the hungry (verse 4:42). We are taught that if a person tells you he/she is hungry, we must drop whatever we are doing and feed him or her at once.

◆ Read and discuss the following Talmudic story (*Ta'anit* 21a) on this subject:

Nahum of Gamzu was blind in both eyes, his hands and legs were amputated, and his body was covered with boils. His disciples said to him, "Master, you're such a righteous man. Why has all this happened to you?"

He answered, "I brought it on myself. Once I was traveling to my father-in-law's house, and I had three donkeys with me. One carried food, one drink, and one all kinds of dainties. A poor man stopped me and asked for something to eat. I answered, 'Wait until I unload my donkey.' I had barely managed to unload something when the man died.

"I laid myself on him and exclaimed, 'May my eyes that did not pity your eyes become blind; may my hands that did not pity your hands be cut off; may my legs that did not pity your legs be amputated.' And my mind was not at rest until I added, 'May my whole body be covered with boils.'"

◆ Explain how this story teaches that you must do everything within your power (with every part of your body) to feed someone immediately if he/she is hungry.

◆ What do you think of this story? Explain your answer.

12 We learned in Connecting the Text To the Sedra #10, p. 195, that God is the source of both food and healing. In addition, we learned in Insights from the Tradition #A, p. 192, that Naaman was used by God to get rid of the wicked king.

◆ There are at least two more examples in the Bible of non-Israelites being used by God to accomplish God's goals. Read the story of the Moabite prophet Balaam in Numbers 22-24

and the story of King Cyrus of Persia in II Chronicles 36:22-23.

◆ Explain how Balaam had no power to curse or bless Israel. God had the power, and Balaam could only say what God wanted. Explain why it is theologically important that God, not Cyrus, redeemed the people.

◆ Are Balaam and Cyrus both willing and enthusiastic "tools" for God?

◆ What does it mean to you that non-Israelites were tools for God?

13 Elisha required Naaman to dunk in the Jordan River seven times. According to *Yalkut HaGershuni*, the number 7 indicates that Naaman did not keep the seven Noachide laws required of all people (Jew and non-Jew alike). Only when he repented from his sins would Naaman be healed.

Derived from the divine commands given to Adam and Noah, the seven Noachide Laws prohibit idol worship, blasphemy, murder, adultery, robbery, and eating flesh cut from a living animal. The seventh law provides for the establishment of courts of law.

◆ Discuss these seven laws and why they might be considered mandatory for all people.

◆ Are there any other laws you think should be mandatory for all people?

◆ For more information on this subject, see *Teaching Torah* by Sorel Goldberg Loeb and Barbara Binder Kadden, Insights from the Tradition #H, Analyzing the Text #2-4, pp. 12-14.

14 While *tzara'at* was explained by some *midrashim* as a punishment for selfishness, Elisha represents for us someone who is selfless in his commitment to God and Israel.

It can be difficult to find a comfortable place between selflessness and selfishness. *Pirke Avot* 1:14 quotes Hillel: "If I am not for myself, who will be for me? And if I am only for my own self, what am I?"

◆ What is the lesson of *Pirke Avot*?

◆ Write a motto for Elisha that reflects selflessness.

15 Naaman, a man of high rank and social stature, takes advice from an Israelite servant girl.

Rabbi Ben Zoma once taught, "Who is wise? The one who learns from everyone" (*Pirke Avot* 4:1).

◆ Do you agree with Ben Zoma? Why or why not?

◆ In the same Mishnah, Ben Zoma also asks, "Who is mighty; Who is rich; and Who is honored?" How would you answer these questions?

◆ Compare your answers with Ben Zoma's, which are, respectively: One who controls his/her passions; One who rejoices in his/her portion; and One who honors others.

16 Naaman's bathing in the Jordan River brings to mind the use of *mikvah* in Jewish tradition. A *mikvah* is a body of natural water used for ritual immersion on various occasions, including conversion. A *mikvah* can be an indoor pool of collected rainwater or a natural body of water, such as an ocean.

◆ Find out if there is a *mikvah* in your community. Arrange a visit and tour for your class.

17 Naaman comes to believe that the God of Israel is the only God. However, he does not go through the ritual of conversion, as there were no specific guidelines for this in biblical times.

◆ The requirements for conversion to Judaism vary from one movement to another within Judaism. Ask your Rabbi to speak to your class about the process of conversion.

◆ Ask a convert in your community to speak to the class about his or her conversion experience.

◆ You can also visit the Conversion To Judaism web site at www.convert.org.

18 Naaman takes with him soil from Israel for his altar at home. The Jewish synagogue in Nehardea, Babylonia was composed solely of stone and earth from Jerusalem. Many Jews, upon landing in Israel, bend down to kiss the soil. It is also customary to keep soil from Israel to place in the coffins of Diaspora Jews.

◆ Why do Jews around the world feel connected to the Land of Israel? Do you?

◆ Make a sand art mural depicting various features of the Land of Israel and their religious significance. You might want to include important sites in Jerusalem, the Galilee, Masada, the Red Sea, and so on.

19 The number 7 is important in the Haftarah. Match the following biblical characters with his or her particular connection with the number 7:

1. Worked seven years for a wife, Genesis 29:20 (g.)
2. Judged Israel for seven years, Judges 12:9 (d.)
3. Dreamed of seven fat and seven lean cows, Genesis 41:2-3 (c.)
4. Her daughter-in-law was better than seven sons, Ruth 4:15 (a.)
5. Became king at age seven, II Kings 12:1 (f.)
6. Had seven locks of hair woven into a web, Judges 16:13 (b.)
7. Condemned by seven ministers to the king, Esther 1:14-16 (e.)

a. Naomi
b. Samson
c. Pharaoh
d. Ibzan
e. Vashti
f. Jehoash
g. Jacob

20 Elisha tells Naaman to "go in peace." Think of other expressions for good-bye that are said around the world, such as "Godspeed," "Go in health," *"L'hitraot,"* "Farewell." What messages do these expressions convey?

◆ Choose several different expressions, and act them out in a game of *Charades* to see if your classmates can distinguish among them.

Personalizing the Text

21 Elisha's first miracle in this Haftarah involves feeding hungry people.

◆ Follow in Elisha's footsteps and volunteer as a class at a soup kitchen or food pantry.

22 Elisha is a role model for selflessness in the service of others.

◆ Think of several real-life situations in which you may be confronted with the choice between your own interests and those of others. Role-play each of the situations twice: once with a selfish outcome and once with concern for others. Discuss the outcomes and how you might have done it the same or differently. Consider these possible topics: personal glory versus team success in sports, telling the principal about a bully in order to save potential victims when doing so puts you at great personal risk, donating a percentage of your Bar/Bat Mitzvah gifts to worthy causes versus keeping it all for yourself because you worked hard and deserve it.

23 Bread is an essential food in the Bible and still today.

◆ Learn how to bake bread.

24 Today many people believe that the mineral-rich waters of the Dead Sea and its surrounding mud have healing properties.

◆ Buy some Dead Sea bath salts and enjoy a mineral bath at home, or do a Dead Sea mud facial masque. (Be sure to check with your parents or doctor before using these products.)

25 Naaman gets good advice from an unlikely source.

◆ Interview your family and friends and ask each person to describe the best advice they ever received. Also ask if they ever received advice from an unlikely person, and what that advice was.

26 Naaman takes the soil of Israel home with him.

◆ Why do people collect souvenirs? Do you collect souvenirs when you travel?

◆ Bring to class a souvenir from your favorite place to share as show-and-tell with the class.

27 Naaman thanks Elisha profusely for healing him, but we never hear again from the Israelite king.

◆ Write a thank-you note from Naaman to Elisha for healing him and thereby saving Israel from conflict with Aram.

◆ Why might Naaman be sincerely grateful to Elisha?

◆ Do you think Elisha's miracle would cause Naaman to stop worshiping idols? Why or why not?

◆ Do you think Naaman would be embarrassed by his prior lack of faith?

Other Resources

28 For a story on a young, selfish princess who learns to open her heart to others, read and discuss "The Princess Who Wanted to See God" in *Who Knows Ten? Children's Tales of the Ten Commandments* by Molly Cone, p. 14-20.

29 For a story about two unselfish men who unwittingly help each other, read and discuss "Challahs in the Ark," as told by Syd Lieberman in *Because God Loves Stories*, edited by Steve Zeitlin, pp. 30-32.

30 For a display of selfish behavior that takes advantage of other people, view and discuss the film *Back To the Future II* (1989, rated PG, 108 minutes).

31 For information on prophecy in general, and on Elisha in particular, read *Messengers of God: A Jewish Prophets Who's Who* by Ronald H. Isaacs.

32 Discuss the illustration of this Haftarah in *The Illustrated Torah* by Michal Meron, p. 119. Who are the people depicted in this illustration? How does verse 5:3 compare with verses 5:10-11?

Involving the Family

33 Naaman took soil as a token of his experience in Israel. Begin a family collection of objects representing places you visit together. Consider collecting rocks, leaves from trees (which you can press in waxed paper), matchbooks, or brochures. Carefully label your items and display your collection on a shelf or in a scrapbook.

Bar/Bat Mitzvah Project

34 AIDS has been compared with the disease of leprosy, in that the victims of both diseases have been ostracized and feared by their communities. There are dozens of organizations dedicated to helping children and families with AIDS. Check with your local hospital or search online (under AIDS and children) to find organizations in your area that support children with AIDS. Find a way to get involved by raising money, visiting patients, or raising community awareness. Or, you can learn to knit or crochet and create lap blankets for AIDS patients.

II KINGS 7:3-20
METZORA מצורע

This Haftarah has been paired with *Parashat Metzora*, Leviticus 14:1-15:33. See "Connecting the Text To the Sedra," pp. 202-203, for an exploration of the many ways the two texts shed light on each other.

SYNOPSIS

Four leprous Israelite men are talking outside the gate of the Israelite city of Samaria in the beginning of this Haftarah. They agree that if they go inside the town, they will die of starvation because of the famine there. Yet they will also die if they remain outside. They decide instead to go to the Aramean camp and put their lives in the hands of the Arameans, who are the enemies of Israel.

When they arrive at the Aramean camp, they find it utterly deserted. It seems that God had caused the Arameans to hear a sound of chariots, horses, and an approaching army. The Arameans figured that the Israelites must have joined forces with the Hittites and Egyptians to attack them, and they fled for safety without taking any of their animals or belongings.

The leprous men go into a deserted Aramean tent, where they eat and drink. They carry away silver and gold and clothing, which they bury. Then they return and ransack a second tent, after which they begin to feel guilty. They go to report the news of the deserted Aramean camp to the Israelite king. When the king hears the report, he suspects the Arameans are simply hiding and waiting to ambush the Israelites. One of the king's advisers suggests that they send some teams to investigate.

When it is determined that the Arameans are truly gone, the Israelites plunder the Aramean camp, bringing to fruition God's prophecy that they would soon find flour and barley to eat.

However, the joyous event is marred by tragedy when, as Elisha the prophet had predicted, the king's aide is trampled to death by the stampeding Israelites. Just the day before the food was found in the Aramean camp, Elisha had told the king and his aide that the next day barley and flour would be sold at the gate of Samaria. When the aide doubts the prophecy, Elisha responds that he would see it with his eyes, but he would never eat it.

Note: *Metzora* is often read as a double portion with *Tazria*, which precedes it. The two Haftarot contain similar material. See *Tazria* for more Insights and Strategies that apply to *Metzora*.

INSIGHTS FROM THE TRADITION

A God causes the Arameans to hear imaginary sounds of chariots and a great army (verse 7:6). According to Malbim, this involved two miracles. Not only did God cause the enemy to hear imaginary sounds, but God also caused them to imagine that the sounds were those of attacking armies.

◆ Does your imagination ever leap to conclusions based on something you think you see or hear? Why do you think this happens?

B The four men feed themselves and loot the Aramean camp before it occurs to them to report the good news to the Israelites, who are dying from starvation in Samaria. *Metsudat David* argues that the men are motivated to report the good news primarily by fear of punishment if they do not.

◆ Does it matter whether a good act is motivated by a good or bad reason?

◆ If a wealthy person or corporation makes a huge charitable contribution in order to get a good tax deduction or to gain fame with the family name emblazoned on a building, does that somehow affect the quality of the contribution?

STRATEGIES
Analyzing the Text

1 The Arameans flee their camp, leaving behind their horses, donkeys, and all their possessions (verse 7:7).

According to Malbim, they purposely left their horses and donkeys to provide a distraction that might cause the attackers not to pursue them.

◆ Why do *you* think they left all their animals and belongings?

◆ If the animals are used as vehicles of transportation, describe the state of mind of the Arameans when they left.

2 The famine and consequent inflation in the prices of any available food, which are referred to in the Haftarah, are a result of a siege on Samaria mounted by the Arameans (II Kings 6:24).

The four leprous men are driven by desperation to take their chances by visiting the Aramean camp.

◆ Explain why lepers, outcasts from society, have little to lose in taking a risk and going to the Arameans.

◆ Do you think the king needs to act more cautiously? Why or why not?

3 King Jehoram questions the report of the four men and sends investigators to find out whether or not it was safe to invade the Aramean camp.

However, the report could not have come as a surprise to the king. On the day before the events in the Haftarah take place, Elisha tells King Jehoram in II Kings 7:1, "This time tomorrow, a [measure] of choice flour shall sell for a shekel at the gate of Samaria, and two [measures] of barley for a shekel." In other words, there will soon be enough flour and barley to drive down the prices of these products.

◆ Based on the fact that the king sent messengers, do you think he believed Elisha's prophecy? If not, why not? If not, what does King Jehoram's lack of faith in Elisha's prophecy tell us about him as a king, a person, and an Israelite? If so, why did he investigate the report?

4 In verse 7:19 the aide says that even if *Adonai* made "windows in the sky," there would not be enough food for the prices to drop and the food to become affordable.

◆ What does the phrase "windows in the sky" mean?

◆ Does the aide's statement seem sarcastic to you? Why or why not?

◆ Some English Bibles translate this phrase as "floodgates in the sky." Does this translation change your understanding of the aide's statement?

◆ This same word, "floodgates" or "windows," appears in Genesis 7:11 when God opens the floodgates of the sky and causes the flood to begin in the time of Noah. Draw a depiction of the open windows or floodgates in the sky as you imagine them in this story or in the story of Noah.

5 The starving Israelites stampeded to the gate to get food, trampling to death the king's aide.

◆ How might the king have planned better to avoid this kind of tragedy?

◆ How does the death of the doubting aide defend the prophet's honor?

◆ Imagine you are a television news reporter. Describe the event in as much detail as you can imagine.

Connecting the Text To the Sedra

6 The Haftarah begins with verse 7:3 because the story of the four leprous men establishes a connection with *Parashat Metzora*, which deals with the ritual purification of someone whose *tzara'at* has healed. (A *metzora* is someone who suffers from the disease.)

However, the first two verses of chapter 7 contain important information regarding Elisha's prophecy to King Jehoram.

◆ Do you think the exclusion of the first two verses strengthens or weakens the story in the Haftarah? Explain your answer.

◆ Do you think this omission was necessary in order to make a clear connection between the Sedra and Haftarah?

7 The four men stricken with *tzara'at* are quarantined outside the city gates, according to the law recorded in Leviticus 13:46: "Being unclean, he shall dwell apart; his dwelling shall be outside the camp."

◆ People with leprosy may have been quarantined for a number of reasons, including medical, social, or a combination of these. Do you think any of these reasons are legitimate? As you ponder this question, consider that the Tent of Meeting, or God's dwelling place, was also set outside the camp or city (Exodus 33:7).

◆ It is possible that sick people were intentionally placed nearer to God's dwelling place. Discuss these possible reasons why:

   a. The community couldn't help them, but hoped that perhaps God could.

   b. God's power was just as scary as some illnesses were, and was thus placed outside the camp.

◆ Can you suggest any other reasons?

8 Leviticus 13:46, our source in Connecting the Text To the Sedra #7, p. 202, is found not in *Parashat Metzora*, but in its sister portion, *Tazria*. In most years, *Tazria* and *Metzora* are read together as a double portion. Certain portions are doubled in order to fit all of them into a liturgical year. The Jewish calendar is based on a lunar cycle of 354 days, or 50 weeks in a year. Since there are 54 weekly Torah readings, plus special readings for major holidays that fall on Shabbat, it is necessary to double some weekly portions so that the whole cycle of Torah readings is completed in a year. In a leap year, when an extra month (Adar II) is added to the Jewish calendar, there are four more Shabbatot. In such years, *Tazria* and *Metzora* are read as separate portions, each with its own Haftarah.

◆ Is this a leap year?

◆ Are *Tazria* and *Metzora* read together or separately this year?

◆ What other portions are combined this year?

9 The Rabbis connected the Hebrew expression for slander or gossip (*motzi shaym ra*) with the word leper (*metzora*). Just as leprosy is a horrific physical disease, the Rabbis believed gossip to be a dangerous social ill.

◆ How do you think the Rabbis would have felt about newspaper gossip columnists, gossip magazines, and television shows, and about our society that hungrily devours gossip about celebrities and other public figures? How do *you* feel about them?

10 *Numbers Rabbah* 7:5 identifies 13 sins which are punishable by *tzara'at*: blasphemy, immodesty, murder, falsely suspecting someone, pride, theft, slander, perjury, stealing someone's rights, idolatry, making God's name look bad, envy, and contempt for Torah.

◆ Arrange these sins in the order of severity. Do you think *tzara'at* is a fitting punishment for any of these crimes? Do you believe that disease is ever contracted as a punishment for sin?

◆ What are the moral difficulties involved with viewing illness as punishment?

11 The Rabbis taught that leprosy (*tzara'at*) was considered to be punishment for, among other things, selfish behavior.

◆ How do the actions of the four men in verses 7:8-9 demonstrate their selfishness?

◆ Can you argue instead that their actions demonstrated their *lack* of selfishness?

◆ Do you see in these same verses a transformation in the characters of the men?

12 In the Sedra we are taught that if someone suspects his or her house is infected with leprosy, the owner of the house should go to the priest and suggest that he/she thinks there *might* be something like leprosy in the house. The priest must then inspect the house to confirm the report, and only after the inspection can the house be declared unclean. The lesson we draw from this is that it is best not to jump to conclusions or to make assumptions, but rather to discover carefully the truth for ourselves.

The same lesson is taught in the Haftarah, when the king's aide scoffs at Elisha's prediction, jumping to the conclusion that it is impossible that they will have enough food to feed the people by tomorrow. Sure enough, the prophecy comes true and the aide is punished for jumping to the wrong conclusion.

◆ Have you ever gotten into trouble by jumping to conclusions or making the wrong assumption?

◆ What steps might we take to avoid making assumptions in the future?

Extending the Text

13 We learn in II Kings just how devastating the famine in Samaria referred to in the Haftarah was. II Kings 6:25-30 recounts a gruesome story of parents eating their own children.

◆ Throughout the world today, famine continues to be a serious and dangerous problem. Use the Internet to collect a list of all the places in the world where there are currently famines caused by nature, politics, and/or economics. Also collect a list of charitable organizations that try to fight famine, hunger, and malnutrition throughout the world.

◆ As a class, prepare a newsletter or brochure on these famine-stricken places. Include a list of charities and their addresses to which people can contribute toward famine relief. Send the newsletter or brochure to all the families in your community.

14 The miracle performed by God, which caused the Arameans to flee for fear of being attacked by the Israelites, recalls the miracle of the story of Joshua and the Battle of Jericho.

◆ Read the Book of Joshua, chapter 6, to discover for yourself the similarity between the two stories. How are they the same, and how are they different?

15 Read the famous cases of *tzara'at* in the Bible. Moses (Exodus 4:1-9), Moses' sister Miriam (Numbers 12:1-16), Naaman and Gehazi (II Kings 5), and King Uzziah (II Chronicles 26) were all stricken with this disease.

◆ Why did each get *tzara'at*?

◆ Were they cured? If so, how?

◆ Discuss how these stories formed the Rabbis' opinion that *tzara'at* was not simply a medical problem, but a punishment from God.

◆ For additional information, see *Teaching Torah* by Sorel Golberg Loeb and Barbara Binder Kadden, p. 185.

16 The four men reported the good news about the deserted Aramean camp to the Israelite officials.

◆ There is a blessing we say upon hearing unusually good news: "Blessed are You, *Adonai* our God, Sovereign of the universe, Who is good and Who does good." Why do you think we recite a blessing when we hear good news?

◆ There is also a blessing we say upon hearing unusually bad news: "Blessed are You, *Adonai* our God, Sovereign of the universe, Judge of truth." Why do you think we recite a blessing when we hear bad news?

◆ Compare the two traditional blessings. Memorize them for future use.

◆ Write your own blessings for hearing good news and for hearing bad news.

17 Today we are reluctant to believe that God uses illness to punish us. Opinions vary greatly on the question of God's role in sickness and in healing.

◆ Organize a panel discussion on this issue. Invite Rabbis from different movements, as well as a Jewish physician. Ask them specific questions (prepared and reviewed ahead of time) on the roles of God and Judaism in sickness and healing.

18 Jewish tradition has always been and continues to be strongly opposed to gossip (see Connecting the Text To the Sedra #9, pp. 202-203).

◆ Read and discuss the following ancient sources:

• "You shall not utter a false report . . . [or] go about as a talebearer among your people." (Leviticus 19:16)

• "Life and death are in the power of the tongue." (Proverbs 18:21)

• "Gossip kills three people at once: the speaker, the listener, and the one about whom they speak." (*Numbers Rabbah* 19:2)

◆ In what ways do you think gossip has the power to "kill"?

◆ Is only false gossip dangerous, or do you think true gossip can be harmful as well?

◆ You can probably imagine how you might stop gossiping if you tried. In many ways, it is more difficult to stop listening to gossip. Brainstorm ways you can stop participating in gossip by refusing to listen.

19 Rabbi Levi Yitzhak of Berditchev told a story of an unkind woman who was accused of starting a rumor. When she was brought before the village Rabbi, she protested that she had only spoken in jest. Besides, she said, her words were spread mostly by others.

The person whose name the woman had ruined with gossip demanded justice. The gossiping woman responded that she would just take back her words, and the whole thing would be over.

The Rabbi observed that the gossiping woman did not understand the severity of her actions. He told her that her words could not be excused until she brought a feather pillow to the market square, cut it, and let the feathers fly through the air. Her gossip would be forgiven when she had collected every last feather. The woman did what he said. However, try as she might, she could not possibly catch every single flying feather.

When she returned to the Rabbi with very few feathers in her hand, she realized that just as the feathers scattered everywhere and could not be retrieved, so, too, was the case with her slanderous words.

◆ How are words like feathers?

◆ What is the lesson of this story?

◆ Flying feathers are a wonderful analogy for rumors. Draw or paint a picture illustrating the story, or think of another analogy (such as flying feathers) and represent it visually in a drawing or painting.

◆ Learn and sing the song "Feathers," based on the tale by Rabbi Lev Yitzhak of Berditchev. It is written by Heather Forest and found in *Chosen Tales*, edited by Peninnah Schram, pp. 95-96.

Personalizing the Text

20 The Arameans let their imaginations get the best of them.

◆ What do you do to quiet your imagination and calm the fears your imagination might cause?

◆ Interview relatives and friends to find out about times when imagination got the best of them and what each does to calm his/her fears.

21 Our tradition advises us strongly against the dangers of gossip.

◆ In your view, would the Rabbis agree that "sticks and stones can break my bones, but words will never hurt me"?

◆ Write a Public Service Announcement (PSA) warning people about the perils of engaging in gossip and slander. For ideas, you may want to read Psalm 12 and Jeremiah 9:1-10. Videotape the class members delivering their PSAs for future viewing.

22 Perhaps the king didn't believe the men because of their leprous appearance.

◆ Do you think that physical appearances affect the way we judge others?

◆ Keep a log of your own reactions to people, based on their appearance. How often are your first impressions accurate?

23 The king's aide was told (before the Haftarah) that he would live to see, but not to eat, the food that would soon be found in abundance.

◆ What precautions might you have taken if you were the aide so as to avert this decree?

◆ Do you believe that each of us has a destiny that cannot be avoided?

◆ Do you believe in free choice?

◆ Can one believe in both destiny and free will at the same time?

Other Resources

24 The leprous men are driven by desperation to visit the enemy camp.

◆ Do you think "desperate times deserve desperate measures"? Give examples.

◆ If you were diagnosed with a terminal disease, would you volunteer for experimental treatment if the risks and results were not yet known? Why or why not?

25 For other insights and activities on gossip, see *Teaching Torah* by Sorel Goldberg Loeb and Barbara Binder Kadden, pp.186-187, or *Teaching Mitzvot* by Barbara Binder Kadden and Bruce Kadden, pp. 83-86.

◆ Complete the Torah Aura Instant Lesson on gossip, *Wounding with Words* by Rabbi Steven Bayar.

◆ The four men who find the deserted Aramean camp do a *mitzvah* by informing the Israelites, albeit somewhat reluctantly. Read and discuss the story "The Car that Ran from Mitzvahs" by Hanna Bandes in *Chosen Tales*, edited by Peninnah Schram, pp. 11-19. This is the story of a woman who encounters all kinds of troubles when she does *mitzvot* reluctantly, but whose life is transformed when she learns to do her good deeds with a full heart.

26 The magical stories of Elijah and Elisha fit into a genre of literature that praises righteous people *(tzaddikim)* and the miracles they do. Traditional Hasidic tales share much in common with the miracle stories of Elijah and Elisha. Read selections from *Tales of the Hasidim* by Martin Buber.

27 *Elephant Man* (1980, rated PG, 124 minutes) and *Edward Scissorhands* (1990, rated PG-13, 100 minutes) are films that deal with the way we treat people who are disfigured in some way. View and discuss one or both of these films.

28 For information on Jewish prophecy in general, and on Elisha in particular, read *Messengers of God: A Jewish Prophets Who's Who* by Ronald H. Isaacs.

29 Discuss the illustration of this Haftarah in *The Illustrated Torah* by Michal Meron, p. 122.

Involving the Family

30 Try this little trick to encourage your family members to limit their gossiping: As a family, decide on a special word or symbol, like "oops" or pulling on your ear. When any family member hears another engaging in gossip, he/she can use the special signal subtly to alert the gossiper, without embarrassing him or her. Upon hearing or seeing the signal, the gossiper can quickly change the subject and resist the temptation to engage in gossip. Remember, it is a *mitzvah* not to embarrass someone, so try to be discrete and polite.

Bar/Bat Mitzvah Project

31 The Haftarah takes place during a time of famine. Fight hunger in our time. Donate a percentage of your Bar/Bat Mitzvah gifts to Mazon: A Jewish Response To Hunger. You can contact them at 12401 Wilshire Boulevard, Suite 303, Los Angeles, CA 90025-1015, or visit their web site at www.Mazon.org. To encourage others to do the same, display on your guests' tables a sign that informs them that you are donating to Mazon and thanking them for making this possible.

II KINGS 12:1–17 Ashkenazim
II KINGS 11:17-12:17 Sephardim
SHABBAT SH'KALIM שקלים

This Haftarah has been paired with *Shabbat Sh'kalim*, on which we read Exodus 30:11-16. See "Connecting the Text To the Special Shabbat," pp. 209-210, for an exploration of the many ways the two texts and the special Shabbat shed light on each other.

SYNOPSIS

Jehoash becomes King of Judah at the age of seven, in the seventh year of King Jehu's reign in Israel, and he reigns in Jerusalem for 40 years. Jehoash, whose mother is Zibiah of Beersheba, is a good king who follows the instructions of the priest Jehoiada. However, because he fails to demolish the shrines that had been outlawed since the building of the Holy Temple, the people continue to sacrifice and worship at those forbidden shrines.

Jehoash instructs the priests to collect all the money that comes into the Temple. The priests would then disburse the funds for both the maintenance of the Temple services and the repairs to the Temple structure. Yet by Jehoash's twenty-third year in power, the priests had not arranged any repairs. Jehoash decides that the priests shall no longer be responsible for the collection of the money or for the repairs to the Temple. Without protest, the priests consent to the new arrangement.

Subsequently, a new system of collection is instituted for the Temple repairs. Jehoiada the priest takes a chest, bores a hole in its lid, and sets it on the right side of the altar for the collection of funds. Whenever the box is full, the priests call the king's scribe and High Priest, who count the money and put it into bags. Once counted, the money is given to the workers who repair and maintain the Temple. So many repairs have to be made that there is no money left over for the creation of new vessels or ritual objects.

The priests continue to collect and use the money brought to the Temple as a guilt offering or sin offering.

INSIGHTS FROM THE TRADITION

A According to Abrabanel, the king's mother Zibia (verse 12:2) was pious and a good influence on Jehoash.

◆ List five ways in which your parents have been good influences on you.

◆ Is it a parent's responsibility to be a good role model for his/her children?

◆ For whom are you a role model? Describe the circumstances.

B According to Rashi, Jehoash was hidden for the first six years of his life after the assassination of his father Ahaziah by King Jehu of Israel. He was hidden in the Holy of Holies, even though it is forbidden for anyone, except the High Priest on Yom Kippur, to enter that most sacred of places.

◆ Imagine what it would be like to spend your first six years hidden in a small room, with only one or two (the commentators disagree on this point) adults nearby. What would you have missed the most?

◆ How do you think such circumstances would affect your development?

C According to *Daath Soferim*, the priests were pleased to be relieved by Jehoash of a duty they regarded as unpleasant (collecting money for the building repairs).

◆ What are some tasks you have to do, but consider unpleasant?

◆ How do you deal with a task you don't like to do? Do you put off doing it as long as possible? Do you do it immediately to get it out of the way?

D In verse 12:16 we are told that "no check was kept on the men to whom the money was delivered to pay the workers; for they dealt honestly." According to Radak, only men who could be trusted were hired for the job.

◆ How important is it for bosses to trust their workers?

◆ How do you know if someone is trustworthy?

◆ Design a questionnaire that can assess someone's trustworthiness.

E We are told that Jehoash was a good king who followed the instructions of the priest Jehoiada. According to Rashi, Jehoash acted properly until Jehoiada died. Then the people came to Jehoash and told him that if he managed to hide as a child in the Holy of Holies, which was otherwise off limits to people, he must be a god. According to Rashia, Jehoash believed the people and declared himself a god. (See also *Exodus Rabbah* 8:2.)

◆ How can excessive praise and flattery harm someone and lead them to trouble?

Recent research, cited in an article in *The New York Times* of October 18, 2000 (p. A18), warns parents not to over praise their children. The experts explain that too much praise might make children "praise junkies," who don't have a sense of their own worth separate from the approval of others. Other experts disagree, saying that children need praise to build their own sense of their abilities and encourage them to feel good about themselves.

◆ Debate this point: Too much praise harms children.

F According to Malbim, Jehoiada the priest made an error in the education of King Jehoash. He instructed Jehoash on issues that arose daily, but he did not teach him Torah so thoroughly that Jehoash would be able to think for himself and decide the right behavior. Without the priest's daily guidance, then, Jehoash was easily misled.

◆ Which of the following do you think are the goals of education: teaching facts and figures to be memorized, teaching students to think for themselves, teaching children to get along with others, instilling in children a love of learning? all of the above?

◆ Can you think of any other goals of education?

STRATEGIES
Analyzing the Text

1 The Sephardic version of the Haftarah includes the last four verses of chapter 11. These verses recount how the priest Jehoiada leads the people of Judah in a revolt against the wicked Athaliah, who for six years usurped power in Judah. Athaliah, the daughter of Ahab and Jezebel (see Haftarah for *Ki Tisa*, p. 164, and for

Pinchas, p. 173), was the mother of King Ahaziah and grandmother of Jehoash. When Ahaziah was assassinated by the Israelite King Jehu, Athaliah murdered all her grandchildren in order that she, the Queen Mother, might ascend the throne herself. Only Jehoash was hidden and saved from her wrath.

In the seventh year, as recorded in II Kings 11:17-20, Jehoiada installs Jehoash as the true King, and the people kill Athaliah.

◆ How does this historical background add to your understanding of the world of King Jehoash?

◆ Imagine you are a newspaper or television news reporter. Interview Jehoiada about the revolution against Athaliah and his hopes for the reign of King Jehoash.

2 You might notice the similarity among the names of Jehoash the king of Judah, Jehoiada the priest, Jehu, the king of Israel, and Jehoahaz, his son. The "Je" in all their English names is one of the names for God, *"Yah."*

Jehoash means "God is strong," Jehoiada means "God knows," Jehu means "God is He," and Jehoahaz means "God has grasped."

◆ What do the meanings of these names indicate about the characters who bear them?

◆ Look up your own English and Hebrew names in a name dictionary to discover what they mean. Does a name for God appear within your name? What does the meaning of your name say about you? It is true? Make a poster with your name at the top and the meaning of your name with illustrations below.

◆ Last names are often clues about what an ancestor of yours did for a living or where he/she lived. Talk to your parents and grandparents to discover what you can learn about your family history from your last name.

3 King Jehoash in verse 12:10 decides to place a box with a hole in it near the door of the Temple. Anyone could slip a half-shekel into the box, but no one could take the money out without completely opening the box.

◆ It is unclear why Jehoash decided to take the job of collection away from the priests. Reread verses 12:7-10 to see if you can determine Jehoash's motivation.

◆ Radak explains that the priests didn't commission any of the Temple repairs because they were waiting until sufficient funds had been collected. The king, however, suspected that the priests were pocketing the money instead of designating it for repairs. Based on the text, what do you think?

4 The system for collection and payment for repairs is outlined in verses 12:10-16.

◆ Review the system. Does the system ensure security? efficiency? work quality? As a class, design a system to collect and disburse funds for Temple repairs. Make a list of every job to be done, and assign one job to each student, including someone to be in charge. What changes, if any, would you make to Jehoash's plan? Would you make sure there was some money set aside for the purchase of new Temple implements?

Connecting the Text
To the Special Shabbat

5 There are four special Shabbatot in the weeks preceding Pesach, the first of which is called *Shabbat Sh'kalim*. These four Shabbatot are distinguished from others by special additional

(Maftir) readings from the Torah and related Haftarot.

In the special Maftir reading for *Shabbat Sh'kalim*, Exodus 30:11-16, God instructs Moses to collect a half-shekel from every adult male Israelite in order to take a census and for the maintenance of the Tabernacle. *Shabbat Sh'kalim* takes place on the Shabbat preceding the first of Adar, recalling the ancient custom of announcing on the first of Adar that the annual Temple dues were due by the first of Nisan. According to Mishnah *Shekalim* 1:1, the shekels collected during Adar were used to repair roads. It was important to repair the roads after the winter season and before the Passover Pilgrimage to Jerusalem.

◆ Why do you think this timing was crucial?

In verse 12:5 of this Haftarah, Jehoash instructs the priests to collect all the money coming into the Temple and use the money for repairs.

◆ Explain how collecting a half-shekel from each adult male was a way to take a census.

◆ Explain how in both Maftir reading and Haftarah, money is used to make repairs. Read the Mishnah to find out what other repairs were done to prepare for Passover.

◆ Deciding when to fix a road is sometimes a question of money, but not always. Research online the controversy over repairing Klingle Road in Washington, D.C. (see the web site www.repairklingleroad.org. Present a report on the financial and other issues involved in the repair of this road.

6 The Torah requires every male from the age of 20 to contribute the mandatory half-shekel (Exodus 30:14). According to some commentators, 20 is the Israelite military age.

◆ At what age do you think individuals should become obligated to pay congregational dues?

◆ Check with your congregation's office to find out the current policy on dues. Does it seem like a fair structure to you?

◆ At what age do you think individuals should be responsible for paying taxes to the government? Find out from your parents if *you* currently pay taxes.

7 According to Hertz, p. 993, "Although the Temple is no more, this special Sabbath continues to stress the thought that each member of the community is under the obligation to give his measure of support to the . . . perpetuation of [our] Religion."

◆ In what ways are you contributing to the perpetuation of Judaism?

◆ Does your responsibility for the perpetuation of Judaism change once you have become a Bar/Bat Mitzvah?

◆ Write a Bar/Bat Mitzvah speech outlining ways in which all members (religious and secular, rich and poor, etc.) of the Jewish community can contribute to the perpetuation of our religion. Include an explanation as to why you think Judaism is worth perpetuating.

Extending the Text

8 Jehoash spent his early childhood hidden away from the world. Many children, including Anne Frank, spent years hiding from the Nazis during the Holocaust.

◆ Read an account of life in hiding and report on it to your class. Recommended sources: *The Diary of Anne Frank* by Anne Frank, *Anna Is Still Here* by Ida Vos, *Hide and Seek* by Ida Vos, and *Jacob's Rescue: A Holocaust Story* by Malka Drucker. *The Diary of Anne Frank* is also available on video (1959, not rated, 150 minutes).

9 Jehoash becomes King of Judah in approximately 837 B.C.E. Saul became the first king of Israel around 1010 B.C.E., followed by David in 1000 B.C.E., and Solomon in 961 B.C.E. The kingdom divided under the leadership of Solomon's son Rehoboam in Judah and King Jeroboam in Israel in 922 B.C.E.

◆ Draw a time line to hang in your classroom, covering the years from Saul through Jehoash's successor. Include the reigns of Judah's kings and Israel's kings (listed below), as well as the prominent prophets Elijah and Elisha.

Judah's Kings:
Abijah – 915 B.C.E.
Asa – 913 B.C.E.
Jehoshaphat – 873 B.C.E.
Jehoram – 849 B.C.E.
Ahaziah – 843 B.C.E.
Athaliah – 842 B.C.E.
Jehoash – 837 B.C.E.
Amaziah – 800 B.C.E.

Israel's Kings:
Nadab – 901 B.C.E.
Baasha – 900 B.C.E.
Elah – 877 B.C.E.
Zimri – 876 B.C.E.
Omri – 876 B.C.E.
Ahab – 869 B.C.E.
Ahazia – 850 B.C.E.
Jehoram – 849 B.C.E.
Jehu – 843 B.C.E.
Jehoahaz – 815 B.C.E.
Jehoash – 802 B.C.E.

(Source: *A History of Israel* by John Bright, Chronological Chart V.)

◆ For advanced study, you can continue the time line through the end of the kingdom of Judah.

10 All Israelites, even outside the Land of Israel, sent a half-shekel to support the Temple.

The modern Zionist movement asked all Jews around the world to pay an annual membership fee to support their cause. For many years, world Jewry complied (from *The Haftarah Commentary* by W. Gunther Plaut, p. 544).

◆ Do you think that mandatory donations from Jews around the world to support Israel is a reasonable idea?

◆ Do you think Israel wants and/or needs our donations?

◆ How would you go about collecting such donations?

◆ Write a letter appealing to all Jews to contribute financially to Israel. Explain why you think they should do so.

11 In Rambam's ladder of *tzedakah*, one rung is most closely related to mandatory giving.

◆ Which rung is it? A listing of the rungs follows:

1. Help someone find employment in order that they will no longer need aid.
2. Give anonymously to an unknown recipient.
3. Give anonymously to a known recipient.
4. Give when your identity is known, but the recipient's is not.
5. Give personally to someone before they ask.
6. Give personally to someone after they ask.
7. Give less than you should, but cheerfully.

8. Give begrudgingly.

◆ Do you agree with Rambam's ranking?

◆ Does *tzedakah* still count as *tzedakah*, even when it is not given voluntarily?

12 Most synagogues have a "Building Fund," which is not necessarily used for building, but rather to repair and maintain the current building.

◆ Find out what your congregation's building fund obligation is.

◆ Interview your congregation's treasurer to find out how much money is needed annually to maintain the physical building and grounds. Were you surprised by the amount?

13 The final verse of the Haftarah (verse 12:17) relates that the money brought as a guilt offering or sin offering was used by the priests and not the Temple building fund.

According to Leviticus 4-5, different groups of people were required to bring different kinds of sin offerings. The High Priest, for example, was to offer a young bull for his sins, while extremely poor individuals were required to offer flour. By laying his hands on his offering, the sinner symbolically identified himself with his sacrifice.

A guilt offering, according to Leviticus 5:7, was a special kind of sin offering required when someone had been denied his due. Crimes that required guilt offerings included cheating, robbery, oppression, and failing to testify (Leviticus 5). In these cases, the sinner was required to confess the sin, make full restitution plus a fine of 20 percent, and offer the guilt sacrifice.

◆ For discussion and activities relating to these sacrifices, see *Teaching Torah* by Sorel Goldberg Loeb and Barbara Binder Kadden, pp. 165-171.

◆ What do you do to atone for your sins?

Personalizing the Text

14 King Jehoash found the Temple in a state of disrepair.

◆ Are there any old synagogues near where you live? Find out if they need repairs or cleaning, and volunteer as a class to help care for them.

15 While the Temple stood in Jerusalem, it was forbidden to offer sacrifices anywhere else. Today we may worship at any synagogue, or anywhere for that matter.

◆ Do you think it is better to have a mandatory worship center or many places to pray?

◆ How does having many places to pray make Judaism more accessible to those of us who don't live in or near Jerusalem?

◆ Where is your favorite place to pray, and why?

16 The Temple is gone, and we can no longer bring sin or guilt offerings.

◆ Without the Temple, how do we now atone for our sins?

Rabbi Eleazar in *Sukkah* 49b taught, "greater is he who performs charity than he who offers all the sacrifices, for it says: 'To do charity and justice is more acceptable to *Adonai* than sacrifice.'" (Proverbs 21:3)

Avot de Rabbi Natan 4:5 also teaches, "It happened once that Rabbi Johanan ben Zakkai was coming out of Jerusalem along with Rabbi Joshua, and he saw the Temple in ruins. Rabbi Joshua cried, 'Woe to us for this house that lies in ruins is the place where atonement was made for the sins of Israel.' Johanan said, 'Do not be grieved. We have another means of atonement, which is as effective, and that means is the practice of loving-kindness.'"

◆ How do acts of loving-kindness *(gemilut chasadim)* and charity *(tzedakah)* help us atone for our sins?

◆ Make your own *tzedakah* box out of clay, by decoupaging a glass container, or by decorating a coffee can. Use it often!

17 There are various kinds of sin offerings specified in Leviticus (see information in Extending the Text #13, p. 212).

◆ Make your own sin offerings for a month. Each time you do something you wish you hadn't, put money into your *tzedakah* box. At the end of the month, donate the money to your favorite cause.

◆ In what ways are these contributions both mandatory and voluntary?

18 Jehoash has to devise a safe system for the collection and disbursement of funds for the Temple. Many charitable organizations today are under scrutiny for their allocation of donated funds, especially with regard to how much money goes into running the charity itself. People object when a charity spends too much money on administrative costs and too little on actually donating to its cause.

◆ Each student should choose his/her favorite charitable organization and research the organization's asset allocations. Students present their findings to the class. They then rank the charities according to how much money collected is allocated solely for running the organization itself. To do your research, you can contact charities directly or visit a charity web site, such as www.Shine.com, which provides information on many charitable organizations.

19 According to Analyzing the Text #3, p. 209, Jehoash had some reason to question the honesty of the priests who were collecting the donations.

◆ Read and discuss the following two stories about trust:

a. Once there was a couple that wanted to save enough money to have *latkes* at Chanukah. They agreed that each of them would put a coin in their locked box everyday. When Chanukah arrived, and they opened it, they found nothing in the box, because each of them had thought there would be enough money if only the other had put money in.

b. A king was to be installed with a grand party. All the townspeople were to pour one gallon of wine into a locked barrel as a gift to their new king. Instead, each person poured in water, thinking that no one would be able to tell if one gallon of water had been mixed into all that wine. When they opened the barrel on the day of the installation, all they found was water.

◆ Form two groups and prepare puppet shows on both these stories to present to the younger students in your school. After the presentations, hold a discussion on the importance of trust.

20 For many families, *Shabbat Sh'kalim*, the first of four special Shabbatot preceding Pesach (see Connecting the Text To the Special Shabbat #5, pp. 209-210) signals that it is time to start preparing for that holiday.

◆ Work with your Rabbi to design a pamphlet outlining and describing all the preparations to be made for Passover. Include a time line to help people prioritize and organize their preparations. Send the pamphlets out to your community in a congregational mailing around the time of Shabbat Sh'kalim.

Other Resources

21 View and discuss the film *Au Revoir Les Enfants* (1987, rated PG, 104 minutes), which tells the true story of a Jewish boy hidden at a school for boys during the Holocaust. The film is in French with English subtitles.

22 Live the message of Shabbat Sh'kalim, as outlined in Connecting the Text To the Special Shabbat #7, p. 210. For ideas on how you can play a part in perpetuating Judaism, read and discuss the ideas outlined in *40 Things You Can Do to Save the Jewish People* by Joel Lurie Grishaver.

23 For information on preparing for Pesach, see *The Jewish Holidays* by Michael Strassfeld, pp. 5-19 and pp. 206-213.

24 For more insights and activities on *tzedakah*, see *Teaching Mitzvot* by Barbara Binder Kadden and Bruce Kadden, pp. 91-94.

25 Discuss the portrayal of this Haftarah in *The Illustrated Torah* by Michal Meron, p. 227.

26 For more information on the special Torah readings and Haftarot before Passover, see *A Guide To Jewish Religious Practice* by Isaac Klein, p. 106.

Involving the Family

27 Preparing for Pesach can be an overwhelming task. To relieve some of the last minute pressure, make a list of everything that must be done. Prioritize the items and decide which items can be done in each of the four weeks preceding the holiday. Once your preparation list is in order, you can assign tasks and prepare cooperatively.

Bar/Bat Mitzvah Projects

28 Organize a collection of Kosher for Passover food items that can be packaged and delivered to the needy and elderly members of your congregation. Alternatively, organize your fellow students to help elderly congregants prepare their kitchens for the holiday.

29 Run for the office of class treasurer, to learn about and become involved with the ways in which money is raised and spent at your school. Encourage some charitable giving to causes important to your classmates.

II KINGS 23:1–9; 21-25
SECOND DAY PASSOVER

 This Haftarah has been paired with the second day of Passover, on which we read Leviticus 22:26-23:44. See "Connecting the Text To the Holiday," p. 217, for an exploration of the many ways the two texts and the holiday shed light on each other.

SYNOPSIS

After decades of religious neglect and wayward practices among the Israelites, King Josiah of Judah holds a great convocation at the Holy Temple in Jerusalem. Joining him are elders and citizens of Judah and Jerusalem, the priests, and the prophets. At the Temple, Josiah reads aloud all the words of the Torah. He then makes a covenant between God and the people, promising to walk in God's ways and to keep God's commandments and laws with all their heart and soul. The people accept the covenant.

In a sweeping reform of the corrupt worshiping practices in Judah, Josiah orders Hilkiah the High Priest, along with the priests and the guards, to bring out of the Temple all the objects made for *Baal* and *Asherah* and other foreign gods. Josiah burns the forbidden objects outside Jerusalem in the fields of Kidron. He suppresses the idolatrous priests throughout Judah and tears down all the places in the Temple that had been used for idolatrous purposes. He furthermore defiles the shrines at which priests had been making offerings throughout Judah because it was forbidden to offer sacrifices anywhere other than at the Holy Temple in Jerusalem. The priests who officiated at these shrines are not permitted to ascend the altar in Jerusalem, but they are entitled to continue to eat the unleavened bread reserved for priests.

At the end of the Haftarah, King Josiah commands all the people to observe the Passover unto *Adonai*, as it is written in the Torah. The Passover sacrifice had not been offered properly since the days of the Judges, even before the time of King Saul. Thus, the Passover celebrated in the eighteenth year of the reign of King Josiah marks the first time in hundreds of years that the Israelites celebrate the holiday.

Fulfilling additional terms of the covenant in the Torah, Josiah bans all necromancers and mediums, idols and fetishes. There was no king before or after Josiah who turned back to the ways of God with all his heart and soul.

INSIGHTS FROM THE TRADITION

A In verse 23:5 King Josiah abolishes pagan priests. According to Radak, these priests wore black in contrast to the priests of the Temple, who wore white.

◆ Watch the film *Star Wars* (1977, rated PG, 121 minutes), in which the good guy is always dressed in white and the bad guy in black. It is easy to tell the bad guys from the good guys in films, but how do you do it in real life? For what clues do you usually look?

B According to Malbim, the king had only to destroy the utensils and tools used by the pagan priests, and then they would stop engaging in idolatry (verse 23:5).

◆ Explain Malbim's idea that if you take away the utensils used in idolatry, the pagan priests, who could no longer practise idolatry, would leave.

◆ Debate: You can eliminate drug abuse by taking away the paraphernalia of drug users.

◆ Debate: You can eliminate violent crimes by taking guns away from would-be criminals.

◆ Debate: You can eliminate terrorism by taking away funds and safe havens from would-be terrorists.

C In verse 23:6 the *Asherah* and other symbols of idolatry were taken, burned, and pulverized. The ashes were then thrown on the graves of those people who had participated in this idolatry during their lives.

According to Radak, the ashes were put on their graves to degrade the deceased.

This practice would have been in sharp contrast to Jewish custom. When we visit Jewish cemeteries, we leave little stones on the grave to show that people have visited and to honor the dead.

◆ How did the ashes degrade the dead?

◆ How do little stones left at a graveside show honor to the dead?

STRATEGIES
Analyzing the Text

1 In the chapter immediately before this Haftarah, King Josiah arranges to have the Temple repaired. The workmen find in the walls a hidden scroll, which is brought to the King and read to him. It contains laws that the King and the people were not following. The King sets out to atone immediately by implementing religious reforms based on the laws of the book.

The book found by Josiah is thought to have been the Book of Deuteronomy for the following reasons:

a. Deuteronomy requires centralized worship in Jerusalem, and Josiah immediately set about destroying local shrines and requiring centralized worship in Jerusalem.

b. Josiah was fearful when the book was read, as Deuteronomy contains lengthy curses for those who do not comply.

c. Deuteronomy seems to have been written in the seventh century B.C.E., Josiah's era.

◆ Compare the version of the story here in II Kings 23 with the version contained in II Chronicles 34.

◆ Which version seems to you to be more authentic, and why?

2 The *Asherah* was a pole or tree used as part of idol worship of *Baal*. To destroy the *Asherah*, Josiah burned it, ground it down, and scattered the dust.

◆ Compare the treatment of the *Asherah* to the treatment of the golden calf in Exodus 32:20 or Deuteronomy 9:21.

3 In verse 23:2 King Josiah read the book to all the people, who accepted the covenant with God contained within the book.

◆ Why is Passover (spring) a fitting time for a new covenant with God? (It marks the beginning of the nation; it marks the new year for kings; it marks Israel's emergence as a nation serving God.)

4 King Josiah followed *Adonai* with all his heart and all his soul and all his might (see verse 23:25). This parallels the language of Deuteronomy 6:5 (recited in the *"Shema"*).

The expression "with all his heart and all his soul" is traditionally understood to mean "with all his intelligence and emotions." The expression "with all his might" is understood to be mean "very much" or "with his wealth." King Josiah truly followed God with all his heart and soul and might.

◆ What might it mean to follow God with one's wealth? Which translation of "with all his might" — "very much" or "with all his wealth" — do you prefer?

◆ Draw King Josiah following God with all his heart and soul.

Connecting the Text To the Holiday

5 Josiah commanded the people to observe Passover based on the scroll found (verses 23:21-23).

Interestingly, the scroll required that everyone bring a paschal sacrifice to Jerusalem (Deuteronomy 16). Therefore, everyone in the kingdom would have had to make the pilgrimage to Jerusalem.

◆ How does this compare to the way Passover was supposed to be observed in every individual home according to Exodus 12:21-27?

◆ Does it seem feasible that all Israelites could have brought a paschal lamb for sacrifice and sacrificed it in the one Temple on the afternoon before Passover?

◆ Imagine what it would be like today if every Jew in the world spent Passover in Jerusalem.

6 The ashes of the burned *Asherah* were scattered outside Jerusalem (see verse 23:6). That way, according to Hertz, Jerusalem would be clean not only of idolatry, but also of the pollution from the ashes of idolatry.

Before Passover, we want to clean our houses of *chametz*. We not only collect the last bits of *chametz* the night before Passover, but we also make a statement declaring *bittul* (null and void) any *chametz* that we might have inadvertently missed:

> "All leaven in my possession which I have not seen or removed or of which I am unaware is nullified and ownerless as the dust of the earth." *(Haggadah)*

The next day, we burn the *chametz* that we found and we again declare (with a slightly modified formula) any remaining *chametz* to be *bittul*.

◆ Why would it be so important to get rid of any trace of idolatry from Jerusalem? Why would it be so important to get rid of any trace of *chametz* on Passover?

7 The Passover Torah reading, Leviticus 23, discusses the festivals of Israel and their observance. It begins in verse 23:1 by saying that the message should be proclaimed to all Israel. Leviticus 23:44 reports that Moses proclaimed all of chapter 23 to the people.

Similarly, Josiah in the Haftarah makes a proclamation by reading the law to all the people and then commanding them to keep the holiday according to the law.

◆ Of what use is a public proclamation of the Law?

◆ What laws of contemporary Passover observance do you think should be proclaimed publicly before Passover in your synagogue?

◆ What impact do you think a public proclamation of Passover laws would have in your community? Explain your answer.

◆ How would you react to such a public proclamation?

OVERVIEW

"In all her history, Israel produced few figures of greater stature than Isaiah," wrote eminent historian John Bright in *A History of Israel* (p. 290).

Isaiah, the son of Amoz, prophesied in Jerusalem during the reigns of Judean Kings Uzziah, Jotham, Ahaz, and Hezekiah. His prophetic career extended from about 742 until 688 B.C.E.

The eighth century brought with it profound changes to both the Southern Kingdom of Judah, in which Isaiah lived and preached, and to the Northern Kingdom of Israel, which was destroyed during Isaiah's life. At the beginning of the century, both kingdoms enjoyed great prosperity and population booms. By the end of the century, however, both kingdoms had been brutally attacked by Assyria. The Northern Kingdom of Israel was destroyed in 722-721 B.C.E. Judah only narrowly escaped destruction after an invasion by King Sennacherib's Assyrian army at the end of the century.

Isaiah believed that Assyria was an instrument of God; God had passed judgment on the sins of the people and was punishing them with attacks by Assyria. Isaiah also believed that the Israelite nation, or at least a remnant of it, would ultimately survive these attacks.

Isaiah prophesied in times that were troubled not only by foreign aggression, but also by internal decay. He counseled four kings in matters of politics, morality, and religion in years that saw war, decadent materialism, and indulgent excesses among wealthy Israelites. He warned against widespread assimilation and faltering faith in God. He condemned idolatry and sacrifices offered by those who lived unrighteously. He exalted charity, compassion, and faith.

Isaiah passionately brought to Israel the message of God's omnipotence and universal rule over all peoples. Furthermore, Isaiah spread his belief that one day an enlightened king of Judah (a descendant of the House of David) would lead the world into an age of peace and justice.

It was the viewpoint of the early Rabbis that the entire book of Isaiah was written by Isaiah, son of Amoz, who lived during the late eighth century B.C.E. However, as early as the twelfth century C.E., Rabbi Abraham Ibn Ezra suggested that the first 39 chapters were written by a prophet who lived in the eighth century B.C.E., while the rest of the book was written by a prophet who lived about 150 years later. Ibn Ezra came to this conclusion because he noticed that chapters 40-66 contained detailed historical information from the sixth century B.C.E. that could not have been known by someone living in the eighth century B.C.E. Today, it is almost unanimously held that chapters 40-66 were written by one or more prophets who were living in exile in Babylon after the destruction of the Southern Kingdom in 586 B.C.E. Chapters 40-66 differ so significantly in tone, language, content, and style from that of chapters 1 to 39 that the second half of the book is referred to as Deutero-Isaiah, or Second Isaiah.

Second Isaiah's message is one of comfort to a people clearly in despair. After the Babylonians destroyed Jerusalem, they carried away the Israelite survivors to Babylon. Second Isaiah speaks to the exiles and reminds them that they have a special relationship with God. He tells them that they have been exiled because of their sins, but assures them that God will forgive them if they repent.

There are scholars who posit a third or Trito-Isaiah, ascribing chapters 55-66 to him. This Isaiah would have preached to the people in Jerusalem about 100 years after they returned from Babylonian exile — 440-420 B.C.E. His message was one of great hope for a future in which Jerusalem shall flourish: "the wealth of nations" shall flow through her, and all "her children" shall return to live within her gates. Work hard and have faith, the prophet says, for your light has come.

ISAIAH 1:1-27
DEVARIM דברים

This Haftarah has been paired with *Parashat Devarim*, Deuteronomy 1:1-3:22. See "Connecting the Text To the Sedra," pp. 223-224, for an exploration of the many ways the two texts shed light on each other.

SYNOPSIS

Many scholars believe that this Haftarah was prophesied by Isaiah around 701 B.C.E., during the campaign of King Sennacherib of Assyria against Judah. Specifically, it is probable that the Assyrians have already invaded Judah and are beginning their siege of Jerusalem. This was especially agonizing for the Israelites of the Southern Kingdom of Judah, because about 20 years earlier the Assyrians utterly destroyed the Northern Kingdom of Israel.

The Haftarah introduces Isaiah, the son of Amoz, who prophesied in Jerusalem during the reign of Kings Uzziah, Jotham, Ahaz, and Hezekiah. Isaiah has a vision from God, in which God laments that Israel, whom God has raised like children, have grown up to rebel against God. Isaiah describes in graphic metaphors the devastation that has plagued Judah. The nation, he says, is like a sickly body, living in a desolate country with burned cities overrun by strange invaders. Jerusalem is as vulnerable as a temporary *sukkah* in a vineyard. Isaiah even says that Israel was only narrowly saved from the same fate as the destroyed cities of Sodom and Gomorrah.

Isaiah criticizes the Israelites for offering sacrifices to God, while they disregard God's moral laws and behave unjustly. God, says Isaiah, no longer wants to listen to the prayers of the hypocritical Israelites. Isaiah urges the people to cleanse themselves of evil and learn to do good, seek justice, relieve the oppressed, and protect the orphans and the widows. He reminds them that God will forgive and even reward them if they repent of their evil ways. But if not, Israel will surely be vanquished by its enemies.

Isaiah laments the sad decay of the Holy City of Jerusalem, in which the rulers are rebels and everyone loves bribes. In conclusion, the prophet announces that God will certainly punish the sinners and restore Jerusalem to its former righteousness.

INSIGHTS FROM THE TRADITION

A We learn in verse 1:3 that Israel does not recognize God as its Sovereign. Hirsch explains that in Isaiah's time, the Israelite nation had no true conception of itself as a holy people and no sense of identity or purpose.

◆ What does a sense of identity do for us?

◆ If an auto mechanic tries to repair a car without knowing what make or model the car is, what problems might he run into?

◆ What might go wrong if a coach tried to coach a team without knowing exactly which sport the team plays?

◆ How does your sense of Jewish identity affect your life?

B In verse 1:4 Isaiah calls Israel a "sinful nation." Rashi points out that this stands in sharp contrast with the "holy nation" Israel was supposed to be.

◆ Do you think it is beneficial when parents have high expectations of their children, or do you think that high expectations set children up for failure?

◆ Schools usually have standards for how students are to dress in school. Which is better: standards for dress or required uniforms?

C Hirsch understands that the Israelites spurned God only after generations had forsaken God and ceased to study Torah and keep *mitzvot*. While former generations had been neglectful and indifferent to God, Isaiah's generation had actually become hostile to God.

◆ Which do you think is worse: indifference or hatred?

◆ Do you think indifference ultimately leads to hatred? Why or why not?

◆ Sometimes parents who had bad Hebrew school experiences send their children to Hebrew school only because they think they must. Do you think their own indifference leads their children to dislike Jewish education? Explain.

◆ In *40 Things You Can Do to Save the Jewish People*, Joel Lurie Grishaver relates the following hypothetical conversation:

Child: I don't want to go to Hebrew School today.

Parent: Forget it, you're going.

Child: Why do I have to go? I hate it — it's so boring!

Parent: Listen to me — you're going. I had to go and I hated it, and I survived. Now, you have to go. Even if you hate it, you'll survive, too.

Grishaver concludes, "For Jewish schools to work for your child, you must break the cycle of 'Hebrew School bashing' which has been imprinted on all of us" (p. 176).

Why is it important for parents to have a good attitude toward their children's religious education?

◆ For solutions to this Hebrew school problem, read and discuss chapter 33 in Grishaver's book, pp. 176-179. With which solutions do you agree, and why? What other suggestions do you have?

D Verses 1:5 and 1:6 describe Israel as an ailing body, with sick head and heart and wounds from head to foot. According to *Targum Jonathan*, "from head to foot" means from the greatest of the people to the least of the people, there is none without sin.

◆ What do you think *Targum Jonathan* meant by "the greatest of people" and the "least of people"?

◆ How are leaders and regular folk all part of the same "body"?

◆ Do you think regular people tend to sin more if their leaders engage in sinful behavior?

E According to Rashi verses 1:16-18 contains ten expressions of repentance corresponding to the ten days between Rosh HaShanah and Yom Kippur. The ten phrases are: wash, clean yourselves, put your evil doings away, cease from doing evil, learn to do good, devote yourselves to justice, aid the wronged, uphold, defend, and come let us reach an understanding.

◆ Do you see a logical order and progression to this list?

◆ Hertz explains that it is not enough to refrain from doing evil, but that one must also do good. Do you agree or disagree with Hertz? Explain.

◆ Which step in Rashi's list of ten is this?

◆ There is a famous saying that goes, "If you're not part of the solution, then you're part of the problem." What do you think this means, and how does it relate to Hertz's message?

F Malbim explains the difference between the two metaphors in verse 1:18. In the first case, if you have sinned by yourself and repent, you will be completely forgiven and be pure as the white snow. In the second case, if you have caused others to sin, your sins will not be completely forgiven, leaving you only as white as wool, which is not as pure in color as snow.

◆ Think of one example in which your sin involves only yourself.

◆ Think of one example in which your sin causes others to sin as well.

◆ Why do you think there is a difference in the degree of forgiveness that can be given for the two types of wrongdoings?

STRATEGIES
Analyzing the Text

1 In verse 1:2 Isaiah calls upon heaven and earth to witness God's judgment on Israel for breaking their part of the Covenant.

◆ Compare this to Deuteronomy 32:1, in which Moses calls heaven and earth to witness the making of the Covenant between God and Israel.

◆ Isaiah called the same witnesses as Moses, our greatest prophet. Explain how the witnesses, heaven and earth, represent the whole universe. What does it mean that the whole world is testifying against you about your sins?

2 As he does in verse 1:4, Isaiah calls God the "Holy One of Israel" 39 times in the Book of Isaiah. This particular name for God rarely appears at all outside the Book of Isaiah. To be קדוש (kadosh) can mean any of the following: holy, set apart, sacred, honored, dedicated, and consecrated.

◆ Which of these definitions best fits your understanding of God?

◆ List five other names you can think of for God. Discuss which of the names you relate to the best, which the least, and why.

3 Isaiah uses several metaphors for sin in this Haftarah: sickness in verses 1:5-6, crimson and red dye in verse 1:18, and tarnished silver in verse 1:22.

◆ Explain what each metaphor means.

◆ What quality of sin does each metaphor convey? For example, do the metaphors indicate the sin is visible to others, suggest the sin hurts the sinner, say the sin weakens the sinner, imply the sin makes the world ugly?

◆ Which metaphor do you like best, and why?

◆ Using these examples, can you think of your own metaphor for sin?

4 Verse 1:8 says that "Fair Zion is left like a booth in a vineyard, like a hut in a cucumber field, like a city beleaguered." Zion is another name for Jerusalem.

◆ What are these similes expressing about the condition of Jerusalem?

These expressions have led our Sages to believe that this prophecy was delivered after the destruction of the Northern Kingdom by Assyria in 721 B.C.E. Furthermore, "a city beleaguered" suggests that Isaiah might have been speaking around 701 B.C.E., during Assyria's campaign against Judah, led by King Sennacherib.

Knowing that their attackers have already destroyed the Northern Kingdom of Israel, the people of Judah must have been especially terrified.

◆ Imagine you are a resident of Jerusalem in the year 701 B.C.E. Write a diary entry about the current events in your city and your reaction to them. Use these similes and the historical information given in the Synopsis, p. 220, and in the Overview of the Book of Isaiah, pp. 118-119, to inform your entry.

5 In verse 1:10 Isaiah refers to the Israelites as people of the cities of Sodom and Gomorrah which were destroyed for their sins in Genesis 19.

◆ Explain what Isaiah meant by this sarcastic characterization.

◆ In the same verse, the prophet seems to place equal blame on the "chieftains" and the "folk." When things go wrong in a community, do you think the leaders and the people are equally to blame?

6 Reread verses 1:11-17. There has been a long debate about the message of this passage.

◆ Do you think Isaiah is saying that God no longer wants any sacrifice or ritual from anyone? Explain your response.

◆ Alternatively, do you think Isaiah is saying that God wants sacrifice and ritual only from people who live righteously and sincerely practice their religion? Explain your response.

◆ In *Numbers Rabbah* 21:25, Rabbi Akiba was asked why Israel continued to celebrate festivals after God says in Isaiah 1:14, "I hate your festivals." Akiva answered that if God had said, "I hate MY festivals," it would be time to stop observing these holidays altogether. However, God said, "I hate YOUR festivals," which meant God hated the way the people

observed them. Explain this *midrash* in your own words.

◆ Which interpretation of verses 1:11-17 does the *midrash* support — that God no longer wants sacrifices, or that God wants sacrifices only from righteous people?

◆ Conduct a debate on the meaning of verses 1:11-17. Use text and interpretation to support your position.

Connecting the Text To the Sedra

7 This Haftarah and Sedra always fall on the Shabbat immediately before Tishah B'Av, the fast day that marks the anniversary of the destruction of both Temples in Jerusalem.

It is believed that many additional tragic events occurred on Tishah B'Av:

• The return of the spies from Canaan with a bad report for Moses (Numbers 13).

• The destruction of First Temple in 586 B.C.E.

• The destruction of Second Temple in 70 C.E.

• The expulsion of the Jews from Spain in 1492.

• The beginning of World War I on August 1, 1914 (corresponding to the 9th of Av).

• The decree to establish the Warsaw ghetto in 1941.

◆ Do you think the occurrence of these events on Tishah B'Av is by divine design, by mere coincidence, or by virtue of the fact that with such a long history, it is inevitable that many events will befall the Jewish people on the same calendar date? Justify your answer.

◆ Look up the Hebrew date of your birthday in *100 Year Jewish Calendar* or visit www. rtlsoft.com/hebrew/calendar/today.html. This web site will provide the corresponding

Jewish date if you enter your secular birthday. Do some research to find other events throughout history that occurred on your Hebrew birth date or secular birth date. You can access information about all the events that happened on your secular birthday on the Internet at www.historychannel.com/tdih/.

8 In the Sedra we read, "and from there you will seek God and will find God" (Deuteronomy 4:29). According to the Baal Shem Tov, "from there" means wherever you happen to be — including in exile.

◆ Given that Tishah B'Av marks the beginning of the 2,000-year exile of the Jewish people, this is a reassuring interpretation. Explain why this is reassuring.

◆ Contrast this message of reassurance with verse 1:4 in the Haftarah, which indicates that because Israel has forsaken and abandoned God, it will be punished.

◆ According to Deuteronomy, punishment can lead to true repentance and then forgiveness by God. Do you believe that God can be found whenever and wherever one honestly seeks God?

9 On Tishah B'Av, we read the Book of Lamentations, called *Aychah* in Hebrew, which recounts the destruction of the Temple. Verse 1:21 of this Haftarah begins with the word *"Aychah,"* which echoes the mournful tone of the Book of Lamentations. *"Aychah"* means "how."

Examine the meaning of the word *"Aychah"* in the first verse of chapters 1, 2, and 4 of the Book of Lamentations and compare them with verse 1:21 of the Haftarah. When something bad has happened, what do you think is the difference between asking "why did this happen" rather than asking "how are we going to go on"?

◆ Ask your Cantor to teach you to chant *Aychah* with the proper cantillation for Tishah B'Av. Learn to sing the penultimate verse of *Aychah*: *"Hashivenu Adonai aylecha v'nashuvah, chadesh yamaynu k'kedem."*

10 On Tishah B'Av, we mourn the loss of the Holy Temple in Jerusalem. In the Haftarah Isaiah mourns the types of behavior that led to the Temple's destruction and ultimate exile of the Israelites.

◆ Reread Isaiah's message and identify the types of behavior that set Israel on the course toward destruction. Discuss how each behavior can contribute to a people's destruction.

Extending the Text

11 Verse 1:1 announces a "vision" of Isaiah. According to *Genesis Rabbah* 44:6, the Bible uses at least ten words to describe prophetic events: prophecy, vision, preaching, speech, saying, command, burden, parable, metaphor, and enigma.

When a particular society has many synonyms for a single word or concept, it usually means that that word or concept has great importance to that society.

◆ What can we learn about Judaism from the fact that the Bible uses ten words for prophecy?

◆ Eskimos who speak Labradoran Inuit have no less than ten words that mean "snow." The Eskimos who speak West Greenlandic use an incredible 49 words meaning "snow" and "ice," revealing the prevalence of these weather conditions in Eskimo life. Visit www.urbanlegends.com/language/eskimo for more on this subject.

◆ Consult a thesaurus to discover words in the English language that have multiple synonyms. (For example, consider the synonyms for liberty — freedom, suffrage, autonomy, sovereignty, franchise, independence, enfranchisement, opportunity, right, privilege, democracy, and autarchy. Consider also the synonyms for money — cash, currency, notes, tender, beans, gravy, dough, lucre, wad, bucks, and bread.) What do these words say about our society's values? Can you think of other important words in our society and their synonyms?

12 Heaven and earth were called as witnesses at the beginning of the Haftarah (see Analyzing the Text #1, p. 222). Jewish law requires witnesses for many legal matters, such as marriage, divorce, and conversion. Two witnesses are required to sign a *ketubah* — the Jewish marriage document.

◆ Ask your parents who signed their *ketubah* and why those particular witnesses were chosen. Did the same witnesses also sign your parents' civil marriage license?

13 As noted in the footnotes, the JPS translation of verse 1:27 differs from most other translations, which read, "Zion shall be saved by justice. Her repentant ones by righteousness." The word "righteousness" in Hebrew is *tzedakah*, which you might recognize as the word we use to mean "charity." There is, in fact, no exact Hebrew equivalent for the English word "charity."

◆ Why do you think the Rabbis might have chosen to equate the act of charity with the concept of righteousness or justice?

◆ Does this mean you are unjust if you don't give charity?

◆ Is it the needy individual's just right to receive charity?

◆ The historian Josephus Flavius wrote, "He who refuses aid which he has the power to give is accountable to justice" (*Against Apion*, II:27). What do you think this means?

14 Isaiah uses the color red as a sign of sin. According to Mishnah *Yoma* 4:2, the priests tied a red thread to the horn of the scapegoat on Yom Kippur.

In Jewish tradition, red also symbolizes life (blood), earth, judgment, and royalty. The color was believed to have powers to keep away the evil eye, thus giving rise to the practices of decorating the skin of Oriental brides with Henna and tying red ribbons to baby cribs to keep demons away.

◆ For more on the symbolism of red in the Jewish tradition, see *The Encyclopedia of Jewish Symbols* by Ellen Frankel and Betsy Platkin Teutsch, p. 137.

◆ Search your synagogue for red objects (e.g., Torah covers, Ark curtains, etc.). What do you think the red in those items symbolizes?

◆ Think of examples of the ways in which red is used in our society to attract attention (e.g., STOP signs, fire trucks). Take photos of those examples and curate an exhibit displaying how red is used in our society to attract attention. You may want to include other colors and how they are used as well.

15 There are many customs associated with the mourning mood of Tishah B'Av. Traditionally, Jews fast an entire day, from sunset to sundown. Other mourning rituals associated with the holiday include sitting on the floor and refraining from singing, greeting one another, and wearing leather shoes.

◆ Discuss how each of these rituals is appropriate to a state of mourning.

◆ In recent years, some Jews argue that we need not fast an entire day in mourning for the Temple and Jerusalem because, since 1948, we have had our own sovereign state in Israel. Hold a debate as to whether Jews should fast and mourn for an entire day, for part of the day, or not at all on Tishah B'Av now that there is a modern state of Israel.

16 President Franklin Delano Roosevelt nicknamed Supreme Court Justice Louis Brandeis "Isaiah" because of the judge's emphasis on social justice. Brandeis once said, "The greatest menace to freedom is an inert people."

◆ Explain this quotation.

◆ Make a poster depicting the quotation by Brandeis or your own favorite quotation about a danger to freedom.

◆ What do you think is the greatest danger to freedom? How can we ameliorate this danger?

◆ For more information on Justice Louis Brandeis, see *Encyclopaedia Judaica*, vol. 4, pp. 1295-1299.

17 Artistic masters Michelangelo and Raphael both painted their interpretations of Isaiah the prophet. View their works at: www.kfki.hu/~arthp/welcome.html.

◆ Compare the renderings of Isaiah by Michelangelo and Raphael. The web site allows you to send a free e-mail postcard of any picture. Choose your favorite picture of Isaiah and send it with a message to someone you consider to be, like Isaiah, a champion for social justice.

Personalizing the Text

18 Isaiah's prophecies were written in poetic form.

◆ Play a poetry game based on one in *The Jewish Experiential Book* by Bernard Reisman, p. 89. An odd number of people, each with paper and pencil, sit in a circle. Each person composes the first line of a poem at the top of the paper and passes it to the next person. The next person should read the first line, write a second line, fold over the first line so that only the second line is visible, and pass the paper to the next person. The papers will be passed around the circle until everyone has made an entry on each sheet and the papers have returned to their starting point. Then read each poem aloud.

19 God calls Israel "rebellious children" in verse 1:2, and laments that they have turned against God.

It is sometimes difficult to meet all of the expectations that our parents have of us.

◆ Why do parents expect so much of us?

◆ How do expectations help us to be better people?

◆ List certain expectations that your parents had for you that you believe helped you.

◆ At what age do you think children should be permitted to make their own lifestyle decisions?

◆ If you choose to lead a life that is different from that of your parents, does it necessarily mean that you are ungrateful and rebellious? Explain your answer.

◆ Perhaps you will be a parent one day. Write a letter to your future children, outlining your expectations of them.

20 According to *midrash* (see Analyzing the Text #6, p. 223), God hated the way the children of Israel observed their holidays.

◆ Describe how you and your family celebrate one holiday and how your festival celebration is pleasing to God.

21 Isaiah and the other prophets preached their ideas to the people. There is a Speakers' Corner in London's Hyde Park that is always available to anyone who wants to preach publicly on any subject.

◆ Set up a podium in your class and allow each student two minutes to preach on the subject of his or her choice.

22 Isaiah portrays Israel as a people that has forgotten who it is.

◆ What does it mean to you to be a Jew?

◆ Create a collage of photos cut out from Jewish magazines and newspapers that portrays your idea of what it means to be Jewish. (The teacher might consider creating his or her own collage prior to class that includes a broad spectrum of Jewish images — from religious Hasidim to Jerry Seinfeld to *kibbutz* farmers in Israel. When the students have completed their posters, they can compare them to the teacher's. Discuss how this comparison challenges you to broaden your perspective on the meaning of Jewish identity.)

23 By comparing the Israelites to the denizens of Sodom and Gomorrah, Isaiah tries to get his point across by using sarcasm.

One dictionary definition of sarcasm is, "a sharply mocking remark intended to wound another."

◆ It is said that parents should never be sarcastic with their children. Do you agree or disagree, and why?

◆ Do you know anyone who is always sarcastic? How do you and others feel about this person?

24 Jerusalem is compared to a fragile booth in verse 1:8, vulnerable to all the ravages of nature.

Houses made of cards evoke the same sense of fragility as the booth to which Jerusalem is compared.

◆ Hold a contest in your class to see who can build the tallest house of cards. Students may work in small teams or individually.

25 Isaiah indicates that both leaders and the general public are equally responsible for the moral behavior of a nation.

The Statement of Principles of the Reform Movement includes the following:

"We are committed to the *mitzvah* of *ahavat Yisrael*, love for the Jewish people, and to *k'lal Yisrael*, the entirety of the community of Israel. Recognizing that *kol Yisrael arevim zeh bazeh*, all Jews are responsible for one another, we reach out to all Jews across ideological and geographical boundaries.

◆ Discuss this aspect of the Principles of the Reform Movement. Give examples of how Jews throughout the world are responsible for each other.

◆ The phrase "all Jews are responsible for one another" is a quotation from *Shevuot* 39a-b. For additional quotations, information, and discussion questions on this topic, see the web site www.uahcweb.org/growth/principles/israel2.shtml.

◆ For a web site dedicated to teaching an understanding of this Talmudic quotation, see www.jajz-ed.org.il/news/mias/02a.html.

◆ To see the rest of the Statement of Principles of the Reform Movement, go to the web site: www.ccarnet.org/platforms/principles.html.

◆ Learn the Hebrew song *"Kol Yisrael Arevim Zeh BaZeh,"* which teaches that all Jews are responsible for one another. The song may be found on the CD *Shir Mi-libeinu: A Song from Our Heart*, recorded at UAHC Swig Camp Institute.

26 Red dye is mentioned in the Haftarah.

◆ Make a natural red vegetable dye and tie-dye T-shirts or other cotton items. Create different shades of red by boiling various fruits in water (pomegranates, grapes, beets, cherries, red plums, etc.). Alternatively, use henna to decorate your hands in the manner of Oriental brides. (Be aware that henna is a semi-permanent dye that will last on skin for several days or weeks!)

27 As we saw in Analyzing the Text #2, p. 222, Isaiah often uses the name Holy One of Israel for God.

◆ Review a comprehensive list of names for God. Find such a list in *Higher and Higher: Making Jewish Prayer Part of Us* by Steven M. Brown. Compare the names and explain how they differ in meaning.

◆ Make a crossword puzzle in which all the answers are different names for God. Design clues for each name.

28 Isaiah compares Jerusalem to a booth in a cucumber field. Cucumbers are a favorite vegetable in Israel.

◆ Learn to make Israeli salad, which is typically comprised of diced cucumbers, diced tomatoes, parsley, lemon juice, olive oil, salt, and pepper. Also learn to make cucumber and yogurt salad. Enjoy these salads with pita bread and falafel as a non-meat meal during the nine days before Tishah B'Av, during which it is traditional not to eat meat.

Other Resources

29 For a story on how one woman is forever marked as a sinner with a red letter "A," read the classic novel *The Scarlet Letter* by Nathaniel Hawthorne.

30 For more on the prophet Isaiah, including history, themes, and notable quotations, read *Messengers of God: A Jewish Prophets Who's Who* by Ronald H. Isaacs, pp. 91-101.

31 There is a delicate balance between meeting our parents' expectations of us and pursuing our own idea of personal fulfillment. View and discuss the Disney film *The Little Mermaid* (1989, rated G, 83 minutes), which deals with the issues that arise when a daughter wants to honor her father and yet live a life that is different from that which he wants for her.

32 Discuss the illustrations of this Haftarah in *The Illustrated Torah* by Michal Meron, p. 186.

33 See the *Encyclopaedia Judaica* entry for Isaiah (vol. 9, pp. 44-71) for more information on Isaiah in the Bible, *midrash*, and the arts. In particular, see the beautiful illustration to the first chapter of Isaiah from a fourteenth century Bible opposite pp. 43-44. Discuss why the artist chose to feature the word *"hazon."*

Involving the Family

34 Experience Tishah B'Av this year by refraining from eating meat during the nine days before the fast day, and/or actually fasting on Tishah B'Av itself.

35 Plan a family trip to Israel to take place over Tishah B'Av, when you can visit the site of the Holy Temple and/or the Model of the Second Temple at the Holy Land Hotel.

36 Grow cucumbers in a vegetable garden. Use them in your Israeli salad (see Personalizing the Text #28 above).

Bar/Bat Mitzvah Project

37 Supreme Court Justice Louis Brandeis said that apathy is a great menace to freedom. Do your part to end indifference! Volunteer for an organization that advocates for the environment or for the homeless or for any cause that is important to you. Plan an event that raises your community's awareness about your cause. Or volunteer to help register voters in your community. Remember, only about 50 percent of eligible Americans exercised their Constitutional right to vote in the historic 2000 Presidential election.

ISAIAH 6:1-7:6; 9:5-6 Ashkenazim
ISAIAH 6:1-13 Sephardim
YITRO יתרו

This Haftarah has been paired with *Parashat Yitro*, Exodus 18:1-20:23. See "Connecting the Text To the Sedra," pp. 233-235, for an exploration of the many ways the two texts shed light on each other.

SYNOPSIS

The historical context for this Haftarah is given within the text itself, in verses 7:1-6. Around the year 734 B.C.E., King Rezin of Aram and King Pekah of the Northern Kingdom of Israel united in a siege upon Jerusalem in order to garner support against Assyria. For the Southern Kingdom of Judah, then, it was a time of great anxiety about external confrontations. At the same time, the Judeans were suffering internally from the ills of idolatry and egregious materialism.

Now that the stage is set, we can understand Isaiah's prophecy in chapter 6, which reportedly takes place in 742 B.C.E., the year that King Uzziah died. The vision is one of the Hebrew Bible's most enduring images of Divine splendor and majesty. Isaiah beholds God seated on a throne, surrounded by angels — *seraphim*. Each *seraph* has six wings: two to cover his face, two to cover his legs, and two for flying. The *seraphim* call out to one another: "Holy, holy, holy! *Adonai* of Hosts! God's presence fills all the earth!"

Frightened by the divine vision, Isaiah worries about his own sinfulness. Just then, one of the *seraphim* flies over and touches a hot coal to Isaiah's lips, declaring that all Isaiah's sins have been washed away. God then asks Isaiah to be a prophet in Israel, and Isaiah immediately agrees.

God proceeds to deliver the divine message to Isaiah, which the prophet is to broadcast to the Israelites. God informs Isaiah that although he will warn the people of their imminent destruction, he will be frustrated by their lack of attention to his words. God describes a future in which the evil majority of Israel will be destroyed, leaving only a small, holy remnant to face the future and carry God's covenant.

The Haftarah concludes on a hopeful note, a selection from chapter 9, in which Isaiah prophesies that a child has been born who will bring peace and justice back to the throne and Kingdom of David.

INSIGHTS FROM THE TRADITION

A Isaiah is called by God in the year of King Uzziah's death (6:1). According to Rashi, King Uzziah sinned by trying to take over the job of the priest in the Temple. The priest's job was reserved for someone born into a priestly family and could not be done by anyone outside the family, even the king.

The founders of the United States rejected the concept that someone had to be born into a particular family to attain a certain social status or perform a certain job. In the U.S., any citizen (who meets certain requirements) can run for office.

◆ There is at least one notable exception to this rule: anyone running for the office of United

States President must be American-born. Do you think this rule is fair?

B *Seraphim* covered their feet with two of their wings (6:2). According to *Leviticus Rabbah* 27:3, *seraphim* feet were the shape of a calf's foot. They kept their feet covered so that the Israelites would not be reminded of the sin they committed by building the golden calf.

◆ Why do you think the angels didn't want to remind the Israelites of the golden calf?

◆ How would you like to be reminded constantly of your biggest mistake? Would reminders help you not to repeat it or just make you feel bad?

C With two wings, the *seraphim* covered their faces to prevent them from looking at God's presence, *Shechinah*, according to *Leviticus Rabbah* 27:3.

◆ What are some things we are not supposed to look at? (Consider other people's mail, pornography, other students' test papers, graphic violence, and so on.)

◆ Why is it sometimes hard not to look at something, even though we know we shouldn't?

D The Hasidic master, Baal Shem Tov, taught a lesson based on verse 6:3, "God's presence fills all the earth!" From this he taught that one ought to enjoy the pleasures of the world, recognizing that God is the source of those pleasures (from *Jewish Literacy* by Joseph Telushkin, p. 216).

◆ What things in life make you happy?

◆ List as many ways as you can for how we might show appreciation to God every time we enjoy these pleasures.

E Radak explains that in verse 6:5 Isaiah feels that his own shortcomings stand in the way of his meeting God's call to service.

◆ Must we be perfect to do God's work? Explain your answer.

◆ The Bible never fails to point out that even our greatest leaders had great faults. Everyone from Abraham to Moses to Solomon made mistakes, big and small. If a person had to be perfect in order to be a leader or do holy work, how many leaders or *mitzvah*-doers would we have?

◆ Since everyone has some faults, what qualities other than perfection does it take for someone to succeed in serving God?

F King Ahaz is identified in verse 7:1 as "the son of Jotham, the son of Uzziah, king of Judah." He is not identified just by his own name. Rashi explains that Ahaz's genealogy is given here because although Ahaz was a wicked idol-worshiping king undeserving of divine help, God does in fact help him because of the merit of his fathers.

◆ Should children be rewarded for the deeds of their parents? How might this happen in today's world?

◆ Should the children of the head of the PTA get special treatment at school? How about the children of big financial contributors to a private school? Should the little league coach's kid get to play the entire game because of his or her parent's special commitment to the team?

STRATEGIES
Analyzing the Text

1 Isaiah describes God in verse 6:1 as "seated on a high and lofty throne; and the skirts of

TEACHING HAFTARAH

God's robe filled the Temple." God, who is surrounded by ministering angels, looks for a representative to deliver God's message of judgment to the people.

◆ God is often represented in the Bible and in our prayers as a king. List five words you might associate with a king. Discuss whether these words also fit the scene of Isaiah's vision of God.

2 The Temple filling with smoke in verse 6:4 is similar to Ezekiel 10:4, in which the Temple also fills with a cloud. Theophanies (divine appearances) throughout the Bible are often accompanied by smoke or clouds, as in Exodus 40:34, I Kings 8:10-11, and Isaiah 4:5, for example.

◆ Why might smoke be present when God appears to Isaiah? Consider the following incidents of smoke in the Bible. Decide which interpretation you like best and least:

- The smoke veils God's presence (Exodus 19:16-18).

- The smoke is the breath of the fiery *seraphim* (Psalm 18:9).

- The smoke is God's anger (Psalm 74:1).

3 Isaiah calls the angels surrounding God's throne *seraphim*. The Hebrew word *seraph* means "burning," and may allude to the angel burning Isaiah's mouth with coal. "*Seraph*" may also be related to the Hebrew word for serpent, perhaps because a serpent's bite feels as if it is burning the skin. In fact, Isaiah connects *seraphim* with serpents in verses 14:29 and 30:6. Interestingly, a bronze serpent, made by Moses in Numbers 21:4-9, was housed in the First Temple, according to II Kings 18:4. Perhaps Isaiah saw this bronze serpent and then it became part of his vision of *seraphim*.

◆ Which interpretation of *seraph* helps you understand the text better?

◆ Have you ever seen anything before you went to sleep that then appeared in your dreams?

◆ Based on the information given here and in verses 6:2 and 6:6-7, draw your own impression of what a *seraph* might look like.

◆ Compare your drawing with the illustration of this Haftarah in *The Illustrated Torah* by Michal Meron, p. 80. What emotions does this illustration convey?

4 In verse 6:6 the *seraph* brings a burning coal to Isaiah's mouth and touches it to his lips. This recalls the famous *midrash* about Moses when he was three years old. Pharaoh was worried that Moses would try to take his power and crown, and so Pharaoh wanted to kill young Moses. Disguised as a wise man of Egypt, the angel Gabriel designs a test to determine for Pharaoh whether the young Moses should be killed or not. Gabriel proposes that an onyx stone (which was shiny like Pharaoh's crown) and a coal of fire be placed before Moses. If Moses grabs the onyx, then he wants to take Pharaoh's kingship and he should be killed. But if he grasps the coal of fire, then he has no wishes for the kingship and he shall live. When the two stones are placed before the child, Moses starts to reach for the onyx, but Gabriel secretly guides his hand away from it and places it on the live coal. The coal burns Moses' hand, which he places in his mouth, burning part of his lips and tongue and making him slow of speech.

◆ How are the two stories similar and how are they different?

5 Isaiah stands out in the prophetic tradition as one who didn't hesitate to answer God's call. After the angel purifies Isaiah, God calls to him in verse 6:8, saying, "Whom shall I send?

Who will go for us?" Isaiah immediately replies, "Here am I; send me."

◆ Read Exodus chapters 3-4 to see if Moses, our greatest prophet, was as willing as Isaiah to accept the job. How do their responses differ?

◆ Compare Isaiah's response with those of some of his fellow prophets (see the following citations for your comparison: Jeremiah 1:4-9; Hosea 1:2-3; and Jonah 1:1-3, 4:2-3). Since Isaiah, unlike other prophets, does not hesitate to respond to God's call here, some scholars believe Isaiah was already a prophet and this chapter was just a request by God that Isaiah go on a specific mission.

◆ Why might the placement of this story in chapter 6 of the Book of Isaiah support this interpretation?

◆ Find other clues in the text to support the idea that this was not Isaiah's first call to be a prophet.

6 God tells Israel to go prophesy to the people.

◆ What does God expect the people's reaction to be to this request?

◆ Reread and discuss verses 6:9-13. What does God expect? Why might God have these expectations?

◆ If God did not expect the people to listen, then why do you think God sent Isaiah to speak to them?

◆ Discuss these possible explanations: God wants to offer hope to the few who might listen; God could not help but show compassion to the people by giving them a warning; God wanted to be on record so the people could not say they were not forewarned. Can you think of other possible explanations?

7 Verse 6:13 contains a hopeful note for the future.

◆ Explain what is hopeful about verse 6:13.

◆ Can you think of any examples from nature in which destruction is necessary for the continuation of life?

8 The Haftarah ends on a positive note when verse 9:5 indicates that a child will be a great leader and will bring peace. Scholars believe Isaiah was referring to King Hezekiah, who proved to be a great and righteous leader in Judah.

◆ The verse teaches that in order to have peace, we need strong leadership that rules with justice and equity. Do you agree that this is how to advance peace?

◆ Review the stories of Hezekiah's reign in II Kings chapters 18-20 and II Chronicles chapters 29-33 to determine for yourself if Hezekiah was worthy of such acclaim.

◆ Write your own tribute to Hezekiah based on what you have learned about him.

Connecting the Text To the Sedra

9 The Sedra relates a public revelation of God to the entire nation of Israel. The Haftarah, on the other hand, is about a personal divine revelation to Isaiah alone. Compare the sights and sounds of the revelation at Sinai in Exodus 19:16-21 to the sights and sounds witnessed by Isaiah in the Haftarah.

A public revelation is especially powerful, in part, because it is witnessed by many people together who help maintain the memory of the event and verify that it did indeed happen. The Israelites in Moses' story accept his prophecy, perhaps because they were able to witness part of the revelation themselves. In contrast, the Israelites in

Isaiah's story rejected his prophecy, perhaps because they were not let in on the revelation itself.

◆ Imagine how difficult it would be to convey a private revelation to a doubting public.

◆ Form groups, each of which should write and perform a skit portraying either a public or private revelation. For the private revelation, act out also how the prophet might convey the revelation to the public.

10 In the Sedra Moses' father-in-law Yitro brings Moses' family to him. Yitro visits a short time, but chooses not to witness the impending revelation of God at Mount Sinai and not to follow God. Yitro, a Midianite priest, leaves before the revelation and returns to his nation (Exodus 18:27).

◆ Theologically, why does it make sense that Yitro leaves before revelation and not after it?

◆ Write a diary entry for Yitro for the day on which he decides to return to his people. Describe what, for him, were the pros and cons of leaving.

◆ Why is it a theological problem that the people hear the word of God, but do not follow it?

◆ Do you think that Yitro comes across better or worse when compared to the Israelites in the Haftarah?

11 The Haftarah closes with an optimistic view of the future (verse 9:6): when there will be a strong leader who rules with justice and equity, and when there will be peace. In the Sedra Moses is advised by Yitro on how to rule over the people to ensure justice and equity (Exodus 18:13-26).

◆ Sketch a flow chart of the system Yitro and Moses set up.

◆ Why might the system devised by Yitro and Moses promote peace among the people?

12 The names of Moses' sons are linked to his life story, just as Isaiah's children's names are linked to the history of the Israelites. Isaiah named his sons *"She'ar yashuv"* (the remnant will remain) and *"Maher-shlal-hash-baz"* (the spoil speeds and the prey hastens). See Exodus 18:3-4 for the names of Moses' sons and their meanings.

◆ The names of many children in the Bible reveal something about their society or the circumstances of their birth. Match the biblical names below with their meanings. (Hint: When you check the verses in the JPS Tanach, you may also have to read the footnotes.)

1. Lo Ami (c.) Hosea 1:9
2. Judah (f) Genesis 29:35
3. Moses (a.) Exodus 2:10
4. Benjamin (h.) Genesis 35:18
5. Isaac (b.) Genesis 17:17
6. Esau (e.) Genesis 25:25
7. Jacob (g.) Genesis 25:26
8. Samuel (d.) I Samuel 1:20

a. Drew him from water
b. Laughter
c. Not my people
d. I asked God for him
e. Hairy
f. I will praise
g. Heel
h. Son of my right hand

◆ What do you think it would be like to have a very unusual name?

◆ If you wanted to give your child a name that described the state of society today, what would the name be?

13 The Haftarah features winged creatures that can fly and do God's work. In Exodus 19:4 God speaks of transporting the Israelites from Egypt on eagles' wings, another flying creature.

◆ Why might flying creatures have been so fascinating to the ancient imagination?

◆ Why do you think we still make associations between God and the heavens above?

◆ Listen to the song "On Wings of Eagles" by Debbie Friedman on the recording *Live at the Del*.

14 God hopes in Exodus 19:5-6 that Israel will be a holy nation, גוי קדוש (goy kadosh). Then, in the Ten Commandments, we are instructed to remember Shabbat and to make it holy. The *seraphim* in the Haftarah call out to one another, saying, "Holy, holy, holy is *Adonai* of hosts."

◆ What does it mean to be holy (see discussion in Analyzing the Text #2 in the Haftarah for *Devarim*, p. 222)?

◆ Who is the holiest person you know, and why do you think so?

15 God is described in the Ten Commandments as "zealous." In the Haftarah the same word appears about God in verse 9:6.

Zealous means: active, ardent, diligent, devoted, fanatic, warlike, fervid, fired, avid, eager, rabid, obsessed, extremist, a crank.

Also, "zealous" is only one way to translate the Hebrew קנא (kana). This word can also mean "jealous," "envious," or "demanding of exclusive service."

◆ Do any of these definitions agree with your ideas about God?

◆ Today, we don't necessarily think about God in the way that God is portrayed in the Bible. For example, do you think of God as a king (as did Isaiah)?

◆ List your own adjectives or metaphors for God.

16 Isaiah fears that he will die because he was unfit to witness God's presence. Similarly, the Israelites are afraid in Exodus 20:16 that they will die if they hear God's voice.

◆ If God is a powerful, zealous, holy king who appears in smoky revelations, why might it be scary to have a close encounter with the Divine?

◆ View and discuss clips from the film *The Wizard of Oz* (1939, not rated, 101 minutes) that show how Dorothy and her friends are afraid to come face-to-face with the Wizard. Of what are they afraid, and why?

Extending the Text

17 In *A Jewish Theology*, Louis Jacobs summarizes some beliefs about angels held by our Sages (pp. 109-110):

• Angels are immortal.

• Angels do not reproduce.

• Angels have no evil inclination.

• Angels are nameless, with the exception of Gabriel and Michael in the Book of Daniel.

• Good people are higher in rank than the angels.

• Israel is dearer to God than the angels.

• Angels possess form without matter (Maimonides).

- There are eleven grades of angels (*seraphim, ophanim,* and *cherubim,* for example), ranked by their spiritual worth and apprehension of God.

- Prophets received communication through angels.

- There are many angels, but only One God.

Genesis Rabbah 10:6 teaches, "There is no blade of grass in the world below that does not have an angel over it, striking it and telling it to grow."

◆ Review these teachings. How many can you apply to the account of Isaiah, chapter 6?

◆ Angels have been the subject of many films and television shows in recent years. Why do you think angels have captured the modern imagination?

◆ What emotional and/or spiritual need do you think is filled by a belief in angels?

18 Rashi taught us (see Insights from the Tradition #A, p. 230) that the job of a priest was reserved only for someone born into a priestly family.

Today there are no such things as priests offering sacrifices in the Jewish religion. However, in some Jewish movements, there still remain three categories of Jews, according to ancient divisions: *Kohayn, Levy,* and *Yisrael.*

Traditional Jewish custom, for example, awards the first *aliyah* to the Torah reading to *Kohanim,* the second to *Levi'im,* and the remaining honors to the Israelites.

In addition, in some Jewish communities, *Kohanim* make the Priestly Blessing in synagogue. On the other hand, *Kohanim* are historically prohibited from making any contact with the dead (they may not enter a cemetery) or from marrying a divorcee or convert.

◆ Ask your parents or grandparents if you are a *Kohayn, Levi,* or *Yisrael.*

◆ Ask your Rabbi if your congregation makes any distinctions among these groups.

19 The Hebrew root word קדש is evident in four words found in prayer: *kadosh* (holy), *Kiddush* (the blessing over wine), "*Kedushah*" (found in the repetition of the "*Amidah*"), and "*Kaddish*" (the prayer said by mourners and others).

◆ Find each of these prayers in your prayer book. Try to determine why they take a form of the word "holy."

◆ Learn to sing the *Kiddush* for Shabbat evening.

◆ Learn the choreography of the "*Kedushah*," which quotes the words of Isaiah's angels.

20 By reciting blessings over ordinary events, we transform them into holy experiences that enrich our lives. To this end, our Sages composed blessings for nearly every occasion that occurs in our daily lives. There are blessings said, for example, when we eat or drink various foods, when we smell plants and herbs, and when we see a rainbow or ocean.

◆ Compile a list of 20 blessings for various occasions in Hebrew and English. Hold a "*Berachah* Bee" in your class or school to see which student has memorized the most blessings. A prize can be awarded to the winner in each class or grade.

◆ For an extensive list of blessings for various occasions, see *Siddur Sim Shalom,* pp. 708-715, or the *Complete ArtScroll Siddur,* pp. 225-231.

21 With two of their six wings, *seraphim* fly around fulfilling missions serving God, according to *Targum Jonathan* (see Insights from the Tradition #B and #C, p. 231, for how *seraphim* use their other wings). It seems as if the angels always hurry to do God's work.

Numbers Rabbah 10:5 teaches us that the righteous always hurry enthusiastically to perform appointed tasks and *mitzvot*. It is customary, then, to perform *mitzvot* as soon as one is able. For example, *Brit Milah* ceremonies are traditionally held early in the morning of the eighth day. According to Jewish tradition, hurrying to do a *mitzvah* indicates that one is doing the *mitzvah* willingly and voluntarily out of joy.

◆ What does rushing to do a *mitzvah* indicate about one's attitude toward the *mitzvah*? Write an angelic motto about rushing to do a *mitzvah,* or design a poster encouraging people not to waste a minute before doing a *mitzvah*.

Personalizing the Text

22 The *seraphim* sing to each other antiphonally or responsively.

◆ Responsive readings and prayers are very common in our liturgy. Ask your Cantor to teach your class to sing an antiphonal prayer (e.g., Psalm 136, the "Great Hallel").

◆ Write your own antiphonal prayer, featuring a refrain that is repeated by the congregation. Write the refrain on a poster that can be held up for the congregation to see.

23 In Isaiah's prophecy he used many metaphors.

◆ Learn more about the prophecy of Isaiah and the metaphors he used. Divide selected verses of his prophecy into three parts. Write each part on a separate card and distribute the cards to participants. Participants should then try to find the other people whose cards help finish their verse (based on the exercise "Complete

the Quotation" in *The Jewish Experiential Book* by Bernard Reisman, p. 95).

24 Isaiah is prepared for his visit with God by the *seraph* that cleanses Isaiah of his sins. In *The Wizard of Oz*, Dorothy, Scarecrow, Tin Man, and Cowardly Lion prepare for their meeting with the Wizard by getting washed, brushed, and polished. Explain how their preparation was like or unlike that of Isaiah.

◆ How do you imagine God (like the Wizard, like Isaiah's "King," or another way)?

◆ Based on your image of God, how would you prepare — mentally and physically — for an encounter with the Divine?

Note: Some students may find it easier to think first about getting ready to meet God and then to infer their view of God from their necessary preparation.

25 God looks for a prophet in verse 6:8, asking, "Whom shall I send? Who will go for us?"

◆ Write a classified advertisement for a prophet. What is the job description? What hours does a prophet work? What qualifications and recommendations are required? What kind of compensation is offered?

26 A prophet is called by God, and is not elected democratically.

◆ Imagine a democratic election of a prophet. Stage a political convention, complete with campaign posters, hats, buttons, and speeches to elect a prophet (based on the exercise "Prophets for President" in *The Jewish Experiential Book* by Bernard Reisman, pp. 220-222).

27 Isaiah prophesies that only a small, holy remnant of Israel will remain to face the future and carry out God's holy Covenant.

◆ Imagine that the world is about to be destroyed. You have the power to choose ten individuals who will be protected from the destruction and given the task of repopulating the world. You can approach this exercise in one of two ways. First, you can choose ten actual people, living or dead, to establish the new world. Alternatively, you can list the qualities that you would like to have represented among your survivors (intelligence, age, skill, etc.).

◆ What does your list reveal about your own values and priorities?

◆ Early in this century, there was a proliferation of "survival" shows on TV. Do you think the survivors of these shows demonstrate good values as they attempt to win the prize? What is the prize that Isaiah's holy remnant will win?

28 Rashi notes that the wicked Ahaz's name is attached to the names of his righteous ancestors (see Insights from the Tradition #F, p. 231).

◆ In our society, we tend to remember the names of villains much more than the names of righteous individuals. What do you think this reflects about our society's values?

◆ Examine a recent newspaper or news magazine. Make a list of names featured in headlines or captions. Are the names associated with mischief or good deeds? Cut out the pictures of the individuals mentioned for doing good things and make a collage of their faces, along with their names and deeds.

29 Television talk show host Oprah Winfrey created her Angel Network to "inspire people to use their lives and to reap the truest rewards that come from giving to others." Every Monday on her show, Oprah awards $100,000 to

an "angel" to enable him or her to continue and expand his or her work.

◆ Visit Oprah's web site at www.Oprah.com and click on "Use Your Life" to find out more about the Angel Network. You can even nominate for Oprah's weekly prize someone you know whose work helps make the world a better place.

30 Isaiah predicts that a holy remnant of Israel will remain after the destruction to carry on the mission of God and Judaism. In many ways, Holocaust survivors can be seen as a holy remnant of the European Jewry destroyed during World War II by Hitler.

◆ Ask a Holocaust survivor to come to your class and talk about what it is like to be a survivor. Prepare questions in advance. Consider asking such questions as: Do survivors feel a special responsibility? Do survivors feel a certain kind of guilt for surviving? What special responsibility do Jews have today to honor the legacy of those who perished?

◆ Read about the difficulties of surviving the war and beginning life again in such books for Grades 4-6 as *Hide and Seek* or *Anna Is Still Here*, both by Ida Vos.

Other Resources

31 View and discuss the film *Angels in the Outfield* (1951, not rated, 102 minutes) or the newer version (1994, rated PG, 103 minutes), in which angels answer a boy's request for divine intervention to help his favorite ball team.

32 Read and discuss the short story, "Nettie Blumenthal," told by Gerald Fierst in *Chosen Tales*, edited by Peninnah Schram, pp. 89-92. Fierst relates the memory of a woman who believes that as a young girl, she (along with her mother and sister) was saved from the Nazis by angels.

33 To learn how to sanctify and truly enjoy the events of everyday life, read *The Extraordinary Nature of Ordinary Things* by Steven Z. Leder.

34 View and discuss the film *Oh, God!* (1977, rated PG, 98 minutes) about an ordinary man called by God to be a prophet, and how hard it is for him to convince people to listen to him.

35 *The Seventh Million* by Tom Segev documents Israel's relation to the Holocaust and to the survivors who settled the new state.

36 View and discuss the classic film *It's a Wonderful Life* (1947, not rated, 132 minutes), in which an angel saves the life of George Bailey and shows him how important he is. Discuss how George's life is prophetic as he fights evil and engages in holy acts.

37 Read and discuss the seventh stanza of the poem "Vacillation" by William Butler Yeats, which is based on the story of Isaiah and the coal. You can find the poem at www.bibliomania.com/0/2/332/2432/28294/1/frameset.html.

38 For more on the Holocaust, read books, such as the following, about righteous non-Jews who saved the lives of Jews: *Raoul Wallenberg: The Man Who Stopped Death* by Sharon Linnea (Grades 6-9); *Rescue: The Story of How Gentiles Saved Jews in the Holocaust* by Milton Meltzer (Grades 7-10); *The Courage to Care: Rescuers of Jews During the Holocaust* by Carol Rittner and Sondra Myers (Grades 7-10); *Rescuers: Portraits of Moral Courage in the Holocaust* by Malka Drucker, with photographs by Gay Block (Grades 6 and up).

39 For more on the prophet Isaiah, including history, themes, and notable quotations, read *Messengers of God: A Jewish Prophets Who's Who* by Ronald H. Isaacs, pp. 91-101.

Involving the Family

40 Make every meal your family shares together a holy occasion by sanctifying it with the *Motzi* over bread. How does making a blessing change the mood of your meal?

41 The angels cover their hoof-shaped feet because they didn't want the Israelites to be reminded constantly of their biggest mistake (the golden calf). Make an effort as a family to refrain from reminding others of the mistakes they have made. Instead, try to offer positive feedback and compliment one another at least once a day.

Bar/Bat Mitzvah Project

42 Danny Siegel's books *Gym Shoes and Irises: Personalized Tzedakah Book Two* and *Munbaz II and Other Mitzvah Heroes* tell the inspiring stories of several *mitzvah* heroes. Read one or both of these books. Then choose one of the featured *tzedakah* projects to support financially, to become involved with personally, or to emulate on your own.

ISAIAH 10:32-12:6
EIGHTH DAY PASSOVER
YOM HAATZMA'UT

 This Haftarah has been paired with the eighth day of Passover, on which we read Deuteronomy 15:19-16:17, and with Israel Independence day. See "Connecting the Text To the Holiday," pp. 242-243, for an exploration of the many ways the two texts and the holidays shed light on each other.

SYNOPSIS

This Haftarah is set in the last years of the eighth century B.C.E. Isaiah lived and preached in Jerusalem, the capital of the Kingdom of Judah. The Assyrians have already conquered the Northern Kingdom of Israel and were now advancing on Jerusalem in the South. The people are understandably very afraid of what lies ahead.

As the Haftarah begins, Isaiah prophesies that, just as a lumberjack cuts the trees of a mighty forest, so will God destroy the Assyrians who threaten Jerusalem.

Isaiah comforts the Israelites (chapter 11) with a vision of an age in which the spirit of wisdom and understanding shall prevail in a world united in peace. In this age, all people will delight in *Adonai* and in righteousness. The wolf will dwell with the lamb, the leopard with the kid, the calf with the lion, and the cow with the bear. Animals will no longer prey upon each other, and even the poisonous serpent will be harmless. The honored remnant of Israel will flourish in its own homeland, safe from enemies who will be destroyed by God.

The six verses of chapter 12 included in the Haftarah contain two hymns to be sung by the community in gratitude for God's deliverance. The Israelites thank God for turning away from anger and toward forgiveness and redemption. God — who is called Israel's deliverance, strength, and might — is to be praised for the glorious acts God has done.

INSIGHTS FROM THE TRADITION

A Isaiah prophesies that a new leader will stem from the family of Jesse and the spirit of God will be on him (verse 11:2).

Radak explains that the spirit of God includes a spirit of wisdom, understanding, counsel, heroism, knowledge, and awe of God.

◆ What do all these qualities have to do with leadership?

◆ Can someone be a leader without some of these qualities?

◆ List some Jewish leaders of the past and discuss whether each had some or all of these qualities.

◆ Play the leadership game listed in the Haftarah for *Korach*, Connecting the Text To the Sedra #16, p. 57.

B Isaiah says that the spirit of wisdom and understanding will be on the new leader. Radak suggests that wisdom is knowing clearly what you learned and being able to recall it at anytime. Understanding is being able to deduce what you have not studied from what you have studied.

- What do you think is the difference between wisdom and knowledge?

- Have you been in situations in which you didn't know what to say or do until it was too late?

C Isaiah praises the future leader saying that he will not judge by sight (verse 11:3). According to Ibn Ezra, this means that he will not judge based solely on appearances.

- When is it wrong to judge someone based on appearances, and when is it right to judge someone based on appearances?

- Role-play both types of scenarios.

- Alternatively, discuss the practice (legality and morality) of racial profiling by police.

D The future leader will not chastise based on what he hears with his ears (verse 11:3). Abrabanel explains that people sometimes hear a rumor and judge a person based solely on that rumor.

- Ask your parents if there was ever a time they heard a rumor about someone they had not yet met and they prejudged that person based on the rumor (e.g., a new boss, a new teacher, a new neighbor).

- Were their judgments right or wrong, once they got to know the person?

STRATEGIES
Analyzing the Text

1 In verse 11:1 Isaiah speaks of a future king from the line of David who will rule wisely, justly, charismatically, and with God's spirit on him. Isaiah lived in a time during which a king of the line of David ruled, and he hoped for the day

when that king would be endowed with God's spirit and wisdom.

However, later commentators, living when there was no Jewish king or kingdom, developed the idea of a restoration of the Davidic line with a charismatic leader who would rule forever in peace: the Messiah.

- Explain how verse 11:1 can be understood to be the wish for a new and better king.

- Explain how some later commentators read into the verse the wish for a Messiah who would be descended from the line of Jesse and David.

- For more information on the interpretation of Isaiah chapter 11, see the article "Isaiah in the Light of History" by H. L. Ginsberg, in *Conservative Judaism*, Fall 1967, pp. 1-18.

2 Isaiah's description of the future king includes many images of power and strength. The king will use strong words effectively, he will be girded by justice and faithfulness, and he will have a king's rod or scepter.

- Find each of these images in the Haftarah.

- Do you think it takes strength and power to create an era of peace?

- How does just rule bring to a king strength and support from the people?

3 In verses 11:6-8 Isaiah describes the wolf and lamb, leopard and kid, calf and lion all living peacefully together. Some commentators explain the passage as an allegory. The wolf, the leopard, and the lion represent evil people who oppress the weak. The lamb, cow, calf, and kid represent the poor and weak people.

The allegory can also be understood to mean that the stronger and weaker nations will coexist in peace.

◆ Explain how this allegory portrays a time of future universal peace and harmony among all people.

◆ Draw your own interpretation of this famous verse.

Connecting the Text To the Holiday

4 Isaiah prophesies in verses 10:32-34 that an assault by the Assyrians on Jerusalem will be stopped by God. This occurred around the years 715-705 B.C.E. when Assyria, under the leadership of King Sargon II, was annexing land and enslaving nations. Sargon II was indeed stopped in the year 705, when he was killed in battle and his body was ignominiously abandoned by his men.

Isaiah uses a metaphor to describe Sargon's army: It is like a big, mighty, arrogant, seemingly indestructible forest that will be quickly and easily chopped down by God.

◆ Explain this metaphor in your own words.

◆ Explain how Pharaoh was a mighty, arrogant tyrant, who in a manner similar to Sargon, was brought down by God.

◆ Make a political cartoon of the enemy army being hacked down to size — use the forest metaphor, please.

5 Passover celebrates the freedom of Israel from Egyptian captivity. The Haftarah hopes for a future return from exile in Assyria. See verse 11:11, in which God will take the people out of exile a second time (the first time was from Egypt, the second time will be the Northerners out of Assyria). In addition, verse 11:15 describes the drying up of a sea and river, allowing the people to escape as at the Reed Sea. In this way, God will make a highway for the people to return home

from exile. Also see verse 12:2, which uses language that is virtually identical to Exodus 15:2, the Song at the Sea, which was sung in thanksgiving after God rescued Israel from the Egyptians.

Later Rabbinic commentators also discuss another Passover: Passover of the Future, which will bring another redemption.

Yom HaAtzma'ut celebrates a similar type of redemption: the Jews were redeemed from being a homeless people to having a home; we were redeemed from lacking our own sovereign state to having one; we were redeemed from being the minority people everywhere we lived to having a place where we are the majority.

◆ Discuss these types of redemptions. Can you identify other ways in which we were redeemed with the formation of the State of Israel? (Hebrew was reborn, survivors of the Holocaust had a new lease on life, etc.)

6 Isaiah, in verse 11:1, may have been hoping for the reign of the next king, Hezekiah. Hezekiah is known for having enacted religious reforms. In particular, he overhauled the observance of the Passover holiday. According to II Chronicles 30, after instituting his religious reforms, Hezekiah also called on the people to come to Jerusalem to celebrate the Passover holiday the way God wanted. They did everything according to the law of Moses, and we are taught that there had never been a Passover like it.

Hezekiah was not alone in being dedicated to the observance of Passover. For example, after him, King Josiah also chose to enact widespread religious reforms at Passover (see II Chronicles 34-35). Before Hezekiah, Joshua instituted a community-wide campaign to circumcise all the Israelite males before Passover, none of whom had been circumcised during the wandering in the desert (Joshua 5).

◆ Today, many people are much more careful about what they eat at Passover than they are the rest of the year. Many people who do not keep kosher during the year do keep kosher at Passover. Why do you think this is so?

◆ Would you consider Passover the most important Jewish holiday to your family? Why or why not?

7 The Holiday Torah reading includes Deuteronomy 15:4, which promises that if you will follow God's laws, there will be no needy people in your land.

However, the same Torah reading also includes Deuteronomy 15:11, which asserts that the poor will never cease to be in the land.

◆ How do you reconcile these two seemingly contradictory statements?

◆ In the Haftarah Isaiah longs for a just and wise king who will judge impartially, giving equal treatment to the poor and meek. Compare Isaiah's vision of an ideal king with the utopian situation described by the Torah in Deuteronomy 15:4.

◆ Consider the following different references to poor and needy people in the traditions of Passover:

• The *Haggadah* instructs us to invite those in need to our *Seder*.

• *Matzah* is called poor people's bread.

• Rabbinic law states that everyone must have four glasses of wine on Passover, even if they must be given funding from a charity fund to pay for the wine and their Passover meal.

8 The Haftarah says in verse 12:3 that you will draw water בששון (b'sason), which is usually translated as "with joy." However, another way to translate the word is "willingly."

◆ What is your understanding of this verse with this alternative translation?

◆ Learn the song *"U'Shavtem Mayim B'sason,"* which may be found in the songbook *B'Kol Echad*, edited by Jeffrey Shiovitz, p. 90, and on the accompanying audiocassettes, *Shirei B'Kol Echad*, both of which may be ordered from the web site of United Synagogue for Conservative Judaism, www.uscj.org/booksvc.

◆ Learn the folkdance that goes with the song, too.

ISAIAH 27:6-28:13; 29:22-23
SHEMOT שמות Ashkenazim

This Haftarah has been paired with *Parashat Shemot*, Exodus 1:1-6:1. See "Connecting the Text To the Sedra," pp. 246-247, for an exploration of the many ways the two texts shed light on each other.

SYNOPSIS

Isaiah preaches to the people of Judah after the fall of the Northern Kingdom of Israel to Assyria in 721 B.C.E. His prophetic message reviews the tragic demise of the Northern Kingdom and the inevitable doom of Judah, yet Isaiah also interjects several strong notes of hope. In fact, the Haftarah begins with the announcement that one day in the future, Israel will sprout and blossom, bringing goodness to the entire world.

Isaiah mourns the loss of the Northern Kingdom and assures his people that Israel's enemy will ultimately suffer far greater punishment. Then, he promises a day when the Israelite exiles in Assyria and Egypt will return to Jerusalem, where they will worship God.

Chapter 28 opens with a sweeping condemnation of the leaders of the Northern Kingdom (Ephraim), who brought their nation down by being drunks and gluttons. Again Isaiah interrupts his grim message of doom with a word of hope, assuring the people that one day *Adonai* will be a crown of beauty and diadem of glory for the remnant of the people of Judah.

Isaiah returns to his main point, in which he likens Judah to destroyed Samaria. Judah's leaders also abuse alcohol, which impairs their judgment. He compares the leaders to children who cannot understand even the simplest instructions. They will fall backward, Isaiah predicts, and be injured and captured.

The Rabbis concluded the Haftarah with an uplifting selection from chapter 29, in which Isaiah predicts a day on which the remnant of Israel will rise above its former shame and sanctify God's holy name.

INSIGHTS FROM THE TRADITION

A Isaiah prophesies in verse 27:6 that "In days to come Jacob shall strike root, Israel shall sprout and blossom; and the face of the world shall be covered with fruit." Soncino explains that this means that when Israel is blessed, the entire world will share in the benefit of that blessing.

◆ What do you think this means?

◆ When a stone is thrown into a pool of water, ripples emanate from the stone and spread to the edges of the water. How do we all benefit from the ripple effect of any one person's success? Jonas Salk, for example, helped us all by inventing the vaccine for polio. At the same time, he inspired a young generation to pursue careers in medicine. His vaccine also spurred research in preventing other diseases.

◆ Think of someone else whose good fortune or success affected the world. What were the ripple effects of his or her contribution?

B According to Soncino, verse 27:12 indicates that when the people of Israel are gathered from dispersion, not a single exile will be forgotten.

◆ Mishnah *Sanhedrin* (37a) teaches that one who saves a single life is as though he/she has saved the entire world. Conversely, whoever destroys a single life is as though he/she has destroyed an entire world.

◆ How does each person represent an entire world?

◆ Often orphanages or foster parents save the life of a child by giving the child a home and raising him/her. Explain how the orphanage or foster parents have saved the entire world if, for example, the child grows up to discover a cure for AIDS, or if the child grows up and has a family. Give other examples which also prove the point the Mishnah was making.

C Isaiah criticizes priest and prophet in verse 28:7 for exercising poor judgment, confused by liquor. Radak explains that because of drinking, they erred and did not judge justly.

◆ Why wouldn't we want a judge to make decisions under the influence of alcohol?

◆ Is it equally important that, say, a bus driver or accountant should never work under the influence of alcohol?

◆ List other jobs that should never be performed under the influence of drugs or alcohol.

◆ Our society has adopted a policy of zero tolerance on many issues, including working or driving under the influence of drugs or alcohol. For example, we have zero tolerance for smoking in many environments and zero tolerance for sexual harassment and racism in the workplace or classroom. Do you think zero tolerance is effective in getting people to change for the better? Alternatively, can you think of instances when zero tolerance might be too extreme? Debate this subject.

STRATEGIES
Analyzing the Text

1 Isaiah asks a rhetorical question in verse 27:7: "Was [Israel] beaten as [Israel's] beater has been? Did [Israel] suffer such slaughter as his slayers?"

◆ What is a rhetorical question? (Usually rhetorical questions in the Bible are given to make a point, and are usually meant to be answered negatively. This is also the case here, according to Ibn Ezra. The message is that Israel's enemies will ultimately suffer more severely than they have caused Israel to suffer.)

◆ What point is Isaiah making in verse 27:7?

◆ Why do you think Isaiah uses rhetorical questions instead of simply stating the fact?

2 In verse 27:9 Isaiah says that the sin of the Israelites (Jacob) can be corrected only by shattering limestone altars, tearing down every *Asherah* (sacred post), and destroying incense stands.

◆ Based on these corrective measures, what is the sin of the Israelites?

3 Isaiah refers to the "fortified city" in verse 27:10. Plaut contends that the city is Samaria, the destroyed capital of the Northern Kingdom. Radak, on the other hand, says the city is Jerusalem, the capital of the Southern Kingdom. The JPS translation reads "fortified cities," although the Hebrew text seems to be in the singular. Other scholars suggest that "fortified cities" means enemy cities now destroyed.

◆ Based on your understanding of the text and the history, which of these interpretations makes the most sense to you, and why?

4 Verses 27:12 and 27:13 both start with the phrase, "And in that day." Radak explains that the repetition of the phrase is for added emphasis.

◆ What message do you think Isaiah is emphasizing in these consecutive verses?

◆ How does the sounding of the ram's horn, described in verse 27:13, add to your understanding of Isaiah's message?

5 Isaiah promises that the exiles will eventually be returned to Israel in verses 27:12-13. Rashi explains that the collection of exiles will be like the collection of scattered olives after they had been beaten off the tree.

◆ How are the Israelites like olives — first beaten out and then carefully collected?

◆ In this metaphor, who is the tree, and what happens to the tree after the olives are collected?

◆ Alternatively, Radak understands from this verse that God will thresh grain and remove the valuable kernel (Israel) from the chaff (other nations). Which metaphor — olives or grain — do you prefer? Make a collage to depict one of these metaphors.

6 Isaiah regrets in verse 28:11 that God's word is not understood by the Israelites. It is as if God "speaks to that people in a stammering jargon and an alien tongue." Isaiah concludes that because they "refuse to listen," the Israelites will be punished.

◆ Reread verses 28:7-13 and identify as many reasons as possible for why the people cannot understand.

7 Verses 28:9-10 may constitute a response by the drunken leaders to Isaiah's reproof, and in their response they mockingly quote Isaiah's own words back to him.

◆ Why are they (the leaders of Israel characterized by Isaiah as drunkards) insulted?

◆ Why is quoting a prophet's own words an effective way to mock him?

◆ Act out these leaders' reaction to Isaiah's message, including the body language.

8 The word "crown" is used four times in the Haftarah, and the synonym "diadem" once.

◆ Find where these words are used. In each case, what does "crown" or "diadem" symbolize? Are the words used the same way or differently each time?

Connecting the Text To the Sedra

9 Isaiah says in verse 27:6 that Jacob (Israel) will eventually flourish and cover the face of the world. In the Sedra we are reminded that Jacob brought his people to Egypt, where they took root, flourished, and now fill the land.

◆ Jews have made contributions to every land in which they have lived. What are some contributions Jews have made in your country? Each student should choose one famous Jewish person and present to the class his or her greatest contribution(s) to your society. (You may wish to consult *The Jewish 100* by Michael Shapiro to help you answer this question.)

10 Isaiah prophesies that Israel's enemies will suffer great punishment in the future (see Analyzing the Text #1, p. 245). In the Sedra Israel suffers at the hands of the Egyptians, who are severely punished in the end.

◆ Do you think the promise that their enemies will ultimately suffer was a source of comfort to the Israelites?

◆ If someone committed a crime against you, would it make you feel better to know they will be punished?

◆ This Sedra and Haftarah are usually read near Martin Luther King, Jr. Day. One of Dr. King's most famous speeches, given on August 28, 1963, included the statement: "I have a dream that one day on the red hills of Georgia the sons of former slaves and the sons of former slave owners will be able to sit down together at the table of brotherhood." Did this speech offer the suffering of one's enemy as a source of comfort? Did this speech offer comfort in another form?

11 The Israelite leaders fail to heed Isaiah's warning, just as Pharaoh fails to listen to Moses. The Israelites were then plagued with war, destruction, and exile. Pharaoh was plagued ten times.

◆ List the ten plagues Pharaoh faced. List modern plagues which threaten our environment and our society.

◆ Make a poster featuring a warning to today's society about the environment, morality, education, or the issue of your choice. Make sure it will catch people's attention and not be ignored. Arrange to take your poster to your Passover *Seder* and, during the *Seder*, discuss our modern plagues.

12 Isaiah says that the Israelite exiles will be gathered and brought to worship *Adonai* on the holy mount in Jerusalem. In the Sedra God tells Moses to gather the Israelites so they can leave Egypt and worship God in the wilderness.

Worshiping God may be at the center of both redemptions, because the Israelites were freed from Egypt and exile in order to serve God and be God's people.

◆ Using a disposable (or even waterproof) camera, take pictures of various people, places and things that remind you of God. Be prepared to explain why you are grateful for each person, place, or thing, and how or why each reminds you of godliness.

13 Both Moses and Isaiah have difficulty getting their message across to others. In the Sedra Moses must prove to the Israelites with visible signs that God has appeared to him. He causes his rod to turn into a snake, and makes leprosy appear and disappear from his hand. In the Haftarah Isaiah laments that he must speak to the leaders like children, murmur by murmur, in order to make them understand his message. Moses wants the people to risk their lives trying to flee Pharaoh, and Isaiah wants the people to stop idolatry.

◆ Why do you think Moses' and Isaiah's messages are so difficult for the people to understand?

◆ Why are the Israelites in both cases portrayed as children incapable of understanding?

◆ Is it fair to compare dazed drunks to children?

Extending the Text

14 We learned above in Connecting the Text To the Sedra #9, p. 246, that Jews have made contributions to every land in which they have lived. Before World War II, Jews constituted a significant percentage of the German population, having settled there hundreds of years earlier. Jews were wrongly blamed for many of Germany's woes, even though from 1901 through 1933, 11 of 37 Nobel Prizes awarded to Germans were given to German Jews.

◆ Choose one of the German Jewish recipients listed below and make a poster highlighting his life and Nobel Prize winning work:

1905 Adolf von Baeyer

1908 Paul Ehrlich

1910 Paul Heyse

1910 Otto Wallach

1915 Richard Willstatter

1918 Fritz Haber

1921 Albert Einstein

1922 Otto Meyerhof

1925 James Franck

1925 Gustav Hertz

1931 Otto Warburg

◆ Alternatively, prepare a report on Nadine Gordimer, a Jewish woman who won the 1991 Nobel Prize in Literature. Gordimer has made important cultural and political contributions to her native country, South Africa, through her writing and political activism against Apartheid.

◆ Research other Jewish (male and female) Nobel laureates. Report on how they, too, contributed significantly to their countries.

15 Isaiah uses the image of a crown five times in this Haftarah. Every day in our morning blessings, we bless God who "crowns Israel with glory."

◆ What do you think it means to be crowned with glory by God?

◆ In the Bible crowns symbolize royalty, power, and honor. God is said to wear a crown made of human prayers. The Sabbath Queen is also said to wear a crown. Shabbat itself is called in the liturgy "a crown of distinction and triumph for Israel." The Messiah, we are taught, will wear a wreath of prayers. The Book of Proverbs 12:4 says a good wife is a "crown of her husband." Choose one of these crown images and draw your interpretation of it.

◆ Alternatively, make crowns for members of your synagogue to wear at a Purim *Megillah* reading.

◆ For more information on the symbolism of crowns, see *The Encyclopedia of Jewish Symbols* by Ellen Frankel and Betsy Platkin Teutsch, pp. 37-38.

16 Isaiah promises that every single exiled Israelite will be returned to Jerusalem. Rambam teaches in the *Mishneh Torah* that if funds are needed to ransom Jews who are being held hostage somewhere, everything should be done to raise the necessary funds. The *mitzvah* of redeeming captives, *pidyon shevuyim*, has been very important throughout Jewish history, most recently in the rescue of Jews from Yemen, Ethiopia, and Russia.

Because *pidyon shevuyim* is one of the few commandments that deal with matters of life and death, it is regarded by Jewish law as one of the most important *mitzvot*. The concept is so central to Jewish thought, in fact, that every day in the *"Amidah"* we pray for the redemption of exiles:

"Sound the great *shofar* for our freedom, raise the banner to gather our exiles and gather us together from the four corners of the earth. Blessed are You, *Adonai*, Who gathers in the dispersed of the people Israel."

◆ Invite a representative of your local Jewish Federation to tell your class about Project Moses and current redemption situations.

◆ For a discussion and activities on this *mitzvah*, see *Teaching Mitzvot* by Barbara Binder Kadden and Bruce Kadden, pp. 105-110.

17 Isaiah uses in verse 28:9 the phrase יורה דעה *(yoreh day'ah)*, which gives its name to one of four sections of the Jewish law code called the *Shulchan Aruch*. Mastery of this section, which literally means "teaching knowledge," is required of all Orthodox Rabbis before ordination. The section deals with complex legal issues requiring a Rabbinic decision, including in part: ritual slaughter of animals, *kashrut, mezuzah, Sefer Torah, Brit Milah, bikkur cholim*, and mourning.

◆ Do a report on one small topic among these legal issues to give you an idea of how extensive a Rabbi's knowledge must be. As a resource for research, use *A Guide To Jewish Religious Practice* by Isaac Klein.

◆ What do you think all Rabbis should be required to know?

◆ Besides knowledge requirements, what other qualifications do you think Rabbis should have?

◆ Imagine you are on the committee to hire a new Rabbi for your congregation. Write a list of interview questions you might want to ask the candidates.

18 Isaiah says in verse 27:13 that the *shofar* will sound on the day the exiles are gathered to Jerusalem.

The *shofar* called the Israelites to the Revelation at Sinai, and on various occasions the *shofar* called the Israelites to war. During the month of Elul, we sound the *shofar* daily to call us to repentance. On Rosh HaShanah, the *shofar* calls us to the throne of God, the Judge. On Yom Kippur, the *shofar* calls us to freedom.

◆ To appreciate the power of the call of the ram's horn, learn to sound the *shofar*. Many synagogues invite all congregants to sound their *shofar* at the close of Yom Kippur. Does your synagogue have this tradition? If so, start practicing so you can be ready to sound a *shofar* next Yom Kippur. If not, talk to the Rabbi and Ritual Committee about instituting it next year.

19 Isaiah promises in 29:22 that one day, "No more shall Jacob be shamed; no longer his face grow pale."

Jewish law prohibits us from embarrassing someone in public. In the *Mishneh Torah (Hilchot De'ot)* 6:7-8, Rambam teaches that whoever shames someone in public has committed a great sin. One must never call someone else a bad name, nor embarrass him in public. If you notice that a person has committed a sin or behaved badly, you must point out what the person did wrong. You should speak gently and nicely, informing him or her that it is for their own good.

◆ Imagine a scene between a child and parent, in which the child behaves badly. Role-play the scene in two ways: the parent embarrasses the child by scolding him or her in public; the parent honors the child by dealing with the situation privately and constructively. How is the child likely to react in each situation?

◆ Alternatively, role-play a scene in which the child embarrasses the parent. Now role-play the scene without embarrassment.

20 Isaiah condemns the leaders of Israel for excessive eating and drinking. The Book of Proverbs 23:20-21 teaches, "Do not be of those who guzzle wine or glut themselves on meat; for guzzlers and gluttons will be impoverished, and drowsing will clothe you in tatters."

◆ What do you think the word "drowsing" means? Look it up in the dictionary. Were you right about the meaning?

◆ In your own words, what lesson is Proverbs teaching?

◆ Form several groups, each of which will have 15 minutes to write their own anti-drinking or pro-healthy eating rap. The groups can present their raps to the class, and the performances can be videotaped for later viewing.

21 In verses 28:5-6 Isaiah prophesies a day when *Adonai* will be a crown of beauty and glory. Some believe that Isaiah is predicting the successful survival of a faithful remnant of Israel who will enjoy the benefits of a life that honors God. Others assert that Isaiah is announcing the coming of a Messianic Age.

The idea of a Messiah remains a controversial belief among Jews. However, in his 13 Principles of Faith, Rambam states, "I believe with perfect faith in the coming of the Messiah, and even though he may delay, nevertheless I anticipate every day that he will come."

◆ Do you believe that a Messiah will come one day? Justify your opinion.

◆ With your classmates, brainstorm what you think the world will be like after the Messiah comes.

◆ Ask your Rabbi about his or her beliefs regarding the Messiah.

◆ Read and discuss the story "Why the Night Watchman Was Denied a Raise" in *The Jewish Spirit: A Celebration in Stories and Art* by Ellen Frankel.

22 During the 1968 Olympics, Kenyan runner Kipchoge Keino won a gold medal in the 1500 meter race. At later Olympic competitions, he won more gold and silver medals. He also served for ten years as the running coach for his country's Olympic teams. However, Kipchoge Keino is a hero in Kenya for another reason. Over the last 30 years, he and his wife have run an orphanage in their home. They raised their own children, as well as dozens of other children in

need of a home. Recently, their orphanage was home to over 70 young people. Keino is quoted as saying, "I think I have been lucky. Now what is important is how I use what I have to help others."

◆ Explain how this story is an example of the ripple effect lesson taught in Insights from the Tradition #A, p. 244.

◆ How is this story also an example of the lesson that saving one life is like saving the whole world, taught in Insights from the Tradition #B, pp. 244-245?

◆ Find other examples of people who have used the good that came to them to help others and save lives.

23 Isaiah refers to the Northern Kingdom of Israel as Ephraim because Ephraim is one of the larger tribes comprising the kingdom.

◆ Draw a map of the territories of the 12 tribes of Israel in both the Northern and Southern Kingdoms. (The teacher can provide enlarged photocopies of the appropriate map from Appendix C of this book. Students can then color this with markers, fill it in with colored sand, or make it into clay relief maps.) This is also a good opportunity to ask the students to memorize the names of the 12 tribes in Hebrew and/or English.

Personalizing the Text

24 Our acts have ripple effects (see Insights from the Tradition #A, p. 244).

◆ Interview your parents, grandparents, aunts, and uncles to collect stories about how they, or people they know, used their good fortune and success to help other people. Write a

D'var Torah that includes some of these stories.

◆ Alternatively, interview family members about having saved a life (Insights from the Tradition #B, pp. 244-245).

25 Isaiah asks a rhetorical question in verse 27:7 to make a point.

◆ Practice your questioning skills by playing a game of verbal tennis. The object of the game is to have a running conversation, without pauses, between two or more participants, during which the players may only ask questions. The first person to make a declarative statement instead of asking a question loses.

A sample conversation might go something like this:

"Do you know what the weather will be like tomorrow?"

"Why do you ask?"

"Can I go to the beach or will it be too cold?"

"Why would you want to go to the beach in November?"

And so on.

26 Isaiah anticipates that he will have great difficulty getting the people to understand his message.

◆ To get a sense of Isaiah's frustration, try this communication exercise: teach the class a simple skill, such as making a sandwich or tying your shoe, without using any words or props. You must demonstrate the skill entirely with hand gestures, body language, and non-verbal communication.

27 Although Isaiah's main message in this Haftarah is one of condemnation, he repeatedly interjects words of hope and comfort into his harsh rebuke of Israel.

◆ Why do you think Isaiah tries to soften his message with a note of hope?

◆ Do you think punishment is easier to bear if the one who is being punished knows there is an end in sight? Explain your answer.

◆ New employees must always "pay their dues" before being awarded good assignments and promotions. Medical interns must work long, hard hours before they open fulfilling and lucrative practices of their own. Athletes must struggle and practice for endless, and often painful, hours before they can compete in the Olympics. Can you think of other examples when hope for a better future helps someone endure times of great difficulty?

28 In Analyzing the Text #5, p. 246, the Israelites in exile were compared to olives beaten out of their olive tree, scattered in all directions, and then collected.

◆ Olives roll far, and it must be very hard to collect all of them. To help imagine how hard it is to collect little pieces thrown into the air, play a game of jacks. Make the game progressively harder by adding more and more jacks.

29 The song *"Uva'u Ha'ovdim"* (And the Wanderers Came) is taken from Isaiah 27:13.

◆ Learn and sing this song, which may be found at www.ohr.org.il/audio/ra/perlman/ pursongs.htm#U'va'u Haovdim or on the recoding *Live in Tel Aviv* by Shlomo Carlebach.

30 The song *"Ani Ma'amin"* (I Believe) is based on Rambam's principles of faith, one of which is the coming of the Messiah. It was often sung by Holocaust victims in the concentration camps.

◆ Learn and sing this song, which may be found on the recording *The Jewish Soul* by Roslyn Barak. For a modern version of this song, see the recording *Ani Ma-amin* by Debbie Friedman.

◆ What was the significance of this song during the Holocaust?

31 The *"Yigdal"* prayer reviews all of Rambam's Thirteen Principles of Faith.

◆ This prayer has a special melody for the High Holy Days. Learn this beautiful melody.

Other Resources

32 To learn "how a tribe of desert nomads changed the way everyone thinks and feels," read portions of *The Gifts of the Jews* by Thomas Cahill.

33 View and discuss the classic film *It's a Wonderful Life* (1946, not rated, 132 minutes), which demonstrates how each person's life touches countless other lives.

34 For more on the prophet Isaiah, including history, themes, and notable quotations, read *Messengers of God: A Jewish Prophets Who's Who* by Ronald H. Isaacs, pp. 91-101.

35 For more information and discussion questions on Isaiah, see the Reform Movement's Shabbat Talk web page, www. uahc.org/shabbat/stt/3shemot.shtml.

36 Complete p. 21 in *Prophets Copy Pak™* by Marji Gold-Vukson.

37 Discuss the illustration of this Haftarah in *The Illustrated Torah* by Michal Meron, p. 64.

38 Redeeming captives is a *mitzvah*. View and discuss the film *Raid on Entebbe* (1977, rated R, 150 minutes) about Israel's daring rescue of captives taken in a hijacking.

Involving the Family

39 We learned in Extending the Text #17, p. 249, that there is a body of information that Rabbis are required to know. As a family, compile your own list of required knowledge. Learn all your family members' birthdays, favorite foods, favorite colors, and favorite things to do. Learn who is responsible to perform which household tasks. Learn important genealogical information about your ancestors and family history. Consider printing this information (and any other knowledge you consider "required") and posting it in a public space in your home.

Bar/Bat Mitzvah Project

40 The Israelites are condemned for their excessively indulgent and destructive habits. With all the temptation facing young adults, it can be difficult for them to make healthy decisions about their lifestyle and habits. The organization Students Against Destructive Decisions (SADD) believes that "effective child-parent communication is critically important in helping young adults make healthy decisions." Visit the web site for Students Against Destructive Decisions (SADD) at www.saddon-line.com. Find out how to join or start a local chapter. While you are online, click on "Contract for Life," which is a pledge by both you and your parents to help you make responsible decisions in your young adulthood. With your parents, consider signing this pledge.

ISAIAH 40:1-26
VA'ETCHANAN ואתחנן

This Haftarah has been paired with *Parashat Va'etchanan*, Deuteronomy 3:23-7:11. See "Connecting the Text To the Sedra," pp. 256-258, for an exploration of the many ways the two texts shed light on each other.

Note: All the Haftarot from Deutero-Isaiah have similar historical context and themes. Many Extending and Personalizing Strategies, as well as Other Resources and Bar Mitzvah Projects, can be shared among them.

SYNOPSIS

This first Haftarah of Deutero-Isaiah finds the Israelites in exile in Babylon after the destruction of Jerusalem (see Isaiah Overview, pp. 218-219). It appears that Persian King Cyrus is about to conquer Babylon (539 B.C.E.), and Isaiah hopes he will be willing to let the exiles return to Israel. Thus, Isaiah prophesies that Israel's punishment will soon end, and tenderly encourages the Israelites to take comfort that God's promise of redemption is near at hand.

Isaiah announces that God's mighty power, which had once been used to chastise Israel, will now be dedicated to redeeming the people from exile. God's awesome and eternal power, portrayed as a devastating desert wind, is contrasted with fleeting human life, which Isaiah compares to grass that withers and fades.

Adonai instructs the prophet to proclaim from the mountain tops that *Adonai* is both Israel's mighty warrior and gentle shepherd who will gather them back to their home. God's awesome and eternal power is once again contrasted with the insignificance of nations, the folly of idols, and the transience of human existence.

This is read as the first Haftarah of consolation following Tishah B'Av, which commemorates the destruction of the First Temple in 586 B.C.E.

INSIGHTS FROM THE TRADITION

A The word "comfort" is repeated twice in verse 40:1. According to some commentators, it is repeated to indicate two different exiles: the first "comfort" refers to the exile in Babylon, and the second "comfort" refers to the exile inflicted 600 years later by the Romans in 70 C.E.
We might assume that prophecy predicts the future. But biblical prophecy is understood primarily as an attempt by a prophet to convince the people to be faithful to God's ways.

◆ Which type of prophecy would be implied if "comfort" refers only to the Babylonian exile?

◆ Which type of prophecy would be implied if "comfort" refers also to an exile that would occur 600 years later?

◆ We often read stories written a long time ago that seem to apply directly to our own situations. Can you think of such a story that you believed was speaking directly to you?

B According to *midrash*, "Comfort My people" in verse 40:1 can also be translated as "Comfort Me, My people," meaning that God needed to be comforted by Israel (see Plaut, p. 449).

One way to understand this *midrash* is that God felt bad after having to punish Israel for its disobedience.

◆ How does this *midrash* remind you of when parents, about to punish their children, say, "This will hurt me more than it will hurt you"?

◆ Have you ever had to make your parents feel better after they have had to punish you? Why?

C Hirsch explains that Isaiah's consolation is meant to fill Israel with strength and courage to meet the hardships it will face on its journey through the treacherous wilderness back to their homeland.

◆ Why might it be difficult for the Israelites to leave their country of exile, which they know, and return to their homeland, which they do not know?

◆ Have you ever moved from one country to another? from one state to another? from one town to another?

◆ What were the best and worst things about moving?

D Isaiah indicates in verse 40:2 that Israel has received double punishment for all its sins. Ibn Ezra explains that Israel received double the punishment any other nation would have suffered for the same sins.

◆ Is it fair to set different expectations for different people, or should everyone be judged based on the same standards? Debate this question.

◆ Should leaders be punished more severely for the same crimes also committed by others?

◆ In what ways is Israel a leader among nations?

E Isaiah says in verse 40:6, "All flesh is grass." Rashi explains that this phrase means that every human being is destined to die. Therefore, even if someone promises to do a kindness for you, you cannot completely trust her/him because he/she may die in the meantime. Only the word of God can be fully trusted.

◆ Did you ever lose someone who was very close to you, such as a grandparent?

◆ Why might you have felt abandoned, cheated, or betrayed by your loved one's death?

◆ Do you think Rashi's message is that we should never trust anyone at all, or is there another message?

F *Midrash* suggests that there is a difference between "reward" and "recompense" in verse 40:10. A reward is often delayed and only received in the future. Recompense, on the other hand, is an immediate payoff. According to this *midrash*, righteous people act anticipating future reward, whereas evil people act only in order to get immediate recompense. (See *The Rabbi's Bible* by Solomon Simon and Abraham Rothberg, vol. 3, p. 33.)

◆ Do you agree?

◆ What is instant gratification, and into which category (reward or recompense) does it fall?

◆ When people save their income instead of immediately spending it all, they delay the enjoyment or reward until the future.

◆ Can you think of examples (other than money) when you might have the choice between an immediate recompense and a future reward?

G According to Radak, the prophet indicates in verse 40:21 that there are three ways to know something:

- Through your own understanding of your own observation

- By learning from others and from books

- By hearing what others have learned through tradition

◆ Give examples of how you learn each day in all three of these ways.

STRATEGIES
Analyzing the Text

1 Isaiah twice repeats the word "comfort" in verse 40:1. Repetition of words is part of the style of the prophet, helping him to convey a sense of urgency.

◆ What other ways can you think of that convey urgency in a written text (e.g., italics, underlining, writing in all capital letters)?

◆ If we could hear Isaiah speaking these words, what could he do with his voice and body to convey urgency?

◆ Memorize the first two verses of the Haftarah, then take turns pretending you are Isaiah speaking these words to the children of Israel. Alternate making the message sound urgent and tender.

◆ Which way of reading — urgent or tender — seems to fit the text best?

2 Isaiah 40:2 says "speak tenderly to Israel," but the literal translation is "speak to the heart."

◆ Ibn Ezra says "speaking to the heart" means to remove anxiety and worry. What does this phrase mean to you?

◆ This expression, "speak to the heart," also appears in Genesis 34:3 and 50:21. Compare its uses in these passages with its use here.

3 The prophet describes in verse 40:3 a highway prepared across the desert for God. Archaeologists have uncovered ancient Babylonian highways prepared for the triumphant entry of the god or king, which appear to have been quite magnificent.

◆ Modern customs recalling these ancient ones include rolling out the red carpet and a ticker tape parade. Can you think of any other similar examples?

◆ The image of a level highway cut through a mountainous wilderness is a powerful one. Using verses 40:3-5 for ideas, draw a mural of what your class thinks the highway might have looked like.

4 In verses 40:7 and 8, the prophet mentions God's breath blowing like a strong, hot desert wind.

◆ How does this create the image that any life form — vegetable, animal, or human — who tries to stop God's plans will be destroyed?

◆ Draw or paint your understanding of the withering grass and fading flowers in contrast to the everlasting word of God.

◆ Compare your drawing with the illustration of this Haftarah in *The Illustrated Torah* by Michal Meron, p. 191. How does the artist depict God's breath blowing like a hot desert wind?

5 In verse 40:10 God is described as a mighty soldier Who comes to destroy Israel's enemy and save the Israelites.

◆ What do you think of when you picture a soldier?

◆ View the last several minutes of the film *Life Is Beautiful* (1997, PG-13, 116 minutes), available with English subtitles or dubbed in English. How are the American soldiers portrayed in this film clip? Is this portrayal consistent with your own picture of soldiers?

6 Another metaphor is used in verse 40:11, which describes God as a shepherd caring tenderly for a flock.

◆ Compare the tasks of a shepherd to those of God leading a tired people from exile to their home.

◆ Which image of God — as soldier (see Analyzing the Text #5, p. 255) or as shepherd — do you like better, and why?

◆ The following biblical characters worked as shepherds: Abel, Abraham, Jacob, Rachel, Joseph, Moses, David, Saul, and Zipporah. Why might shepherding be good training for a future national leader?

7 God's power over the natural world is described in verses 40:12-24.

◆ In what ways is nature more powerful than humans?

◆ What does it mean, then, for God to be more powerful than nature?

◆ For advanced study, read God's response in the Book of Job 38-39, and compare the images there with those in this Haftarah.

Connecting the Text To the Sedra

8 This Haftarah, which delivers a message of consolation and hope that the enemy would be defeated and the exiles would return home, is the first of seven read on the Shabbatot from Tishah B'Av to Rosh HaShanah. It is always read on the Shabbat immediately following the fast of Tishah B'Av, coupled with *Parashat Va'etchanan*.

◆ The prophet delivered this message of comfort in a climate of great despair. Consider the following factors that might have made the prophet's job more difficult. Then discuss which of the following factors you think would pose the largest obstacle to the prophet.

• Idol worship may have decreased belief among the Israelites that God could truly free the people.

• Powerful enemy empires may have seemed undefeatable.

• The forces of nature (such as the hot desert between Babylon and Israel) may have made home seem too far away.

• The exiles might have been physically weakened by their stay in a foreign land.

• The Israelites might have distrusted God and prophets alike.

• After a long exile, the Israelites might have long since given up the desire of returning to their homeland.

◆ If a prophet preached today to all Jews to return to Israel, what would be the largest obstacle to them in accepting that message?

9 Isaiah uses rhetorical questions in verses 40:12-14, 18, and 21. A rhetorical question, in modern usage, is typically a question to which no answer is expected. In the Bible, rhetorical questions are given to make a point, and are usually meant to be answered negatively.

◆ What are the obvious answers to Isaiah's questions in this Haftarah?

◆ The Sedra also uses rhetorical questions in Deuteronomy 4:32-34. What are the obvious answers to Moses' questions?

◆ Which set of questions are hopeful and uplifting, and which are stern and full of warning?

◆ Do you think the questions get their message across?

◆ In your class discussion today, try using as many rhetorical questions as you can.

10 The Haftarah appears to contradict the Sedra. The Sedra begins with God refusing to forgive Moses' transgression and refusing to reduce the punishment, thereby preventing Moses from ever entering the Promised Land. In sharp contrast, the Haftarah announces that God is ready to forgive Israel and end Israel's punishment, allowing the people to return to the Promised Land.

◆ Review the two stories and explain how God's attitude differs in the two texts.

◆ Keeping in mind that both the Sedra and Haftarah are read on the Shabbat immediately following Tishah B'Av, which text would provide more comfort?

◆ Why do you think the Rabbis wanted to convey on the Shabbat of Consolation that forgiveness from God may be expected, but never taken for granted?

◆ What is the difference between expecting something and taking it for granted?

◆ Moses failed to accomplish one goal in his life — entering the Promised Land. Yet he was nonetheless a productive, successful person. One may fail to achieve all one's goals and face failures in life, but that does not diminish the successes that have been achieved. How might this notion be comforting to the Israel-ites, to the Rabbis in exile

after the destruction of the Second Temple, and to us?

11 The Sedra refers several times to God's strong arm (Deuteronomy 3:24, 4:34, and 7:8). The Haftarah says, "Behold, *Adonai* comes in might, and God's arm wins triumph" (verse 40:10).

◆ Do you think God actually has an arm? If not, what might this image mean?

12 In Deuteronomy 6:18 Moses says to the Israelites, "You will do that which is right and good in the sight of *Adonai*." The Hebrew for "right" or "straight" is ישר (*yashar*). The same word is used in verse 40:3 of the Haftarah: "Clear in the wilderness the way of *Adonai*! Level (make straight) in the desert a highway for our God."

Another name for Israel comes from the same root word ישר *B'nai Jeshurun*, meaning "the upright children."

◆ Why do you think Jews are called *B'nai Jeshurun*?

◆ Do you know of any synagogues that bear the name B'nai Jeshurun?

13 Isaiah criticizes those who craft idols in verse 40:20, while the Sedra speaks out against graven images in the Ten Commandments (Deuteronomy 4:16-19, 23-24, 28, 5:7-9).

◆ How can money, fame, or youth be considered idols?

◆ What are other idols that people worship today?

◆ Write and deliver a speech criticizing those who worship any of today's idols.

14 Isaiah 40:2 says, when translated literally, "speak to the 'heart' of Jerusalem". In the Sedra we read the *"Shema"* in which we say that we should love God with all our heart and should keep these words on our heart.

◆ According to tradition, one shows love for God by clinging to God's teachings and keeping God's commandments. In what ways are these actions an expression of love?

15 The *"Shema"* urges us to study and keep these teachings on our heart.

◆ How will this help us to keep God's ways? Against what does the heart have to fight to enable us to continue to follow God's ways?

◆ How do you understand Isaiah's "speak to the heart" in light of the Sedra?

◆ How do you understand the *"Shema"* in the Sedra in light of Isaiah's "speak to the heart"?

Extending the Text

16 The song *"Nachamu Ami"* (Be Comforted, My People) is sung by the group Safam on the album *Safam on Track.*

◆ Ask your Cantor to teach you this beautiful song.

17 This first Haftarah of Consolation offers hope to a despairing people in exile.

◆ Choose your favorite among the following quotations on hope, or find others that you like.

"Hope springs eternal in the human breast." (Alexander Pope)

"Discipline your son while there is hope, and do not pay attention to his moaning." (Proverbs 19:18)

"Hope deferred makes the heart sick; but desire fulfilled is a tree of life." (Proverbs 13:12)

◆ Do you think any of these thoughts would be encouraging to the Israelite exiles in the Book of Isaiah?

◆ Design a banner featuring your favorite quotation about hope for the returning exiles to carry on their way home.

◆ For more quotations on hope, see *Two Jews, Three Opinions*, edited by Sandee Brawarsky and Deborah Mark, p. 242, or *Treasury of Jewish Quotations* by Leo Rosten.

18 Hirsch teaches that making a straight path (Isaiah 40:3) means to find the right path between extremes.

In his *Mishneh Torah (Hilchot De'ot,* chapters 1-2), Rambam, who was both a physician and a Rabbi, taught, "The right way is the middle course in each set of human traits." He explained that people should be neither hilarious nor gloomy, neither hot tempered nor without feeling, neither tightfisted nor lavish, neither a workaholic nor lazy. "The person who avoids extremes and follows the middle course in all things is wise," he says.

◆ Review each of these traits and why it would be wise to avoid the extremes.

◆ Make a list of opposite extremes in behavior or personality. Then, describe the middle course between them.

◆ Do you agree with Rambam that the middle course is always best?

◆ Is it ever appropriate to behave in an extreme way (such as political radicalism or extreme ambition)?

◆ The U.S. Army has an advertising slogan: "Be All That You Can Be." Discuss whether Rambam's teaching would deter you from being all that you can be or would help you accomplish that goal.

◆ List ways by which one might train oneself to avoid extremes.

19 Isaiah offered consolation to Israel. Providing consolation is an important role for members of the community when someone among them is in mourning. According to Isaac Klein in *A Time to Be Born, A Time to Die* (p. 39), "Jewish tradition involves the whole Jewish community in helping a mourner overcome the shock, trauma, and sorrow of bereavement. Thereby it not only helps the mourner overcome a most painful and tragic experience . . . but it also helps bring out what is best and most human in us."

◆ Consolation begins before death, when community members visit the sick and support their family. After a death has occurred, community members can perform the *mitzvah* of consoling the mourners, which begins immediately after burial. Why do you think we don't try to comfort mourners until after the burial?

◆ Mourners should be welcomed home to a meal of consolation at their home, prepared and served by friends and neighbors who show the mourners that they care about them. It is customary to serve symbolic foods, such as eggs, lentils, and chickpeas, whose roundness reminds the mourners that life is a circle. Eggs are also a symbol of new life and hope. Why do you think the community should make sure the mourners are fed?

Visiting the mourners when they sit *shivah* (the seven days of mourning) is a very important part of consoling mourners. Visitors help the mourners not to feel so alone in their loss. They can also help with chores in the house of mourning and make a *minyan* so the mourner can recite "*Kaddish*."

We are taught that condolence calls are meant to express sympathy to the mourners, though visitors should always let the mourner speak first. Close friends may bring or send food, while it is appropriate for others to make donations to the favorite charity of the deceased.

◆ Why do you think mourners should speak first?

◆ When mourners enter the sanctuary on a Friday night, it is customary for the congregation to greet them with the words, "May *Adonai* comfort you among the others mourners for Zion and Jerusalem." (Source: *A Time to Be Born, A Time to Die* by Isaac Klein, pp. 39-44.) Do you think a mourner would find these words comforting? Why or why not?

20 Isaiah promised the exiles that soon they will be able to return home to the Land of Israel.

For 2,000 years following the destruction of Jerusalem by the Romans in 70 C.E., the Jewish people dreamed of returning to their homeland. The modern Zionist movement, founded in 1897 by Theodor Herzl, resolved to turn this dream into a reality. Finally, on May 14, 1948 the State of Israel declared its independence, followed immediately by an attack by six Arab nations vehemently opposed to the Jewish state. Israel won the War of Independence, losing nearly one percent of its population in battle.

Israel has continued to grow and thrive, despite continual war and threats from its hostile neighbors.

◆ Groups of students can each complete a research project on an aspect of the road to Israeli independence. Choose from such topics as: the First Zionist Congress, *Chalutzim*, the Balfour Declaration, the Haganah and Irgun, the British White Paper, the United Nations

Partition Plan, and the War of Independence. The groups can make oral and visual presentations to the class based on their research. The *Encyclopaedia Judaica* is a useful resource for researching these topics (as is the Internet).

21 Israel is the Jewish homeland, and living in it is considered a *mitzvah*. For 2,000 years of exile, and especially in the decades leading up to and since the establishment of the State of Israel in 1948, Jews from all over the world have voluntarily chosen to make *aliyah* and return "home."

Interestingly, a Russian Zionist organization founded in 1882 based its name on verse 2:5 from the Book of Isaiah. The name, BILU, was an acronym based on the verse *"Bayt Ya'akov Lechu V'naylcha"* (Let the house of Jacob go).

◆ Invite someone who made *aliyah* from your community to speak to the class when they are in town visiting (or alternatively, a member of their family who is in your town). Ask about their decision to move to Israel and their experiences in the Jewish homeland.

◆ Write your own lists of pros and cons regarding making *aliyah* to Israel.

◆ For more information on the *mitzvah* of *aliyah*, see *Encyclopaedia Judaica*, vol. 2, pp. 633-635.

Personalizing the Text

22 God asks the prophet to comfort Israel.

◆ In the film *The Sound of Music*, Maria comforts the frightened children with the song, "My Favorite Things." Make a list of the things that give you comfort when you are sad or afraid. Listen to a recording of the song (on the original cast album) and compare Maria's list with your own.

◆ Note all the "comfort foods" on your lists. Compile a recipe collection of comfort foods that you can distribute among your classmates. Hold a "Comfort Food Feast," with each student contributing his or her favorite comforting dish.

◆ Why do you think particular objects, places, songs, or foods give people comfort?

◆ It may have been comforting for the Israelites just to know that God was thinking of them and had concern for them.

◆ How might it be comforting just to know someone is thinking about you or praying for you?

◆ How might such knowledge give courage to someone who is ill?

◆ Describe a time when you comforted someone. Did you use words, a gift, or just your caring presence?

23 Isaiah is trying to strengthen the exiled people with words of hope and encouragement. Cheerleaders use cheers to give hope to fans and players of a struggling team.

◆ Using the images in the Haftarah, write your own cheer to boost the morale of the Israelite exiles.

24 Israel's independence was declared on May 14, 1948 in Tel Aviv.

◆ Hold a theme party. Imagine it is May 14, 1948, and you are celebrating Israel's declaration of Independence in Tel Aviv. Based on what you learned in Extending the Text #20, p. 259, design posters and decorations for your party, play the part of historical characters, choose food and music to reflect the event. Be as creative as you can.

♦ Listen to David Ben Gurion's speech announcing Israel's independence. The speech may be found on the CD-Rom edition of *Encyclopaedia Judaica* under "Media" and on the web site www.mfa.gof.il/mfa/go.asp? MFAH00k90.

25 The Israeli national anthem is called *"Hatikvah,"* (The Hope). Study a translation of the words, then learn to sing *"Hatikvah"* in Hebrew. The song can be found on the album *My Favorite Hebrew Songs* by Nancy Linder or at www.mfa.gof.il/mfa/go.asp?MFAH00k90.

26 Artistic masters Michelangelo and Raphael both painted their interpretations of Isaiah the prophet. View these works at the web site www.kfki.hu/arthp/welcome.html.

♦ Compare the renderings by Michelangelo and Raphael. The web site allows you to send a free e-mail postcard of any picture. Choose your favorite picture of Isaiah and send it with a message of gratitude to someone who has given you comfort, encouragement, or hope.

27 Studies show that young people who visit Israel develop a stronger connection with Judaism than those who do not. Some organizations, in fact, are even sending young people to Israel free of charge.

♦ Visit the web site www.israelexperience.org to find out about subsidized and free trips to Israel. Encourage a friend or relative of the right age to apply for a free trip to Israel.

Other Resources

28 Read and discuss *The Power of Hope* by Maurice Lamm.

29 View and discuss the classic film *Exodus* (1960, not rated, 208 minutes), which captures the mood and moments leading up to Israel's independence in 1948.

30 Read and discuss the story "How I Learned to Study Torah" by Doug Lipman in *Chosen Tales*, edited by Peninnah Schram, pp. 205-209. In this retelling of a Hasidic story, a Rebbe teaches a boy the importance of studying Torah by "speaking tenderly to his heart."

31 For more on the prophet Isaiah, including history, themes, and notable quotations, read *Messengers of God: A Jewish Prophets Who's Who* by Ronald H. Isaacs, pp. 91-101.

32 See the commentary, discussion questions, and project for this Haftarah on the UAHC's Family Shabbat Table Talk web page: www.uahc.org/shabbat/stt/3vaetchanan.html.

33 According to Insights from the Tradition #B, pp. 253-254, God is suffering and needs to be comforted. To study more about God's suffering, see Psalms 91:15, Talmud *Hagigah* 15b, and *Exodus Rabbah* 2:5.

Involving the Family

34 People have many different attitudes toward saving and spending money (see Insights from the Tradition #F, p. 254). Discuss your family's philosophy toward long-term savings. What percentage of your family income do you save per year? For what do you expect your savings will eventually be used?

35 Most North American Jews will never visit Israel and cannot envision Israel being "home" to them. If you have not been to Israel, begin planning a family trip to Israel (and start a long-term savings plan toward this goal). If you have already been to Israel, start planning your next trip.

Bar/Bat Mitzvah Project

36 In the Haftarah God will lead the exiles on a long journey home. Take a relatively short journey. Organizations throughout the country sponsor walk-a-thons and other events to raise money for research to find cures for diseases. These events also give hope to patients and families of patients who suffer from the diseases. Participate in or even help to organize a walk-a-thon or other event that raises money to cure cancer, AIDS, breast cancer, birth defects, etc.

ISAIAH 40:27-41:16
LECH LECHA לך לך

This Haftarah has been paired with *Parashat Lech Lecha*, Genesis 12:1-17:27. See "Connecting the Text To the Sedra," pp. 266-269, for an exploration of the many ways the two texts shed light on each other.

SYNOPSIS

After decades of exile in Babylon, the Israelites despair of ever returning home. However, it appears that King Cyrus of Persia is about to conquer Babylon (539 B.C.E.), and Isaiah hopes he will be willing to let the exiles return to Israel.

In the first section of the Haftarah (40:27-31), the prophet assures the people that *Adonai* remains faithful and will not forget them. He urges them to trust in *Adonai*, who will renew their strength.

God invites the nations to a trial at which God's supreme omnipotence is contrasted with the weakness of nations in verses 41:1-7. *Adonai* can raise up nations and beat down leaders, turn swords into dust and bows into straw. *Adonai* was the first and will be the last. Fearing the judgment of *Adonai*'s great power, the nations vainly create idols to protect themselves.

But Israel, who has been chosen as God's servant, has nothing to fear, says Isaiah in verses 41:8-16. God will strengthen and help Israel, even though Israel seems helpless and meek as a worm. Furthermore, Isaiah assures, God will punish Israel's captors, who will be reduced to dust and scattered into oblivion by God's whirlwind.

Note: All the Haftarot from Deutero-Isaiah have similar historical context and themes. Many

Extending and Personalizing Strategies, as well as Other Resources and Bar Mitzvah Projects, can be shared among them.

INSIGHTS FROM THE TRADITION

A According to Radak verse 40:28 defends what Israel might perceive as God's inaction on its behalf. God's inaction is not due to any lack of Divine power because "God never grows faint or weary." It's not, therefore, that God *can't* help. God's actions are simply beyond our understanding because "God's wisdom cannot be fathomed."

◆ Can you accept that we cannot understand God's ways? Explain your answer.

◆ Does this commentary remind you of a parent defending his or her actions by saying, ". . . because I'm the parent"?

◆ Are you now or have you ever been willing to accept your parents' authority on the sole basis of their being your parents?

◆ In what ways does your view of your parents' authority change as you grow older?

◆ In what ways does your view of God's authority change as you grow older?

B In verse 41:5 the coastlands are afraid, according to Hirsch, because all the might and power in the world cannot guarantee peace and security. The only way to ensure true peace and security is through the mutual support of people. That is to say, I can be secure only if you are secure.

◆ Politicians tell us that a strong police force and legal code control crime. Does this philosophy agree with Hirsch's?

◆ Debate the following statement: There would be no violent crime, theft, or terrorism if society ensured that all people live well.

C Hirsch further explains that the people in verse 41:6 help only those who will benefit them. To all others they just say, "Take courage," meaning "Be strong yourself – help yourself." We learn from Hirsch's interpretation that, unlike the people in 41:6, a truly righteous person seeks to help all people.

◆ What is altruism?

◆ Give some examples of altruistic behavior, then see if you can find any stories about altruism in your local newspaper.

◆ Is it altruistic to live by the principle of "I'll scratch your back if you scratch mine"?

◆ List five reasons why you might want to help an enemy? How many of these are altruistic reasons?

D Ibn Ezra explains that the idol worshipers try to seek help by intensifying their worship of idols, which they think perhaps might help them (verse 41:6).

We often resort to superstition and rituals to help us in difficult situations. Baseball players are famous for their superstitious rituals, such as wearing their lucky shirt or eating the same food before each game.

◆ List other types of superstitious rituals people follow (e.g., carrying a rabbit foot or putting horseshoes on the wall).

◆ Do you ever count on lucky charms or superstitious rituals? Explain.

◆ Do you really trust that they are helping you? How?

E Radak teaches that the Israelites are compared to a worm in verse 41:14 because just as a soft worm can cut through a hard cedar tree using only its mouth, so, too, are the people of Israel because all their strength is in their words of prayer from their mouths with which they can defeat great adversity.

◆ In which of the following ways do you think the words of prayer can make us strong? Defend your choices.

• Teach Jewish values

• Explain how God behaves and serves as a role model for us

• Remind us that we are not alone with our problems

• Remind us that others have similar needs

• Encourage us to overcome hardship in our lives

• Help us to acknowledge and express what we are feeling inside

◆ Can you think of other ways prayer helps to make us strong?

STRATEGIES
Analyzing the Text

1 The prophet indicates in verse 40:28 that God never wearies. On the other hand, the exiles — even the young and strong — do grow tired, and need God to give them strength (40:30-31).

◆ Why might a people that has no hope of returning home think God has become tired and impotent?

◆ How can a total lack of hope weaken even the physically strong? Conversely, how can hope strengthen the physically weak?

2 Most interpreters understand that the "victor from the East" in verse 41:2 is Cyrus the King of Persia, who reigned from 559 to 529 B.C.E. As Isaiah hoped, Cyrus eventually freed the Israelites from Babylonian exile and let them go home.

◆ It is always interesting to know what historical events were taking place in biblical times, both in the Middle East and elsewhere. Prepare posters highlighting events that happened in various places around the world in the sixth century B.C.E. Form groups, each of which can research the century in a particular area. (For two good resources, consult *The Timetables of Jewish History* by Judah Gribetz, Edward Greenstein, and Regina Stein, or the time line in the CD-Rom edition of *Encyclopaedia Judaica*.)

3 God summons the nations to a court trial in verse 41:1-7, according to commentators. The question to be addressed at the trial is: Who rules the world, God or the idols? God seeks to prove the superiority of divine omnipotence over the inadequacy of human power and the utter sham of idols.

◆ What evidence is brought to prove that God rules supreme?

◆ Can you make any arguments against God's evidence?

4 In verse 41:7 the other nations try to strengthen their idols in order to be better protected and safer.

◆ Reread verses 41:6-7. With what do the other nations strengthen their idols?

◆ Compare what Isaiah says here to a similar portrayal of people strengthening and decorating their idols in Jeremiah 10:4 and Isaiah 40:19-20. In contrast, God strengthens Israel (verses 41:9-10); Israel does not need to try to strengthen God.

◆ Draw cartoons depicting the contrast between these two scenes.

5 God reassures the Israelites in verse 41:10 that they are not alone and should not fear, for God is with them and will strengthen and help them, even in exile.

◆ Do you find it easier to go through a difficult time or situation when others are there to support you? Why or why not?

◆ Why might someone prefer to face a difficult situation alone?

6 Isaiah assures the Israelites in verse 41:11-12 that in the future their enemies will be punished and even obliterated by God. This is a theme the prophet repeats throughout the Book of Isaiah. See, for example, the Haftarah for *Shemot*, Analyzing the Text #1, p. 245, and Connecting the Text To the Sedra #10, pp. 246-247.

◆ Do you think the promise that their enemies will ultimately suffer was a source of comfort to the Israelites?

◆ If someone committed a crime against you, would it make you feel better to know they'll be punished? Explain your answer.

◆ Do you think the family of a murder victim is entitled to witness the execution of the perpetrator?

7 God calls Israel a "worm" in verse 41:14.

◆ Do you understand God's tone to be critical, condescending, or affectionate, and why?

◆ Consider the helplessness of a worm facing predators. Isaiah could have used any number of images other than "worm." List some alternatives.

◆ Eat gummy worms.

8 The mountains in verse 41:15-16 are symbols of haughtiness, power, and pride.

◆ Compare the characteristics of mountains (a symbol for Israel's enemies) with those of worms (a symbol for Israel).

◆ In what ways does the prophet imagine the mountains will stand up to God?

◆ What do you think is Isaiah's message here about the perceived position and power of human beings?

9 Isaiah calls God the "Holy One of Israel" in verses 41:14 and 41:16. This name for God is used 39 times in the Book of Isaiah. This particular name for God rarely appears at all outside this book.

◆ To be קָדוֹשׁ (kadosh) can mean any of the following: holy, set apart, sacred, honored, dedicated, and consecrated. Which of these definitions best fits your understanding of God?

◆ Using a disposable camera, take pictures of people, places, or things that best exemplify for you the term "holy."

Connecting the Text To the Sedra

10 In the Sedra God commands Abram to leave everything behind and go to a new place that he does not know.

◆ List reasons why any move might be hard for any person.

◆ List reasons why this move might be hard for Abram.

◆ Sometimes strength of character or planning and preparation can help overcome the difficulties. For each aspect of his move that might

be hard, suggest a character trait for Abram that might help him overcome the difficulty.

◆ Alternatively, suggest a way Abram could prepare so as to make the move easier.

◆ How does God help make Abram's move easier?

◆ In the Haftarah the people are being prepared for a difficult move. List the reasons why their move might be hard.

◆ How has God tried to make their move easier for the people?

◆ Imagine a time you moved to a new home or left home to go somewhere unfamiliar (for example, the first day in a new school or camp). What was hard about that experience for you? What helped make the day easier for you? Did anyone give you extra courage to deal with the experience?

◆ Because moving can be difficult, help to form a committee at your synagogue that delivers care packages to families moving away from your community and welcome baskets to families moving to it. Contents might include phone books, basic toiletries, snacks, items necessary for a first Shabbat in a new community (candles, wine, *challah*), a copy of the Jewish newspaper, and a directory of Jewish organizations and resources in the new community.

11 Some of the most famous stories about Abram are not in the Bible, yet they are related to the Sedra because they explain why Abram left his homeland and his father's house. There are several *midrashim* that teach that Abram's father was an idol maker. One day, Abram was minding the store when a man came to buy an idol. Abram talked the man out of buying the idol by asking how old the man was. When the man answered that he was 50 years old,

Abram asked how could a 50-year-old bow down to an idol that Abram had just made that day. Then a woman came to buy a new idol because her old one had been stolen. Abram argued with her, asking that if the idol could not save itself, how could it help her at all? Abram also tied a rope around the necks of two idols and dragged them face down in the street, calling out to people "who would like to buy an idol which serves no profit?" (For more *midrashim* of this type, see *The Legends of the Jews,* by Louis Ginzberg, vol. 1, pp. 195-198.)

◆ How do these stories explain why Abram left his father's home?

◆ Reread verses 41:6-7 in the Haftarah (also see Isaiah 40:18-20). How are idols and idol makers portrayed in the stories about Abram and in the Haftarah?

◆ Why, in your opinion, do the Bible and *midrash* mock idols and idol makers?

◆ In our multicultural age, we avoid mocking the traditions of others. Can you give examples? Review the reaction of governments and religious leaders following September 11, 2001. In what ways did they work hard to prevent the public from denigrating Islam?

12 The Haftarah begins with the Israelites asking why their way has been hidden from God and why their cause has been ignored.

◆ What were the Israelites feeling, and why were they feeling this way?

◆ How does the prophet answer them?

◆ In the Sedra God tells Abram that his descendants will spend 400 years in exile serving other people. God is referring to the time the children of Israel will spend as slaves in Egypt. While the children of Israel were slaves in Egypt, did they know that their slavery would end after 400 years? How do you think they felt? In what ways were their feelings similar to the way the Israelites felt in Isaiah's time?

◆ Have you ever been in a seemingly never ending situation and you were not sure you could endure it (for example, a long car ride or a medical or dental procedure)? Were there others who knew when the situation would end who tried to reassure you? Did their reassurances help you?

13 Isaiah calls Israel in verse 41:8 "My servant, Jacob, whom I have chosen, seed of Abraham, My friend."

In the Sedra God selects Abraham from all the people of the earth to father a new nation dedicated to God. In both texts, it is clear that God chose Israel, whose fate depends on its allegiance to God.

Chosenness carries great promise, but in our texts it leaves Abraham and Israel isolated in a world that does not understand them. Being chosen requires long-term patience for the promise to be fulfilled.

Joseph Telushkin, in *Jewish Literacy* (p. 421), asserts that the Reconstructionist Movement has rejected the concept of Jews being God's chosen people, in part because of the views of the movement's founder, Mordecai Kaplan. Kaplan felt it was arrogant for Jews to feel that God had singled them out from all other nations and given them a special mission on earth.

◆ Do you think being the chosen people is an honor, privilege, burden, and/or obligation?

◆ Do you think the concept of chosen people is meant to make Jews feel superior to other people? Explain your view.

◆ Do you agree with Kaplan that the concept should be rejected altogether? Why or why not?

14 Abram approaches God to argue over the decision to destroy Sodom and Gomorrah in the Sedra. In the Haftarah God invites the nations to try to argue who controls history (verses 41:1-5).

◆ Do you think it is appropriate to argue or disagree with God? List the types of subjects about which you believe it would be reasonable to argue with God.

◆ In the following story, Hasidic Rabbi Levi Yitzhak of Berditchev taught that it was appropriate to argue with God:

There once was a man who could not read the High Holy Day prayer book. Following Yom Kippur services, Rabbi Levi Yitzhak asked the man what he did all day during services. The man explained that he sat and argued with God. He told God about the minor sins he may have committed during the year (by not saying all his prayers), and then he chastised God for the major sins God committed during the year (such as allowing children to die young or to be orphaned). So he reached an agreement with God — he would pardon God for all God's sins if God would pardon him. Rabbi Levi Yitzhak angrily scolded the man for having let God off too easily.

◆ Discuss this story, which may be found in *The Yom Kippur Anthology* by Philip Goodman, p. 118.

15 In the Sedra (Genesis 15:1), God tells Abram, "Fear not, Abram, I am a shield to you." Abram, a newcomer to Canaan, is afraid that the kings he just defeated (Genesis 14) will seek revenge against him.

◆ Review Genesis 14:1-16 to see why Abram felt compelled to fight the kings.

◆ In the Haftarah God tells the Israelites twice, "Fear not" (see verses 41:10 and 41:14). What do the Israelites fear? Reread the Haftarah and list all the military images in the Haftarah.

◆ Imagine standing up to a bully who was picking on someone smaller. Would you be afraid afterward that the bully might seek revenge on you?

◆ If you stand up to the bully in spite of your fear, you are helping to make your community a more ethical, compassionate, and just one. How were Abram's actions in Genesis 14 also an effort to make his new home more ethical, compassionate, and just?

◆ Abram is told in Genesis 15:13 that his descendants will be slaves in a foreign land. We learn from the Exodus from Egypt not to oppress the stranger, for we were once strangers in a strange land. Similarly, before the Israelites went into exile, their prophets chastised them for not seeking justice, equity, and compassion for the weak in their society (the orphans, widows, and destitute). How might their experiences in Babylon and their fear to fight for their own freedom help the Israelites learn about creating a just society when they returned to their land?

◆ Debate: In order to build a just and ethical society, one must first have experienced the opposite.

16 While the word צדק (tzedek) in verse 41:2 of the Haftarah is generally read as "victor" or "victory," it can also be translated as "righteousness."

◆ How can being righteous bring us success or victory in life?

◆ Early commentators interpreted "a victor from the East" in verse 41:2 of the Haftarah as Abraham. Abraham came from Ur in Mesopotamia, which is east of the Land of Israel. He is seen as the champion from the

East, because in the Sedra (Genesis 14) he saves his nephew Lot from four kings who invaded the country and kidnapped people. How was this a righteous act?

◆ List other righteous acts performed by Abraham in the Sedra.

◆ In what ways can you today emulate Abraham's righteous behavior?

17 *Ta'anit* 21a explains that the dust and straw of Isaiah 41:2 refer to Abraham's ability to throw dust and straw stubble into the air and have them turn into swords and arrows. This *midrash* supports the Sedra, which teaches in Genesis 14:14 that Abraham went to battle against the four kings, taking with him his army of 318 men. It offers one explanation as to how Abraham provided weapons to his troops.

◆ It is interesting that an image about Abraham which is in the Sedra and in much of Rabbinic tradition is not our focus today. Describe Abraham as you have learned about him in school. Is military warrior one of the images you associate with Abraham?

◆ Describe a Jew. Is military warrior one of the images you associate with a Jew? It is interesting that until Jews made *aliyah* to Israel in the twentieth century, Jews were not usually thought of as soldiers or as farmers. Yet in modern day Israel, Jews have excelled in both roles.

◆ Cut out pictures of Israeli soldiers and/or farmers from newspapers and Jewish magazines and make a collage of these modern images of Jews.

◆ Tell about one of your traits or abilities of which you are proud, and which might surprise people.

Extending the Text

18 Study the morning blessings, which include the use of verse 40:29. These include:

Blessed are you God, Sovereign of the universe Who:

• gives the rooster the knowledge to separate day and night.

• made me in Your image.

• releases prisoners.

• straightens up those who are bent over.

• provides me with all my needs.

• guides the steps of people.

• wraps Israel in strength.

• crowns Israel with pride.

• gives strength to the weary.

◆ Review Insights from the Tradition #E, p. 264, for the many things prayer can do for us. Now explain how each of these prayers might teach a Jewish value, or teach that God is a role model for us, or express our gratitude.

19 The Synopsis to this Haftarah and Analyzing the Text #2, p. 265, point out that Cyrus, a foreigner, helped free the Israelites from their exile. In fact, Cyrus was held in such high esteem for his liberation of the Israelites that the Bible contains a tribute to him in II Chronicles 36.

The Talmudic Sages also presented righteous non-Jews as moral role models. Today the term "righteous gentile" is closely associated with non-Jews who actively saved Jews during the Holocaust. At Yad Vashem, the Holocaust memorial in Jerusalem, there is a grove of trees planted to honor those righteous gentiles. The names of many such righteous people have become well-known: Raoul Wallenberg, Oskar Schindler, King Christian X of

Denmark, and Miep Gies, who hid the family of Anne Frank in Amsterdam.

♦ Research what each of these people did.

♦ View and discuss the film *Schindler's List*, (1993, rated R, 197 minutes). Analyze and discuss the various aspects of Schindler's motivation to save "his" Jews.

♦ Find out about the organization founded by Rabbi Harold Schulweis that supports with monthly stipends needy rescuers of Jews during the Holocaust. Contact them at The Jewish Foundation for the Righteous, 305 7th Ave., 19th floor, New York, NY 10117-0994, 888-421-1221, www.jfr.org.

20 God assures the Israelites that the Divine Presence would be with them.

There is a Hasidic story (attributed to Baruch of Medzebozh, the grandson of the Baal Shem Tov) of a young boy who was playing *Hide-and-Seek* with a friend. After some time, the young boy came out of his hiding place and went crying to his grandfather. The grandfather asked why was the boy crying, to which he replied that his friend played with him until it was his turn to hide. He found such a good hiding place, that his friend gave up trying to find him after a short time. The boy said it was unfair that instead of continuing to look, the friend gave up and left.

The grandfather kissed the boy and began to cry, too. The boy wondered why his grandfather was crying. The grandfather explained, "Like you, my grandson, God, too, is unhappy because God is hiding and humanity does not put much effort into looking for God. Humanity has stopped its search and that is unfair to God."

♦ What do you think it means that God is hiding?

♦ What do you think it means that humanity is not trying to look for God?

♦ Imagine how the world would be different if God's presence could be felt by everyone all of the time.

21 Isaiah assures the Israelites that their oppressors will be duly punished. Many Holocaust victims took comfort when 21 Nazi leaders were tried for their crimes at the Nuremberg Trial in 1946. Eleven of the Nazis were sentenced to death.

In the years following the Nuremberg Trial, and even to this day, Nazi hunters have continued the search for Nazi criminals who have managed to escape justice. In 1960, Adolf Eichmann was kidnapped by Israeli agents off the streets of Buenos Aires, Argentina, and brought to trial in Israel. He was sentenced to death.

♦ Why do you think Nazi hunters continue to search for war criminals so many years after World War II?

♦ Many Jews, even today, refuse to buy German cars or manufactured goods in protest against the Holocaust. Debate whether or not Jews should drive German cars.

22 Isaiah characterizes the Israelites as a helpless worm. Primo Levi, a Holocaust survivor, wrote the following about his time in the camps (*The Drowned and the Saved*, p. 114):

"Clothes, even the foul clothes which were distributed, even the crude clogs with their wooden soles, are a tenuous but indispensable defense. Anyone who does not have them no longer perceives himself as a human being, but rather as a worm; naked, slow, ignoble, prone on the ground. He knows he can be crushed at any moment."

♦ Levi compares a person stripped of his or her dignity to a worm. Why would the Nazis have wanted to make the Jews feel like worms?

◆ How might the Israelites in Babylonian exile have felt like worms (see Insights from the Tradition #E, p. 264)?

◆ In what ways is dignity like hope?

◆ Winston Churchill, Britain's Prime Minister during World War II, once said: "We are all worms, but I do believe I am a glowworm." Explain this comment. Do you think Churchill was expressing an optimistic or pessimistic view of life?

23 In the Haftarah the Israelites are anticipating their long, arduous journey home.

◆ The Travelers' Prayer, or *"Tefilat HaDerech,"* is traditionally recited by anyone who sets out on a journey. It can be found in most *Siddurim* (for example, in *Siddur Sim Shalom*, p. 713), and goes something like this: "May it be your will, *Adonai*, our God and the God of our ancestors, that You lead us toward peace, place our footsteps toward peace, guide us toward peace, and make us reach our desired destination for life, gladness, and peace. May You rescue us from the hand of every foe, ambush, bandit, and evil animal along the way, and from all manner of danger . . . Blessed are You, *Adonai*, who hears prayer." With a new awareness of the possible dangers of travel today, do you think you might feel more secure on a journey if you say *"Tefilat HaDerech"*?

◆ Many people carry a small card containing the words of *"Tefilat HaDerech"* in their wallets, in order that they have the words of the prayer always at hand. Write your own version (or the traditional one) of this prayer on a small piece of paper about the size of a credit card. The teacher can have the cards laminated for years of use. Don't forget to illustrate the back side of the card.

Personalizing the Text

24 Isaiah indicates in verse 40:30 that even the young and vigorous will weaken and stumble. Everyone faces obstacles in their lives, including aging and illness.

Booker T. Washington, a former slave who became an outstanding Black educator, once said: "Success is measured not so much by the position that one has reached in life as by the obstacles which [one] has overcome while trying to succeed."

◆ Can you think of a famous athlete or celebrity (or, better yet, Jewish hero) who has overcome great obstacles to achieve success? What lesson can we learn from his/her example?

◆ The Booker T. Washington National Monument is in Hardy, Virginia. (You can visit the web site at www.nps.gov/bowa/home.htm.) Design such a national monument for the athlete, celebrity, or Jewish hero you thought of in answer to the previous question.

25 God demonstrates that "youths may grow faint and weary, and young men stumble and fall," while God remains strong and steady.

◆ Our society worships youth and vigor above almost all else. Make a collage of advertisements that promote this ideal.

◆ Based on God's viewpoint, what is problematic about worshiping youth? Do you agree or disagree?

26 We may understand the contrast between youths and God as a metaphor for our bodies and souls. In our lives, we tend to pay much more attention to our physical selves, which grow weak and weary, than to our spiritual selves, which can remain strong despite what happens to our bodies.

◆ What do you do to take care of your body?

◆ What do you do to take care of your soul?

◆ Make a list of ways you can use your body to nourish and fortify your soul.

27 Hirsch teaches the importance of helping our neighbors (see Insights from the Tradition #C, pp. 263-264). Sforno taught, "to love your fellow human being means putting yourself in his or her position. For instance, in thinking of a friend who is ill, one must say, 'If I were ill myself, what would be the choicest blessing I could seek from God?' and then pray that the other should receive that blessing" (quoted in *Exploring Jewish Ethics and Values* by Ronald H. Isaacs, p. 90).

◆ How does Sforno's lesson define altruism?

◆ Write a true story about someone you know who is truly altruistic. Present the story to the class.

28 Israel is called "God's servant" in verse 41:8. Strangely, this subservient position empowers them.

◆ How might submitting to God's superior power make one stronger?

◆ It stands to reason that submitting oneself to rules and regulations takes away one's freedom. However, if you think about it, how can rules and regulations actually increase one's freedom?

◆ In a lawless society, people do what they want without regard for the rights and freedoms of others. Just laws help to protect everyone's rights by restricting everyone's behavior. How does submitting to rules at home actually empower you to be a better family member? How do rules at school help you to be a better student? How do your local laws help to make you a better citizen?

◆ How do *mitzvot*, which might take away some of our freedom of choice, actually help to make us stronger Jews? Make a list of ten *mitzvot*, and describe how submitting to their authority empowers us (e.g., observing Shabbat empowers us to spend time with our family and enables us to be more productive during the work week).

29 Silkworms spin cocoons and turn into moths that can fly away freely into the distance.

◆ Purchase and care for some silkworms, and witness their magnificent growth and metamorphosis.

◆ What lessons about life can we learn from the humble silkworm, which creates one of the world's most precious fabrics?

30 In Analyzing the Text #5, p. 265, we considered how some people feel better not being alone when they are sick or have troubles.

◆ Consider the story of a young boy named Andy who was sick with cancer. Daily, Andy would hope to get mail, but there was rarely anything for him. His mother decided to start writing him letters as a secret pen pal. Andy loved getting the letters and writing back to his secret pen pal. One day, he made a special drawing for his secret pal and wouldn't let his mother see it. He left it on the table after going to bed and his mother opened it to see it. In the corner he left a message: P.S. Mom, I love you.

After Andy died, his mother cleaned out his closets and found an address book with names of his friends from a summer camp he had attended for kids with cancer. Andy's mother began writing to each child in the address book. The children began to write letters back.

More than ten years later, she is still writing letters to kids with cancer and other serious illnesses. Her volunteer organization, Love Letters Inc., sends out about 7,000 cards, letters, and packages every month. She says she keeps writing so that these kids are not standing alone at the mailbox.

◆ How do you think the secret letters helped Andy?

◆ How do you feel when you receive mail?

◆ Send get well cards to the ill children at a local hospital (the nurses on the pediatric ward can help you with this project).

Other Resources

31 Discuss the illustration rendered for this Haftarah in *The Illustrated Torah* by Michal Meron, p. 22. How does the illustration convey the relationship between prophet and people? Does the illustration convey a prophecy of hope, consolation, despair, or wrath?

32 Read and discuss *You Never Know: A Legend of the Lamed-Vavniks* by Francine Prose.

33 View and discuss either the classic film *Judgment at Nuremberg* (1961, not rated, 186 minutes), or the newer A&E production on the subject, *Nuremberg — Tyranny on Trial*.

34 Read and discuss *The House on Garibaldi Street* by Isser Harel, which tells the story of how Israel's spy network captured and brought to trial in Israel hated Nazi war criminal Adolf Eichmann. Consider how bringing him to justice for his war crimes was a source of comfort to all Jews.

35 For a beautiful account of the connection between body and soul, read and discuss "Story of a Soul" in *Minding the Temple of the Soul* by Tamar Frankiel and Judy Greenfeld.

36 Review the craft *midrashim* related to this Sedra in *Handmade Midrash* by Jo Milgrom, pp. 93-113. Which of the images can be interpreted as also applying to the Haftarah? Draw or design ones for the Haftarah.

37 God's "hand" is mentioned several times in the Haftarah. See *The Encyclopedia of Jewish Symbols* by Ellen Frankel and Betsy Platkin Teutsch, pp. 106-107, for information on "hand" in the Bible.

38 Search a CD containing the Bible in English for the words "right hand" and "your right hand." What can you conclude about God's right hand? Why does God hold Israel's right hand? (Clue: God holds Israel's right hand with God's left hand.) Write a new entry for *The Encyclopedia of Jewish Symbols* for "right hand."

39 See the *Encyclopaedia Judaica* entry for Isaiah (vol. 9, pp. 44-71) for more information about Isaiah in the Bible, *midrash*, and in the arts. Also, see p. 45, a beautiful illustration to the first chapter of Isaiah in a fourteenth century Bible. Choose a representative word from our Haftarah and illuminate it in the fashion of this illustration.

Involving the Family

40 Being supportive of our friends and family should not be limited to bad times. Make an extra effort to show support for your family members by being present at events that are important to them, such as athletic competitions, recitals, plays, and so on. Celebrate the achievements of your family members, such as victories, promotions, good report cards, etc.

41 Learn about altruism. Spend one week not being altruistic — only do things for other family members if they agree to do something for you. Then spend the next week being very altruistic — going out of your way to find things to do for other family members without expecting anything in return.

Finally, as a family, compare how you feel about those two weeks (see Insights from the Tradition #C, p. 264).

Bar/Bat Mitzvah Projects

42 Isaiah gave the Israelites hope of redemption and a feeling that they were not alone. For the year of your Bar/Bat Mitzvah, reach out to seriously ill children by becoming a volunteer letter writer. Spend this year writing let-

ters to lonely kids who need your support and friendship. Contact Linda Bremner, Andy's mom (see Personalizing the Text #30, p. 272-273) by writing to Love Letters, 837 S. Westmore, Lombard, IL 60148.

43 Find out about the Bar/Bat Mitzvah Program of the Jewish Foundation for the Righteous (see Extending the Text #19, pp. 269-270). Consider fulfilling the *mitzvah* of *tzedakah* by becoming linked, or "twinned," with one of the Righteous Gentiles supported by the Foundation. You can select a particular rescuer, and will be asked to make a donation to the JFR. The Foundation will send a Twinning Certificate, which can be presented on the day of your Bar/Bat Mitzvah from the *bimah*. Perhaps you will want to speak about the rescuer you are honoring in your *D'var Torah*.

ISAIAH 42:5-43:10 Ashkenazim
ISAIAH 42:5-42:21 Sephardim
ISAIAH 42:5-43:11 Reform
BERESHEET בראשית

This Haftarah has been paired with *Parashat Beresheet*, Genesis 1:1-6:8. See "Connecting the Text To the Sedra," pp. 278-281, for an exploration of the many ways the two texts shed light on each other.

SYNOPSIS

The Israelites have spent long decades of exile in Babylon. Now, with the defeat of the Babylonians by King Cyrus of Persia, it seems that their punishment may be drawing to an end. Isaiah hopes Cyrus will give them the opportunity to return home to Israel.

The prophet affirms *Adonai's* support for Israel, whom *Adonai* has chosen to share in the Covenant and to be a light to the other nations. *Adonai* will not be undone by idols and those who worship them. Just as events predicted by God in the past have come true, so will Israel's promised redemption from exile.

Adonai is described as a warrior, who will charge and defeat the enemy. Screaming like a woman in labor, *Adonai* will destroy the enemy and their land and lead the Israelites from darkness to light. Since Israel was blind and deaf, it was then plundered and imprisoned for failing to follow God. The Israelites are called upon now to open their eyes and ears and to listen and pay attention to the prophet's message of redemption. The prophet promises that God will save Israel, protecting them through water and fire. God, the Savior,

loves Israel, and will gather all the dispersed into the Holy Land.

The Haftarah concludes as Israel is called to witness *Adonai's* power, faithfulness, and eternity.

Note: All Haftarot from Deutero-Isaiah have similar historical context and themes. Many Extending and Personalizing Strategies, as well as Other Resources and Bar Mitzvah Projects, can be shared among them.

INSIGHTS FROM THE TRADITION

A Rashi explains that when God gives breath to the people on the earth in verse 42:5, it means that God gives a soul to every person (the Hebrew for breath and for soul is the same word, נשמה *(neshamah)*. Rashi adds that the phrase "to the people on the earth" indicates that souls are given to all people equally.

◆ If souls are given equally to all people, is there a place in the world for prejudice or racism? Explain your answer.

B According to Radak, Isaiah describes God as Creator of the Heavens (verse 42:5) because some people erroneously thought the world always existed. The prophet wants to emphasize that the world was, in fact, created by a Creator. Isaiah focused on the heavens because the heavens appear to remain the same, unlike the earth, which is constantly changing. When something is always the same, such as the heavens, it is especially hard to believe that it did not always exist.

◆ Make a list of things you use or benefit from regularly that you believe did not exist 50 years ago.

◆ Make a list of things you use or benefit from regularly that you believe always existed.

◆ Check your lists with your parents or grandparents and find out from them what life was like without the items you consider modern necessities.

◆ True or False: It is easier to take for granted something we think has always existed. Justify your answer.

C Being exiled from the Land of Israel was tremendously painful for the Jewish people. They tried to console themselves by believing there was a greater purpose to their exile. For example, we were sent to live all around the world instead of in our homeland, in order that we might share our Torah with other people and become a light to the nations (see *Pesachim* 87b).

◆ Do you agree that the Israelites were exiled in order to be a light to the other nations? Why or why not?

◆ How is this teaching an example of making lemonade out of lemons (i.e., making something good out of adversity)?

◆ Can you think of a time in your own life when you or a family member made lemonade out of lemons?

◆ In what ways can it be good to put a positive spin on an event that is outside your control?

◆ Interview family members for examples from their lives of times when they made lemonade out of lemons.

◆ Create a lemonade stand. Donate the proceeds to *tzedakah*.

D The prophet reiterates the harsh circumstances of Israel's exile. Hirsch teaches regarding verse 42:6 that Israel's sufferings are a discipline imposed by God to prepare Israel to do God's work for the benefit of humanity.

◆ In what ways do your parents discipline you in order to prepare you to be a moral, upstanding adult?

◆ In what positive ways (not through punishment) might children be molded into moral adults?

E In verse 43:10 God declares to Israel, "You are My witnesses." There is a Rabbinic teaching (*Midrash Tehillim* 123:2) that says, "If you are My witnesses I am God, but if you are not My witnesses, then I would not be God."

◆ What do you think this teaching means?

◆ Did you ever realize that parents wouldn't be parents if they didn't have (you for) kids?

◆ How can children help to make their parents better parents?

◆ Ask your parents in what ways you have made them better parents.

STRATEGIES
Analyzing the Text

1 God says in verse 42:6, "I have summoned you." Rashi believes that God here is speaking directly to the prophet regarding his calling as a prophet. However, the rest of the verse seems to indicate that God is addressing the people Israel, in general.

♦ Which interpretation of "you" seems to make the most sense?

♦ For advanced study, check the Hebrew suffix for "you" in this phrase to determine whether it is singular or plural.

2 It is unclear in verse 42:7 who will be opening the eyes of those deprived of light and who will be rescuing prisoners from confinement.

♦ Do you think this will be God's role? Why or why not?

♦ Do you think this will be Israel's role? Why or why not?

♦ Can you make an argument for both points of view?

3 God is described in human images in verses 42:13-17. Attributing human characteristics to God is called "anthropomorphism."

Anthropomorphisms help us explain God and godly behavior to ourselves, since human behavior and human terms are the only ones we understand.

♦ List different anthropomorphisms about God (e.g., God has a strong right arm, God is a king) that are found in Tanach or *tefilah*.

♦ What do you learn about God from these anthropomorphisms?

♦ What do you learn about God when God is described as screaming like a woman in labor?

♦ What do you learn about God when God is described as vengefully destroying the enemy?

♦ Do you prefer a different kind of image of God, and why?

4 "Listen, you who are deaf; You blind ones, look up and see!" the prophet declares in verse 42:18. Ibn Ezra and Radak explain that deafness and blindness here are figurative terms for the mental and spiritual obtuseness possessed by the Israelites.

♦ What have the Israelites failed to see or hear?

♦ We often spend our days running around without noticing the beautiful world around us. Take a walk outside, paying very close attention to the sights and sounds of God's creations. Make a list of all the beautiful sights and sounds God has created.

♦ How does this awareness affect your mood?

♦ Better yet, take a camera and photograph some of the beautiful sights on your list. Put together an album of these pictures.

5 In the Book of Isaiah, the words "Jacob" and "Israel" are used interchangeably.

♦ To learn why this is so, read Genesis 32:23-33. Jacob means "heel," as Jacob was born holding his older brother's heel, as if trying to catch up with him. Israel means "struggling with God." Draw your own artistic interpretation of the meanings of both names.

6 Verse 43:2 contains several metaphors for dangerous situations through which God will accompany Israel. Identify the metaphor. How do they convey the idea that God will be with the Israelites no matter what the circumstances? Metaphors generally transcend specific situations, yet some of these metaphors can be suggestive of actual events. Match the following metaphors with the situations below:

a. An example from history when the people passed through water. (3)

b. An example from history when the people passed through streams. (4)

c. An example from history when the people walked through fire. (1, 2)

1. The Holocaust
2. The destruction of Jerusalem
3. The Exodus from Egypt
4. The entry into the Promised Land

7 God says in verse 43:10 that Israel will be God's witnesses.

◆ The word "witness" has many meanings. Check a dictionary or thesaurus for meanings for "witness." Explain how you understand this verse based on some of the meanings you found. (Many commentators believe that Isaiah means that by Israel's presence, Israel will attest to something to the other nations. Israel's presence will certify to the other nations that God's many predictions about Israel came true. Israel's presence will serve as a witness, a sign, and a token to the other nations that God is in charge of history — God has the power to deliver a nation from exile, and the good prophecies will come true, too, now as the bad prophecies came true earlier.)

◆ Pretend that you are being called upon in a court as a witness to God's involvement in the world God created. Think of a time when you were convinced that God helped you or otherwise made the Divine Presence known in your own life. Take turns testifying about God's Supreme Power.

Connecting the Text To the Sedra

8 In the Sedra God alone is the creator of the world. However, in Genesis 1:27, God says, "Let us create human beings in our image."

◆ Based on this verse, how many gods are there, and how many gods created the world?

◆ Many Rabbinic explanations have been offered to demonstrate that, in spite of the plu-ral language, God alone created; no other gods or angels helped God in the act of creation. One example of these explanations is that God was using royal language, like a king would use in saying "we" to refer to himself. Alternatively, *Genesis Rabbah* 8:3 says God took counsel with God's own heart about creating human beings. Or, *Genesis Rabbah* 8:4-7 suggests that God consulted with angels or the souls of the righteous who had not yet been born. Explain how these various explanations solve the problem (arising in Genesis 1:27) of more than one god having created the world. Which of these explanations do you prefer, and why?

◆ In the Haftarah God complains that the people have refused to acknowledge God as the sole creator and director of all that happens (see verses 42:5, 8, 10-12, 17, 23-24). Describe God's reaction to people who actually call idols "god" and give these idols some of the credit due God. How would you feel if someone else got credit for your efforts?

◆ Put on a skit in which one person gets credit for another person's accomplishment.

9 Like the Sedra, the Haftarah begins with a description of God as the creator of the heavens and earth.

◆ Compare the language of Genesis 2:7 with that of Isaiah 42:5. Genesis 2:7 says. "*Adonai* God formed man from the dust of the earth. He blew into his nostrils the breath of life, and man became a living being."

◆ Explain how God is the source of life in both Genesis 2:7 and Isaiah 42:5.

◆ How might understanding that God is the source of life affect someone's opinions regarding: the death penalty, euthanasia, slavery, violence, terrorism, use of drugs or alcohol, eating meat?

◆ Do you think someone might consider life more precious if God is the source of life? Why or why not?

10 When the Haftarah was written, Israel was in exile. In the Sedra Adam and Eve were exiled from Eden, and then Cain was sentenced to exile.

◆ In what ways is exile considered a punishment for Israel, Adam and Eve, and Cain?

◆ Do you think exile is an appropriate punishment in any of the above situations? Justify your answer.

◆ If you were doling out punishments, what might you have inflicted on Adam and Eve, Cain, and the Israelites during the time of Isaiah, and why?

11 In the Sedra God sets Adam and Eve in the garden. God gives them one law to keep. They break that one law and are sent into exile. According to a Rabbinic teaching (see *Tanhuma Lech Lecha 9*), the events that take place in the lives of one generation serve as a sign to a later generation. Similarly, the children of Israel live in the Land promised to them. God had given them a Torah of laws to keep, but they broke those laws and were sent into exile.

◆ Explain how the same type of pattern that happened once, happened again.

◆ Interview your parents to find out if they see you doing things in your life that they did, too. Are your similar patterns of behavior good ones or bad ones? How are your parents trying to help you to change bad patterns that they had, too? Does it help you to learn from their experience, or do you feel you must learn from your own successes and mistakes?

12 The Sedra is about the creation of the world. The first human beings are given a command and fail to keep it. Their two sons fight, and one kills the other. Yet, God does not despair; God allows Adam and Eve to have a third child. Their third son has such wicked descendants that by the end of the Sedra (Genesis 6:5-7), God wants to destroy humanity. But instead, God does not despair. God chooses Noah to continue humanity, hopefully on a more successful path.

◆ What do you think God's attitude teaches about hope and despair?

◆ How hard must it be to be God?

◆ How would you feel if everything you tried to do for an entire year failed? The Haftarah views the future as the opportunity to create the world anew. Since the future does not yet exist, the people can hope that God will create for them a new and better existence in the future.

◆ How is the future like a new creation?

◆ Why must Israel have hope in God for the future?

◆ Why must God have hope in Israel for the future?

◆ The Haftarah indicates, however, that one thing stands in the way of hope — blindness. Explain blindness as a metaphor for the inability to see potential in the future.

◆ We read the Sedra and Haftarah at the beginning of our new year when we are creating our lives anew. Design a new year's card featuring your thoughts about hope for a better future. Send your card to a friend or family member who has had a particularly difficult year.

13 Adam and Eve are given just one law to obey. When they break it, God holds them accountable and punishes them. Isaiah recounts how Israel has a Covenant with God (which includes many laws), but is paying the price for breaking it.

◆ Do you think it is easier to obey just one law or an entire system of laws? Explain your answer.

◆ If you had to decide on one law for all of humanity to obey, what would it be?

◆ What would be the punishment for breaking the law?

◆ Establish a list of rules (or just one rule) governing behavior in your classroom.

14 The Haftarah opens with two names for God, *El* and *Adonai*. According to Rashi, the first represents God's attribute of justice, and the second represents God's attribute of mercy.

◆ Describe how in the Haftarah God shows mercy for Israel after imposing justice by exiling her.

◆ The Sedra, too, juxtaposes these two names for God. The Rabbis teach that the world cannot exist on the basis of either justice (strict application of the law) or mercy (leniency and forgiveness) alone, but only with a combination of the two. Identify examples in the Sedra of God acting mercifully. For example, see Genesis 4:13-15 and Genesis 6:5-8.

◆ Do you think the punishment of exile combines both justice and mercy? Why or why not?

◆ Do you think our system of jurisprudence should always combine justice and mercy? Explain your response. Consider the death penalty versus life sentences in terms of justice and mercy.

◆ For more on this topic, see *Teaching Torah* by Sorel Goldberg Loeb and Barbara Binder Kadden, *Parashat Beresheet*, Extending the Text #10, p. 7.

15 God asks a series of questions in the Garden of Eden, although God obviously already knows the answers (where are you? who told you? did you eat?). In the Haftarah God asks rhetorically in 42:19, "Who is so blind as My servant, So deaf as the messenger I send?"

◆ Why do you think God asks questions the answers to which God already knows?

◆ Do you ever ask questions to which you already know the answers? If so, why?

16 Michael Fishbane teaches in the *Etz Hayim Chumash*, p. 36, that darkness comprises the original state of the world, which is transformed by the creation of light in the Sedra. In the Haftarah, images of darkness represent exile and despair, while light symbolizes the promise of God's redemption of the people and hope for a brighter future.

◆ Using black and white construction paper, make a positive-negative picture depicting images of despair on one side, and of hope on the other.

17 In the Sedra God creates light, separating it from the darkness that already existed. In the Haftarah God reminds us that Israel was created as a light to remove darkness from other nations (verses 42:6-7).

◆ In the Sedra darkness is not destroyed, just separated. What does darkness represent, and why do we need it?

◆ In contrast to the separation of darkness in the Sedra, we see that in the Haftarah, darkness is to be eliminated. What do you think the darkness in the Haftarah represents?

◆ One could posit that in the creation of the world, God can separate light and darkness, but in the operation of the world, God needs *us* to remove darkness. What does this indicate to you about our role as God's partner?

18 As the Creator of the world, God reserves the right to destroy creation, according to Isaiah 42:15.

◆ As the appointed caretakers of God's earth, do we also have such a right? Explain your answer.

◆ What is our responsibility for saving God's creation?

◆ For more on this issue, see *Teaching Torah* by Sorel Goldberg Loeb and Barbara Binder Kadden, *Parashat Beresheet*, Personalizing the Text #15, p. 8.

Extending the Text

19 The Haftarah excludes the first four verses of Isaiah 42. It is important to note, however, that Isaiah 42 begins with the phrase, "My servant," over which there has been much theological debate.

The text of the Haftarah was most likely written in the sixth century B.C.E. by a prophet in exile in Babylon concerned with the return of his people to Israel.

◆ Which of the following options do you think best explains the phrase "My servant":

• Cyrus the Great, King of Persia and Media, who would serve God by freeing Israel from Babylon

• Israel, a people who serve God

• Isaiah, a prophet who serves God

• The Messiah, who will come one day in the future (even though the Bible does not specifically contain the idea of Messiah)

20 Rambam, a Rabbi and physician who lived in the twelfth century, wrote in chapter 3 of *The Regimen of Health* (as quoted in

The Medical Legacy of Moses Maimonides by Fred Rosner, pp. 200-201):

". . . emotional experiences produce marked changes in the body which are apparent and manifest to all. I will prove this to you in that you may see a man of robust build whose voice is strong and pleasant and whose face shines. When news suddenly reaches him that causes him great anxiety, his facial expression falls and loses its glitter . . . His strength weakens and sometimes he trembles from his great weakness. His pulse becomes small and weak, his eyes change, and his eyelids become too heavy to move . . ."

"Similarly, the situations of hopeful and fearful people and of those who expect security and tranquility are known; so, too, the emotional reactions of the desperate and the successful are manifest. Sometimes a desperate person may be so disheartened by his misfortune that he cannot see because of the diminution of his visual power and its gloominess. On the other hand, the light in the eyes of a successful person markedly increases to the point that the light of the day has increased and grown."

◆ What are psychosomatic illnesses?

◆ Could Rambam's description of desperate, hopeless people explain those people in the Haftarah who were blind? Why or why not?

◆ Rambam concludes that an important part of maintaining good health is the removal of anxiety. What are your favorite ways of dealing with anxiety?

◆ Listen to the words of the hit song, "Don't Worry, Be Happy" by Bobby McFerrin, which can be found on the CD of the same name. Do you think McFerrin's advice is good? How do you feel when you listen to this song? Write an original verse for the song and sing it to your classmates.

21 Cyrus is a very important figure in the Book of Isaiah.

◆ Do some research on Cyrus, King of Persia, and present an oral report on him to the class. (You may want to consult the *Encyclopaedia Judaica*, vol. 5, pp. 1184-86.)

22 Isaiah refers to the people as being blind and deaf.

◆ Review the blessings that we say at the opening of our morning service. One blessing says that we thank God for giving sight to the blind. When we say it, we mean that we thank God in the morning for restoring vision to our eyes that seemed not to work while we slept.

According to a number of Jewish legal commentators, even if one is not obligated to say a particular blessing (perhaps because one is blind), one nevertheless does say the blessing. One says the blessing because blessings do not apply to each person specifically; rather they praise God for providing for the needs of the world. Perhaps blind people cannot thank God for their own eyesight, but they can thank God for the benefit they get when people (or seeing eye dogs) use their eyesight to help them.

Another answer to the same question understands "sight" metaphorically. Even people who cannot see can have "insight" into difficult matters, can have a "vision" of what they want to do with their lives, can be "enlightened by education." This answer reflects an understanding that there are different types of sight for which we should be thankful.

◆ Do you think that blind people, who do not have their vision restored in the morning, say this blessing thanking God for giving sight to the blind?

◆ Among the other morning blessings, find some that do not seem to apply to all people.

Why might these blessings be said nonetheless by everyone? (For example, some may suggest that a person who cannot walk, might not say, "Blessed is God Who guides the steps of people," because a person who cannot walk does not take steps. However, they, too, benefit from other people having the ability to walk. In addition, being guided on a path in life is a metaphoric reading of this blessing. If we live in the city, we do not hear roosters in the morning, yet still we say, "Blessed is God Who gives the rooster understanding to distinguish day from night." This is said even though we do not hear roosters because it also has a more general meaning of expressing gratitude for our intelligence. Even if particular blessings do not seem to apply, one might still say them in order to teach empathy for others, to feel a sense of community, to encourage us to be appreciative.)

23 The word "light" (verses 42:6-7) is used to symbolize many things.

◆ Make a list of all the symbolic meanings of "light." To get you started, think of the idea light bulb from cartoons, the torch in the Statue of Liberty, the phrase "sweetness and light."

◆ See an exhaustive list of the symbols of light in *The Encyclopedia of Jewish Symbols* by Ellen Frankel and Betsy Platkin Teutsch, pp. 96-98.

◆ Collect as many "light bulb" jokes as you can. Share them with your classmates.

24 In the Haftarah light must remove darkness. View and discuss the film *Star Wars* (1977, rated PG, 125 minutes), in which Luke must fight the dark side. What does the dark side stand for — is it evil in general, is it Luke's evil inclination, or is it hopelessness?

25 Verses 42:6-7 indicate that the role of Israel is to be a light to the nations, rescuing prisoners from confinement.

Instead of working in congregations, some Rabbis work as chaplains for the greater Jewish community. Often chaplains make weekly visits to local prisons to visit Jews who are incarcerated.

◆ Invite a Rabbi who works as a prison chaplain to come to your class and discuss his or her experiences. Find out what religious items the Jewish prisoners might need, then collect and send those things.

26 The Prophet Elijah was once asked who, of all the people milling around in the town market, was deserving to go to heaven. Elijah responded that the prison guard was the most deserving because he was always considerate to his prisoners and never used unnecessary cruelty. When asked if anyone else present deserved to go to heaven, Elijah pointed to two clowns who were amusing people walking by. Elijah explained that the two clowns approach anyone, even one who is suffering with grief, and by merry talk and joking help the people to forget their grief (from *Ta'anith* 22a).

◆ Explain why the prison guard was deserving.

◆ There are many metaphorical prisons that imprison us. Explain in what ways each of the following are prisons: financial worry, illness, stress, depression, a bad job.

◆ Explain how clowns help free people from some of these metaphorical prisons.

27 Rabbi Henry Cohen was well-known in Texas for showing kindness to non-Jews, as well as to Jews. He was especially concerned about the treatment of prisoners in Texas — prisoners' rights and prison reform.

One day, Rabbi Cohen heard about a prisoner named Sidney Porter who was falsely arrested. The Rabbi researched the subject, and proved to the governor of Texas that Porter was innocent. When Porter was freed, he promised Rabbi Cohen that he would find a way to repay the Rabbi's kindness by helping his people.

Years later, Rabbi Cohen read a short story, written by O. Henry (Sidney Porter's pen name), about a Rabbi who saved an innocent man from jail. (This story can be found in the book *A Treasury of Jewish Anecdotes* by Lawrence J. Epstein, p. 51.)

North Americans who live in places where there aren't many Jews learn about Jews from stories such as this, from films, and from television.

◆ What did Sidney Porter and the Governor of Texas learn about Jews from Rabbi Cohen?

◆ What do people learn about Jews from the television series *Seinfeld*, or from the films of filmmaker Steven Spielberg?

◆ If you could teach someone who didn't know any Jews about what Jews are like, what would you say?

Personalizing the Text

28 As we learned in Insights from the Tradition #A, p. 275, God gives breath (a soul, according to Rashi) to every person.

◆ Make an anti-racism poster demonstrating that all people equally have souls, given by God.

29 We learned in Insights from the Tradition #E, p. 276, that children can make their parents better parents.

◆ As a class, develop a "Parenting Report Card." Decide categories and criteria for grading parents on their parenting skills. Ask your parents if they would be willing to be graded and to discuss the resulting "Parent Report Card" with you.

30 Hirsch explains that verse 42:5 says that God "creates" the heavens in the present tense (not the past tense) because God continues to be the creator and continually wills everything into existence. Should God decide to stop creating, the world would cease to exist.

◆ *Midrash* teaches that with each child, the world begins anew. As a class, design a *"mazal tov"* card for parents of new babies, and include in it this *midrashic* thought. Keep up with the new births and adoptions in your congregation, and send the card to each happy family.

31 In verse 42:10 Isaiah says, "Sing to *Adonai* a new song." The phrase "new song" appears frequently in the Bible.

◆ Find and compare these references (see Psalm 40:4, 96:1-2, 98:1, and 149:1-2).

32 We are taught to appreciate the fact that all the conveniences we enjoy today did not always exist (see Insights from the Tradition #B, pp. 275-276).

◆ List five items invented in the last 100 years that you think you could not live without.

◆ Role-play a scene using these five things.

◆ Then, role-play the same scene without the five items. Discuss how your life would be different without these items.

◆ Finally, role-play any scene from the Bible, incorporating the five items that did not exist back then.

◆ Imagine how history might have been different if your five items existed in biblical times.

33 One argument for God's existence goes like this: Since it is true that sculptures have a sculptor and paintings have a painter, it must also be true that creations have a Creator.

◆ Can you think of other examples of this linguistic argument for God's existence?

◆ Do you find this argument convincing?

34 The Baal Shem Tov once wrote, "From every human being there rises a light that reaches straight to heaven. And when two souls that are destined to be together find each other, their streams of light flow together, and a single brighter light goes forth from their united being" (from *Living a Jewish Life* by Anita Diamant and Howard Cooper, p. 266).

◆ In what ways are your parents, together and/or individually, a "light" for you?

35 "I love you," says *Adonai* to Israel in verse 43:4.

◆ How do we know that God loves us?

◆ How does it feel to be loved by God?

◆ Write a poem expressing your love for God and gratitude for God's love for you.

◆ Alternatively, design a billboard that reminds us of God and God's love.

36 God loves Israel (verse 43:4). Research the organization called God's Love We Deliver. (Access their web site at www.godslovewedeliver.org.) Define "God's love" based on what this organization does.

Other Resources

37 Read and discuss the poem, "How Long Have We Forgotten How to Listen" by Nelly Sachs, which is based on Isaiah 42:9. The poem may be found in her book *Shirim: A Jewish Poetry Journal*, and is reprinted in *A Jewish Book of Comfort* by Alan A. Kay, p. 144.

38 God admonishes Israel, but at the same time reminds Israel that God loves them. Love can be a powerful tool. Read and discuss the story "How I Learned to Study Torah" by Doug Lipman in *Chosen Tales*, edited by Peninnah Schram, pp. 205-209.

39 See the commentary for this Haftarah in the Haftarot commentary of the Fuchsberg Center for Conservative Judaism in Jerusalem. Find it on their web site at www.uscj. org.il/haftarah/index.html.

40 For more on witnesses, see the book *The Jewish Religion: A Companion* by Louis Jacobs, pp. 591-592, or the *Encyclopaedia Judaica*, vol. 16, pp. 584-590.

41 For more proverbs, parables, and lessons on light, see *A Different Light: The Big Book of Hanukkah* by Noam Zion and Barbara Spectre, pp. 194-213.

42 For more discussion on darkness, see Extending the Text #19 and #20 in the Haftarah for *Ekev*, pp. 300-301.

43 Join J-CLOWN LIST, the online e-mail discussion list for Jewish clowns, at www.geocities.com/jgirlscout/j-clown.html (see Extending the Text #26, p. 283, for Elijah's view of clowns). Subscribers share ideas and explore how to reinforce religious activities and Hebrew school curriculum through clowning. Find out how to start a Mitzvah Clown Group.

Alternatively, check the web page of *mitzvah* clowns, Sue and Michael Turk: www. mitzvahclowns.com.

Involving the Family

44 Insights from the Tradition #E, p. 276, and Personalizing the Text #29, pp. 283-284, suggest that children can help their parents become better parents. Parents can help their children be better people. However, for this to happen, parents and children need to talk to each other regularly. According to recent research, the average American parent and child spend 14 minutes per day talking to each other. Moreover, most of the time is spent on insubstantial chitchat.

For a month, keep a record of how much time you spend with a parent (with the television off) discussing subjects other than whether or not you have you finished your homework. Make a plan for how you can double your weekly time spent talking parent-child.

Bar/Bat Mitzvah Projects

45 Isaiah spoke of giving light to those in the dark and sight to the blind. Volunteer for the Jewish Braille Institute by reading books on tape, typing Jewish books in large print on your computer, or doing a variety of other very important tasks. To become a JBI volunteer, call them at 1-800-433-1531 or visit their web site: www.jewishbraille.org.

46 Collect old eyeglasses for the organization New Eyes for the Needy. They refurbish eyeglasses for those who cannot afford new ones. Find more information about this organization by calling 973-376-4903. They also collect old hearing aids.

ISAIAH 43:21-44:23
VAYIKRA ויקרא

This Haftarah has been paired with *Parashat Vayikra*, Leviticus 1:1-5:26. See "Connecting the Text To the Sedra," pp. 288-290, for an exploration of the many ways the two texts shed light on each other.

Note: All the Haftarot from Deutero-Isaiah have similar historical context and themes. Many Extending and Personalizing Strategies, as well as Other Resources and Bar Mitzvah Projects, can be shared among them.

SYNOPSIS

Worn down by exile, many Israelites have lost their faith in God and turned to idolatry. Isaiah is appalled by this lapse, and attacks the Israelites for their idolatrous sins. Still, he assures Israel that God will ultimately forgive them and give them a fresh start in their homeland.

First, the Haftarah describes how instead of honoring God by offering sacrifices, Israel has burdened God with its sins. Yet, we are told, God will bless the Israelite future just as God pours rain on the thirsty ground. God is eternal and there is no god but *Adonai*. Israel should not fear, because all God's predictions come true.

Then God's eternal and supreme power is contrasted with the impotence of idols. The makers of idols will be shamed. The prophet ridicules idol makers for creating so-called gods out of the same wood they use for mundane purposes, such as building fires. He likewise criticizes misguided idolators for foolishly bowing down to blocks of wood.

Isaiah finally exhorts the Israelites to forget about the idols and turn back to God, Who will redeem them. The prophet calls upon the heavens, the depths of the earth, the mountains, and the forests to rejoice together over the redemption of the people Israel.

INSIGHTS FROM THE TRADITION

A Hertz explains that when the people sing God's praise through prayer (verse 43:21), the prayer should inspire them to do deeds of righteousness. Those deeds, in turn, shower more praise on God.

◆ How do our good deeds make God look good?

◆ How do our bad deeds make God look bad?

◆ Do you think children's behavior reflects somehow on their parents, or students' behavior on their school? Why is this fair or unfair?

B Isaiah explains that God erases the sins of Israel for God's own sake (verse 43:25). According to Radak, if God did not erase the sins, God would have to punish and eventually destroy Israel. Destroying God's own chosen people might make God look bad to other nations because God could defeat Egypt and take Israel out of Egypt, but God could not get Israel to keep the laws of Torah and behave according to God's wishes.

◆ Explain in your own words why God would look bad to the other nations if God destroys Israel.

◆ Why might it matter to God what other nations think and say about God?

◆ Do you think it should matter to you what other people think and say about you? Why or why not?

C Although an idolator plants a sapling to be used for idolatrous purposes (verse 44:14), he or she is nonetheless dependent on rain from God to help the sapling grow. If trees grown with God's rain are used to worship other gods instead of God, this might be considered a type of theft. This is like the Talmudic teaching (*Avodah Zarah* 54b), which says that if someone steals wheat and plants it, one might think that the wheat should not grow because it was stolen. However, because the world goes on according to the laws of nature, we should just know that the thief who sinned will one day have to account for his wrongdoing.

◆ Why is it so unsatisfying when a crime goes unpunished?

◆ Do you think all sinners, punished and unpunished, will one day have to account for their wrongdoing, or will some just get away with their sins?

D The prophet says in verse 43:28 that God profaned the holy princes. According to Radak, the holy princes are righteous people who are often profaned, attacked, or killed by the enemy who is sent to destroy the wicked. Radak explains that when the wicked are large in number compared to the righteous, the righteous will be killed with them.

◆ After September 11, 2001, the United States demanded that Afghanistan turn over the criminals responsible for the terrorist acts. When the Taliban government refused, the United States and NATO attacked Afghanistan in order to destroy the Taliban government and capture the criminals. In the process of the U.S. bombing of Afghanistan, many innocent people were hurt or killed. In your opinion,

was the hurting of innocent people in this situation inevitable?

◆ Imagine other situations in which innocent people are harmed when punishment is inflicted on guilty people.

STRATEGIES
Analyzing the Text

1 God says in verse 43:26, "Help Me remember." Radak explains that God says to Israel, as a person says to a friend, if I forgot any of your merits, remind me. Furthermore, if God has overstated Israel's sins, Israel should correct the record. As the verse says, "Tell your version that you may be vindicated."

◆ Describe God's emotional state, according to Radak's interpretation.

◆ Why might God be in such an emotional state?

2 The prophet points out in verse 43:27 that Israel's "earliest ancestor sinned." It is unclear who this earliest ancestor was.

◆ To which "earliest ancestor" do you think Isaiah is referring? Make your choice among the following possibilities. Defend your answer.

• Adam may or may not be Israel's first ancestor. Read about Adam's sin in Genesis 3:6, 17ff.

• Abraham may or may not be Israel's first ancestor. Read about Abraham's sin in Genesis 15:8.

• Jacob may or may not be Israel's first ancestor. Read Hosea 12:3-5.

• The first generation of Israel brought out from Egypt by God may or may not be

Israel's first ancestors. Read about the Exodus generation's sin in Exodus 32.

3 In verses 44:14-17 Isaiah explains the history of the wooden idol from its origin as a tree in the forest. Isaiah pictures the idol maker cutting down a tree and using part to make a fire to warm himself and to cook his meals (particularly secular, mundane uses) and using the rest to make a god.

◆ Explain the sarcasm in this scene.

◆ Draw a political/theological cartoon depicting this futile scene.

◆ List other things that people worship other than statues (e.g., money, fame, success). Now make a cartoon depicting the futile worship of these things.

4 God reminds Israel several times that they were created by God (see verses 43:21, 44:2, 44:21). Contrast this statement with the prophet's sarcastic criticism of idol makers forming gods out of wood themselves.

◆ The message seems to be that God can create people, but people cannot create gods. What is the difference?

5 In verse 44:5 we are given four names for the Israelite people: "I am *Adonai's*," "Jacob," "of *Adonai*," and "Israel." Earlier, in verse 44:2, the name *"Jeshurun,"* which means "upright," is mentioned.

◆ What do you think these names indicate about the Israelite people?

◆ List as many names as you can for the Jewish people. Which do you like best, and why?

◆ Could any of the names be considered anti-Semitic?

6 God is called a "rock" in verse 44:8.

◆ What does it mean that God is a Rock?

◆ Consider how a rock might be a place of safety, a high point, or a source of strength. Are there other images a rock conveys to you?

◆ For a discussion of what a rock might mean to us, see the Haftarah for *Ha'azinu*, Connecting the Text To the Sedra #10, pp. 94-95.

Connecting the Text To the Sedra

7 The Sedra outlines the sacrifices to be made in the Temple. In contrast, Isaiah speaks to the people in Babylon after the Temple was destroyed. Sacrifices were no longer possible.

◆ Why might the Israelites have believed that, without a Temple, they could no longer serve God?

◆ The Israelites were wrong to believe that they could no longer serve God without a Temple. Isaiah explained to them how to continue to serve God. Reread verse 43:21 to learn how God wants to be worshiped by Israel.

◆ What does praising God mean to you?

◆ Just as the first verse of the Haftarah explains that God wants Israel to praise God, so the last verse of the Haftarah offers a picture of all creation praising God. What do you learn from this verse about how to praise God?

8 Deuteronomy 11:13 says you are "to serve God with all your heart." The word for "serve" is the same word used for serving God in the Temple by offering sacrifices. The Rabbis ask what it means to serve God with your heart. They answer, with prayer. Thus, prayer became another way to serve God. After the destruction of the Second Temple in 70 C.E., prayer replaced sacrifice. Judaism adapted to the traumatic loss of the Temple by devising a new system for serving God. We now have three services a day to replace the daily sacrifices.

- In place of the morning sacrifices, we have a morning service called Shacharit.

- In place of the afternoon sacrifices, we have an afternoon service called Minchah.

- In place of the evening sacrifices, we have an evening service called Ma'ariv.

- In addition, we have replaced Shabbat and holiday sacrifices with special Shabbat and holiday services.

- Moreover, our prayers are sometimes called "service of the heart."

◆ Invite your Cantor to speak to your class about the structure of the worship services.

◆ Alternatively, work with your Cantor to design a creative service in which your class can truly shout aloud in praise of God.

◆ There is a small movement among the Orthodox in Israel to reinstate sacrifices. What is your view of this?

9 According to the Sedra, one type of sacrifice is offered when a person trespasses against God. Read Leviticus 5:15-16, which explains that a trespass against God means using a sacred thing of God's sanctuary for an unrelated purpose.

◆ Why do you think using a sacred thing of God's sanctuary for an unrelated purpose is considered a sin?

◆ In the Haftarah, God complains that God provides rain to make the trees grow, but people use the trees to worship idols (see verse 44:14 and Insights from the Tradition #C, p. 287.

Does this seem to you to be misuse of God's assets?

◆ As a class, brainstorm ways to use trees that would be in service to God.

10 The Sedra sets up a ritual system for offering sacrifices and drawing near to God. The word for sacrifice — *"korban"*— comes from the Hebrew root "to draw near." According to Rambam, offering sacrifices is a primitive form of religion designed for human beings. God designed it for human beings in order to wean them from idol worship. Rambam explains in *Guide of the Perplexed* (3:32):

"It is, namely, impossible to go suddenly from one extreme to the other; it is therefore according to the nature of man impossible for him suddenly to discontinue everything to which he has been accustomed . . . The Israelites were commanded to devote them to His service 'and to serve Him with all your heart' (Deuteronomy 11:13) . . . But the custom which was in those days general among men, and the general mode of worship in which the Israelites were brought up, consisted in sacrificing animals in those temples which contained certain images, to bow down to those images and to burn incense before them . . . It was in accordance with the wisdom and plan of God . . . that He did not command us to give up and to discontinue all these manners of service; for to obey such a commandment it would have been contrary to the nature of man, who generally cleaves to that to which he is used."

◆ Explain Rambam's theory in your own words.

◆ How does this theory depict God (e.g., wise understanding, patient, sympathetic)?

◆ According to this theory, does God need sacrifices?

◆ Alternatively, the Haftarah describes what God wants. Reread the following verses and describe how God feels: 43:21, 22, 26, 27-28; 44:1-5, 21-23.

◆ Discuss the following possibilities for how God feels. Justify your choice(s).

- God feels abandoned.

- God wants to have a close relationship with the people God formed.

- God is unhappy that the relationship is one-sided.

- God feels unappreciated.

◆ As mentioned above, the meaning of the word for sacrifice — *"korban"* — is actually "to draw near." Perform a skit which depicts the need of God to feel near to human beings.

◆ Alternatively, write a letter from God to a "Heavenly Dear Abby," expressing God's need to feel near to human beings and asking for advice on the matter.

11 Leviticus 5:1 teaches that a person who can serve as a witness to a crime, but fails to do so, is guilty of avoiding social responsibility. In the Haftarah, Isaiah speaks of Israel's role as witnesses to God's power and ability to fulfill divine promises (verse 44:6-8). In the *Etz Hayim Chumash* (p. 607), Michael Fishbane writes, "This remarkable teaching presents theology as a form of human testimony to religious experience." In other words, the study of God is really an analysis of the experiences of God.

◆ Describe a time you have experienced God.

◆ Ask your Rabbi to speak to the class about his/her role as a witness to religious experience. Has he or she had a personal experience of God? What would he/she like to teach your community about God and/or Judaism?

◆ For more discussion on being a witness, see the Haftarah for *Beresheet*, Analyzing the Text #7, p. 278.

Extending the Text

12 We learned in Insights from the Tradition #A, p. 286, that our acts are a reflection on God.

A story is told in the Palestinian Talmud (*Bava Metzia* 8a) about Rabbi Shimon ben Shatach. Shimon wanted a donkey, so he sent his students to buy one for him. They returned with a donkey and when the Rabbi inspected it, he found a valuable jewel hidden in one saddle bag. Of course, he could have kept it legally (since the donkey and its saddle bags were now his), but he decided to return the jewel to the donkey's previous owner because it was not intentionally part of the sale. The first owner was grateful to get his jewel back, and praised the Israelite God.

◆ Why did the first owner praise not just the Israelite, but the Israelite God as well?

◆ What lessons do you learn from this story?

◆ Debate this dilemma: You bought a book at a garage sale for $1, took the book home, and found five $100 bills in it. Do you return the money?

13 Verse 43:25 says, "It is I, I who — for My own sake — wipe your transgressions away and remember your sins no more." This verse is included in the *"Amidah"* of our Yom Kippur services.

◆ Find verse 43:25 in the High Holy Day prayer book (see for example the *High Holiday Prayer Book* by Morris Silverman, pp. 220, 268, or 453).

◆ Why do you think we remind God to forgive our sins for God's own sake on Yom Kippur?

◆ Make your own list of reasons why God should forgive our sins.

14 A parable is told to explain why God acts for God's own sake:

A king had a small key for his palace. "If I leave it as it is, it will be lost," said the king. "I shall, rather, make a chain for it, for if it would get lost, the chain will be attached to it." So said the Most Holy, "If I leave Israel as they are, they will be swallowed up among the nations. I shall, rather, incorporate My great Name in them, and they will remain alive."

◆ What does it mean that God's name is the chain to which Israel is attached?

◆ What does it mean to be swallowed up among the nations?

◆ How does God's name keep Israel from getting swallowed up among the nations?

◆ Many people collect key chains as good luck charms or for other reasons. Bring in your favorite key chain for show-and-tell.

15 God declares in verses 44:6-7, that there is only one God and no other. If there is only one God and one law coming from the one God, then all nations can be held accountable under that one law.

In theory, the United Nations attempts to hold all nations to one legal standard of morality. However, the United Nations tends to be as fallible as its members. Review Resolution #3379, know as the "Zionism Is Racism" resolution, which was passed by the U.N. in 1975, and retracted only in 1991. This Resolution called Zionism a form of racism and racial discrimination. The resolution may be found at www.cdn-friends-icej.ca/un/3379.html.

◆ Debate: The United Nations sets one standard of behavior for all nations equally.

16 We learn in verse 44:6 that God is the first and God is the last. This idea is echoed in the words of the hymn with which many religious services are concluded.

◆ Read a translation of *"Adon Olam"* and find a verse of the prayer which paraphrases this idea.

◆ Since *"Adon Olam"* (Eternal Sovereign) is written in iambic pentameter, it can be sung to many, many different tunes. Choose your favorite tune and sing *"Adon Olam"* to it.

17 The prophet predicts in verse 44:5 that one day the Israelites will make a mark on their arms, declaring their allegiance to *Adonai*.

◆ Can you think of a Jewish religious ritual that parallels this image? (In Exodus 13:9 and 13:16 and in Deuteronomy 6:8 and 11:18, a law commands the placement of a symbol "on the hand and between the eyes" as a reminder of God's commandments. These verses gave rise to the *mitzvah* of wearing *tefillin*. *Tefillin* are leather boxes containing pieces of parchment on which biblical verses are written. Leather straps attached to the boxes are used to fasten them around the head and upper arm of Jewish adults during weekday prayer.)

◆ Look up the verses contained in *tefillin*: Exodus 13:1-10, Exodus 13:11-16, Deuteronomy 6:4-9, and Deuteronomy 11:13-21.

◆ The straps on the arm *tefillin* are wound around the arm seven times. The end of the strap is wound three times around the hand and three times around the ring finger and middle finger, forming the letters of the Hebrew word *Shaddai* (a name for God). The numbers three and seven have special significance in Jewish tradition. Ask your Rabbi, Cantor, or teacher to teach you how to put on *tefillin*.

18 God is called a "rock" in verse 44:8. Read the following lines from the Proclamation of the Independence of the State of Israel from May 14, 1948, and consider its use of the image of God as a rock:

"We hereby proclaim the establishment of the Jewish State in Palestine, to be called *Medinat Yisrael* (The State of Israel) . . . With trust in the Rock of Israel, we set our hand to this Declaration, at this Session of the Provisional State Council, on the soil of the Homeland, in the city of Tel Aviv, on this Sabbath eve, the fifth of Iyar, 5708, the fourteenth of May, 1948."

◆ Other than the use of the word "rock," what is most striking to you in this proclamation?

19 A total of 20 Haftarot are taken from the Book of Isaiah. The first Sedra from four of the five books of the Torah (excluding Numbers) is paired with a Haftarah from Isaiah. All but two of the Haftarot for the Book of Deuteronomy are taken from the Book of Isaiah.

◆ Based on what you know so far about the Book of Isaiah, why do you think the ancient Rabbis liked the book and its message so much? Remember, these Rabbis lived in exile, too, after the destruction of the Second Temple by the Romans in 70 A.D.

◆ Write a book review of the Book of Isaiah, describing its general content, its overall message, and historical contexts. Write what you like and dislike about the book.

20 The Jewish people spent 2,000 years in exile after the destruction of the Second Temple in 70 A.D. Some Jews ended up in the remotest regions of the world.

◆ Do a research project and prepare a presentation to the class on the Jews of China or on the Jews of India. For information about the Jews of China, see *Legends of the Chinese Jews of Kaifeng* by Xin Xu and Beverly Friend. To learn about Jews in India, see *Encyclopaedia Judaica*, vol. 8, pp. 1349-1360.

Personalizing the Text

21 In verse 43:21 God says that people were created for the purpose of declaring God's praise.

◆ Have a class party in celebration of all the blessings God has given you. Decorate with posters and banners declaring God's praise. Perform songs, raps, cheers, and skits declaring God's praise. Serve a big sheet cake with "Thank you" written on it, and don't forget to make the appropriate blessings, praising God for the foods that you will eat.

◆ Alternatively, have a class party to celebrate the existence of the State of Israel. Make a poster of the Independence Proclamation, decorations in the blue and white colors of Israel, and lots of Israeli food and music.

22 Isaiah chastises the Israelites for turning to idolatry.

◆ Make a list of all the things people worship today (e.g., money, fame, thinness). Be a modern day prophet. Choose one modern "idol," then write a speech criticizing those who worship it. Include reasons why only God should be worshiped. Try to incorporate some of Isaiah's words in your message. Consider wearing an ancient prophet-like costume when you deliver your sermon. Alternatively, imagine what a modern day prophet would wear and make such a costume. The speeches can be videotaped for later viewing by the class.

23 Before virtual pets came onto the scene, "pet rocks" were very popular among young Americans.

◆ Ask your parents if they owned a pet rock.

◆ Since God is called a "rock" in this Haftarah, make your own pet rock, as a symbol of God's solid presence in your life. Decorate your rock any way you wish, with fuzzy hair or googly eyes, with markers or paint, glitter or fabric.

24 Although they suffer, the Israelites are comforted by the hope that they will soon be freed from their exile in Babylon. Hope can bring us comfort in almost any situation.

Anne Frank wrote to her famous diary, "I hope I will be able to confide everything to you, as I have never been able to confide in anyone, and I hope you will be a great source of comfort and support." (*The Definitive Edition of the Diary of a Young Girl* by Anne Frank, p. 1)

◆ How might writing your thoughts be a source of comfort and support?

◆ Everyone's life has in it times of trouble. Keep a diary in which to express your fears, hopes, and desires.

25 The title of the song *"Ma'oz Tzur"* means "Rock of Ages."

◆ Learn and sing *"Ma'oz Tzur"* in Hebrew or "Rock of Ages" in English. This song may be found on the recording *Lights* by the Zamir Chorale of Boston.

Other Resources

26 Read and discuss the essay on "The Chosen People" by Plaut in *The Haftarah Commentary*, pp. 239-240.

27 Israel suffers a great loss with the destruction of the Temple, yet commentators agree that it could have been worse. For a story about preferring the problems you already have to something that could be worse, read and discuss "The Pekl Story" by Helen Mintz in *Chosen Tales*, edited by Peninnah Schram, pp. 222-225.

28 Discuss the illustration of this Haftarah in *The Illustrated Torah* by Michal Meron, p. 108. What transgression does this illustration highlight? Why do you think the artist chose this transgression?

29 For more information on the prophet Isaiah, see *Messengers of God: A Jewish Prophets Who's Who* by Ronald H. Isaacs.

30 For a commentary on this Haftarah and its connection to the Sedra, see the web site of the Fuchsberg Center for Conservative Judaism in Jerusalem, www.uscj.org.il/haftarah.

31 Alternatively, see The Haftarah Commentary of CLAL — The National Jewish Center for Learning and Leadership, at their web site, www.clal.org/h27.html.

32 For more on prayer and worship services, see *Service of the Heart: A Guide To the Jewish Prayer Book* by Evelyn Garfiel.

33 Instead of sacrifices, we now hold prayer services to worship God. Our morning services contain a description of the sacrifices instead of the sacrifices themselves. Read some of these prayers (see, for example, the *ArtScroll Siddur*, pp. 31-49, or the first paragraph on p. 468).

34 Rambam explains the reason for the commandment of sacrifices. For more on the reasons behind the commandment, see the *Encyclopaedia Judaica*, vol. 5, pp. 783-792.

Involving the Family

35 Purchase a special set of *tefillin*, which you will be entitled to wear as a Jewish adult. If your parent(s) already have *tefillin*, take this opportunity to have them inspected and/or repaired. If your parent(s) or older sibling(s) do not already have *tefillin*, consider purchasing a set for them as well.

36 Based on Analyzing the Text #3, p. 288, and Personalizing the Text #20, p. 292, it is important to be aware of times when we worship false idols. Discuss as a family what things your family may idolize, and make a plan to end this idolatry.

Bar/Bat Mitzvah Projects

37 Alexander Pope wrote, "To err is human, to forgive Divine." Isaiah taught that God is always willing to forgive our sins. How willing are you to forgive others? Make a special effort to forgive your friends and loved ones for any wrongdoings they might have committed, either knowingly or unknowingly.

38 Be a rock for the State of Israel. Use your Bar/Bat Mitzvah gifts to buy a State of Israel Bond.

ISAIAH 49:14-51:3
EKEV עקב

This Haftarah has been paired with *Parashat Ekev*, Deuteronomy 7:12-11:25. See "Connecting the Text To the Sedra," pp. 297-300, for an exploration of the many ways the two texts shed light on each other.

Note: All the Haftarot from Deutero-Isaiah have similar historical context and themes. Many Extending and Personalizing Strategies, as well as Other Resources and Bar/Bat Mitzvah Projects, can be shared among them.

SYNOPSIS

This unusually long Haftarah is again set in the sixth century B.C.E., during the Babylonian exile of the Israelites. The prophet comforts and reassures the people, who doubt if they will ever return to their homeland. He explains that even if a mother could forget her child, God will never abandon Israel. Soon the Israelites will return to Jerusalem, the ruins will be rebuilt, and their population will increase.

When God decides the time is right, the nations of the world will join together to help the Israelites return safely home. The most powerful and tyrannical nations will be humbled by God, Who will inflict horrific punishments on them.

Though the Israelites have sinned and paid the price for their evil ways, God has neither divorced them nor sold them off. As such, God will welcome them back into the Covenant.

The prophet shares his own personal experience as proof that God will help the Israelites who revere *Adonai*.

The Israelites, who seem to be walking around in darkness, are instructed to remember their ancestors, Abraham and Sarah. Just as they (who had been childless) were blessed and grew into a mighty nation, so Israel will be restored to greatness, surrounded with gladness and joy, thanksgiving and music.

INSIGHTS FROM THE TRADITION

A Israel has been engraved on the palms of God's hands (verse 49:16). Rashi explains that this verse means that God always sees and remembers Israel.

◆ What does it mean to know someone as well as the palm of your hand?

◆ Palm prints are as unique to an individual as fingerprints. Explain how if Israel is engraved on God's palm print, Israel is unique for God.

◆ List people with whom you have unique relationships (for example, only sibling, best friend, and so on).

B According to Hirsch, verse 49:17 indicates that the worst enemy, the one that harmed Israel most severely, was Israel itself.

◆ How was Israel its own worst enemy in the sixth century B.C.E. (Read the previous Haftarot for guidance.)

◆ How can someone be his or her own worst enemy? Give examples.

◆ In what way(s) are you your own worst enemy? Interview family members to see how each of them has been his/her own worst enemy.

C God called out to Israel in verse 50:2, but no one responded. According to Hirsch, God comes into our lives by calling us to do *mitzvot*. When we do not do the *mitzvot*, it is as if we fail to answer God's call.

◆ Explain how the doing of *mitzvot* might be viewed as answering God's call to us.

◆ Does this explanation in any way change your view of *mitzvot*?

◆ Choose one *mitzvah* and describe how its performance brings God into your life.

D The prophet is given a "skilled tongue" in verse 50:4. According to Hirsch, this means that he has been given the understanding and ability to know how to speak the right word at the right time to those who need to listen.

◆ What does it mean to speak the right word at the right time?

◆ Who do you know who has a "skilled tongue"?

◆ Hirsch explains that there are different moments in life that require different types of words. Consider how you might:

• Urge someone who is feeling lazy.

• Warn someone who is driven by passion.

• Instruct someone who is in error.

• Encourage someone who is struggling.

STRATEGIES
Analyzing the Text

1 Zion speaks in verse 49:14 as the spurned wife of *Adonai*. Zion is another name for Jerusalem, and biblical literature often represents her as the wife of God, whose children are Israel. The metaphor continues for several verses, as Israel is compared to children who will return to Zion, adorning her as jewels adorn a bride. Again in verse 50:1, *Adonai* speaks of Israel's mother, who has been estranged, but not divorced.

◆ What does it mean to you that Jerusalem is "married" to (and estranged from) God?

◆ What does it mean to you that the Israelite people are Jerusalem's children?

2 *Adonai* asks the rhetorical question in verse 50:1, "Where is the bill of divorce of your mother whom I dismissed?" Like most biblical rhetorical questions, this one is meant to be answered in the negative: God has not divorced or disowned the Israelite people, despite their reprehensible behavior. This is important because the Covenant with God (agreement with God that we are God's people) is often viewed as a symbol for the certificate of our marriage with God.

◆ Why does God emphasize so strongly that the people have not been disconnected?

◆ If God did not divorce Israel, what does this imply for the continued existence of the Covenant?

◆ Find three more sets of rhetorical questions in the Haftarah. Confirm that these, too, are to be answered in the negative.

3 Verses 50:4-9 constitute one of the Book of Isaiah's four so-called "Songs of the Servant of *Adonai*." The four songs, which greatly resemble one another, are oddly out of place wherever they appear.

◆ Reread the Servant Song. In what ways are these verses different from the rest of the Haftarah?

◆ Scholars have debated the identity of the "servant," suggesting many possibilities: it might refer to Isaiah himself; the prophet Jeremiah; the Messiah; the Children of Israel collectively or individually; Moses; or even Cyrus the

King of Persia, who released the Israelites from Babylonian captivity. Christian scholars identify the servant as Jesus. Discuss which answer makes the most sense to you.

◆ For more information on the Song of the Servant, see the essay in *The Haftarah Commentary* by W. Gunther Plaut, pp. 458-459, or *Encyclopaedia Judaica*, vol. 9, p. 66.

4 In verses 50:5-7, the servant says that he did not disobey, run away, or let his tormentors stop him.

◆ If the servant is the prophet, why does he say this? (See Jeremiah 1:5-8 and Jonah 1:1-2.)

◆ Who do you think his tormentors were, and why were they tormenting him?

5 Isaiah accuses the Israelites of being "kindlers of fire" in verse 50:11. Rashi says that this means that the Israelites were igniting God's anger through their defiant behavior.

◆ How is misbehaving like playing with fire?

◆ Write a story or skit demonstrating that you might get burned if you play with fire, i.e., misbehave.

6 "Look to the rock you were hewn from, to the quarry you were dug from," instructs the prophet in verse 51:1.

◆ Can you think of other expressions that convey the idea that children are often very much like their parents?

◆ How are you a "chip off the old block"?

Connecting the Text To the Sedra

7 This Haftarah is the second Haftarah of Consolation following Tishah B'Av, the day of fasting and mourning that commemorates the destruction of both Temples in Jerusalem. This Haftarah asserts that although relations between God and Israel are strained due to Israel's sinfulness, nevertheless the Covenant between Israel and God still stands. (See also Analyzing the Text #2, p. 296.)

◆ Why is this a comforting and consoling message following Tishah B'Av?

◆ Read verse 51:3. Notice the use of the verb "comforted" twice.

◆ In the Sedra Moses recalls Israel's repeated sinfulness and defiance in the desert, which parallels Israel's sinfulness in the time of Isaiah. Yet the Covenant remains in existence for those who will keep it. The Hebrew word for Covenant, *brit*, appears throughout the Sedra, as the Israelites are reminded again and again of their Covenant with God. Try to locate all six occurrences of the word "covenant" in the Sedra.

◆ How might the realization of an enduring Covenant give hope to the hopeless exiles?

8 In this Haftarah, Isaiah uses three different images of items being worn.

◆ In verse 50:9 who is like a garment? Who is wearing the garment? What does the wearing out of the garment represent?

◆ Contrast this image to verse 49:18. Who are the jewels, and who will wear the jewels? What meaning does this image convey?

◆ Now, contrast these images with verse 50:3. What does the darkness or sackcloth represent? Why does God decide to clothe the skies in sackcloth?

◆ Compare these images to items being worn in the Sedra (Deuteronomy 8:4, 10:18, 11:18).

◆ Illustrate these metaphors.

9 Isaiah compares Israel to Abraham, whom God blessed and multiplied (Isaiah 51:2). Moses promises in Deuteronomy 7:13-14 that God will love, bless, and multiply Israel.

◆ Throughout the Bible God repeatedly promises to multiply the Israelite people. If there is strength, economic prosperity, and stability in greater numbers, explain the importance of this promise.

◆ Today, do we think of exploding population growth as positive or negative? What is your view of "zero population growth"? Is your view of it different for the Jewish people? Why or why not?

◆ Write alternative blessings that we might need today.

10 Commentators explain that "the rock you were hewn from" in verse 51:1 refers to Abraham.

◆ Reread verse 51:1-2 to see how "the rock" is equated with Abraham (consider the parallel language). In the Haftarah God reminds Israel to think back to Abraham for inspiration in acting with justice.

◆ Why might the people have forgotten how to act justly?

◆ The Sedra mentions Abraham in Deuteronomy 9:27. Read this verse in the Sedra. In the Sedra Moses reminds God to think back to Abraham in order to inspire God to act with mercy. Why do you think God seems to need to be reminded to act mercifully? Explain your answer.

◆ The Jewish ideal is to temper strict justice with appropriate mercy. For another discussion of balancing justice and mercy, see the Haftarah for *Noah*, Connecting the Text To The Sedra #9, p. 317.

11 As stated above, commentators thought that "the rock you were hewn from" in Isaiah 51:1 refers to Abraham.

◆ Do you think being descendants of Abraham means that we have the same genetic potential to be as worthy as Abraham? Or, do you think the verse means that the lives of great people can inspire us to greatness, and just knowing we are descendants from Abraham gives us extra inspiration? Or, do you think that Jewish culture in general promotes worthy behavior?

◆ On the subject of emulating our forebears, the great American poet Henry Wadsworth Longfellow wrote a poem entitled "A Psalm of Life." Find the poem on the Internet at http://fullmoongraphics.com/psalm.html. Read and discuss the meanings of this poem. (Note that the poem uses the word "footprint," which in Hebrew is the same as the Sedra, *Ekev*.)

◆ Preceding the Longfellow poem on the web site listed above is a drawing, perhaps a woodcut, depicting one of the verses. Create your own woodcut for one of the verses from the Haftarah. Organize an art exhibit or bulletin board display of all the woodcuts from the class.

◆ Which Jewish heroes (since biblical times) inspire you to walk in their great footsteps, and why?

◆ Write a *D'var Torah* about someone in whose footsteps you hope to follow.

12 Both Haftarah and Sedra employ clothing metaphors. In the Sedra Moses points out the miracle that "the clothes upon you did not wear out . . . these 40 years" of wandering in the desert (Deuteronomy 8:4).

In contrast, in the Haftarah the prophet declares that Israel's enemies "shall all wear out like a garment; the moth shall consume them" (Isaiah 50:9).

◆ What are clothes being used to demonstrate in each case?

◆ See Connecting the Text To the Sedra #8, p. 297, for additional clothing metaphors.

◆ Can you think of any clothing metaphors or similes used in our language today? (For example, "it fits like a glove.")

◆ Do a rag art painting project using worn out, threadbare clothes.

13 Abraham, Isaac, and Jacob are mentioned repeatedly throughout the Sedra, which is from the last book of the Torah — long after the death of the third Patriarch. Abraham is also mentioned as the father of the Israelites in the Haftarah (Isaiah 51:2).

◆ The Patriarchs have lasting power in the Jewish experience, and their names are used repeatedly in our *Siddur*. Find places in the *Siddur* where their names appear.

◆ What themes are associated with the Patriarchs in the *Siddur*?

◆ Which prominent Americans or Canadians are similarly invoked most frequently in daily discourse? (For example, George Washington could not tell a lie!)

◆ Reflect on people you know or knew personally (family, congregation leaders, friends). What quality did they exemplify, and how do you remember them or mention them on a daily basis?

14 The prophet condemns the Israelites for being "kindlers of fire" (verse 50:11). Hertz believes that this may be a reference to idol worship. The Sedra similarly contains several statements against idolatry (Deuteronomy 7:16 and 25, 8:19, and 11:16).

◆ Idolatry was viewed as a threat to biblical religion because it interfered with Israel's loyalty to God and their one-to-one relationship.

◆ Have a class debate over what you think is the most serious threat to Judaism today (consider assimilation, intermarriage, anti-Semitism, etc.).

15 In the Haftarah (verses 51:1-2), God wants to teach the Israelites a lesson that they are to remember forever. God commands them both to listen and to look.

◆ Read in the Sedra, Deuteronomy 11:18-21. List the commandments contained in these verses. Which commandments involve sight, and which involve hearing? Are other senses also used in these commandments?

◆ Some people learn better by seeing a lesson, and some learn better by hearing a lesson. In which group are you? To find out, try this exercise: One student teaches the class how to do a simple task, such as making a peanut butter and jelly sandwich, by describing the process verbally. Another student teaches the same task by way of visible demonstration. Which lesson was easier for you to follow, and why?

16 The Haftarah indicates that God keeps us engraved on God's palm as a reminder (see Insights from the Tradition #A, p. 295). The Sedra, in Deuteronomy 11:18, indicates that we are to keep the words of Torah on our hearts and on our hands. This commandment has been interpreted to mean that we are to wear *tefillin* when we pray weekday mornings.

◆ See the Haftarah for *Vayikra*, Extending the Text #15, p. 291, for more information on *tefillin*.

◆ What are some other ways we use our hands to remember things (e.g., tying strings around our fingers, writing notes on our palms, etc)?

Extending the Text

17 The Haftarah speaks of Zion as the estranged, but not divorced, wife of *Adonai*.

On the subject of divorce, the Torah says, "When a man takes a woman, and marries her, then it shall come to pass, if she find no favor in his eyes, because he has found something unseemly in her, that he shall write her a bill of divorcement, and give it into her hand" (Deuteronomy 24:1). The "bill of divorcement" is a legal divorce document known as a *get*. It must be written by either the husband or by his representative and handed personally by the husband to his wife. According to Jewish law, a man or woman who has been married in a Jewish ceremony, and then has a civil but not a religious divorce, is still considered married. The Reform Movement maintains that a civil divorce alone is adequate.

◆ Many of our families today are affected by divorce. Ask your Rabbi to speak on the subject of Judaism's view of marriage and divorce.

18 God has Israel engraved on the palms of God's hands in verse 49:16 in order that God will always see and remember the people. The Torah teaches us how to use fringes as reminders.

Numbers 15:39 says: "And you shall see [the fringes at the corner of the garment] and remember all the commandments of *Adonai*, and observe them."

From this we have adopted the custom of wearing *tzitzit* attached either to a garment worn under the shirt or to a *tallit*. Each of the *tzitzit* is made of four strings doubled over to make eight. They are tied with five knots and four groups of windings between the knots. After the first knot, seven windings are made, after the second knot, eight windings, after the third knot, 11 windings, after the fourth knot, 13 windings, and the fifth knot concludes the *tzitzit*.

The numbers of strings and knots are highly symbolic. The five knots are said to represent the Five Books of the Torah. Some say the five knots symbolize the five senses, which should all be dedicated to God. The combination of the eight strings and five knots can remind us of God's Thirteen Attributes. The numerical value of the Hebrew word ציצית (*tzitzit*) is 600. When you add to this the five knots and eight strings, the total is 613 — the number of commandments in the Torah.

◆ For more information on making *tallitot* or *tzitzit*, see *The First Jewish Catalog* by Richard Siegel, Michael Strassfeld, and Sharon Strassfeld, pp. 51-57. Practice knotting and winding *tzitzit*.

◆ Devise your own meanings behind these symbolic numbers. Also, what symbolism can you find behind the fact that *tzitzit* are connected to four corners of a garment?

19 The people are described in verse 50:10 as walking in darkness and having no light. Our tradition teaches that life without Torah is darkness, but that Torah brings light into our lives.

◆ What does darkness symbolize for you?

◆ Proverbs 6:23 says, "For the commandment (*mitzvah*) is a lamp and the teaching (Torah) is a light." Discuss this famous quotation, which is often displayed in synagogue sanctuaries. Then, see if you can find it anywhere in your synagogue.

◆ Make and decorate a banner featuring this quotation, and display it in a prominent place in the building.

20 Darkness is a powerful symbol of God's absence.

◆ Look up the following biblical incidences of darkness. In what way is darkness portrayed in each?

- Darkness in creation (Genesis 1:2 and 1:5)
- The plague of darkness (Exodus 10:21-23)
- Samson's blindness (Judges 16:21-30)
- Zedekiah's blindness (II Kings 25:1-7)
- Psalm 107:10, 14.

◆ Draw one of these portrayals of darkness. Display all the pictures together as an exhibit of darkness in the Bible. Consider drawing with milky pens on black paper, or cutting out the picture on black paper and mounting your paper-cut on a white background.

◆ Why do you think we sit in darkness on Tishah B'Av?

◆ On the other hand, we are instructed to light Shabbat candles every Shabbat specifically so we can enjoy ourselves and our families. Imagine what it must have been like before electricity, trying to eat dinner after the sunset. Experiment one night by eating Thursday night dinner with your family in the dark (wait until after sunset and use no lights or candles). The next night, eat Shabbat dinner with candles. Report back to your class on your experiment.

21 Zion (Jerusalem) is presented as the estranged wife of *Adonai*, whose children are the Israelite people. Isaiah predicts one day that the entire family will be happily united.

This theme runs through the final third of the Book of Isaiah. It is also reflected in the fourth of the seven Jewish wedding blessings: "Bring intense joy and exultation to the barren one through the ingathering of her children amidst her in gladness. Blessed are You, God, Who gladdens Zion through her children."

◆ How is a Jewish wedding a time of joy for all the Jewish people (symbolized by Zion)?

◆ Study the other six blessings recited at a Jewish wedding. Hold a mock wedding. (See the Haftarah for *Noah*, Personalizing the Text #26, p. 321, for more information, or see *The First Jewish Catalog* by Richard Siegel, Michael Strassfeld, and Sharon Strassfeld, pp. 158-166).

Personalizing the Text

22 The Jewish people are imprinted on God's palm.

◆ Make a handprint by covering the palm side of your hand with yellow paint and pressing your hand onto paper. Draw a dark outline around your print. In each finger of the print, write a value you consider important in your life. In the palm of your hand, write the value you consider most important in your life.

23 The song *"Sisu et Yerushalayim"* (Rejoice in Jerusalem) takes one of its verses from Isaiah 49:18. (Note: This verse also appears as Isaiah 60:4.) This song may be found in the songbook *B'Kol Echad*, edited by Jeffrey Shiovitz, pp. 113-114, and on the accompanying audiocassettes, *Shirei B'Kol Echad*, both of which may be ordered from the web site of United Synagogue for Conservative Judaism, www.uscj.org/booksvc.

◆ Ask your Cantor to teach this song.

24 The prophet knows how to speak the right word at the right time to those who need to listen (see Insights from the Tradition #D, p. 296).

There is a *midrashic* story about God speaking to Moses at the burning bush. God considered, "If I reveal Myself to Moses in loud tones, I shall alarm him, but if I reveal Myself with a subdued voice, he will hold prophecy in low esteem." Consequently, God chose to speak to Moses in the voice of his father Amram. Moses was overjoyed to hear his father speak. When God explained that it was God and not Amram who spoke, Moses was pleased and ready to listen to what God had to say (*The Legends of the Jews* by Louis Ginzberg, 2:305).

◆ Why would a parent's voice be the best voice for God to use?

In the film *The Ten Commandments* (1956, rated G, 220 minutes), the director, Cecil B. DeMille, found the hardest part to cast was the actor to be the voice of God. He was dissatisfied with all the actors who read the part. For some of the scenes, Charlton Heston (he played Moses) recorded God's lines, and then his recording was electronically altered and used for the voice of God.

Furthermore, in the important scene when God gave the Ten Commandments to Moses, the director wanted a different voice for God. He found an actor to read the part, but that actor's identity is still a secret, even today.

◆ Explain how the decision for how to create God's voice in this film seems to reflect the above *midrash* about God speaking to Moses at the burning bush.

◆ Explain the significance of keeping secret the identity of the actor reading God's lines.

◆ View and discuss the film *The Ten Commandments*. Find out how many in the class have been to Universal Studios in Los Angeles, and experienced the "parting of the Reed Sea" from the film.

25 God clothes the sky in blackness in verse 50:3, which some commentators explain to mean a total eclipse of the sun.

◆ Does it help you to understand the text if biblical events are explained in terms of natural phenomena? Does it hinder your understanding? Explain your answers.

◆ List other examples of biblical events that scholars have attempted to understand in terms of natural events.

◆ Natural or miraculous or both, eclipses are awesome events. To view eclipses and learn everything you ever wanted to know about eclipses, visit the Earth View Eclipse Network at their web site: www.earthview.com.

◆ See if you can stage an eclipse, based on what you have learned, using a flashlight, a tennis ball, and a beach ball.

Other Resources

26 Read and discuss Elie Wiesel's Holocaust memoir, entitled *Night*. How does the title of the book reflect the darkness of the time?

27 View and discuss the film *Breaking Away* (1979, 100 minutes, rated PG), which involves the children of quarry cutters (see Analyzing the Text #6, p. 297). Are the children "chips off the old block"? Where do they find the hope and strength to overcome the obstacles they face?

28 View and discuss the film *The Miracle Worker* (1979, not rated, 106 minutes), in which Annie Sullivan struggles to communicate with the blind and deaf Helen Keller.

29 Read *Tzitzith: A Thread of Light* by Aryeh Kaplan, which delves into the spiritual and symbolic significance of wearing *tzitzit*.

30 Read the classic book *Heart of Darkness* by Joseph Conrad, which explores the dark places of the human soul and the capacity of human beings for both good and evil.

31 Read and discuss *Emma Ansky-Levine And Her Mitzvah Machine* by Lawrence Bush, about a girl who receives a special gift that helps her discover her Jewish identity and the true meaning of becoming a Bat Mitzvah.

32 *The Always Prayer Shawl* by Sheldon Oberman tells the story of a *tallit* that is passed down from generation to generation. Read and discuss this book. Ask your father and/or grandfather if there is an interesting history concerning his *tallit*. If your mother and/or grandmother wears a *tallit,* ask them, too.

33 For books on how to talk about God with children, read excerpts from *When Children Ask about God* by Harold S. Kushner, *Where Does God Live?* by Marc Gellman and Thomas Hartman, or *Teaching Your Children about God: A Modern Jewish Approach* by David Wolpe. Which author's philosophy is most compatible with yours?

34 Discuss the illustration of this Haftarah in *The Illustrated Torah* by Michal Meron, p. 194.

35 See the *Encyclopaedia Judaica*, vol. 16, pp. 1030-1031, for more information on Zion.

36 See the *Encyclopaedia Judaica*, vol. 5, pp.1012-1022, for more information on Covenant. Alternatively, see *Exploring Exodus* by Nahum M. Sarna, pp. 134-144.

37 See a commentary for this Haftarah on the UAHC Family Shabbat Table Talk web site, www.uahc.org/shabbat/stt/3ekev.shtml.

38 For more on this Haftarah, see the commentary of the Fuchsberg Center for Conservative Judaism in Jerusalem, which may be found at www.uscj.org.il/haftarah.

Involving the Family

39 The Israelites are to take heart that they are the descendants of Abraham. Do some genealogical research and make your own family tree. Find out at least one positive thing about each of your ancestors. How does knowing about your heritage make you feel about your family and yourself?

40 Based on Connecting the Text To the Sedra #13, p. 299, write an epitaph (e.g., George Washington could not tell a lie) for one or more people on your family tree.

Bar/Bat Mitzvah Projects

41 The exiled Israelites are as if they are walking in darkness and have no light. Bring hope to those who really do walk around in the dark due to blindness. Volunteer to run errands for or read to the visually impaired in your community. Consider raising a puppy to be a Seeing Eye dog.

42 Organize a used clothing drive to collect clothing that was gently worn and does not show wear and tear (see Connecting the Text To the Sedra #12, p. 298). Donate the clothing to a local shelter for the homeless or other organization of your choice.

ISAIAH 51:12-52:12
SHOFETIM שופטים

This Haftarah has been paired with *Parashat Shofetim*, Deuteronomy 16:18-21:9. See "Connecting the Text To the Sedra," pp. 307-309, for an exploration of the many ways the two texts shed light on each other.

SYNOPSIS

As the Israelites languish in exile (586-536 B.C.E.), the expected victory of the Persians over the Babylonians brings them hope that King Cyrus of Persia will allow the captive Israelites to return to the Land of Israel.

With redemption close at hand, the prophet reminds the people that it is the immortal God who will comfort them and redeem them from the tyranny of mere mortals. God's awesome power is contrasted with the relative weakness of humans, however powerful they might seem.

The prophet instructs Israel to rouse itself from its miserable situation, caused by God's wrath against them. He assures them that just as God caused their suffering, so will God redeem them and turn the Divine wrath upon Israel's enemies.

In chapter 52, Zion (another name for Jerusalem) is promised that she will never be invaded again. She is called upon to prepare for the return of her children, Israel. God predicts that on the day they are returned to Zion, the Israelites will know that God is their faithful King. The reunion of Zion and her people will be an occasion of unparalleled happiness and joy, as God's might is revealed to the nations.

The concluding verses summon the Israelites to prepare themselves spiritually and emotionally for their imminent return home.

Note: All the Haftarot from Deutero-Isaiah have similar historical context and themes. Many Extending and Personalizing Strategies, as well as Other Resources and Bar/Bat Mitzvah Projects, can be shared among them.

INSIGHTS FROM THE TRADITION

A Throughout the Bible and in our prayer liturgy, there are many names for God, each signifying a particular aspect of the Divine. The first word of the Haftarah, "*anochi*," designates, according to Hirsch, God's characteristic of Mercy.

◆ Each of us has many distinct and varied qualities that make us who we are, and each of us plays many different roles in our lives. Make a list of all your roles (sister, son, student, athlete, friend, etc.). Think about the particular aspects of your personality that are highlighted in each role you play, and about the responsibilities that go along with each one.

B Hirsch explains that verse 51:13 should be translated literally as, "God Who is still making you." Because the verb is in the present and not the past tense, we can understand that God is not finished working on the Israelites. It just wouldn't make sense for God to plan Israel's total destruction if God is still working on creating them.

◆ In what ways are all people growing and changing every day?

◆ Does constant change represent for you a strength or weakness in human nature? Explain your answer.

◆ Buzz Aldrin, one of the first astronauts to land on the moon, was frustrated years later because he could not top the experience of landing on the moon. Explain how his situation is an example of the human need to be continually growing and changing.

C Based on verse 51:16, Hertz teaches that we plant Heaven on earth whenever we teach a child — by word or example — a noble, godly idea, action, or way to live.

◆ What do you think Hertz means?

◆ Give examples of the type of lesson taught to a child that would help plant heaven on earth. For example, when a parent teaches a child to lose graciously, or even to let someone else win, how is that planting heaven on earth?

◆ Steven Spielberg tells a story about how he was an uncoordinated and unpopular kid. One day in gym class, the whole class had to run a mile. He was barely able to finish the mile, and he saw that there was only one kid behind him. The kid behind him was a developmentally disabled boy who was working as hard as he could to run the mile. Spielberg compassionately slowed down and let the other boy pass him in spite of the humiliation it cost him. How was his act godly? How did his act plant heaven on earth?

◆ Think of a godly lesson your parents have taught you. Write the lesson on a poster and hang every student's poster on a bulletin board, with the heading, "Parents Plant Heaven on Earth."

D The prophet urges the people to snap out of their drunken stupor (verse 51:21). Radak and Ibn Ezra explain that the Israelites are drunk not from wine, but from "drinking" too much of God's anger and fury.

◆ Describe the behavior of someone who is drunk.

◆ Describe the behavior of someone who is overwhelmed by trouble and sorrow.

◆ In what ways are the behaviors similar?

◆ Just as alcohol impairs someone's judgment, so can deep sorrow. What other situations and emotions could affect someone's judgment and behavior?

E The Israelites are instructed in verse 52:11 to turn away from the unclean. Hirsch teaches that it is the duty of every Jew to be a strict judge of his/her own conduct (that is, turn away from anything wrong). We must judge ourselves by our own conscience and never use the excuse that we do something because everybody else does it.

◆ Can you think of a time when your conscience was in conflict with what everyone else seemed to want you to do? Give examples.

◆ How did you handle the conflict?

◆ How did your parents expect you to handle the conflict? Did your parents help you in any way with the conflict?

◆ Is it noble — or snobbish — to set higher standards for yourself than everyone else might set for you? Ask your Rabbi to answer this same question.

F According to Radak, the phrase "vessels of *Adonai*" in verse 52:11 means that God alone will be the Israelites' weapon. In other words, the holy power of kindness and mercy, and not that of spears and swords, will redeem them.

◆ In what ways can kindness be more powerful than violence and hatred?

◆ Read your local newspaper for a few days looking for stories about powerful acts of kindness or mercy.

STRATEGIES
Analyzing the Text

1 In verse 51:12 human beings are compared to grass, a comparison also used elsewhere in Deutero-Isaiah.

◆ What do you think this comparison is trying to demonstrate?

◆ Can you think of three additional metaphors that convey the same notion about the mortality of human beings?

2 Israel has drunk from the cup of God's wrath, draining even the dregs, according to verse 51:17. Dregs are the sediment left over from liquid.

According to Radak, the verse means that Israel suffered the full measure of God's punishment — down to the last drop.

Dregs, which don't taste good, represent God's punishment and wrath.

◆ If dregs are the last drop, explain how this metaphor demonstrates that Israel was totally and completely punished.

3 Israel's tormentors have said, according to verse 51:23, "Get down, that we may walk over you."

◆ What is this image trying to convey?

◆ Some people tend to allow others to "walk all over them." What would be your advice to such a person?

◆ The motto of the first flag of the American Revolution, raised on Paul Jones's ship in 1776, was, "Don't Tread on Me." Why was this an appropriate motto for the American revolt against the British?

◆ Displayed on the Revolutionary flag was a pine tree with a rattlesnake coiled at its foot. Design a freedom flag for the Israelites exiled in Babylonia, with the motto, "Don't Walk over Us."

4 Zion, or Jerusalem, is portrayed in Isaiah 52 as a woman who has been abused in the past, but will be restored to splendor.

◆ Compile a list of adjectives that describe an abused woman.

◆ Compile a list of adjectives that describe a woman restored.

◆ Did you list just physical traits, or did you also include psychological, economic, and other traits? Give a rationale for your list.

5 We read in verse 52:10 that *Adonai* will bare God's holy arm in the sight of all the nations. What does it mean when a human rolls up shirtsleeves to show powerful muscles to an enemy?

◆ If God has no actual arm to reveal, then what do you think is the symbolic meaning of verse 52:10? What do you think God is feeling when rolling up the "sleeves"?

◆ Anthropomorphisms give God human characteristics (physical and emotional) that God doesn't really have; they are used in order to convey an idea. Suggesting that God has an arm is an anthropomorphism meant to teach that God is powerful. Identify other anthropomorphisms in this Haftarah and determine what ideas they convey.

6 The prophet says in verse 52:12 that the Israelites will not leave Babylon in haste. According to the story of the Exodus from Egypt, the Israelites left Egypt in a hurry with the Egyptians chasing them into the Reed Sea.

◆ According to the rest of verse 52:12, is it better or worse that this time they will not leave hurriedly? Explain your answer.

Connecting the Text To the Sedra

7 This is the fourth of the seven Haftarot of Consolation following Tishah B'Av. In what ways is its message comforting?

◆ Reread the first verse of the Haftarah (51:12) and one of the last verses (52:9), both of which say that God comforts Israel. What do you think God feels for Israel in this Haftarah, and why?

◆ In part, the Haftarah portrays the future reunion of Jerusalem with her exiled children. Read and discuss *Anna Is Still Here* by Ida Vos, which includes a post-World War II reunion.

8 Jerusalem is also portrayed in this Haftarah as a Queen.

◆ In the Book of Lamentations, which is read on Tishah B'Av, Jerusalem is called a "princess," and "perfect in beauty, the joy of all the earth."

◆ Write a poem in honor of Jerusalem, using these images, as well as those used in our Haftarah.

◆ Alternatively, put together a picture collection of modern day Jerusalem. Include captions that describe Jerusalem as a queen or princess.

9 The Sedra teaches in Deuteronomy 16:20, "Justice, justice you shall pursue." Scholars have long argued about the repetition of the word "justice."

Possibly the repetition is for emphasis or to sound poetic. The Rabbis teach that the repetition may have been intended to teach ethical or moral lessons. For example, perhaps justice is mentioned twice in order that you learn to treat (a) your own people justly, and (b) all other people justly as well. Alternatively, perhaps justice is mentioned twice in order that you learn that justice must be pursued to right wrongdoings both in (a) minor cases, and (b) major cases. Or perhaps justice is repeated in order that you learn that justice is the responsibility of (a) judges in courtrooms, and (b) all of us in everyday life.

◆ Give examples that might support the Rabbis' teachings about the repetition of the word "justice."

◆ Why do you think the word "justice" is repeated twice in a row?

◆ This Haftarah contains at least three other examples of word repetitions. Can you find them? Do you think these repetitions were intended for emphasis or for poetry?

◆ Can you draw any moral lessons from these repetitions?

10 We learn in verse 51:16 of the Haftarah that God "made firm the earth." Some explain this to mean that the true foundation of the earth consists of truth, justice, and peace (not swords and blood). This echoes the Sedra's instruction to pursue justice.

Pirke Avot 5:8 teaches, "The sword comes into the world because of justice delayed and because of justice perverted."

◆ What does the phrase "justice delayed" mean? What does the phrase "justice perverted" mean? Give examples of each phrase from stories you have read or from the news.

◆ Why might justice delayed or perverted lead to frustration and violence?

◆ Do you believe there would be no violence in our world if everyone were treated justly and fairly?

◆ Why do you think some teenagers become involved in gangs, and how does this relate to the words of *Pirke Avot*?

11 The Sedra discusses a future time when the children of Israel will dwell in the Promised Land, and will choose to have a human king rule over them (Deuteronomy 17:14-20).

◆ List the laws pertaining to the establishment of a king of Israel.

◆ What do you think of these laws? What in your view is the main concern of these laws?

◆ Debate: It is inevitable that power corrupts human beings and leads to abuse of power.

◆ In the Haftarah the Israelites are told "Your God is King" (verse 52:7). How does this message relate to the laws in Deuteronomy 17:14-20?

12 The Sedra discusses just punishments for offenses committed. For example, Deuteronomy 19:16-19 teaches that if a witness offers false testimony with the purpose of causing harm to another person, the witness is to be punished with the penalty that would have been imposed on the other person.

◆ Is this a punishment that fits the crime (that is, measure for measure)? Explain your answer.

◆ What is the purpose of the punishment (see Deuteronomy 19:20)?

◆ Interview a lawyer or judge to find out what type of penalties are imposed today on witnesses that give false testimony. Are the punishments measure for measure? Do they serve their purpose?

◆ Read Deuteronomy 19:21. Explain how this famous verse also teaches that punishments should be measure for measure.

◆ In the Haftarah, God promises to punish those who have oppressed and tormented Israel measure for measure. Read verses 51:13-14 and 51:22-23. Make an illustration of what Israel's enemies have done to her and how they will be punished in the same fashion.

13 Both Sedra and Haftarah claim that there is no need to be afraid as long as God is with you. In Deuteronomy 20:3 we are told that the priests will speak to the people before a battle and tell them not to be afraid because God will be going to fight with them.

The Haftarah begins by asking the Israelites why they are afraid and ends by assuring them that they will not have to rush out of Babylonia in fear because God will be their escort.

Is it realistic to tell a person emigrating or a soldier not to be afraid?

◆ What good can come from expressing one's fears?

◆ A phrase from the Israeli song *"Kol Ha'olam Kulo"* (The Whole World) reads, "The whole world is a narrow bridge, but the main thing is not to fear." Describe a time in your life when you were afraid. What helped you get across that scary bridge?

◆ Learn and sing the song *"Kol Ha'olam Kulo,"* which may be found in the songbook *B'Kol Echad*, edited by Jeffrey Shiovitz, p. 88, and on the accompanying audiocassettes, *Shirei B'Kol Echad*, both of which may be ordered from the web site of United Synagogue for Conservative Judaism, www.uscj.org/booksvc.

Extending the Text

14 Verses 51:17, 52:1, and 52:2 are featured in the Shabbat song, *"L'Cha Dodi,"* written by a Jewish mystic.

"L'Cha Dodi" is an acrostic poem which spells out the author's name. The poem was written by Rabbi Shlomo ben Moshe Alkabetz. He was born in Salonica in 1505, emigrated to the Land of Israel in 1535, and died in Safed in 1584. A famous Kabbalist, he was conscious of the degradation of exile on the Jewish people and eagerly looked forward to their redemption.

◆ Read a translation of *"L'Cha Dodi."* Discuss how it describes the suffering of the Jews and their hope to be redeemed and to return to Israel.

◆ Learn and sing this hymn using various melodies. One version may be found in *The Harvard Hillel Shabbat Songbook*, pp. 100-101.

◆ Compare *"L'cha Dodi"* on the recording *Friday Night Live* by Craig Taubman with the version on *Bittersweet* by Safam or with the melody your congregation usually sings.

15 Israel will be redeemed by the holy power of kindness and mercy (see Insights from the Tradition #A, p. 304).

◆ Read and discuss the following story from *Small Miracles II* by Yitta Halberstam and Judith Leventhal, pp. 244-255.

In 1991, Michael and Julie Weisser received their first telephone call from Larry Trapp, the Grand Dragon of the Nebraska Ku Klux Klan.

Trapp harassed Jewish people, immigrants, and people of color. He made threatening phone calls, sent hate mail, and encouraged his followers to commit vandalism and acts of violence against non-white or Jewish people. Trapp received an unexpected response from the Weissers. They decided to fight his hatred with love. Michael Weisser began leaving caring, friendly messages on Larry Trapp's answering machine. When the Weissers learned that Trapp was a blind, wheelchair-bound diabetic, they offered to run errands for him. Finally, so moved by the Weisser's kindnesses, Larry Trapp left the Ku Klux Klan and converted to Judaism. He gave to the police and FBI valuable insider information on local and national hate organizations. He also called up every person he had ever harassed and apologized. As Larry's diabetes worsened, the Weissers took him in and cared for him until his death.

◆ How does this story show the true power of gentleness and mercy?

◆ How would you have handled this situation? Would you have had as much patience as the Weissers had you received threatening phone calls, or would you have reacted out of fear?

16 Zion signifies Jerusalem in particular and the Land of Israel in general.

◆ Find these other places where Zion is mentioned:

  • Israel's national anthem, *"Hatikvah."*

  • The blessings after the Haftarah.

◆ Write your own poetic tribute to Zion.

◆ For more on Zion, read the article by Plaut in *The Haftarah Commentary*, pp. 477-478, or look up the article in vol. 16, pp. 1030-1031, in the *Encyclopaedia Judaica*.

17 Although the State of Israel considers Jerusalem to be its capital, many countries around the world object to this and, in fact, the United States of America keeps its embassy in Tel Aviv (a foreign embassy is supposed to be in the capital city).

◆ Did you know that the American embassy was in Tel Aviv, not in Jerusalem? Do you agree with this decision?

◆ Learn the capitals of countries around the world, especially of those in the Middle East. Hold a college bowl or play other games (such as *Geography*) involving the capitals.

18 We are taught that the holy power of kindness and mercy is more powerful than spears and swords.

◆ Learn and sing the song *"Lo Yisa Goy el Goy Cherev"* (Let Nation Not Lift up Sword against Nation), which is about peace and is based on the words of Isaiah 2:4. The song may be found in the songbook *B'Kol Echad*, edited by Jeffrey Shiovitz, pp. 89-90, and on the accompanying audiocassettes, *Shirei B'Kol Echad*, both of which may be ordered from the web site of United Synagogue for Conservative Judaism, www.uscj.org/booksvc.

19 There is a Hasidic teaching on the subject of personal growth and change (see Insights from the Tradition #B, pp. 304-305) titled "The Growing Tree," found in *Tales of the Hasidim: Early Masters* by Martin Buber, p. 148:

A human being is like a tree: If you stand in front of a tree and watch it constantly to see how it grows and to see how much it has grown, you won't see anything at all. But if you care for it at all times, prune the runners, and keep bothersome insects away from it, then — all in good time — it will come into its growth. It is the same with a human being: a human being must overcome

obstacles to be able to thrive and grow. But if you examine him/her every hour to see how much growth has taken place, you will see nothing.

◆ Discuss how these obstacles might prevent a human being's growth: closed mindedness, lack of self-confidence, financial difficulties, war, racism, illness, depression. Can you list other obstacles? Why do we not see change if we watch incessantly?

◆ We often think of our parents as completed human beings. Interview your parents and their friends to find out ways in which they still see themselves as growing.

Personalizing the Text

20 The word *"Menachem,"* meaning "one who comforts," is found in verse 51:12, and is a popular Hebrew name.

◆ Consult a Jewish name book to discover the meaning of your Hebrew name.

◆ Write a short essay explaining why your Hebrew name is appropriate for you.

21 Part of verse 51:13 appears in the *"Alaynu"* prayer.

◆ Can you find the verse in the *"Alaynu"*? Learn to sing and lead this prayer.

22 The prophesied reunion of Zion and her people will be an occasion of unparalleled happiness. The joy of future triumph is also expressed in Isaiah 12:3, the words of which have been set to music in the well-known folk song *"U'Shavtem Mayim B'sason"* (And You Shall Draw Water in Joy). The song may be found in the songbook *B'Kol Echad*, edited by Jeffrey Shiovitz, p. 90, and on the accompanying audiocassettes, *Shirei B'Kol Echad*, both of which may be ordered from the web site of United Synagogue for Conservative Judaism, www.uscj.org/booksvc.

◆ Learn both the song and the dance that goes with it. Consider performing the song and dance for the other classes at your school.

23 Human beings are likened to grass in the Book of Isaiah.

◆ Make a grass head: Pour a handful of grass seed into a nylon knee-high stocking. Then fill the stocking with enough potting soil to make a ball the size of a softball. Tie the stocking to keep the soil inside. Dampen the soil and keep it moist and in a sunny spot for about two weeks, when you should see the grass head's hair begin to grow. You can make a face on your grass head by gluing on eyes and a felt nose and mouth. Assess how fragile the grass head is.

◆ Alternatively, learn how to make flower arrangements using dried grasses instead of flowers. Decorate your synagogue with these arrangements for your Bar/Bat Mitzvah.

24 At all ages we are still growing and being created.

◆ To see how your parents have grown and changed, ask them to share with you the following things about their childhoods. (Source of this exercise: *The Jewish Experiential Book* by Bernard Reisman, pp. 312-313.)

- Most significant memory of school
- Most significant memory of Religious School
- Worst punishment as a child
- Best friend as a child
- Favorite Jewish holiday as a child
- Favorite childhood game or toy
- Childhood ambition

- Worst childhood fear
- Most admired person as a child
- Least favorite thing as a child
- Most embarrassing experience as a child

Now, to see how their opinions and experiences have changed over time, ask your parents to answer the same questions from their adult perspective. You may also wish to take a turn answering the questions from your own perspective.

Together with one of your parents, play with the game or toy that was his/her childhood favorite. Is the game or toy just as your parent remembered?

25 Jerusalem is a city of great beauty and majesty, with a very famous skyline of minarets, domes, and spires.

◆ Make your own stylized Jerusalem silhouette by cutting familiar architectural shapes out of colored foil sheets and pasting them onto a black background. You might want to look at Jewish greeting cards or Jewish periodicals for ideas or search the Internet at http://gallery.yahoo.com for pictures of Jerusalem. On the top of your silhouette, write the immortal words from Psalm 137:5: "If I forget you, O Jerusalem, let my right hand wither; let my tongue stick to my palate if I cease to think of you, if I do not keep Jerusalem in memory even at my happiest hour."

◆ Consider using your design of Jerusalem as decoration on your Bar/Bat Mitzvah invitations or as decoration on a *tallit* you make for yourself.

26 At the end of the Haftarah, the prophet admonishes the people to prepare themselves both spiritually and emotionally to return home.

◆ Imagine you are planning to make *aliyah* to Israel in six months. Make a list of all the things you need to do to wrap up your life here and to prepare for your new life in Israel. Make a list of all the things in your present country that you will miss. Make a list of all the things you look forward to in Israel.

27 There are many resources available for those considering *aliyah* to Israel.

◆ Invite a speaker from your local Jewish Federation or your community *Shaliach* from Israel to speak to your class about *aliyah*. Have questions prepared ahead of time for your speaker to address.

Other Resources

28 View and discuss the feature film version of the classic *Les Miserables* (1998, rated PG, 134 minutes), in which kindness is more powerful than hatred.

29 For more information on Isaiah, see *Messengers of God: A Jewish Prophets Who's Who* by Ronald H. Isaacs.

30 Discuss the illustration of this Haftarah in *The Illustrated Torah* by Michal Meron, p. 202. How is the artist's depiction of the herald a source of hope and comfort?

31 For more on this Haftarah, see the UAHC Family Shabbat Table Talk web site at www.uahc.org/shabbat/stt/3shofetim.shtml.

32 For a commentary on this Haftarah, see the web site of the Fuchsberg Center for Conservative Judaism in Jerusalem, www.uscj.org.il/haftarah.

33 Learn more about the hymn *"L'Cha Dodi"* in *Service of the Heart* by Evelyn Garfiel, pp. 132-133.

34 Kindness and mercy touch our souls with holy power. For more inspiring stories of kindness and mercy, read selections from *Chicken Soup for the Jewish Soul: Stories to Open the Heart and Rekindle the Spirit*, edited by Jack Canfield, Mark Victor Hansen, and Dov Peretz Elkins.

35 Learn more about Cyrus, the king of Persia, who freed the Israelites from exile (see the *Encyclopaedia Judaica*, vol. 5, pp. 1184-1186).

36 Isaiah prepares the people spiritually for a return to their land. Discuss selections from *Israel — A Spiritual Travel Guide: A Companion for the Modern Jewish Pilgrim* by Lawrence A. Hoffman.

Involving the Family

37 During the year before their child's Bar or Bat Mitzvah, parents can enroll in adult education classes to continue their own Jewish growth (see Insights from the Tradition #B, pp. 304-305).

38 Collect toiletries for a shelter for abused women (see Analyzing the Text #4, p. 306, in which Jerusalem is described as an abused woman who would one day be returned to her former splendor).

39 Forge your own personal connection with Israel by becoming a pen pal with an Israeli student. Contact the Israel program department of your local Jewish Federation for information. Make a long-term plan to visit your pen pal in Israel.

Bar/Bat Mitzvah Projects

40 Jerusalem and Israel are our spiritual home. Bank Leumi and some local Jewish Federations have teamed up to offer American families the Gift of Israel Savings Plan, in which the local Federation will match a family's savings (up to a certain amount) toward

sending their children on a group trip to Israel. Contact your local Federation about starting your own Gift of Israel Savings Plan and start researching teen trips to Israel.

41 Prepare yourselves spiritually for your upcoming Bar or Bat Mitzvah by reading and discussing together the book *Putting God on the Guest List: How to Reclaim the Spiritual Meaning of Your Child's Bar or Bat Mitzvah* by Jeffrey Salkin.

ISAIAH 54:1-55:5 Ashkenazim
ISAIAH 54:1-54:10 Sephardim
NOAH נח

This Haftarah has been paired with *Parashat Noah*, Genesis 6:9-11:32. See "Connecting the Text To the Sedra," pp. 317-319, for an exploration of the many ways the two texts shed light on each other.

SYNOPSIS

The victory of the Persians over their Babylonian captors brings the Israelites hope that King Cyrus of Persia will allow them to return to the Land of Israel. In this Haftarah Isaiah emphasizes that the time of redemption is near at hand.

Zion (Jerusalem) is described both as a mother, who will be blessed with numerous children, and as a wife, who will be joyfully reunited with her husband, *Adonai*. God's momentary anger is contrasted with God's vast and eternal love for Zion and Israel. Just as God swore to Noah that the world would never again be flooded, so God swears never again to be angry with Israel and Zion, whom God loves.

In Zion's glorious future, she will be adorned with rubies, sapphires, and other gems. Her children will be happy and devoted to *Adonai*.

In the day of salvation (verse 55:1-5), Israel will enjoy plentiful water, bread, milk, and wine — free of charge. As in the days of King David, Israel will once again be a mighty nation, glorified by God and glorifying God.

Note: This Haftarah and the two that follow it (*Ki Taytzay* and *Re'eh*) are based on the same passages in Isaiah. Accordingly, this Haftarah will contain Insights from the Tradition, Analyzing the Text, Extending the Text, and Personalizing Strategies, and Other Resources. The next two Haftarot will contain only Connecting the Text To the Sedra, Involving the Family, and Bar/Bat Mitzvah Projects — which may be shared among the three Haftarot. The Insights from the Tradition and Analyzing, Extending, and Personalizing Strategies found in this Haftarah apply to the next two as well.

INSIGHTS FROM THE TRADITION

A Radak understands the message of verse 54:4 to be that we should not be embarrassed out of fear that we will experience exile and its humiliations again.

◆ In today's terms, we can understand Radak's message to mean something like: if you fall off a horse, you must get right back on it. Do you agree or disagree with this advice?

◆ Why might fear of failure prevent us from striving for success?

◆ President Franklin D. Roosevelt said on the day after Pearl Harbor was bombed, "We have nothing to fear but fear itself." What did he mean by this? Do you agree with this statement? Is the statement true today, when we are fighting terrorists and bio-terrorists?

B Also regarding verse 54:4, Radak explains that "you will no more remember the shame of your widowhood" means that when Israel returns from its exile from God and Jerusalem, the bounty of all that will be lavished upon them will make them forget their earlier troubles.

◆ Do you think people who have survived difficult times should completely forget about those times when life becomes good again? Do you think they are able to forget completely?

◆ What lessons might we be able to learn from life's difficult times that will help us be better people in the future?

C Radak explains that the mountains and hills in verse 54:10 represent the kings of other nations, which certainly cannot be counted on as God can.

◆ On which people in your life can you always count, no matter what?

◆ Do you feel you can always count on God to help you?

D Verse 54:13 says, "And all your children shall be disciples of *Adonai*, and great shall be the happiness of your children." *Berachot* 64a makes a famous word play on this verse: "Read not *banayich* (your children) but *bonayich* (your builders)."

◆ In what ways are children like builders?

◆ Why will children who learn God's teachings be happy?

E Ibn Ezra understands verse 54:14 to mean that once free, Israel will act righteously and not oppress others. Israel will, therefore, not have to fear ruin because God will have no cause to punish them as long as they behave righteously.

◆ Do you believe that bad things happen only to people who deserve them?

◆ Do you believe bad things are punishments from God? Why or why not?

◆ Why do you think bad things also happen to good people?

F In a differing view, Rashi explains that verse 54:14 means that, in the future, Israel will refrain from oppressing other people because only those in fear of ruin or poverty resort to oppression. Because God will protect Israel, they will have no such fear and, therefore, no reason to oppress anyone.

◆ List the different types of fears people have.

◆ Discuss how some of these fears might lead people to oppress or treat badly other people.

G Verse 55:1 says that all who are thirsty should come for water. *Sukkah* 52b explains that if your evil inclination is stubborn and hard as rock, the teachings of Torah will eventually wear down that evil inclination, just as water can wear away rock over time.

◆ How might studying Torah help someone to be a better person?

◆ What are other ways someone might wear down his or her evil inclination?

STRATEGIES
Analyzing the Text

1 Throughout chapter 54 Jerusalem is portrayed as God's abandoned (but not divorced) wife, and the Israelites are portrayed as the wayward children of God and Jerusalem.

◆ Explain how it is reassuring to Israel to hear that God and Jerusalem are only temporarily separated, not divorced.

◆ See the article on divorce as a metaphor in *The Haftarah Commentary* by W. Gunther Plaut, p. 486.

2 In verse 54:2 the prophet instructs Jerusalem to "enlarge the size of your tent."

◆ Why do you think the prophet gives this instruction?

◆ See the illustration to this Haftarah in *The Illustrated Torah* by Michal Meron, p. 18. What emotions does the illustration convey from the Haftarah?

◆ How do families today "enlarge the size of their tents" for new babies or children?

3 Verse 54:7 says that it was only for the briefest moment that Israel was abandoned by God, because God's love for Israel is eternal.

◆ Why is this an important message for people in exile or just returning from exile?

◆ How do you feel when your parents are angry with you? Does it feel like it might be forever?

◆ How is God's unconditional love for Israel like a parent's unconditional love for his/her children?

◆ Compare this verse to verse 54:8, which seems to convey the same idea.

4 The metaphor, "I hid My face from you" in verse 54:8 conveys God's anger with the Israelites.

◆ Why do you think these words represent God's anger?

◆ Can you think of other expressions for anger or abandonment? For example, explain how these expressions convey anger or abandonment: turn my back, turn a deaf ear, give a cold shoulder.

5 The precious stones mentioned in verses 54:11-12 include carbuncles, sapphires, and rubies. Carbuncle is another word for garnet.

◆ Describe each of these gemstones. Definitions or descriptions are available in most dictionaries or on the Internet.

◆ Paint an abstract picture using brilliant gemstone colors.

6 Verse 55:4 is translated as "As I made him a leader of peoples." The Hebrew, however, says literally, "As I made him a witness to peoples."

Deutero-Isaiah's idea about witnessing is as follows: *Adonai* reveals an event that will take place in the future. The event occurs, and the Israelites live through it. The Israelites then serve as witnesses able to offer firsthand testimony as to both the earlier revelation and to the event itself. As a result of their testimony, *Adonai's* divinity is established; both Israel and the other nations have confirmed evidence that *Adonai* is God.

◆ Explain how Israel's testimony proves God had foreknowledge of the event.

◆ Explain how Israel's testimony proves that events in history are controlled by God. Commentators and translators have offered various interpretations for the word "witness" in this verse. They have suggested that "witness" may mean: leader, prince, one who rebukes, one who warns, one who forewarns, summoner, witness, or commander. Which of these interpretations makes sense to you, and why?

◆ It is difficult to be a reliable witness. Try this exercise: Look around your classroom for one minute. Attempt to notice what is on the walls, what everyone is wearing, etc. Then close your eyes while other students ask you questions about the classroom. How accurate is your testimony?

Connecting the Text To the Sedra

7 In the *Etz Hayim Chumash* (p. 65), Michael Fishbane points out that the Sedra and the Haftarah offer two complementary models of righteousness. In the Sedra Noah's righteousness is based on personal purity and God-centered living. On the other hand, for Isaiah, followers of God who establish their city through *tzedakah* are the models of community and collective righteousness.

◆ What is the difference between personal righteousness and community-minded righteousness? Can you think of examples of each? Do you think one is more valuable than the other? Why or why not?

◆ Fishbane explains that Maimonides used Isaiah 54:14 as the scriptural basis for the *mitzvah* of *tzedakah*, "underscoring the importance of personal piety for collective religious life" (*Etz Hayim Chumash*, p. 65). Create a *tzedakah* box that features a quotation of part or all of Isaiah 54:14, as well as decorative motifs from the Noah story (e.g., ark, rainbow, dove, olive branch).

8 In the Sedra God forewarns Noah about the impending flood. The flood happens, and Noah survives to tell about it.

◆ Why do you think that Noah does not tell anybody about the flood before it happens?

◆ What responsibility do you think Noah has to tell his children, grandchildren, and great grandchildren about the flood afterward?

◆ In the Haftarah Israel is in exile, but God predicts their imminent return to their land. Israel will live through the events and survive to witness/testify to God's prediction and God's control of the events. Explain verses 54:15-16. How do these verses support the idea that God controls history?

◆ Explain verse 54:5: *Adonai* is "God of all the earth."

◆ Find other verses in the Haftarah that say that God controls the events that happen. What responsibility does Israel have to tell about the events?

◆ Imagine you are a television reporter doing a story on either the flood or the Israelites' return from exile. Interview witnesses and experts, and tell the story as accurately as you can for future generations. If desired, you can videotape your broadcast.

◆ Alternatively, make a diorama depicting either the flood or the return from exile. Remember, your diorama will tell the story to future generations.

9 God acts with justice tempered with mercy in both Sedra and Haftarah.

In the story of Noah, God destroys the world with the great flood, but God spares Noah and his family and promises never to destroy the world again.

In the Haftarah God exiles the Israelites and allows Jerusalem to be destroyed, but is now ready to return the people to a rebuilt city.

◆ Should justice always be tempered with mercy?

◆ Can you think of any exceptions to this rule?

10 In the Haftarah Israel is compared to Noah (see verses 54:9-11). Israel is about to return from exile, and God has to comfort Israel and reassure her (see verses 54:4-5, 14).

◆ Do you think Noah was afraid to leave the ark when the flood subsided? What might he find, and why might it be scary to walk around in a world of destruction? How did God reassure and comfort Noah?

◆ Role-play the scene surrounding the end of the flood and emerging from the ark. You can base your skit on the play entitled "Who Will Stop the Rain?" in *Parashah Plays: For Children of All Ages* by Richard J. Allen, pp. 9-16. Be sure to add more details about life and concerns after the flood — and about God's efforts to comfort Noah and his family.

11 God promises in Isaiah 54:9, "For this to Me is like the waters of Noah: As I swore that the waters of Noah nevermore would flood the earth, so I swear that I will not be angry with you or rebuke you."

God's promise to Noah in Genesis 8:21 says, "Never again will I doom the earth because of humankind . . . nor will I ever again destroy every living being, as I have done."

◆ Why would God's promise to Noah have been comforting to the exiled Israelites?

◆ God produced the rainbow as a sign of God's promise never to destroy the world again. What might be an appropriate sign of God's promise to restore the exiled Israelites to their homeland? For example, might a magic carpet, a winged eagle, or map of the route home be appropriate symbols? Give a rationale for your answer.

◆ Draw or otherwise demonstrate a rainbow or the sign you choose.

12 An interesting contrast exists between Sedra and Haftarah.

In the story of Noah, water is the agent of destruction, and wine is the vehicle of sin. In the Haftarah however, water, wine, and milk are represented as life-giving liquids (verse 55:1). Rashi equates water with Torah.

◆ How can a substance be both good and destructive, depending on how it is used?

◆ Alfred Nobel was a scientist who invented dynamite to assist in building and construction. His invention, however, proved very useful for war and destruction. Nobel became a peace activist and, in his will, left his fortune to be used to reward peacemakers and scientists of various kinds. How is dynamite an example of something that can be used for both good and devastation?

◆ Can you think of other examples of things that can be used for both good and devastation?

◆ Why might Nobel have wanted his name associated with the Nobel Prizes and not with the invention of dynamite?

◆ Find out more about Alfred Nobel and the Nobel Foundation by visiting www. Nobelchannel.com.

13 In the Sedra water causes death, although typically water is needed to sustain life. In the Sedra wine is the vehicle of sin, although typically in Judaism wine is considered a source of joy.

◆ Consider the following story, then explain it in your own words (based on *Ta'anit* 19a).

There was a drought in the Land of Israel. The Jews, desperate for water, went to Honi the Circlemaker and asked him to pray for rain on their behalf. Honi drew a circle and stood in it praying, insisting that he would not leave the circle until rain came. Rain did come. However, there were only little drops of sporadic rain. The Jews hurried back to Honi and said that they needed rain that was given willingly, with blessing and voluntarily. The rains then increased to be just the amount the people needed to sustain life and be a blessing.

◆ The rain needed to be given willingly, with blessing, and voluntarily, in order to be the proper quantity and the proper rate so as not to be too little nor too much, and therefore life threatening. What happens when you do something unwillingly? Apply this lesson to how you do your homework.

◆ If water is provided by God unwillingly, what might go wrong? If wine is drunk by people improperly, what might go wrong?

14 The Sedra includes the story of the tower of Babel, in which different languages developed as a way to scatter the people (Genesis 11:1-9).

◆ Reread this story and discuss why you think God chose different languages — the inability to communicate and understand each other — as a way to distance people from one another? How does the inability to communicate make people separate and less powerful?

◆ In the Haftarah the nations of the world are to be reunited in common belief. They will all understand that God is the only god. What do you think the world would be like if everyone agreed that there is only one God?

◆ Even if everyone agreed that there is only one God, it would still be possible to worship that one God in different ways. As your Rabbi to invite local clergy of other faiths to hold a panel discussion on how the worship of God in each of their faiths differs. See if the panelists agree that these different traditions can all be used in the service of the same God.

Extending the Text

15 In verse 54:7 God promises to be angry only slightly and only temporarily. God is to be a role model for us in how to be angry. According to Rambam (*Mishneh Torah, De'ot* 1:4): "One should not be wrathful, easily angered; nor be like the dead, without feeling; rather one

should adopt an intermediate course; one should display anger only when the matter is serious enough to warrant it, in order to prevent the matter from recurring."

◆ Do you agree with Rambam's statement about anger?

◆ Give examples of when it would be right to be angry.

◆ In addition, Rambam wrote (*Mishneh Torah, De'ot* 2:3): "The early Sages said: Anyone who becomes angry is like one who worships idols. They also said: Whenever one becomes angry, if he is a wise man, his wisdom leaves him; if he is a prophet, his prophecy leaves him. The life of the irate is not true life." Why might anger cause one's wisdom or prophetic abilities to depart?

◆ Next time you get angry, try this: count to ten before you react or say anything. How does this technique help you to keep your wisdom, even in anger?

◆ For more texts and exercises on the issue of handling anger, see *Teaching Jewish Virtues* by Susan Freeman, pp. 85-101.

16 God hides God's face in verse 54:8. Theologians have developed the doctrine of the "hidden God," based on this verse from Isaiah. This doctrine serves to explain that, at certain periods of history, God hides and allows history to take its own course (from Martin Buber, quoted in *The Haftarah Commentary* by W. Gunther Plaut, p. 30.)

◆ Can you list periods of time that God appeared to be hidden from history?

◆ Why do you think God hides and lets history happen?

◆ According to Rambam (*Guide of the Perplexed* 3:12), evil things happen to people for three reasons: (a) people choose to hurt other people; (b) a person does harm to him/herself; and (c) nature causes harm to people (for example, illnesses or disability that is part of a person's constitution or changes in the environment, such as earthquakes). Into which of these categories would you put the following events: war, cancer, robbery, cigarette smoking, drought?

◆ Give other examples of evil things for each of the categories.

◆ When bad things happen in history, into which of the above categories does it fall?

◆ What do you think God feels when bad things happen in history? Why might God feel like hiding?

◆ Write a letter from God to humanity explaining why God sometimes hides and how God feels about being hidden.

◆ How might we coax God back into being involved in our lives?

17 Jerusalem will be adorned with jewels (verses 54:11-12). The limestone known as Jerusalem stone is very beautiful, and it shines dramatically in sunlight. According to zoning laws, all buildings built in Jerusalem must have Jerusalem stone as their facade. Jerusalem stone is available at some American stone and tile retailers, as it is growing in popularity for use in people's homes.

◆ What does it mean to you that God wants to rebuild Jerusalem beautifully?

◆ Visit a store where you can see and touch Jerusalem stone.

◆ Jerusalem stone is commonly used to make beautiful *mezuzot* cases. Design a *mezuzah* case made from Jerusalem stone, or buy one to adorn your home.

18 We are taught in verse 54:13 that our children will study God's Torah and their consequent happiness will be great.

Berachot 64a teaches: "Rabbi Eleazar said in the name of Rabbi Chanina, 'The disciples of the wise increase peace in the world.'"

◆ How does wisdom result in peace?

◆ Learn the song, *"Amar Rabbi Eleazar"* (Rabbi Eleazar Said), which features this verse of Talmud. The song can be found on the recording by the group Safam, *Peace by Piece*.

19 The name for God, *"Kadosh Yisrael"* (The Holy One of Israel), is used several times in this Haftarah and many times throughout the Book of Isaiah. The blessing before the morning *"Amidah,"* which praises God for redeeming Israel, features the same name, "Holy One of Israel." It says, "Rock of Israel, rise to help your people Israel and loyally redeem Judah and Israel. Our redeemer's name is *Adonai* of hosts, *Kadosh Yisrael*."

◆ Read verse 55:5 and compare phrases or terms describing God to those that appear in this blessing.

◆ What do you think the name "Holy One of Israel" means as we thank God for redeeming Israel?

◆ Memorize this blessing in Hebrew and English.

◆ Using any of these names for God (or other names), play a game of *Hangman*.

Personalizing the Text

20 God will adorn Jerusalem with sapphires, rubies, and other precious stones.

◆ Make jewelry with colored beads with which to adorn yourself.

◆ Alternatively, make a *tallit* for yourself and decorate it with shiny gems.

21 The Shabbat song "*L'Cha Dodi*," written by Jewish mystics, contains parts of verses 54:3-4.

◆ Ask your Cantor to teach your class this beautiful hymn. Sing it to several different melodies.

◆ For more information about this hymn, see the Haftarah for *Shofetim*, Extending the Text #14, p. 309.

22 In this Haftarah God swears never again to be angry with Israel and Zion.

◆ Make a covenant with a friend, emphasizing that even if you get angry at one another, you will still love each other and remain loyal to one another.

23 God instructs Jerusalem to "enlarge the size of your tent" (see Analyzing the Text #2, p. 316).

◆ Interview one family that is large and one family that is small. Find out what the joys of each may be.

◆ Describe the size family you want to have one day, and why.

24 God instructs Jerusalem to enlarge her tent to accommodate all her children.

◆ Design a tent representing a safe haven for all Jewish people.

25 Insights from the Tradition #A, p. 314, warns us not to fear.

◆ Consider this story:

Edmund Hillary and his guide were the first people ever known to climb Mount Everest, reaching the top on May 29, 1953. The climb was steep, snowy, icy, and dangerous. Fifty years after the climb, Hillary acknowledged that he was often frightened during the climb. He said, "I experienced fears on many occasions. I often thought, 'What the heck am I doing here when I could be on the beach?' But I always considered fear to be a stimulating factor. It makes you able to perform beyond what you thought was physically possible."

◆ List times when you have been afraid.

◆ Identify times when fear helped you accomplish more, and times when fear hindered you.

◆ Do you agree with Edmund Hillary that fear can be a stimulating factor?

◆ Create a puppet show or storybook that teaches young children not to be afraid.

26 God is married to Jerusalem.

◆ Stage a Jewish wedding between God and Jerusalem. Learn all the traditional wedding rituals. Make a *chupah*, write a creative *ketubah* and vows. Last, but not least, celebrate the wedding with a big party and *Seudah Mitzvah*. For information on weddings, see *The First Jewish Catalog* by Richard Siegel, Michael Strassfeld, and Sharon Strassfeld, pp. 158-166.

27 Psalm 23, like the Haftarah, asserts that there is no need to fear because God is with us.

◆ Learn and sing Psalm 23. One melody may be found in *The Harvard Hillel Sabbath Songbook*, pp. 73-79. You will also find it on the recording *In Spite of It All* by Safam.

28 Torah is compared to milk. In the 1990s, there was a national advertising campaign for milk, featuring prominent celebrities drinking the calcium-rich beverage. Another milk advertising campaign featured the slogan, "Got milk?"

◆ Make your own advertisement for Torah, featuring the slogan, "Got Torah?" or famous people studying Torah. (Your advertisement can be print or video.)

29 The words of the song *"David Melech Yisrael"* (David King of Israel) relate to the Haftarah.

◆ What do the words of the song have to do with the Haftarah?

◆ Learn and sing the song with hand motions.

◆ Teach the song and hand motions to a first or second grade class. (Be sure to explain to them what the words mean.)

◆ For a different tune, listen to the recording entitled *Neshama shel Shlomo* by Neshama Carlebach and Shlomo Carlebach.

Other Resources

30 Read and discuss the theological and moral issues in *When Bad Things Happen To Good People* by Harold Kushner (see Insights from the Tradition #E, p. 315).

31 Read and discuss *Gabriel's Ark* by Sandra R. Curtis, which is about the Bar Mitzvah of a developmentally disabled boy.

32 Read and discuss *The Narrowest Bar Mitzvah* by Steven Schnur, which is about a flood in the synagogue on the day of someone's Bar Mitzvah.

33 Read the classic book *A Little Princess* by Frances Hodgson Burnett, or view the film version (1939, not rated, 91 minutes). This is the story of a little girl (Shirley Temple) who goes from riches to rags and back to riches, much like the Jerusalem that is symbolized in the Haftarah.

34 View a videotape of someone's traditional Jewish wedding. Watch especially for all the rituals and customs. A professionally made film, *A Seal upon Thy Heart* (Ergo Media, 30 minutes) can be a substitute if desired.

35 For a commentary on this Haftarah, see the web site of The Fuchsberg Center for Conservative Judaism, www.uscj.org.il/haftarah/ noah5762.html.

36 Read Psalm 30 and compare the images of God's hiding God's face and God's anger being for but a moment. Alternatively, read Psalm 113 and compare images of God being worshiped universally, making the weak mighty and the barren a mother.

37 Listen to the song "Noah and the Ark" on the recording *Dreams of Safam* by Safam.

Involving the Family

38 According to verse 54:10, even grand mountains and hills may be shaken or collapse from natural forces, but God's loyalty will be unshakeable forever (see Insights from the Tradition #C, p. 315). In an ideal world, family members will also be unquestionably loyal and supportive. Design a family logo or crest to signify your family's loyalty for its members. Discuss ways to make family members feel more securely supported.

39 The prophet teaches that once free, Israel will act righteously and not oppress others, because they will remember what oppression feels like. Check out the web site www. socialaction.com for articles, resources, and opportunities for Jewish social activism. Become involved as a family in a group that promotes social justice.

Bar/Bat Mitzvah Projects

40 The exiled Israelites in the Haftarah are comforted by the promise that there will be an abundant supply of water, wine, milk, and food waiting for them at home. Hold a food drive in the weeks preceding your Bar/Bat Mitzvah. Notify congregants of your drive through the synagogue bulletin, and notify your community by putting posters in store windows around town. Set up receptacles in your synagogue in which people can deposit non-perishable food items. Before your Bar/Bat Mitzvah, bring the food to a local shelter or organization that assists the homeless and/or hungry.

41 Collect used wedding dresses for brides who cannot afford new ones. Send them to The Rabbanit Bracha Kapach, 12 Lod St., Jerusalem, 02-624-9296. Or, send monetary contributions to further the work of this *mitzvah* hero (see *Gym Shoes and Irises* by Danny Siegel, p. 142) to PEF-Israel Endowments, Inc., 317 Madison Ave., New York, NY 10017. Rabbanit Kapach does much more than collect and distribute wedding dresses, she also distributes 4500 food packages at Passover, and clothing for men, women, and children all year round. She was recently the recipient of the coveted Israel Prize, which is comparable in status to the Nobel Prize.

ISAIAH 54:1-10
KI TAYTZAY כי תצא

This Haftarah has been paired with *Parashat Ki Taytzay*, Deuteronomy 21:10-25:19. See "Connecting the Text To the Sedra," pp. 324-326, for an exploration of the many ways the two texts shed light on each other.

SYNOPSIS

The victory of the Persians over their Babylonian captors (539 B.C.E.) brings the Israelites hope that King Cyrus of Persia will allow them to return to the Land of Israel. In this Haftarah Isaiah emphasizes that the time of redemption is almost here.

Zion (Jerusalem) is described both as a mother, who will be blessed with numerous children, and as a wife, who will be joyfully reunited with her husband, *Adonai*. God's momentary anger is contrasted with God's vast and eternal love for Zion and Israel. Just as God swore to Noah that the world would never again be flooded, so God swears never again to be angry with Israel and Zion, whom God loves.

Note: This Haftarah and the next one *(Re'eh)* are based on the same passages in Isaiah as the one before this *(Noah)*. See the Haftarah for *Noah* (pp. 314-323) for the Insights from the Tradition, Analyzing the Text, Extending the Text, and Personalizing Strategies, as well as Other Resources, Involving the Family, and Bar/Bat Mitzvah Projects. See below for Connecting the Text To the Sedra, Involving the Family, and Bar/Bat Mitzvah Projects that are specific to this Haftarah.

INSIGHTS FROM THE TRADITION

See pp. 314-315.

STRATEGIES
Analyzing the Text

See pp. 315-316.

Connecting the Text To the Sedra

1 This is the fifth Haftarah of Consolation following Tishah B'Av.

◆ Why do you think this text is suitable as a message of consolation?

◆ Jerusalem is depicted in the Haftarah as a barren, desolate woman because her children are gone and her husband has left her. What emotions in you does this image of Jerusalem evoke?

◆ Who are Jerusalem's metaphorical husband and children?

◆ The Book of Lamentations is read on Tishah B'Av. Read it to discover how the same metaphor of Jerusalem as a barren woman is used there as well.

2 In this Haftarah of Consolation, God tells Israel to shout for joy and to expand their tents.

◆ Does singing ever change your mood? If so, describe such times.

◆ Does taking action and planning for positive events ever make you feel better? If so, describe such times.

◆ Interview family and friends about times when they were sick or troubled. Did planning for a better future ever serve as consolation for them? What did console them?

◆ Try whistling a happy tune the next time you feel troubled. What happens?

◆ Listen to the song "Whistle a Happy Tune" on the original cast recording of *The King and I*.

3 The Sedra contains various directives to remember. Deuteronomy 24:9 instructs us to remember that God punished Miriam for speaking badly about Moses' wife. Deuteronomy 24:18 and 22 command us to prevent injustice, because we remember that we were unjustly treated as slaves in Egypt. Finally, we are commanded in Deuteronomy 25:17-19 to wipe out the memory of Amalek.

◆ See those verses to refresh your memory on these subjects.

◆ In contrast, the Haftarah instructs Zion in verse 54:4 to forget the "reproach of your youth" and "the shame of your widowhood," and to remember (verses 54:7-10) God's everlasting love for Israel. Why might you want to remember some things from your life and forget other things?

◆ Does remembering your own bad times help you empathize and put yourself in another person's shoes?

◆ List three things you always want to remember and three you would rather forget.

4 As the fifth Haftarah of Consolation, *Ki Taytzay* is read during the month of Elul, which precedes Rosh HaShanah. Every Elul weekday morning, Jews recite the *"Selichot"* prayer and hear the blast of the *shofar* in preparation for the High Holy Days.

◆ Why would we spend an entire month remembering and repenting for the sins we committed during the year?

◆ It is also customary for Jews to visit their deceased loved ones at the cemetery during Elul. Why do you think people might want to remember their deceased loved ones before the High Holy Days?

◆ How might visits to the cemetery help us to take stock of our lives?

◆ Visit the cemetery and, with paper and pencil, make rubbings from the tombstones of your deceased loved ones. If necessary, get help translating the Hebrew.

5 Both the Sedra and Haftarah argue for individual responsibility, not collective responsibility.

◆ Find an example of this in the Haftarah (see verse 54:10).

◆ Find examples of this in the Sedra (see Deuteronomy 24:16).

◆ For more biblical examples of incidents in which groups were held responsible for the actions of individuals, see the essay by Plaut in *The Torah: A Modern Commentary*, pp. 1502-1503.

6 Following are examples of laws from Deuteronomy 21-25. These indicate the important role the value of mercy plays in both Sedra and Haftarah:

• We are taught to be merciful toward women taken captive in war (21:10-14).

• We are taught to shoo away the mother bird before taking her eggs (22:6-7).

TEACHING HAFTARAH

- We are prohibited from plowing with an ox and donkey yoked together, to avoid cruelty to the weaker animal (22:10).

- We are taught that fugitive slaves who seek asylum in Israel must not be returned to their masters (23:16-17).

- We are forbidden to muzzle an ox while it is plowing (25:4).

- What do these situations and laws all have in common?

- How do you think human beings learn to be merciful? Give examples from current events that portray people being merciful.

- The Haftarah is permeated with a sense of God's mercy toward Israel and Zion, and God's kindness is specifically highlighted in verse 54:8. Human beings can learn to be merciful by remembering similar personal experiences or putting themselves in the other's place. But God is not human. How can God feel mercy?

- Do you think that God can put God's self in our place to see how we feel?

7 The laws of divorce are outlined in chapter 24 of the Sedra, while the metaphor of God's divorce from Zion is employed by the Haftarah (verses 54:4-10).

- For more discussion and information on the subject of Jewish divorce, see the Haftarah for *Ekev*, Extending the Text #17, p. 300.

Extending the Text

See pp. 319-320.

Personalizing the Text

See pp. 320-322.

Other Resources

See p. 322.

Involving the Family

8 The year of your Bar or Bat Mitzvah is an important one for you and your family — one you will always want to remember.

- Make a memory book or collage (which you can frame) of the year of your *simchah*. Discuss as a family whether you want to include memories of good things and bad things, or only of good things from your year. Include photographs, newspaper clippings, personal anecdotes and information, and other mementos in your collection.

Bar/Bat Mitzvah Projects

9 A "memory *tallit*" features, instead of a blessing on the *atarah*, a favorite quotation or verse from the Sedra. Make a memory *tallit*. First, research how to make a *tallit* in *The First Jewish Catalog* by Richard Siegel, Michael Strassfeld, and Sharon Strassfeld, pp. 51-57. Then, choose a favorite quotation or verse from the Sedra. Make the *tallit*, then write the quotation on the *atarah*. On the *tallit* itself, have family, friends, and teachers use fabric paints or markers to write something complimentary about you (as they might write in a yearbook or on someone's cast).

10 Keep a daily diary for the year of your Bar/Bat Mitzvah. Include entries about events in which you put yourself in other people's places and felt mercy and compassion toward them.

ISAIAH 54:11-55:5
RE'EH ראה

This Haftarah has been paired with *Parashat Re'eh*, Deuteronomy 11:26-16:17. See "Connecting the Text To the Sedra," pp. 327-328, for an exploration of the many ways the two texts shed light on each other.

SYNOPSIS

The victory of the Persians over Babylon (539 B.C.E.) brings the Israelites hope that King Cyrus of Persia will allow them to return to Land of Israel. In this Haftarah Isaiah emphasizes that the time of redemption is near.

In Zion's glorious future, she will be adorned with rubies, sapphires, and other gems. Her children will be happy and devoted to *Adonai*.

In the day of salvation, Israel will enjoy plentiful water, bread, and wine, free of charge. As in the days of King David, Israel will once again be a mighty nation, glorified by God and glorifying God.

Note: This Haftarah and the preceding one *(Ki Taytzay)* are based on the same passages in Isaiah as the Haftarah for *Noah*. See the Haftarah for *Noah* (pp. 314-323) for Insights from the Tradition, Analyzing the Text, Extending the Text, and Personalizing Strategies, as well as Other Resources. See below for Connecting the Text To the Sedra, Involving the Family, and Bar/Bat Mitzvah Projects that are specific to this Haftarah.

INSIGHTS FROM THE TRADITION

See pp. 314-315.

STRATEGIES
Analyzing the Text

See pp. 315-316.

Connecting the Text To the Sedra

1 This Haftarah, which is the third Haftarah of Consolation after Tishah B'Av, begins with the statement that Israel is "unhappy" and "uncomforted" (verse 54:11).

◆ Explain how the Rabbis emphasized our need for consolation by choosing to start the Haftarah with this statement.

◆ List the ways the Haftarah goes on to offer consolation to the "uncomforted."

Jewish tradition recognizes different phases of mourning that occur after someone loses a loved one. The first phase, *aninut*, is the time between the moment of death and the burial of the body. The second phase, *avaylut*, refers to the time from burial, through the period of *shivah* and on to the subsequent period of mourning.

Pirke Avot 4:18 teaches, "Do not comfort a person while his dead lies before him." Recognizing that a new mourner should be left to the full experience of his/her despair, Jewish law prohibits someone in *aninut* from performing any religious obligations (such as reciting the morning and evening prayers) that might distract him/her from the emotions and practical obligations associated with the new death.

◆ Once the period of *avaylut* begins, it is the community's responsibility to comfort the mourner. Discuss the following ways to offer comfort to a mourner: delivering food, sending a note, visiting. List other ways to comfort a mourner. For more information, see *A Time to Mourn, A Time to Comfort* by Ron Wolfson.

◆ Isaiah's words offer comfort, and so can yours. Practice writing a sympathy note for someone in mourning. For guidance, see *To Comfort the Bereaved* by Aaron Levine, pp. 80-85.

2 This Haftarah contains many verses that comfort.

◆ Chose a comforting verse from this Haftarah and depict it artistically.

◆ Compare your artwork with the illustration of this Haftarah in *The Illustrated Torah* by Michal Meron, p. 198. Which verse did the artist chose to highlight and why?

3 Both Sedra and Haftarah teach us to do what is right because it will be good for our children (see Deuteronomy 12:25 and 12:28 and Isaiah 54:13).

◆ Why might knowing their children will benefit help people make good decisions?

◆ What decisions and actions have your parents made that have benefited you directly or indirectly? Talk to them about this.

◆ List five things you have done, or may decide to do in the future, from which your own future children might benefit.

4 The Sedra warns against false prophets in Deuteronomy 13:1-4. False prophets are those who tell us to do things that are contrary to the Torah. In addition, Isaiah 54:13 says in the Haftarah, "Your children shall be disciples of *Adonai*." Being disciples of *Adonai* also implies studying and following the Torah.

◆ Agree to continue your Jewish studies after this life cycle event. With the help of your Rabbi, plan Jewish studies tailored to you and commit yourself to this plan.

Extending the Text

See pp. 319-320.

Personalizing the Text

See pp. 320-322.

Other Resources

See p. 322.

Involving the Family

5 An important part of comforting mourners is providing food for them to eat.

◆ This year, with your family, prepare and deliver a meal for the mourners whenever a family in your community suffers a loss.

6 A parent should be mindful that his or her actions are good for his/her children.

◆ Spend some time every Shabbat evening (or another night you choose) reading Jewish stories together. Stories help teach lessons and spur discussions that you might not otherwise have. Some good sources for such stories are: *A Treasury of Jewish Bedtime Stories* by Shmuel Blitz; *Chosen Tales*, edited by

Peninnah Schram; *A Treasury of Sholom Aleichem Children's Stories* or *Miriam's Tambourine: Jewish Folktales from around the World*, both by Howard Schwartz.

Bar/Bat Mitzvah Project

7 Throughout his prophecy Isaiah strives to bring hope to the hopeless. Many years ago, Yad Lakashish (Lifeline for the Old) was opened in Jerusalem to provide hope and a reason to "choose life" for the city's needy, elderly, and disabled citizens. Lifeline for the Old offers work opportunities, support services, and intergenerational programming. Whenever you go to Jerusalem, you will want to visit this truly remarkable place. However, if you are not planning a pre or post Bar/Bat Mitzvah trip to Israel, you can visit their web site at www.lifeline.org.il. There you can find out how to help support this fine organization. More importantly, you can order Bar/Bat Mitzvah gifts for your friends from the online store, which sells the beautiful handicrafts created in Lifeline's workshops. By purchasing the works created by Lifeline's artisans, you remind them that, indeed, their lives are worthwhile.

ISAIAH 55:6-56:8
VAYAYLECH וילך Some Ashkenazim
FAST DAY AFTERNOONS

 This Haftarah has been paired with both *Parashat Vayaylech*, Deuteronomy 31:1-30 and the reading on fast day afternoons of Exodus 32:11-14, 34:1-10. See "Connecting the Text To the Sedra," pp. 332-333, for an exploration of the many ways the different texts and occasions shed light on each other.

SYNOPSIS

This Haftarah appears to be set near the end of the Israelites' long exile in Babylonia (536 B.C.E.). The last verse even suggests that some of the exiles appear to have already begun their journey home.

In the opening verses, the prophet urges the Israelites to seek *Adonai* while *Adonai* is near. He pleads with the wicked to turn from their evil ways toward *Adonai*, who will pardon them. He reminds the people that God's ways are not like human ways and cannot, therefore, be understood. God has promised that the people will return home, and so they shall — and soon.

The prophet charges Israel with the task of observing God's laws, and especially the Shabbat. Those who hold fast to God's ways will be rewarded. The door to salvation is even opened to any foreigners who will enter into the Covenant with God.

Finally, *Adonai* declares that all the dispersed of Israel will be gathered, joining those who have already been gathered.

INSIGHTS FROM THE TRADITION

A Verse 55:7 calls on the evil person to give up his/her ways and plans, and to turn back to *Adonai*. Radak explains that the wicked must give up their evil deeds, speech, and even thoughts, because otherwise the act of repentance cannot be felt sincerely.

According to alcoholics and addicts, it is not enough to repent their drinking and addiction in order to overcome their bad habits. They must also give up their old friends, their old way of thinking, and their old habits that led them to drink — in order not to drink again.

◆ What other bad habits (besides drinking and drugs) do people have?

◆ Why do you think addicts might have to change their entire lives to stay clean and sober?

B Radak adds to the commentary on verse 55:8 that when humans forgive, there is still the memory of the event. But when God forgives, there is no hidden trace of a grudge. God forgives completely.

◆ Are you able to forgive and forget?

◆ Is it always best to forgive and forget, or is it sometimes right to forgive, but not forget? List some of these times.

C God's salvation is promised in verse 56:1. Ibn Ezra explains that the only thing keeping messianic salvation from coming is our sins.

◆ List ways in which human beings undermine their own best interests.

◆ Interview your parents or grandparents to find out about times in which they prevented themselves from accomplishing their own goals.

D "Happy is the man who . . . keeps the Sabbath," teaches verse 56:2. Radak explains that not profaning Shabbat means that we must elevate that day over other days in every possible way: by consuming elaborate food and drink, by wearing clean and special garments, by freeing ourselves spiritually from mundane thought.

◆ What frame of mind do you think you would be in when eating your favorite foods, wearing special clothes, and not thinking about school and work?

◆ List your favorite foods and friends.

◆ Arrange with your parents to have these favorite foods at the next *Erev* Shabbat dinner, and get their permission to invite those friends to join you for dinner that evening.

E Hirsch adds to the commentary on verse 56:2 that it is not enough to keep Shabbat. You must also refrain from sinning during the rest of the week. "The hand that conscientiously refrains from doing any work on Shabbat but during the week does evil, desecrates both the keeping of the previous Shabbat as well as the next one."

◆ Do you agree with Hirsch that it is not enough to be religious and moral just some of the time? Why or why not?

◆ Find stories in the newspapers of religious people who commit immoral acts.

F Radak explains that Shabbat is mentioned in verse 56:6 because Shabbat was given to the people first, before the Torah. Shabbat had to be given to them first as a sign that God is Creator of the world. Only after they accepted Shabbat and accepted that God is Creator was it fitting for God to command them — as a master commands his

servants — concerning the whole Torah and the commandments.

◆ How does Shabbat remind us that God is Creator of the world?

◆ How are we imitating God by resting on Shabbat?

◆ Do you agree that you have to believe in God as Creator to observe all the laws of the Torah?

◆ What are other reasons someone might observe the Torah's laws? (For example, to remember that we are not slaves, to express community identity.)

STRATEGIES
Analyzing the Text

1 The prophet explains in verse 55:8 that God's plans are not your plans, God's ways are not your ways.

◆ Sheldon Blank writes in *Prophetic Faith in Isaiah*, p. 140: "Biblical man thought and spoke of [God] in human terms — as of a personality with positive attributes and strong emotions, and with virtues and weaknesses, comparable to the attributes and emotions, virtues and weaknesses of men." Explain the different anthropomorphic ideas about God (i.e., that God has human characteristics) contained in verses 55:6-8.

◆ What does a human being mean if he/she says, "My plans are not your plans"? What do you think God means when God says this?

◆ Can you think of an example of when someone might say, "God works in mysterious ways"?

◆ Do you believe that things in life, although we might not understand why, always happen for the best, according to God's plan? Justify your belief.

2 In verse 55:13 thorns are to be replaced by strong trees, such as cypress and myrtle. There are many different interpretations of this verse. Rashi understands the thorns as wicked people to be replaced by good people. *Megillah* 10b posits that the thorns were Haman and Vashti, who were replaced by Mordecai and Esther. Radak says that when the Israelites return from exile, God will replace the desert thorns in the Land of Israel with trees. And Abrabanel explains that the thorns are Israel's troubles during exile, while the trees represent its future prosperity in freedom.

◆ Which explanation do you like best, and why?

◆ Draw an illustration of Isaiah 55:13 that conveys your interpretation of this verse.

3 God says in verse 56:7, "My House shall be called a house of prayer for all peoples."

◆ Explain how this verse indicates God is a universal God.

◆ Does your synagogue ever participate in interfaith services?

◆ Check with your Rabbi about planning an interfaith service. Since this Haftarah is typically read during September, perhaps plan an interfaith service for Labor Day weekend.

4 It is generally agreed that the Book of Isaiah was written by three different authors at different periods of time (see Overview, pp. 218-219). While chapters 40-55 were written by Deutero-Isaiah in Babylonia, chapters 56-66 may have been written a century later in Jerusalem by Trito-Isaiah.

◆ Read the first part of Trito-Isaiah, 56:1.

◆ What does the prophet say can help bring salvation faster?

◆ Does the tone of 56:1-8 sound polemical, anticipatory, hopeful, depressed, optimistic, other? Explain your answer.

Connecting the Text To the Sedra

5 Some Ashkenazim read this Haftarah when *Vayaylech* falls on the Shabbat before Rosh HaShanah.

The prophet's call at the beginning of the Haftarah, to "seek *Adonai* while *Adonai* can be found" makes this Haftarah an appropriate one with which to begin the High Holy Days.

◆ How might you prepare for the introspection and repentance that is required of Jews on the High Holy Days?

◆ Design a creative pre-High Holy Day worship service in which you seek *Adonai*.

◆ List all the reasons you would want to be close to God, especially before the High Holy Days.

6 This Haftarah is also chanted at the afternoon services of fast days, such as Tishah B'Av. The Torah reading for fast days is Exodus 32:11-14 and 34:1-10, which begins with Moses pleading with God to turn from anger and repent from the evil God wanted to do to the people. The Haftarah begins with Isaiah telling the wicked people to return to God Who would have compassion and pardon them (verse 55:7).

◆ How might fasting help us recognize our errors and more sincerely seek to change and be forgiven?

◆ Write a note to God expressing your regret over an error you have made and asking forgiveness. (You need not show the note to anyone.)

7 Isaiah's message throughout his book is much like that of Hirsch, who says above

(Insights from the Tradition #E, p. 331) that Judaism requires us to be moral and aware of God every day of the week.

- Why do you think this is an appropriate message to ponder both on fast days and before Rosh HaShanah?

8 The Haftarah says in verse 55:6 that God is near and can be found by those who call on God. In contrast, *Vayaylech* teaches in Deuteronomy 31:17-18 that God hides from those who disobey the *mitzvot*. Similarly, in Exodus 34:9 Moses pleads with God to be in their midst even though the people have not followed God's orders.

- List some of the *mitzvot* that you observe.

- Describe how each of these *mitzvot* might help you feel the Divine — God's presence. (For example, wearing a *tallit* might make you feel wrapped in God's presence, or visiting the sick might make you feel like God's partner in making the world a better place.)

Extending the Text

9 The Holocaust memorial in Israel, Yad Vashem, takes its name, which means "a monument and a name," from Isaiah 56:5: "I will give them, in My House and within My walls, a monument and a name better than sons or daughters. I will give them an everlasting name which shall not perish."

- How has Yad Vashem given the victims of the Holocaust "an everlasting name which shall not perish"?

- Visit the web site of Yad Vashem at www.yadvashem.org.

- Invite to class someone who has visited Yad Vashem to speak about the experience, and perhaps show some slides.

10 The Rabbis taught in *Shabbat* 118b that if the Jewish people would faithfully keep Shabbat two weeks in a row, they would be redeemed immediately by the Messiah.

- Explain this Rabbinic teaching in your own words. Why does it seem impossible for all the Jewish people in the whole world to keep Shabbat?

- Ask your Rabbi to speak to your class about your Movement's views and recommendations on Shabbat observance.

- With your Rabbi, organize a special Shabbat campaign in your community during which everyone is specially encouraged to light Shabbat candles at the same time.

11 Isaiah had a universal outlook (see verses 56:3-8). Invite a Christian Sunday School class to visit your class and ask you and your teacher (and perhaps your Rabbi) anything they want to know about Judaism. On a following week, visit the same Sunday School class at their church, where you can ask them everything you want to know about their religion.

- Consider starting an interfaith task force to: collect food for a local food bank, keep a neighborhood park clean, etc.

12 Israeli author and thinker Ahad Ha'am (1856-1927) once wrote, "More than the Jewish people has kept Shabbat, Shabbat has kept the Jewish people."

- Discuss what Ahad Ha'am meant by this. Do you agree or disagree with his statement?

- Does Isaiah 56:2 and 56:6-7 support Ahad Ha'am?

13 A Shabbat story is told in Talmud *Shabbat* 119b that on Friday night, when a person leaves services at the synagogue to walk home in the dark, two angels accompany that person. One angel is good and one angel is bad. When they arrive at the person's home, the angels look around. If they find that the person had prepared the table with tablecloth and fine dishes, cleaned the house, and the Shabbat candles were burning, then the good angel blesses the person with a good Shabbat, and declares that it will be so next Shabbat, too. However, if the angels find the house unprepared and the candles were not lit, the bad angel is delighted and promises that next Shabbat will be the same.

◆ Explain this story.

◆ How can the angels be sure that things will be same the next week?

◆ Notice that the worshiper returns home to enjoy Shabbat dinner after services. Does your synagogue typically have Friday night services before or after dinner? Which do you prefer, and why?

◆ Notice that the two angels accompany the person walking home from synagogue. If you live near enough, try walking one Shabbat to and from services. Does walking on Shabbat instead of driving change the day for you?

◆ In the story, when the person arrives home, the candles are already lit. Traditionally, Shabbat candles are lit before sunset because once the sun has set and Shabbat has begun, we are not supposed to create fire. However, different families have developed different customs. Does your family light candles before the sun sets, when everyone has arrived home, or when you are ready to sit down for dinner?

Personalizing the Text

14 Yad Vashem, the Holocaust memorial in Jerusalem, takes its name from verse 56:5.

◆ Create a classroom Holocaust memorial, using photographs, drawings, poems, stories, etc. Invite other classes to view your memorial.

15 The High Holy Days are a time when we apologize to others for any wrongdoing. We ask forgiveness from them, and we also forgive those who have wronged us.

◆ In preparation for the High Holy Days, make a list of grudges you have been holding throughout the year. Write letters of forgiveness to the people who have committed the wrongs for which you hold the grudges. Free yourself of the bad feelings by throwing those letters away, either in a class ceremony or privately.

16 Israel is assured in verse 55:11 that God's word is always fulfilled. In Exodus 32:13-14 Moses begs God to keep the promise made to the Patriarchs.

◆ Make two Rosh HaShanah or fast day resolutions that you will definitely fulfill.

17 In this Haftarah Isaiah charges Israel to observe the Shabbat, one of the Ten Commandments on Moses' tablets (Exodus 34:4).

◆ Conduct a model Shabbat dinner for your class. In preparation, students can learn to recite "*Kiddush*" and "*HaMotzi*," as well as "*Birkat HaMazon*." They can also decorate the room with posters welcoming the Shabbat Queen. Make *challah* covers ahead of time for use at the dinner. Students may later take their *challah* covers home to use at family Shabbat dinners. At the dinner, everyone should wear nice clothing, and traditional Shabbat fare should be served.

18 Shabbat means different things to different people.

◆ Play a Shabbat values clarification game. The objective of the game is to aid individuals in clarifying their views regarding Shabbat, and to create an atmosphere of active participation and open communication. (Source: *Slow Down and Live: A Guide To Shabbat Observance and Enjoyment*, edited by Stephen Garfinkel, p. 83).

In front of the room, the leader posts a sign that says, "To Me, Shabbat Is . . . " In each of the four corners of the room, the leader posts one of four signs representing various responses: "A time of joy and warm experiences," "Unimportant in modern times," "The central institution responsible for uniting the Jewish people," and "A day which I am required by God to observe."

Participants are asked to move physically to that corner of the room which most closely approximates their view. They can initially choose only one. Once they have chosen a corner, the leader opens up the discussion across groups, asking a representative from one corner at a time to speak. Participants are allowed to switch corners if they find an argument or statement particularly convincing.

◆ Have a discussion with those who chose the same corner as you as to why each person made the decision to go there. Then, debrief the exercise with the class as a whole. What did you learn from it?

19 A guide for Shabbat observance is a helpful aid for families.

◆ Make a class guidebook for enjoying and observing Shabbat. Choose subjects (laws, customs, songs, services, stories) that you and the other students can research individually or in groups. Once the research is completed, all the information can be compiled into your guidebook. (Some good resources for research are: *A Guide to Jewish Religious Practice* by

Isaac Klein, *Gates of Shabbat: A Guide for Observing Shabbat* by Mark Dov Shapiro, *The Shabbat Seder* by Ron Wolfson, and *Teaching Mitzvot* by Barbara Binder Kadden and Bruce Kadden.)

20 On Shabbat, we sing *zemirot*, Shabbat songs.

◆ Ask the Cantor to teach your class two Shabbat *zemirot* that you don't already know.

◆ Alternatively, learn to sing *"Shalom Alaychem,"* (Peace To You), which is reflective of the story of the two angels who accompany worshipers home from synagogue on Friday night (see Extending the Text #14, p. 334). This song may be found in the songbook *B'Kol Echad*, edited by Jeffrey Shiovitz, p. 2, and on the accompanying audiocassettes, *Shirei B'Kol Echad*, both of which may be ordered from the web site of United Synagogue for Conservative Judaism, www.uscj.org/booksvc.

21 Israelite exiles who lived in Babylonia for most of their lives faced uncertainty as they were uprooted a second time.

◆ Imagine you are such an Israelite exile. You can hardly remember your former home. Write a journal entry describing how you feel at this very crucial juncture. Also write about what you and your family have been doing to prepare for the long journey home.

Other Resources

22 This Haftarah is read on fast day afternoons: The Fast of Gedaliah, 10th of Tevet, the Fast of Esther, 17th of Tammuz, and Tishah B'Av. To understand why each is a fast day, do research using *A Guide To Jewish Religious Practice* by Isaac Klein or the *Encyclopaedia Judaica*.

23 For ideas on how Shabbat can enhance a liberal Jewish lifestyle, read *Living a Jewish Life: Jewish Traditions, Customs and Values for Today's Families* by Anita Diamant and Howard Cooper, pp. 33-67.

24 Read and discuss the chapter on Shabbat in *40 Things You Can Do to Save the Jewish People* by Joel Lurie Grishaver, pp. 26-58.

25 For curricula and resources on the Holocaust, visit the Holocaust teaching resource center at www.holocaust-trc.org.

26 Read and discuss *An Orphan in History*, in which author Paul Cowan describes one assimilated man's search for and ultimate return to his Jewish roots.

27 See additional activities and discussion on Shabbat in *Teaching Mitzvot* by Barbara Binder Kadden and Bruce Kadden, pp. 1-6.

28 Discuss the illustrations of this Haftarah in *The Illustrated Torah* by Michal Meron, p. 216 and 246.

Involving the Family

29 It may not be immediately possible for your family to visit the Yad Vashem Holocaust Memorial in Israel. However, it may be more practical to plan a Bar/Bat Mitzvah trip to the United States Holocaust Memorial Museum in Washington, D.C. Visit their web site at www.ushmm.org to find out how to plan your visit, how to become a museum member, and more. While you are in Washington, be sure to visit all the other memorials and monuments that are designed to give various people and events "an everlasting name which shall not perish."

30 Enhance your Shabbat dinner by including a discussion topic suitable for your family. For example, everyone can be asked to tell one good thing that happened to them that week. Or, everyone can take a turn telling a good deed they did that week. Parents can take the opportunity Shabbat offers to tell each child one thing each did that week that made them proud of that child.

Consider also making Friday night a Family Games Night. After a family dinner, take out each family member's favorite game and play a round of each game.

Bar/Bat Mitzvah Project

31 Your Bar/Bat Mitzvah year offers you an excellent opportunity to intensify your own personal Shabbat observance. In preparation for your service, you have probably become accustomed to attending services regularly. Don't view your Bar/Bat Mitzvah as the conclusion of the process, but rather as the beginning of making Shabbat a more important feature in your life. Make a plan to add one Shabbat observance a month for the entire year of your Bar/Bat Mitzvah. For example, you might want to stay at home with your family on Friday evenings, to light Shabbat candles, to make Havdalah on Saturday evening, to have a nice family dinner with *Kiddush* and *Motzi*, to attend services regularly, to not shop on Shabbat, etc. Your ultimate goal should be to make the most of your Shabbat experience. Be patient, add observances slowly, and see where it takes you.

ISAIAH 57:14-58:14 TRADITIONAL
ISAIAH 58:1-14 REFORM
YOM KIPPUR MORNING

 This Haftarah has been paired with the holiday Yom Kippur, on which we read Leviticus 16. See "Connecting the Text To the Holiday," pp. 339-341, for an exploration of the many ways the two texts and the holiday shed light on each other.

SYNOPSIS

After many years of exile in Babylon, the Israelites have apparently adopted a lifestyle that has compromised their religious devotion to God. This Haftarah is a challenge to the people to change their ways and win God's favor.

God promises comfort and peace for the humble and contrite, whom God is ready to forgive and return safely to Jerusalem. For the wicked, God promises continued punishment.

God calls upon the prophet in the beginning of chapter 58 to cry out to the people and urge them to reform their sinful ways. The prophet goes on to condemn Israel's exploitation of the poor and failure to care for the needy. He says that their fasting and religious observances are meaningless as long as they continue to live such wicked lives. He pleads with them to free the oppressed, to feed the hungry, and to house and clothe the needy.

When they do, the prophet says, God will rush to their side and protect them from every enemy. When Israel earnestly calls upon *Adonai*, *Adonai* will surely answer. When Israel cares for the poor and hungry, God's light will shine on Israel and strengthen the nation like a watered garden.

Finally, the prophet calls upon Israel to honor the Shabbat and refrain from pursuing business affairs on that most holy day. Only then will *Adonai's* favor fall upon Israel.

INSIGHTS FROM THE TRADITION

A In verse 57:14 God orders that all obstacles be removed from before God's people. Rashi explains that "all obstacles" means the wicked thoughts or evil inclinations that cause one to stumble and sin.

◆ Explain with examples how wicked thoughts are stumbling blocks.

◆ Debate: It is possible to prevent all wicked thoughts from entering your mind.

B Shabbat observance, according to verse 58:13, requires that we observe Shabbat by acting differently from the way we usually do. Radak says this means not wearing the same clothes we wear all week, not eating the same foods as the rest of the week or at the same set mealtimes, and not even walking the same way to the same places.

◆ What is an opposite day?

◆ Do we learn anything by doing things opposite?

◆ Describe how you might spend Shabbat doing everything in a way opposite from how you might ordinarily do things (e.g., eat dessert first at Shabbat dinner or share a meal together when you usually do not).

◆ Why would treating Shabbat differently from the rest of the week be a way of honoring it?

◆ Plan with your family an opposite day Shabbat.

C Ismar Schorsch, the chancellor of the Jewish Theological Seminary in New York City, explains that at the opening breakfast each year at the school, he greets the Rabbinical students with the literal translation of Isaiah 57:19: "Peace, peace unto those from afar and near." Schorsch explains that he learned this tradition when he was a student at the Seminary. The then chancellor, Louis Finkelstein, recited this verse at the opening breakfast. It is thought that this tradition originated with the first chancellor of the school, Solomon Schechter.

◆ Explain why this is an appropriate verse with which to welcome students who have traveled to New York to study.

◆ Do you think students in a school who come from various backgrounds need to be encouraged to get along peacefully? Explain your answer.

◆ Write a slogan to welcome newcomers to your school.

D According to Radak verse 58:7 teaches that we must help everyone who needs food and clothing and shelter. But the verse also reminds us that we should help our own relatives first (before helping strangers).

◆ Do you agree that "charity starts at home"?

◆ Review the following law written by Joseph Karo in *Yoreh De'ah* 251:3:

A person should give to relatives before giving to anyone else . . . The poor in a person's household come before the poor in the town in which the person lives. The poor of the town come before the poor of another town, and the poor of the Land of Israel come before the poor in lands outside Israel.

◆ What explanations can you give for the priorities established in this law?

◆ Do you agree with the priorities?

◆ Review with your parents the recipients of their *tzedakah* contributions. What are their giving priorities (for example, relatives first, Jews second, general third)?

STRATEGIES
Analyzing the Text

1 In verse 57:14 God instructs the prophet to remove all obstacles for the people's return.

◆ What might the obstacles be, and how is the prophet removing the obstacles? For example, if the obstacle is despair, explain how verses 57:15, 16, and 18 might offer hope to remove the despair.

◆ Make an obstacle course in your classroom. Record the time it takes for each student to complete the course. Remove one obstacle at a time, and see how much faster students can then complete the course.

2 God says in verse 57:19, "It shall be well with the far and the near." The Israelites had been scattered to other countries, in exile. Far and near may refer to countries where they live, far and near.

"Far and near" may refer to those who have already returned from exile (near) and those not yet returned (far).

◆ Write and design an advertisement to appear in all local papers throughout the ancient Near East, calling all Israelites "far and near" to return from Exile to the Promised Land.

3 God does not appreciate religious rituals and fasting unless the people doing the rituals and fasting are also behaving in just and godly ways (see verses 58:3-7).

◆ Based on these verses, what types of behavior does God consider just?

◆ Find out if your synagogue works to do any of these just and godly deeds.

◆ Can a Jew be "religious" and underpay his employees, steal from her boss, or not give charity?

4 Verse 58:5 depicts a fast day that includes fasting and wearing sackcloth and ashes.

The Bible does not require the wearing of sackcloth and ashes for Yom Kippur. The only other biblical reason to fast was as a sign of mourning, and the wearing of sackcloth and ashes was also a sign of mourning.

◆ What do you think the Israelites were mourning in the Haftarah?

◆ Explain, based on verses 58:5-7, 9-10 and 13, how their fast was unsatisfactory to God. (Their fast was all form — giving things up for show; and no substance — giving up food, clothes, and money to help those in need.)

◆ In your opinion, does this Haftarah mean that we do not have to fast on Yom Kippur if we fight social injustices?

5 Verses 58:7-8 explain that if the Israelites act righteously, they will be brought out of exile. The "vindicator" will lead the way and God will protect them from behind. According to the Hebrew, "vindicator" is an interpretation of the

word צֶדֶק (*tzedek*), which is generally translated as righteousness.

◆ Compare this image to Exodus 13:21-22.

◆ Draw a caricature or cartoon strip that features a Jewish Super Hero called "Righteous Vindicator." Show how righteousness has the power to make the world a better place.

Connecting the Text To the Holiday

6 Different words for sinning are used in verses 57:17 and 58:1.

פֶּשַׁע (*pesha*) is often translated as "purposeful, rebellious transgression."

חֵטְא (*chayt*) is often translated as "inadvertent sins."

עָוֹן (*avone*) is "iniquity."

◆ Look for these words in the confessional prayers of the Yom Kippur *Machzor* (High Holy Day prayer book). For example, before the *"Al Chayt"* confessional is a statement:

"Therefore may it be Your will, *Adonai* our God, to forgive all our sins, to pardon all our iniquities, and to grant us atonement for all our transgressions."

◆ The three words used for sin in our Haftarah are all here in this prayer. Identify them and compare the uses. Which of the sins in the *"Al Chayt"* prayer that follow it do you think are purposeful, which inadvertent, and which a sign of iniquity? Assign each sin to a category.

7 According to *Berachot* 34b, when Isaiah 57:19 uses the words "afar and near," he is not discussing geography. Rather, the words refer to distance from God due to sinning, and nearness to God due to following of God's ways. This interpretation suggests that "those from afar" are mentioned before "those from near" because we believe that those who have sinned and repented are religiously more elevated and should come before those who have never sinned.

◆ Debate: Which is harder to achieve: a life without any sin or a life of sin and sincere repentance?

◆ Explain the maxim: "In the spot where penitents stand, there is no room for the perfectly righteous."

◆ Rambam wrote, "The merit of penitents is higher than that of the perfectly righteous, because the former have struggled harder to subdue their passions." Do you agree or disagree with Rambam?

◆ Do you know anyone who has never sinned at all?

8 The Talmud offers a contradictory reading for verse 57:19, suggesting that "those from afar" means those who have kept themselves far from sin and "those from near" are those who have been near evil and sinned. According to this interpretation, it is better never to have sinned and, therefore, "those from afar" precedes "those from near."

◆ Compare this interpretation with that in Connecting the Text To the Holiday #7, p. 339. Which reading do you prefer?

◆ Which reading seems more encouraging for human beings likely to sin?

◆ Which reading seems most appropriate for Yom Kippur?

◆ Create and illustrate a Jewish New Years card featuring your favorite interpretation of the first part of verse 57:19.

9 The prophet is told to raise his voice and cry out loud like a *shofar* and proclaim the sins of Israel (58:1).

On Yom Kippur, we all act like the prophet: we all proclaim aloud communal sins in the *"Al Chayt"* prayer.

Notice that this prayer is stated in the first person plural: We all sinned.

Notice that we all recite every sin, even if it does not apply to us personally. By proclaiming aloud the sins of all Israel, no one need be embarrassed by being the only one to recite a particular item.

◆ Hold a contest: Contestants cry out part of the *"Al Chayt"* prayer, trying to make their voices sound like a *shofar*. A panel will select the one who sounds most like a *shofar*.

10 God promises in verse 57:16 not to be angry always for our sins. On Yom Kippur, we believe that if we truly repent, our sins against God will be forgiven; God will not be angry forever.

◆ Why is this a comforting message on Yom Kippur?

◆ Following the Yom Kippur recitation of *"Kol Nidre,"* we quote three verses from the book of Numbers which indicate that God forgives: 15:26, 14:19, and 14:20. Compare the message of those three verses to verse 57:16 in the Haftarah.

◆ Are we reminding God that God is forgiving, or are we reassuring ourselves, or both?

◆ There is a category of sins for which we do not get automatic forgiveness: if we have sinned against other people, we will only be forgiven if we have apologized to them and paid them for any damage done.

◆ Review Mishnah *Yoma* 8:9, or see an explanation of *"Kol Nidre"* in most *Machzorim*. These explain that Yom Kippur does not bring atonement for sins against another person until the other party has been appeased.

◆ It is a tradition to seek forgiveness for anything you may have done, knowingly or unwittingly, from family and friends during the Ten Days of Repentance leading up to Yom Kippur. Institute this tradition in your family this year.

11 According to verse 58:6, God wants to undo the fetters of wickedness. According to Radak, when a person gets used to sinning in a certain way, it becomes "tied" to the person, and it is very hard to undo those ties.

◆ Describe types of misbehavior that people get so used to doing that they can't stop (for example, smoking, fighting with siblings, lying).

◆ On Yom Kippur, we ask to be forgiven for sins we committed knowingly and unknowingly. To which of these categories do you think belong the sins that are tied to us? Why do you think so?

12 God says in verse 57:14 that we are God's people.

◆ Learn from the Cantor the Yom Kippur prayer *"Ki Anu Amecha,"* (We Are Your People). This is a hopeful, lively Yom Kippur prayer that reminds us (and God) that we are God's people. A few of the verses are:

Our God and God of our ancestors

Forgive us, pardon us, grant us atonement.

For we are Your people, and You are our God.

We are your children, and You are our Father.

We are Your flock, and You are our Shepherd.

We are Your treasure, and You are our Protector.

◆ If Yom Kippur is a day of atonement, why do you suppose we sing an upbeat prayer? After the confessional listing all our sins, do you think we have to remind God that we are God's people, or do we need to reassure ourselves?

◆ Imagine you are publishing a new *Machzor.* Prepare an illustration of the prayer *"Ki Anu Amecha"* for inclusion in your *Machzor.* If you wish, you can also add your own interpretive lines to the prayer in the same parallel style (e.g., We are Your <u>noun</u>, and You are our <u>noun</u>").

ISAIAH 60:1-22
KI TAVO כי תבוא

This Haftarah has been paired with *Parashat Ki Tavo*, Deuteronomy 26:1-29:8. See "Connecting the Text To the Sedra," p. 344, for an exploration of the many ways the two texts shed light on each other.

SYNOPSIS

In this Haftarah Isaiah paints a bright future for the despairing exiles. He promises that God's light will shine upon Jerusalem, and her resulting radiance will illuminate the world.

Jerusalem's children — the Israelites —will return to her, and Jerusalem will be blessed with gifts of silver and gold, of flocks and rams, and of spices and wood from all the nations of the world. All of Israel's former oppressors will be assembled to serve them and their Holy City. The supply of wealth and service to God will be endless. Those nations unworthy of helping Jerusalem will be destroyed.

Returned to a city of splendor, Jerusalem will be the pride and joy of the world forever, as *Adonai* is recognized as her Savior and Redeemer. Jerusalem will enjoy eternal well-being and prosperity, and the cry of violence shall never again be heard within her borders.

The light of sun and moon will no longer be needed, due to the sheer radiance of Jerusalem. God's light will shine, and the days of sadness will be done.

The righteous people of Israel will possess the land for all time and become a mighty nation, at a time to be determined by God.

INSIGHTS FROM THE TRADITION

A According to verse 60:3, Israel will be in the light, and the rest of the world will be in the dark but guided by Israel's light. Ibn Ezra points out that the person who sits in the light cannot see those in the dark, but people in the dark can see others in the light.

Sometimes, when you have to do something, you have to block out what everyone else in the world is doing in order to focus completely on what it is you have to do.

◆ List things that require a person's undivided attention.

◆ List things that might distract a person.

◆ What techniques might people use to prevent distractions from ruining their ability to focus?

◆ Choose one technique to try for a week. Keep a log describing times you needed to focus, what distractions arose, and how the technique helped you.

B Radak teaches concerning verse 60:5 that you will be startled and full of wonder because of the abundance and goodness lavished on you.

◆ Have you ever been startled by a kindness someone has done for you?

◆ Why might such goodness be startling?

C Verse 60:8 describes doves flying home. Radak suggests that doves fly faster when they are carrying food home for their young than they do when flying away from home.

When people do a task for someone they love (e.g., the doves flying home with food), they rush to do it. They seem to do it without effort or complaint, no matter how hard it is.

◆ Interview your parents and grandparents for examples from their experience of difficult tasks they did without complaint for the benefit of their loved ones.

D Verse 60:9 suggests that nations will bring home to Zion her children and will also bring her many riches; all this will be done "in the name of God." To Rashi, this means that when other peoples hear about God and God's might, they will come.

◆ What does it mean to jump on a bandwagon?

◆ How do you know when the bandwagon is a good one to join?

◆ What is the difference between joining a bandwagon and giving in to peer pressure?

◆ When can peer pressure be a good thing?

STRATEGIES
Analyzing the Text

1 The prophet says in verse 60:2 that in spite of darkness all around, God's light will shine about Jerusalem. Ibn Ezra emphasizes that that light will be solely upon Jerusalem.

◆ Do you think it is a blessing or a curse to be in the spotlight? Explain your answer.

◆ What privileges come with being in the spotlight?

◆ What responsibilities come with being in the spotlight?

◆ Would you prefer to be the exception, or to be the same as those around you? Why?

2 It is said in verse 60:5 that Jerusalem will "glow." Why do we say that when someone is extremely happy, they are "glowing" or "radiant"?

◆ In what other ways does happiness inside affect the way someone looks (or behaves) on the outside?

3 Verse 60:18 states, "And you shall name your walls 'Victory' and your gates 'Renown'" (literally, Praise).

◆ What do you think this means? (One explanation is that Jerusalem will call out or proclaim on her walls and her gates Victory and Praise of God.)

◆ Compare this verse to verse 54:11-12, then make a mural of the restored Jerusalem walls.

4 Well-being will be the government of Jerusalem, and prosperity (literally, righteousness) will be her officials, according to verse 60:17, which ascribes a utopian vision of the future of Jerusalem.

◆ Compare this verse to verses 52:1-2. Create and present a skit or puppet show in which Jerusalem changes her clothes of dust and mourning for those of power, righteousness, and splendor.

◆ What is a utopia?

◆ Write a description of your own vision of the perfect world.

5 There is an apparent contradiction in verse 60:22 which says, "I *Adonai* will speed it in due time."

◆ In "due time" sounds like the event will happen as expected no matter how long it takes, but the verse also says that God will speed its happening. Can you suggest resolutions to the contradiction, or can you explain how it might not be a contradiction? (One explanation is that if they are worthy, then the time for their redemption will come sooner, but if not worthy, redemption will take longer. Another explanation is that it may be a long time until the time of salvation arrives, but when it does, it will happen quickly.)

Connecting the Text To the Sedra

6 This is the sixth of seven Haftarot of Consolation, recited in the weeks following Tishah B'Av.

◆ Why do you think this Haftarah was chosen as a message of comfort?

◆ List the many messages in this Haftarah that are comforting and hopeful.

◆ Draw your understanding of one of these hopeful messages.

◆ Compare your drawing with the illustration of this Haftarah in *The Illustrated Torah* by Michal Meron, p. 210. Which verse or verses did the artist depict, and why?

7 Deuteronomy 26:1-11 provides a summary of Israel's history, including the exile in Egypt and the deliverance from that captivity. The Haftarah highlights what life will be like once the Israelites are freed from their exile in Babylonia.

◆ How might the communal memory of the Exodus from Egypt have brought comfort to the exiled Israelites in Babylonia?

◆ Write a diary entry by a young Israelite exile in Babylonia who has just been taught about the Exodus from Egypt. How does your new knowledge about Israel's history affect your view of the current situation?

8 The Haftarah ends with the assurance in verse 60:22 that the smallest remnant of

Israel will grow into a mighty and numerous nation. In the Sedra (Deuteronomy 26:5), Moses reminds the Israelites that they were few when they went down to Egypt, but grew to be many.

◆ Check in the most recent *American Jewish Year Book* to find out the current world Jewish population, or find out at the web site www.sites.huji.ac.il/jcj/dmg_worldjpop.html.

◆ In which country do the largest number of Jews live?

◆ Would you consider Jews worldwide to be "a mighty nation"?

◆ In what ways, other than sheer numbers, can a people be great and mighty?

Extending the Text

9 The song *"Sisu et Yerushalayim"* (Rejoice in Jerusalem) includes verses 60:4 and 21.

◆ Learn and sing this song, which may be found in the songbook *B'Kol Echad*, edited by Jeffrey Shiovitz, p. 113, and on the accompanying audiocassettes *Shirei B'Kol Echad*. These may be ordered from the web site of United Synagogue of Conservative Judaism at www.uscj.org/booksvc.

10 The nations that harbor Israelites will transport their Israelite inhabitants to the Holy Land.

During the Holocaust, the Nazis planned to round up all the Jews of Denmark on October 1, 1943, the second day of Rosh HaShanah. Ordinarily, it would have been easy to find all the Jews in synagogue, but the Danish underground had uncovered the Nazi plan and hid all the Jews. Then the Danes transported virtually their entire Jewish community by rowboats and fishing boats to safety in Sweden. Since World War II, Denmark has become for Jews a symbol of righteousness.

◆ How might Hitler's plan to exterminate the Jews have worked out differently had more European nations acted like the Danes?

◆ What lessons can we learn from Denmark's behavior during World War II?

11 Many ancient nations are mentioned in verses 60:6-13, including Midian, Ephah, Sheba, Kedar, Nebaioth, Tarshish, and Lebanon.

◆ Choose one of these nations and prepare a presentation on it for your class. Consult the *Encyclopaedia Judaica* for information and further references.

◆ Alternatively, prepare a word scramble of these places for your classmates to solve.

12 The enemy nations will be made to build and glorify Jerusalem. Since 1952, Germany has been paying financial reparations to the State of Israel. When the Israelis and Germans officially met in 1952 to discuss reparations, citizens of the new Jewish state were divided on the issue. Violent clashes even broke out among disagreeing Israelis. Finally, the Knesset approved the reparations by a slim margin of 61-50.

◆ Debate whether or not Israel should have accepted reparations payments from West Germany. (Remember that a significant percentage of Israelis were Holocaust survivors.)

13 Jerusalem recently celebrated its 3000th anniversary.

◆ Prepare a "Jerusalem Bowl." You and your classmates can do research about Jerusalem's history, culture, neighborhoods, etc. Compile all the information into a fact sheet to study before competing in a Jerusalem trivia contest. This competition can be just for your class or administered by your class for the whole

school. Great resources for this project may be found at your local public library: travel guidebooks to Israel.

14 Both the Passover *Seder* and the Yom Kippur liturgy conclude with the cry, "Next year in Jerusalem!"

◆ Look in a *Machzor* to find this phrase. (We say it following the acceptance of our last prayers and the final sounding of the *shofar* with a *Tekiah Gedolah*.) Look in a *Haggadah* for the phrase. We say this phrase following the prayer *"Nirtzah"* (which means "acceptance").

◆ Why do you think the *Seder* concludes with "Next Year in Jerusalem"?

◆ Why does being in Jerusalem signify "acceptance"?

◆ Why does Jerusalem continue to be at the heart and soul of Jewish existence?

◆ Write a story about what it might be like to celebrate Yom Kippur or Passover in Jerusalem.

◆ For more on the prayer *"Nirtzah,"* see *The Art of Jewish Living: The Passover Seder* by Ron Wolfson, pp. 229-231.

15 In Insights from the Tradition #B, p. 342, we learn about unexpected acts of kindness. Do a newspaper search looking for articles about acts of kindness. Compile these into a storybook that can be read to younger kids.

◆ Design and make a sign proclaiming your school a "Kindness Zone." The sign can be posted at all entrances, reminding people how to act in your school.

◆ For more projects related to random acts of kindness, check the web site www. actsofkindness.org, or contact the Random Acts of Kindness Foundation at 1801

TEACHING HAFTARAH

Broadway, Denver, CO 80202, 303-297-1964. This foundation, which now has offshoots in 135 countries, helps people organize their projects, teaches them how to deal with the media, enlist volunteers, and raise money. All their services are free; their money comes from an anonymous Denver philanthropist, who provides $5 million annually, and through the sale of lapel pins, bumper stickers, T-shirts, banners, balloons, and other items carrying the Random Acts slogan, "Practice Random Acts of Kindness."

Personalizing the Text

16 The song "By the Waters of Babylon," based on Psalm 137, recalls the Babylonian captivity. The Hebrew version of this song, *"Al Naharot Bavel"* (By the Waters of Babylon) is mournfully sung on Tishah B'Av. The song "Rivers of Babylon" may be found on the recording *Greater Scheme of Things* by Safam.

♦ Learn to sing both of these songs.

17 Insights from the Tradition #A, p. 342, deals with the matter of concentration.

♦ Participate in this concentration exercise. One student estimates how long a minute takes without counting the seconds. The teacher can try to distract him/her from guessing correctly by asking questions, telling stories, being silly, etc. Repeat the exercise with all the students, and see which student comes closest to guessing an actual minute. Find out how the winner was able to concentrate despite the distractions.

18 Different types of items were brought to Jerusalem by the foreign nations.

♦ Curate a classroom exhibit of these types of items. Collect, for example, something made of cypress wood and pine, something made

of wool, a ram's horn, gold, copper, iron, stone, frankincense or similar exotic spice, and so on. Paint a mural to be used as a backdrop to your exhibit. The mural can depict camels laden with goodies brought by people from the various nations.

19 Verse 60:20 states: "Your sun shall set no more, your moon no more withdraw; For *Adonai* shall be a light to you forever, and your days of mourning shall be ended."

♦ Explain the meaning of this verse in your own words.

♦ Design a sympathy card using this verse. Why might this verse be appropriate for such a card?

20 Israel is described in verse 60:21 as the shoot that God planted.

♦ Germinate some seeds of your choice and plant the saplings in a windowsill container. When they are strong enough, you can transplant the saplings to a spot outside.

♦ How do you feel about this sapling for which you have cared?

♦ For advanced study, read the Haftarah for Yom Kippur afternoon (The Book of Jonah, p. 569), to learn the lesson God teaches to Jonah about caring for other living creatures.

21 In this Haftarah (verse 60:18), the city walls have unusual names. In the Bible there are also many unusual names for people, places, and things.

♦ Make up your own version of the game Twenty Questions. Using the following list, make up rules for a game in which players must identify whether the item is a person, place, or thing.

Midian – Isaiah 60:6 (place)

Hadadezer – II Samuel 8:3 (person)

Nebaioth – Isaiah 60:7 (place)

Harnepher – I Chronicles 7:36 (person)

Tarshish – Isaiah 60:9 (place)

Ephah – Amos 8:5 (thing)

Dodo – II Samuel 23:9 (person)

22 Israel is described in verse 60:21 as God's handiwork.

◆ Crafts and special articles of clothing often come with care instructions. Write out instructions on how to care for such a fine piece of work as a human being.

◆ Create your own fine handiwork: a soap carving of Jerusalem.

Other Resources

23 Read and discuss the children's picture book *Designed by God So I Must Be Special* by Bonnie Sose.

24 The textbook *Welcome To Israel!* by Lilly Rivlin and Gila Gevirtz is a lively introduction to Israel, with a nice section on Jerusalem.

25 For additional activities on Jerusalem, see *Teaching Israel* by Josh Zweiback and Adam Zweiback, forthcoming in 2003 from A.R.E. Publishing, Inc.

26 Read and enjoy the beautiful illustrations in the non-sectarian book *The Golden City: Jerusalem's 3,000 Years* by Neil Waldman.

27 For more information on Isaiah, see *Messengers of God: A Jewish Prophets Who's Who* by Ronald H. Isaacs.

28 See the commentary for this Haftarah at the Fuchsberg Center for Conservative Judaism in Jerusalem at www.uscj.org.il/haftarah.

29 For commentary, discussion questions, and activities, see the UAHC Family Shabbat Table Talk web site at www.uahc.org/shabbat/stt/3kitavo.shtml.

30 Listen to the song "Where Is the Light" on the recording *Safam on Track* by Safam.

31 For more on random acts of kindness, read *Chicken Soup for Little Souls: The Goodness Gorillas* by Jack Canfield and Mark Victor Hansen (ages 4-8).

Involving the Family

32 Subscribe to the *Jerusalem Post* or the *Jerusalem Report* and keep up with the Israeli perspective on current events in Israel. You can also access their web sites: www.jpost.com and http:www.jrep.com.

Bar/Bat Mitzvah Projects

33 Spend this year doing one random act of kindness per week for strangers (see Insights from the Tradition #B, p. 342). For example, leave a friendly note in a schoolmate's locker. Call a friend or relative and read them your favorite poem. Walk through town putting dimes in parking meters that have expired so people don't get parking tickets. Do your brother's/sister's chores one day without asking anything in return.

Keep a log of what you did, the recipient's reaction (if known), and how you felt during and after the kindness.

ISAIAH 61:10-63:9
NITZAVIM נצבים

This Haftarah has been paired with *Parashat Nitzavim*, Deuteronomy 29:9-30:20. See "Connecting the Text To the Sedra," p. 350, for an exploration of the many ways the two texts shed light on each other.

SYNOPSIS

Now that King Cyrus of Persia has defeated Babylonia, hopes are running high among the Israelites for freedom from exile and the return to Zion. This hope is expressed in the beginning of the Haftarah, as the prophet describes being dressed in garments of triumph and victory.

Adonai pledges never to rest until Zion (Jerusalem) emerges victorious and resplendent. Jerusalem will be God's crowning glory on earth and will never again be called "forsaken" or "desolate." God will rejoice over her as a bridegroom rejoices over his bride.

Adonai further promises that the Israelites will enjoy the food and wine they produce and that they will be called "The Holy People."

In the first six verses of chapter 63, God is painstakingly described as a mighty warrior Whose majestic attire is stained red with the blood of Israel's defeated enemies.

The Haftarah concludes with a call to recount the kind acts *Adonai* has done for Israel. The prophet praises *Adonai* as Israel's merciful deliverer, whose love and pity exalts Israel above its troubles.

INSIGHTS FROM THE TRADITION

A God appoints watchmen on the walls of Jerusalem in verse 62:6. There has been great discussion among the Rabbis as to who these watchmen are.

Targum Jonathan suggests that the watchmen are the ancestors who were righteous and protect us like a wall.

◆ How do our ancestors and our moral traditions offer us protection, and from what?

◆ Listen to and discuss the famous song "Tradition," found on the original cast recording of *Fiddler on the Roof*. What role does tradition play for Tevye and the other villagers?

B Hirsch believes that the watchmen are those who are loyal to our heritage. He contrasts these loyal Jews with those who destroy Israel because they do not have a Jewish education and completely neglect Jewish tradition. Hirsch argues that redemption will occur only when all Jews are faithful to the *mitzvot*.

◆ Do you agree or disagree with Hirsch? Justify your answer.

◆ Debate Hirsch's idea that Jews without a Jewish education and commitment to *mitzvot* are destroyers of Israel.

C Verse 62:11 indicates that God will bring a reward. Radak explains that the reward is for those who have clung to God's Torah and *mitzvot* throughout the years of exile and despite great persecution.

◆ Do you think it is harder to be a Jew when Jews are being persecuted or when we are free from persecution? Explain your answer.

◆ List ways in which people express their Jewish identity. Which of these ways are more difficult in times of oppression?

D We are taught in verse 63:9 that an angel saved the Israelite people.

Radak understands that Israel was saved through a series of events, one leading to the next. One might see these events as a series of mere coincidences. But here the prophet assures us that all the events were planned and set into motion by God.

◆ Can you think of any amazing coincidences that have occurred in your life?

◆ Do you think these coincidences were mere accidents, or were they somehow planned and destined to happen? Explain your answer.

◆ If these coincidences were somehow planned, in what ways does that change your understanding of the event (and the world)?

STRATEGIES
Analyzing the Text

1 There is a disagreement about who is speaking in verse 61:10. *Targum Jonathan* asserts it is Jerusalem, but Radak suggests it is the Israelite people.

◆ Defend both interpretations. Which do you prefer?

◆ Compare this verse to Jeremiah 2:32.

◆ Verse 61:10 speaks of being wrapped in a robe of victory. Chose one of these images and create a design for a *tallit* bag. If possible, really make the bag.

2 Israel will flourish "in the presence of all the nations" (verse 61:11). The idea that Israel's redemption will prove God's supremacy to the nations of the world is repeated throughout the book of Isaiah.

◆ Why might it matter so much that everyone should recognize God's greatness and mercy toward Israel?

◆ Should we do good things only so that we may be recognized for them? Explain your answer.

◆ Do you think God redeemed Israel only to be recognized by the other nations? Explain your answer.

3 Israel's new growth, development, and success is compared in verse 61:11 to a seed planted in the garden that the earth nurtures and brings forth.

◆ Compare this metaphor to the parable in Isaiah 5:1-8.

◆ Illustrate both the parable's failed vines and this verse's successful seed.

4 In verses 63:1-5 God is described as a valiant warrior, bloodied from battle with the enemy. This description of God is an anthropomorphism.

◆ According to Jewish tradition, God has no shape or form, making it impossible for God to actually be a warrior covered with blood. If this is only an imaginary depiction of God, what message is it trying to relay?

◆ What does God feel that makes God ready to be bloodied in battle?

◆ How does this description compare with the way you usually imagine God?

◆ Do you find this image disturbing or comforting? Explain.

◆ See the Haftarah for *Beresheet*, Analyzing the Text #3, p. 277, and the Haftarah for *Shofetim*, Analyzing the Text #5, p. 306, for more information and examples of anthropomorphisms.

5 Verse 63:9 states that God is troubled by Israel's troubles.

◆ What does this mean? How can the Supreme Power in the world be troubled by anything, and why wouldn't the Supreme Power just change or fix the source of the trouble? W. Gunther Plaut explains in *The Haftarah Commentary*, p. 506, that "God appears to be both powerful and vulnerable." How can anyone, including God, be both powerful and vulnerable at the same time? (For more discussion on this verse, see the essay in Plaut's book, pp. 506-507.)

Connecting the Text To the Sedra

6 This is the last of the seven Haftarot of Consolation, which is read on the Shabbat immediately before Rosh HaShanah.

◆ Describe five images of hope and consolation in this Haftarah (such as the glorious crown in *Adonai*'s hand in verse 62:3).

◆ Isaiah talks a lot in this Haftarah about the redemption of the people, God's love and pity, God's watchfulness, and rejoicing and exultation in the name of *Adonai*. How can these ideas also relate to Rosh HaShanah?

◆ How is Rosh HaShanah itself a kind of redemption for the Jewish people? (Consider that on Rosh HaShanah we rid ourselves of sin and start a new year with a clean slate, effectively saving ourselves from our past mistakes.)

◆ Which of these ideas do you find inspiring? Explain your choices.

7 The Sedra teaches in Deuteronomy 30:1-2 that when the Israelites do not follow God's laws, they will be driven into exile. It further states that when Israel repents and returns to God, God will return them from where they had been scattered. The clear message is that exile is a temporary punishment meant to teach Israel a lesson.

◆ How and where does the Haftarah make this same point?

◆ List a variety of punishments. Describe what you think the main purpose of each punishment is (e.g., jail is to protect society from the criminal, fines are to restore stolen property, time-outs protect a young child from dangerous activity).

◆ Do you usually consider punishment's purpose to be to encourage repentance and atonement? Explain your answer.

◆ If punishments were meted out to encourage repentance and atonement, how might the nature of the punishments be different?

8 The Haftarah describes how God will rejoice משוש (*m'sos*) — with Jerusalem, just as a bridegroom rejoices with his bride in verse 62:5. (The same word is also used in the first verse of the Haftarah.)

The Sedra describes in Deuteronomy 30:9 how God will rejoice (delight) in us as God had rejoiced in our ancestors.

◆ What do you think it means for God to rejoice?

◆ Who and what causes you to rejoice, and why?

Extending the Text

9 According to some *midrashim*, God is Watchman over Israel.

It is written in Psalm 121:4 that "The guardian of Israel neither slumbers nor sleeps."

◆ Why is important for a guard or protector to be awake and alert at all times?

◆ Furthermore, the *Zohar* teaches concerning this verse that God, the guardian of Israel, is like a deer. Just as a deer sleeps with one eye closed and the other eye open, so does God always have one eye open (*kevayachol*) as God watches over Israel. God, who needs no sleep, is nonetheless compared to a deer. Explain the comparison in your own words.

◆ This verse has been used in signs and posters for bedrooms, as it reminds us that even as we sleep, God vigilantly protects us. Make an illustrated poster for a child's room, using verse 62:6 or Psalm 121:4.

◆ Compare your illustration to the illustration of this Haftarah in *The Illustrated Torah* by Michal Meron, p. 213.

10 Ibn Ezra says the watchmen in verse 62:6 are the mourners of Jerusalem who pray for Israel day and night. Rashi says they are the angels reminding God to rebuild the destroyed city. In Radak's view the watchmen represent God, Who will protect the rebuilt city.

◆ Put on a skit involving each of these interpretations.

11 In Insights from the Tradition #A, p. 348, we learn that our ancestors and traditions are like a wall that protects us.

There is a concept in Jewish law about building a fence (or wall) around the Torah. A fence in Jewish law is a Rabbinic construct (*gezerah*) which is enacted in order to prevent a Jew from inadvertently breaking a law commanded by the Torah. For example, the Torah prohibits the cooking of meat and milk together. The Rabbis require that separate pots be used for the cooking of meats and the cooking of dairy items in order to build a fence around the Torah. By not being allowed to use the same pot for a meat meal as for a dairy meal, we are prevented from inadvertently mixing the two together.

◆ What is the purpose of the Rabbinic fence?

◆ If the Torah says that we are not to add to or subtract from the laws of the Torah, how can we justify adding laws that are fences? (Answer: according to many scholars, laws which act as fences are not considered laws from the Torah and therefore nothing has been added to the laws of the Torah.)

◆ Here is a corny joke: How do you make a *Sefer Torah*? Put a fence around it! Explain the pun involved with this joke.

12 Verses 63:2-3 describe God's clothing as being soaked with the red blood of Israel's enemies.

Pesachim 25b asks the question, "Whose blood is redder? We cannot know if someone's life is more important than another's."

Joseph Telushkin points out in *Jewish Literacy*, p. 508, that this principle can be applied to common situations. "For example, we have no right to push ahead of other people waiting in line, because who says we are better than they and entitled to go first?"

◆ In what other everyday situations can we apply the principle of "who says your blood is redder"?

◆ How does this principle teach us to be better people?

13 Julia Ward Howe composed "The Battle Hymn of the Republic" in 1862. The first verse (about God trampling out the vintage where the grapes of wrath are stored) uses the imagery written by Isaiah in 63:3.

◆ Learn and sing the first two verses of this song, which can be found at the web site www.contemplator.com/folk2/battle.html. The music can be downloaded from this web site.

◆ Make up a different second verse that uses other imagery from this Haftarah.

14 God could find no help to free the Israelites in verse 63:5. The following was written by Pastor Martin Niemöller, a German minister who did not intervene against the Nazis to help save the Jews. He later came to regret his inaction. His famous statement about the guilt he felt for his inaction may be found at www.hoboes.com/html/FireBlade/Politics/niemoller.shtml.

First they came for the Jews.
I was silent. I was not a Jew.
Then they came for the Communists
I was silent. I was not a Communist.
Then they came for the trade unionists.
I was silent. I was not a trade unionist.
Then they came for me.
There was no one left to speak for me.

◆ What is the lesson we learn from those who do not help those in need?

◆ Can you give examples from recent news stories of people who might need our help?

◆ Design a newspaper advertisement that uses the Niemöller quotation and some recent news stories to encourage people to take action when their help is needed.

15 The phrase, "powerful to give triumph," from verse 63:1, is quoted in the second blessing of the *"Amidah."* Like the Haftarah, the *"Amidah"* also contains many references to redemption, the gathering of exiles, and the rebuilding of Jerusalem.

◆ Find and study these references in the *"Amidah,"* and compare the tone of each to the tone of the Haftarah.

◆ Create a rebus for each of the blessings in the *"Amidah"* that refers to these ideas.

16 The Haftarah says that God's clothing will be red when God redeems Israel.

◆ The color red appears often in the Bible. Match up these events that involve red with the person listed below:

a. Fed his brother red pottage (1)
b. Was born red all over (5)
c. Was commanded to kill the red heifer (6)
d. Saw water as red as blood (3)
e. Was born with a red thread on his hand (2)
f. Put a red thread on her window (4)

1. Jacob (Genesis 25)
2. Zerah (Genesis 38)
3. Moabites (II Kings 3)
4. Rahab (Joshua 2)
5. Esau (Genesis 25)
6. Eleazar (Numbers 19)

Personalizing the Text

17 Once she is restored to glory, God will call Zion by a new name that broadcasts her majesty to all the nations.

◆ What does your name broadcast to the world about you? Check a Hebrew and English name dictionary for the meaning of your Hebrew and English names.

◆ If you could choose a new name for yourself, one that revealed something about your character or personality, what name would you choose, and why?

◆ Make an acrostic with the letters of your name that reveals something about your personality.

18 The wedding song, *"Yasis Alayich"* (May He Rejoice Over You), comes from Isaiah 62:5.

◆ Learn and sing this song, which may be found in *B'Kol Echad*, edited by Jeffrey Shiovitz, p. 99, and on the accompanying audiocassettes *Shirei B'Kol Echad*, both of which can be ordered from the web site of United Synagogue of Conservative Judaism at www.uscj.org/booksvc.

19 The song, *"Sisu et Yerushalayim"* (Rejoice in Jerusalem) is taken in part from verse 62:6.

◆ Learn and sing this song, which may be found in *B'Kol* Echad, edited by Jeffrey Shiovitz, pp. 113-114, and on the accompanying audiocassettes *Shirei B'Kol Echad*. Both of these may be ordered from the web site of United Synagogue for Conservative Judaism at www.uscj.org/booksvc.

20 According to Hertz verse 63:7 should not be understood simply as "I will talk about the kind acts of *Adonai*," but as "I will commemorate the kind acts of *Adonai*."

◆ What is the difference between merely mentioning something and commemorating it?

◆ Have you ever been to a commemoration ceremony (on Independence Day or Veterans Day, for example)? If so, describe it.

◆ Plan a commemoration ceremony for the kind acts *Adonai* has done for you personally, for the Jewish people, and/or for the world in general. Design a seat for the guest of honor (God). Write speeches to be delivered. Create a plaque to be awarded at the commemoration. Perform *"Yasis Alayich," "Sisu et Yerushalayim,"* and/or "Battle Hymn of the Republic."

21 We are told in verse 63:9 that an angel saved the Israelite people. Some conclude that it was rather a series of coincidences that saved them.

◆ View and discuss the film *The Truman Show* (1998, rated PG, 103 minutes). The creator of Truman's world tries to tell Truman that it is better for him to stay in the world that has been created for him, a world in which everything has been planned for his needs. Why did Truman want to leave? Would you want to live in Truman's world? Why or why not?

22 God emerges victorious from Edom and Bozrah in verse 63:1. According to *midrash*, Edom is a term for Roman tyrants and oppressors who are descendants of Esau. Bozrah is a fortified city within the Edomite territory.

◆ Explain how this interpretation indicates that God fights against tyrants and oppressors. How is this like fighting for the underdog?

◆ Watch sporting events and root for the underdog and against the more powerful, favored team. Keep a log of how it feels to root for the underdog.

Other Resources

23 View a home video of someone's traditional Jewish wedding, pointing out all the key elements of the ceremony. See how bride and groom are rejoicing, just as Isaiah portrays God rejoicing over Israel.

24 For more information on Isaiah, see *Messengers of God: A Jewish Prophets Who's Who* by Ronald H. Isaacs.

25 See the UAHC Family Shabbat Table Talk web site for a commentary on this Haftarah, discussion questions, and project at www.uahc.org/shabbat/stt/3nv.shtml

26 See the commentary for this Haftarah at the web site of the Fuchsberg Center for Conservative Judaism in Jerusalem, www.uscj. org.il/haftarah.

Involving the Family

27 The rebirth of Israel is compared in verse 61:11 to nature. The Jewish National Fund is dedicated to making Israel's deserts come to life. Donate the money you would have spent on centerpieces at your Bar/Bat Mitzvah celebration to JNF. In the middle of your tables, where the centerpieces would have gone, you can place a card that explains your decision to donate to JNF. (You can contact JNF at 800-542-TREE or www.JNF.org.)

28 According to Insights from the Tradition #A, p. 348, our ancestors give us our traditions and protect us. As a family, compile a family tree. Discuss traditions, customs, sayings, and philosophies that ancestors have taught the members of your family. Add these traditions to your tree. You might even want to include recipes as well.

Bar/Bat Mitzvah Projects

29 God says in verse 62:1 that for Jerusalem's sake I will not be silent.

The American Israel Public Affairs Committee (AIPAC) is, according to *The New York Times*, "the most important organization affecting America's relationships with Israel." Visit their web site at www.AIPAC.org to keep up with current events and learn how to become a member and support AIPAC.

30 According to Insights from the Tradition #B, p. 348, the watchmen of our people keep us safe because of their loyalty to our heritage and their good Jewish education. Commit yourself to continue your Jewish studies through high school. Write your Bar/Bat Mitzvah speech on this subject. Try to convince at least one friend to join you.

ISAIAH 66:1-24
SHABBAT ROSH CHODESH

This Haftarah has been paired with Rosh Chodesh when the beginning of the month falls on Shabbat. We read a special Maftir Torah reading, Numbers 28:1-15. See "Connecting the Text To the Special Shabbat," pp. 357-358, for an exploration of the ways the texts and the Special Shabbat shed light on each other.

SYNOPSIS

This Haftarah comes from the section of the Book of Isaiah that has been attributed to a Third Isaiah. Cyrus, King of Persia, permitted the exiles to return to Judea and Jerusalem. The setting for this Haftarah appears to be decades after they returned and met with many frustrations, such as famine and poverty. As a result of their despair, they developed an eschatological, or "end of time" outlook.

This last chapter of the Book of Isaiah opens with a declaration of God's transcendence; God is not on earth but in heaven. No mere man-made Temple could serve as home to God, who created the heavens and earth. Moreover, God does not care about splendid buildings; rather God cares that people act humbly and with awe for God's commands. Those who engage in abominable acts of worship and idolatry, in violation of God's words, will be mocked and punished by God.

Throughout most of the prophecy, Jerusalem is the focus; the prophet describes a glorious future for Jerusalem. Jerusalem will one day be as a joyful, young mother who painlessly gives birth to her newborn, revived nation. Jerusalem will be as a loving mother feeding her children, consoling them for their pains. The nation will tenderly be carried on her shoulders, bounced on her knees, and comforted from their troubles by her and by God. They, in turn, will delight in her presence, grow and flourish. All this, however, will come to be only for the faithful, and it will occur only after God's enemies will have met with a violent end.

The Haftarah closes with the gathering of all the nations to behold and declare God's glory. All the nations will gather the Israelite exiles among them and return with them to Jerusalem where they will be assured a great future. Those who rebelled against God shall endure eternal punishment, while the faithful will worship *Adonai*, the God of Israel, every New Moon and every Shabbat.

INSIGHTS FROM THE TRADITION

A God says in verse 66:1, "The heaven is My throne and the earth is My footstool." Radak explains that the Temple was not built to contain or house God, nor were sacrifices commanded to feed God. The Temple was commanded only so that Israel would come to a designated place to pray. Sacrifices were required not to feed God, but to stir the hearts of the people to eliminate evil thoughts and burn them like sacrifices on an altar.

◆ Explain how Israel ostensibly built the Temple for God, but really built the Temple for itself.

◆ Describe times when people think they are doing something for someone else, but it is really the doer who benefits from the act.

◆ Give examples of times when a person seemingly does something for someone else, but is actually the real beneficiary of the action. (For example, we say that we are saying *"Kaddish"* for the deceased, but in many ways it is the mourner who benefits; we do homework for our teachers, but we are the ones who benefit; an apprentice helps a carpenter, but actually the carpenter could have done the work twice as fast and is training the apprentice.)

B Verse 66:3 compares the sacrifice of an ox with the slaying of a human being. Radak explains that this means that if someone slaughters an ox for sacrifice without repenting for his/her sins, it is as useless an act as if he/she tried to sacrifice a human being — an unacceptable sacrifice.

◆ Explain how until a person has apologized to God for wrongdoings, God won't appreciate receiving an offering from that person.

◆ True or false: If someone deeply hurts your feelings or wrongs you and refuses to apologize, you will not like getting a gift from that person. Will you want to thank them politely for the gift? Why or why not? Can gifts replace sincere words of apology?

C Verse 66:4 indicates that God spoke, but no one responded. Rashi understands this to mean that no one said, "I heard."

◆ Explain how Rashi's interpretation attributes to God certain human traits, such as the desire to be taken seriously and listened to.

◆ Role-play the following related situation in two different ways: two people who know each other well (family members or friends) have a conversation in which one wants to tell the other about an important event. The first time, the listener should not speak at all. The second time, the listener should respond to all the speaker's sentences with, "I hear you."

◆ What do you learn from this role-play about human beings and about Rashi's view of God?

D Verse 66:19-20 indicates that the Israelites who remain in exile in distant lands will be brought by animals or chariots to Jerusalem as an offering to God.

According to Radak, just as a sacrifice to God is brought to the Temple in a pure vessel, so, too, the Israelites returning to Jerusalem will be attired in beautiful clean clothes and will be riding in wonderful new wagons.

◆ Does your synagogue have a dress code for Shabbat and holiday services? What are reasons for such a dress code? Does your family have expectations for your attire on those special days? Are the reasons the same? Are you in favor of such dress codes? Why or why not?

STRATEGIES
Analyzing the Text

1 Verse 66:1 says that God's throne is the heavens, and the earth is merely God's footstool.

◆ Explain how this verse teaches that God is transcendent: one should not expect to find God physically present in the Temple or on earth.

◆ Explain how this verse teaches that the Temple is merely a symbolic dwelling place for God.

◆ For advanced study, compare this verse with Jeremiah 3:16-17, I Kings 8:27, and Deuteronomy 4:36.

2 In verses 66:2-5 God contrasts two different types of people. One group is humble (translated as poor), shows great concern for following God's wishes, and trembles at God's word. The other group ignores God's words and engages in abominable behavior.

◆ Find the descriptions of each group in these verses.

◆ Draw pictures or cartoons of these two groups.

◆ If you draw those who scoff at God and ignore God, include their sarcastic words in verse 66:5: "Let *Adonai* be manifest so we may see your joy!"

3 Verses 66:7-14 contain a metaphor of Jerusalem or Zion giving birth to the rejuvenated nation, Israel.

◆ What is amazing about this birth? (It is without pain, a whole nation is born in one day.)

◆ What type of mother is Jerusalem? (She nurtures, consoles, delights in her offspring, plays with her children, comforts them, watches them grow and flourish.)

◆ Explain how this metaphor of a loving mother is also applied to God in verse 66:13.

◆ Do you find it unusual to think of God as a mother figure?

4 In verse 66:12 God uses a metaphor to describe peace. Prosperity will be like a river bringing with a flood the wealth of other nations.

◆ Describe a flooding river. Does the prosperity come quickly, dangerously, washing everything from upstream downstream?

5 In the distant future that Isaiah discusses, all peoples will worship the One God. In addition, serving in the Temple will not be limited just to Priests and Levites; even foreigners will serve in the Temple (verses 66:21-23).

◆ Explain which phrases in these verses describe all peoples worshiping God and serving in the Temple (this outlook is universalistic because it implies that God is the God of all).

◆ Is it surprising to you that non-Israelites would be able to serve in the Temple when previously this was limited to certain Israelites (those born to priestly or Levitical families)? Explain your answer.

◆ Make a banner welcoming all peoples to Jerusalem or to the new Temple.

Connecting the Text To the Special Shabbat

6 The most obvious connection between the Haftarah and the holiday of Rosh Chodesh is that the Haftarah mentions the New Moon (verse 66:23).

The New Moon occurs every 29 or 30 days without fail; it is regular, reliable, unchanging. The prophet seems to say in verse 23 that people will be like the New Moon: like clockwork, every Shabbat and New Moon, the people will come to worship God.

◆ Interview someone who attends services every Shabbat (for example, the president of your synagogue or the *Gabbai*). What is it like for him/her to attend services like clockwork? How does he/she benefit from it?

7 The New Moon is called in Hebrew a *nolad*, newborn. Similarly, in the Haftarah, a metaphor is used which describes the nation as a newborn (see verses 66:7-14, and Analyzing the Text #3, p. 357).

Why are the New Moon and the nation the same? The moon emerges from total darkness at the beginning of the month (is born), grows big, and arrives at full brightness at mid-month. Similarly, Israel was in exile and dark despair even after returning from exile. But Israel will one day, in the prophet's view of the future, be brought back to full brightness.

◆ What happened on the fifth day of the month of Iyar in the year 5708 that was a new birth? (The State of Israel was born — May 14, 1948.)

8 The prophet describes a universal worship of God in verses 66:21-23. On Rosh Chodesh, we recite *"Hallel"* (Psalms 113-118), which, in part, may be understood to include a universal outlook on the worship of God (see Analyzing the Text # 5, p. 357).

◆ Read, for example, Psalm 117:

"Praise *Adonai*, all you nations;
extol God, all you peoples,
for great is God's steadfast love toward us;
the faithfulness of *Adonai* endures forever.
Hallelujah."

◆ The message of the above Psalm is a universal one. Plan an interfaith service for Rosh Chodesh. Invite a class from a local church and/or mosque to share in the universal experience of a New Moon. Emphasize interfaith messages from Isaiah and Psalms.

Extending the Text

9 In some months, Rosh Chodesh is one day long, and in some months, it is two days long. It all depends on the length of the previous month.

In the Jewish calendar, a month is either 29 or 30 days long (just as the secular calendar has months that are either 30 or 31 days long). Rosh Chodesh is two days long when the month before has 30 days instead of just 29 days. The thirtieth day of the previous month is called the first day of Rosh Chodesh, although the first day of the new month is not until the next day.

The months of the Jewish calendar alternate between 29 and 30 days (with exceptions in some years). The general pattern looks like this:

Nisan	30
Iyar	29
Sivan	30
Tammuz	29
Av	30
Elul	29
Tishre	30
Cheshvan	29
Kislev	30
Tevet	29
Shevat	30
Adar	29

There are, however, many exceptions to this general pattern. One exception is the addition of an extra month of Adar II in leap years. Also, in some years, Cheshvan has 30 days or Kislev will have only 29 days. These adjustments of one day more or less are meant to help the holidays fall on the right days of the week.

◆ For more information on the calendar and exceptions, see *A Guide To Jewish Religious Practice* by Isaac Klein, pp. 257-260.

◆ Based on the above table, identify in which months we observe two days of Rosh Chodesh.

10 On Rosh Chodesh, we add an extra paragraph to the *"Amidah"* and to the *"Birkat HaMazon"* (Blessing after Meals).

◆ Consider this translation of the blessings which can be found in *Siddur Makor Hayyim:*

The Source of Life by Henry M. Shreibman, p. 57:

"Our God and God of our ancestors, may our prayers rise up, come and reach You, appear, be desired and heard by You. May our blessings and prayers be counted and remembered. Please remember us and our ancestors, the Messiah, the son of David, Your servant. Remember Jerusalem your sacred (special) city, all of Your people Israel before You. Remember us for survival, for good, for beauty, for kindness and caring, for life, for peacefulness, on this day of the New Moon. Remember us *Adonai*, our God for good, count us for a blessing, help us throughout our life. According to Your promise of help and caring, spare, favor, care for, and help us, for our eyes are directed toward You, because You are a kind, caring leader. May we see Your return to Jerusalem with caring. Blessed are You *Adonai,* Who returns Your spirit to Zion."

◆ Based on this translation, what are our hopes for the new month?

◆ Design a serving plate that illustrates the wishes expressed in the prayer.

◆ Make your own plate to use on Rosh Chodesh either at a paint-your-own pottery store or with a plate and marker kit.

11 Mishnah *Rosh HaShanah* 2:5-8 explains the ritual for receiving witnesses in Jerusalem who testified that they saw the sliver of the New Moon and the questions the witnesses would be asked:

There was a large courtyard in Jerusalem called Bet Yaazek, where all the witnesses used to gather and eat the tasty food that was prepared for them. The court questioned the witnesses in this same courtyard. The pair that came first was questioned first. The elder of the pair was questioned first:

"Tell us, in exactly what position did you see the moon? turned toward the sun? away from it? to the north? to the south? How high in the sky was it? Toward what point of the compass did it incline? How thick was the crescent?" Then, the younger witness of the pair was questioned. If the two accounts were the same, their evidence was considered accurate. After that, the other pairs were questioned, but only briefly, as their evidence was not really needed. In this way, they would not leave the courtyard disappointed, and would, therefore, return to testify again.

◆ What were these questions trying to verify?

◆ Describe the different ways that the witnesses were treated carefully so that they would be willing to come and testify in the future. Can we learn any lessons about how to treat people from this story?

◆ The next time there is a New Moon, come to class prepared to testify about it. Do the testimonies of all the students match?

12 Each New Moon is an opportunity to start over and shine brighter. The Haftarah's universalism reminds us to work with other people, and the Haftarah's transcendental idea of God reminds us it is up to us to do the work required on earth.

◆ Learn the Hebrew song *"Ani V'Atah"* (You and I) which translates into English as follows:

"You and I will change the world, then everyone will join us. It's been said before, it doesn't matter, you and I will change the world. You and I will try from the beginning — it will be difficult — but never mind . . . It doesn't matter, you and I will change the world."

The words and guitar chords may be found at the Teva Learning Center web site, www. tevacenter.org/home/voices. asp?page=song.

Or listen to the NFTY recording *The Time of Singing*, available from Transcontinental Music, 800-455-5223, www.eTranscom.com. The song is also on the recording *The Bridge* by Kol B'seder.

13 This Haftarah is the last chapter in the Book of Isaiah. *Makkot* 24a teaches that Isaiah reduced the commandments from Moses' 613 to six: honesty in dealing, sincerity in speech, refusal of illicit gain, absence of corruption, aversion for bloody deeds, and contempt for evil. Isaiah later reduced them to just two: keeping justice and doing righteousness (56:11).

◆ Compare these six commandments to the Ten Commandments. Are all ten included somehow in Isaiah's six? Are all ten in Isaiah's two?

◆ Make a crossword puzzle featuring lessons from the Ten Commandments or Isaiah's.

Personalizing the Text

14 Partaking of a festive meal is an appropriate way to observe Rosh Chodesh.

◆ Organize and hold your own festive meal for the New Moon. Based on the Haftarah's metaphor of Jerusalem and God as mothers, make this meal a Mother Appreciation Party. Be sure to include special foods, special prayers or speeches, decorations, and so on.

15 A silly ritual exists for the first day of April — April Fools Day.

◆ Invent a ritual to celebrate the first day of any month in the secular calendar.

16 The poet Marcia Falk, in *The Book of Blessings*, p. 360, wrote a service for the welcoming of the New Moon that includes the following Blessing of Children:

"[Insert name of child], be who you are — and may you be blessed in all that you are."

◆ Write a blessing for your parent(s).

17 One of the best known Jewish prayers is *"Avinu Malkaynu"* (Our Father Our King.) This Haftarah, however, describes God as a mother.

◆ Rewrite the *"Avinu Malkaynu"* prayer as "Our Mother Our Queen." Be creative with your imagery.

18 One of the chief merits of Isaiah's prophecies is their ability to console others.

◆ Collect Isaiah quotations from this and other Haftarot to include in consolation cards that your class can make and sell to raise money for *tzedakah*. You can find notable quotations in *Messengers of God: A Jewish Prophets Who's Who* by Ronald H. Isaacs, pp. 99-101.

19 As stated previously, verse 66:23 mentions the New Moon.

◆ For an entire Jewish month, chart the growth and diminution of the moon in the sky. Draw what you see and learn what the moon looks like on any given day of the month.

Other Resources

20 For more information and exercises on the *mitzvah* to sanctify the New Moon, see *Teaching Mitzvot* by Barbara Binder Kadden and Bruce Kadden, pp. 27-31.

21 For a Rosh Chodesh study guide, see *Moonbeams: A Hadassah Rosh Hodesh*

Guide, edited by Carol Diament, which contains a history of Rosh Chodesh observances, as well as study topics suited to each month of the Jewish calendar.

22 Read and discuss the article "This Month Is for You: Observing Rosh Chodesh as a Women's Holiday" by Arlene Agus in *The Jewish Woman*, edited by Elizabeth Koltun, pp. 84-93.

23 A *midrash* explains why the moon is smaller than the sun and why Jews use a calendar based on the moon. See the *midrash* in the Haftarah for *Machar Chodesh*, Connecting the Text To the Holiday #8, p. 74.

24 Discuss the portrayal of this Haftarah in *The Illustrated Torah* by Michal Meron, p. 225.

Involving the Family

25 Go on a special Rosh Chodesh outing. On the evening of the New Moon, take a telescope to a good spot for moon gazing, and check out the new sliver.

26 The New Moon is viewed as a newborn, bringing with it hopes for the future. Together as a family, look at the baby pictures of family members. Parents can tell stories that the kids may not have heard about their infancy and can relate their hopes and dreams for each child. If you don't already have an album of baby pictures, assemble one.

Bar/Bat Mitzvah Project

27 Every month represents a new start. For the year of your Bar/Bat Mitzvah, make one resolution each month. Keep a log of your resolutions and how they helped you.

OVERVIEW

Jeremiah was the son of a priestly family living in a town called Anathoth near Jerusalem. He was born around the year 640 B.C.E., the same year that King Josiah's reign over the Southern Kingdom of Judea began. When Jeremiah was about 12 or 13 years old, he was called by God to be a prophet (chapter 1); this was the year 627 B.C.E. It is thought that Jeremiah began his career as a prophet in 622 B.C.E., the same year in which a scroll was found in the Temple and read to King Josiah, who began to institute religious reforms based on that scroll.

Jeremiah supported the religious reforms and centralized worship of King Josiah, and was critical of Josiah's successors who abandoned the reforms. Religiously, Jeremiah preached loyalty to God and the pursuit of justice instead of the pursuit of idolatry and the abuse of the poor. Jeremiah had a grueling and thankless task. He spent his life lonely, unmarried, unhappy, and unpopular. He was unpopular not just for his religious preachings; he was also threatened and arrested for his political proclamations.

During King Josiah's reign, the political situation in the region shifted. Assyria, the previous superpower, lost influence to Babylonia, which had become the new superpower of the region. Egypt and Assyria joined forces against Babylonia, and Judah was caught in the middle. King Josiah became involved, and was mortally wounded in 609 B.C.E. Judah soon came under the control of King Nebuchadnezzar of Babylonia, who put one of Josiah's sons, Jehoiakim, on the throne. Jehoiakim swore allegiance to Nebuchadnezzar, but soon broke his allegiance, which led to the invasion and conquest of Jerusalem by Babylonia in 597 B.C.E. The Babylonians sent the leaders of Judah into exile in Babylonia (the first exile).

Zedekiah next assumed the throne and also swore allegiance to Babylonia, but he, too, soon joined an anti-Babylonian coalition with other nations. Finally, Babylonia crushed Jerusalem, destroyed the Temple, and exiled the king and the people in 586 B.C.E. For the few who remained, Nebuchadnezzar appointed an Israelite governor in Judah named Gedaliah, but the Israelites assassinated him as a traitor. The remaining Israelites fled to Egypt, forcing Jeremiah to go with them. It is presumed that Jeremiah died in Egypt.

As a prophet in these most difficult of times, Jeremiah preached peace and submission, while the leaders wanted only war and rebellion. Jeremiah dictated his prophecies to his personal scribe, Baruch, and had them read to King

Jehoiakim, who had the scrolls burned. Jeremiah had Baruch rewrite the prophecies, but both of them had to go into hiding from the king.

The Book of Jeremiah is filled with historical data and emotional confessions by the lonely and depressed prophet. Jeremiah wrote in both prose and poetry, and his words and thoughts are clear and concise. His images are graphic. Jeremiah loved his country, but he had the difficult job of preaching submission to their conquerors.

JEREMIAH 1:1-2:3
SHEMOT שמות Sephardim
MATOT מטות

This Haftarah has been paired with *Parashat Matot*, Numbers 30:2-32:42, and by Sephardim to *Shemot*, Exodus 1:1-6:1. See "Connecting the Text To the Sedra," pp. 367-369, for an exploration of the many ways the texts shed light on each other.

SYNOPSIS

This Haftarah records the young Jeremiah's call to prophecy. The son of the priest Hilkiah, Jeremiah receives his call in the thirteenth year of King Josiah of Judah at the end of the seventh century B.C.E. He continues to prophesy through the two Babylonian sieges on Jerusalem in 597 and 586 B.C.E., after which he is exiled to Egypt.

Adonai tells Jeremiah that he was selected to be a prophet even before he was born. Jeremiah, who is still a boy, does not think he is up to the task of bringing *Adonai*'s word to the world, but *Adonai* reassures him.

Jeremiah sees a vision of a branch from an almond tree, and is assured by God that God's word will come to pass. Jeremiah then envisions a steaming pot, which represents the devastation that will come from the north to the Kingdom of Judah. *Adonai* explains that the destruction is punishment for the Israelites' wickedness and rejection of God. Jeremiah also learns that his job will be very difficult. The people will attack him for his words, but the prophet will prevail, for *Adonai* will be with him.

The Haftarah concludes with a reminder that Jerusalem is loved as a bride by *Adonai*. Further-more, Israel is holy to God, and its enemies shall be punished.

INSIGHTS FROM THE TRADITION

A In verse 1:5 God says that even before Jeremiah was created in his mother's womb, *Adonai* had selected him as a prophet. Radak quotes Rambam, saying that no one can be a prophet without being properly prepared, from before birth to later training.

◆ Identify some professions for which skills must be developed from birth. For example, consider what type of early training (or indeed, innate gift) might be essential for these careers: musician, dancer, linguist, scientist, or gymnast.

◆ Do you know people who were sure of their future profession from an early age? Ask them how they prepared for their careers at various stages of their lives.

B Jeremiah says in verse 1:6 that he cannot speak to the people because he is "still a boy." Rashi explains that this means Jeremiah does not think he is worthy of chastising the people. Moses, for example, chastised the people only late in his life, after he had done many miracles for them. Jeremiah, on the other hand, is still young, and has not earned the peoples' esteem and respect.

◆ In your opinion, do adults take young people seriously or not?

♦ If young people are not taken seriously, it may be due to lack of respect. It frequently takes time to earn respect. Which of the following command respect in our society: earning a lot of money, doing heroic acts, professional achievements, age, good looks, athletic ability? Can you think of other qualities that command respect?

C Ibn Nachmiash comments on verse 1:17 that if Jeremiah strengthens himself, God will add to his strength. But if Jeremiah allows himself to be afraid and breaks down, God will add to his breakdown.

♦ Explain the old expression: God helps those who help themselves.

♦ Do you agree with this expression?

♦ Does this mean other people don't have to help someone in need because God will help that person?

♦ Debate: There is no need for government assistance programs, such as welfare or food stamps, because God will help those who help themselves.

D In verse 1:11 Jeremiah is asked what he sees, and he responds, "I see a branch of an almond tree." God responds, "You have seen right." Radak explains that what Jeremiah saw was a bare branch of an almond tree with no leaves or blossoms on it. It is very difficult to identify what type of tree a branch has come from if it has no leaves or blossoms.

♦ Has it ever happened to you that you meet someone in an unusual location and do not recognize him/her, although you would have recognized him/her in a familiar location?

♦ Have you ever failed to recognize someone because his/her appearance had changed (haircut, weight loss or gain, new beard or moustache, etc.)?

E Verse 2:2 speaks of the love of a bride and groom. According to Radak, this is like the love of Israel and God, and it refers to the giving of the Torah to Israel when Israel was like a bride and God was like the groom. The Torah was, therefore, like a wedding present.

♦ Discuss what makes something a good gift. Consider whether it is something he always wanted, whether it is something she never knew about, whether it is something the person would never buy for herself, whether it is practical, whether it is something to grow into. Add other qualities.

♦ What made (and still makes) the Torah a good gift?

STRATEGIES
Analyzing the Text

1 According to verse 1:1, Jeremiah is from the town of Anathoth. We learn from the Book of Anathoth Joshua (21:18) that Anathoth is a citygiven to Levites from the tribe of Benjamin. (See I Kings 2:26, in which the Priest Abiathar was exiled to Anathoth by Solomon for supporting Adonijah's campaign to be king.) We know, therefore, that Jeremiah was from a priestly family that lived in Anathoth, about three miles from Jerusalem. In addition, Jeremiah was first called to serve God in the thirteenth year of King Josiah (see verse 1:2), which we can date to 627 B.C.E., shortly before Josiah began his religious reforms. He served as a prophet during the reigns of several different kings.

Jeremiah was appointed by God to be a prophet to the nations in verse 1:5. This means that Jeremiah was a universal prophet, and not just a prophet for Israel.

♦ Based on this information, make a business card for Jeremiah, prophet to the nations.

2 Jeremiah felt inadequate to speak. God helped him by touching Jeremiah's mouth and putting God's words in his mouth (see verse 1:9). Jeremiah was not the only one to feel this way. Isaiah felt inadequate to speak as a prophet, and angels *(serafim)* touched a coal to Isaiah's mouth purifying it (see the Haftarah for *Yitro*, Analyzing the Text #5, pp. 232-233). Also, Moses complained to God that he was slow of speech and, therefore, could not talk to Pharaoh. Consequently, God told Moses to take Aaron along as his spokesperson (see Exodus 4:10-14).

◆ List the talents and characteristics you would most expect a prophet to have.

◆ What characteristics of prophets do these three stories about prophets seem to portray? Discuss how each prophet seems humble, concerned about the need to speak persuasively, receptive to assistance, and sensitive. How important do you think these particular characteristics are in a good prophet?

3 There is a word play in verses 1:11-12. The Hebrew for the almond tree that Jeremiah sees is שָׁקֵד *(shakayd)*. Then God says, "I am watchful to bring my word to pass." The Hebrew word שָׁקֵד also means to be watchful.

◆ What does it mean to you when God says, "I am watchful to bring my word to pass"?

◆ Draw a picture of an almond tree that also conveys a sense of watchfulness. When doing your drawing, remember that we learned in Insights from the Tradition #D, p. 365, that an almond tree has distinctive leaves and blossoms. You can research their distinctive features at search.gallery.yahoo.com/search/cobis?p=almond+tree&r=all.

4 There is a second word play involving the word שָׁקֵד *(shakayd)*. According to Rabbinic tradition, the almond tree has a quick ripening period from flower to ripe fruit. Therefore, the Rabbis also teach that שָׁקֵד means "quickly." Just as the fruit ripens quickly, so does God's word quickly come to pass.

◆ According to Radak, "God's word will come to pass quickly" means that God will bring punishment on Israel swiftly as God promised.

◆ What do you think God might have been feeling at this moment before inflicting punishment on Israel?

◆ Make up your own short story with symbols that use English word plays (for example, pear, pair, and pare, or a baseball bat, the animal bat, and batty behavior).

5 In verses 1:13-15 Jeremiah describes a steaming, bubbling pot. According to Radak, the pot symbolizes Jerusalem, and those putting it on the fire are the enemies from the North coming to destroy Jerusalem (i.e., Babylonians).

Alternatively, Hirsch suggests that a pot protects its contents and makes them feel secure. In the case of Judah and Jerusalem, they felt too secure in the pot, unaware of trouble about to descend on them from the North.

◆ Which interpretation of the parable of the steaming pot do you prefer, and why?

◆ Make a collage of torn paper depicting this image.

◆ Compare your depiction of the steaming pot with the illustration of this Haftarah in *The Illustrated Torah* by Michal Meron, p. 178.

6 In verse 1:17 God warns Jeremiah to be strong when doing what God has commanded him, and in verse 1:18 God promises to strengthen Jeremiah.

◆ What made what God asked Jeremiah to do so difficult?

7 In verse 2:3 Israel is described as holy, and as God's first fruit.

◆ Firstfruits cannot be eaten, but must be donated to God (Deuteronomy 26). In addition, "holy" is understood to mean separate or set aside. Read Leviticus 22:10-16 to learn about holy donations to God.

◆ Why might Jeremiah the priest be familiar with these laws?

◆ Explain the metaphor comparing eating and being devoured in war (verse 2:3).

Connecting the Text To the Sedra

8 This Haftarah is the first of three Haftarot read between 17 Tammuz and 9 Av (Tishah B'Av). The three are known by an Aramaic name *t'lat d'fur'anuta* (the three Haftarot of affliction). They discuss the punishment that was brought upon the people because they abandoned their Covenant with God. Two of the three Haftarot are from the prophet Jeremiah, who is also, according to tradition, the author of the Book of Lamentations, which is read on Tishah B'Av.

This Haftarah is typically read with Sedra *Matot*. However, *Matot* is often read on the same Shabbat as the next Sedra, *Mas'ay*. When the two are read together, this Haftarah is read one Shabbat earlier when Sedra *Pinchas* is read.

During the three weeks before Tishah B'Av, there are supposed to be no weddings or celebrations, and one is not to get a haircut — just as if in mourning.

◆ Review the warnings of punishment in this Haftarah.

◆ Choose a national tragedy you want to commemorate (the bombing of Pearl Harbor; the Oklahoma City bombing; the killings at Columbine High School in Littleton, Colorado; the assassination of President Kennedy; the September 11, 2001 terrorist attacks; etc.). Outline the observances you believe would be appropriate for an annual week of mourning. What activities would you include or prohibit?

9 In verse 1:11 Jeremiah sees a branch of an almond tree.

◆ The word for branch is often translated as "rod." How is a rod a symbol of punishment?

◆ Explain the expression "Spare the rod and spoil the child." Do you agree with this philosophy of child rearing? Why or why not?

◆ The destruction of the Temple and Jerusalem has been explained as a punishment for the Israelites' wrongdoings. As an experiment, take a tree twig and beat it on a tree or rock as if punishing the rock. What happens to the leaves? If a branch is bare, might it mean that it was already used for punishment?

10 Several times, the Haftarah repeats the phrase, "the word of *Adonai* came to me": ויהי דבר יי אלי לאמר, (*Vayehe d'var Adonai aylie laymore*).

The Torah reading from *Matot* begins with the phrase, "This is the thing that *Adonai* commanded: זה הדבר אשר צוה יי (*Zeh hadavar asher tzivah Adonai*).

◆ When Moses or Jeremiah (or any prophet) starts a statement by saying, "These are the words *Adonai* told me," they are invoking God's authority to support their statement. Explain how this is so.

◆ Explain how authority is being invoked in the familiar statement, "Because I'm your mother/father and I say so."

◆ If you are baby-sitting and need to convince a young child to go to bed, how might you verbally assert your authority?

◆ Scramble the Hebrew words that Jeremiah uses that mean "The word of *Adonai* came to me." Ask your classmates to unscramble them and memorize them.

11 In the Haftarah (verse 1:12), God says, "I am watchful to bring my word to pass." God's word is like a vow, and God will see to it that the vow will come to be.

The Torah reading teaches cases in which people make vows and must keep them (unless there are special circumstances).

◆ Review how both these texts remind us of the importance of keeping one's word.

◆ If God would vow to punish Israel and then not punish Israel when punishment is deserved, would this constitute an empty threat?

◆ Why might God feel torn about punishing Israel? Why do you think God appointed Jeremiah to be a prophet at this moment?

◆ Have your parents ever threatened a punishment they could not (or did not) carry through? What stopped them?

12 Moses is told by God to avenge the children of Israel for the harm done to them by Midian in Numbers 31:2. In the Haftarah (verse 2:3), God promises that evil will come to all who hurt (devour) Israel.

◆ Design a battle shield for God, Who avenges Israel on her enemies.

13 In Sedra *Matot*, Numbers 32:17, the Torah mentions fortified cities. In the Haftarah Jeremiah is told that he will be a fortified city (verse 1:18).

◆ Go to the beach (or sandbox) and build a sand castle with moat, bridges, and fortification walls for defense.

◆ Alternatively, make a fortified city of clay.

14 According to Sephardic custom, Jeremiah 1:1-2:3 is the Haftarah for *Shemot*. God's call to prophesy in the Haftarah is met with the same kind of hesitation by Jeremiah as was God's call to prophesy to Moses in *Shemot*. Compare Jeremiah's response in verse 1:6 to Moses' response in Exodus 3:11-14, 4:1, 4:10, and 4:13.

◆ Based on the text and what you know about the kind of work God had in store for them, why do you think Jeremiah and Moses are so reluctant to accept their call to prophesy? Write a journal entry for either prophet that records his reaction to God's call.

◆ In the *Etz Hayim Chumash* (p. 347), Michael Fishbane observes, "The prophets, who sense the enormity of their task and their personal inadequacy, are strengthened by divine reassurances as they set out to confront the resistance of others." How does God alleviate the fears of Moses and of Jeremiah (see Jeremiah 1:7-10 and Exodus 3:13-22, 4:2-9, and 4:11-12, and 4:13-17)?

◆ View and discuss scenes in the film *Oh, God!* (1977, rated PG, 104 minutes) when God, in the person of George Burns, recruits John Denver as God's herald in God's plan to save the world. Denver, at first skeptical, keeps faith and is rewarded.

15 The Israelites seem to be in an opposite position in the Haftarah from their position in the Sedra. In the Sedra the Israelites are outside of the Land of Israel about to enter it. In the Haftarah they are in the Land about to be attacked and exiled. In the Sedra they are hopeful that they will do well in the Land of Israel, but there is some doubt because the generation before them was repeatedly disloyal to God following the Exodus (see, for example, Numbers 11, 13-14, 16-17, 20, 21). In the Haftarah God is going to bring punishment on Israel, but there is hope they will ultimately be avenged (see verse 2:3).

When we read this Sedra and Haftarah just before Tishah B'Av, we must wonder whether we have been loyal to God.

◆ For a week, read the *Jerusalem Post* or the Israeli daily newspaper *Ha'aretz* (in English) online. Make a list of the main issues facing the international Jewish community. Then, for a month, read your local community's Jewish newspaper. Make a list of the main issues in your community. How do you think your local community and the international Jewish community are doing in terms of maintaining loyalty to God? Explain your conclusions.

16 According to Hertz, the final verses of the Haftarah poetically recall the wanderings in the wilderness, and thus form another link with the Sedra.

Extending the Text

17 Jeremiah 1:1 says that Jeremiah was the son of Hilkiah, one of the priests in the town of Anathoth in the territory of the tribe of Benjamin.

Alternatively, *Megillah* 14b suggests *midrashically* that Jeremiah was descended from Joshua. There is, however, no biblical support for this tradition, according to which Joshua married Rahab (see the Haftarah for *Shelach Lecha*, p. 6) after she converted, and they had descendants who were both priests and prophets. Jeremiah was one such descendant. The others were: Neriah,

Baruch, Serayah, Mahseyah, Hilkiah, Hanamel, Shallum, and Hulda.

◆ Dress in costume and come to a Joshua-Rahab family reunion. (Remember that many of the descendants were both priests and prophets.) Have a sign-in board, take family photos, and deliver speeches in tribute to your ancient ancestors.

18 Verse 1:3 mentions that Jeremiah prophesied until the fifth month. This was Av, when the Temple was destroyed on the ninth day. There is another holiday in Av that contrasts greatly with the tragedy of Tishah B'Av. That holiday is Tu B'Av, the 15th of Av. About this day *Ta'anit* 30b says:

"There never were in Israel greater days of joy than the fifteenth of Av and the Day of Atonement. I can understand the Day of Atonement because it is a day of forgiveness and pardon and on it the second set of Tablets of the Law were given, but what happened on the fifteenth of Av?"

◆ Discuss why the Rabbis considered Yom Kippur to be a day of great joy. Is this how you think of Yom Kippur?

◆ According to tradition, on Tu B'Av (a night of a full moon), girls would go out to the fields and vineyards to dance and to meet boys. Naturally, they would want to look their best, but *Ta'anit* 31a describes what they did instead:

"The daughter of the king borrows garments from the daughter of the High Priest, the daughter of the High Priest from the daughter of the deputy High Priest, and the daughter of the deputy High Priest from the daughter of the army chaplain, and the daughter of the army chaplain from the daughter of an ordinary priest, and all Israel borrow from one another, so as not to put to shame any one who may not possess suitable garments."

◆ Why, according to this passage, was Tu B'Av a day of great joy?

◆ Explain the purpose of borrowing garments from each other. What lesson is taught by this custom? When you go to a school mixer or dance, is it a joyous occasion for you? How much effort do you put into your appearance for such an event?

◆ Plan a hike and picnic for Tu B'Av.

19 According to Insights from the Tradition #B, p. 364, Jeremiah doubted whether people would take him seriously because of his youth. The following story is told by Abraham J. Twerski in *From Bondage To Freedom: The Passover Hagaddah*, pp. 102-3:

Rabbi Heschel of Cracow was a child prodigy, and when a community interviewed candidates for a Rabbinic position, he applied, brilliantly outperforming older scholars. The community leaders told him that while he was more learned than the other candidates, he could not expect the community to hire an 11-year-old boy as their Rabbi.

Rabbi Heschel responded, "Why not? Every person has some defect. I am the only one who can guarantee to improve upon his defect every single day."

◆ How is age in this case a "defect"?

◆ How is age in the case of Jeremiah a "defect"?

◆ Do you ever feel your own age is some kind of "defect"? Explain your answer.

◆ What is ageism?

◆ Invite someone from the American Association of Retired People (AARP) to speak to the class about ageism.

20 According to verse 1:5, Jeremiah was selected as a prophet while still in the womb.

◆ Do you think this means Jeremiah had no free choice over how to spend his life?

◆ *Pirke Avot* 3:15 teaches, "All is foreseen, yet the right of free choice is granted." Explain the apparent contradiction in this statement. How would you resolve it? How does it apply to Jeremiah's situation?

◆ Debate whether "all is foreseen" or "free choice is granted."

21 The name Jeremiah is spelled: ירמיה. It is unclear what this name means, but there are theories. One suggestion is that it is related to an ancient Semitic phrase meaning "whose womb is loosened." If so, then his name means "*Adonai* loosened (the womb)."

Another theory is that it is from the verb "to throw," and means that "*Adonai* hurls."

It may also come from the verb "to raise up" and means "*Adonai* is exalted."

◆ Reread verse 1:5 and discuss the appropriateness of each possible definition of Jeremiah's name in regard to his history.

◆ Make an acrostic of Jeremiah's name, using each letter to begin a word you think describes the prophet.

22 Jeremiah depicts the relationship between Israel and God in terms of marital love. Rabbinic tradition has expanded the metaphor. For example, when Israel was freed by God and taken out of Egypt, it was the beginning of their engagement period. Our Passover holiday, therefore, celebrates the engagement of Israel and God. The wedding is said to have taken place on the next holiday, Shavuot, when God gave the Torah to Israel. The Torah is often described as a wedding present God gave Israel. The third major holiday, Sukkot, is also tied into this metaphor. Sukkot can be described as the occasion on which the newlyweds, God and Israel, set up their home.

◆ For more information on this metaphor, see *The Jewish Holidays: A Guide and Commentary* by Michael Strassfeld, p. 75.

◆ Make a mural representing the three holidays and the three stages of development of the relationship of God and Israel.

23 Jeremiah says in verse 1:6 that he is too young to be a prophet. God tells him in the next verse not to worry — all the words he is going to have to say will be God's words and not Jeremiah's own.

◆ According to Rabbinic teachings, the prophets used their own creativity and emotions to find the way to express God's message. Does this mean the prophets' statements were God's words or the prophets' words?

◆ In the film *Oh, God! Book 2* (1980, rated PG, 94 minutes), God asks Tracy, an elementary school student, to write an ad slogan for God in her own words. God thought that her words would be better at convincing other kids to believe in God than an adult's words. Tracy came up with the slogan "THINK GOD."

◆ Explain why Tracy's slogan is clever.

◆ Write your own slogan for God.

◆ Discuss whether it is easier to say someone else's words than to present your own (for example, is it easier to read a Haftarah or to give your Bar/Bat Mitzvah speech?).

Personalizing the Text

24 Verse 1:1 says that these are "the words of Jeremiah." Radak explains that the

book includes not just what Jeremiah said, but also what happened to him as a result of his prophecies.

◆ The Sedra and Haftarah are the words of your Bar/Bat Mitzvah. Choose one verse from either text and write a speech about how your life has been affected by the meaning of the verse.

25 *Megillah* 14b suggests that Jeremiah was descended from Joshua.

◆ Using Extending the Text #17, p. 369, as a basis, choose a biblical character whom you wish had been one of your direct ancestors. Write an essay explaining why you chose that person.

26 We see in Analyzing the Text #2, p. 366, that one of the important qualities of a prophet is sensitivity. Jeremiah was sensitive to everything around him. He saw important, holy messages in the most ordinary objects (such as an almond branch or a boiling pot).

Additionally, Jeremiah's sensitivity may have helped make him a great prophet, but it also may have caused him to be terribly hurt by people who rejected his messages. God promised to make him strong and fortified (verse 1:18-19).

◆ Bring to class an ordinary object that for you is somehow holy. Tell the class why it is holy to you.

◆ Have you ever had to do or say something that was scary or unpleasant? Did someone else give you courage before you did it?

27 God instructs Jeremiah in verse 1:10 to uproot, pull down, destroy, and over-throw, and then to build and to plant.

◆ What do the first four verbs all have in common?

◆ What do the last two verbs have in common?

◆ Give examples of occasions (natural, man-made, psychological, or other) on which something must first be destroyed or ended before a new start may be made.

◆ Interview family members and friends for examples in their lives of times when they first had to end something before they could build something better.

28 There is a saying in *The Book of Ahikar* 2:7: "Do not be in a hurry, like the almond tree, first to blossom and last to ripen. Rather be like the mulberry tree, which is last to blossom and first to ripen."

◆ Explain the reasoning behind this statement. Why do you think the author says the mulberry is better?

◆ Do you agree with the author? Which type of tree are you most like, and why?

29 Jeremiah was destined to grow up to be a prophet. His job involved many difficulties (for example, being ignored by the people and being threatened by the people and the king). His job also provided great satisfaction (for example, he helped guide his people through a terrible time in their history).

◆ What do you want to do when you are an adult?

◆ Interview adults in various professions about what is most rewarding and most difficult about their job. Do any of their responses surprise you?

30 The song *"Ko Amar HaShem: Matza Chayn Bamidbar"* (Thus Said God: The People Found Favor in the Desert) is from Jeremiah 31:1. It refers to the love of God for Israel when Israel was in the desert. Similarly, verse 2:2 speaks of the love between Israel and God in the desert.

◆ Learn and sing this song, which may be found in *B'Kol Echad*, edited by Jeffrey Shiovitz, pp. 87-88, and on the accompanying audiocassettes, *Shirei B'Kol Echad,* both of which may be ordered from the web site of United Synagogue for Conservative Judaism, www.uscj.org/booksvc.

Other Resources

31 For more on the prophet Jeremiah, including history, themes, and notable quotations, read *Messengers of God: A Jewish Prophets Who's Who* by Ronald H. Isaacs, pp. 102-120.

32 Complete p. 22 in *Prophets Copy Pak™* by Marji Gold-Vukson.

33 For additional information on the prophet Jeremiah, as well as on the writing of the Book of Jeremiah, see *Encyclopaedia Judaica*, vol. 9, pp. 1345-1361.

34 Discuss the illustration of this Haftarah in *The Illustrated Torah* by Michal Meron, p. 64.

35 See Rembrandt's painting of Jeremiah lamenting over Jerusalem at www.archive.com. Try painting your own portrait of Jeremiah.

36 For additional information on the almond tree and other vegetation growing in the Land of Israel, see *Encyclopaedia Judaica*, vol. 2, pp. 665-666 (almond, including pictures of blossoms); vol. 13, pp. 614ff (plants in the Land of Israel); and vol. 9, pp. 225-236

(Israel, fauna). Make a poster illustrating Israel's plants.

37 For additional information on the observance of Tishah B'Av and the three weeks preceding it, see *The Jewish Holidays: A Guide and Commentary* by Michael Strassfeld, pp. 85-94, and *A Guide To Jewish Religious Practice* by Isaac Klein, pp. 246-251.

38 Read about the role of the prophet in *Love and Joy* by Yohanan Muffs, pp. 27-31.

Involving the Family

39 Organize a family testimonial dinner at which every family member will pay tribute to one ancestor (see Extending the Text #17, p. 369).

40 Plant an almond tree in your yard to commemorate your Bar or Bat Mitzvah.

Bar/Bat Mitzvah Project

41 Support the March of Dimes to help fight birth defects and care for fetuses in their mothers' wombs (see Insights from the Tradition #A, p. 364).

JEREMIAH 2:4-28; 3:4 Ashkenazim
JEREMIAH 2:4-28; 4:1-2 Sephardim
MAS'AY מסעי

This Haftarah has been paired with *Parashat Mas'ay*, Numbers 33:1-36:13. See "Connecting the Text To the Sedra," pp. 377-378, for an exploration of the many ways the two texts shed light on each other.

SYNOPSIS

Jeremiah was called to prophesy in the thirteenth year of the reign of King Josiah of Judah in 627 B.C.E., and he prophesied until after the destruction of the Temple in 586 B.C.E. It is unclear at what point the prophecy in this Haftarah was delivered, but scholars believe it was between the years 622, when Josiah began his religious reform, and 616, when Assyria and Egypt became allies.

In a brief history of Israel's infidelity to *Adonai*, Jeremiah recalls the people's complaints in the wilderness after the redemption from Egypt. He remembers that the Israelites defiled the Land of Israel and that the priests, teachers, rulers, and prophets repeatedly rebelled.

Jeremiah sadly notes that even the idol worshipers of the other nations have been more loyal to their so-called gods than Israel has been to *Adonai*. Israel, on the other hand, has continuously betrayed the one real God for any number of false ones.

Israel is so deeply stained with sin that it no longer resembles the noble nation God established. It has been and will continue to be punished for running after every temptation. Jeremiah challenges Israel to call upon its idols of stone and wood to help them weather the storm of *Adonai*'s wrath.

It was Rabbinic custom to avoid ending Haftarot on a negative note. Consequently, the Sephardic version ends with a reminder that God is always willing to forgive a repentant people, and the Ashkenazic version concludes with a reassuring image of God as a loving Father.

INSIGHTS FROM THE TRADITION

A God complains in verse 2:8 that "the guardians of the Teaching (Torah) ignored Me." Radak understands from this verse that the sages who learned Torah did not learn it in order to know God and to keep the Torah's precepts willingly. Rather, they learned it with their lips but not their hearts.

◆ What is meant by the term "lip service"?

◆ Explain how Radak's interpretation means one should not just learn Torah and do lip service to Torah, but really live by Torah.

◆ Consider modern examples of people just doing lip service: there are people who say they are in favor of protecting our environment, and yet they unnecessarily drive sport utility vehicles, which are gas guzzlers and sources of pollution. How is this an example of giving lip service to an idea? Can you give other examples?

B According to verse 2:19, "Let your misfortune reprove you." In other words, once you have erred and been punished, at least learn from the punishment not to err in that way again. Kara teaches that this is how most people learn — only after they have been punished do they correct their ways. However, he suggests that truly wise people can change their behavior even without being punished.

◆ Do you tend to learn only after you get hurt from your mistakes, or do you also learn from warnings beforehand?

◆ Debate: People who learn from warnings beforehand do not take enough risks in life.

C In verse 2:22 Jeremiah describes wrongful behavior as a stain that, if it becomes completely ingrained, cannot be removed, even with soap or bleach. The *Zohar* comments that if a person sins once before God, there is just a mark. If a person sins a second time, the mark becomes more intense. If a person sins a third time, the stain spreads. Similarly, it is taught in *Sifre* that "Sin at its beginning is as thin as a spider's web, and at the end as thick as a rope."

◆ What do these images of sin suggest to you?

◆ Consider the example of lying: a person may begin lying with some fear and difficulty. Yet, if not caught, that person may continue to lie as it becomes easier and easier to do. Can you suggest other examples of bad behavior that become easier with "practice"?

D Verse 2:22 also informs the Israelites that their guilt is before God. What does it mean that one's guilt is before God? According to the *Zohar*, if someone sins, the sin goes up to Heaven and presents itself before God. The sin introduces itself to God as having been committed by that specific person. The sin then stands before God watching for an opportunity to do harm to the committer of the sin.

◆ Explain the expression, "It will come back to haunt you."

◆ Do you believe that your actions can come back to haunt you? Give examples.

E Why do the Israelites love the strangers in verse 2:25? According to Radak, they see strangers prospering, so they hope also to prosper by imitating their neighbors and loving and following them.

◆ Why does the grass always seem greener on the other side of the fence? What does this expression mean?

◆ Do you think the grass truly is greener on the other side? What do you think makes some people long to be on the other side of the fence and other people content to stay on their own side?

F In verse 2:25, the response given by Israel is, "It is no use."

◆ What is no use? According to Kara, some people despair of ever rectifying their sins. Why might this be?

◆ Imagine you have a friend who is deeply involved in destructive behavior (for example, lying, drugs, eating disorder, etc.). What advice would you give to your friend if he/she wanted to begin the process of stopping the behavior, but felt overwhelmed by the challenge?

STRATEGIES
Analyzing the Text

1 Verse 2:7 refers to a country of farmland. The word in Hebrew — כרמל *(Carmel)* — is an abbreviation of the words כרם אל *(kerem el)*, which mean "vineyard of God." "*El*" is a form of God's name that is often a part of people's names, such as Michael and Gabriel.

◆ Does your name contain God's name in it? Consult a name dictionary to be sure.

◆ Learn where the Carmel is in Israel and why it got its name. Serve wine from Israel's Carmel Mountain region on *Erev* Shabbat (this is not the same thing as the Carmel brand of wine).

2 A metaphor involving water is used in verse 2:13 to describe God. God and God's Torah are compared to a fount of living waters (sometimes translated as a spring of water). Israel is chastised for having abandoned a plentiful, never ceasing source of fresh, available, life-giving water in exchange for a system of broken cisterns. Cisterns are large storage devices dug in order to gather and hold rainwater — and Israel's cisterns leak.

◆ Explain the metaphor: why are idols like broken cisterns?

◆ Jeremiah also uses this metaphor in the Haftarah for *Bechukotai* (see verses 17:7-8). For a similar image, see Psalm 1:3. Notice that this metaphor draws on images in nature. How many other images from nature did Jeremiah use in this Haftarah? Explain how seeing meaningful messages in nature and in ordinary objects may be an important prophetic teaching talent.

◆ Be a prophet: learn and teach a valuable life lesson from an ordinary object, creature, or phenomenon of nature.

3 Jeremiah introduces another metaphor in verses 2:14-19. Israel is compared to a homeless slave searching among ferocious lions for a place to live. The lions represent foreign nations with whom Israel has formed alliances rather than trusting in God.

◆ Explain this metaphor: why are foreign nations like powerful lions?

◆ Notice that in verse 2:18, the metaphor of the slave searching for help in foreign nations merges with the previous metaphor describing God as living water. What will happen to them when they go to Egypt or Assyria for water instead of to God? Illustrate one of these images.

4 Jeremiah says in verse 2:13 that the people have done two wrongs. In verses 2:13-19 he identifies those wrongs.

◆ Identify both in the text. (Answers: idolatry and forming alliances with foreigners.)

◆ Today, people still put their trust in the wrong things and the wrong allies. Can you give examples?

◆ Create your own metaphor, either poetically or artistically, for one of these two wrongs.

5 Idolatrous Israel is compared to a thief caught in the act (verse 2:26).

◆ Israel was not stealing. What sin were the people committing?

◆ How does a thief feel when caught — embarrassed, frustrated, ashamed, chagrined, not chagrined, angry, resentful, other? How does Israel feel?

6 God speaks very sarcastically in verses 2:27-28.

◆ Identify the sarcasm. (Answer: Let the idols come and save them, their idols are as numerous as their towns.)

◆ Put on a skit in which sarcasm is used.

Connecting the Text To the Sedra

7 This Haftarah is the second of three Haftarot that precede Tishah B'Av (see also the Haftarah for *Matot*, p. 364, and for *Devarim*, p. 220). The Haftarah, like the holiday, contains a grim message.

The addition of text from another chapter of Jeremiah enables the Haftarah to end on a positive note. However, various Jewish communities differ regarding which verse (or verses) to add. Ashkenazim add verse 3:4, but Sephardim add verses 4:1-2 instead of verse 3:4.

◆ Compare verses 3:4 and 4:1-2.

◆ Explain how both offer hope. Which ending do you prefer?

8 Jeremiah is said to have been an eyewitness to the destruction of Jerusalem and burning of the Temple, which occurred on Tishah B'Av. According to Rabbinic tradition, Jeremiah was also the author of the Book of Lamentations, which we read on Tishah B'Av.

◆ "Jeremiad" is an English word. What do you think it means? Check your definition against the definition in a dictionary.

◆ Read selections from the Book of Lamentations.

◆ Write your own lament for a national disaster.

9 Verse 2:6 of the Haftarah mentions the wanderings in the desert after leaving Egypt. This parallels the Sedra, where in Numbers 33 a detailed description is given of the wanderings of Israel in the desert after leaving Egypt. In a further parallel, Tishah B'Av commemorates the destruction of the First Temple, Jerusalem, and the Judean kingdom, resulting in Israel's wandering in the desert toward a Babylonian exile.

Jews, unfortunately, have vast experience with homelessness.

◆ Compile a history of your family for the last 100 years and review how many times your family has had to move, especially moves from one country to another.

◆ Run an event to support a local shelter for homeless people. (For example, collect money, toiletries, clothing, or children's toys, or sponsor a walk-a-thon or read-a-thon to raise money for the cause.)

10 Numbers 33:50-56 in the Sedra warns that if the Israelites follow the ways of the people in Canaan, God will punish them. Similarly, the entire Haftarah seems to warn Israel not to run wild after foreign nations, other sources of water, and other gods.

◆ What is assimilation?

◆ In what ways has assimilation helped Jews in North America? In what ways has assimilation hurt Jews in North America?

11 In verse 2:25 of the Haftarah, Jeremiah warns the people about being without shoes. To Jeremiah, being barefoot symbolized running wild after idols. To Rashi, it was also a warning that they would be punished by being forced to march barefoot into exile. On Tishah B'Av, it is our tradition not to wear comfortable leather shoes. You may see people wearing canvas sneakers or sandals made from man-made materials. This tradition applies to Yom Kippur as well. The prohibition from wearing leather does not apply to all clothing (such as belts, *kipot*, jackets), but specifically to shoes. By not wearing leather shoes, we increase our discomfort on these two fast days and hopefully reflect a little harder on our behavior and our future.

◆ Shoes are valuable commodities, and during World War II they were taken from Jewish concentration camp prisoners and stored. At the peak of the killings at Auschwitz, as many as 25,000 pairs of shoes were taken from prisoners each day. Go to the web site http://remember.org/jacobs/ShoeHeap.html to see photos of a mountain of shoes taken from prisoners at Auschwitz.

Extending the Text

12 We learned in Insights from the Tradition #F, p. 375, that the Israelites seem to feel that it is too late to return to God because they have been sinning so much and for so long. Rabbi Tarfon taught in *Pirke Avot* 2:16, "It is not your obligation to complete the task, but neither are you free to desist from it."

◆ What do you think is the lesson of Rabbi Tarfon's words?

◆ Do you think that a little repentance is better than none at all, or do you think that if you can't do something all the way, then why bother?

◆ Design a daily reminder of this lesson for yourself. Jeremiah often taught lessons using everyday objects (see Analyzing the Text #2, p. 376). Try to use an ordinary object as your reminder. Explain to the class how your reminder will work.

13 God states in verse 2:19 that "awe for Me is not in you." The Hebrew word translated as "awe," however, is usually translated as "fear."

God seems to be saying in this verse that the Israelites do not have enough fear/awe of God to control their behavior and act according to God's laws.

◆ Look up the definition of "awe" in a dictionary. What is the relationship between fear and awe?

◆ Which translation of the verse do you prefer?

◆ According to *Berachot* 33b, "Everything is in the hands of heaven except the fear of heaven." What do you think is the fear of heaven? Explain the paradox. Make an abstract painting of either fear or awe.

14 The Haftarah suggests that Israel's troubles were due to sins committed by Israel.

◆ Do you believe that ancient Israel's troubles were really due to its sins?

◆ For a discussion of why the troubles were not due to Israel's sins, see *The Haftarah Commentary* by W. Gunther Plaut, p. 425.

15 Jeremiah describes Israel as a thief in verse 2:26. Jewish law makes a distinction between the thief and the robber. A thief is defined as one who steals during the night when no one is able to see his actions, whereas a robber steals during the day when someone might see what he has done. The thief has to pay a fine equal to the full value of the goods (in addition to returning the stolen goods). In contrast, the robber has to return the stolen goods and pay a fine of only 20 percent of the value of the stolen goods.

The explanation given for the difference in punishment is that the thief steals at night, obviously out of fear that people will catch him and stop him. While he fears other people, he apparently has no fear of God. The robber, on the other hand, seems to fear neither God nor humans.

◆ Is Jeremiah's Israel better described as a thief or as a robber (see verse 2:26)? Defend your answer.

16 The following quotations concern thieves.

• Not to teach your child a trade is like teaching him or her to steal. (*Kiddushin* 29a)

• To rob a friend even of a penny is like taking his life. (*Baba Kamma* 119a)

• He who shares with a thief is his own enemy. (Proverbs 29:24)

• If you steal from a thief, you also taste of thieving. (*Berachot* 5b)

• When courage fails a thief, [the thief] becomes virtuous. (*Sanhedrin* 22a)

◆ Read and discuss these quotations.

◆ What encourages a thief most? Hunger? Envy? Extravagant life style? Laziness? Those who buy stolen goods? (*Leviticus Rabbah* 6:2).

17 After the fall of Jerusalem on Tishah B'Av, the Babylonian officers offered to take Jeremiah to Babylonia and treat him well there, but he refused to leave Judah (chapter 40). Although Jeremiah wanted to stay in Judah, he was taken, against his will, to Egypt by those Israelites who fled from their Babylonian conquerors (chapters 42-43). According to tradition, the Babylonian king ordered his general to treat Jeremiah with consideration and kindness, but the prophet chose to share the hardships inflicted on his people (see *Legends of the Jews* by Louis Ginzberg, vol. 4, pp. 310-311).

◆ What lesson can leaders (and all of us) learn from Jeremiah's choice to stay in Judah instead of going to Babylonia? What lesson can leaders (and all of us) learn from Jere-miah's choice to be treated no differently from the rest of his people? Do you think you would have made the same choice?

◆ Imagine you are Jeremiah faced with the choice between special treatment or sharing the fate of your people. Make a list of pros and cons for each choice.

◆ Research the story of Dr. Janusz Korczak, the teacher in Warsaw during the Holocaust who chose to go to Treblinka with his orphan students. Would you have made the same choice? Why or why not?

◆ Read *A Voice for the Child*, edited by Sandra Joseph, a collection of writings by Janusz Korczak.

Personalizing the Text

18 In verse 2:27 Israel says to wood and stone, "You are my father" and "You gave birth to me."

◆ Reread the delightful children's book *Are You My Mother?* by P.D. Eastman. Write a parody of this book involving adult Israelites who cannot tell the difference between wood, stone, and *Adonai*.

19 Radak asserted that the Israelites saw strangers prospering, and imitated them (see Insights from the Tradition #E, p. 375).

◆ Interview your family members about times they did something because things appeared to be greener on the other side of the fence. What were the end results?

20 In Insights from the Tradition #D, p. 375, a *midrash* was presented that suggests that your sins go to heaven and introduce themselves to God, then wait to come back to haunt you.

◆ Write and act out a skit in which a character's actions come back to haunt him/her. Alternatively, enact a skit based on the scene in the *Zohar* in which the sin presents itself to God in heaven.

21 Jeremiah indicts the leaders of Israel — priests, teachers, rulers, and prophets — for repeatedly rebelling against God and leading the people astray (verse 2:8).

◆ Leaders are supposed to be role models. Write and deliver a short speech about a teacher or other positive role model and how they have influenced your life.

22 Stains become ingrained in fabric, just as sins become ingrained in us.

◆ Try tie-dying a white shirt red, then see if you can return the shirt to its original whiteness with bleach. Like Jeremiah, learn a life lesson from this experiment.

Other Resources

24 View and discuss a film version of Charles Dickens' classic book *A Christmas Carol* (one version was made in 1951, not rated, 86 minutes), in which a man's actions come back to haunt him (based on Insights from the Tradition #D, p. 375).

24 View and discuss the film *Defending Your Life*, (1991, rated PG, 112 minutes), in which a man dies and must defend his actions in life.

25 For more on the prophet Jeremiah, including history, themes, and notable quotations, read *Messengers of God: A Jewish Prophets Who's Who* by Ronald H. Isaacs, pp. 102-120.

26 See Rembrandt's painting of Jeremiah lamenting over Jerusalem at www.archive.com. Try painting your own portrait of Jeremiah.

27 Discuss the illustrations of this Haftarah in *The Illustrated Torah* by Michal Meron, p. 182.

28 For additional information on the prophet Jeremiah as well as the Book of Jeremiah, see *Encyclopaedia Judaica*, vol. 9, pp. 1345-1361.

29 Jeremiah learns important lessons from nature. For more such lessons, read *Just So Stories* by Rudyard Kipling.

30 For additional information on the observance of Tishah B'Av and the three weeks preceding it, see *The Jewish Holidays: A Guide and Commentary* by Michael Strassfeld, pp. 85-94, and *A Guide To Jewish Religious Practice* by Isaac Klein, pp. 246-251. For Haftarah commentary, discussion questions, and project, see the UAHC Family Shabbat Table Talk web site at www.uahc.org/Shabbat/stt/3mm.shtml.

Involving the Family

31 Make your Jewish education more than lip service (see Insights from the Tradition #A, p. 374). Each month incorporate one lesson from Hebrew school into your family's life.

32 Everyone makes resolutions to improve behavior, but few people actually manage to stick to such resolutions. As a family, help and encourage each other to keep resolutions that would improve your behavior, your health, and your lives. Ask each family member to make one resolution. Then, as a family, identify little steps to take to accomplish the resolution, and make a commitment to help get each person going on their new course. At a family meeting once a week, check on the progress being made and support offered.

Bar/Bat Mitzvah Project

33 See Connecting the Text To the Sedra #11, pp. 377-378. We can prevent people from having to go without shoes. The "Shoe Lady" of Denver (Ranya Kelly) got her start distributing shoes when she found 500 pairs of new shoes in a dumpster outside a shoe store. Although she was threatened with arrest, she reclaimed the shoes in order to donate them to those in need. Years later, the Shoe Lady continues to divert would-be throwaway shoes — and many other useful items — for charitable purposes. Begin redistributing shoes and other valuable items to those in need.

You can contact and send donations to Ranya Kelly, c/o The Redistribution Center, 7736 Hoyt Circle, Arvada, CO 80005, 303-431-0904, Fax: 303-424-3368.

JEREMIAH 7:21-8:3; 9:22-23
TZAV צַו

This Haftarah has been paired with *Parashat Tzav*, Leviticus 6:1-8:36. See "Connecting the Text To the Sedra," pp. 385-386, for an exploration of the many ways the two texts shed light on each other.

SYNOPSIS

This prophecy is set in the years shortly before the first Babylonian siege of Jerusalem in 597 B.C.E. As the political situation worsens for the people of Judah, they cling tightly to the belief that the Temple and its sacrificial rites will protect them from disaster.

Jeremiah informs the people that their sacrifices will do no good to appease *Adonai*, who wishes only that they will repent and lead righteous lives. Instead, the people have grown more and more wicked with each passing generation. *Adonai* warns the prophet that just as the people have refused to listen to good advice before, they will not listen to him either.

Jeremiah announces that *Adonai* is fed up with such behavior as desecrating the Temple and building shrines for burning children. He tells the Israelites that doom is their fate. The towns of Judah and the streets of Jerusalem will be devastated and the people killed. The suffering will be unbearable, and the dead will decay above the ground.

It was Rabbinic custom to avoid ending a Haftarah on a negative note. Thus, this grim Haftarah ends with Jeremiah in verses 9:22-23 exhorting the people to trust only in God, who acts with and treasures kindness, justice, and equity.

INSIGHTS FROM THE TRADITION

A Jeremiah says in verse 7:24 that the Israelites went backward not forward. According to Hirsch, this is an indication that human civilization can make great progress and become more culturally sophisticated, yet at the same time go backward according to God's standards.

◆ Explain how the industrial and technological advances of the twentieth century were used by Nazi Germany in backward, inhumane ways.

◆ Explain how the Internet, a symbol of modern progress, can be used for holy purposes and for unholy purposes.

◆ Give other examples of how modern culture and progress can lead us either forward or backward (for example, sophisticated terrorist acts).

B According to verse 7:25, God sent prophets to warn Israel "daily and persistently." Radak understands the verse more literally: that God sent prophets early every morning because most warnings were made before people went to work.

◆ Describe your morning routine. Does it include reminders about how to act that day?

◆ Are prayers included in your morning routine?

◆ If prayers teach us about how to be better people, why might it be most beneficial to recite morning prayers before we start our day?

◆ Alternatively, would you be more receptive to messages about how to behave at other times of the day?

C God proclaims in verse 7:28: "Faithfulness has perished, vanished from their mouths." According to Radak, this means that often people will speak honest and faithful words even if they have no intention of following them and even if they don't truly believe them. However, in the time of Jeremiah, Israel acted unfaithfully and didn't even pretend to speak faithfully.

◆ People often say the right thing but do not always follow up by acting as they preach. Can you give examples?

◆ Explain Radak's interpretation that, in the case of Israel, the people did not even pretend to express loyalty to God.

◆ Debate: It is worse to be a hypocrite (say one thing and do another) than a flagrant violator (say and do the same, albeit wrong, thing).

D Verse 9:22 warns against boasting about your wisdom. Kara teaches that if someone learns Torah and doesn't practice it, he deserves no praise, for it is a disgrace.

Kara seems to be saying that it is not good enough to have knowledge of Torah; one must use knowledge to make the world a better place.

◆ Explain Kara's outlook in your own words. Do you agree with him?

◆ Collect stories from the newspaper or news magazines about people who have used their knowledge, wealth, resources, talent, or fame to improve the world.

E According to Hirsch, verse 9:23 means that every person who does acts of kindness, justice, and equity is working in God's service as messengers or angels.

◆ Interview your family members for times when they did acts of kindness and felt like messengers or angels.

STRATEGIES
Analyzing the Text

1 In verse 7:21 God orders Israel to add burnt offerings to its other sacrifices and eat the meat. Burnt offerings are sacrifices meant to be entirely consumed by fire and completely dedicated to God. Other sacrifices are only partially offered to God, with the rest of the meat consumed by the one bringing the sacrifice. Jeremiah seems to show contempt for their burnt offerings when he tells Israel to eat the meat of those offerings.

It is a common theme in the prophets that God does not want sacrifices from the people unless they are also following God's ways and living just lives. It is not a rejection of the entire sacrificial system, but rather a rejection of the way in which the people are living.

◆ The verse is said ironically: the people should stop making sacrifices, but the prophet tells them to make more. What tone of voice might Jeremiah have used for this verse?

◆ According to Radak, the prophet is really saying, "Do whatever you want, but it will be of no use." In what tone of voice might this have been said?

◆ Explain how the opening statement of this Haftarah is a rejection by God of the Israelites' sacrifices.

◆ For more information on this theme, see the Haftarah for *Devarim*, Analyzing the Text #6, p. 223.

2 The offerings of verse 7:21 were part of Israel's sacrificial system. Sacrifice is called *korban* in Hebrew (see Leviticus 6:12), which means "draw near." It was intended as a system to help the Israelites draw near to God.

◆ Explain the following statements. Then make a drawing in the style of a political cartoon that illustrates one of the statements.

- God's statement that the people should eat the meat themselves reminds them that God has no need for sacrifices. People need the sacrifices to feel closer to God.

- If the sacrifice is meant to draw the people nearer to God, it is hypocritical to participate in sinful activities that push them away from God.

- God doesn't need sacrifices, but God does need the people to follow God's teachings.

3 Verses 7:24-26 describe how Israel would not heed God.

◆ Describe how the Israelites failed to use each of the following body parts to listen to God: ear, heart, and necks.

◆ The phrase "stiff-necked people" appears in the Torah, particularly concerning the golden calf (Exodus 32:9). What do you think "stiff-necked" means?

◆ Make two clay figures: one of a person failing to listen, and one of a person listening.

4 Verse 7:28 says, "This is the nation that would not obey *Adonai* their God, that would not accept rebuke." The Hebrew word translated as "rebuke" is מוסר *(musar)*. The word *musar* is often translated as discipline of a moral nature, chastening, correction, warning, example, admonishment.

◆ What does it mean to refuse to accept rebuke?

◆ How does God's refusal to accept their sacrifices (see Analyzing the Text #1, p. 383) mirror the Israelites' refusal to accept rebuke concerning immoral or unacceptable behavior?

5 According to verses 7:30-31, the people are engaging in child sacrifice. Twice God denies having commanded them to sacrifice their children. Malbim explains that God did not command child sacrifice, because God thinks such a practice is abominable.

◆ Explain how God's twice repeated denial emphasizes God's disgust at such an abomination.

6 Read verses 8:1-2. If the sun, moon, and the host of heaven were worshiped by the Israelites instead of God, it is ironic that the Israelites' unburied corpses will be exposed before these supposed gods that couldn't save them.

◆ Explain the irony in these verses.

◆ Read verses 7:17-19 (just before the Haftarah begins), in which the Israelites prepare offerings for other gods. Compare the images of those verses to those in verses 8:1-2. How does this comparison intensify the irony?

7 Explain how verses 9:22-23 end the Haftarah on a positive note. These verses indicate that one's wisdom, strength, and riches are not important in and of themselves, but only when used for kindness, justice, and equity.

◆ Do you agree that this is so? Why or why not?

◆ Do you see a parallel between these verses and the earlier statement about sacrifices? Sacrifices are not automatically acceptable to God; they are acceptable only when offered by people who do acts of kindness, and seek justice and equity.

◆ Design a prayer book cover that extends this message to our prayer services.

Connecting the Text To the Sedra

8 The Sedra specifies the laws of the burnt offering in Leviticus 6:2-5. Other sacrifices are also detailed in the Sedra.

God rejects Israel's burnt offerings at the beginning of the Haftarah. We learn in the Haftarah that sacrifices offered by someone who is unethical are not desirable to God.

Do you think modern day charitable organizations have the same criteria? In other words, should charitable organizations accept donations made by someone who acquired the money unethically?

◆ Debate what you think your synagogue should do if one million dollars is given to it by someone who made his/her money by defrauding innocent people out of their life savings.

◆ Alternatively, find out from your synagogue's treasurer whether your synagogue could manage financially if first the board had to check out the ethical conduct of every donor and where their money came from.

9 The word נֵזֶר (nezer), meaning "diadem," appears in Leviticus 8:9 in the Sedra. It was worn by Aaron when he conducted a sacrifice.

In verse 7:29 of the Haftarah, God commands the people to cut off their נֵזֶר, which is translated as "hair locks." According to Plaut, cutting off their hair may be a sign of mourning for what is to come. Alternatively, he suggests that they were letting their hair grow long as do those dedicated to God's service (like Nazirites). However, because these people were not serious about their dedication to God, this was just a way to appear publicly as if they were religious people when, in fact, they were not.

◆ Based on verse 7:29, which interpretation of cutting off their hair do you think fits the Haftarah better, and why?

◆ What do you think of people who outwardly pretend they are something that they really are not?

10 In the Haftarah (verses 7:24 and 7:26), Jeremiah says that the Israelites did not give ear.

◆ What does it mean to "give ear"?

◆ In the Sedra (Leviticus 8:23-24), Moses consecrates Aaron and his sons by dabbing blood from a consecration offering on their right ears, right thumbs, and big toe of their right feet. Why were these parts of the body chosen for anointing? Some say they represent the whole priest being anointed from head (ear) to toe. Others suggest that the ear indicates the priest is prepared to listen to God's commands, the thumb (hand) indicates the priest is ready to perform God's tasks, and the toe (foot) indicates that the priest will walk in God's holy ways.

◆ Which interpretation of the Leviticus anointment scene do you prefer? Can you argue that both interpretations make sense?

◆ Reread verses 7:23-26 of the Haftarah. Which parts of their bodies did the Israelites refuse to use in service of God?

◆ List *mitzvot* we are expected to keep, then identify a part of the body that is associated with each *mitzvah*. For example:

• Torah reading is associated with our ears.

• Keeping kosher is associated with our mouths.

• Visiting the sick is associated with our feet.

• *Tefillin* is associated with our head and arm.

11 Leviticus 8:23 has an unusual cantillation note on the first word ("it was slaughtered"). Perhaps the unusual note (which is often interpreted as representing hesitation or regret) is there because this is the last sacrifice Moses will offer. (After this consecration offering, Aaron will replace Moses as chief sacrificer.) Perhaps the note is there because even as the Sedra recounts the offering made to consecrate Aaron and his sons, the Torah reader hesitates with this note, remembering that Aaron also built the golden calf.

◆ Why would Moses hesitate at his last sacrificial offering?

◆ Why would Aaron's involvement with the golden calf make one hesitate about his selection as High Priest?

◆ The Haftarah tells us that a sacrifice may be made only by those who behave properly and righteously. Explain how this rule applies to Aaron's early behavior in the golden calf incident.

◆ Should people running for elected office be called to account for their past wrongdoings? What does the example of Aaron becoming High Priest teach us on this subject?

◆ Learn to sing this cantillation.

Extending the Text

12 In Analyzing the Text #4, p. 384, we considered the meaning of the word *"musar."*

In nineteenth century Lithuania, Rabbi Israel Lipkin Salanter was worried about Jewish life and studies. He was concerned that too much emphasis was placed on the study of Talmud and Jewish Law. He did not want to abolish the study of Talmud and Jewish Law, but he worried that some people were becoming too competitive about their studies. He also worried that some people who devoted themselves to Jewish texts did not also lead ethically pure lives. He believed Talmud scholars must set an example of the purest ethical lives. He, therefore, set out to change Jewish education.

◆ Explain Rabbi Salanter's concerns. How did his concerns about dedication to Talmud study parallel Jeremiah's concerns about the sacrifices?

◆ Rabbi Salanter changed Jewish education by introducing the study of ethical works *(musar)* into the curriculum. For more information on the Musar Movement and Rabbi Salanter, see *Encyclopaedia Judaica*, vol. 12, pp. 534-537 or vol. 11, pp. 279-280.

◆ Rabbi Salanter never published a collection of his writings, but he is famous for certain sayings. Read and discuss the following ones (found in *The Jewish Religion: A Companion* by Louis Jacobs):

"One must not be pious by standing on another's shoulders" (i.e., by being inconsiderate of other people's feelings in the pursuit of piousness).

It is told that Rabbi Salanter once met a pious Jew engrossed in reflection during the penitential period. The man was so deep in thought, he did not greet Salanter. Salanter chastised the man saying, "Because you are so pious, does this give you the right to deny me my 'Good Morning'"?

◆ What moral theme underlies both of the above sayings?

13 Jeremiah preaches against the hypocrisy of offering sacrifices while not simultaneously living ethical lives. According to some modern scholars, the Ten Commandments were posted at the entrance to the sacrificial shrine. Their purpose was to remind everyone entering the shrine that they had to follow those ethical laws to qualify to offer a sacrifice.

◆ Read and discuss the Ten Commandments.

◆ Why would these rules be important for anyone bringing a sacrifice to God?

◆ Compare these rules to Jeremiah 7:5-9, in which God says the people must follow certain laws.

◆ Emblazon the Ten Commandments on a large poster to hang in your classroom.

For more on the subject of sacrifices and ethical living, read the commentary by Michael Fishbane in the *Etz Hayim Chumash*, p. 626.

14 According to Michael Fishbane in the *Etz Hayim Chumash*, p. 627, "It may have been just this critique of sacrifices that attracted the Sages to Jeremiah's word." The ancient Rabbis, living in the years after the destruction of the Second Temple in 70 C.E., must have worried about the future of their religion without a Temple and sacrifices. Jeremiah's words about the supreme importance of ethical living (kindness, justice, and equity) might have shown them that Judaism did have a future. Yochanan ben Zakkai followed in Jeremiah's footsteps when he taught that acts of loving-kindness would even bring about atonement (just as ancient sacrifices did).

◆ In the ancient world, specific sacrifices were prescribed to atone for sins. Make a list of possible wrongdoings and prescribe a particular act of loving-kindness that might effect atonement for each. When you find yourself guilty of one of the wrongdoings, make sure you "atone" with the prescribed remedy.

15 The Haftarah (verse 7:29) uses the word קִינָה (*kinah*), which means "a lament."

A lament is defined as an expression of grief or sorrow, an elegy or dirge. On Tishah B'Av, we recite poems called *kinot* (the plural of *kinah*) to express sorrow and grief over the destruction of Jerusalem and the Temple.

The most famous of these *kinot* is called *"Eli Tzion,"* and it is sung to a well-known melody. In part, *"Eli Tzion"* says:

"Weep for the Temple which was destroyed Because of the sins of the people!

Weep because the enemies of God have despoiled the Temple."

◆ Discuss the excerpt from *"Eli Tzion."* How does it reflect similar ideas expressed in the Haftarah and especially in verse 7:29?

◆ Ask your Rabbi or Cantor to teach you to sing *"Eli Tzion."* The music only is available on the St. Petersburg School audiocassette *"Beit Hatfutsot."* You may listen to an excerpt at www.jewishmusic.com.

16 According to Insights from the Tradition #E, p. 383, each person who does acts of kindness, justice, and equity is working as God's messenger or angel.

Rabbi Lawrence Kushner teaches that we may all have opportunities to be messengers of God and not even know it. In *Honey from the Rock*, pp. 68-75, he writes about an incident that happened to him.

Kushner tells the story of owning a pair of *tefillin* that he never used; they just sat in a drawer. Interestingly, every time he went on a trip, he packed his *tefillin*. He took them just in case he might need them, but over many years, he never used them once. He kept packing them anyway. On one trip, he met a friend who tearily mentioned that his mother had been cleaning out drawers in her house and had thrown away his old set of *tefillin*. Kushner reached into his bag and gave his friend the *tefillin* he invariably had with him. It was then that he realized why he had always carried the *tefillin* with him on trips — one day he was going to be a messenger from God, healing the hurt this friend suffered.

◆ Kushner interprets his act of kindness to his friend as working for God as a messenger or angel. Explain this interpretation. In what way is God in this story the source of justice or kindness?

◆ Debate: The *tefillin* would have been a more meaningful gift if Rabbi Kushner had used it himself regularly versus the *tefillin* was a meaningful gift because Rabbi Kushner went to the effort to carry it with him for a purpose not even he knew.

◆ A Denver teenager carries with him at all times a little pouch containing a clown nose and a set of imitation false teeth. "So many people walk around upset and depressed," says Josh Fixler, "anything I can do to cheer them up is well worth the effort." In a sense, Josh is acting as a messenger or angel. Make a list of things you could do to become such a messenger. Pick one of the things on the list and do it. Report your experiences back to the class.

17 The Haftarah describes the terrible end that will come to those who commit abominations against God. In verse 7:33 God threatens that these people will die and not be buried, and that their corpses will lie on the ground exposed to the elements and the animals.

The horrible end threatened by God stands in sharp contrast to the way Judaism requires that we treat the human body after death. The *mitzvah* of caring for the body is called *kevod ha-mayt*.

According to tradition, a body must be accompanied at all times between death and burial. Guardians, called *shomrim*, accompany the body from hospital or home to the funeral home. They

take turns sitting with the body and reciting Psalms before the funeral.

The body is physically prepared for burial. The ritual, called *taharah*, includes a ceremonial washing of the body, dressing it in shrouds, and placing it in a coffin. Sometimes the *mitzvah* of *taharah* is done by the funeral home staff and sometimes by a group of volunteers called a *Chevrah Kadisha*, a burial society.

Open caskets and viewing of the body are forbidden in Judaism, as this practice is considered to be the opposite of *kevod ha-mayt*. One honors the deceased by remembering him or her as he/she was when alive, not as an artificially arranged and dressed corpse.

Attending the funeral, accompanying the body to the cemetery, and even shoveling dirt onto the casket after it has been lowered into the grave are all ways to show respect for the dead.

◆ Discuss these rituals and how they show respect for the dead. Ask students who have been to funerals to describe what they saw that honored the deceased.

◆ For more on the concept of *kevod ha-mayt* and other Jewish burial customs, see *Saying Kaddish: How to Comfort the Dying, Bury the Dead and Mourn as a Jew* by Anita Diamant.

18 The following quotations are about the importance of listening to good advice:

• "They did not listen or give ear; they followed their own counsels, the willfulness of their evil hearts." (Jeremiah 7:24)

• "They have eyes to see but see not, ears to hear but hear not; for they are a rebellious breed." (Ezekiel 12:2)

• "He whose ear heeds the discipline of life lodges among the wise." (Proverbs 15:31)

- "The ear that hears, the eye that sees — *Adonai* made them both." (Proverbs 20:12)

- "Like a ring of gold, a golden ornament, is a wise man's reproof in a receptive ear." (Proverbs 25:12)

- "Truly, the ear tests arguments as the palate tastes foods." (Job 12:11)

◆ Read and discuss the quotations. Which is your favorite one, and why?

◆ Make a sign for the entrance (or exit) of your chapel or sanctuary reminding people that all who come to pray should also live ethical lives outside the sanctuary.

Personalizing the Text

19 We learned in Insights from the Tradition #A, p. 382, that technological advances can be used either to further or damage human culture.

◆ Conduct a survey of your friends, schoolmates, teachers, and family. Ask them whether they think the following technological advances have greater potential to hurt or to help:

- the Internet

- genetic engineering of animals

- genetic engineering of food

- cellular phones

- organ transplants

- mechanical organs

◆ Compile your data according to the age of the respondent. Can you find any patterns in response?

20 The Israelites refused to listen to the prophet's good advice — and paid the price.

◆ The great Rabbi Akiva gave seven pieces of advice to his son Joshua (*Pesachim* 112a):

- Do not live and study in the busy district of the city.

- Do not dwell in a town whose leaders are scholars.

- Do not enter your own house unexpectedly, much less your neighbor's house.

- Do not withhold shoes from your feet.

- Rise early and eat.

- Do not be dependent on the charity of others.

- Strive to be on good terms with a man upon whom the hour smiles.

◆ Discuss the meanings of these pieces of advice.

◆ With which do you agree, and why? With which do you disagree, and why?

◆ Write your own seven pieces of advice for someone trying to live a kind and just life in today's world.

21 Every time we do an act of kindness, justice, or equity we are working as a messenger of God. Indeed, since we know God loves kindness, justice, and equity, whenever we work to achieve these goals, we are actually imitating God.

◆ Play the game "Clay," which is described in *Jewish Identity Games* by Richard J. Israel, p. 51. Divide the class into two groups. One group will be the sculptors and the other will become the sculpture. The sculptors pose the sculptures performing acts of kindness, justice, and equity. View and photograph the sculpture when you are finished, and then switch groups.

22 We no longer offer sacrifices to God, but offer prayers instead. We have learned that God desires sincere devotion and not just "lip service."

◆ Sometimes it is difficult to pray with sincerity from the prayers in our prayer books. Write your own prayer in prose or poetry. Remember, prayers can offer thanksgiving to God, or can praise God, or can sincerely request something from God.

◆ For an example of a prayer that acknowledges that we offer prayers instead of sacrifices and that our prayers must be worthy, see *The Complete ArtScroll Siddur*, pp. 40-43.

23 Insights from the Tradition #B, p. 382, explains that God sent prophets to warn Israel every day.

◆ Decide on one way that you can improve yourself, function better at school, or treat others better. Then make a resolution to carry this out. Design a reminder that will cue you each morning to carry out your resolution. For example, it could be a symbolic reminder drawn with lipstick on your bathroom mirror, or it could be a particular recording that wakes you with your alarm clock. Keep a diary of how it feels to see or hear the reminder every morning, and whether you change your behavior during the day because of it.

24 The Israelites grew their hair long to prove they were pious when they were not, and then were told to cut it off (verse 7:29).

◆ Research the organization called Locks of Love. It encourages people to grow their hair long and then cut off at least ten inches to donate for hairpieces for financially disadvantaged children suffering from long-term hair loss due to a medical condition. You can write or call them at 1640 S. Congress Ave.,

Suite 104, Palm Springs, FL 33461, 888-896-1588, or access their web site at www.locksoflove.org. Start a group for students who are willing to try to grow their hair long enough for Locks of Love. Decide how to publicize your cause.

Other Resources

25 For more on the prophet Jeremiah, including history, themes, and notable quotations, read *Messengers of God: A Jewish Prophets Who's Who* by Ronald H. Isaacs, pp. 102-120.

26 Discuss the illustration of this Haftarah in *The Illustrated Torah* by Michal Meron, p. 112. Note that, although Meron indicates Malachi is the standard Haftarah for this Sedra, other Haftarah commentators (Hirsch, Hertz, Plaut, and Rosenberg) mention only Jeremiah.

27 For additional information on the prophet Jeremiah as well as the Book of Jeremiah, see *Encyclopaedia Judaica*, vol. 9, pp. 1345-1361.

28 See Rembrandt's painting of Jeremiah lamenting over Jerusalem at www.archive.com. Try painting your own portrait of Jeremiah.

29 Read and discuss the story "The Car That Ran from Mitzvahs" by Hanna Bandes in *Chosen Tales*, edited by Peninnah Schram, pp. 11-19. It is about how one woman's life is changed when she decides to listen to some good advice.

30 There are many popular short books that contain advice for living a good life.

Read and discuss selections from *Life's Little Instruction Book* by H. Jackson Brown, Jr., or *A Short Guide To a Happy Life* by Anna Quindlen. Also, consider reading the Book of Proverbs. Then, with your classmates, create an original short book of advice on living a good life.

31 For a commentary on this Haftarah, see UAHC's Family Shabbat Table Talk web site, www.uahc.org/torah/stt/2tzav.html.

Involving the Family

32 Write a family code of conduct that promotes ethical behavior, kindness, justice, and equity. All family members might sign an agreement to comply with the code.

33 Check out the web site of National Youth Service Day at www.SERVEnet.org or by writing Youth Service America, 1101 15th St. NW, Washington, DC 20005. With your siblings, choose a volunteer opportunity and participate in this annual community service event.

Bar/Bat Mitzvah Project

34 Becoming a Bar or Bat Mitzvah makes you a son or daughter of the commandments. Don't just pay lip service to the commandments. Practice what you have been studying and engage in a *mitzvah* activity of your choice in the months before and after your Bar/Bat Mitzvah. For example, volunteer at a nearby nursing home, tutor younger children, help an elderly congregant with shopping, or clean up litter on a highway or in a local park. Consider donating part of your Bar/Bat Mitzvah gifts to *tzedakah*.

JEREMIAH 8:13-9:23
TISHAH B'AV

 This Haftarah has been paired with the holiday Tishah B'Av, on which we read Deuteronomy 4:25-40. See "Connecting the Text To the Holiday," pp. 394-395, for an exploration of the many ways the two texts and the holiday shed light on each other.

SYNOPSIS

Jeremiah was very unpopular because he predicted that Jerusalem would be destroyed if the people did not change their sinful ways. However, when the Babylonians attacked the city in 598 B.C.E., Jeremiah was proven right. The Babylonians did leave for a short time, but would return 12 years later to conquer Jerusalem completely, destroy the Temple, and exile the people. This prophecy most likely was made in those 12 years between the first Babylonian siege and the destruction of Jerusalem.

In the first ten verses of the Haftarah, a vengeful *Adonai* promises to punish Israel for its sins. Israel mourns its agonizing present and its doomed fate. Jeremiah, who is sick with grief, yearns for comfort for himself and his people, but finds none.

Adonai accuses the people of treachery, evil, baseness, cheating, lying, and deceit. Even brothers and friends take advantage of one another. *Adonai* feels there is no choice but to punish the people for such evil. Yet *Adonai* is saddened that the destruction will also bring harm to the mountains and pastures, cattle and birds, Jerusalem and the towns of Judah. Even Jeremiah has difficulty understanding why the land must be reduced to ruin. *Adonai* responds that because the Israelites ignored the Torah and followed idols instead, they

must be punished and scattered among the nations, where the sword will pursue them.

In the final verses of the Haftarah, *Adonai* calls for dirge singers and wailing women to sing a lament for Israel's shame and humiliation. Death is at their doors, and the carcasses of their people will lay unburied in the fields.

The Haftarah concludes with the prophet's exhortation to the people to trust not in wisdom, strength, or riches, but only in *Adonai*, who acts with kindness, justice, and equity in the world.

INSIGHTS FROM THE TRADITION

A In verse 8:22 Jeremiah asks if there is no balm in Gilead. This has been interpreted by Rashi to mean: isn't there one righteous person there whose behavior they can learn to copy so they will improve their ways?

◆ Who is a role model in your school from whom the other students learn good behavior?

◆ Can you imagine what a school or world would be if there were no role models from whom to learn good behavior?

B Verse 8:22 is interpreted by *Targum Jonathan* to mean that Jeremiah asks if he does not have good deeds that would help Israel. If his own good deeds aren't enough to pray for Israel, then perhaps Israel can't be cured because they have not repented.

◆ Do you agree with *Targum Jonathan* that a person has to be ready to change in order for someone else to be able to help them? Why or why not? What does it mean to be ready to change?

C In verse 9:18 the people express shame that they will have to leave their homes. Radak teaches that there is no greater shame than that of a person forced to leave his/her home.

◆ Why is being forced out of one's home a cause of shame?

◆ Why is being homeless a source of shame?

◆ What might we be able to do to help people in a homeless shelter feel less shame?

D Hertz teaches concerning verse 9:22 that strength means the moral strength to resist temptation.

◆ How do you measure strength?

◆ Do you consider people who resist temptation to be the strongest people you know?

E Radak explains in regard to verse 9:23 that knowing God means practicing kindness, justice, and righteousness.

Since we can't ever really know God, the best we can hope for is to know God's qualities and to try to act like God.

◆ Give examples of ways in which people could know God by imitating God's kindness, justice, and righteousness in our world.

STRATEGIES
Analyzing the Text

1 Verse 8:13 is difficult to translate because the verb translated as "make an end of them" can also mean "harvest them."

◆ How might this be a harvest that Israel will not like?

◆ Compare the imagery here to Jeremiah 2:3, 21 and Isaiah 5:1-7. Draw one of these images of

the vineyard God planted and how it turned out.

2 In verse 8:14 the Israelites say that God has forced them to drink a bitter draft. This verse is ambiguous, and thus has several possible meanings. Consider the following possible meanings and decide which you prefer. Justify your choice.

• A bitter draft symbolizes the bitter punishment that the people will receive from their enemies.

• A bitter draft may refer to wartime when the enemy would cut off their water or poison their water supply.

• A bitter draft may refer to the water of bitterness given to a woman who was suspected of being disloyal to her husband (Numbers 5:11-31).

• A bitter draft may refer to a curse contained in ancient treaties: if the treaty vassal broke the treaty agreement, the gods would give him poisoned water to drink.

3 In verses 8:16-17 enemy warhorses are coming from the north and serpents are attacking. God warns that the serpents cannot be charmed.

◆ Explain how this warning indicates that there is no hope against the serpents and that there will be no hope against the enemy.

4 Jeremiah, like other prophets before and after him, often uses rhetorical questions. However, Jeremiah is known for using a series of three questions in a row. The first two questions begin simply with "is" or "do," and both have obvious answers. The third question begins with "why" and points out a contradiction based on the first two questions.

◆ Read verse 8:22. Identify the first two questions. The obvious answer to these questions is "yes." As a result of these two questions, would you expect there to be healing? What is the third "why" question? How does its answer contradict the expected answer based on the firsts two questions?

◆ Make a flow chart that diagrams the information gathered in these questions and then the expected outcome versus the actual outcome.

◆ Compare this triple set of rhetorical questions with the other ones in Jeremiah (2:14, 2:31, 8:4-5, 14:19, and 49:1). Make a flow chart for these verses, too.

5 In verses 9:1 the prophet wishes he could leave and live in an inn in the wilderness.

◆ Explain how, even though the wilderness is dreary, lonely, and unsafe, it would be better for Jeremiah than having to see the people's wickedness anymore.

◆ Could God be the speaker in this verse?

◆ Make a newspaper or television advertisement for this wilderness inn.

6 Hyperbole is used in verse 8:23.

◆ Identify the instances of hyperbole in this verse.

In ancient Ugaritic poetry, a similar image is used. Discuss the following passage in which King Keret is visited by his son and tells his son not to cry so much over the king's illness:

"Do not, my son, empty the fount of thine eye, the water of thy head with tears."

◆ What is the hyperbole that expresses the son's feeling for King Keret and the prophet's feeling for Israel?

◆ For more on the relationship between ancient Ugarit and Israel, see the *Encyclopaedia Judaica*, vol. 15, pp. 1501-1506.

7 In verse 9:11 Jeremiah tries to save the people from punishment. He argues that none of them are wise enough to have understood God's teachings and none will understand or learn from God's punishment. Jeremiah uses this argument to intercede with God and try to stop God from punishing the people.

◆ Do you think it is unjust to punish someone who will not learn from the punishment?

◆ Read more about the prophet as an intercessor on behalf of the people in the book *Love and Joy* by Yohanan Muffs, pp. 9-48.

◆ In verse 9:12 God responds to Jeremiah. Does God accept Jeremiah's argument?

◆ In a progress report, evaluate Jeremiah's performance as an intercessor. Keep in mind his particularly difficult situation.

Connecting the Text To the Holiday

8 The Haftarah (see Hertz's translation) uses the expression "daughter of my people" in 8:19, 8:21, 22, 23; 9:6.

The Book of Lamentations (see a literal translation), which is read in synagogue on the evening of Tishah B'Av, refers to Jerusalem as "the daughter of Zion" or "the daughter of Judah" (see 1:6, 2:1, 2, 4, 5, 8, 10, 13, 18), or "daughter of my people" (2:11, 4:3, 6, 10).

◆ What emotions does the expression "daughter of my people" evoke? How does Jeremiah feel about the people? Draw a picture of this distraught "daughter."

9 The Haftarah uses the word *"kinah"* (verses 9:9 and 9:19), which means a lamentation. On Tishah B'Av, we recite *kinot* — mournful poems of lamentation for Jerusalem.

◆ Study and learn to chant one of the most well known of all *kinot, "Eli Zion."* (see the St.

Petersburg School audiocassette *Beit Hatfutsot).* You may listen to an excerpt at www.jewishmusic.com.

10 Jeremiah says (verse 8:23) that he wishes he had a head full of water so that he could cry over his people. In the Book of Lamentations, Jerusalem weeps for the destruction, for the loss of her children, and because there is no one to bring her comfort.

◆ Read the following verses from the Book of Lamentations, then interpret them through movement or drama.

• "Alas! Lonely sits the city once great with people! She that was great among nations is become like a widow; The princess among states is become a thrall [slave]. Bitterly she weeps in the night, her cheek wet with tears. There is none to comfort her of all her friends. All her allies have betrayed her; They have become her foes." (1:1-2)

• "Silent on the ground the leaders of Fair Zion; They have strewn dust on the heads and girded themselves with sackcloth; The maidens of Jerusalem have bowed their heads to the ground. My eyes are spent with tears, my heart is in tumult, my being melts away over the ruin of my poor people, as babes and sucklings languish in the squares of the city." (2:10-11)

• "Remember, O *Adonai,* what has befallen us; Behold and see our disgrace! Our heritage has passed to aliens, our homes to strangers. We have become orphans, fatherless; Our mothers are like widows. We must pay to drink our own water, obtain our own kindling at a price . . . Gone is the joy from our hearts; our dancing is turned into mourning. The crown

has fallen from our head; Woe to us that we have sinned!" (5:1-4, 15-16)

11 There is something of a controversy surrounding the observance of Tishah B'Av. Plaut writes in *The Haftarah Commentary,* p. 756, "The ninth of Av has been a recurrent day of calamity for the Jewish people . . . There was thus enough reason to mourn, and, indeed, in past centuries the unhappy day and the three weeks before were scrupulously observed by our people. Not so today. With the emergence of Israel as an independent Jewish state, the whole idea of a God-enforced exile appears obsolete."

◆ Read and discuss Plaut's essay on "The Controversy about Tishah B'Av" on pp. 756-757 of *The Haftarah Commentary.* Do you think Yom HaShoah has replaced Tishah B'Av? Do you think we should forget about tragedies because they no longer seem to be relevant to us? Can you imagine a day when the Holocaust will lose its relevance, or when September 11, 2001 will be forgotten?

◆ Design a billboard reminding people to remember the Temples and observe Tishah B'Av.

◆ Write a letter to the editor of your local Jewish newspaper urging people to be grateful for the State of Israel and to forget the observance of Tishah B'Av.

12 Tishah B'Av commemorates the destruction of Jerusalem. According to a *midrash* (see *The Legends of the Jews* by Louis Ginzberg, 4:303-5), Jeremiah was commanded by God to return home to Anathoth because his merits were so great that God could not destroy Jerusalem as long as Jeremiah was in the city. In Jeremiah's absence, Jerusalem was conquered and the city set on fire. When Jeremiah returned, he saw smoke rising from the Temple and rejoiced, thinking that the people had repented and were offering sacrifices. He wept bitterly when he realized his error.

JEREMIAH 16:19-17:14
BECHUKOTAI בחקתי

This Haftarah has been paired with *Parashat Bechukotai*, Leviticus 26:3-27:34. See "Connecting the Text To the Sedra," pp. 398-399, for an exploration of the many ways the two texts shed light on each other.

SYNOPSIS

Jeremiah was called to prophesy in the thirteenth year of the reign of King Josiah of Judah in 627 B.C.E., and he prophesied until after the destruction of the Temple in 586 B.C.E. This Haftarah seems to be a collection of several distinct messages from various times throughout Jeremiah's turbulent prophetic career.

In the first message, Jeremiah declares that all the nations will ultimately recognize that *Adonai* is the one true God and that idols are not gods at all.

Jeremiah next informs Israel that the stains of its sins are indelible. Because the people have forfeited their divine inheritance, an infuriated God will make them slaves to their enemies in a foreign land.

Jeremiah contrasts those who trust in *Adonai* with those who trust in man. The one who trusts in man will be cursed like a bush in the dry desert. The one who trusts in *Adonai* will be blessed like a tree planted by waters, which never suffers and always yields fruit.

The human heart is described as devious, but *Adonai* probes our hearts and searches our minds to know our true ways.

Those who become rich through unscrupulous means are condemned, and those who abandon *Adonai* are doomed.

The Haftarah ends with Jeremiah's prayer to be healed and saved through God's glory.

INSIGHTS FROM THE TRADITION

A In verse 16:20 Jeremiah says, "Can a man make gods for himself?" Hirsch understands this verse to mean that human beings cannot make gods; God can make humans. Sometimes we forget that we are only human and of limited ability, unlike the God who created us.

◆ Often we like to believe we have control over things in our lives and in nature. List five examples of things that we might like to control, but cannot.

◆ Discuss the following examples or suggest your own: one person thinks that if he wears a special baseball cap while he watches his favorite team play, they will win, but if he does not wear the cap, they will lose. Another thinks that if she eats her favorite, lucky sandwich, she will do well on a test, but if she eats a different sandwich, she will fail.

B Verse 16:21 says that God will teach the Israelites about God's power and might. According to Hirsch, they learn that God's power destroyed the Temple as punishment for their sins. However, they learn from God's might that as an act of love and mercy, God did not destroy the people at the same time the Temple was destroyed.

From this we learn that might is willingness to restrain our power and ourselves.

◆ One of our challenges in life is to know when to use our might and when to use our power. List three real-life situations in which restraint (might) is in order. List three other situations in which forceful action (power) is in order. Role-play some of the situations.

C In verse 17:1 Jeremiah condemns the people for sinning in their hearts and on their altars. *Metsudat David* explains that the sin has both penetrated deep into their innermost nature and has been openly flaunted.

◆ Which is worse: sinning even though you know it is wrong, or sinning and convincing yourself that it is not a sin?

◆ Which implies that the sin has penetrated one's innermost self?

D Hertz says that the "fruit of his deeds" mentioned in verse 17:10 indicates that good intentions are not enough. A person is judged by the outcome of his/her actions, whether foreseen or unforeseen.

◆ Debate whether it is intentions or actions that matter most.

STRATEGIES
Analyzing the Text

1 Verse 17:1 describes Israel's sins as having been written on the tablet of their hearts with a pen of iron.

◆ Explain the metaphor that the hearts of Israel are as hard as stone tablets and that a very hard pen of iron engraved their sins there so they can never be erased. What do you think it means that their hearts are hard as stone tablets? What do you think it means that their sins are permanently engraved on their hearts?

◆ Compare this metaphor to the "*Shema*," which says, "And these words which I command you today will be on your heart" (Deuteronomy 6:4-9).

2 The prophet warns against trusting in people instead of trusting in God (verse 17:5).

◆ What happens to people who trust in people?

◆ Reread verse 17:6. Explain why those who do not follow God are compared to a scrawny bush, and living without God is like living without water. Will it survive the drought to see good times?

3 Verses 17:7-8 in Jeremiah and Psalm 1:1-3 are very similar texts.

◆ Reread these verses. Explain how each text compares the righteous to a tree and God to life-giving water.

◆ Which would you prefer to be: the tree that is described here, or the bush described in verse 17:6?

◆ Find pictures of desert trees or shrubs and of trees from a rain forest. Make a collage with these two contrasting images.

4 It was a belief of the biblical era that the partridge took over other birds' nests and eggs and hatched them (see verse 17:11). The baby birds, however, would desert the false mother.

◆ Explain how the prophet is suggesting that dishonestly acquired wealth will abandon the one who collected it, just as the baby birds abandon the false mother.

◆ Make up your own proverbs that teach that dishonesty never pays.

5 In verse 17:14 the prophet asks God for healing. From what does the prophet need to be healed?

◆ Read Jeremiah 15:17-18. Also see verses 8:21-22. Write a journal entry of Jeremiah's that conveys the depth of feeling he has for his people and the pain he suffers when they suffer.

◆ Advanced study: See Jeremiah 31:33-34 and 33:6-9, in which God promises to replace the sins on their hearts with God's teaching (see Analyzing the Text #1, p. 397), and to heal them. Illustrate the inscribed heart before (17:1) and after (31:33).

Connecting the Text To the Sedra

6 The Sedra begins in Leviticus 26:3-5 by saying that if you choose to follow God, you will get sufficient rain in the right seasons and will have plenty of crops.

The Haftarah compares those who choose to follow God as nourished by sources of water and having plenty of fruit (verses 17:8,13).

◆ How does Judaism nourish you?

◆ We learn from the Torah reading and Haftarah that without the nourishment of Jewish teachings, life would be somehow lacking. What might be missing from your life if you chose not to practice Judaism at all?

7 The Torah reading (see Leviticus 26:3 and 26:14) is about the choices we make and the consequences of those choices. The Haftarah (see, for example, Jeremiah 17:5 and 17:7) is about the same thing.

◆ Interview your Rabbi, teacher, and parents about an important choice each made, how it affected his/her life, how he/she went about making it, and whether or not each would make that same choice again.

8 It seems significant that the word security, בטח (betach), appears in both the Sedra (Leviticus 26:5) and in the Haftarah (verses 17:5, 7, translated as "trust").

◆ Review these verses.

◆ Does trust in God mean that you are guaranteed a "secure" life?

◆ Can any life be completely secure?

◆ Does security mean that nothing bad will ever happen to you? Or does security mean you will somehow get through difficult times?

9 God's sanctuary is mentioned in Jeremiah 17:12 and in Leviticus 26:11. A sanctuary is at the heart of any synagogue today.

◆ Tour the sanctuaries of other synagogues in your area. Compare their features. Which do you like best, and why?

◆ Alternatively, learn about your own sanctuary, then give guided tours to the younger classes.

10 The Sedra recalls in verse 26:13 that God took the Israelites out of Egypt, freed them from slavery, and helped them to walk upright. In the Haftarah verse 17:6, the Israelites are compared to a stunted, bent over tree growing in the desert.

◆ What events in our lives can stunt us and bend us?

◆ What kinds of things can we do to strengthen ourselves to walk upright?

◆ How can our viewpoint or our faith help to make us strong?

11 The Sedra discusses the uncircumcised heart that does not listen to God in Leviticus 26:41.

◆ What do you think the figurative uncircumcised heart is? (Consider the following possible meanings: closed to God's call, unconsecrated, unclean, sinning, stunted or not fully developed, stubborn, thick, unfeeling.) Have you ever felt as if your heart was stubbornly leading you to err? If so, describe such a time. Ask your parents if this has ever happened to them.

- Verses 17:9-10 of the Haftarah mention how weak and deceitful the heart is and how God can search the heart and know its secrets. Explain how the Haftarah seems to be saying that even our deepest, most awful secrets can be known by God.

- Would you be less likely to do bad things if you remembered that your secrets could be read from the depths of your heart?

- Read Jeremiah 31:33-34, in which God promises to cure the Israelites by writing God's laws on their hearts. Think of one thing you would like to change about yourself, but your stubborn heart won't let you. Write it on a heart-shaped card and wear it close to your heart. Does it help you change?

Extending the Text

12 The last verse of the Haftarah is included in the weekday *"Amidah."* It reads:

"Heal us, *Adonai*, and we shall be healed; save us and we shall be saved, for to You we offer praise. Grant complete healing for all our ailments, for You, O God, are our Sovereign, our faithful and merciful Healer. Praised are You, *Adonai*, who heals the sick among Your people Israel."

- Compare the wording of this blessing to the last verse of the Haftarah.

- Find all the places where the wording has changed from the singular to the plural.

- Suggest explanations for why the wording was changed to "we." (For example, on any given day, a particular person saying the prayer might not be ill and in need of healing, but

will say the prayer on behalf of everyone in the community. The person will thus be reminded that there are sick people in the community in need of assistance. In addition, when someone in need of healing says the prayer in the plural, it helps that person think about others and not dwell on just his/her own problems.)

- Learn to recite this paragraph in the *"Amidah"* in Hebrew and/or English.

13 God inspects the heart and kidneys (verse 17:10). In the ancient world, the heart was thought to be the seat of intelligence, and kidneys (often translated as "mind") were understood to be the source of emotion.

In the High Holy Day prayer *"L'El Orech Din"* (To God Who Is the Judge), we describe God as not only the judge of our deeds, but as the detective who collects the hidden evidence by examining the depths of our hearts:

"To God who orders judgment
Who searches the hearts on the Day of Judgment;
Who uncovers deep things in judgment,
Who ordains righteousness on the Day of Judgment."

- Discuss this prayer and perhaps read the whole prayer as it is found in a *Machzor*.

- What do you think it means to inspect, search out, or look into the heart and mind?

- For advanced study, note that this concept appears several times in the Book of Jeremiah. See these three cites: Jeremiah 11:20, 17:10, 20:12. It does not appear elsewhere in the Bible.

14 The meaning of Jeremiah's name is unclear; it may mean "may God lift up."

◆ How is this an appropriate name for a prophet of God? Is Jeremiah's name also reflective of his message to Israel?

◆ For more information on the possible meanings of the name Jeremiah, see the Haftarah for *Matot*, Extending the Text #20, p. 370.

15 Following are some quotations about hearts.

Do you think any of the quotations about hearts reflect the image of a heart in the Sedra or the Haftarah?

- "The people's heart is the foundation on which the land will be built." (Ahad HaAm)

- "The Holy One wants the heart." (*Sanhedrin* 106b)

- "It is the same whether a person offers much or little, provided his heart is directed to heaven." (*Mishnah Menahot* 13:11)

- "The heart is the tabernacle of the human intellect." (Rambam, *Shaare HaMusar*)

- "The heart sees better than the eye." (Yiddish proverb)

- "When the heart is full, the eyes overflow." (Shalom Aleichem)

- "The heart is king. Wherever it leads, the organs follow." (M. H. Luzzato)

- "It is absurd that a man should be forbidden to enter the Temple save after washing his body . . . and yet attempt to sacrifice and pray with a heart still polluted and disordered." (Philo)

- "Purify our hearts that we may serve You in truth." (Shabbat prayer)

◆ Discuss the quotations. Using the images from one of them, or from the Haftarah or Sedra,

write a prayer that expresses the desire to have an open and receptive heart.

Personalizing the Text

16 Jeremiah predicts in verse 16:19 that one day people will realize that their ancestors were wrong about idols. Each successive generation learns that their parents were wrong about something, e.g., slavery or women's rights or smoking or recycling.

◆ What does your generation know that your parents did not?

17 Jeremiah compares the sinful Israelites to a scrawny bush living without the nourishment of God's water.

◆ Maintain a healthy class plant. Be sure to water it enough and give it the right amount of sunlight. Watch how it develops.

18 God wants the spiritually "malnourished" Israelites to drink the life-giving water of Torah.

◆ Pantomime a skit in which a withered desert bush becomes a strong and healthy, well watered tree.

19 God inscribes Israel's sins with an iron pen upon hearts of stone.

◆ Declare your belief in God by writing the words of the *"Shema"* in indelible ink on a plaque of cardboard, wood, stone, or ceramic tile. You can use the stone or tile as a paperweight on your desk.

20 Jeremiah says in verse 17:11 that whoever succeeds by unjust means hasn't really succeeded at all.

◆ Do you agree with Jeremiah's statement?

◆ Does his statement apply to your activities? For example, in sports or academics or music, one must master the fundamentals first, building a strong base for future success that is real and lasting. Is it possible to succeed in these endeavors by unjust means? Is it really success?

◆ In contrast, have you slowly built up your skills in your favorite sport, or instrument, or school subject in an effort to earn success?

◆ What advice would you give to a younger athlete or student or musician who wants to succeed right away?

21 Jeremiah prays for healing in verse 17:14. *"Mi Shebayrach"* is a prayer some congregations recite for people who are ill. (For a discussion on this prayer, see Extending the Text #20 in the Haftarah for *Chayay Sarah*, p. 107.)

◆ Learn to sing the popular version of the *"Mi Shebeirach"* prayer for healing by Debbie Friedman, which may be found on her recording *Debbie Friedman at Carnegie Hall.*

Other Resources

22 For a commentary, discussion questions, and project, see the UAHC Family Shabbat Table Talk web site at www.uahc.org/torah/stt/3bechukotai.shtml.

23 For more on the prophet Jeremiah, including history, themes, and notable quotations, read *Messengers of God: A Jewish Prophets Who's Who* by Ronald H. Isaacs, pp. 102-120.

24 For additional information on the prophet Jeremiah as well as the Book of Jeremiah, see *Encyclopaedia Judaica*, vol. 9, pp. 1345-1361.

25 See Rembrandt's painting of Jeremiah lamenting over Jerusalem at www.archive.com. Try painting your own portrait of Jeremiah.

26 Discuss the illustration of this Haftarah in *The Illustrated Torah* by Michal Meron, p. 142.

27 For a commentary on this Haftarah, see the web site of the Fuchsberg Center for Conservative Judaism in Jerusalem, www.uscj.org.il/haftarah/beharbehukotai5761.html.

28 For another resource, see the chapter on Jeremiah in *The Gift of Wisdom* by Steven F. Steinbock, pp. 147-157.

Involving the Family

29 In Analyzing the Text #5, pp. 397-398, we learned that Jeremiah prayed to be healed from the pain he suffered from humiliation and threats. No one can flourish in a threatening environment. Make a family pledge to refrain from humiliating and threatening one another and to create a safe and nurturing home environment, where everyone can grow and flourish.

Bar/Bat Mitzvah Project

30 Jeremiah calls God "my strength and my stronghold, my refuge in a day of trouble" (verse 16:19). Homeless shelters and women's shelters also give "refuge in a day of trouble." Do God's work by volunteering at a local shelter.

JEREMIAH 31:2-20
SECOND DAY ROSH HASHANAH

 This Haftarah has been paired with the second day of Rosh HaShanah, on which we read Genesis 22. See "Connecting the Text To the Holiday," pp. 404-405, for an exploration of the many ways the two texts and the holiday shed light on each other.

SYNOPSIS

Jeremiah prophesied at a time (the end of the seventh century B.C.E.) when Babylonia threatened to conquer the Southern Kingdom of Judah. The Northern Kingdom had been destroyed by the Assyrians about 100 years earlier.

In this Haftarah Jeremiah assures his people that one day the exiles from the north will be returned. God, says Jeremiah, will strengthen Northern Israel, who will plant vineyards on the hills of Samaria. Then the two kingdoms will be reunited and worship together at the Temple in Jerusalem. It will be a time of great rejoicing, when God compassionately guides the remnant of Israel to Jerusalem. As the Father of the nation, God loves Israel eternally. God will guard them as a shepherd guards his flock and save them from the powers that seek to destroy them. God will return them to Zion, where they will flourish like a fertile garden. Everyone will dance as their mourning is turned into joy.

Meanwhile, Israel's mother Rachel can be heard bitterly weeping for her lost children. But *Adonai* promises that her children will return to their country. Ephraim (another name for Israel) can be heard repenting and begging *Adonai* to let him return. He accepts *Adonai* as his God, and is filled with humiliation at his youthful behavior as he returns to *Adonai*.

Note: The verses in the JPS translation of this Haftarah are numbered differently from that of many other translations. The verses are numbered one ahead. For example, verse 15 in JPS is identified as verse 14. If you are using a different translation, use the verse numbers indicated in parentheses. The verses listed above for the Haftarah are according to most translations.

INSIGHTS FROM THE TRADITION

A The cry heard in Ramah in verse 31:15 (14) is that of Rachel weeping for her children. According to *Lamentations Rabbah*, Proem 24, God was really angry about the idolatry in the Temple. All the Patriarchs and Matriarchs went to try to calm God down and keep God from destroying the people. None could calm God. Finally, Rachel came before God and said,

"Whose mercy is greater: yours or a human being's? Yours must be greater. Look what happened to me: Jacob worked to earn the right to marry me. Then my father gave my sister, my rival, to Jacob as a wife instead of me. If I have been able to live with a rival and keep my silence, so can you."

God responded that Rachel defended the people well, and God decided not to destroy Israel based on the example set by Rachel.

◆ What was the point of Rachel's story, in your own words?

◆ How was Israel able to benefit from God's ability to control anger?

◆ How do we all benefit by our own ability to control anger?

B Jeremiah predicts in verse 31:17 (16) that "your children shall return to their country." Hirsch understands this to mean that the children will return to "their own sphere," to God.

◆ Hirsch equates God with home. What does this comparison mean to you?

◆ Do you ever feel that Judaism is somehow your home base where you feel welcome and protected?

C In verse 31:18 (17) Ephraim says he is chastised like a "calf that has not been broken."

Rashi explained that because Ephraim was unbroken, he sinned against God.

According to Radak, "like an untrained calf" means that Ephraim doesn't learn until he is whipped and taught. Now that Ephraim has been chastised, he is ashamed of his past behavior and ready to return and behave well.

◆ Do you agree that punishment is an effective way to encourage good behavior? Why or why not?

D In verse 31:20 (19) God calls Ephraim "a dear son to Me." According to Radak, God is saying, "Why is it that I remember him always as if he were a dear son to me, who never sinned against me?"

◆ What is unconditional love and how does it affect the way we think about someone?

◆ What does it mean when parents tell you that they love you even when they are angry or disappointed in you?

◆ What does it mean that God has unconditional love for us?

STRATEGIES
Analyzing the Text

1 In verse 31:9 (8) the redeemed people weep. Why do the redeemed people weep? Rashi says they will be redeemed through tears and prayers of penitence. Radak says there will be tears of joy for returning to their land. Abrabanel says they will weep over the trials they have been through.

◆ The three commentators mention tears of penitence, of joy, and of sorrow. What other emotions can tears symbolize?

◆ Which interpretation do you think fits the text the best, and why?

2 Compare verses 31:9-10 (8-9) to Psalm 23: 1-3. What similarities can you find? What are God's role, responsibilities, and feelings toward the children of Israel?

3 Mother Rachel weeps for her lost children even as *Adonai* promises to return them safely to her in verse 31:15 (14).

◆ Do you think Rachel is skeptical, or overcome by emotion, or both? How might Rachel symbolize the people of Judah in her emotion and/or skepticism?

4 The popular Hebrew song *"Ko Amar HaShem"* is taken from verse 31:2 (1).

◆ Learn and sing this song, which can be found in *B'Kol Echad* edited by Jeffrey Shiovitz, p. 87, and on the audiocassettes *Shirei B'Kol Echad*, available from United Synagogue of

Conservative Judaism at www.uscj.org/booksvc.

5 There is a tension between God's love for Israel and God's wrath at Israel. Read verse 31:20 (19), in which God describes feeling both love and anger toward Israel. Which sentiment prevails in this verse?

Connecting the Text To the Holiday

6 Verse 31:8 (7) states that God will gather and return the exiles — the blind and lame, those with child, and those in labor among them.

◆ Why are these groups of people mentioned by name? (Commentators explain that even people for whom the journey would be difficult will be returned — God will make the journey slow enough or the road smooth enough for the physically challenged.)

◆ For whom might repentance on Rosh HaShanah be most difficult? What could make repentance easier?

◆ What is the message of this Haftarah for them, and for anyone who fears his or her repentance might not be good enough to "make the journey" to redemption?

7 The people will return with weeping and supplication in verse 31:9 (8). *Baba Metzia* 59a teaches that "even if the gates of prayer are shut, the gates of tears are not."

On Rosh HaShanah, all who wish to repent sincerely will be heard. It is difficult to examine our behavior over the past year and to face our shortcomings and failure to be as good as we can be.

◆ How might true repentance *(teshuvah)* cause tears to fall?

◆ How might tears cause true repentance to happen?

8 In verse 31:9 (8) God will lead the people to streams of water, by a level road, because God is a Father to Israel.

Parents help their children. God helps us.

God is called "Father" in the prayer *"Avinu Malkaynu,"* which for many is a haunting centerpiece of the Rosh HaShanah service. It is recited just before the Torah service. Its famous last lines say:

"Our Father, Our King, graciously answer us, although we are without merits; deal with us charitably and lovingly save us."

◆ Read the prayer *"Avinu Malkaynu"* in any High Holy Day *Machzor*, then learn to sing the last lines using the traditional melody. Ask your Cantor to teach it to your class. *"Avinu Malkaynu"* may be found on many recordings, including the songbook and cassette *Shiron L'Gan — Songs for Children* (Transcontinental Music).

9 Ephraim expresses deep regret and humiliation for his wicked ways in verses 31:18-19 (17-18).

Radak taught that a penitent sinner has not performed complete repentance unless he regrets his sins.

According to Shimon Apisdorf in *Rosh Hashanah Yom Kippur Survival Kit*, pp. 78-79, there are four steps to true repentance *(teshuvah)*.

a. Regret what you have done.

b. Abandon all rationalizations for what you have done.

c. Verbalize your regret to the one wronged.

d. Resolve never to repeat the same mistake.

◆ Discuss how each of these steps is essential for true *teshuvah*.

10 Verse 31:20 (19) of this Haftarah is included as one of the *Zichronot* verses in the Musaf *"Amidah"* for Rosh HaShanah.

The *Zichronot* verses remind God of all the times God remembered Israel and helped us. On Rosh HaShanah, we pray that God will be compassionate once again and remember us for a good year to come.

◆ For advanced study, review these *Zichronot* verses: Genesis 8:1; Exodus 2:24; Leviticus 26:42; Psalms 111:4-5; 111:5, 106:45; Jeremiah 2:2; Ezekiel 16:60; and Jeremiah 31:20. What do they all have in common?

11 In verse 31:18 (19), Ephraim asks God to "receive me back, let me return."

◆ What inspires Ephraim to return to God, shame for his deeds of the past or God's love?

◆ In what ways does the Rosh HaShanah service inspire you to return to God? (For example, the sounding of the *shofar* at Rosh HaShanah is meant to do just that: inspire repentance.)

◆ Discuss this teaching from Rambam about the effect the *shofar* should have on us:

"Awake from your slumber, and rouse yourselves from your lethargy. Scrutinize your deeds and return in repentance. Remember your Creator, you who forget eternal truth in the trifles of the hour, who go astray after vain illusions that can neither profit nor deliver. Carefully examine your souls; mend your ways and your actions; forsake the evil path and unworthy purposes. Return to God, so that God may have mercy upon you."

◆ How does the *shofar* inspire us to repent?

◆ What parts of the Rosh HaShanah service or rituals do you find inspiring?

12 Rosh HaShanah is known as *Yom Harat HaOlam*, the birthday of the world. In this Haftarah, the rebirth of Israel is promised.

◆ How is Rosh HaShanah an opportunity for all of us to be "re-born" and start the year with a clean slate?

JEREMIAH 32:6-27 Ashkenazim
JEREMIAH 32:6-22 Sephardim
BEHAR בהר

This Haftarah has been paired with *Parashat Behar*, Leviticus 25:1-26:2. See "Connecting the Text To the Sedra," p. 409, for an exploration of the many ways the two texts shed light on each other.

SYNOPSIS

The setting for this Haftarah is given in the first five verses of chapter 32. It is the tenth year of the reign of King Zedekiah of Judah (587 B.C.E.), which also makes it the eighteenth year of the reign of the enemy King Nebuchadnezzar of Babylonia. Jerusalem is under siege by the Babylonians, and Jeremiah has advised Zedekiah to surrender. Perceived as a traitor for his advice, Jeremiah is imprisoned by Zedekiah.

A personal event in Jeremiah's life takes on important symbolic meaning for all of Israel. God predicts that his cousin Hanamel will come to Jeremiah to sell him land in the besieged territory of Benjamin. Sure enough, Hanamel visits Jeremiah in prison to sell him the land. Jeremiah buys the land for 17 shekels of silver and exchanges all the legal papers in a procedure that is given in great detail. According to *Adonai's* instructions, the deed and the texts regarding the sale were to be placed in an earthen jar, so that they would last a long time. Jeremiah gives the deed of purchase to Baruch, his personal secretary and scribe.

But even Jeremiah has his doubts. After all, the land he just bought is located in a territory that is about to fall to the enemy. He prays to God for an explanation. Jeremiah acknowledges in his prayer that nothing is too wondrous for *Adonai*, who created heaven and earth and freed Israel from slavery in Egypt. Still, he wonders what God's intentions are.

Adonai responds to Jeremiah, asking rhetorically, "Is anything too wondrous for Me?" Jeremiah is reassured that God has a plan, and Israel is reassured that all will be well.

INSIGHTS FROM THE TRADITION

A Why does Jeremiah say in verse 32:8, "Then I knew that it was indeed the word of *Adonai*"?

Radak asserts that Jeremiah never doubted that he had experienced a true prophecy in verse 32:7. Rather, the phrase in verse 32:8 indicates that Jeremiah understood that when God told him in verse 32:7 that Hanamel would come to sell his land to Jeremiah, God was telling Jeremiah to buy the land. God did not actually command Jeremiah in verse 32:7 to buy the land. Rather, it dawned on Jeremiah that there was no reason for God to tell him about Hanamel unless God wanted him to buy the land. In other words, it seems that Jeremiah had a "light bulb" go on in verse 32:8 when he understood God's unstated command.

◆ Have you ever had a "light bulb moment" when you suddenly understood something you previously could not comprehend?

◆ Draw a caricature of Jeremiah having his "light bulb moment" that enabled him to understand God's wish.

B Hirsch explains that everyone was amazed that Jeremiah would throw away money for worthless land when they were about to go into exile. But Jeremiah went ahead with the land deal because he knew that it came from God.

◆ Have you ever done something you knew was right, even though everyone else thought you were making a big mistake? What made you do it? Were you right?

◆ What does it mean to "trust your instincts"?

C *Adonai* says in verse 32:15 that "houses, fields, and vineyards shall again be purchased in this land." *Metsudat David* explains that this implies that the Israelite people will survive its current tragedy and live to buy houses and dwell in the land.

◆ Did you ever feel like you would not get through a tough time in your life?

◆ Ask your parents or other relatives if there was ever a tough time in their lives that they thought they might not get through.

◆ What were the factors and beliefs that pull(ed) you or them through?

◆ There is an expression, "Whatever doesn't kill you makes you stronger." What do you think this expression means? Do you agree with it? Ask your parents or relatives if surviving their difficult experience made them stronger.

STRATEGIES
Analyzing the Text

1 The Haftarah begins in verse 32:6 with the statement, "Jeremiah said." This sounds like someone else is telling Jeremiah's story, but to whom might Jeremiah have told the story of buying his cousin's land? Since this story took place while Jeremiah was imprisoned by the king for

predicting Jerusalem's doom, it is possible that he told the story to King Zedekiah, to his fellow prisoner, to those who witnessed the transaction, or to all Israelites as a prophecy of hope.

◆ Discuss each possibility. Which do you think is most likely?

◆ Read verses 32:1-5 to learn about Jeremiah's imprisonment.

◆ Draw your understanding of Jeremiah's purchase of the land while in prison. Compare your drawing to the illustration of this Haftarah in *The Illustrated Torah* by Michal Meron, p. 138.

2 Jeremiah bought his cousin's land even though Chaldean (Babylonian) invaders were on the verge of destroying the country and he would have to flee. It was clear that he might never inhabit the land he was buying.

His purchase of the land was not intended as a well researched financial investment, but rather as a symbolic act meant to give hope that the Israelites would one day return.

◆ Explain how his purchase of a worthless piece of land might have given hope to the despairing Israelites. Write and deliver a television news story on the important event.

3 Hanamel, Jeremiah's uncle's son, asked Jeremiah to buy his land. Hanamel said, " . . . for the right of inheritance and obligation of redemption is yours, so buy it yourself" (verse 32:8). Hanamel is referring to two laws: inheritance laws and land redemption laws. The inheritance laws, found in Numbers 27:8-11, provide the order of inheritance among relatives.

◆ Read the laws of inheritance in Numbers 27:8-11.

◆ According to Hanamel, Jeremiah, his cousin, was his nearest relative for purposes of inheritance. Does it appear that Hanamel has sons, daughters, or brothers?

◆ The land redemption laws are found in Leviticus 25:23-28. Review these laws. These laws recognize that God gave the land to specific tribes, which divided it among its members. Since the land belongs ultimately to God and was given according to God's will, the land should not leave those owners. If someone is financially desperate and must sell his land, his family must buy it back (redeem it).

◆ Read a copy of the deed to your house or a standard deed used in your community. Are there any conditions limiting the sale of the house?

4 In verse 32:17 Jeremiah is unsure why he is buying the land and wants reassurance from God. He says that nothing is "too wondrous" for God. God responds to Jeremiah's inquiry in verse 32:27 by repeating Jeremiah's words back to him: "Is anything too wondrous for Me?"

◆ What do you think "too wondrous" means — too hard to do, too hard to know? Something else?

◆ Have you ever asked a question and been given the question back as an answer? Was it reassuring?

◆ How reassured do you think God's response made Jeremiah feel?

5 The Hebrew text of verse 32:23 contains the word ובתרותך (u'vetorot'cha). The word, as it is written, means "Your teachings." The written form of a biblical word is called a *ketiv*. However, in some places of the Bible, Rabbinic scholars determined that a word was spelled wrong. They did not want to change the spelling of the word because the text is sacred. However, they wanted to indicate to the reader that there is a more correct way to read the text. The Rabbinic scholars noted in the margins an alternative reading, called a *keri*. According to these scholars, the word ובתרותך in verse 32:23 should be changed by moving one letter to ובתורתך (u'vetorat'cha) — "Your teaching" (singular).

◆ How is the word written in your copy of the Haftarah? If it has been written as ובתורתך, it was changed in order to make it easier for you to learn.

◆ What do you think is the difference between saying "Your teachings" (literally, your Torahs) and "Your teaching" (literally, your Torah)?

6 According to verse 32:24, siege mounds were in place and ready to assist in storming the city.

Siege mounds were hills, embankments, or ramps built by an enemy up against a city's defense walls in order to assist attacking soldiers who needed to climb over the city walls.

◆ The most famous of all ancient siege mounds in Israel was that of the Romans against the Jewish zealots on Masada. You can read about the history of Masada and see a photo of the earthen ramp built by the Romans (and their Jewish slaves) at http://mosaic.lk.net/g-masada.html.

7 In verse 32:27 God says, "Behold I am *Adonai*, the God of all flesh. Is anything too wondrous for Me?" This statement acknowledges that God is omnipotent.

◆ Explain why this means that all people and all of nature are at God's disposal to achieve God's will, and history reflects God's will.

◆ Explain why this is a soothing viewpoint for a nation about to be defeated by enemies. Does it deny that the enemies' gods are stronger than Israel's God?

◆ Cut out wondrous photographs from nature magazines, such as *National Geographic*, and make a collage entitled, "Is anything too wondrous for God?"

Connecting the Text To the Sedra

8 Leviticus 25:25-28 requires that one redeem (buy) the land of one's relative if the relative is in financial difficulty and needs to sell it.

◆ Reread these verses.

◆ In the Haftarah Jeremiah was asked by his cousin to buy his land because "you have a duty of redemption." Reread verses 32:6-15.

◆ Based on what you learned from Leviticus 25, explain Jeremiah's duty of redemption.

◆ Do you think family members should have a legal responsibility to help each other out of financial trouble? Do you think family members have a moral responsibility to help each other out of financial trouble?

◆ Interview family and friends to find out if there was ever a time they had to help family members financially, or if they ever received financial help from family. How did the help get them back on their feet and "redeem them"?

9 God teaches Israel in the Sedra (Leviticus 25:18) that if they follow God's laws, they will dwell safely in the Land. In the Haftarah (verses 32:22-23) Jeremiah reviews how God brought the people into a land flowing with milk and honey. However, because the people did not listen to God or follow the laws of Torah, God has caused misfortune to befall them.

◆ This concept of reward and punishment was more acceptable to ancient peoples than it is to us today. What event(s) happened in the twentieth and twenty-first centuries that forced many of us to change our thinking about Divine reward and punishment? Why is it so difficult now to think that bad things happen because people deserve them?

Extending the Text

10 In verse 32:12 we are introduced to Baruch, Jeremiah's scribe and personal secretary. Earlier, during the reign of Jehoiakim, Jeremiah dictated his prophecies to Baruch, who wrote them on a scroll of leather. Jeremiah was in hiding at that time, so he sent Baruch to read his prophecies to the people at the Temple. The prophecies angered King Jehoiakim, who slashed and burned the scroll. Baruch had to join Jeremiah in hiding, where Jeremiah ordered him to rewrite the scroll.

◆ Read the whole story in Jeremiah 36.

◆ For more information on Baruch, see *Encyclopaedia Judaica*, vol. 4, pp. 266-267.

◆ To learn about the *sofer's* (scribe's) art, visit the web site: www.geocities.com/athens/9587/alephbet.html. Try your hand at writing the letters as shown on the web site.

11 Baruch ben Neriah was Jeremiah's scribe. The next great scribe mentioned in the Bible was Ezra. According to *Megillah* 16b, Baruch was the teacher of Ezra. This is not likely literally; Baruch lived during the fall of Jerusalem (586 B.C.E.), and Ezra is thought to have lived after the return from exile (around 440 B.C.E.). Nonetheless, tradition connects them, because scribal skills are a valued part of our tradition and require great training from one generation to the next.

◆ Invite a scribe (*sofer*, in Hebrew) to your class to speak about and demonstrate the important job a *sofer* performs. Ask about the training needed. Is an apprenticeship required?

◆ Scrolls should be checked periodically for errors. Exposure to the elements and simple usage can damage the text in a scroll. Ask the scribe to check one of your synagogue's *mezuzot* so that you can see how a *mezuzah* scroll is checked, and so that you can find out how often to have it checked.

◆ Read and discuss *Sofer, The Story of a Torah Scroll* by Eric Ray (Grades K-7). The book teaches through photos and text how an actual *sofer* (Ray) makes *mezuzot, tefillin,* and a Torah scroll.

12 Jeremiah gave the deed to his new land acquired from Hanamel to Baruch, and ordered Baruch to seal the deed in an earthen jar so that it might last a long time (verse 32:14). In the twentieth century, earthen jars containing scrolls were discovered in caves near the Dead Sea in Israel.

◆ For pictures of some of these earthen jars and their contents, see the *Encyclopaedia Judaica*, vol. 5, pp. 1396-1418.

◆ Make a pottery jar with a lid to hold your private papers and letters.

13 We learned in Analyzing the Text #5, p. 408, about scribal errors.

Perhaps the best-known possible scribal error is the omission of the line beginning with the Hebrew letter *nun* from the *"Ashray"* (Psalm 145). The *"Ashray"* is an acrostic — with each line beginning with consecutive letters of the Hebrew *alef-bet*, but the *nun* line is missing. In the Greek translation of the Hebrew Bible, called the *Septuagint*, there is a verse beginning with *nun*. It says, "Faithful is *Adonai* in all His words and loving in all His deeds." The word "faithful" in Hebrew is נאמן (ne'eman).

The Rabbis (*Berachot* 4b) had a different explanation for why there was no *nun* verse in *"Ashray."* They suggested that the verse beginning with the letter *nun* foretold bad news, and so it was dropped. They thought the verse might have been "Fallen (*naflah*) is the young woman Israel, she shall rise no more."

◆ Explain how a scribe might have mistakenly skipped a line when copying this Psalm, which caused the verse to be missing from that time on.

◆ Identify the line of *"Ashray"* that begins with the same letter as your Hebrew name. Memorize that line and its English translation. Can you suggest any special significance this verse has for you?

14 This Haftarah takes place during a terrible era of Israelite history. But God promises better days are to come. Such days are described in the next chapter of Jeremiah in 33:10-11. These words of promise have been set to music in the song *"Od Yishama"* (Again Will Be Heard), which is traditionally sung at joyous Jewish weddings.

◆ Learn and sing *"Od Yishama."* Sing it and dance the Hora! The words, translation, and transliteration may be found in *B'Kol Echad*, edited by Jeffrey Shiovitz, p. 92, and the song may be found on the accompanying audiocassette, *Shirei B'Kol Echad*. Both can be ordered from the United Synagogue for Conservative Judaism at www.uscj.org/booksvc.

15 Jeremiah was imprisoned for his political and religious beliefs. In most democratic countries, it is illegal to punish someone for their beliefs, and we are all granted the right of free speech.

◆ Read the First Amendment to the Constitution of the United States, protecting the right to free speech. You can find it online at http://pacific.discover.net/~dansyr/billrigh.html.

◆ Invite someone from the American Civil Liberties Union to talk about free speech.

Personalizing the Text

16 Jeremiah dictated his prophecies to Baruch (verse 36:4).

◆ Play a dictation game. The teacher reads a short selection from the Book of Jeremiah to the class. The students write down what they hear. Then, compare all the versions to see if they came out exactly the same.

17 Jeremiah's prophecies were written on scrolls (verse 36:2).

◆ Make a Bar or Bat Mitzvah scroll. To make the scroll, tape pieces of paper together and attach the ends to the cardboard rolls from paper towels. On your scroll handwrite part of your Haftarah portion, then try to read it from your scroll.

◆ Alternatively, write your *D'var Torah* on the scroll, then deliver it to the congregation from your scroll. Does reading a speech from a scroll make it seem more important?

18 We learned in verses 32:17 and 27 that nothing is too wondrous for God.

◆ Think of a modern day miracle that you have either witnessed, heard about personally, or learned about in the news. As a class, share these "wondrous" events and discuss God's role in each.

19 Since Jeremiah was imprisoned at the time of this particular prophecy, he must have had some difficulty getting the message out to the people.

◆ Imagine you are a newspaper or television reporter covering the controversial imprisonment of the prophet. You have been granted a rare interview with Jeremiah, and he takes the opportunity to tell you the story and its message. Write the interview in question and answer format for your newspaper, or videotape the interview for your viewing audience.

20 Jeremiah put his real estate documents in a jar for safekeeping.

◆ Make a class time capsule. Collect objects, newspaper clippings, and photos, and compile lists of favorite songs, films, television shows, etc., to include in your time capsule. Seal these in a glass jar and bury the jar in your synagogue yard (get permission first) for safekeeping. As a class, agree on a future date to come together and open your time capsule.

Other Resources

21 For more on the prophet Jeremiah, including history, themes, and notable quotations, read *Messengers of God: A Jewish Prophets Who's Who* by Ronald H. Isaacs, pp. 102-120.

22 For additional information on the prophet Jeremiah as well as the Book of Jeremiah, see *Encyclopaedia Judaica*, vol. 9, pp. 1345-1361.

23 See Rembrandt's painting of Jeremiah lamenting over Jerusalem at www. archive.com. Try painting your own portrait of Jeremiah.

24 For more on the trial of Jeremiah, see *Defending the Faith: Trials and Great Debates in Jewish History* by Ronald H. Isaacs.

25 For more information on *Ketib* and *Keri* (see Analyzing the Text #6, p. 408), see *The Masorah of B.H.S.* by Page H. Kelley, Daniel S. Mynatt, and Timothy G. Crawford, or the entry "Masorah" in the *Encyclopaedia Judaica*, vol. 16, pp. 1419-1421.

26 For a commentary to this Haftarah, see the UAHC Family Shabbat Table Talk web site at www.uahc.org/torah/stt/3bb.shtml.

Involving the Family

27 We are not permitted to touch a Torah scroll with our hands because the oils in our hands can damage the text. It is customary to read from the Torah using a pointer called a *yad*. Buy a beautiful *yad* for your Bar/Bat Mitzvah, and start a family tradition of purchasing a special *yad* for each child who becomes (or has already become) a Bar/Bat Mitzvah. Having your own personal *yad* might just encourage you to continue reading Torah in the future.

Bar/Bat Mitzvah Project

28 Jeremiah was able to help his relative out of financial ruin. Find out if there is any relative who cannot come to your Bar/Bat Mitzvah because of financial or physical hardship. Do whatever you can to help that person share your day with you.

JEREMIAH 34:8-22, 33:25-26
MISHPATIM משפטים

This Haftarah has been paired with *Parashat Mishpatim*, Exodus 21:1-24:18. See "Connecting the Text To the Sedra," pp. 415-418, for an exploration of the many ways the two texts shed light on each other.

SYNOPSIS

When the Babylonians invaded Judah and Jerusalem in 589 B.C.E., the Israelite elite tried to win God's forgiveness by releasing all Hebrew slaves who, according to biblical law, should have been released long before then. But when the siege is lifted a year later, the former slave owners cancel the release and demand that the slaves return to their previous status. In this scathing Haftarah, Jeremiah pronounces judgment on Israel's elite and predicts the harsh consequence.

Jeremiah reminds the people that after the redemption from Egypt, God established with Israel that Hebrew slaves must be released after six years of service. First, the Israelites neglected the law altogether, and now they released the slaves only to enslave them once again! They will be punished, says Jeremiah, with sword, pestilence, and famine. The officials and priests and people of Judah and Jerusalem will be killed, and their carcasses will become food for the birds and beasts. Babylonia, which has temporarily retreated from Judah, will return to utterly destroy it.

Because the Rabbis did not want to end any Haftarah on a negative note, they included verses 33:25-26 at the end of this particularly devastating one. Jeremiah's concluding words reassure Israel that God will not reject the offspring of Jacob and David, but will restore them and take them back in love.

INSIGHTS FROM THE TRADITION

A Hertz suggests that the people who owned slaves agreed to let them go in compliance with the law (verse 34:10). In the face of destruction, they thought they would be more worthy of salvation if they complied with the law.

◆ In your own words, explain Hertz's interpretation of why the people decided to let their slaves go free.

◆ What do you think is the difference between people who do the right thing just because it is right and people who do the right thing because they want to be rewarded for it?

◆ Investigate instances of slave labor by companies who manufacture or assemble their products in third world countries. Start a letter writing campaign to those companies against these practices.

B In verse 34:16 we are told that the people who have taken back the slaves have profaned God's name. Hertz explains that God's name is made holy by acts of justice and is profaned by acts of inhumanity.

◆ List three acts of justice and three acts of inhumanity.

◆ Explain how acts of justice make God look good and how acts of inhumanity reflect badly on God.

◆ For more information on profaning God's name, see the Haftarah for *Kedoshim* (Sephardim), Connecting the Text To the Sedra #10, p. 438, and the Haftarah for *Shabbat Parah*, Analyzing the Text #1, p. 460.

C *Daath Soferim* suggests the emancipation of slaves was accompanied by an enormous celebration.

◆ Explain why both slaves and slave owners might have celebrated this emancipation.

◆ List the Jewish and American holidays that in some way celebrate freedom from slavery.

D In verse 33:25 God says that a covenant has been established with day and night. Rashi (*Pesachim* 68b) wonders what it means to have a covenant with day and night, and concludes it must be an allusion to studying Torah day and night.

◆ How often do you go to Religious School?

◆ How often do you practice for your Bar/Bat Mitzvah?

◆ Why do you think Rashi suggests that we should study Torah day and night?

◆ Do you think this suggestion applies to adults as well as to children?

E In the concluding verse 33:26, God says, "I will never reject the offspring of Jacob and My servant David." According to Ibn Ezra, Jacob is mentioned to teach that it is prohibited to have a non-Israelite as king over Israel.

◆ According to American law, a president must have been born in the United States. Do you agree with this law? Why or why not?

◆ Find out if other countries share the same condition for their president or prime minister. How about Israel?

STRATEGIES
Analyzing the Text

1 Jeremiah 34:9 includes the first use of the word יהודי (*yehudi*) in the Bible. The word is translated as "Judean." It is also the root of the names Judah, Judith, Judaism, and Jewish.

Notice that verse 34:9 also contains the word עברי (*ivri*), translated as "Hebrew." The meaning and origin of the word *ivri* is uncertain, but it is most often used in the Bible when foreigners refer to Israelites. *Ivri* could, therefore, be used interchangeably with Israelite.

It is not clear why today Jews are called Jews and not Hebrews. There is, however, a *midrash* that attempts to explain this. In Genesis 36, Joseph was sold into slavery at the suggestion of his brother Judah. Many years later, Joseph was a powerful man in Egypt, and his younger brother Benjamin was about to be imprisoned. Judah offered his own life in exchange for Benjamin's freedom. The *midrash* suggests that due to Judah's willingness to sacrifice himself for the freedom of another, we are all called by his name — Judeans, or Jews.

◆ Make an acrostic of the word "Jewish" or "Judaism," using each letter to begin a word that describes the Jewish people.

2 The Torah contains specific laws about how to treat Israelite slaves and when they must be released. See Exodus 21:2-11, Deuteronomy 15:1-18, and Leviticus 25:39-43 for these laws about how to treat fellow Israelite slaves.

According to modern scholars, Jeremiah 34:14-15 suggests that the law requiring that Israelite slaves be released after six years was probably never enforced. It was probably a utopian, idealistic law that was never in practice.

◆ Explain why Jeremiah 34:14-15 might be a clue to us that the law regarding Israelite slaves was never kept.

◆ Can you think of other laws (such as the one prohibiting jaywalking, for example) that should be followed, but are not really enforced?

◆ Compared to a law freeing slaves, are the laws you listed important? Explain your answer.

3 In an ironic twist, God says in verse 34:17 that since the Israelites would not release their slaves, God would release the Israelites, God's servants. God proclaims their release "to the sword, to pestilence, and to famine."

◆ Explain the irony of this verse.

◆ Do you agree that God is speaking ironically? What emotions do you think God is expressing?

◆ Explain how the Israelites wanted the protection that comes from being God's servant, but did not want the obligation to follow God's laws and release their own servants. Why can't they have it both ways?

4 Verses 34:18-20 refer to an ancient covenantal custom. When making a covenant, the two parties indicated that the covenant would be binding upon them by cutting up an animal and walking between the halves of the animal. This was a symbolic action that meant: may this happen to me (i.e., may I be drawn and quartered) if I don't keep my part of the deal.

◆ Why might this custom have been effective?

◆ For an example of a biblical agreement that was completed in accordance with this custom, see Genesis 15:10-21.

◆ Ask a lawyer if contracts today contain a clause that stipulates what will happen if someone breaks the agreement.

5 The Haftarah concludes with verses 33:25-26 from earlier in the Book of Jeremiah, which connect very well to the end of chapter 34. Chapter 34 discusses the consequences to Israel for having broken its Covenant with God. Verses 33:25-26 include God's assertion that God will never fail to keep the Covenant: "As surely as I have established My Covenant with day and night — the laws of heaven and earth — so I will never reject the offspring of Jacob and My servant David."

◆ Just as God considers the laws of physics unbreakable, so God considers the Covenant with our ancestors to be unbreakable. Why might this have been a reassuring analogy for the ancient Israelites?

◆ Write your own alternative upbeat ending to this Haftarah that would offer reassurance to the Israelites.

Connecting the Text To the Sedra

6 The Haftarah condemns the Israelites for failing to release their Hebrew slaves.

◆ The Sedra begins with a law code, the first law of which concerns slavery. Read the laws concerning slavery in Exodus 21:2-11, 20-21, and 26-27.

◆ These laws were written for the protection of slaves. Do you consider these laws to be protective of slaves? Explain your answer.

◆ Typically, when a law code is composed, the first law stated in the code is considered to be the most important. Do you think a law requiring the release and protection of slaves is more important than all the other laws in this law code?

◆ If this law is the most important law, explain why God was so upset in the Haftarah that the Israelites did not keep the law.

◆ In the *Etz Hayim Chumash* (p. 482), Michael Fishbane observes that "Jeremiah's rebuke suggests that the people's disregard for human freedom violates their ancient Covenant with God, who 'brought them out of . . . the house of bondage.'" Do you think a society that approves of slavery (no matter how regulated) can be a truly just society? Explain.

◆ Imagine one student is God's press secretary or spokesperson. Hold a press conference on freedom and slavery. Other students pose as reporters, attempting to ascertain God's position on both subjects.

7 The Haftarah says in verse 34:14 that there was a law to free slaves after six years, but the Israelites did not obey the law — they did not "give ear." The expression "to give ear" means to listen, heed, or obey.

◆ Explain why this figure of speech makes sense.

◆ In the Sedra ears are mentioned at least twice. For example, if a slave refused to go free, the owner had to pierce the slave's ear and the slave remained with the owner for life (Exodus 21:6). The piercing may have been a mark of ownership on the slave. Explain why a slave — who must heed his owner at all times — would be marked on his ear.

◆ Rashi also comments on Exodus 21:6 that the ear is marked because the Israelites stood at Mount Sinai and, with their ears, heard God say, "The children of Israel are slaves to Me." In spite of what it heard from God, this ear went and acquired a different master for itself.

Make a cartoon depiction of the ears at Mount Sinai.

◆ The Sedra (Exodus 24:7) also requires that the Covenant with God be read into the ears of the people. For more information on biblical quotations related to ears, see the Haftarah for *Tzav*, Extending the Text #17, pp. 388-389.

8 The idea that punishment should be measure for measure is an important biblical concept. In the Haftarah (verse 34:17), God is angry that the Israelites broke the law by not freeing their slaves. The punishment proclaimed by God is that they will be freed from their relationship with God: "You would not obey Me and proclaim a release . . . I proclaim your release."

◆ Explain how God's proclamation is "measure for measure."

Similarly, in the Sedra, there are examples of measure for measure punishment. Exodus 21:12-13 requires capital punishment for intentionally causing a death. Exodus 21:24 requires a monetary penalty based on the type of damage done. Contrary to popular belief, "an eye for an eye" does not mean that the one who causes another to lose an eye must also lose an eye in punishment. Rather, it means the guilty party must pay the monetary value of an eye.

◆ Explain how these laws in the Sedra provide a measure for measure punishment.

◆ Modern day laws and punishments are also measure for measure, because they are weighted to the severity of the crime, but are usually paid in jail time or financial fines. For example, the penalty for driving above the speed limit and littering involves a fine, whereas the penalty for perjury is jail time.

◆ Suggest other penalties for these and other crimes that would not involve money or jail time, but would still be measure for measure.

For example, someone who litters might have to clean a town park, and a speed limit violator might have to serve as a school crossing guard.

◆ Do you think measure for measure penalties are appropriate? How might they deter crime?

9 According to Malbim, when the people reneged on their declaration of freedom for their slaves and forcibly took them back in verse 34:16, it was equivalent to theft or kidnapping. The Sedra also contains laws for dealing with theft in Exodus 22.

◆ Why do you think Malbim considered the forced return of the slaves to be equivalent to theft or kidnapping? Who or what was stolen?

10 Exodus 22:27 teaches us not to revile God or curse the ruler. In verse 34:16 of the Haftarah, God complains that the Israelites "have profaned My name" by taking back their slaves. In other words, by taking back their slaves, the Israelites have cursed their Divine Ruler. It may seem obvious that it is forbidden to curse God publicly, but one *midrash* goes a step further.

Leviticus Rabbah 32:2 teaches that one ought not to curse the king — even when one is alone in the privacy of the bedroom — for a bird of the air shall carry the voice. Rabbi Levi commented, "The road has ears, ay, the wall has ears!"

◆ What does the expression, "the wall has ears" mean?

◆ What does this lesson teach about talking about other people, even in private?

◆ List reasons why gossip is dangerous, even in private.

11 The Torah reading forbids holy people from eating *trayfah* (flesh torn in the field) and instructs us to cast it to the dogs to eat (Exodus 22:30).

◆ The Haftarah threatens that those who broke God's Covenant would die and their carcasses would lie in the field as food for the birds and beasts. How does this image demonstrate that God's holy people would themselves become *trayfah*?

◆ Why is this such a powerful image?

◆ The word *"trayfah"* has evolved to mean any food that is not kosher. Ask your Rabbi or other knowledgeable person to speak to your class about the rules of *kashrut*. You can also surf the Internet; search under kosher and *kashrut* for a huge selection of resources on the subject.

12 The expression "My name" is used by God in both Exodus 23:21 and Jeremiah 34:15. While God has many names in the Bible and in Jewish tradition, God is often referred to simply as "The Name," or *"HaShem,"* in Hebrew. Some consider it a sign of respect to refer to God this way when we are not praying.

◆ Practice using *HaShem* when you are talking about God during this lesson.

13 In verse 34:13 *Adonai* castigates the Israelites for breaking "a Covenant I made with your fathers when I brought them out of the land of Egypt."

A covenant is a contract between two groups that spells out their responsibilities toward each other. The Haftarah refers to the Covenant made between God and the children of Israel at Mount Sinai. God gave the people the Torah, the people agreed to keep it, and God promised to maintain the Israelites as a special people (Exodus 24). In the Sedra (Exodus 24), Moses presents the conditions of the Covenant with God to the people, and the people respond, "All the things that *Adonai* has commanded we will do!"

- In your opinion, does God have legitimate grounds to be so angry at the violation of the Covenant?

- Imagine you are a defense attorney representing Israel in a trial against God. What are your best arguments in Israel's defense for violating the Covenant?

Extending the Text

14 Freedom is proclaimed for all Hebrew slaves in verses 34:8-9.

Over 2,000 years later, the Thirteenth Amendment of the Constitution of the United States granted freedom to America's slaves. It says, "Neither slavery nor involuntary servitude, except as a punishment for crime whereof the party shall have been duly convicted, shall exist within the United States, or any place subject to their jurisdiction. Congress shall have power to enforce this article by appropriate legislation."

- How does this compare with God's decree in 34:8-9?

- Visit the web site www.nps.gov/ncro/anti/emancipation.html to read President Lincoln's Emancipation Proclamation. Can you detect any Jewish influence in the President's words?

- The Emancipation Proclamation was delivered to the nation on September 22, 1862. Do you think September 22 should be a national holiday?

- Design a ceremony to commemorate the end of slavery in the United States.

15 Jeremiah abhorred slavery and man's injustice to man. In the twentieth century, Rabbi Abraham Joshua Heschel stood out as a Jewish leader for civil rights, equal justice, and peace. He once remarked, "We are commanded to love our neighbor: this must mean that we can." Heschel, who was a professor of ethics and mysticism at the Jewish Theological Seminary in New York, marched for civil rights with Martin Luther King, Jr. He also spoke at the National Conference of Religion and Race in Chicago in 1963, helped to found the organization Clergy and Laity Concerned about Vietnam, and was a leader in the struggle for Soviet Jewry. He believed it was a Jewish responsibility to be politically active in humanitarian causes.

- You can learn more about Rabbi Heschel from an article reprinted at www.crosscurrents.org/heschel.htm.

- Do a reading of or perform the play "Abraham Joshua Heschel: A Modern Prophet" in *Extraordinary Jews: Staging Their Lives* by Gabrielle Suzanne Kaplan, pp. 71-89.

- Prepare a class exhibit on Rabbi Abraham Joshua Heschel, champion of human rights. Invite other classes to view and learn from your exhibit.

16 The Haftarah begins with the release of all Hebrew slaves.

- What does Jewish tradition have to say about slavery? Consider these quotations:

  - "[Slavery is] the greatest possible crime against God. " (Rabbi David Einhorn)

  - "God requires that your servant be your equal. You should not eat white bread and he black bread; you should not drink old wine and he new wine; you should not sleep on a feather bed and he on straw. Therefore it is said that whoever acquires a Hebrew slave, acquires a master." (*Kiddushin* 20a)

  - "Love a wise slave as yourself, and withhold not his freedom!" (*Ben Sira* 7:21)

- "A slave cannot be disciplined by words alone." (Proverbs 29:19)

◆ Perhaps you can see a progression in Judaism's attitude toward slaves and slavery. Try to put the quotations into their proper historical order (reverse them).

17 In verse 34:20 God threatens that the Israelites will die and their corpses will remain ignobly unburied. In Judaism we are taught to honor the dead by caring for and guarding the body from the moment of death until burial is complete. This *mitzvah* is called *kavod ha-mayt*.

The Talmud compares a corpse to a scroll of Torah that has been destroyed. While the person lived, he/she used his/her body to fulfill the commandments and teachings of the Torah. Once dead, the body must be buried with the same care and respect accorded to a destroyed scroll of Torah (which we are enjoined to bury).

◆ Discuss this comparison and what it teaches about the sanctity of human life.

◆ Imagine the soul of a deceased person could write a thank-you note for treating his/her body with respect. Be the soul and write the note.

◆ For more information on the *mitzvah* of *kavod ha-mayt*, see the Haftarah for *Tzav*, Extending the Text #16, p. 388. See also the book *Exploring Jewish Ethics and Values* by Ronald H. Isaacs, pp. 120-124.

18 The Haftarah occurs during the reign of King Zedekiah of Judah. The name Zedekiah means "*Adonai* is righteousness."

◆ Do you think this is an appropriate name for the king in this story?

◆ The Haftarah says that Zedekiah will be handed over to his enemies. What ended up happening to King Zedekiah?

◆ Read II Kings 25 and Jeremiah 52. Then write an obituary for King Zedekiah.

Personalizing the Text

19 The law to free Hebrew slaves was first in the Sedra's law code.

◆ If the whole world had one big law code, what law would you put first because you thought it is most important?

◆ Emblazon your most important law on a poster to hang in class.

20 Jeremiah was "enslaved" in prison because of his controversial views.

◆ Imagine you are a newspaper editor in Jeremiah's time. Half the class can write an editorial about why Jeremiah should be freed. The other half can write about why Jeremiah should stay in jail.

21 Artistic illustrations of text often provide answers to ambiguous parts of the texts.

◆ Choose a verse of the Haftarah that you think needs explanation and depict it by painting, drawing, or collage. How does your illustration answer a question in the text?

◆ Compare your illustration with the illustration of this Haftarah in *The Illustrated Torah* by Michal Meron, p. 84. Why is the angel is this illustration crying? What other emotions are conveyed by your illustration or Meron's illustration?

22 In Insights from the Tradition #A, p. 413, Hertz suggests that some people do the right thing not because it is right, but because they hope to be rewarded for their behavior.

◆ Interview your family and friends to find out if there are laws that they obey not because they think the laws are important to obey, but because they don't want to get in trouble or they want a reward.

23 In Insights from the Tradition #D, p. 414, we learn that Torah should be studied day and night.

◆ Choose one verse from the Torah reading or one from the Haftarah. Make a plaque with this verse to hang on your refrigerator so that you will reflect on it at breakfast and at dinner (i.e., day and night).

24 In verse 34:16 God complains that the Israelites profaned God's name by the way they acted. Most people do not realize that the synagogue is not the only place to be religious; our behavior in the outside world can be holy or profane.

◆ Design an exit sign for your synagogue that reminds people as they are leaving that their actions for the rest of the day can either sanctify or profane God's name.

25 Freedom is an important Jewish value. Write and perform a rap about the importance of freedom and the injustices of slavery.

Other Resources

26 Jews have been very involved in the fight against slavery and racism in the U.S. View and discuss the film *Mississippi Burning* (1988, rated R, 128 minutes), which tells the true story of the deaths of three civil rights workers (two of them Jewish) in the summer of 1964. Warning: this film is graphic and disturbing. Teacher should preview first to determine whether it is appropriate for viewing.

27 Public television produced a series called "Africans in America" that chronicles the history of slavery in the United States. Visit the PBS web site to learn more about this subject and to get teaching material on it: www.pbs.org/wgbh/aia/home.html.

28 For more discussion on measure for measure punishment, see *Teaching Torah* by Sorel Goldberg Loeb and Barbara Binder Kadden, *Mishpatim*, Insights from the Tradition #E, pp. 122-123.

29 For more on the prophet Jeremiah, including history, themes, and notable quotations, read the book *Messengers of God: A Jewish Prophets Who's Who* by Ronald H. Isaacs, pp. 102-120.

30 For additional information on the prophet Jeremiah as well as the Book of Jeremiah, see *Encyclopaedia Judaica*, vol. 9, pp. 1345-1361.

31 See Rembrandt's painting of Jeremiah lamenting over Jerusalem at www.archive.com. Try painting your own portrait of Jeremiah.

32 For a commentary on this Haftarah, see the UAHC Family Shabbat Table Talk web site at www.uahc.org/torah/stt/3mishpatim.shtml.

33 View and discuss the film *Spartacus*, about a slave in Roman times (1960, PG-13, 196 min.) or the comedy *A Funny Thing Happened on the Way To the Forum* (1966, not rated, 100 min.).

Involving the Family

34 In Connecting the Text To the Sedra #11, p. 417, we learn about *trayfah*. For the month of your Bar/Bat Mitzvah, avoid *trayfah* foods at home and/or when eating out of the house. Ask your Rabbi to explain which foods are considered *trayfah*, or consult a book such as *The Jewish Dietary Law*s from the Rabbinical Assembly of America.

Bar/Bat Mitzvah Projects

35 America still suffers the pains of the legacy of slavery in strained relations between the races. Become involved in school or community efforts to improve race relations.

Alternatively, help your Religious School/Day School teacher to arrange a project or discussion with a group of local African-American teenagers.

36 In Insights from the Tradition #B, p. 413, we learned that God's name is made holy by acts of justice. Each week of your Bar/Bat Mitzvah year, do one act of justice, keeping a diary of your deeds. Consider, for example, writing a letter to your Congressperson to stop an injustice, taking groceries to a sick neighbor, or making someone new at school feel welcome. Alternatively, support an organization that is concerned about doing justice by fighting hunger and poverty, such as the Jewish Fund for Justice. For more information about this organization, see their web site at www.jfjustice.org.

JEREMIAH 46:13-28
BO בא

This Haftarah has been paired with *Parashat Bo*, Exodus 10:1-13:16. See "Connecting the Text To the Sedra," pp. 424-425, for an exploration of the many ways the two texts shed light on each other.

SYNOPSIS

Jeremiah witnessed many major international wars and changes in the balance of power. This Haftarah consists of the second half of chapter 46. The first half of chapter 46 is made up of a poem, probably written in 605 B.C.E., just after Pharaoh Necho of Egypt was vanquished by Babylonian forces under King Nebuchadnezzar at the battle of Carchemish. Carechemish was on the Euphrates River, at a great distance from Egypt.

This Haftarah considers the implications of that military defeat: now that the Egyptians have lost to the Babylonians at a foreign location, the Babylonians will probably proceed to invade Egypt and defeat them also on their home territory. Jeremiah says that *Adonai* will punish Egypt for its treatment of Judah by delivering that country into the hands of the Babylonians. Fair Egypt shall be shamed, Jeremiah proclaims, and her people exiled.

But Israel has no need to fear, Jeremiah concludes, because although they will be chastised, *Adonai* is with them and will restore them and destroy all their enemies.

This Haftarah is the first of Jeremiah's prophecies against foreign nations, which comprise the remainder of his book.

INSIGHTS FROM THE TRADITION

A According to Rashi, "they fell over one another" in verse 46:16 means they joined one another and said, "let's go home."

It seems there were non-Egyptians living in Egypt who sensed that Egypt was no longer a safe place to live. With the threat of impending invasion and Egypt's imminent defeat, these foreigners felt they must leave.

◆ What would make your country unsafe for Jews?

◆ Do you imagine we would join together and all leave together? Or, do you imagine that some Jews would leave and some would stay?

B Hirsch explains concerning verse 46:16 that "they fell over one another" in fear. He explains that fear is infectious; the minute one person loses courage, others do, too.

◆ What does it mean that fear is contagious?

◆ Are courage and hope also infectious? Explain your answer.

C Concerning verse 46:17 *Metsudat David* teaches that Pharaoh made a lot of noise boasting that he could defeat the Babylonians, but on the day set for battle, Pharaoh was too afraid to confront the enemy.

◆ In what way is boasting really a cover-up for fear and insecurity?

◆ Does a truly confident person need to broadcast his or her abilities to others?

D Jeremiah tells Egypt in verse 46:19 to "equip yourself for exile." Fearing the Babylonians, Egyptians may flee and go into exile. Rashi explains that when a person leaves on a journey, he/she packs a flask and a cup from which to drink.

◆ Why do you think Rashi specified these two items?

◆ If you were leaving home and were unlikely to return, what five (portable) objects would you carry with you (excluding people and animals)? Compare your list to those of your classmates. What items were the same? How were the lists different?

STRATEGIES
Analyzing the Text

1 Verse 46:14 mentions these Egyptian cities. Noph is modern day Memphis, just south of Cairo. Tahpanhes is a border city called Tel Defneh on the Nile River. Migdol means "tower," and was a frontier town in Northern Egypt.

◆ Find these cities on a map of the region as it appeared in Jeremiah's time.

2 In verse 46:17 Pharaoh is said to be a braggart, but literally the verse says he "made a lot of noise" and allowed the hour to go by.

◆ What does it mean to make a lot of noise? Consider these explanations and decide which makes the most sense to you:

• He was a braggart.

• His large army made a lot of noise.

• He boasted with his armies (Rashi).

• He was king over a huge noisy population (Radak).

3 Tabor and Carmel are referred to in verse 46:18. Both of these places are in Israel. Tabor towers over the surrounding plains, and Carmel is a mountain by the sea.

Tabor and Carmel stand out clearly because they are both mountains adjacent to very flat terrain. Similarly, God's message should be as obvious to the viewer as are these two mountains.

◆ Identify both Tabor and Carmel on a map of Israel.

◆ How is the simile about God's message like today's expression, "plain as the nose on your face"?

4 According to verse 46:20, Egypt was a lovely heifer about to be stung by a gadfly from the north. A gadfly is an annoying fly that persistently bites farm animals.

◆ Explain how the gadfly represents the Babylonian enemy in the north.

◆ In addition, verse 46:21 says that Egypt's mercenaries are like fat calves that will only turn and run and not fight. What are mercenaries?

◆ Why would it be insulting for a mercenary to be compared to a fat calf?

5 Egypt is said in verse 46:22 to make the sound of the snake. There are a variety of explanations for what this might mean:

Kara says a snake sheds its skin yearly by sliding between two trees that pull off its old skin. The snake cries out in pain from this maneuver, as does Egypt. *Targum Jonathan* explains the sound of the rustling snake is like the sound of Egypt's rattling weapons. Freedman says that the silent slithering away of the defeated snake is in contrast to the stomping sound of a marching, victorious army.

◆ Which explanation do you like best, and why?

◆ Draw a picture representing ancient Egypt as a rattling, slithering snake.

6 Radak explains that her "forest" in verse 46:24 is figurative for the "people" of Egypt.

◆ According to this verse, what will happen to Egypt?

7 According to Radak God will punish Pharaoh (verse 46:25) in part because Pharaoh Neco II killed the Judean King Josiah in 609 B.C.E. (Note: the King was instituting a great religious reform and convincing the people to follow God.)

◆ See the Overview, pp. 362-363, for a summary of these events.

◆ Why would this assassination be particularly disturbing to God?

◆ Write an inscription for King Josiah's tomb - stone.

Connecting the Text To the Sedra

8 Both the Sedra and Haftarah involve Pharaoh. The Sedra deals with the ancient Pharaoh of Moses' time, who refused to let the Israelites go free, but eventually complied. The Haftarah discusses the modern Pharaoh of Jeremiah's time, who made a lot of noise, but was eventually defeated by the Babylonians.

◆ What characteristics and personality traits do these two Pharaohs seem to share in common? Based on what you know about these two, write a humorous want ad for Pharaoh of Egypt and include undesirable characteristics and traits.

9 There is a lengthy word play in the Haftarah and Sedra. The Sedra is named בא (Bo — to go) because in the first verse God orders Moses to

go to Pharaoh. This verb also reappears repeatedly in the Sedra (Exodus 10:3, 4, 26, 12:25, 13:5, 11). The word also appears repeatedly in the Haftarah.

◆ See the following verses from Jeremiah:
  • 46:13 לבוא (lavo)
  • 46:18 יבוא (yavo)
  • 46:20 בא (ba)
  • 46:21 בא (bo)
  • 46:22 באו (ba'u)

◆ In addition, the Haftarah contains a word that sounds just like בא, "to go," but means "in it." (See 46:25 בו.) It seems that this word may be emphasizing the word play.

◆ What must it have been like for a prophet, Moses or Jeremiah, to go before the mighty Pharaoh? (For example, was it difficult, exciting, or scary?) Perhaps the repetition of this word "go," בא, is meant to emphasize that difficult task.

◆ Write a short story in which you repeat the same word several times; choose any word you want that seems to highlight the point of your story.

10 Michael Fishbane notes in the *Etz Hayim Chumash*, p. 395, that Nebuchadnezzar's coming in judgment against Pharaoh in the Haftarah parallels Moses' coming in supplication before Pharaoh in the Sedra (Exodus 10:1).

◆ How is one Pharaoh paying the price for an earlier Pharaoh's wrongdoings? How is this an example of divine justice?

◆ Fishbane also points out another example of Divine Justice shared between the Sedra and Haftarah. In the Sedra (Exodus 12:12), God promises to visit judgment on the gods of Egypt for Egypt's enslavement of the Israelites. In the Haftarah, this judgment is about to come to pass in verse 46:25. Compare these two verses.

◆ How do Haftarah and Sedra come together to show that God always fulfills God's promises? How do they come together to show that justice will prevail in the world? Do you agree with these two premises? Explain your response.

11 The first plague mentioned in the Sedra is the plague of locusts (Exodus 10:12-19). Similarly, the Haftarah refers to the enemy from the north coming down and destroying Egypt's forests like innumerable locusts (see 46:23).

◆ Describe the damage done by the locusts in both the Sedra and the Haftarah.

◆ Why would locusts be such a threat to an agricultural society like the ancient Middle East?

◆ Make locusts for your next *Seder*. Use clay and pipe cleaners, dates and toothpicks, or paint Styrofoam packing peanuts.

12 The children of Israel flee Egypt in a panic in Exodus 12:38. They do not have time to prepare provisions for the journey.

In the Haftarah (verse 46:19), foreigners in Egypt want to flee and must furnish provisions for themselves for going into exile.

◆ Do you prefer to leave somewhere in a hurry, or do you take your time to prepare for your departure? Explain.

◆ Do you prefer long good-byes or brief ones? Why?

◆ If you had five minutes to prepare to leave your home forever, what would you do in that time? What few items would you take with you, and why?

Extending the Text

13 Jeremiah refers to Mount Tabor and Mount Carmel in verse 46:18. For a small country, Israel is topographically rich and diverse. Learn your way around Israel's many hills and valleys. Make a relief map of Israel using clay or papier mâché, or even ice cream!

14 The Haftarah speaks of people going into exile. The Hebrew word for exile is *galut*.

Consider the following quotations about exile, then use them in a dramatic presentation on *galut*.

• "How can we sing *Adonai*'s song in a foreign land?" (Psalm 137:4)

• "The three great causes of exile: lack of courage, of honor, of government." (Abrabanel)

• "I am from Jerusalem, but because Titus destroyed the Temple, I was born in Poland." (S. Y. Agnon, Israeli writer on winning the Nobel Prize for literature in 1966)

• "Exile is not only a punishment, but a sin." (Abraham Cahan)

• "Wherever Jews live as a minority is *galut*." (Hayim Greenberg)

• "When a person is in exile, nothing fits." (Elie Wiesel)

• "Israel can accomplish its task better in exile than in the full possession of good fortune." (Samson Raphael Hirsch)

• "Exile is a form of imprisonment. The refugee is like a plant without soil or water." (Moses Ibn Ezra)

• "Woe to the children, for whose sins I destroyed My house, burnt My Temple, and exiled My people among the nations! Woe to the father who had to banish his children, and woe to the children who had to be banished from the table!" (*Berachot* 3a)

- "My Heart is in the East, and I am in the ends of the West. How then can I taste what I eat, and how can food to me be sweet?" (Judah Halevi)

15 In the morning service, just before we say the *"Shema,"* we recite a prayer in hope that our people will be gathered from their exile:

"Bring us in peace from the four corners of the earth and lead the homeless of our people triumphantly to our land, for You are the God who grants deliverance."

- ◆ Explain the expression "four corners of the earth."

- ◆ It is a custom that while reciting this passage, we gather together in one hand the *tzitzit* from the four corners of our *tallit.* Explain how our act prepares us to recite the *"Shema,"* and also represents symbolically God gathering together our people. (Hint: See the third paragraph of the *"Shema"* for the answer to the first part of this question.)

- ◆ It has become a custom in recent years to sing this passage to the same melody as *"Hatikvah,"* the national anthem of the State of Israel. Explain how that melody is appropriate for these words.

- ◆ Learn to sing this prayer to the melody of *"Hatikvah."*

16 Pharaoh did a lot of talking, but could not stand up to his enemy. Shammai taught in *Pirke Avot* 1:15, "Say little and do much."

- ◆ What do you think Shammai meant?

- ◆ Can you think of a time when it is important to speak up? Can you think of a time when it is important to keep quiet and take action? Role-play examples of each.

17 The last several chapters of the Book of Jeremiah include prophecies against foreign nations, including Egypt, the Philistines, Moab, Ammon, Edom, Damascus, Kedar, and Babylonia.

- ◆ Make and play a word game (unscramble, *Hangman,* crossword puzzle, or word search) with the names of these nations. You can check Jeremiah 46-51 for more names and information for clues.

Personalizing the Text

18 Jeremiah says that the Egyptians will fall over one another.

- ◆ Play the lap game, and try not to fall over each other. Stand in a circle. Everyone face right and move very close together. Now, each person should sit on the knees of the person behind him or her, until the entire circle is "sitting."

19 The world outside of Israel is called Diaspora in English and *galut* (exile) in Hebrew.

- ◆ Debate this statement: Jews who live outside Israel today are choosing to live in exile.

20 Jeremiah lived in a time of great political and military turbulence.

- ◆ The 1960s were a turbulent time in the United States (Cuban Missile Crisis, Vietnam War, racial tension). Interview a parent or grandparent about what life was like during the 1960s.

21 In Insights from the Tradition #B, p. 422, Hirsch explains that fear is contagious. A Hebrew song, *"Kol Ha'Olam Kulo"* (The Entire World) says, "All the world is a narrow bridge. The main thing is not to be afraid."

◆ Learn and sing this song, which may be found in *B'Kol Echad*, edited by Jeffrey Shiovitz, p. 88, and on the companion audiocassettes *Shirei B'Kol Echad*. Order both from the United Synagogue for Conservative Judaism, www.uscj.org/booksvc.

22 In this Haftarah, and for the remainder of the Book of Jeremiah, Jeremiah prophesies about foreign nations. He predicts doom for all of Israel's enemies. This must have made the exiled Israelites feel some hope for the future.

◆ Imagine you are a child your own age during the exile in Babylonia. You have just heard Jeremiah prophesy the destruction of your enemies and the restoration of your people to Israel. Write Jeremiah a note expressing your feelings and gratitude. (Remember, being a prophet was a thankless job. Jeremiah would be delighted to get some positive feedback.)

Other Resources

23 Read and discuss the story "The Shoebox" in *Because God Loves Stories*, edited by Steve Zeitlin, p. 244. It tells the story of a boy who had to pack quickly when fleeing Europe.

24 For texts and activities related to having courage, see *Teaching Jewish Virtues* by Susan Freeman, pp. 195-210.

25 For more on the prophet Jeremiah, including history, themes, and notable quotations, read *Messengers of God: A Jewish Prophets Who's Who* by Ronald H. Isaacs, pp. 102-120.

26 For additional information on the prophet Jeremiah as well as the writing of the Book of Jeremiah, see *Encyclopaedia Judaica*, vol. 9, pp. 1345-1361.

27 See Rembrandt's painting of Jeremiah lamenting over Jerusalem at www.archive.com. Try painting your own portrait of Jeremiah.

28 Discuss the illustration of this Haftarah in *The Illustrated Torah* by Michal Meron, p.72.

29 For discussion questions and exercises, see *Understanding the Hebrew Prophets* by Ronald H. Isaacs.

30 For commentary, discussion questions, and project, see the UAHC Family Shabbat Table Talk web site at www.uahc.org/torah/stt/3bo.shtml.

Involving the Family

31 The ancient Israelites yearned to return to their land, but were forced to remain in exile. Make plans for a family trip to Israel to see our land that is both ancient and quite modern.

Bar/Bat Mitzvah Project

32 The Israelite exiles longed to return to their land. Today, there are Jewish people all over the world who are trying to return to Israel, but cannot for various reasons (political, economic, etc.). Donate a part of your Bar/Bat Mitzvah gifts (or organize a fund-raiser) to an organization that helps people make *aliyah*, such as Hadassah (their Youth Aliyah department), North American Conference on Ethiopian Jewry, or the United Jewish Communities: The Federations of North America.

OVERVIEW

Ezekiel was both priest and prophet, who preached in the early part of the sixth century B.C.E. His prophecies span the period of roughly 592-572 B.C.E. and seem to have all been prophesied while he was living in exile in Babylonia.

Ezekiel was among those Israelites exiled to Babylonia following its invasion of Jerusalem. Jerusalem surrendered to Babylonian King Nebuchadnezzar in 597 B.C.E. To prevent rebellions, the Babylonian King exiled the royal, priestly, and elite leaders of Jerusalem (Ezekiel among them) to Babylonia. In addition, he installed on the throne in Jerusalem a new king, Zedekiah, whom he hoped would be loyal to him. Less than ten years later, however, Jerusalem rebelled against the Babylonians. The rebellion led to another lengthy siege of Jerusalem that ended in defeat in the summer of 586 B.C.E. King Zedekiah was taken as a prisoner to Babylonia, and Jerusalem and the Temple were burned.

Ezekiel most likely died in Babylonia around 571 B.C.E., since no event after that year is reflected in his prophecies. In addition, from the Book of Ezekiel (chapter 24) we learn that the prophet's wife died in the final siege of Jerusalem.

The Book of Ezekiel contains a wide variety of topics, literary styles, moods and themes. Ezekiel, addressing both those already in exile with him and those who remain in Jerusalem, covers many topics including: the siege and fall of Jerusalem, the exile of the population, blame for the destruction on the sins of the nation, calls for repentance, prophecies against the foreign nations and their rulers, messages of comfort and consolation, and prophecies of the eventual revitalization of the Israelite people. His prophecies of renewal go so far as to give intricate descriptions and measurements of a new Temple and detailed accounts of the new order of Temple service.

The Book of Ezekiel is probably best known for a number of vivid images, rich symbols, parables, and allegories. First is the vision of God's heavenly chariot in the opening chapter, which features a combination of a machine on wheels and multifaced, winged, living creatures. In addition, his famous description of the valley of dry bones (chapter 37) serves as a symbol of the restoration of Israel. Moreover, in order to convey his message, Ezekiel often engages in symbolic actions (as did Isaiah and Jeremiah). Occasionally, however, Ezekiel uses troubling imagery, such as the murder of a wife by her enraged husband. These sometimes violent, misogynistic portions of his book should be seen as metaphors for God's troubled relationship with Israel and not as a realistic manner of solving marital strife.

Throughout his book, Ezekiel emphasizes individual responsibility, holiness, and the importance of repentance. He believes in divine justice and divine retribution for sin. Even though he speaks to a people who had suffered the humiliating disaster of captivity, he is quite assured of Israel's eventual restoration.

EZEKIEL 1:1-28; 3:12
FIRST DAY SHAVUOT

 This Haftarah has been paired with the first day of Shavuot, on which we read Exodus 19 and 20. See "Connecting the Text To the Holiday," pp. 433-434, for an exploration of the many ways the two texts and the holiday shed light on each other.

SYNOPSIS

Ezekiel lived in the days immediately before and after the destruction of Jerusalem by the Babylonians. He prophesied in exile, and this Haftarah (circa 592 B.C.E.) describes Ezekiel's personal revelation of God. His vision is one of the most intriguing passages in the entire Bible.

A huge cloud and flashing fire, surrounded by radiance, appeared before Ezekiel. In the center of the vision was an amber glow and the figures of four creatures. They had the shape of human beings, but each had four faces, four wings, a single rigid leg, and feet like a single calf's hoof. They sparkled like burnished bronze. Below their wings were human hands. Each had faces and wings on all four sides. Their wings touched one another and made a sound like water when they moved. They did not turn, but could move in the direction of any of their four faces.

Of their four faces, one was human, one was a lion's, one an ox's, and the last was an eagle's face. Two wings stretched above their heads, touching the wings of the neighboring figures, while the two bottom wings covered each figure's body.

The figures were accompanied by something that looked like burning coals of fire, like torches that kept moving among the creatures. Lightning came from the fire. Next to each of the four-faced creatures was a gleaming wheel, the rim of which was covered with eyes. The wheels moved with the figures.

Spread above the heads of the creatures was a glowing form. And above the glowing form was a sapphire throne. And above the throne was a human form, glowing like amber and fire and surrounded by a radiance. When Ezekiel saw this presence of *Adonai*, he fell on his face and heard the voice of someone speaking.

The Haftarah concludes with a blessing that proclaims the presence of *Adonai*.

INSIGHTS FROM THE TRADITION

A Ezekiel saw the color of amber in the center of the fire (verse 1:4). The Hebrew word translated as amber is *chashmal*; it is unclear how to translate it. According to *Chagigah* 13a-b, *chashmal* is a type of angel who is silent when God speaks and speaks when God is silent.

◆ What a talent it is to know when to speak and when to be silent and just listen! Describe a situation when you have not known whether or not to speak and, if so, what to say. Why is it hard?

B In verse 1:14 the living beings would run and return quickly, like sparks (lightning). *Metsudat David* explains that the living beings run to perform their missions and return as quickly as lightning.

◆ According to Jewish tradition, we are to rush to fulfill *mitzvot*. What does the running to perform our *mitzvot* express about our attitude toward the *mitzvot*?

◆ Which daily tasks do you rush to perform, and why? Which do you delay, and why?

C In verse 3:12 Ezekiel hears God's chariot depart from the Temple and simultaneously he hears heavenly beings say, "Blessed is the Presence (glory) of *Adonai*." Radak argues that when God was with Israel, Israel constantly provoked God by not following God's laws and made God angry and jealous by engaging in idolatry. God's glory was thus reduced because of the association of ugly jealousy with God. Therefore, when God left Israel, God stopped being jealous and God's glory increased.

◆ Explain why Radak thinks God was angry and jealous.

◆ Explain why it may have tarnished God's image to associate God with jealousy.

◆ Think about a time when you were jealous. Did it bring out the best or worst behavior in you?

D In verse 3:12 Ezekiel hears God's chariot depart from the Temple, and simultaneously he hears heavenly beings say, "Blessed is the Presence (glory) of *Adonai*." According to Radak, being "blessed" means having more goodness and honor.

◆ Fill in the blank: I am blessed because I have _____. List all the answers that are true for you. Then analyze how many of your things you listed are material items, and how many are non-material items? Which involve "goodness" and which "honor"?

E According to Eliezer of Beaugency, the departure of God's chariot from the Temple (verse 3:12) is like when a king leaves his city. The inhabitants rush out to stand and bow as he passes and bless him.

◆ What do people do today when dignitaries come to their city? For example, in New York City, a ticker tape parade is held. How is this the same or different from townspeople standing, bowing, and blessing the passing king?

STRATEGIES
Analyzing the Text

1 The Haftarah begins by saying that Ezekiel was standing along the Chebar Canal with the exilic community in Babylonia in the thirtieth year. The thirtieth year may represent 30 years since a new scroll was found in the Temple and presented to King Josiah. Josiah instituted a sweeping religious reform based on the scroll in an attempt to return to proper worship of God.

Josiah was king from 640-609 B.C.E. According to II Kings 22-23, a book was found in 622 B.C.E. that prompted Josiah to institute a reformation.

◆ What year was the thirtieth anniversary of the finding of the scroll by Josiah?

◆ Ezekiel probably went into exile in 597 B.C.E. How long had he been in exile when he had this vision? How does this latter calculation tie into information given in verse 1:2?

2 Ezekiel saw a gleam of amber from the fire (verse 1:4). The Hebrew word that has been translated as amber is *chashmal*, and it is very difficult to understand and to translate.

Chashmal has been understood to have dangerous and holy qualities and may be related to an ancient mythical precious stone that was brilliant. Others have understood it to mean a polished, shiny metal. In modern Hebrew it means "electricity." Rabbinic tradition suggests that it is a type of angel. It seems to have been bright, with a color like fire.

◆ Discuss how these different ideas of *chashmal* might fit the text.

3 In verse 1:7 Ezekiel describes the beings of the chariot as having legs that were fused into one rigid leg. The idea that their legs were fused straight has been understood in a number of ways:

• Their legs did not have knee joints because they did not need to bend them when they walked, as they only flew.

• Their legs could bend, but at the moment of the vision the legs were straight because they were standing erect, not crouching.

• Their legs were in a proper position, close together and facing straight ahead (as our feet are supposed to be when we pray).

◆ Play *Charades* with this additional rule; you must keep your legs together and straight at all times!

4 Each of the beings that carried the chariot had a four-sided head. The four sides were: human, lion, eagle, and bull. Human beings rule all animals. Lions are the mightiest of all animals. Eagles are the swiftest and most majestic of all birds, and the bull is the most valued of all domestic animals.

◆ Explain how the faces chosen for the heads of the beings teach that only the most proud and majestic of animals are fit to be bearers of *Adonai*.

5 The four beings moved wherever the "spirit" moved them to go (verse 1:12). The "spirit" is the will or desire of the one sitting in the chariot; that is, they moved according to the will of God.

◆ How does this portray the beings as being responsive and obedient to every wish of God?

◆ In chapter 2, Ezekiel will be told to prophesy to the rebellious children of Israel. How are these beings the opposite of the rebellious Israelites?

6 In verse 1:18 the rims of the wheels were frightening; they were covered with eyes. Here are the three possible explanations for the eyes:

• The eyes indicate that the wheels were alive and were intelligent.

• The eyes enabled the wheels to go in any direction and see where they were going without turning (like the beings could see in all four directions without turning).

• The eyes symbolize God's constant watchfulness.

◆ Which of these explanations for the eyes would make them frightening? Why do you think so?

7 The vision Ezekiel had of the chariot and God was a personal revelation and a calling for him to prophesy.

◆ Read chapter 2 for the words of encouragement that God spoke to Ezekiel before sending him on the mission.

Although we do not read chapter 2 in the Haftarah for Shavuot, advanced study of the Haftarah could compare the warning that Ezekiel received (that the people would not listen to him) to: Moses being warned that Pharaoh would not listen to him (Exodus 3:19), Isaiah being warned that the people would ignore him (Isaiah 6:9), and Jeremiah being warned that the people would resist him (Jeremiah 1:19).

◆ How do you think the prophets felt knowing that people would not want to listen to them? Stage a prophets support group meeting during which the prophets share complaints, concerns, support, and advice.

8 Ezekiel's description of his vision is ambiguous to most modern readers.

◆ See the painting of Ezekiel's vision by Raphael at www.sunsite.dk/cgfa/raphael/raphae26.jpg and/or a sixteenth century drawing at www.prs.org/images/mviseze.jpg. How do these artists understand the various issues in the text (i.e., *chashmal*, angel's legs, four-headed beings, wheels with eyes, the spirit)? Draw your own interpretation of these issues or complete p. 23 in *Prophets Copy Pak™* by Marji Gold-Vukson.

Connecting the Text To the Holiday

9 The Torah reading for Shavuot begins by establishing the date of the revelation to be described. The date is "the third new moon after the Israelites had gone forth from the land of Egypt." The date is with reference to a major event.

Similarly, the Haftarah begins with the date of the revelation experienced by Ezekiel. This date is also established with reference to an earlier major event: the thirtieth year (although scholars can only guess what the event was 30 years before — see Analyzing the Text #1, p. 431).

Similarly, Shavuot is our only holiday that is marked by counting from an earlier event (counting 50 days from the first grain offering made on the first day of Passover).

◆ Explain why each of these (Exodus, a scroll revealing God's laws, and the first grain offering) is an important occasion by which to mark future events.

◆ Are there events in your life, the life of your family, or your country that you often use as a marker of time? (For example, before Bar/Bat Mitzvah or after Bar/Bat Mitzvah, before having children versus after having children, before the Six Day War or since the September 11, 2001 attacks, etc.)

10 Both the Haftarah and the Torah reading describe a revelation of God. Compare these aspects of the two revelations:

• There was lightning and torches at Mount Sinai (Exodus 19:16, 20:15). Ezekiel saw something like torches coming from the midst of the creatures. (verse 1:13)

• At Mount Sinai there was thunder, the sound of the *shofar*, and God's voice (Exodus 19:16, 19; 20:15-18). In the Haftarah Ezekiel was alone witnessing the noise of the wings of the bearers of the chariot, which was like the sound of *Shaddai* (verse 1:24), and from above them came a noise (1:24-25). Ezekiel heard a voice of God speaking (1:28) and fell on his face.

• A throne was visible to Ezekiel that was like sapphire. Moses, Aaron, and the elders had a revelation from God (in a later Torah reading) in which they, too, saw sapphire pavement under God's feet (Exodus 24:10).

◆ Create dioramas of these two similar, but distinct, revelations.

11 According to the Torah reading, when God took the Israelites out of Egypt, it was as if they had been carried out on eagles' wings (Exodus 19:4)

In the Haftarah an eagle is one of the faces of the winged being that carried God and God's chariot.

◆ Listen to the song "On Wings of Eagles" by Debbie Friedman, which may be found on the recording *Debbie Friedman Live at the Del.*

12 In the Torah reading, it is understood that the people were standing at Mount Sinai (Exodus 20:15).

◆ When we read the Ten Commandments, it is a tradition to stand and imitate the experience at Sinai, as if we were there. What do you think is the significance of reenacting the scene at Sinai when we received the Ten Commandments?

◆ In the last verse of the Haftarah, when Ezekiel heard the voice of God, he fell on his face. However, we do not fall on our faces during the reading of the Haftarah. How might we personally and privately be reenacting for ourselves Ezekiel's experience of being called to serve God?

◆ What might it mean to each of us to be called on Shavuot to serve God?

◆ As you read or hear the Haftarah, try to imagine Ezekiel's vision in your own mind.

13 In the Haftarah we do not actually hear the words God says to Ezekiel (these words are in chapter 2, and they were omitted by the Rabbis who selected this Haftarah). God sends Ezekiel to go and speak to the rebellious children of Israel.

In contrast, in the Torah reading, we hear the words God spoke to the Israelites and to Moses. We hear the Ten Commandments. What we do not hear, however, is what happens a short time later — the children of Israel rebel and build a golden calf.

◆ Is there a tension on Shavuot between the revelation we reenact with reverence and the knowledge that those revelations were followed by a rebellion against God?

14 Ezekiel's revelation of God takes place in Babylon. God is obviously not confined to the Land of Israel, but that is not a special or new message being offered here; many times in the Bible, God takes action outside of the Land of Israel. Consider two examples of this from the Shavuot readings.

a. In the Torah reading, revelation at Mount Sinai happened outside the Land of Israel just after God had rescued the Israelites from Egypt.

b. On Shavuot, it is tradition to read the Book of Ruth after finishing *"Hallel"* and before the Torah service begins. The Book of Ruth begins in the land of Moab. An Israelite family had moved there from Israel. One son married a Moabite woman named Ruth. After her husband died, Ruth insisted she would return to Israel with her husband's widowed mother; she adopted Israel as her people and accepted Israel's God as her God. Ruth, never having set foot in Israel, chose God.

In each of these stories there is a longing to be back in the Land of Israel and, at the same time, a recognition that God is accessible no matter where the people are.

◆ What role does the Land of Israel play in your Jewish identity? Does a longing to live in Israel define being Jewish for you?

◆ If you have been to Israel, did you feel God's presence was somehow stronger there? Explain your answer.

◆ What new way will you choose to access God and keep God's laws this year?

◆ Write a Shavuot resolution about making God's presence felt more in your life.

EZEKIEL 20:2-20 Sephardim
KEDOSHIM קדשים

This Haftarah has been paired with *Parashat Kedoshim*, Leviticus 19:1-20:27. See "Connecting the Text To the Sedra," pp. 437-439, for an exploration of the many ways the two texts shed light on each other.

SYNOPSIS

This prophecy is given in 591 B.C.E., about five years before the fall of Jerusalem and the burning of the Temple. The elders of Ezekiel's exiled community have come to Ezekiel to inquire about the fate of their far-off, beloved city.

Believing that Jerusalem's destruction was inevitable, Ezekiel describes that fate as a consequence of Israel's wicked past behavior. Ezekiel's scathing response traces the persistent sinfulness of the Israelite people from the time of slavery in Egypt to the present time (although only part of this long history is included in the Haftarah). He condemns the Israelite ancestors for failing to be faithful to God. Ezekiel explains that the unfaithful Israelites were freed from Egypt only for God's own sake, lest the other nations think that God was powerless to redeem the Israelites from slavery.

The shameful history continues through the 40 years of wandering in the wilderness with Moses. Ezekiel recalls how God gave Israel the *mitzvot* and Shabbat as a sign of the covenant between Israel and the Holy One. Again, the Israelites rejected God's laws and profaned Shabbat, and again, God stayed with the Israelites only for God's own sake. Although the freed slaves never lived to enter the Promised Land, God urged their children to turn from their parents' evil ways and follow in God's path.

INSIGHTS FROM THE TRADITION

A Ezekiel warns the Israelites in verse 20:7 to resist the temptation of the detestable things they see with their eyes. Radak explains that a person's eyes bring him/her to sin.

◆ The rating system for films, television, and now music is intended to help parents keep their children from seeing or hearing things that might be inappropriate. Do you agree that what we see or hear can be harmful and can lead us to sin? Do you believe the rating system is helpful, and for whom? How would you rate the contents of this Haftarah, and why?

B Verse 20:11 is generally translated as, "I gave them My laws and taught them My rules, by which a person shall live." The Aramaic translation, known as *Targum Jonathan,* translates the second part of the verse like this: "He shall live through them in everlasting life."

The standard translation expresses the command that one should live life by following these laws, while the *Targum* is saying that following the laws entitles us to an afterlife.

◆ Which interpretation do you like better, and why?

◆ Do you think it is better to observe laws because they make the world a better place *now*, or because you may be rewarded *later* for doing so?

C Ezekiel says in verse 20:12 that God gave Shabbat to Israel as a sign of the sacred Covenant between them. *Shabbat* 10b relates the following story.

The Holy One said to Moses, "In My treasury I have a precious gift — it is called Shabbat, and I wish to give it to Israel."

◆ What makes a gift precious?

◆ Survey 25 adults to find out if they ever have enough time for seeing their family and friends, relaxing, reading, or having a good meal. Ask them if free time would be a precious gift to them. Suggest a few ways they might gain more free time.

D Ezekiel recalls that the Israelites did not keep God's laws in the wilderness. *Dorot HaRishonim* (concerning verse 20:13) argues that although the prophet's accusations applied only to a very few people, it nevertheless shows the importance of "collective responsibility."

◆ Should the many be punished for the actions of the few? Do the teachers in your classes hold all students responsible for the actions of some?

◆ Alternatively, should the many be rewarded for the righteousness of a few, as Abraham argues in the story of Sodom and Gomorrah?

STRATEGIES
Analyzing the Text

1 The Hebrew expression *"ben adam,"* translated in the JPS translation as "mortal," is often translated literally as "son of man." It is a phrase used over 80 times in the Book of Ezekiel! Jewish tradition generally explains the phrase as a reminder to Ezekiel that he was only human, even though he was privileged to be a prophet who saw supernatural visions.

◆ Why do you think God might have wanted to remind Ezekiel that he was a mere mortal? (Plaut suggests that perhaps prophets needed this reminder so they wouldn't think of themselves as superior to other humans.)

◆ There are many professions today that might lead those in them to believe that they are better than mere mortals. Can you think of any?

2 In verse 20:1 the elders of Ezekiel's exiled community come to him and ask him to inquire of *Adonai* concerning the fate of their beloved city. *Adonai* tells the prophet in verse 20:3 to ask the elders if they came to inquire of God, and God tells the prophet that *Adonai* will not respond to the elders' inquiry. The cessation of messages from God is a sign of God's displeasure with sinners. (See similar occurrences: Ezekiel 7:26 and I Samuel 14:37.)

◆ Reread verses 20:7-13. List the ways in which Israel sinned, causing God to be so angry that God didn't want to talk to them anymore.

◆ Do you ever resort to using "the silent treatment"?

◆ Debate: "The silent treatment" can be an appropriate way to express anger or displeasure.

3 The Hebrew expression "lift up My hand" appears repeatedly in the Haftarah and is translated in verses 20:5, 6, and 15 as "to swear" or "to give My oath."

Raising one's hand can also mean to hit, to threaten, or to help.

◆ Can you think of any other meanings for the phrase?

◆ Which meaning(s) do you think are intended in the Haftarah?

◆ Read Ezekiel 20:21-22 (these two verses are not in the Haftarah but seem to be restatements of verses 8-9 and 13-14). What does the image of God's raised hand convey in these two verses?

4 Scholars wonder why Shabbat is mentioned both as a sign of the Covenant and as the prime example of Israel not obeying God. Many answers are suggested: Hertz explains that Shabbat is a sign of the Covenant because, for those in exile in Babylonia, there was no longer a Temple or sacrifices through which to worship God, but they could observe Shabbat in exile. Others suggest that it is a later addition by a Shabbat-zealous editor.

Modern Bible scholar Moshe Greenberg suggests that emphasis is given to Shabbat in this exilic oracle because of Israel's tendency to assimilate. In other words, keeping Shabbat may have become a major sign of one's loyalty to God and resistance to assimilation while living in exile in Babylonia.

◆ Which answer makes most sense to you, and why?

◆ Diaspora Jewry today faces challenges similar to those of Ezekiel's exiled community. What observances do you think distinguish those Jews who hold fast to their tradition from those who are less connected to their heritage?

◆ What observances distinguish you?

Connecting the Text To the Sedra

5 Ezekiel condemns Israel's ancestors for failing to observe the laws and customs.

◆ Leviticus 19 in the Sedra outlines many fundamental moral and ritual laws. Read Leviticus 19. See if you can identify all of the Ten Commandments (from Exodus 20 or Deuteronomy 5) intermingled with the other laws of this chapter.

◆ Select one law from Leviticus 19 (other than one of the Ten Commandments) that you think is the most important law in the chapter. Be prepared to argue your case.

6 In both Haftarah and Sedra (Leviticus 19:3), Shabbat is presented as a central *mitzvah*.

◆ Read and discuss the following *midrash* concerning Israel and Shabbat.

When the world was created, Shabbat said to the Holy One, "Ruler of the Universe, every living thing created has its mate, and each day has its companion, except me, the seventh day. I am alone!" God answered, "The people of Israel will be your mate" (from *Genesis Rabbah* 11:8).

◆ What does it mean that every living thing has a mate?

◆ What does it mean that every day has a companion except Shabbat? (Hint: There are an odd number of days if you count Shabbat, but an even number without Shabbat.)

◆ How can Israel be a partner with Shabbat?

◆ We know from other Haftarot that Ezekiel liked to use props to act out his prophecy and to help people understand his message. (For more on Ezekiel engaging in a symbolic action to demonstrate the meaning of his prophecy, see the Haftarah for *Vayigash*, Analyzing the Text #2, p. 471.) Plan how you would proclaim this *midrash* as a prophetic message using ordinary props and symbolic actions.

7 Both texts warn against idolatry. By idol worship the Bible means the worship of sun, moon, stars, other gods, or images of wood, stone, or metal representing gods.

The worship of idols is no longer a prevalent practice, and idolatry has been reinterpreted to include the holding of any value above God and God's laws. Modern dictionary definitions of idol worship include: the blind admiration, adoration, or devotion of any person or thing.

◆ Make a list of things that people worship today (wealth, nation, fame, physical appearance).

◆ What are the dangers of worshiping such things?

◆ Make a collage from magazine pictures of things our society idolizes, which could serve as a warning against modern idolatry.

8 The term *hillul* appears in both texts (see Leviticus 19:8, 12; 20:3 and Ezekiel 20:9, 14, 16). It means to profane or desecrate and is used in warnings against desecrating sacrifices, oaths, God's name, and Shabbat.

When the word *hillul* is used regarding Shabbat, it means that one has engaged in activity on Shabbat that is allowed only on workdays, but is prohibited on Shabbat. Examples of such work include discussing business matters, handling money, or lighting a fire or candles.

◆ List other ways one might desecrate Shabbat by doing non-*Shabbesdik* activities.

◆ For each example given, explain why the activity might detract from a day of rest to be spent in reflection, study, worship, and enjoyment of family and friends.

9 The term *hillul* applies not only to Shabbat, but also to the desecration of an oath. When one testifies in court, one is swearing by God that the statement one is about to make is true. If the statement turns out not to be true, the third commandment of the Ten Commandments (not to take God's name in vain) has been broken.

Not wanting to desecrate an oath and take God's name in vain even inadvertently, some Jews refuse to make any oaths. When they testify in court or serve on a jury, they are unwilling to swear that they are telling the "truth, the whole truth, and nothing but the truth." Instead, American courts allow witnesses and jurors "to affirm" that what they are about to say is true.

However, other Jews see nothing wrong with taking an oath in court in support of a statement that one believes to be true.

◆ Would you choose to swear or to affirm in court?

◆ Find out from family and friends if any have served as witnesses or jurors in court. Ask if they were offered the opportunity to affirm instead of swear, and which option they chose.

10 The term *hillul* applies also to God's name. According to Jewish tradition, God's name is desecrated or profaned whenever a Jew acts dishonorably, because the action not only causes harm to the victim but may cause the victim to blame God. An example of a *hillul* of God's name is given in *Yoma* 86a:

If someone studies Bible and Mishnah (Jewish law), but is dishonest in business and rude in his interaction with other people, what do people say about him? "Woe to him who studied the Torah, woe to his father who taught him Torah, woe to his teacher who taught him Torah."

◆ Explain how such a person's actions reflect badly on God, God's Torah, and the teachers of Torah.

◆ Can you give a modern day example of a *hillul* of God's name? (For example, a person wearing a *kipah* drives her car aggressively, cutting off other cars; a person leaving a synagogue throws garbage in the street.)

◆ How might your examples reflect poorly on our religion?

11 Both Haftarah and Torah reading call Israel the "land of milk and honey" (Ezekiel 20:6, 15; Leviticus 20:24). The phrase is meant to evoke an image of agricultural wealth and abundance in the Land of Israel.

In modern times, we are quite proud of how the Jewish settlers in Palestine and the modern State of Israel have brought agricultural prosperity back to the Land of Israel.

◆ Find out about agriculture in Israel by visiting www.agri.gov.il/Depts/Spokesperson/Fieldminds.html. Or access http://library.Thinkquest.org/2683/agriculture.htm.

◆ Furthermore, find images of agricultural production in Israel by going to: http://search.gallery.yahoo.com/search/corbis?p=israel.

◆ Interview the produce manager of your local grocery store. Find out what fresh, canned, and packaged products from Israel are carried by the store. Buy a selection of the products, then hold an exhibit (or Israeli export food festival) at school.

◆ Learn and sing the song about Israel's milk and honey, *"Eretz Zavat Chalav"* (The Land of Milk and Honey). The song may be heard at www.bus.ualberta.ca/yreshef/pesach/audiopesach/zavatchalav.ram. Directions for accompanying the song with an Israeli folkdance may be found at www.recfd.com/dancenotes/eretzzav.htm.

Extending the Text

12 In Insights from the Tradition #A, p. 435, Radak said that people are lured to sin through their eyes. Read and discuss the following *midrash* from *Genesis Rabbah* 67:3 related to this subject:

Rabbi Levi said, "Six organs serve humanity: over three we are master, and over three we are not. We are not master over the eye, ear, and nose, for we see, hear, and smell what we do not wish to see, hear, and smell. Over the mouth, hand, and foot we are master. If we desire, we study Torah, while if we wish, we engage in slander. With the hand we can dispense charity, while we can also rob and murder if we so desire. With our feet we can go to the theaters and circuses, while if we wish we can go to synagogues and houses of study."

◆ What are the six organs that human beings have according to the *midrash*?

◆ Over which three organs does it seem that we have no control, and why? Over which three does it seem that we do have control, and why?

◆ Draw cartoons illustrating both positive and negative uses for the mouth, hand, and foot.

◆ With what parts of this *midrash* do you agree or disagree, and why?

◆ What lesson do you learn from this *midrash*?

13 Eyes are mentioned several times in the Haftarah. In verses 20:7 and 8, the eyes of Israel are mentioned in the phrase "the detestable things of your eyes" (translated as "the detestable things you are drawn to"). In verses 20:9 and 14, the eyes of the other nations of the world are mentioned. In verse 20:17 God had pity; the verse says literally, "but my eye had pity on them and did not destroy them."

Eyes also appear frequently in many *midrashim*. For example, eyes are said to be windows of the person's soul into the world; eyes also function as windows into the person's soul. *Midrashic* traditions say eyes may be flirtatious, envious, greedy, desirous, aspiring, protective, shining, and glaring to inspire fear.

◆ Find a portrait of a human being painted by a famous artist. (Find these paintings in art books in your local library or on the Internet.) Compare how the eyes are treated by different artists (consider if the subject of the portrait is looking at you or away, do the eyes look happy, sad, tired, etc.). Share your findings with the class.

◆ Find a portrait with eyes that show pity, like God's in the Haftarah. You can look either at fine art portraits or simply at photographs of faces in magazines and newspapers.

◆ Alternatively, invite a psychologist to talk to your class about what he/she can tell about people from their eyes.

14 In this Haftarah, Ezekiel singles out Shabbat from among all God's laws.

Shabbat begins in the home with the lighting of Shabbat candles. It is a *mitzvah* to light candles on the eve of Shabbat in the room in which Shabbat dinner will take place. The commandment applies to men as well as to women, although in the past women were more likely to light candles for their family because women were associated with the preparation of the home and dinner for Shabbat. Traditionally, candles should be lit before sunset. Many Jewish calendars indicate the time for candle lighting on Fridays — 18 minutes before sunset, to allow a little leeway in case one is running late.

Customs vary as to how many candles to light. Though only one candle is required to be lit, it is traditional to light two candles. One explanation for the two candles is that in the Torah the Ten Commandments appears twice (see Exodus 20:8 and Deuteronomy 5:12). In one version of the Ten Commandments, we are instructed to remember the Sabbath, and in the other we are taught to observe the Sabbath. Traditionally, then, one candle stands for the command to remember and the other for the command to observe. However, many families light more than two candles. Some light one candle for every member of the family, others light seven because it is a special number or in honor of the seventh day of the week.

When one lights Shabbat candles, one first lights the candles, then covers one's eyes, recites the blessing, and then uncovers one's eyes to see the light. Shabbat is considered to have begun when the blessing is recited, after which fires cannot be made.

◆ For more information on the lighting of Shabbat candles and the ushering of Shabbat into the home, see *Gates of Shabbat: A Guide for Observing Shabbat* by Mark Dov Shapiro, pp. 15-17; *The Shabbat Seder* by Ron Wolfson, pp. 98-111; and/or *Teaching Mitzvot* by Barbara Binder Kadden and Bruce Kadden, pp. 1-6.

◆ Teach a lesson on how to read all the information about Shabbat contained in a Jewish calendar.

15 Every Shabbat, we sing verses (Exodus 31:16-17) that remind us that Shabbat is a sign between us and God.

◆ Ask your Cantor to teach your class to sing *"V'shamru"* (They Shall Observe).

16 Mishnah *Shabbat* 7:2 lists 39 categories of work that are forbidden on Shabbat:

Sowing, plowing, reaping, binding sheaves, threshing, winnowing, cleansing crops, grinding, sifting, kneading, baking, shearing wool, washing or beating or dyeing wool, spinning, weaving, making two loops, weaving two threads, separating two threads, tying a knot, loosening a knot, sewing two stitches, tearing in order to sew two stitches, hunting a gazelle, slaughtering or flaying or slaying it or curing its skin, scraping it or cutting it up, writing two letters of the alphabet, erasing in order to write two letters, building, pulling down, putting out a fire, lighting a fire, striking with a hammer, and taking anything from one domain into another.

◆ Illustrate these types of forbidden work on flash cards and use the cards to quiz your classmates.

◆ It is taught that the types of work forbidden on Shabbat were the types of work required to build the Tabernacle. How might these 39 categories all be required for building a Tabernacle?

◆ Driving a car on Shabbat is considered forbidden work. Into which one(s) of the 39 categories do you think it falls?

◆ If work is forbidden on Shabbat, ask your Rabbi why he/she is allowed to work on Shabbat.

◆ For more information on forbidden work on Shabbat, see the web site www.jewfaq.org/shabbat.htm.

17 In the Haftarah Ezekiel condemns Israel's ancestors for their behavior during the 40-year wanderings in the wilderness.

◆ Review some stories from Exodus and Numbers (the golden calf, Exodus 32; food, Numbers 11; the spies, Numbers 14; Korach's rebellion, Numbers 16; and complaints about water in Numbers 20:2-12) to discover why God might have been so disappointed.

◆ With a group of your classmates, write and perform skits about these rebellions. Skits may also be found in *Parashah Plays* by Richard J. Allen: the golden calf, pp. 136-141; complaints about food, pp. 219-224; the spies, pp. 225-231; Korach's rebellion, pp. 232-237; and complaints about water, pp. 238-243.

Personalizing the Text

18 This Haftarah reviews the grim details of Israel's sinful past. Ezekiel, like other prophets, had the unfortunate task of telling the people things they need to hear, but don't want to hear. In other words, Ezekiel had to deliver the bad news. However, what the people wanted to hear was the good news about the future restoration of Jerusalem. Ezekiel does eventually (later in his book) soften the blow of the bad news with the good news promise of Jerusalem's revival.

◆ Which do you prefer to hear first, the good news or the bad news?

◆ Do newspapers and magazines and television provide more good news or more bad news? Why do you think this is the case? Make a list of current headlines and determine which describe good news and which describe bad news.

◆ We often find ourselves searching for good news in the world. Log on to the web site www.goodnewsnetwork.org to hear some positive news from around the world.

19 According to *The Encyclopedia of Jewish Symbols* by Ellen Frankel and Betsy Platkin Teutsch, p. 151, some scholars believe that Jews introduced the seven-day week to the world.

◆ If you could change the length of a week, how long would you make it, and why? Compare the advantages and disadvantages of your week with the seven-day week.

20 The milk and honey of which the Torah speaks is actually date honey and goat's milk.

Since this Haftarah is often read near Passover, learn to make Passover recipes that use dates, honey, or goat cheese.

A Persian version of Passover *charoset* is made as follows:

    10 dates, pitted and diced
    1/4 cup pistachio nuts chopped fine
    1/4 cup almonds, chopped fine
    1/4 cup yellow raisins, diced
    1 apple, peeled, cored, and diced
    1/2 cup sweet red wine
    1/4 teaspoon cayenne pepper
    1/4 teaspoon cloves
    1/2 teaspoon cinnamon

Combine and mix well all the above ingredients. Then gently stir in one peeled and sliced banana and one peeled and diced orange.

21 Ezekiel claims that the Israelites desecrated Shabbat.

◆ Make a beautiful *challah* cover to help you sanctify Shabbat. Alternatively, draw an abstract picture describing how Shabbat makes you feel.

22 Based on Insights from the Tradition #A, p. 435, we learned that one's eyes can lead one astray.

◆ Draw a silly picture illustrating the saying, "See no evil, hear no evil, speak no evil."

23 God mentions repeatedly in this Haftarah that God refrains from destroying Israel and is kind to Israel for God's own sake. What does "for God's own sake" mean? God meant that, if Israel had been destroyed, it would have appeared to people that God wasn't as powerful as the gods of other nations and couldn't protect Israel. God wanted to protect God's reputation and, therefore, did not destroy Israel.

◆ Have you ever done something nice for someone just for your reputation and how you would look?

◆ It is possible that being nice to others can ultimately benefit the one who is being nice in ways other than just making that person look good.

◆ Make an effort to engage in random acts of kindness for others, such as putting money in parking meters, opening doors, etc. How does your kindness make others feel? How do your kind acts make you feel?

◆ Find out about the nonprofit program called Do Something "Kindness & Justice Challenge" co-founded in 1993 by actor Andrew Shue. Its annual challenge to students in Grades K-12 is based on the values of Dr. Martin Luther King Jr.: tolerance, responsibility, compassion, nonviolence, and moral courage. The Do Something web site is http://coach.dosomething.org.

24 Israel has trouble remaining faithful to its Covenant with God.

◆ Make a covenant with your best friend, describing how you will treat each other and listing the things you will regularly do for one another. Discuss what will happen should either of you break the agreement.

TEACHING HAFTARAH

Other Resources

25 Ezekiel portrays God to be constantly disappointed in our failure to act as faithful partners. Read and discuss ideas on this matter presented in *Living as Partners with God* by Gila Gevirtz.

26 For resources on what to do on Shabbat, read *The Shabbat Seder* by Ron Wolfson or *Gates of Shabbat: A Guide for Observing Shabbat* by Mark Dov Shapiro.

27 Read the chapter on Ezekiel in *Messengers of God: A Jewish Prophets Who's Who* by Ronald H. Isaacs, pp. 121-133.

28 See the painter Raphael's painting of Ezekiel and his vision in chapter 1 at: www.abcgallery.com/R/raphael/raphael84.html. Paint a portrait of Ezekiel based on this Haftarah.

29 Discuss the illustration of this Haftarah in *The Illustrated Torah* by Michal Meron, p. 130.

Involving the Family

30 Ezekiel reviews some Israelite family history. Spend time together collecting photos, stories, and mementos with which to make a family history scrapbook.

31 In order to help support the rebirth of agriculture and forests in the Land of Israel, make a contribution this year to support The Society for the Protection of Nature in Israel (known as SPNI). SPNI was founded in 1953 in order to protect the environment and promote education and eco-tourism. The organization operates field schools and offers guided hikes, tours, and speakers (in countries other than Israel, too). For more information, access their web site at www.teva.org.il/e.

Bar/Bat Mitzvah Projects

32 Choose one *mitzvah* associated with Shabbat and observe it. Or, spend one entire Shabbat observing all the laws to see what it's like to be *Shomer Shabbat* (one who is Shabbat observant).

33 God gave Shabbat as a precious gift to the Israelites. Try to make all the Bar and Bat Mitzvah gifts you give personal and meaningful. Consider making donations to the Bar or Bat Mitzvah's favorite cause in his/her honor instead of giving a material gift.

EZEKIEL 22:1-19 Ashkenazim
EZEKIEL 22:1-16 Sephardim
ACHARAY MOT אחרי מות

This Haftarah has been paired with *Parashat Acharay Mot*, Leviticus 16:1-18:30. See "Connecting the Text To the Sedra," pp. 446-447, for an exploration of the many ways the two texts shed light on each other.

SYNOPSIS

Ezekiel was exiled with many of his compatriots sometime around 597 B.C.E., when Nebuchadnezzar first occupied Jerusalem. This Haftarah records a vision he had between that time and the destruction of Jerusalem in 586 B.C.E. In it, Ezekiel describes a Jerusalem that is marred by the appalling transgressions of its leaders and inhabitants. He prophesies that because of its heinous sins, Israel will be made the mockery and scorn of all the nations.

Ezekiel indicts every Israelite leader for shedding blood, humiliating fathers and mothers, cheating strangers, and wronging orphans and widows. He accuses them of despising holy things and profaning Shabbat. In his disturbing litany of accusations against the Israelites, Ezekiel cites bloodshed, idolatry, depravity, sexual impropriety, adultery, bribery, usury, and fraud.

Adonai will be sure to punish Israel for its sins, scattering the Israelites among the nations, cries Ezekiel. Just as copper, tin, iron, lead, and silver must be smelted to be purified, so, too, will Israel be burned and purified in the furnace that will be Jerusalem.

INSIGHTS FROM THE TRADITION

A Radak says that verse 22:8 indicates that the Israelites showed contempt for God by bringing sick or injured animals for sacrifice.

◆ Sometimes we go through the motions of doing the right thing without paying enough attention to the details or having the proper attitude while doing them. In what ways can inattention to detail and attitude adversely affect our (well intentioned) action?

◆ Did your parents ever make you repeat an apology and "say it like you mean it"? Why?

◆ Consider this story: A customer service representative from a large turkey producer once received a call from a woman who asked, "Can you eat a turkey if it's been frozen for 20 years?" The representative responded that the turkey would not be spoiled, but the texture would not be of the same quality as a fresh turkey. "That's what I thought," responded the woman. "I was going to give it to a food bank, so the texture doesn't matter." How was the woman in this story going through the motions of doing the right thing, without paying attention to details or having the right attitude?

◆ Do you think details and attitude matter in a situation like this? In any situation?

B According to Rashi, verse 22:12 indicates that the princes of Israel took wealth from the poor Israelite population. Radak explains that they paid the wealth to their foreign friends,

Egypt and Assyria, for military protection, forgetting that Israel's true protection was up to God. It seems as if the Israelite leaders neglected the needs of their own people in order to please their new friends.

◆ What do you think of kids who drop their old friends when it seems that new ones can do something for them?

◆ What is the value of remaining loyal to old friends?

C The sins mentioned by Ezekiel in the Haftarah (verse 22:7) are, according to Radak, the serious wrongdoings that a person would automatically know to avoid even if the Torah had not specifically prohibited them. In other words, everyone knows that stealing and killing are wrong without having to be told so.

◆ Make a list of crimes (sins) that you think people innately know not to commit.

◆ Make a list of sins that you think people might not normally know to avoid unless they were taught about them (violating Shabbat, for example).

STRATEGIES
Analyzing the Text

1 The Hebrew expression *"ben adam"* is used over 80 times to refer to the prophet in the Book of Ezekiel.

◆ For a discussion on this interesting term, see Analyzing the Text #1 in the Haftarah for *Kedoshim*, p. 436.

2 How many sins do you think Ezekiel lists in this Haftarah? Some commentators count as many as 24.

◆ Which is the first sin listed by Ezekiel, and which is the last?

◆ Some scholars suggest that the first sin listed — bloodshed —is considered the worst. Do you agree?

◆ In contrast, our Sages believed that robbery was left for last because it is the worst. Can you argue for their position?

3 Compare the list of sins in Ezekiel 22:6-12 with the Ten Commandments.

◆ Which of Ezekiel's sins are included in the Ten Commandments, and which are not? Regarding those that are not included, do you think any should have been?

4 Israel's princes are castigated in verse 22:6 for spilling blood. According to Plaut in *The Haftarah Commentary*, p. 286, shedding blood is used here figuratively, in the same sense as the phrase "bloodsucker" is used to mean someone who engages in economic exploitation.

◆ What is economic exploitation?

◆ How is exploiting someone economically like shedding their blood?

5 The parable of silver and dross in verses 22:18-19 continues into the next three verses, which have been excluded from the Haftarah. They read, "As silver, copper, iron, lead, and tin are gathered into a crucible to blow the fire upon them, so as to melt them, so will I gather you in My fierce anger and cast you [into the fire] and melt you. I will gather you and I will blow upon you the fire of My fury, and you shall be melted in it. As silver is melted in a crucible, so shall you be melted in it. And you shall know I *Adonai* have poured out My fury upon you."

◆ Now that you have read the whole parable, can you explain its message?

♦ What impending historical event in ancient Israel was Ezekiel likening to a burning (but purifying) furnace?

6 The Rabbis took great pains to make sure that Haftarot never end on a negative note.

♦ What is positive about the way this Haftarah ends? Hint: take the parable of the smelting furnace to its logical conclusion.

♦ How does proper punishment (in theory) make us better people in the end?

♦ Do you agree that, indeed, the Rabbis ended this Haftarah on a positive note? Justify your response.

Connecting the Text To the Sedra

7 Both Sedra (Leviticus 18:6-18) and Haftarah list which marriages are forbidden and which are permitted. Under Jewish law, in addition to marrying completely unrelated people, a man may marry a stepsister, a niece, a cousin, his deceased wife's sister. A woman may marry a step-brother, a cousin, her deceased sister's husband, an uncle.

♦ Review these lists. (For more information on prohibited and permitted marriage partners, see *The Jewish Way in Love and Marriage* by Maurice Lamm, pp. 95-96).

♦ Each state in the United States has legislated its own rules about permitted and forbidden marriages. Find out from a local judge, government official, or social studies teacher the rules concerning marriage in your state.

♦ Write your own list of laws regarding marriage. Consider at what age people should be permitted to marry, which relatives may or may not marry each other, how many times an individual should be allowed to get mar-

ried, how many spouses any individual may have, and so on.

♦ Write a want ad for your perfect marriage partner. Include qualifications, personality traits, and a job description.

8 Both Sedra and Haftarah outlaw idolatry.

♦ What kinds of "idols" do people in our society worship (see a discussion of this topic in the Haftarah for *Kedoshim*, Connecting the Text To the Sedra #7, p. 438)? What is the danger of worshiping each of the "idols" on your list?

♦ A Public Service Announcement (PSA) is a message in the public interest delivered on television or radio. Write a PSA warning people about the dangers of worshiping one of the "idols" of modern society. Videotape the PSAs and view them later as a class.

9 Blood plays an important role in both Sedra and Haftarah. Ezekiel condemns the Israelites for shedding blood in the Haftarah; in the Torah reading, Moses describes a blood ritual involved in the Yom Kippur sacrifice (Leviticus 16:14, 18). Moses further explains that Israelites are never to consume the blood of an animal, for blood represents life itself (Leviticus 17:10-14).

♦ In the Bible, blood symbolizes life, death, and holiness. What does blood symbolize to you?

♦ To the American Red Cross, blood symbolizes life and healing. Find out if your synagogue sponsors a blood drive for the American Red Cross. If so, volunteer to do publicity for the blood drive and to serve juice and cookies to donors. If not, work with your synagogue president to start such a drive.

♦ Read more about the symbolism of blood in *The Encyclopedia of Jewish Symbols* by Ellen Frankel and Betsy Platkin Teutsch, pp. 21-22.

10 God declares in Leviticus 18:24-28, "Do not sin in ways I have forbidden. If you do, the land will spew you out for defiling it." In Ezekiel's time, the Israelites are exiled from their land. The prophets teach that the exile was punishment for Israel's sins.

◆ In order to endure and thrive, a community must have moral foundations. The Ten Commandments are one such set of moral foundations. Write your own Ten Commandments necessary for a healthy society. You may include any of the traditional Ten Commandments and add any of your own. Discuss why the laws you have chosen are absolutely essential for the success of a society.

11 In the Sedra Moses describes the Yom Kippur ritual for atonement and purification from sin. In the Haftarah Ezekiel says that Israel will be purified in the "furnace" of exile.

◆ Compare the process of purging sins in Leviticus 16 with the furnace of the Haftarah.

◆ Why must the sins of the past be eliminated?

◆ We don't just seek to atone for our sins and purge ourselves of their negative effects once per year. Rather, every day we seek atonement. For example, in the traditional daily *"Amidah,"* we say, "Forgive us, for we have sinned. Pardon us for we have transgressed. For You forgive and pardon. Blessed are You, merciful *Adonai,* Who forgives abundantly." What opportunity for self-improvement does this daily blessing offer us?

12 Both the Torah portion and Haftarah discuss the "stranger." The Sedra indicates that any stranger who lives among the Israelites must live by Israelite standards of behavior (Leviticus 17:8, 17:10, 17:13, 17:15, and 18:26).

In verse 22:7 of the Haftarah, Ezekiel condemns the Israelites for oppressing the stranger. According to *Bava Metzia* 59b, the Torah repeats this prohibition at least 36 times.

◆ Read the following excerpt from the Talmud:

"Why did the Torah warn against the wronging of a stranger in 36, or as others say, in 46 places? . . . It is taught: Do not taunt your neighbor with the blemish that you yourself have."

◆ The explanation given by the Talmud means that since we were once strangers, we should not taunt someone else about being strangers. Can you give other reasons for not wronging a stranger (for example, it is unjust to take advantage of anyone, especially a stranger)?

◆ Interview your parents and grandparents to find out if there was ever a time when they felt like strangers in your country. Did anyone ever take advantage of them because they were strangers? What changed to make them feel at home?

◆ Who would you consider to be strangers today in your society? How do you think those people are treated?

Extending the Text

13 Among Israel's sins is the contemptuous treatment of mothers and fathers (verse 22:7). *Kiddushin* 31b teaches that in order to honor one's parents, a child must give them food and drink, clothe and shelter them, and lead them in and out.

◆ To what stage in life does the Talmud's list refer?

◆ Why do you think the Talmud focuses on honoring one's parents in their old age?

◆ List three ways you might honor your parent at your current stage in life.

◆ Discuss ways your parents honor (or honored) their parents.

14 The prophet in verse 22:8 castigates the Israelites for profaning Shabbat. Shabbat is intended to be a day of rest and enjoyment, and it is important to share this day with others. The book *Gates of Shabbat: A Guide for Observing Shabbat* (p. 97) says:

"It is a *mitzvah* to invite guests to join in the celebration of Shabbat. Ideally, no one should have to observe Shabbat alone. Therefore, one should pay particular attention to newcomers in the community and others who are alone. Although every Jew is obligated to celebrate Shabbat whether at home or away, the joy of Shabbat is increased by joining with others. The *mitzvah* is called *hachnasat orchim*."

◆ Explain this lesson in your own words.

◆ Find out what your synagogue and your Rabbi do to help welcome newcomers for Shabbat services and meals. If there is no program to accomplish this, join with your classmates to start one. Be sure to include opportunities for congregants to invite newcomers to a Chanukah dinner and/or their Passover *Seder*.

15 The Israelite leaders are accused of usury, which is charging excessive interest on loans (verse 22:12). For hundreds of years, Jewish communities have had Free Loan Societies that offer interest free or low interest loans to help keep community members out of financial trouble.

◆ Does your synagogue or greater Jewish community have a Free Loan Society? If so, interview the director to find out what they do, whom they help, and where they get their funding.

◆ Visit the web site of the International Association of Hebrew Free Loans at www.freeloan.org, where you can read their mission statement and newsletter and find your local affiliate.

16 Ezekiel indicts the Israelite leaders for cheating, stealing, and committing fraud. According to the Talmud (*Baba Metzia* 49b), an overcharge of a sixth or more of the market price of the good sold constitutes "wronging" the consumer.

The *Shulchan Aruch* (*Chosen Mishpat, Hilkot G'neivah*, Sec. 228) prohibits additional types of fraudulent business practices:

"One is forbidden to beautify an item being sold in order to create a false impression. One is forbidden to dye a slave's hair or beard in order to make him appear young. One is not allowed to give an animal bran to drink, which makes her hair brown and upright, creating the impression that she is fat and sleek. One may not comb the animal artfully in order to create that same impression. One is not allowed to paint old baskets to make them look new, nor is one allowed to soak meat in water to make it white and look fat."

◆ Can you think of other, modern day, dishonest business practices? For example, consider fruit that has been waxed so it looks shiny or items packaged in larger boxes than warranted.

◆ Have you or a family member ever been a victim of such a fraudulent practice?

17 Jewish tradition is quite serious about the prohibition against stealing. Joseph Caro writes in the Jewish law code called *Shulchan Aruch* (*Chosen Mishpat*, sec. 348): "In order not to become accustomed to stealing, one is forbidden to steal even as a practical joke or even with the intent of later returning the stolen article."

◆ Do you think Caro's prohibitions are necessary to teach good lessons, or do they go too far?

◆ Caro further adds that Jews are not permitted to buy stolen goods, lest we encourage thieves to continue stealing. How might you ascertain whether or not merchandise has been stolen? Invite a local police officer to teach your class about identifying stolen merchandise.

18 Verse 22:12 seems to indicate that bribes were given that distorted judges's decisions. In the eleventh blessing of the weekday *"Amidah,"* we ask to have our judges restored. The prayer says:

"Return our judges as before and our advisors as they once were, remove from us sorrow and sadness and rule over us *Adonai* alone, with kindness and mercy and righteousness and justice. Blessed are you *Adonai* who loves righteousness and justice."

◆ What things other than monetary bribes might improperly influence a judge?

◆ How might party affiliation affect a judge's decisions?

◆ Write a prayer expressing our concern for justice and our hopes for our civil judicial system.

Personalizing the Text

19 Ezekiel condemns the Israelites for their sins. Today, educators believe in using positive reinforcement to emphasize the things that people do right rather than the things they do wrong.

◆ Conduct the following exercise: The teacher gives each student a sheet of paper that contains a list of every student in the class. Each student, as homework, writes one complimen-

tary thing about each other student on the list. The teacher then compiles for each individual student a personalized list of all the nice things written about her/him by the other students (without identifying who wrote what).

20 Ezekiel indicts the Israelites for failing to care for their orphans and widows, and for exploiting one another. This was far from the Jewish ideal, which calls for all Jews to care for one another.

◆ Ask your Cantor to teach you the song *"Kol Yisrael Arevim Zeh BaZeh,"* which means all Jews are responsible for one another. Or learn it from the audiocassette *Shir Mi-libeinu: A Song from Our Heart*, recorded by UAHC Camp Newman/Camp Swig.

21 Ezekiel warns (verse 22:16) that Israel will be dishonored as a result of all the dishonorable deeds they committed.

◆ *Pirke Avot* 4:1 asks, "Who is worthy of honor?" The answer given is, "One who honors others."

◆ Make posters to hang in your classroom or school that describe ways to honor others.

22 The Israelites committed fraud, bribery, and all kinds of social crimes.

◆ Play the game *Scruples* to test your moral limits.

23 Ezekiel criticized the Israelites for taking bribes.

◆ Do your parents bribe you to get you to do certain things?

◆ Do you think bribes are ever an acceptable means of "behavior modification"?

TEACHING HAFTARAH

Other Resources

24 The Israelites had a bad attitude even when they were doing the *mitzvah* of making sacrifices to God. Read and discuss the story "The Car that Ran from Mitzvahs" by Hanna Bandes in *Chosen Tales,* edited by Peninnah Schram, pp. 11-19.

25 Complete the Torah Aura Instant Lesson *Wounding with Words* by Rabbi Steven Bayar, which begins with a Rabbinic discussion of what is the worst sin in the world.

26 To explore children's responsibilities to their parents, complete the Torah Aura Instant Lesson *What Must Parents Do? — What Must Children Do?*

27 View and discuss selected scenes from the film *Annie* (1981, rated PG, 127 minutes), or *Oliver* (1968, rated G, 145 minutes), both of which lightly portray the worst kind of treatment of orphans (see verse 22:7).

28 Read the chapter on Ezekiel in *Messengers of God: A Jewish Prophets Who's Who* by Ronald H. Isaacs, pp. 121-133.

29 Discuss the illustration of this Haftarah in *The Illustrated Torah* by Michal Meron, p. 127. Which portion of the Haftarah is conveyed in this illustration? What emotions does the artist express?

30 For resources on what to do on Shabbat, read *The Shabbat Seder* by Ron Wolfson or *Gates of Shabbat: A Guide for Observing Shabbat* by Mark Dov Shapiro.

31 For a commentary, discussion questions, and project, see UAHC's Family Shabbat Table Talk web site at www.uahc.org/shabbat/stt/3am.shtml.

Involving the Family

32 Care for the orphans, widows, and strangers of your community by volunteering at a local homeless shelter or soup kitchen, especially on holidays.

33 Choose one Friday night per month and invite guests to share in your Shabbat dinner (see Extending the Text #14, p. 448). Don't worry about having to perform every Shabbat ritual the first time you invite guests. Choose one ritual (lighting candles, making *Motzi* over the *challah*, etc.), and start by doing just that one. Add more rituals as you feel comfortable.

Bar/Bat Mitzvah Projects

34 The Israelites are condemned for insulting God by offering second-rate sacrifices. Honor the guests at your Bar/Bat Mitzvah by writing first-rate sincere and personal thank-you notes to them.

35 Since this Haftarah is usually read near Passover, hold a food drive to collect kosher for Passover foods for the needy members of your community.

EZEKIEL 28:25-29:21
VAERA וארא

This Haftarah has been paired with *Parashat Vaera*, Exodus 6:2-9:35. See "Connecting the Text To the Sedra," pp. 453-454, for an exploration of the many ways the two texts shed light on each other.

SYNOPSIS

There are two distinct prophecies contained within in this Haftarah. According to Ezekiel's own words, the first prophecy was delivered in the tenth year of the reign of Judean King Zedekiah (587 B.C.E.), which was well into the Babylonian exile and just before the fall of Jerusalem in 586 B.C.E. In it, Ezekiel condemns Judah's supposed ally, Egypt, for failing to help the Southern Kingdom when it was attacked by the Babylonians. It contains an allegory, comparing Pharaoh and Egypt to an arrogant monster, which will be destroyed and humiliated by *Adonai* because of its guilt and dishonesty.

The second prophecy is dated about 16 years later, and is considered to be one of Ezekiel's last. In it Ezekiel predicts that Babylon, which has abandoned its siege of Tyre, will now turn its sights on Egypt. In Babylon's invasion of Egypt, Ezekiel sees just punishment for Egypt's failure to defend Israel.

The Haftarah ends as it begins — with words of comfort for the despairing Israelite exiles. Ezekiel assures them that *Adonai* has promised to gather them and return them to safety and prosperity in their homeland and to punish their oppressors.

INSIGHTS FROM THE TRADITION

A Verse 29:3 condemns Egypt for its arrogance. Rashi explains that since Egypt was fortunate enough to have its Nile River — which provided it with everything it needed — the Egyptians felt no need for God's beneficence. In other words, as long as the Egyptians had all the water, food, and other resources they needed, they could arrogantly act any way they wanted.

- Explain in your own words how being fortunate and well-off might lead someone to be unappreciative, spoiled, or arrogant.

- Do you believe that one has to experience hardship before one can appreciate well-being?

- Think of a time in your life that made you especially thankful for your health, your friends, your family. Share this experience with your classmates.

B Ezekiel declares in verse 29:16 that Israel will never again depend on Egypt. Malbim explains that because the Israelites associated themselves with Egypt, they learned to follow Egypt's ways and turned away from God.

- Why do you think we are so influenced by the people with whom we associate?

- List three ways in which your friends have been good influences on you, and three ways in which you have been a good influence on them.

C Verse 29:21 is hard to translate. It literally says that "God will give you an opening of the mouth." Rashi explains that when Israel sees that all of Ezekiel's prophecies have been fulfilled, they will give the prophet free speech.

◆ How do you know whether or not you should believe what someone tells you?

◆ Do you think free speech should be denied to people who preach unpopular ideas? Why or why not?

D Plaut translates the phrase "opening the mouth" as "courage to speak" (verse 29:21). He explains that Israel had not felt free to speak as long as it was a guest in exile. When the Israelites return home, they will again have the courage to speak.

◆ In what situations do you feel comfortable speaking your mind? What situations make you uncomfortable, and why?

◆ Do you think Jews are truly at home in democratic countries, to the extent that we can speak freely about issues that concern us?

STRATEGIES
Analyzing the Text

1 Ezekiel delivers the first prophecy in this Haftarah in the tenth month of the tenth year (of the reign of Judean King, Zedekiah). The tenth month refers to the month of Tevet, which was seven months before the destruction of Jerusalem and the Temple.

◆ List the Hebrew months.

◆ Learn about the dates on the Jewish calendar that signify important events before, during, and after the destruction of Jerusalem by the Babylonians: 10th of Tevet, 17th of Tammuz, 9th of Av, and 3rd of Tishre. For information, see the *Encyclopaedia Judaica*, vol. 3, pp. 936ff.; vol. 6, pp. 1195-1196; vol. 15, p. 789.

2 In verse 29:2 Ezekiel is told to set his face toward Pharaoh. The phrase "set your face toward" occurs in several of Ezekiel's prophecies (see Ezekiel 6:2, 21:2, 25:2, 35:2, 38:2 for a few of these). Since Ezekiel is not located near Pharaoh (Ezekiel is in Babylon, and Pharaoh would be in Egypt), the phrase may mean:

• address the topic

• symbolically turn in the direction of the subject

• express anger toward (see Rambam's *Guide of the Perplexed* 1:37 or Leviticus 20:3-6)

◆ Make up a skit on any subject that uses the phrase "set your face toward" and one of the above meanings. Extra bonus points if you use the phrase more than once with more than one meaning!

3 Ezekiel describes Egypt as a "mighty monster," which has also been translated as "crocodile."

◆ Follow the metaphor in verses 29:3-5 to discover what the fate of the "mighty monster" will be.

4 After Egypt has been described as a great sea monster sprawled in its river, verse 29:4 continues by prophesying that the great monster will be hooked and dragged ashore. The image is that of a greatly humbled sea monster that drags all his little fellow fish down with him. This metaphor is described by one commentator as a "grotesque literary cartoon."

◆ Draw a cartoon of Pharaoh, the great sea monster, being destroyed by God as described in the Haftarah. Include the graphic images in verses 29:3-5.

◆ Compare your drawing with the illustration of this Haftarah in *The Illustrated Torah* by Michal Meron, p. 68.

5 In verses 29:6-7 Egypt and Pharaoh are described as a "staff of reed" that splintered and broke whenever Israel leaned on it for support.

◆ How was the "mighty monster" revealed to be only a "staff of reed"?

◆ List other things that appear to be strong, but are weak in reality.

◆ What characteristics do you look for in someone you turn to for support?

6 Ezekiel predicts in verse 29:10 that *Adonai* will reduce the land of Egypt to utter ruin and desolation in verse 29:10. The word חרב *(chorev)* can mean "destruction." It is also suggested by Eliezer of Beaugency that חרב may mean "dry."

◆ Explain how this translation/word play is especially appropriate for the metaphor of Egypt as a river.

7 According to Ezekiel, Egypt will lie desolate for 40 years. What might be the particular significance of 40 years? (Remember that the Israelites wandered in the wilderness for 40 years and that the rain fell on Noah's ark for 40 days and 40 nights.)

◆ For more on the Bible's use of the number 40 and symbolic numbers, see the Haftarah for *Terumah*, Analyzing the Text #4, p. 130.

◆ Choose a symbolic number (for example, 3, 5, 7, 10, 12, 13, or 40). Research some of the ideas associated with your number either in *The Encyclopedia of Jewish Symbols* by Ellen Frankel and Betsy Platkin Teutsch or in the *Encyclopaedia Judaica*, vol. 12, pp. 1254-1260. Present a report on your research or illuminate your number and the ideas related to it.

Connecting the Text To the Sedra

8 The Haftarah begins with Ezekiel's promise that God will gather the Israelite people from the places to which they have been scattered. In the Sedra God inflicts the plagues on Egypt in an attempt to end the Israelite captivity there.

Throughout the ages, we Jews have longed to return to our homeland in Israel. The modern Zionists decided to stop hoping and start acting to make their hopes come true. The wheels of Jewish statehood were set into motion in 1897 when the First Zionist Congress was called by Theodor Herzl, who is known as the father of modern Zionism

Theodor Herzl wrote, "If you will it, it is no dream." The Hebrew translation of this quotation became a powerful Zionist slogan that motivated generations of activists.

◆ Why is this slogan fitting for Zionists?

◆ Learn these words, which have been put to music by Debbie Friedman in her song *"Im Tirzu, Ayn Zo Agadah."* Try to find someone to teach you the hand motions that go along with the song. The song may be found on the recording *Not by Might, Not by Power* by Debbie Friedman.

9 The phrase "and then they shall know that I am *Adonai*" appears four times in the Haftarah (verses 28:26 and 29:6, 16, and 21). Variations of the same phrase also appear six times in the Sedra (Exodus 6:7, 7:5, 7:17, 8:6, 8:18, and 9:14).

◆ Who do you think is the "they" that shall know that God is *Adonai*? Do you think "they" refers to Israel? Do you think "they" means Egypt? Do you think "they" means the whole world?

◆ What did God want them to know?

10 Ezekiel is ordered by God in verse 29:2 to prophecy against Pharaoh. In the Sedra (Exodus 6:11, 7:26, 7:15, and 9:1) Moses is told to go to Pharaoh and announce the next plague.

◆ Imagine how hard it must have been for these two prophets to prophesy against the great Pharaoh. Form two groups. One group stages a skit in which Moses plans with Aaron, Miriam, and others what he will say before Pharaoh. The other group puts on a similar skit concerning Ezekiel and Pharaoh. Make sure to use quotations or key words either from this Haftarah or from Exodus 1-4. Remember that Moses actually had to face Pharaoh, but Ezekiel prophesied from a distance. In your view, who had the tougher job?

11 Ezekiel describes a water-based plague that will destroy Egypt. Some of the plagues in *Parashat Vaera* are also centered around water. Which are they?

◆ Identify modern plagues (water or non-water based) that threaten our environment, our health, and our society (for example: pollution, drought, AIDS, bigotry, poverty, illiteracy, etc.).

12 Ezekiel describes Pharaoh as being arrogant. Suggest an example from the Sedra (or other portions of the Torah, such as Numbers 12:3) of Moses acting humbly (not arrogantly).

◆ Why might humility be an important trait for a leader or a nation?

◆ Select a national or international leader of your choice, and give examples of his/her humble demeanor. Alternatively, suggest a leader who you believe has acted arrogantly, and give examples of how his/her leadership was hurt by that attitude.

13 Moses and Ezekiel are all well-known biblical prophets from the Haftarah and Sedra.

◆ Match the prophets below with their prophecy. To make this an interactive activity, the teacher can write the prophets' names and quotations on cards. Distribute one card to each student. Each student with a name card finds the person holding the card with the matching message.

1. Moses (c.)
2. Samuel (a.)
3. Nathan (f.)
4. Isaiah (d.)
5. Jeremiah (g.)
6. Ezekiel (h.)
7. Hosea (e.)
8. Jonah (b.)

a. "The day will come when you [Israel] will cry out because of the King whom you yourselves have chosen." (I Samuel 8:18)

b. "Forty days more until Ninevah is overthrown." (Jonah 3:4)

c. "Every firstborn in the land of Egypt shall die." (Exodus 11:5)

d. "Nation shall not lift up sword against nation." (Isaiah 2:4)

e. "I will espouse [betroth] you to me forever." (Hosea 2:21)

f. "The sword shall never depart from your [David's] house." (II Samuel 12:10)

g. "Can the leopard change his spots?" (Jeremiah 13:23)

h. "I will sprinkle clean water upon you, and you shall be clean." (Ezekiel 36:25)

Extending the Text

14 After the first Babylonian advance into Judah and the deportation of King Jehoiachin in 597 B.C.E., Zedekiah became king of the besieged Judah. The first deportation left Israel short on able leadership. Zedekiah himself was a weak leader, unable to stand up to the remaining nobles who would lead Judah to its ultimate destruction in 586 B.C.E. Zedekiah's reign was marked by repeated — and unsuccessful — popular rebellions against Babylonia. In the end, Zedekiah was brought before Nebuchadnezzar. The Judean king was blinded and taken in chains to Babylon, where he died. A month later, Jerusalem was torched and razed to the ground. Zedekiah was the last biblical king of Judah (see II Kings 25).

◆ Imagine you are reporters at a press conference held by Zedekiah, shortly after Ezekiel started prophesying in 592 B.C.E. Interview the king about his hopes for saving Judah from destruction by the Babylonians. Ask him about his plans to rebel against the Babylonian occupation, form an alliance with Egypt, and even redeem the Israelite exiles. Ask him what he thinks of Ezekiel's warnings against rebelling and forming alliances with Egypt, and find out his predictions of the destruction of Jerusalem.

15 Israel depended on the wrong friends and was adversely influenced by them in the process. Rambam recognized that we are all influenced by the people with whom we associate. In the *Mishneh Torah* (*Hilchot De'ot* 6:1), he wrote, "It is our natural instinct to think and act like our friends and colleagues. Therefore, one should associate with good and wise people."

◆ Do you agree that we are influenced by our friends?

◆ How do we know if the people with whom we associate are good and wise?

◆ What other qualities do you value in a friend? How does your list compare with Rambam's qualifications?

16 Israel and Egypt have a long and complicated history. Review these facts and present them on an illustrated time line that you can hang in your classroom:

a. Israelites were freed from slavery in Egypt in the thirteenth century B.C.E. (probably between 1275 B.C.E. and 1225).

b. An engraving from around 1210 B.C.E. commemorates an Egyptian war against Israel.

c. King Solomon, who reigned over a united Israel from about 961-922 B.C.E., married Pharaoh's daughter (I Kings 3:1 and 7:8).

d. Shortly after Solomon's death in 922 B.C.E., Pharaoh Sheshonq I (Shishak) invaded Judah and stole royal and Temple treasures collected by Solomon (I Kings 14:25-6).

e. Eighth century Egypt, having been taken over by Ethiopia, tried to form an alliance with Israel, but Isaiah warned against it (II Kings 18, Isaiah 36).

f. Egypt feared Assyria, which was growing in power. In 609 B.C.E., Judah's King Josiah went out to fight the Egyptian Pharaoh who was on his way to battle Assyria. Josiah was killed in the battle that ensued (II Kings 23:29-30).

g. After Josiah died in 609 B.C.E., the Pharaoh placed a puppet king by the name of Jehoiakim on Josiah's throne in Judah (II Kings 23:35).

h. Against King Nebuchadnezzar of Babylon, Judean King Zedekiah (reigned from 597-586) wavered over whether or not to get help from Egypt.

17 Tyre, Judah, Egypt, and Babylon are ancient nations mentioned in the Haftarah.

◆ Make your own map of the ancient kingdoms of Israel and Judah and their neighbors, based on the maps in the *Encyclopaedia Judaica*, vol. 9, pp. 116-118.

18 Ezekiel, like the other prophets, promises that the oppressors will be brought low, while the oppressed Israelites will be restored to greatness. Consider this biblical quotation (Ecclesiastes 9:11), "The race is not won by the swift, nor the battle by the valiant; nor is bread won by the wise, nor wealth by the intelligent, nor favor by the learned. For the time of mischance comes to all."

◆ Explain how this lesson applies to the mighty sea monster (verses 29:3-5) losing the battle.

◆ Discuss what this lesson means, and whether you agree or disagree with it.

Personalizing the Text

19 Egypt took the blessings of the River Nile for granted. This made the Egyptians spoiled and the Pharaohs arrogant.

◆ List ten blessings in your life for which you are grateful. Write a thank-you note to three people who have always supported you.

20 The Israelites mistakenly depended on Egypt for help. In this case, their "crutch" hurt them more than it helped.

◆ Interview your parents, grandparents, and family friends to find out what types of crutches people have in their lives. Can they tell you stories from their personal experiences?

◆ What types of crutches do you have? Do your crutches always help you, or do they sometimes hamper you? Explain your answer.

21 Egypt turned out to be a poor source of support for Israel.

◆ Make a human pyramid, being very careful to choose your supports well.

◆ Alternatively, form small groups, each of which builds a pyramid of blocks. After an allotted amount of time, analyze which pyramid is the tallest, and why.

22 Prophets felt empowered to speak freely about things that mattered to them. Choose a topic or cause that matters to you. Prepare a two-minute speech on that subject, and deliver it to the class. Consider videotaping the speeches for later viewing.

23 Ezekiel delivers the first prophecy in this Haftarah in the tenth month, which is Tevet.

◆ Memorize the Hebrew months in order. The teacher can award prizes to those who master the list, those who can say the months the fastest, those who correctly answer questions regarding holidays within each month, etc.

24 The Israelites spend about 50 years in Babylonian exile.

◆ Imagine you have just had a grandchild who is born in exile. You don't know whether or not the child will ever return to Israel, but you want your grandchild to know all about life in "the old country." Write a letter to your grandchild, describing the good ol' days when Israelites lived in Israel.

Other Resources

25 For a Haftarah commentary, discussion questions, and project, see the UAHC Family Shabbat Table Talk web site at www.uahc. org/shabbat/stt/3vaera.shtml.

26 For a Haftarah commentary, see the web site for the Fuchsberg Center for Conservative Judaism in Jerusalem, www.uscj.org.il/ haftarah/vaera5762.html.

27 Insights from the Tradition #A and #B, p. 451, deal with people unable to appreciate what they have. These Insights also consider the influence on us by those with whom they associate. View and discuss the film *Trading Places* (1983, rated R, 118 minutes), which explores what happens when a rich man and a poor man switch places.

28 View and discuss the film *Life Stinks* (1991, rated PG-13, 93 minutes), in which a rich landowner learns firsthand what it's like to be a poor tenant in one of his buildings.

29 Read and discuss the classic book *The Prince and the Pauper* by Mark Twain, which is also about learning to appreciate what you have after you seem to lose it.

30 Read the chapter on Ezekiel in *Messengers of God: A Jewish Prophets Who's Who* by Ronald H. Isaacs, pp. 121-133.

Involving the Family

31 Learn to appreciate the warmth and conveniences of your home by taking a wilderness camping or fishing trip with your family. What other things (about nature, family, peace and quiet) do you learn to appreciate while you are camping?

Bar/Bat Mitzvah Project

32 The Israelites were political refugees in Babylonia. Hold a fund-raiser for a relief organization, such as Magen David Adom, Hadassah, or United Jewish Appeal, which helps people who are refugees from natural disasters or political oppression.

EZEKIEL 36:16-38 Ashkenazim
EZEKIEL 36:16-36 Sephardim
SHABBAT PARAH

 This Haftarah has been paired with *Shabbat Parah*, on which we read a special Maftir Torah reading, Numbers 19:1-22. See "Connecting the Text To the Special Shabbat," pp. 460-462, for an exploration of the many ways the two texts and the Special Shabbat shed light on each other.

SYNOPSIS

Ezekiel delivers this prophecy to the exiled Israelites, who despair of ever returning to their homeland. The prophet explains that disaster befell Israel as divine retribution for the nation's sins. Yet it turns out that the nations think badly of God, saying (verse 36:20): "These are the people of *Adonai*, yet they had to leave *Adonai's* land." Seeking to restore the divine name, *Adonai* will gather Israel from its dispersion, cleanse the people from their impurity, and restore them to their homeland.

For God's own sake, *Adonai* will give the Israelites a new heart and new spirit, and they will be ashamed of their past behavior. In the Land of Israel, food will be abundant, settlements will be populated, and ruined places rebuilt. Desolate land will be fertile as the Garden of Eden, and the cities will be strong.

For the sake for the House of Israel, *Adonai* will multiply the people like sheep.

INSIGHTS FROM THE TRADITION

A According to Hirsch, Ezekiel is called "mortal" (or literally, "son of Adam") in verse 36:17, because in the aftermath of national catastrophe he is one of only a very few Israelites left. He could only look to the future (like Adam, who could look only to the future, as there was no past).

◆ What do you imagine it would be like to be one of just a few survivors of a national catastrophe (such as a nuclear accident or war)?

B Hertz explains that the phrase "for the blood which they shed upon their land" in verse 36:18 refers to child sacrifices.

◆ In what way(s) does child sacrifice represent the worst possible sin?

◆ Part of being a parent is putting one's child's interests first, and sometimes that means sacrificing one's own. Can you think of a situation in which a parent's interests might be in conflict with a child's? In this situation, whose interests should be sacrificed for the other, and why?

◆ Interview your parents and grandparents for examples of people they have known who made sacrifices for their children.

C According to *Midrash Lamentations Rabbah* (Proem 15), God went with the Israelites into exile and listened to what their captors were saying. God heard them say that while these are the people of *Adonai*, they had nonetheless to leave the Land. This, of course, would be a black mark on God's reputation, as it would seem that God was not powerful enough to protect them there.

◆ What kind of action might leave a black mark on the reputation of a teacher? a friend? a synagogue? your country? Israel?

◆ How easy or difficult is it to restore a tarnished reputation?

D Malbim explains that God accompanied the Israelites into exile to make sure that they were punished only according to the measure of their sin but no more (verse 36:20).

◆ How do your parents determine what is an appropriate punishment?

◆ What is the danger of over-punishment?

◆ What is the danger of under-punishment?

◆ Discuss and determine what would be appropriate punishments for the following wrongdoings:

• Talking back to your parents

• Cheating on a test

• Lying to your best friend

• Stealing a pack of gum from a store

• Pulling the fire alarm at school

E Kara says that the heart of stone in verse 36:26 means a heart that is tempted to worship idols.

◆ What do you do when your heart tempts you to do something you know you shouldn't do?

F *Targum Jonathan* says that the heart of flesh in verse 36:26 is a fearing heart that desires to do the will of God.

◆ Do you generally do what is right because you are afraid of the consequences of doing something wrong? Or, do you generally do what is right because you know in your heart it is the right thing to do? What is the difference between the two?

G Kara explains that the phrase "My spirit" in verse 36:27 means the inclination to do good.

◆ If God's spirit is our inclination to do good, then what do you think could be the definition of God?

◆ One definition of God may be "Justice," because when we are inclined to do good, Justice (God's spirit) can be felt in the world. Collect newspaper clippings of people doing good in the world. How does each act increase justice — and God's presence — in the world?

◆ Alternatively, if God's spirit is the inclination to do good, God could be defined as the force that impels us to improve ourselves. Give examples of ways in which people improve themselves. How does each way increase God's presence in the world?

H Ezekiel says in verse 36:29 that after Israel is saved from its uncleanness, God will bless it with material well-being. According to Hirsch, once the Israelites are morally healed, they will no longer be led astray by material wealth.

◆ How might material abundance affect peoples' values and lead them astray?

◆ Newspapers, talk radio, television shows, and even Jewish organizations have recently been concerned about raising morally good children in an era of prosperity. Sometimes they refer to a condition called "affluenza." What do you think the tongue-in-cheek term "affluenza" means? What does it mean to be affluent?

◆ What advice would you give to parents in order that they raise their children with good values, even if they are surrounded by great material wealth?

◆ For more on the subject, read *Too Much of a Good Thing: Raising Children of Character in An Indulgent Age* by Daniel Kindlon.

STRATEGIES
Analyzing the Text

1 In verse 36:20 God claims that Israel caused God's name to be profaned. Rashi explains the desecration of God's name:

"What was the dishonor? When their enemies said about them, 'These are *Adonai's* people, but from *Adonai's* land they went out, and *Adonai* did not have the power to save *Adonai's* people or land.'"

◆ What did Ezekiel and Rashi think was the real cause of the Israelites' exile?

◆ What would other nations say was the cause of their exile?

◆ How would God's name be desecrated?

◆ For more on profaning God's name, see the Haftarah for *Kedoshim*, Connecting the Text To the Sedra #8, #9, #10, pp. 438-439.

2 Moshe Greenberg offers a second way to understand the desecration of God's name caused by the exile of the Israelites (Ezekiel 21-37, p. 729). When the surviving Israelites go into exile, they will talk about their terrible behavior. The other nations with whom the Israelites are now living will be horrified that the Israelites were so depraved and that God would associate with such awful people. God's name will be desecrated by association with the corrupt Israelites.

◆ Do you think this explanation of the desecration of God's name reflects verses 36:20, 21,

22, 23? Consider also Ezekiel 5:6-7 and 12:15-16.

◆ Can you offer other explanations?

3 God promises to give the people a new heart in verse 36:26. The Bible understands the heart to be the seat of one's intelligence and emotions (today we think of these as coming from the brain).

According to verse 36:26, Israel has a heart of stone. A heart of stone may be hard, cold, tough, stubborn, unyielding, or inflexible.

Israel will receive from God a new heart of flesh. It is implied that with their new heart, the people will be given new emotions of gratitude, submissiveness, obedience, loyalty, steadfastness, reverence, tenderness, sensitivity, and a willingness to be molded in God's image.

◆ Define and discuss each emotion.

◆ Make a poster with facial expressions representing each of these new emotions. Label the faces.

◆ Why did God want Israel to have these new emotions instead of remaining in their old state?

◆ Are these emotions that you generally associate with being "religious"?

4 The Ashkenazim conclude the Haftarah with verse 36:38, but the Sephardim end two verses earlier at 36:36.

◆ Discuss which ending is more upbeat and which conclusion you prefer.

Connecting the Text To the Special Shabbat

5 *Shabbat Parah* is the third of four special Sabbaths before Passover. The Maftir reading for this Special Shabbat is Numbers 19:1-22, which deals with the subject of ritual purification involving the red heifer. The Haftarah focuses on the future moral purification of the Israelites.

Why is ritual purification a relevant subject to be discussed before Pesach? According to Deuteronomy 16:1-6, all Israelites were required to come to the Jerusalem Temple on Pesach in order to offer the paschal lamb sacrifice. In order to bring this offering to the Temple, they first had to be purified in case anything had happened to them during the past year causing them to become impure (such as having contact with a dead body). The passage from Numbers 19:1-22 reminds us of the need for purification.

◆ Learn more about the red heifer in *Teaching Torah* by Sorel Goldberg Loeb and Barbara Binder Kadden, Insights from the Tradition #A, #B, #C, pp. 260-261.

6 In the Haftarah Ezekiel tells the people that they must rid themselves of their sins. Before Passover, we clean our houses to remove all traces of *chametz*. Along with the literal meaning of "leaven," *chametz* is often interpreted to mean "sins" and "arrogance." By cleaning out our spiritual *chametz*, we purify ourselves of the bad thoughts and the bad habits to which we have been enslaved all year.

◆ Explain in your own words what spiritual *chametz* is. How is ridding one's house of *chametz* similar to Ezekiel's call to the people to rid themselves of their sins?

While the house should be thoroughly cleaned of *chametz* in the weeks and days preceding the holiday, there is a ritual removal of *chametz* that is done on the evening of the 14th of Nisan. It is customary to place small pieces of bread in obvious places around your home. After reciting the blessing about being commanded to remove leaven, we search the house by candlelight, picking up

the bread with a wooden spoon and feather. After the search, a statement annulling all remaining leaven is said. The following morning, the bread is burned.

◆ Hold a *chametz* hunt at school so students will know how to hold one at home. You can find out how to search for *chametz*, the blessing recited before hunting for *chametz*, the statement annulling all remaining *chametz*, and the blessing for burning the *chametz* at the beginning of most *Haggadot*.

7 Concerning verse 36:38, Rashi says that the phrase "sacrificial sheep during her festivals" refers to the flocks that come for sacrifice at Passover. *Shabbat Parah* reminds us that every household must be purified to bring its own Pesach sacrifice.

The paschal sacrifice is symbolized on our Passover *Seder* plates by a roasted bone. Interestingly, the Rabbis of the Talmud suggested that the paschal sacrifice need not be represented only by a roasted bone (*Pesachim* 114b). They also used to roast a beet or fish. These might make suitable substitutes for the roasted bone in vegetarian homes.

Make your own *Seder* plate. Choose whether to designate one section of the *Seder* plate for the roasted bone or roasted beet/fish. Also, there is a modern tradition of putting an orange on the *Seder* plate. Find out about it at www.geocities.com/yiddishemaydl/orange.html. Alternatively, go to the Internet and search for an explanation by entering "orange *seder* plate." Then, decide if you will add an orange to your own *Seder* plate.

8 Ezekiel tells the Israelites in the Haftarah that they have a heart that is hard as stone (verse 36:26). He assures them that God will replace it with a soft heart of flesh. Conversely, at Passover, we remember how God hardened Pharaoh's heart.

◆ Can you think of a situation in which a soft heart might serve you well? Can you think of a situation in which a hard heart might be better?

◆ Role-play some situations that represent each case.

9 Verses 36:27-28 of the Haftarah emphasize that the Jews are expected to observe the *mitzvot* and be God's people after they are brought out of exile in Babylonia and returned to the Promised Land.

At Passover, we remind ourselves that we were freed from slavery in Egypt in order to serve God.

◆ With freedom comes responsibility. Before Passover, chose one *mitzvah* that you are not accustomed to keep. Learn about it. Then keep that *mitzvah* for the seven weeks between Passover and Shavuot to symbolize that on Passover you were freed in order to keep God's laws. The following are examples of the types of *mitzvot* you might observe for seven weeks: say the *"Shema"* every night at bedtime, do not eat milk and meat at the same meal, have guests every Friday night at a festive Shabbat meal.

10 Ezekiel says in verse 36:25 that the people will be purified with water. The Maftir reading also mentions purification by water (Numbers 19:7-21). Jewish tradition gives to water the power of moral and physical cleansing and even of spiritual renewal.

The embodiment of this power is found in the *mikvah*, or ritual bath. A *mikvah* is a body of natural water (an indoor pool of collected rainwater, an ocean, a river, pond, or lake) used for ritual purification. Immersion in a *mikvah* is often required for conversion to Judaism. Some married Jewish women visit the *mikvah* every month, and

some observant Jewish men visit the *mikvah* before Shabbat.

◆ Find out if your community has a *mikvah*, and see if you can arrange a visit. If not, ask your Rabbi to speak to your class about the rituals and blessings associated with *mikvah*.

Extending the Text

11 Throughout the Haftarah, God is concerned about the divine name and reputation. Consider these statements about the importance of a good name:

• The name of the wicked will rot. (Proverbs 10:7)

• A good name is preferable to great riches. (Proverbs 22:1)

• Who glorifies his own name loses it. (*Pirke Avot* 1:13)

• Every person has three names: one his father and mother gave him, one others call him, and one he earns himself. (*Midrash Ecclesiastes Rabbah* 7:3)

• Win a fair name and go to sleep peacefully. (Ladino folk saying)

• God will accept repentance and grant forgiveness for all sins except one: giving a person a bad name. (*Zohar*)

◆ Which of these statements do you like best, and why?

◆ Make a poster with one of these statements on it to hang in your classroom.

12 In Ezekiel's world, Jerusalem — and the Israelite nation — has been destroyed, and only a small community of survivors has gone into exile.

◆ If you ever found yourself in this kind of situation, do you imagine you would remain hopeful that you would return to your homeland?

◆ Although they could not know how long they would remain in exile or if they would ever return to their homeland, many Israelites did remain faithful to their hope of return and the restoration of Jerusalem. If you were living in exile then, how would you preserve your community's traditions and prepare for your eventual return?

Some historians have suggested that the Torah was compiled by the Israelites in Babylon during this period of exile, for the explicit purpose of serving as a guidebook for setting up their new society when they returned to the Land of Israel. The Torah, therefore, provides an historical basis for exile and return, as well as important religious teachings, laws about civil administration, and laws for the sacrificial ritual in a restored Jerusalem. (Source: *Early Judaism* by Martin S. Jaffee, p. 66.)

◆ Explain how this is an example of a great good coming out of a great tragedy.

◆ In what ways do you think the Torah still serves today as a guidebook for the Jewish people?

◆ Design a mantle for a Torah scroll that conveys the Torah's role as guidebook or as a great good emerging from a tragedy.

13 Having a new heart will enable the Israelites to return to God's ways. Returning to God's ways (i.e., observing the *mitzvot*) can be a gradual process.

The modern Jewish philosopher Franz Rosenzweig is a perfect example of a Jew who slowly returned to God's ways. Rosenzweig was once a non-observant Jew who even considered conver-

sion to Christianity. However, after experiencing a moving Yom Kippur service, he decided to return to Jewish ways. Once he returned, he was asked whether he put on *tefillin*. He answered, "Not yet." Although he was not currently observing that particular *mitzvah*, he could envision a day when he might be ready to accept the obligation of *tefillin*. He recognized that observance is always evolving.

◆ What can Rosenzweig's answer teach us about a new heart and returning?

◆ Make a list of *mitzvot* that you think are interesting or valuable, but do not yet observe. Choose a new *mitzvah* to observe as you become a Bar/Bat Mitzvah. Consider adding one new Jewish observance every year.

◆ For information on *mitzvot,* see *The How-To Handbook for Jewish Living* by Kerry M. Olitzky and Ronald H. Isaacs, or *Teaching Mitzvot* by Barbara Binder Kadden and Bruce Kadden. For more on Franz Rosenzweig, read *Franz Rosenzweig: His Life and Thought* by Nahum N. Glatzer or log on to divinity. library.vanderbilt.edu/rosenzw/rosintro.html.

Personalizing the Text

14 Ezekiel is called "son of Adam," the first man on earth. Commentators explain that knowing where we come from helps us to know where we are going.

◆ On the top of a piece of poster board, write your name. On the next line write "son of" or "daughter of" and fill in your parents' names. Beneath that, write what it means to you to be the child of your parents, what they have taught you, and how they are helping to guide you into the future.

15 *Shabbat Parah* heralds the coming of Pesach.

◆ Begin to prepare for your *Seder* by asking your Cantor to teach you how to sing the order of the parts of the *Seder*.

16 *Shabbat Parah* is about purification.

◆ Organize a pre-Passover *chametz* dinner party to help clean out your cabinets and eat all your *chametz*.

17 Regarding verse 36:32 Hirsch explains that self-examination and repentance can prevent future sin and suffering.

◆ Keep a diary of your day, paying special attention to any mistakes you have made. Does noticing and analyzing your mistakes help you to prevent making similar mistakes in the future?

18 Based on Analyzing the Text #2, p. 460, God's name is desecrated when we wrong other people and don't follow God's laws. God's name is sanctified when we live by God's laws and make this world a more just place.

◆ Write an essay about three acts you have committed in the last year that you believe desecrated God's name. Include in your essay three things you hope to do in the next year that will help to sanctify God's name.

19 God promises to give the people a new heart of flesh.

◆ Based on Analyzing the Text #3, p. 460, describe a person you know (or know of) who has a "heart of flesh." Does this person also have a "warm heart," "heart of gold," and a "big heart"? Alternatively, find a newspaper article about such a person and report on the article to your class.

20 Time after time in the Bible, God is disappointed in the Israelites for failing to uphold the *mitzvot*. And time after time, God forgives them.

◆ Do you think your parents/your school/your community expect too much of you? How do you respond when there are high expectations of you? Do you strive to meet them, feel it is impossible and give up, try your best and know your best is good enough, or do something else altogether? If the latter, describe what you do.

◆ How do your parents respond when you don't meet their expectations?

◆ Ezekiel says that God will give Israel a new spirit.

◆ Listen to and learn the song *"Im Tirtzu"* by Debbie Friedman on the recording *Not by Might, Not by Power*.

Other Resources

21 View and discuss the film *Joe's Apartment* (1996, rated PG-13, 80 minutes), which documents the hardhearted environment of New York City.

22 View and discuss the scenes in the classic film *The Wizard of Oz* (1939, not rated, 101 minutes), in which the Tin Man sings about how much he wants a heart and the Wizard awards him a heart. Discuss the Wizard's wise words to the Tin Man.

23 Read the chapter on Ezekiel in *Messengers of God: A Jewish Prophets Who's Who* by Ronald H. Isaacs, pp. 121-133.

24 Discuss the portrayal of this Haftarah in *The Illustrated Torah* by Michal Meron, p. 228.

25 For better understanding of the red heifer in the *Maftir* for *Shabbat Parah*, see the skit in *Parashah Plays* by Richard J. Allen, pp. 238-243.

26 Compare Ezekiel's idea of a new heart (36:26) to Jeremiah's idea of God's teaching being inscribed on Israel's hearts (Jeremiah 31:32-34) and to the requirement in the *"Shema"* to keep God's teaching on one's heart (Deuteronomy 6:4-6).

27 For quotations involving the heart, see Sedra *Bechukotai*, Extending the Text #15, p. 400.

28 Study the poem "The New Ezekiel" by Emma Lazarus, which may be found at www.bartleby.com/248/1018.html. Write your own poem about a new heart for humanity.

29 For more on Ezekiel, see the *Encyclopaedia Judaica*, vol. 6, pp. 1078-1098.

Involving the Family

30 Make cleaning your home for Pesach a family project, making sure that everyone contributes to the effort. Start a family tradition by doing the ritual search for *chametz* and burning *chametz* together.

Bar/Bat Mitzvah Project

31 We discussed in Insight from the Tradition #B, p. 458, that sacrificing children (or their needs) is a grave sin. Support your local Jewish Family Service. To find out where it is and how to contact them, check out www.ajfca.org.

EZEKIEL 37:1-14 TRADITIONAL
EZEKIEL 36:37-37:14 REFORM
SHABBAT PASSOVER

 This Haftarah has been paired with the Shabbat that falls during Passover, on which we read Exodus 33:12-34:26. See "Connecting the Text To the Holiday," pp. 468-469, for an exploration of the ways the two texts and the holiday shed light on each other.

SYNOPSIS

With this prophetic vision, Ezekiel is able to give hope of redemption to the exiled Israelites in Babylonia. He promises that the ruined cities will once again be filled with flocks of people.

Ezekiel describes his vision of a valley full of dry bones. God asks the prophet if he thinks the bones will ever live again, and Ezekiel responds that only God knows. God instructs Ezekiel to tell the bones that *Adonai* will cover them with flesh, put breath into them, and cause them to live again. Ezekiel does as he is told.

The prophet hears a rattling sound and sees the bones come together and become covered with flesh and skin. He watches them come to life again, as they are filled with breath and stand on their feet.

God explains to Ezekiel that the bones are the House of Israel. Just as the bones have been lifted out of their graves and revived, so will the exiled Israelites be restored to their homeland and returned to their former vigor.

INSIGHTS FROM THE TRADITION

A In verse 37:6 God describes the different layers that will be put back on the bones. The last layer to be removed (i.e., the sinews next to the bone) is the first to be put back. *Genesis Rabbah* 14:5 compares this to a person getting dressed after taking a bath who puts the clothes on in the reverse order of how they were taken off.

A human being must put clothes on in the correct order because otherwise he/she cannot make them fit properly (i.e., it would be impossible for a human being to put on outer clothes first and then underclothing and have the underclothing actually be under). However, one would think that God could dress a human being (with sinews, flesh, and skin) in any order and have it come out right.

◆ Why, in your opinion, did God follow the conventional order (inner items and then outer ones) instead of rebuilding the bones into bodies in any order?

◆ Why do you think the physical components of the body preceded the soul?

B According to *Genesis Rabbah* 14:5, when God redressed the bones, it was like a person getting dressed in the exact reverse order of having "undressed." God could, however, have the power to put the person back in any order and it would have come out right. Sometimes we do something one certain way and never think about trying to do it another way.

◆ Explain the expression "think outside the box."

◆ Draw nine dots in three rows to make a three-by-three grid. Try connecting all nine dots by drawing only four straight lines and without lifting pen/pencil from the paper.

◆ Discuss whether it is better to do things differently for the sake of variety or better to do something in the same way as always.

C In verse 37:14 God promises to breathe into the people and that they will then live again. Radak explains this means God would fill them with God's spirit so that they will be infused with knowledge, understanding, and wisdom. As a result, they will no longer transgress.

◆ Debate: The only reason human beings make mistakes is because they have inadequate knowledge, understanding, and wisdom (make sure you define these terms for your debate).

STRATEGIES
Analyzing the Text

1 God shows Ezekiel a valley full of bones in verses 37:1-3. Note that he does not describe skeletons lying everywhere, but rather disconnected bones.

◆ Why would disconnected bones seem to indicate more complete devastation and deterioration than dried up skeletons?

2 In verse 37:3 God asks Ezekiel if the bones will live again and Ezekiel answers that only God knows that.

◆ Why does God ask if the bones will live again?

◆ With his answer, is Ezekiel avoiding God's question?

◆ Rabbi Eliezer of Beaugency understands that Ezekiel's response means: "You know since

you are their Creator. The craftsman who made it has the expertise to know if it can be mended or not."

◆ Do you agree with Rabbi Eliezer that Ezekiel is affirming God's power?

◆ Look for another reference to the story of Creation. (For example, in verse 37:6 God will breathe into the newly formed human beings so that they may live.)

3 There was noise and quaking in verse 37:7 that accompanied movement by the bones. At least two explanations for the noise and movement have been suggested: (1) the prophet's words made the bones move and they made noise banging together and shaking the ground with their movement, and (2) an earthquake shook the ground, made noise, and caused the bones to start moving.

◆ Which explanation makes most sense to you, and why?

4 Two metaphors are used to describe the hopeless exiles: they are dried up bones lying in a field, and they are dead in their graves (verse 37:12). In the second metaphor, the exiles are so depressed with their situation in exile, it is as if they have sunk low, sunk into a grave. God promises to open their graves and raise them up, just as God brought the dry bones back to life.

◆ Just as Ezekiel was inspired by God and relocated by God's spirit (ruach) (verse 37:1), so will all the people be revived for a new life and will be relocated to their land with God's breath (ruach, verses 37:12-14). Make matching illustrations of Ezekiel being moved by God's ruach and the hopeless Israelites being renewed by God's ruach.

Connecting the Text To the Holiday

5 Ezekiel's vision of the dry bones is meant to be an allegory that Israel spent so long in exile that they despaired of ever being redeemed and sent back to their land. That their bones were dried up means their hope was lost.

In verse 37:11 God says the bones represent the whole house of Israel. God means both Northern Kingdom, which had been destroyed and carried off long before, and Southern Kingdom, which had recently been destroyed and taken into exile in Babylonia.

◆ Explain why someone in exile, despairing of going home, might express his/her feelings as being dead.

◆ The point of Ezekiel's prophecy seems to be to encourage belief in eventual redemption in spite of the endless exile. Explain how this is relevant to Passover, which is our festival of redemption.

◆ At the Passover *Seder*, we say, "Next year in Jerusalem." Make a banner with this saying. Hang it in the room where your *Seder* takes place. Alternatively, make a button featuring the saying and wear it at your *Seder*.

6 Both the Torah reading and the Haftarah are about knowing God.

In the Haftarah (verse 37:6), God will bring the dry bones back to life and then they will know "I am *Adonai*." In verses 37:13-14 God says further that after opening the graves of the people, they will know that "I am *Adonai*."

There is also a statement in verse 36:38 that after God has multiplied the population of Israel, then they will know that "I am *Adonai*." (Note: that verses 36:37-38 are not read as part of the Haftarah by all communities.)

Similarly, the Torah reading involves knowing about God. In Exodus 33:12-14 Moses asks to know about God and God's ways, and in 33:18 Moses asks to see God's glory. God responds that Moses cannot see God's face, but God will pass by and Moses will see God's back. Additionally, in 34:6-7 God passes by Moses, and Moses learns God's attributes.

God is known to us by the acts God does: freeing slaves, returning exiles to their homeland, giving hope, being merciful and slow to anger.

◆ By what deeds and acts do you generally define God?

◆ By what deeds and acts do you hope to be known? Write a short biography (or résumé) that reviews your own great acts.

7 There is an interesting phrase in the Haftarah (verse 37:14): God promises to revive the dead from their graves and set them on their own land. Then, God says, " . . . you shall know that I am *Adonai* Who spoke and did this." This phrase, "I am *Adonai* Who spoke and did this," appears several other times in Ezekiel (see 22:14 and 36:36).

◆ The statement by God indicates God's reliability; what God promises, God will carry out. Explain how this is a relevant message for Passover.

There is a similar phrase in the Torah reading. God had promised to take the children of Israel out of Egypt and up to the Promised Land. Then the children of Israel anger God with the golden calf. God announces in Exodus 33:1-2 that God would not go with them, but would send an angel instead. In Exodus 33:17 Moses argues that God should not abandon the people who have sinned with the golden calf. Rather, because Moses has found favor with God, God should continue to accompany the people to the Land of Israel.

Moses further argues that he should not be humiliated by having to deal with an intermediary angel instead of dealing directly with God. God agrees, saying, "What you said, I will do."

◆ What does God's statement say about God's reliability? about Moses' reliability?

◆ How would you characterize your own reliability?

◆ Many businesses pride themselves on being reliable. Make up an advertising slogan for yourself, Moses, or God that conveys reliability.

8 Although Ezekiel speaks metaphorically about reviving the dead, this Haftarah was later reinterpreted to support the concept of resurrection of the dead in the time of the Messiah. Similarly, at the Passover *Seder,* we open the door for Elijah the Prophet, who is expected to herald the coming of the Messiah when the dead will be resurrected.

◆ For a discussion of resurrection and this Haftarah, see the UAHC Family Shabbat Table web site at www.uahc.org/shabbat/stt/3pesach.shtml.

◆ Outside the Knesset in Jerusalem is a *menorah* sculpted by Benno Elkan that features Ezekiel's vision of the dry bones. See a photograph of this *menorah* in the *Encyclopaedia Judaica*, vol. 6, p. 1096. Why is this a fitting symbol for the modern State of Israel's parliament?

◆ Alternatively, see the painting "Vision of Ezekiel" by David Bomberg, which is reprinted in *The Illustrated Hebrew Bible* by Ellen Frankel, p. 215.

9 One theme of Shabbat Passover is the idea of a future messianic redemption. According to *midrash*, this Haftarah predicts such a messianic redemption, complete with resurrection of the dead.

◆ How do you think we will treat each other in such a messianic future? And more important, how can we change the way we treat each other now to make this world more like the imagined messianic future?

◆ Read the following story and analyze the ways it is a lesson for how we can choose to treat each other.

A story is told about heaven and hell. The inhabitants of hell sit around a magnificent banquet table, overflowing with sumptuous food. However, no one is eating because they cannot bend their elbows and cannot, therefore, get the food into their mouths. The inhabitants of heaven are likewise sitting around a magnificent banquet table, overflowing with sumptuous food. They, too, are unable to bend their arms at the elbows. Yet they are able to enjoy the delicious food because they realized that they could feed one another.

◆ In Insights from the Tradition #B, pp. 466-467, we learned about "thinking outside the box." How might this story also teach us to think outside the box?

EZEKIEL 37:15-28
VAYIGASH ויגש

This Haftarah has been paired with *Parashat Vayigash*, Genesis 44:18-47:27. See "Connecting the Text To the Sedra," pp. 472-473, for an exploration of the many ways the two texts shed light on each other.

SYNOPSIS

In this Haftarah Ezekiel shares an encouraging vision of a restored and reunited kingdom of Israel with the dejected Israelite exiles. Using two sticks as props, Ezekiel demonstrates his prophecy symbolically. One stick represents the Northern Kingdom of Israel that had been destroyed by the Assyrians in 721 B.C.E. The other represents the Southern Kingdom of Judah, which was destroyed by the Babylonians in 586 B.C.E.

Holding both sticks together in one hand, Ezekiel declares that just as the sticks are as one, so will the divided and conquered kingdoms of Israel be reunited into one strong and powerful nation. On that day, the Israelites will turn away from idolatry and sin. They will be cleansed and led as God's people by a descendant of King David. They will live in the Promised Land forever, increasing their numbers and enjoying peace and prosperity. *Adonai* will be their God and the other nations will know that *Adonai* dwells with them.

INSIGHTS FROM THE TRADITION

A Hirsch explains that the text in verse 37:25 literally says that the Israelite ancestors lived "in" the land, but the returning exiles will live "on" the land. Hirsch explains that when the disobedient ancestors lived "in" the land, they were subject to the conditions of the land (famine, drought, and so on). In contrast, when the obedient Israelites return to live "on" the land, the land will support and serve them.

While we certainly do not want to be controlled by the land and its conditions, there are also dangers that come with relentlessly subjecting the land to our control (erosion, mineral depletion, exhaustion of natural resources, etc.). Perhaps it is best to aim to live together with the land.

◆ Discuss how each of the following measures can help us to strike a balance between our own needs and those of the land: recycling, using fuel efficient automobiles, walking and riding bicycles instead of driving cars, buying food in bulk (rather than in small packages), and composting.

B The "covenant of peace" mentioned in verse 37:26 means — according to *Metsudat David* — an opportunity to live in their land in peace. Living in the Land of Israel in peace may mean both external peace with neighbors, as well as internal peace among all of Israel.

◆ Debate: It is harder to achieve internal peace among all Jews than to attain external peace between Jews, Christians, and Moslems.

C Verse 37:27, according to Hertz, indicates that God's presence will be evident among the people as soon as they live up to their responsibility to be a holy people. In other words, we feel God's presence when we act in a godly way.

◆ Ask your Rabbi or Cantor to speak to your class on the topic of "holy acts I did this year and how they made me feel connected to the Holy One."

D According to Plaut, the reference in verse 37:27 to God's presence hints at the future rebuilding of the Temple, in which the presence of God will be manifest.

◆ Debate the following statement: God's presence can be felt only within the confines of a synagogue building.

◆ Discuss whether being religious is something you do only at synagogue or in your everyday life.

STRATEGIES
Analyzing the Text

1 The prophet is called *"ben adam"* more than 80 times in the Book of Ezekiel.

◆ For a discussion of this term, see Analyzing the Text #1 in the Haftarah for *Kedoshim*, p. 436.

2 Ezekiel uses the demonstration of the two sticks to serve as a sign of his prophecy.

◆ What does the uniting of the two sticks represent?

◆ Review the first half of chapter 37, which describes another visual image of the future restoration of Israel (see the Haftarah for the Shabbat of Passover, p. 466). See verses 4:1, 4:4, and 12:3 for more examples of Ezekiel dramatically and symbolically demonstrating his points. How do visual demonstrations help to teach a lesson?

3 Commentators have speculated about what type of wood Ezekiel used for his demonstration. Some suggest he used plain pieces of wood into which he carved the names. Others

think he used a kind of wooden writing board that was covered with beeswax, which could be wiped clean.

◆ The wooden writing board sounds a lot like the plastic covered board (called a Magic Slate) on which one writes with a stylus. You can buy one at most toy stores or drugstores. Use a Magic Slate to play *Pictionary*. The teacher and/or students can prepare cards with topics. You and your classmates can take turns drawing and guessing pictures illustrating Jewish people, themes, holidays, and events.

4 First, Ezekiel holds sticks symbolically in his hand. Then God says (verse 37:19) that the two sticks will become one "in My hand."

◆ If "in My hand" means by God's power, explain Ezekiel's message (that God will restore the two peoples).

5 Ezekiel indicates in verse 37:22 that God will make Israel into one גוי *(goy)* — nation. The term "nation" implies a group of people associated with a particular land or territory having, or wishing to have, its own government (political state) independent from other peoples. It is significant that he chooses the word *"goy"* as opposed to the word עם *(am)* — people. The term "people" implies a community, tribe, family, or other group united by common heritage, culture, or religion.

◆ Explain in your own words the difference between *"am"* and *"goy."*

◆ The Israelites in exile with Ezekiel were still a "people," even though they were in exile. What is Ezekiel promising them about their status as a "nation" in the future?

◆ We can identify ourselves as part of several different communities, peoples, or even nations. Are you a "Jewish American" or an "American Jew"? In other words, are you an

American who happens to be Jewish, or a Jew who happens to be an American? Discuss your conclusion with others in the class.

Connecting the Text To the Sedra

6 In Genesis 45:14 Joseph and Benjamin have a tearful reunion. In the Haftarah (see especially verse 37:22), Ezekiel proclaims the reunion of the two halves of Israel, symbolized by the two sticks. On one stick is engraved the name "Judah" (which included the tribe of Benjamin in the Southern Kingdom) and on the other is the name "Ephraim" (Joseph's son who represents the Northern Kingdom). Ezekiel's reunion of Judah-Benjamin and Ephraim-Joseph parallels the Sedra's reunion of Benjamin and Joseph.

♦ Jewish law considers reunions to be a special event. According to the *Shulchan Aruch, Hilchot B'rachot* 225:1, when you meet a friend or family member whom you have not seen for at least 30 days, it is tradition to say the *"Shehecheyanu"* blessing: Blessed are you, *Adonai*, Sovereign of the world, Who gave us life, and kept us strong and brought us to this moment.

♦ Explain how this blessing expresses your happiness in seeing a dear friend or relative whom you have missed.

♦ If, however, you have not seen the person for 12 months, *Shulchan Aruch* says that you should say a different blessing: Blessed are You, *Adonai*, Sovereign of the world, Who brings back to life the dead. What do you think this blessing means? How is a person you haven't seen in over a year like a dead person brought back to life?

♦ Which blessing would Joseph and Benjamin (or members of the Northern and Southern Kingdoms) say when they see each other? How would they feel seeing each other again?

7 The phrase "see for yourselves" appears in Genesis 45:12. It seems to mean that in order to understand fully what is happening, Joseph's brothers cannot just hear an explanation, but must see evidence that supports it. They require a visual sign, just as the Israelites do in the Haftarah.

Again, in Genesis 45:26-27, Jacob does not believe that Joseph is alive until he sees the wagons that Joseph sent to carry his family to Egypt.

♦ Do you generally agree that "seeing is believing"? Why or why not?

♦ Are there times when your eyes mislead you? Describe such times.

8 The Haftarah includes an action that symbolizes a lesson. In the Sedra Joseph makes his brothers go through the action of going home to get Benjamin and bringing him to Egypt, in order to help them relive the time they were alone with Joseph and sold him. This time, the enactment is supposed to teach them to protect the weaker and younger brother.

On face value, Ezekiel's stick demonstration and Joseph's brothers' task do not seem to be very meaningful. It is only upon further explanation and reflection that these actions teach us something.

♦ Give examples of symbolic actions you do. For example, are any of the following symbolic actions meant to teach you something and, if so, what do they teach: science lab, Mother's Day or Father's Day, Little League, getting an allowance.

9 The Haftarah concludes with the statement that the other nations will know that *Adonai* dwells with the people of Israel. This can be understood to mean that God cares about what the other nations think about God's reputation. If God does not save the Israelites, God might be perceived as weak.

In the Sedra Joseph sends his attendants away so they will not see him lose emotional control when he reveals his true identity to his brothers.

◆ It seems that neither God nor Joseph wants to be perceived as weak by others. Why do you think this might be so?

◆ Describe how you would like to be perceived by others.

10 Joseph tells his family in Genesis 46:32-34 to say they are shepherds, because Egyptians hate shepherds and will want them to dwell at a distance in the land of Goshen. Apparently, Joseph thinks it would be good for the family to live at a safe distance from the Egyptians.

◆ The Egyptians hated shepherds. Why do you think this was so? (Perhaps because shepherds were considered very low on the social scale. Or perhaps it was because "shepherds" may have been understood as a group of hated, foreign shepherds who temporarily ruled Egypt.)

◆ In the Haftarah (verse 37:24), Ezekiel says that the Israelite community that returns will have one shepherd. Compare the tasks of a shepherd to those of God leading a tired people from exile to their home.

◆ Do you like the image of God as a shepherd? Why or why not?

◆ Draw a picture of a shepherd caring for his/her flock.

Extending the Text

11 Ezekiel refers to the 12 tribes of the Northern and Southern Kingdoms. Learn the names of the 12 sons of Jacob/Israel: Reuben, Simeon, Levi, Judah, Issachar, Zebulun, Gad, Asher, Dan, Naphtali, Joseph, and Benjamin.

The 12 landholding tribes, however, are slightly different from the 12 sons. Ephraim and Manasseh, Joseph's only two sons, are included as sons of their grandfather instead of Joseph. In addition, the tribe of Levi (the priests) is not included with the 12 landholding tribes because the priests (Levites) had no territory of their own.

◆ Write a revised list that includes only the 12 landholding tribes.

◆ Study pictures of the Chagall windows at Hadassah Hospital in Jerusalem. These windows depict the 12 tribes, and can be seen at www.hadassah.org.il/chagall.htm.

◆ In addition to pictures, this web site includes a detailed description of the symbols representing each tribe in the Chagall windows, biblical quotations explaining the symbols, modern Israeli postage stamps depicting the tribes' symbols and the tribes' gem stones.

◆ Do the windows depict the 12 sons of Jacob/Israel, or do they depict the 12 landholding tribes?

◆ For each tribe, the windows portray a symbol that is associated with the tribe. What is the main symbol used to represent each tribe? We learn from Ezekiel that symbols are important for communicating messages and meanings. What does each symbol represent about each tribe?

12 Ezekiel predicts in verse 37:22 that Israel will be a "single nation in the land," implying that the people would be united.

The 12 tribes were separate entities until the time of Saul and David, when they may have enjoyed some unity. However, by the end of Solomon's reign, the kingdom divided into two distinct parts. Throughout Jewish history, factions and groups have opposed one another over many issues (Pharisees and Sadducees, Hasidim and Mitnagdim, Religious and Secular, etc.).

◆ Study one of these pairs and the issues that divided them. Use such resources as the *Encyclopaedia Judaica* and *A History of the Jews* by Solomon Grayzel.

◆ Do you think the Jewish people is a united group today?

◆ How might diversity make a group stronger and more resilient to change? How might diversity weaken a group?

◆ The motto of United Jewish Communities used to be "We Are One." Do you agree with this motto? Can you write a better motto?

13 In Insights from the Tradition #B, p. 470, we understood "peace" as having more than one meaning. What do the following expressions mean to you?

• Inner peace

• Peace and quiet

• Rest in peace

• Peace of mind

• World peace

• *Sh'lom bayit* (peace in the home)

◆ Using all the phrases you can think of that include the word "peace," play a game of *Hangman*.

14 Ezekiel prophesies that on its return, the nation will be ruled by one king from the House of David. In actual fact, Israel never

had a Davidic king again. Yet in our weekday *"Amidah"* prayer, we say a prayer for the return of the Davidic line as our rulers. Prayer books vary greatly in how they translate this particular blessing. Here is a traditional translation:

"Cause the dynasty of David soon to flourish and may it be exalted through Your saving power, for we daily await Your deliverance. Blessed are You, *Adonai*, Who causes salvation to come forth."

◆ This traditional rendering of the prayer assumes that the dynasty of David means the Messiah who should come soon and save us. Do you believe that there will be a Messiah?

◆ Read the following modern translation of the same prayer, adapted from *Siddur Mikor Hayyim: The Community Siddur* of Brandeis Hillel Day School in San Francisco California:

"May we, the ancestors and followers of David, quickly blossom and flourish, for we count on your help every day. Blessed are You, *Adonai*, the source of all strength and growth."

◆ Explain how the second translation assumes that if we, the descendants of David, are flourishing, then it is as if David has been restored and is flourishing. Does this translation include the idea of a Messiah?

◆ Which translation works better for you, and why?

◆ Read and discuss the story "Why the Night Watchman Was Denied a Raise" in *The Jewish Spirit: A Celebration in Stories and Art* by Ellen Frankel, p. 235.

15 Ezekiel demonstrates Israel's predicted reunification with two sticks. The author of the Book of Ecclesiastes states in 4:9-12, "Two are better off than one, in that they have greater benefit from their earnings. For should they fall, one can raise the other; but woe betide him who is alone and falls with no companion to raise him! Further, when two lie together they are warm; but how can he who is alone get warm? Also, if one attacks, two can stand up to him."

◆ Do you agree or disagree with Ecclesiastes?

◆ Do you always prefer to have a partner for school projects, or sometimes to work alone?

◆ In what ways do you imagine the two kingdoms would be stronger if they were reunified?

◆ In pairs and individually, build houses out of popsicle sticks and glue. Discuss which each group liked better — working alone or with a partner.

16 Ezekiel's prophecy about the kingdom of Israel being reunited never came to pass. When the Northern Kingdom was invaded in 721 B.C.E. by the Assyrians, most of the Israelite inhabitants were exiled. Because nearly all of those exiled Jews assimilated into the societies to which they were sent, they are commonly called the "Ten Lost Tribes." Some groups in Africa, including the Ethiopian Jews, claim to be descendants of one of those tribes.

The Jews of the Southern Kingdom of Judah, on the other hand, were eventually able to return from exile. It is with them that our Judaism was born. Jews are known in Hebrew as *Yehudim* because we are descendants of the southern tribe of *Yehudah* (Judah).

◆ Research one of many topics related to Ethiopian Jews (including a lengthy time line) by going to this web site: www.us-israel.org/jsource/Judaism/ejtoc.html.

17 Ezekiel's vision of peace for Israel has yet to be realized.

◆ Invite an expert on the political situation in the Middle East to speak to your class on the history and current state of Israel's relations with her Arab neighbors.

◆ Alternatively, Ezekiel's vision of Israel united under a Davidic monarchy has also not been realized. Today, Israel's government is not run by a king, but by a prime minister, parliament, and president. Invite your community's *Shaliach* from Israel to class to speak about the way elections and government work in Israel and how it is different from a monarchy.

18 We learn the difference between living "in" the land and "on" the land in Insights from the Tradition #A, p. 470. A story is told in *Pirke de Rabbi Eliezer* that the earth trembled with fear when God decided to make a human mate for man. The earth said to God, "I do not have the power to feed the multitude of humanity." The Holy One responded, "I and you will together feed the multitude of humanity."

The earth and God agreed to divide the task between themselves; the night was for the Holy One, and the day was the responsibility of the earth. God created sleep, so that human beings lie down and sleep while God sustains us and heals us and gives us life and rest. With God's help, the earth yields fruit and food for all creation.

◆ Explain why the earth was afraid in this *midrash*.

◆ Explain how God's solutions to the problem helped the earth.

◆ It can be difficult to be kind to the earth while we try to meet the needs of an ever-growing human population. As a class, write ten things you can do to save the environment. Distribute your list to all the students in your school.

Personalizing the Text

19 Ezekiel liked to demonstrate his visions using dramatic props.

◆ Tell the story of the destruction of Jerusalem and the exile of the Israelites using puppets. Alternatively, play a game of paper bag dramatics. To do paper bag dramatics, every student brings to class several items from home to use as clothing or props. Place the items into large paper bags from which the groups randomly pick props for their skits.

20 Joseph and Benjamin had a tearful reunion. Ezekiel predicted that northerners and southerners would have a long awaited reunion (see Connecting the Text To the Sedra #6, p. 472).

◆ Write a personal account of a reunion you have had with a family member or friend who has moved away. If you have not had such a reunion, write about the first time you met a relative or friend you particularly like.

21 Ezekiel used sticks to demonstrate a point.

◆ You can use sticks to have some fun. Play *Pick-up Sticks*.

22 Ezekiel envisions a future blessed with peace for Israel.

◆ Learn and sing the song *"Shalom al Yisrael"* (Peace To Israel) which shares the same hope. The song may be found on the NFTY recording *Shiru Shir Chadash*.

23 Jews are both a nation and a people.

Learn the songs *"Am Yisrael Chai"* (The Jewish People Lives) and *"Lo Yisa Goy el Goy Cherev"* (Nation Shall Not Lift up Sword against Nation),

both of which may be found in *B'Kol Echad*, edited by Jeffrey Shiovitz, pp. 78 and 89, and on the accompanying audiocassettes *Shirei B'Kol Echad*. Order from United Synagogue of Conservative Judaism, www.uscj.org/booksvc.

24 Ezekiel predicts that Israel will once again be under the leadership of King David (or one of his descendants).

The song, *"David Melech Yisrael"* (David King of Israel) asserts that David, King of Israel, lives forever. Learn the song and the hand motions. Better yet, teach the song to younger students who don't already know it. For an alternative melody, listen to the recording *Neshama Shel Shlomo* by Shlomo Carlebach and Neshama Carlebach.

Other Resources

25 For a commentary on the Haftarah, discussion topics, and project, see the UAHC Family Shabbat Table Talk web site, www.uahc.org/shabbat/stt/3vayigash.html.

26 Read the chapter on Ezekiel in *Messengers of God: A Jewish Prophets Who's Who* by Ronald H. Isaacs, pp. 121-133.

27 Discuss the illustration of this Haftarah in *The Illustrated Torah* by Michal Meron, p.56.

28 Ezekiel predicts the reunion of all Israelites and Judeans. Read *Anna Is Still Here* by Ida Vos, which includes a post-World War II reunion.

29 For lessons on Judaism and ecology, see *Spirit in Nature* by Matt Biers-Ariel, Deborah Newbrun, and Michal Fox Smart.

30 For a *D'var Torah* on this Haftarah, see the web site for the Fuchsberg Center for Conservative Judaism in Jerusalem, www.uscj.org/haftarah/vayigash5762.html.

Involving the Family

31 Your Bar or Bat Mitzvah is the perfect time to organize a family reunion. Invite as many family members as you can to share your occasion, and hold a special family reunion Shabbat dinner.

Bar/Bat Mitzvah Project

32 Ethiopian Jews may be descended from one of the ten lost tribes with which the Jews of Ezekiel's time hoped to be reunited. The North American Conference on Ethiopian Jewry (NACOEJ) aids Ethiopian Jews already in Israel and works to bring to Israel those remaining in Ethiopia. Donate a portion of your Bar/Bat Mitzvah gifts to this worthwhile organization, which may be contacted at www.nacoej.org or www.circus.org/nacoej.htm.

EZEKIEL 38:18-39:16
SHABBAT SUKKOT

 This Haftarah has been paired with the Shabbat that falls during Sukkot, on which we read Exodus 33:12-34:26. See "Connecting the Text To the Holiday," pp. 479-480, for an exploration of the ways the two texts and the holiday shed light on each other.

SYNOPSIS

With his people in exile, the prophet Ezekiel seeks to bring hope of future redemption and a return to the Land of Israel. In this prophetic vision, Ezekiel actually sees his nation restored to its land, but not free of trouble from aggressor nations.

Using the name Gog of Magog to represent the king of an enemy nation, Ezekiel prophesies that Gog will set foot on the soil of Israel, inflaming the rage of *Adonai*. On that day, Ezekiel asserts, a terrible earthquake will shake the Land of Israel, forcing the enemy from Israelite territory.

Ezekiel describes in gory detail the fate of Gog, who dares to challenge *Adonai* and the Israelite people. The Israelites will plunder and despoil those who have come to plunder and despoil them. The weapons of the defeated enemy will be used by the Israelites as fuel for seven years. The Israelites will spend seven months burying all the dead of Gog's armies. Finally, for an additional seven months, the Israelites will appoint sentries to inspect the land for the unburied casualties and bury them, cleansing the land of their memory.

INSIGHTS FROM THE TRADITION

A When the children of Israel observed the first Shabbat in the desert, they didn't all keep Shabbat properly. Moses told them that if they would keep Shabbat, they would get various rewards. One reward would be that they would be free from suffering through the times of Gog and Magog (see *The Legends of the Jews* by Louis Ginzberg, vol. 3, p. 47).

◆ Why do you think rewards are offered for commandments that Israel is obligated to keep?

◆ Why do you think people need to be given a bribe to take a day of rest?

B In verse 39:13 God says that the people of Israel will bury all the corpses of their enemy that are scattered in their land, and the people will be renowned. According to Rashi, all the other nations will speak praise about Israel for the kindness they did to bury the enemy who had tried to kill them.

◆ When a school bully has been hurt, how do kids usually respond?

◆ What does Rashi's teaching say about one of the bully's former victims who helps the bully?

◆ Sometimes terrorists go to another country to kill innocent people in terrorist acts, but are caught in the act. Should the terrorists receive a fair trial, complete with all the legal protections provided to citizens of that country? What does it say about a country if it does (or does not) give terrorists a fair trial?

STRATEGIES
Analyzing the Text

1 Gog, the leader of the imaginary country Magog, plans to bring his people to fight against Israel, but God will defeat Gog.

God will get angry and cause a great shaking (verses 38:19-20). Everything will shake; with great exaggeration, the prophet says even the fish, the birds, beasts, and creeping things will shake.

◆ Hyperbole (obvious and intentional exaggeration) is a literary technique used in modern poetry and literature as well as in the Bible. Discuss whether the hyperbole used here is meant to show how intense the earthquake was or to show how scared all the creatures were at the immense shaking of earth and God's anger.

◆ Describe an event from your own life using hyperbole.

2 The meaning of verse 38:21 is unclear. It seems to indicate that each of the enemy's swords will be against his own brother due to the confusion and panic God will cause.

◆ Write a newspaper headline describing the situation portrayed in verses 38:21-22.

3 According to verse 39:13, all the people of Israel will bury the dead when God finishes destroying Gog and Magog. The verse then says they will be renowned for it. At least two explanations have been suggested for the renown:

a. They will be famous due to the vast number of dead and the length of time it took to bury them.

b. They will be famous due to Israel's willingness to honor the dead of their enemy by giving them a proper burial.

◆ Which explanation fits the text better? Which explanation do you prefer, and why?

◆ The first explanation reflects fame earned for violence. The second reflects fame based on kindness and decency. In today's society, do you think more people are famous for having done good things or having committed crimes? Why do you think this is so?

Connecting the Text To the Holiday

4 There is an old Rabbinic tradition that the war of Gog, preceding the messianic era, would take place during Sukkot.

◆ For more on Gog and Magog, see the *Encyclopaedia Judaica*, vol. 7, pp. 691-693.

◆ Gog represents all the enemies of the Israelite people. The modern State of Israel has many enemies that continue to threaten its existence. Write a prayer for peace for Israel. Include the phrase "*sukkah* of peace."

5 In the Haftarah (verse 38:19), when acting to protect Israel, God was קַנָּא *(kana)*, which is translated as either "jealous," "zealous," or "vindictive." God's jealousy was working for Israel, but made for very scary and ugly times.

The same word is used in the Torah reading (Exodus 34:14): God will be קַנָּא and will seek vengeance if the Israelites engage in idolatry. In the Sedra God's jealousy was against Israel and led God almost to abandon Israel to a scary future.

◆ Is jealousy always a volatile emotion leading to necessarily unpleasant circumstances? Can jealousy ever be useful?

6 On Shabbat during Sukkot, it is a tradition among the Ashkenazim to read Kohelet

(Ecclesiastes) after *"Hallel"* and before the Torah service. The connection between Kohelet and Sukkot is unclear, but here are some possible explanations:

- Kohelet preaches the enjoyment of life while we can and Sukkot is called "the time of our joy."

- Kohelet preaches that worldly possessions are a vanity and are transitory. On Sukkot, we live in our rickety huts that remind us that in reality our worldly possessions offer us no security.

One wonders why the Rabbis did not choose as the Haftarah a text that mentions a *sukkah* or the enjoyment of life. An example of one such text is Amos 9:11, which refers to a *sukkah* that is wobbly and needs to be made stronger. Other verses also allude to agricultural products, and the holiday of Sukkot is an agricultural festival.

- ◆ Read the Haftarah for *Kedoshim* (Ashkenazim), which comes from the ninth chapter of Amos (p. 553). With your classmates, compare the texts. Then decide by vote which Haftarah you like better for the Shabbat of Sukkot. What messages are conveyed by each text?

EZEKIEL 43:10-27
TETZAVEH תצוה

This Haftarah has been paired with *Parashat Tetzaveh*, Exodus 27:20-30:10. See "Connecting the Text To the Sedra," pp. 483-485, for an exploration of the many ways the two texts shed light on each other.

SYNOPSIS

One of Ezekiel's last prophecies, this Haftarah dates to approximately 572 B.C.E. The Israelite exiles, and Ezekiel with them, have already spent almost 25 years in Babylonia. It has also been about 15 years since the Babylonians destroyed the Temple in Jerusalem.

The prophet is commanded to reveal the detailed plan of the future Temple to be rebuilt in Jerusalem, which certainly must have brought the Israelites hope of a future return home. First, however, Ezekiel must be sure that the people are truly sorry for their sinful behavior of the past.

Ezekiel's description begins with detailed measurements (in cubits and handbreadths) of the altar for burnt offerings at the Temple. Measurements are given for the trench surrounding the altar, for the hearth, for the bases, and for the rims of the altar.

The dedication ceremonies of the altar are described in the next nine verses. A young bull should be given for a sin offering to the Levitical priests descended from the Priest Zadok. The bull's blood should then be applied to the four horns of the altar, to the four corners of the base, and to the surrounding rim. Then the bull must be burned outside the Sanctuary.

On the next day, a goat without blemish must be offered as a sin offering. Its blood should be applied just as the bull's blood was. Following this procedure, the priests must offer to *Adonai* a bull and a ram by pouring salt on them and burning them. For seven days, these offerings, which will consecrate the altar for future use, must be repeated.

From the eighth day onward, the priests may use the altar for burnt offerings and offerings of well-being. In return, God will be favorable to Israel.

INSIGHTS FROM THE TRADITION

A In verse 43:10 Ezekiel is commanded to tell the Israelites about the Temple, including its exact dimensions. *Midrash Tanhuma (Tzav* 14) teaches that Ezekiel wondered why he should tell the people all these details, since they were in exile in Babylonia and had no immediate hope of returning to Jerusalem to rebuild the Temple.

God answers that studying the Temple's design was as valuable as actually rebuilding the Temple.

◆ Do you agree that learning about something might be as important as actually doing it?

◆ Alternatively, is this true only when the activity is actually impossible to do (e.g., building the Temple while they were in exile)?

◆ Can you think of an example in which this (studying about something is as valuable as doing it) might not be true? For example, is studying about charity as valuable as giving charity?

B God instructs Ezekiel to let the Israelites be ashamed of their sins (verse 43:10). Rashi explains that when the people see that God has not rejected them despite their sins, they will be ashamed.

◆ Do you agree with Rashi? Explain why you do or don't agree with him.

◆ Are you more ashamed of disobeying a teacher or parent when they get very angry and won't forgive you, or when they are nice about it? Explain your answer.

C Verse 43:11 goes on to say that only when the people are truly ashamed of what they did should Ezekiel tell them about the new Temple.

◆ According to *Metsudat David*, if the people are unaffected and unashamed of the evil deeds they did that lead to the destruction of the First Temple as a punishment, then do not tell them about the new Temple. Why not?

◆ Why must one admit and regret past mistakes in order to avoid making them again?

D Verse 43:24 says to let the priests throw salt on the offering. *Yoma* 66a focuses on the word "let" (i.e., it does not say that it must be priests who throw the salt). Some argue that anyone could throw the salt, but it was an honor for the priests to do it.

◆ Why might you want to give an honor to someone else, even though you could do the job yourself?

◆ Describe a time when you let someone else do something that you could have done in order to make them happy or give them honor?

◆ Are you honoring people when they participate in your *simchah*, or are they honoring you?

STRATEGIES
Analyzing the Text

1 Each component of the altar is given a special name: *Ari'el* (God's lion) is the hearth, or place for firewood; *Har'el* (God's mountain) is the roof of the altar; *Haq* (bosom) is the base of the altar; *Karnot* (horns) are the corners of the altar; *Sovav* (surround) is the rim.

Based on these names, it seems that Ezekiel describes the altar as going from the bosom of the earth to the mountain of God. What do you think this image is trying to convey?

◆ Draw or make a model of your best impression of the altar described in the Haftarah.

2 All the measurements in the Haftarah are given in cubits, which was the prevailing unit of measure at the time. A cubit is the distance from the elbow to the end of the middle finger. The standard cubit is somewhere between 18.9 inches and 22.7 inches.

◆ Calculate the dimensions of the altar in inches/feet, then compare these dimensions to those of your synagogue's *bimah* or Torah table.

3 In the Haftarah and throughout the Torah, animals to be offered as sacrifices are to be unblemished.

◆ Why do you think only physically perfect animals are fit for sacrifice to God?

◆ How might giving up something of great value be a bigger and better sacrifice than giving up something of mediocre quality?

◆ What life lessons can we learn from this standard?

4 The עלה (*olah*) in verse 43:24 is an offering that is completely burned, as opposed to other offerings that are partially burned and partially eaten. The King James Bible, first published in 1611, translated עלה as "holocaust."

There are several dictionary definitions for "holocaust," including total destruction (especially by fire), disaster, massive slaughter, and a sacrificial offering that is consumed entirely by flames.

◆ Which of these definitions do you think agree with the Bible's use of the word עלה, burnt offering?

◆ When you hear the word "holocaust," you most likely think of World War II. Why do you think the name "Holocaust" was given to the attempted genocide of the Jews by Hitler?

◆ It is impossible, however, to compare Hitler's murder of the Jews to a "sacrificial offering," in part because the murder of six million people could never be acceptable before God. Explain why this might make the word "holocaust" unsatisfactory to some Jews.

◆ The Hebrew word for the Nazi war against the Jews is "Shoah," which means destruction, ruin, catastrophe, disaster, cataclysm, pit, and abyss. Do you think this word better describes the events of World War II?

◆ Make an abstract painting of your vision of the word "holocaust." Make another abstract painting of your vision of the word "Shoah." In what ways are the paintings similar or different?

Connecting the Text To the Sedra

5 Both the Sedra (Exodus 27:20) and the Haftarah begin with the word "You," which is a very unusual introduction in the Bible. The "you" seems to place emphasis on the role of the prophets — of Moses in the Sedra and of Ezekiel in the Haftarah. In both cases, the prophets are being told by God to tell the Israelites what to do.

◆ The prophets had a very important job in relating God's word to the people. How does Ezekiel help people feel shame, accept responsibility, and be consecrated?

◆ How does Moses make the people realize who God is — make them want to try to follow God's laws and unite them?

◆ Dramatize Ezekiel's efforts, based on the Haftarah, and the efforts of Moses, based on the Sedra.

6 The Haftarah gives a detailed description of the altar in the Temple, and the Sedra (Exodus 28) provides a detailed description of the Priest's clothing. The Sedra concludes in Exodus 30:1-3 with a description of an altar for burning incense, which contains similar terms for the dimensions and parts of the altar.

Today, as in ancient times, there are "uniforms" and special tools required for synagogue worship. For example, the following items are all uniforms or tools we need for our worship: *Tallit, tefillin, Siddur, yad, Sefer Torah*, Torah table, *kipah, Chumash, Ner Tamid*, and *Aron Kodesh*.

◆ Do a survey of your synagogue building. Locate and report on the condition of the above items in the building. If necessary, review with the Rabbi or Ritual Affairs Committee Chair plans for refurbishing and replenishing your uniforms and tools.

◆ If something is in need of repair or replacement, research with your classmates the possibility of making it a Bar/Bat Mitzvah gift from the class to the synagogue (see the Haftarah for *Emor*, Insights from the Tradition #F, p. 490).

TEACHING HAFTARAH

7 The phrase מלא יד *(milay yad)* appears in the Sedra (Exodus 28:41, 29:9, 29, 33, 35), and is translated as "consecrated." In addition, in the Haftarah (verse 43:26), the altar is cleansed and consecrated. The Hebrew for "consecrate" is the same phrase מלא יד. Literally, *milay yad* means "fill a hand."

Rashi (Exodus 28:41) explains this expression: when you place a responsibility into someone's hands, you consecrate that person to do the task.

◆ Based upon this idiomatic expression, מלא יד, what do you think the word "consecrate" means?

◆ In your opinion, does "filling one's hand" imply that one's hand is filled to the exclusion of all else?

◆ How is Bar or Bat Mitzvah like a priestly consecration?

◆ With what responsibilities are your hands being filled as you become a Jewish adult? List some.

◆ Does your synagogue (or community) have an education program for post-Bar/Bat Mitzvah students? Ask your Rabbi to speak to your class about it and to explain how you can stay consecrated to your role as a Jewish adult.

8 The term קדש קדשים *(Kodesh Kodashim)* means "Holy of Holies," which usually refers to the special inner sanctum of the Temple. However, when it appears in this Haftarah (verse 43:12) and Sedra (see Exodus 29:37, 30:10), it means "most holy."

According to dictionaries: to be קדוש *(Kadosh)* can mean any of the following: holy, set apart, sacred, honored, dedicated, and consecrated.

◆ Which of these definitions best fits your understanding of what it means to be holy?

◆ What do you think it means to be the most holy?

◆ What do you think is more holy: a Rabbi's *tallit* or a cardiac surgeon's scalpel?

◆ What would you consider the most holy object in Judaism?

◆ Have a holy object show-and-tell in class. You and the other class members can bring in holy objects (or photos of them) from home.

9 In Ezekiel 43:20 the priest is instructed to make atonement for the altar. In Exodus 30:10 the High Priest is told to make atonement for the altar once every year on Yom Kippur.

According to the dictionary, to atone means to make amends, to make reparations for an offense or a crime, to make satisfaction for a wrong or injury, to make up for errors or deficiencies, to expiate, to bring back harmony and accord, to make reconciliation or agreement, to create unity.

◆ Which of these definitions best matches your idea of atoning on Yom Kippur?

◆ Try to make different definitions work for Yom Kippur atonement.

◆ On Yom Kippur, we generally think about atoning for the wrongs done by people. What do you think it means to atone for a place? (Answer: In both cases, it seems that atonement helps us to elevate something or even ourselves from a secular level to sacred status. Perhaps when we atone for a place, we are making up for times when the place was erroneously used for secular purposes instead of holy ones.)

◆ In modern times, secular places become holy because of something that happened there. Design a ritual or ceremony to sanctify the Pentagon or the site of the World Trade Center or a local spot worthy of sanctification.

484   EZEKIEL 43:10-27

10 According to Michael Fishbane in the *Etz Hayim Chumash*, p. 522, "Ezekiel's prescription of sacrifices for the seven-day consecration contradicts the laws of the Torah" in the Sedra (Exodus 29:37) and also in Leviticus 8:33, 35. This conflict with Torah, and several others in the Book of Ezekiel (verse 43:22, for example) nearly kept the early Sages from including Ezekiel's writings in the Tanach. But a story is told in the Talmud (*Shabbat* 13b) about a man named Chananyah ben Chizkiah, who shut himself up in a room in the top story of his house. He had 300 barrels of oil brought to him (enough for light throughout the night) in order to compile a commentary to reconcile the differences between Torah and Ezekiel. He may have been the one who invented the term "burning the midnight oil"!

◆ Why was Ezekiel almost excluded from the Tanach?

◆ Who saved the day, and how?

◆ Chananyah ben Chizkiah spent a very creative night reconciling the differences between Tanach and Ezekiel. Do you ever "burn the midnight oil" to complete assignments for school? If so, are the results of your efforts creative, or are they uninspired?

◆ Write a thank-you note from Ezekiel to Chananyah ben Chizkiah for rescuing his work from probable oblivion and for securing its spot in the Hebrew Bible.

Extending the Text

11 The sacrificed meat was to be generously salted on the altar. A Torah law addressed to all humanity forbids the consumption of an animal's blood because, according to the Torah, "the blood is the life." The laws of *kashrut* require that a slaughtered animal's blood is drained as completely as possible. It is further required that the meat be salted until all traces of blood are removed.

◆ What do you think the prohibition against eating blood reflects about Judaism's general feeling about the sanctity of life?

The Hasidic master Baal Shem Tov was a vegetarian, as were Adam and Eve, Franz Kafka, and Isaac Bashevis Singer. *Hullin* 84a teaches, "A person should not eat meat unless he has a special craving for it."

Rabbi Shlomo Riskin was quoted in *The Jewish Week* on August 14, 1987, saying, "The dietary laws are intended to teach us compassion and lead us gently to vegetarianism."

◆ Invite a vegetarian to speak to the class.

◆ Prepare a vegetarian feast for your class. Be sure to use kosher salt in some of the recipes.

◆ For more information on vegetarianism and Judaism, see *Judaism and Vegetarianism* by Richard Schwartz. Also see his web site, www.schwartz.enviroweb.org.

12 Although "holy" is used in Jewish tradition to describe objects, it is more often used to describe the actions of God or of human individuals (See Connecting the Text To the Sedra #8, p. 484.)

◆ Read and discuss the following quotations about holiness. Then, choose your favorite quotation and use it on your Bar/Bat Mitzvah invitation and/or on synagogue announcements related to *Tetzaveh*.

• "If you sanctify yourself a little, you are sanctified much." (*Yoma* 39a)

• "As a Reform Jew, I look at *kedushah* [holiness] as a process. We are never there, but always reaching." (Rabbi Michael L. Kramer, in "A Personal Statement" in

Rabbis and Vegetarianism: An Evolving Tradition, 1995)

- "Man is a holy Temple, and his heart is the holy of holies." (Jonathan Eibschutz, *Yaarot Dvash*)

- "Holiness toward God and justice toward men usually go together." (Philo, *Abraham* 37)

- "If you sanctify yourselves, it is as though you sanctified Me." (*Sifra, Kedoshim* 1)

- "Everything created by God contains a spark of holiness." (Baal Shem Tov, *Dybbuk* by Solomon Anski, 1918, Act 1, quoted in A *Treasury of Jewish Quotations* by Joseph L. Baron)

- "There is nothing in the universe absolutely secular." (Rav Kook, *Orot Hakodesh*, 1938, p. 143)

- "Not what a man does, but how he does it, is profane or sacred." (Steinthal, *Ueber Juden und Judentum*)

- "When the Bible says, 'be holy,' it means exactly the same as if it said, 'do My commandments.'" (Maimonides, *Sefer HaMitzvot*, 4)

13 When the Jews returned from exile in Babylon, they did build a Second Temple, but they did not build it according to Ezekiel's description. There are several explanations given:

- Rashi says that the exiles had not acknowledged their sins adequately and, therefore, could not follow Ezekiel's description.

- According to Rambam, Ezekiel's description was clear to him but not to the people to whom he had explained it. Consequently, they rebuilt the Second Temple according to the model of the First Temple.

- Radak suggests that Ezekiel was not describing the Second Temple, but the Third Temple, to be built in the days of the Messiah (see Plaut, p. 201).

◆ Which explanation do you like best, and why?

14 Some prayer books include at the end of the *"Amidah"* a special prayer for the rebuilding of the Holy Temple: "May it be Your will, *Adonai* our God and the God of our ancestors, that the Holy Temple be rebuilt speedily in our days. Grant us our share in Your Torah, and may we serve You there with reverence, as in days of old and in former years. Then the offering of Judah and Jerusalem will be pleasing to *Adonai*, as in days of old."

◆ Does the prayer book your congregation uses include this prayer?

◆ Do you hope for a new Third Temple? Why or why not?

◆ How would you feel about the return of sacrifices as an acceptable form of worship? Debate the pros and cons of a restored Temple. Consider social, political, and religious implications.

15 The priests must offer to *Adonai* a bull and a ram by pouring salt on them and burning them (verse 43:24). Salt plays an important part in many biblical stories. Match the incidents below with the people involved in them:

1. His wife became a pillar of salt. (d)
2. He sowed the city of Shechem with salt. (f)
3. He told the Israelites to put salt on the sacrifices. (c)
4. He was guaranteed the kingdom of Israel through a covenant of salt. (e)
5. They were warned that their land would be filled with brimstone and salt if they abandoned God's laws to follow their hearts. (b)

6. He used a dish of salt to heal a spring of bad water. (a)

a. Elisha (II Kings 2:20)
b. Israelites (Deuteronomy 29:22)
c. Moses (Leviticus 2:13)
d. Lot (Genesis 19:26)
e. David (II Chronicles 13:5)
f. Abimelech (Judges 9:45)

16 The Temple in Jerusalem has been at the center of Jewish consciousness for thousands of years. Since Jerusalem was reunited in 1967, Jews have been able to pray at the Western Wall, or *Kotel*, which is considered one of our holiest sites. The Temple Mount is also considered a holy site for Muslims, who built a mosque called El Aksa and a shrine called the Dome of the Rock where the Temple once stood. The Temple Mount remains a critical issue in peace negotiations between Israel and the Palestinians.

♦ Learn about the complex history of the Temple Mount in Jerusalem, different theories about the exact location of the Temple, and current tensions over excavation on the Temple Mount by exploring the web site of the journal *Biblical Archaeology Review*, http://biblicalarchaeology.org or by accessing www.templemount.org.

17 According to tradition, since the Temple was destroyed, words of prayer may be offered to God instead of sacrifices.

♦ What does this lesson teach about the quality of our prayers?

♦ Consider how the following aspects of prayer affect the quality of our prayers: words pronounced properly, words understood, acceptable translations, beautiful melodies, frame of mind.

♦ Write, compile, and conduct a meaningful and creative prayer service with your class or school.

Personalizing the Text

18 Before describing the Temple, Ezekiel had to be sure the people were truly sorry for their sinful ways.

♦ Imagine you are an exiled Israelite in Ezekiel's time. Write him a letter demonstrating that you are repentant, and are prepared to live a better life in your homeland.

19 Ezekiel outlines his plan for a new Temple in Jerusalem to the Israelites in exile.

♦ Imagine you are one of the exiles in Babylonia. Write a poem in reaction to Ezekiel's prophecy about a new Temple in a rebuilt Jerusalem. Are you skeptical or hopeful?

20 The song, *"Lo Alecha Ham'la'cha Ligmor"* (It Is Not for You to Complete the Work), expresses the traditional desire for the rebuilding of the Temple.

♦ Learn and sing this song, which may be found in the songbook *B'Kol Echad*, edited by Jeffrey Shiovitz, p. 89, and on the accompanying audiocassettes, *Shirei B'Kol Echad*, both of which may be ordered from the web site of United Synagogue for Conservative Judaism, www.uscj.org/booksvc.

21 Ezekiel describes the altar and dedication ceremonies in minute detail.

♦ Give a brief talk to the class, providing a detailed description of something you once saw (the Statue of Liberty, an adorable dog, a great baseball catch, etc.). After each student talks, see if the others in the class can draw the object, based on the details they were given.

Other Resources

22 For a story about regular objects becoming holy ones, read and discuss "The Story of Bryan" by Tsvi Blanchard in *Chosen Tales*, edited by Peninnah Schram, pp. 47-49.

23 Hollywood filmmaker Steven Spielberg established the Survivors of the Shoah Visual History Foundation to "chronicle first-hand accounts of survivors, liberators, rescuers, and other eyewitnesses of the Holocaust." To learn more about this amazing video project, visit their web site at http://vhf.org. Try to find someone local who was interviewed by the Foundation, then view and discuss the videotape he/she made. Alternatively, contact one of the local interviewers for the Foundation and invite that person to class to speak about his/her experiences.

24 Ezekiel hoped for the rebuilding of the Temple in a restored Jerusalem. His hopeful sentiment is echoed in the film *Field of Dreams*, (1989, rated PG, 116 minutes). View the film, then discuss in particular Ray's belief that, "If you build it, they will come."

25 Read the chapter on Ezekiel in *Messengers of God: A Jewish Prophets Who's Who* by Ronald H. Isaacs, pp. 121-133.

26 Discuss the illustration of this Haftarah in *The Illustrated Torah* by Michal Meron, p. 91.

27 For a commentary, discussion questions, and project, see the UAHC Family Shabbat Table Talk web site, www.uahc.org/shabbat/stt/3tetzaveh.shtm.

Involving the Family

28 In the absence of sacrificial altars, we are taught to make our dinner tables into holy altars to God. We do this by making proper blessings over our food and by always discussing some teaching of Torah at our meals. Rabbi Simeon taught in *Pirke Avot* 3:3 that when people sit at a table and discuss Torah, it is as if they ate at the table in the presence of God.

◆ Choose one night every week (Friday night, if possible) to make your dinner table into a holy altar. Make the blessings over the food you eat, and assign one family member the task of teaching some wise words from our tradition. For a resource, use any of the Insights from the Tradition entries in this book that correspond to the weekly Haftarah.

Bar/Bat Mitzvah Projects

29 Consecrate yourself to a program of post-Bar/Bat Mitzvah Jewish study, whether it is at a local Hebrew high school, in your synagogue's high school program, or a home study course that you can develop with your Rabbi or school director.

30 Make a commitment to become a vegetarian for three months before your Bar/Bat Mitzvah. See if a vegetarian lifestyle leads you to be more compassionate to all living things. Consider writing about your vegetarian experience in your *D'var Torah* (see Extending the Text #11, p. 485).

EZEKIEL 44:15-31
EMOR אמור

This Haftarah has been paired with *Parashat Emor*, Leviticus 21:1-24:23. See "Connecting the Text To the Sedra," pp. 491-492, for an exploration of the many ways the two texts shed light on each other.

SYNOPSIS

The last section of Ezekiel's book is marked with a determination to convince the exiled Israelites that they will, indeed, one day return to their homeland. In this Haftarah, Ezekiel gives the Israelites a real taste of that return by providing minute details about the priestly service in the rebuilt Holy Temple in Jerusalem.

Ezekiel announces that the descendants of Zadok, the High Priest, will be the legitimate officers of the new Temple. Ezekiel enumerates the rules and regulations by which priests must live: While in the Temple, they will wear linen garments, including turbans on their heads. When they leave the inner court of the Temple, they must remove their special garments and wear regular ones instead. The priests should wear their hair neatly trimmed, but not shaved. They shall drink no wine within the inner court of the Temple. They may not marry divorcees or widows (of any man other than another priest). Priests may not come into contact with the dead (unless it is a member of his immediate family). Lastly, priests are not to eat anything, bird or animal, that died of natural causes or was killed by another beast.

The priests' responsibilities will include the determination of what is clean and what is unclean. They will also act as judges in lawsuits among the Israelites. They shall preserve and promote the teachings and laws of the Torah regarding holidays and Shabbat.

The priests will eat the meal offerings, sin offerings, guilt offerings, first fruits, special gifts, and contributions brought by the people to the Temple.

INSIGHTS FROM THE TRADITION

A Radak suggests that verse 44:19 teaches that the priests' linen garments might transmit holiness to anyone who touches them.

◆ Can you think of anything (other than holiness) that can be transmitted by touch? (For example, an electrical charge passes from one conductor to another; smell, heat, germs, and magnetism are also transferred by contact.)

◆ Today we might say that holiness can be transmitted from person to person by the examples we set with our behaviors. Explain how seeing someone doing holy acts of kindness, justice, and mercy teaches us to do similar acts and thereby transmits a sense of holiness to us.

B Rashi interprets verse 44:19 differently. He explains that the sanctity of the priestly clothing might be compromised if the priests wear their special garments when they might come into contact with lay people wearing ordinary, impure clothes.

◆ Do you have special clothes that you wear for particular purposes (e.g., sports, synagogue, scouts, etc.)?

◆ How do your special clothes help prepare you (physically and emotionally) for what you have to do?

◆ Do you wear your special clothes when you are out in the general public, or do you reserve them for their particular purpose? Explain your answer.

C The Rabbis taught in *Sanhedrin* 22b (based on verse 44:20) that the priests were required to get a haircut once every 30 days.

◆ How often do you get your hair cut?

◆ Do you think your hair length or hairstyle reflects anything about your personality?

◆ What message about the priests might their constantly trimmed hair convey?

D Verse 44:31 teaches that the priests should not eat anything thing that dies on its own or is killed by another beast. According to Radak, this law applies to all Israelites (see Exodus 22:30, Leviticus 7:24, and Deuteronomy 14:21). Radak explains that Ezekiel emphasizes it here because the priests are under special obligation to remain pure for Temple rituals.

◆ Can you think of any reasons why it is forbidden to eat anything that dies on its own or is killed by a beast?

◆ Some people also object to eating animals that were treated cruelly, like calves (veal), caged chickens, or tuna that were caught in nets that might also have captured dolphins. Do you have any rules of your own regarding what animals you will or will not eat?

◆ What does the expression "You are what you eat" mean? Do you believe that you are what you eat? Explain your answer.

E Ezekiel forbids all priests to wear wool while they perform their Temple service (verse 44:17). On the other hand, the Torah prohibits the wearing of wool only by the High Priest and only on Yom Kippur. According to Malbim, Ezekiel extends the prohibition from wearing wool to all priests, in order to raise everyone's level of holiness.

◆ Does your school, or your parent's workplace, have a dress code? Does your school have a separate dress code for teachers?

◆ In what ways do you think a dress code helps or hinders people from doing their jobs at your school and at your parent's workplace?

◆ Debate the value of dress codes, either at school or in the workplace.

F According to Rashi, any priest who is serving his first time in the Temple must bring an offering as a consecration offering (verse 44:27).

◆ Why do you think a gift might be in order on such an occasion?

◆ Becoming a Bar/Bat Mitzvah is the first time that that person is serving his/her congregation as a Jewish adult. What type of gift or offering might be appropriate for the Bar/Bat Mitzvah to give to his/her community?

STRATEGIES
Analyzing the Text

1 Priests are told what to wear, what to eat, how to wear their hair, when to drink and not to drink, whom to marry, and so on.

◆ Why do you think priests were so strictly regulated?

◆ List occupations that have strict regulations. How do the regulations help them perform their job better? (For example, hospital employees and train conductors must wear uniforms, which may be designed for safety, hygiene, or ease of identification.)

◆ Propose regulations pertaining to teachers and students at your school.

2 Ezekiel declares in verse 44:18 that the priests may not wear anything that might cause them to sweat. *Metsudat David* explains that the sweat would soil the priestly garments.

◆ Why might the priests serving in the Temple before God want to look their best?

3 Priests must not drink any wine when they enter the inner court of the Temple. Ezekiel's prohibition is in accordance with the law stated in Leviticus 10:9-10, "Drink no wine or other intoxicant . . . when you enter the Tent of Meeting, that you may not die. This is a law for all time throughout the ages, for you must distinguish between the sacred and the profane, and between the unclean and the clean . . . "

◆ List five professions in which it would be dangerous to drink before working. Give other reasons why people should never drink while on the job.

4 In verse 44:28 God says, "This shall be [the priests'] portion, for I am their portion; and no holding shall be given them in Israel, for I am their holding."

When the 12 tribes of Jacob are each given a portion of the Promised Land, the Levites (priests) are given none (Deuteronomy 10:8-9 and 14:27-29). Instead, they are given the privilege and responsibility of service to God, with the promise that they would be sustained by the offerings of the other Israelites.

◆ What does it mean to you that God is their portion (their inheritance)?

◆ Imagine you are an ancient Levite. Write your reaction to this deal. Compare your reaction to those of your classmates.

Connecting the Text To the Sedra

5 Both the Sedra and Haftarah provide rules by which the priests must live. Review the rules and notice the differences between them.

You might notice that Ezekiel holds all priests to the stricter standards of the High Priest. This might be because he is talking about an ideal Temple of the future.

◆ When planning for the future, is it better to hope, imagine, and aim for a hard to achieve ideal or for a more practical, easier to accomplish goal?

◆ If a goal is out of reach, does it make you try harder so as to accomplish more than you might have, or are you more likely to feel frustrated and not try at all?

6 Ezekiel explains that priests cannot defile themselves by being in the same house with a dead person, except if the deceased was a close family member. The same instructions are given in Leviticus 21:1-3.

◆ Read the lists of permitted relatives in Ezekiel 44:25 and Leviticus 21:2. Which obvious relative was left off both lists? (Hertz explains that the wife is not mentioned because husband and wife are regarded throughout the Torah as "one flesh," according to Genesis 2:24. Therefore, the wife's inclusion in the list should be automatically assumed.)

◆ Would you add any other categories of relatives or friends to the list?

7 Ezekiel warns that if a priest doesn't follow the laws of keeping himself away from the dead, he must be excluded from the sanctuary for seven days. The reasons for this are clear. If a priest goes near a dead person, he brings impurities on himself. And if those impurities are brought into the Temple, the community's holy site is compromised.

Leviticus 23:29 teaches that if a person does not follow the laws of Yom Kippur, he/she will be excluded from the community. By not fasting, by working, or by failing to observe the other laws of Yom Kippur, a person threatens to undermine a community's observance of Yom Kippur.

◆ One might wonder why a community can tell a priest or an ordinary person how to behave and threaten them with exclusion from the community. Read and discuss the following story from *Leviticus Rabbah* 4:6).

Rabbi Simeon Ben Yochai told this story: Some people were in a boat, and one of them took a drill and began to bore a hole in the bottom of the boat. Noticing, the others said, "What are you doing?" The one drilling replied, "What business it is of yours? I am drilling under my own seat and not under yours!" The others responded, "It is our business. When the water comes in, it will sink the boat with us in it."

◆ What lesson about community is Ben Yochai teaching in this story?

◆ How does this *midrash* relate to the person who does not keep the laws of Yom Kippur or to the priest who doesn't keep away from the dead?

◆ Explain how this lesson might apply to different groups to which you belong (e.g., sports teams, clubs, scouts).

◆ Listen to the song "Sit Down You're Rocking the Boat" on the original cast recording of *Guys and Dolls*.

8 Ezekiel says the priests will be responsible for preserving God's teachings and laws about the holidays and Shabbatot. Leviticus 23 outlines the appointed holidays and how to observe them.

◆ While the priests are responsible for preserving the laws concerning the holidays and Shabbat, they are not the only ones responsible for observing these special days. How does this situation compare to modern day Rabbis and Cantors in congregations?

◆ Arrange a panel of Rabbis and Cantors in your area to discuss whether their observance of holidays and Shabbat differs from that of their congregants and, if so, how they feel about it.

Extending the Text

9 According to Radak, the priests wore hats or turbans for adornment.

Today, some Jews wear a *kipah* (*yarmulke*, in Yiddish), a small head covering. The *kipah* reminds us that there is always a power above us, reminds us of our Jewish identity, and reminds us to behave in a holy manner at all times and in all places. Some observant Jews wear a *kipah* all the time as a sign of their devotion to God, while others wear one only during religious services, study sessions, and meals. Some wear *kipot* only, while others alternate between *kipot*, hats, and baseball caps. Similarly, women Rabbis often choose between wearing *kipot*, hats, or other head coverings. Ultra-Orthodox and Hasidic Jews cover their heads with a variety of different hats, which identify them as part of a particular group. In contrast, some married Orthodox women wear head coverings for a different reason; they cover their heads with wigs, scarves, or hats out of modesty.

◆ How do you think a *kipah* helps us to remember that there is always a power above us?

◆ Try wearing a head covering (*kipah*, hat, or baseball cap) for one week. How did it affect your sense of Jewish identity? Analyze whether or not the experience was different for the boys and for the girls in your classes.

10 The Rabbis taught in Insights from the Tradition #C, p. 490, that priests had to have a haircut every 30 days. The Rabbis also taught that the High Priest actually had to cut his hair every Friday, before Shabbat (*Sanhedrin* 22b).

Jews who observe Shabbat must do many things to prepare for the day of rest. Homes must be cleaned. Shopping must be done, and the Shabbat meals must be cooked. The Shabbat table must be set. The candlesticks must be polished and set up. *Challah* must be baked or bought. Family members must shower. Clothing might have to be ironed. Guests might be invited.

According to *Gates of Shabbat: A Guide for Observing Shabbat* by Mark Dov Shapiro, p. 97, "It is a *mitzvah* to prepare for Shabbat. According to the Rabbis, this *mitzvah* is implied in the Exodus version of the Ten Commandments, 'Remember Shabbat and keep it holy' (Exodus 20:8). Preparations may begin well before Shabbat by buying special food or waiting to wear a new garment for Shabbat. Wherever possible, all members of the household should be involved in Shabbat preparations."

◆ Explain how you might enjoy Shabbat more if you experienced part of the preparation for it.

◆ For an entertaining account of how one family prepares for Shabbat, read *How to Run a Traditional Jewish Household* by Blu Greenberg, pp. 51-57.

11 Today we do not have priests offering sacrifices in a Temple. However, some Jewish movements still recognize three strata of Jews, according to ancient divisions: *Kohayn* (priest), *Levi*, and *Yisrael*.

Traditional Jewish custom, for example, awards the first *aliyah* to the Torah to *Kohanim*, the second to *Levi'im*, and the remaining honors to the Israelites.

In addition, some Jews generally honor the biblical privileges and restrictions placed upon *Kohanim*. *Kohanim* offer the Priestly Blessing in synagogue and receive the redemption of the firstborn (*Pidyon HaBen*). On the other hand, *Kohanim* are prohibited from making any contact with the dead (they may not enter a cemetery) or from marrying a divorcee, a convert, or most widows.

◆ Ask your parents or grandparents if you are a *Kohayn*, *Levi*, or *Yisrael*.

◆ Ask your Rabbi if your congregation makes any distinctions among these groupings.

12 Verse 44:30 reminds us of the law that a small portion of any dough must be burned in memory of the bread that was to be dedicated to the priests. That portion is called *challah*.

◆ As a class, bake *challah* and burn (right in the oven) a small portion as required by Jewish custom. Don't forget to say the appropriate blessing: Blessed are You, *Adonai* our God, Sovereign of the universe, Who has sanctified us with commandments and commanded us to separate *challah*."

◆ Be sure to eat your *challah*, too!

◆ For more information on how to make *challah*, see *The First Jewish Catalog* by

Richard Siegel, Michael Strassfeld, and Sharon Strassfeld, pp. 37-41.

13 Contact with a dead body was thought to cause uncleanness, which could not be brought into the Temple. This belief was not peculiar to the Israelites, but shared by other ancient peoples as well. It may stem from repugnance to the decay that follows death, or even traced to fear of demons that were thought to accompany the dead.

Today, when returning to a house of mourning after a burial, it is customary to wash one's hands before entering the home. Generally, a pitcher of water is left at the front door for this purpose.

◆ How might the symbolic act of washing one's hands help people make the transition from the sadness of the cemetery back to the realities of life?

◆ Create from clay or other material a pitcher for this special purpose.

14 A priest may violate the prohibition of contact with the dead only to honor his deceased wife, father, mother, son, daughter, brother, or unmarried sister. According to Jewish law, a "mourner" is someone who has suffered the loss of a mother, father, son, daughter, brother, sister, husband, or wife. All mourners observe a period of seven days of intense mourning, called *shivah* (sometimes *shivah* is delayed or shortened by a Jewish holiday). The next phase of mourning, which is called *shloshim* because of its 30-day duration, is less intense and helps ease the mourner into the routine of regular life. Mourners recite "*Kaddish*" daily through *shivah* and *shloshim*, and they are discouraged from attending festive occasions and enjoying music and entertainment. The mourning period for someone who has lost a parent is extended to a full 11 months, during which they continue to say "*Kaddish*" daily.

◆ Ask your Rabbi to speak to your class about Jewish mourning customs and their reasons.

◆ Why do you think the mourning period for parents is longest?

◆ How many days of *shivah* do you think a convert to Judaism should observe if his/her non-Jewish parent dies? To research this question, see www.learn.jtsa.edu/topics/diduknow/responsa/hatesh_cnvmourn.shtml.

◆ For more information on the subject of death and dying in the Jewish tradition, see *The Jewish Book of Why* by Alfred J. Kolatch, pp. 49-83, or *A Time to be Born, A Time to Die* by Isaac Klein.

15 According to Ezekiel, priests may not eat *trayfah* — meat that has been torn by beasts. Actually, this law applies to all Jews not just to priests. The word "*trayfah*" has evolved to mean any food that is not kosher.

◆ Arrange a visit to a local kosher butcher or invite a kosher butcher (*shochet*) to speak to your class about the rules of *kashrut*.

16 Comforting mourners is a very important *mitzvah*.

◆ Read and discuss the following story about a woman who could not be comforted (from *A Time to be Born, A Time to Die* by Isaac Klein, pp. 41-42):

A bereaved woman asked a wise man for help. Because of her loss, she no longer had peace of mind, and when her friends tried to comfort her, it just made her sadder. The wise man instructed her to stop at each house in her city and ask for a grain of wheat. When she had enough wheat, she was to use it to bake a cake and then eat it. Then she would be cured of her sadness. The wise man also told her that she could accept donations of wheat only from houses that have had no sorrow. The woman did as she was told. Everyone was willing to help, but when she asked if there had been sorrow in that house, the answer was always yes, and she had to leave empty-handed. When she saw that all people have their share of sadness, the woman realized that she was not singled out for sorrow and was cured.

◆ Why do you think this woman's realization made her feel better?

◆ Do you think it would be easier to endure a difficult time in your life if you lived alone, or if you had a community to share your burden?

◆ Why do you think community is such an important aspect of Judaism?

◆ Put on a dramatic presentation of this story.

17 According to Ezekiel, priests are told precisely how they should wear their hair. Jewish law also dictates that all Jews should refrain from such ancient practices as tattooing, shaving one's head, and cutting oneself.

◆ How do you feel about these prohibitions?

◆ See activities on the subject of "Taking Care of Your Body" in *Teaching Jewish Virtues* by Susan Freeman, pp. 269-282.

18 According to Ezekiel, priests were to be responsible for maintaining God's appointed seasons and Shabbatot. Learn how to use a 100-year calendar so that you will know how to determine when the appointed holidays will fall and which Torah readings will be read on which Shabbatot.

Alternatively, download from the Internet a free Jewish calendar and learn how to use it to determine when the holidays will be in any given year. For a free Mac calendar, go to the web site www.apple.com/downloads/macosx/business_finance/jewishcalendar.html. For a free PC calendar, go to www.tichnut.de/jewish/index2.htm.

Personalizing the Text

19 Conduct a survey of the students, teachers, and parents in your school. Ask them what assumptions they might make about a boy and a girl with:

- neat, short hair
- long, neat hair
- long, messy hair
- a shaved head
- hair dyed blond
- hair dyed pink or blue
- hair cut into a mohawk
- tattoos
- body piercing

◆ Can you determine any generalities or stereotypes based on your survey results?

20 Ezekiel describes the priests with linen head coverings.

◆ Make personalized *kipot* using fabric paints on suede or fabric *kipot*. Instructions can be found on the fabric paints.

◆ Alternatively, bring to class your favorite *kipah*, hat, or other head covering for show-and-tell. Tell why it is your favorite. Describe any special memories associated with it.

21 In verse 44:28 God explains that the members of the tribe of Levi will not receive territory in the Promised Land, rather they will all work for God (see Analyzing the Text #4, p. 491).

◆ Imagine what it must have been like not to be able to choose a career, but to be obligated to go into your family profession.

◆ Write a letter a young priest might have written to a friend, expressing either his frustration or pleasure at having to go into the family profession.

◆ Do you think you have total freedom to choose your own career as an adult, or do you think your parents have expectations of you that you will feel obligated to fulfill?

◆ Why do you think it might be difficult for some people to choose a career?

22 Ezekiel outlines many rules for the ancient priests.

◆ Make your own list of rules governing the behavior of today's Rabbis.

23 Why might it be forbidden to eat an animal that has been killed by other beasts?

Pinchas Peli said in *Torah Today*, p. 118, "The laws of *kashrut* come to teach us that a Jew's first preference should be a vegetarian meal. If, however, one cannot control a craving for meat, it should be kosher meat, which would serve as a reminder that the animal being eaten is a creature of God, that the death of such a creature cannot be taken lightly, that hunting for sport is forbidden, that we cannot treat any living thing callously, and that we are responsible for what happens to other beings (human or animal) even if we did not personally come into contact with them."

◆ Design posters featuring the preceding list of reminders about the food we eat. For example, one poster could convey the message that "hunting for sport is forbidden," and another that "we are responsible for what happens to other beings."

24 Any priest who is serving his first day in the Temple must bring a gift offering (see Insights from the Tradition #F, p. 490).

◆ Plan a party for an imaginary young priest who has just spent his first day in Temple service. Speakers might include the young priest, his parents, his teachers, his best friend, and the High Priest. Don't forget to describe the gift the priest will bring for his first day.

Other Resources

25 View and discuss the classic film *It's A Wonderful Life* (1947, unrated, 132 minutes). The story revolves around a character named George Bailey who must abandon his dreams when he gets "trapped" into his family business. Eventually, George comes to understand that his family's business involves holy work.

26 Read the chapter on Ezekiel in *Messengers of God: A Jewish Prophets Who's Who* by Ronald H. Isaacs, pp. 121-133.

27 Discuss the illustration of this Haftarah in *The Illustrated Torah* by Michal Meron, p. 134.

28 See the commentary of the Fuchsberg Center for Conservative Judaism in Jerusalem at www.uscj.org.il/haftarah/emor5761.html.

29 For discussion and activities relating to the various kinds of sacrifices offered at the Temple, see *Teaching Torah* by Sorel Goldberg Loeb and Barbara Binder Kadden, pp. 165-171.

30 For commentary, discussion topics, and project, see the UAHC Family Shabbat Table Talk web site at www.uahc.org/shabbat/stt/3emor.shtml.

Involving the Family

31 Engage in a family discussion about *kashrut* and/or vegetarianism. Consider buying kosher meat or having one or more vegetarian meals every week.

Bar/Bat Mitzvah Project

32 During your Bar or Bat Mitzvah year, take time every Friday afternoon to get ready for Shabbat. Get a haircut, take a shower, do all your homework for the weekend, and dress in nice clothes. You might even want to bake a *challah* for your family.

33 Become a role model of holiness by volunteering to be a tutor to younger students.

EZEKIEL 45:16-46:18 Ashkenazim
EZEKIEL 45:18-46:15 Sephardim
SHABBAT HACHODESH

 This Haftarah has been paired with *Shabbat HaChodesh*, on which we read a special Maftir Torah reading, Exodus 12:1-20. See "Connecting the Text To the Special Shabbat," pp. 500-502, for an exploration of the many ways the text and the Special Shabbat shed light on each other.

SYNOPSIS

In this Haftarah, Ezekiel continues to bring hope of a return to Jerusalem to the exiled Israelites in Babylonia. This time, he describes the sacrifices that will be brought for Passover, Shabbat, the New moon, other occasions, and daily worship.

Ezekiel refers several times to the prince, who will apparently be the leader of the Israelites once they return home. The prince's responsibilities for observing the holidays are outlined: he is to make sin offerings, grain offerings, whole burnt offerings, and peace offerings on all the appointed festivals on behalf of the general population of Israel. He may also bring freewill offerings at any time. With his detailed description of these sacrifices, Ezekiel also provides information about which Temple gates should be used, when, and by whom.

The Haftarah concludes with Ezekiel's explanation of the inheritance laws, as they apply to the prince. The prophet emphasizes that the prince must never take property away from the people for his own use.

INSIGHTS FROM THE TRADITION

A We learn in verse 45:18 that the prince is to sacrifice an unblemished bull on the first day of Nisan. One might think that it should be a fresh and youthful lamb offered in service to God as a reminder of the Pesach lamb. Hirsch teaches that a bull is brought because a lamb is passive, surrendering its fate to others. A bull, in contrast, is a strong, active animal that will work to cultivate the field of humanity for the service of God.

◆ Explain why Hirsch felt a bull was a better model for how Israel was to act in the world.

◆ Are you more like a bull or a lamb? Why?

◆ Are the Jewish people more like a bull or a lamb? Why?

B Hirsch also teaches with regard to the Passover offerings that each person individually brings a lamb, because as individuals we have few choices and little power. But when the prince brings an offering for the whole community, it is a bull, which represents the strength of the community and the ability to be a co-worker with God as part of a community.

◆ Think of five ways in which a community is stronger than any individual.

C Hirsch explains the difference between the unwitting and ignorant people mentioned in verse 45:20. "Unwitting," he says, means to do wrong through thoughtlessness. "Ignorant," on the other hand, refers to someone who is mentally immature, open to every external influence, and unable to make his or her own independent judgment.

◆ Give examples of unwitting errors and ignorant errors.

◆ How might you try to help someone who unwittingly does the wrong thing through carelessness?

◆ How might you help someone who is mentally immature and unable to make independent judgments about things?

D Verse 46:7 requires many sacrifices. It is taught: what if the prince has enough money to buy the animals for the sacrifice, but not enough for the required grain or oil? In this case, the prince should buy only as many animals as he can afford, making sure to leave enough money left over to buy the grain and oil as well (Rashi, *Menahot* 45a-b).

◆ Many people note that it is expensive to be a committed Jew. List the things necessary for Jewish life that cost money.

◆ Rank the list in order of priority, in case one cannot afford to pay for all of them.

E Verse 46:8 teaches that the prince must go in and out through the same vestibule. Rashi says he must go in and out through the very same gate because the prince is not commanded to take a short cut through a sacred place.

◆ How might a short cut show disrespect?

◆ Can you think of any short cuts that might be inappropriate to take in homework, household chores, personal relationships, and so on?

STRATEGIES
Analyzing the Text

1 The Hebrew word *"nasi,"* used in this Haftarah, has been interpreted in a number of ways. Most translations use "prince" or "monarch," while *Metsudat David* explains that it refers to the Messiah. In an early translation of the Bible, *"nasi"* means a person of great learning, and in modern Hebrew it means "president."

◆ What underlying theme do all these interpretations have in common? Which translation do you think fits the text best, and why?

◆ Learn about all the presidents of the State of Israel at www.knesset.gov.il/main/eng/engframe.htm.

2 Ezekiel uses measurements such as an *ephah* and a *hin*. An *ephah* is a dry measure equal to about three-eighths to two-thirds of a bushel. A *hin* is a liquid measure, generally thought to be about a half quart.

◆ Demonstrate for the class the size of an *ephah* and a *hin*.

3 The offerings of well-being mentioned in verse 45:17 are called *"sh'lamim"* in Hebrew. They share the same root word (שלם) as the Hebrew word *"Shalom,"* which is used as a greeting, and means both "peace" and "complete." These offerings (described in Numbers 15:3 and Deuteronomy 16:10-11) are always voluntary, and are given in gratitude for some good fortune. They are spontaneous offerings prompted by a joyous occasion. The offering was not completely burned on the altar, but was consumed by the one who brought it.

◆ Do you think this kind of offering is appropriately named *sh'lamim*?

◆ What do you think would be an appropriate modern version of a *sh'lamim* offering?

4 As Plaut points out in *The Haftarah Commentary*, p. 570, Ezekiel envisions in verses 46:8-12 a stately procession of people in and out of the Temple, rather than a disorganized crowd milling about.

◆ What mood does an orderly procession create? Try such a procession around your classroom to see what kind of mood it creates.

5 Ezekiel's instructions in verse 46:18 seem to be intended to prevent a leader from abusing his power and stealing property from his subjects.

The First Book of Kings, chapter 21, relates the story of King Ahab, who steals a vineyard from Naboth the Jezreelite (and has Naboth killed in the process). For his wrongdoings, Ahab is condemned by Elijah the Prophet and punished by God.

◆ Why might a leader want to take the property of his people for himself?

◆ Why must this kind of thing not be tolerated?

Connecting the Text
To the Special Shabbat

6 The Shabbat before Nisan, Shabbat HaChodesh, gets its name from the special Maftir Torah reading from Exodus 12:1-20, which starts with the phrase "this month." This Haftarah also refers to the first month of the year (verse 45:18), which is Nisan.

According to Mishnah *Rosh HaShanah* 1:1, there are four Jewish new year days: the first of Nisan is the new year for kings and for establishing the order of holidays, the first of Elul is the new year for taxes, the first of Tishre is the first day of the

calendar year and a spiritual new year, and the fifteenth of Shevat is the new year for trees.

◆ Which of these new years do we still celebrate?

◆ We know that the secular calendar year begins on January 1 and ends on December 31. But we also count years according to other dates. Ask someone who runs a business when his/her fiscal year starts and ends.

◆ From when do you count school years?

◆ Find out how the age of people in China is counted. Why do they do it this way?

◆ Do you count years according to your birthday?

◆ Can you think of any other milestones or dates by which you keep track of time, from year to year?

7 There is a lengthy section in the Haftarah concerning the prince or leader of the restored Israelite people. Remember that the first of Nisan is the new year for kings (Connecting the Text To the Special Shabbat #6, above).

According to commentators, the new year for kings means that the first of Nisan marks the anniversary of an Israelite king's reign (no matter what date he actually started). The custom in ancient times was to date legal documents by the year of the current monarch's reign as a sign of respect for the king.

◆ Randomly choose any five years in American history. For each year, determine who was president and what year of his term he was in. For example, 2001 was the first year of the term of President George W. Bush. For your calculation, use Inauguration Day (January 20) as the new year for presidents.

8 Verse 45:19 of the Haftarah mentions putting the blood of the sin offering on the doorposts of the sanctuary, while the Sedra mentions putting the blood of the Pesach offering on the doorposts of the house.

In the Sedra the blood was to be a sign so that God would protect the homes of the Israelites (Exodus 12:22-23).

Today, we hang a *mezuzah* on our doorposts, as commanded in the *"Shema"*: "You shall write [the commandments] on the doorposts of your house."

The *mezuzah* is a piece of parchment inscribed with verses from Deuteronomy 6:4-9. The parchment is rolled up, inserted in a case, and attached to the upper third of the right-hand doorpost, pointing in. *Mezuzot* remind us of the *mitzvot* and identify our houses as Jewish homes. In ancient times, people believed that the *mezuzah* had magical powers that could ward off evil spirits. One of God's names, *Shaddai*, is often written on the back of the *mezuzah* scroll. Some people explain that *Shaddai* is an acronym for the Hebrew phrase meaning, "protector of the doors of Israel."

It is customary to touch a *mezuzah* with your fingertips and then to kiss your fingertips, much as we kiss the *Sefer Torah* as it is paraded around the synagogue.

Mezuzot can be hung on the doorpost of any entrance to your home, as well as on the doorposts of any room within your home (excluding bathrooms, closets, storerooms, and other areas in which people do not actually "live").

When one hangs a *mezuzah*, one recites two blessings:

> Blessed are You, *Adonai* our God, Sovereign of the universe, Who has sanctified us with commandments and commanded us to affix the *mezuzah*.

> Blessed are You, *Adonai* our God, Who has kept us alive and sustained us and permitted us to reach this moment.

◆ Visit your synagogue gift shop or local Judaica store to see the wide variety of *mezuzah* cases available. Also ask to see a scroll and try to read what is on it.

9 Scholars believe that Pesach (mentioned in the Haftarah and Maftir) and *Chag HaMatzot* (mentioned in the Maftir) were originally two different holidays that were ultimately merged together into what we know as Passover. It seems that the original Pesach was a feast observed by shepherds in the spring. They would sacrifice a sheep in order to secure prosperity for their flock and to attain protection from their gods over the dangers that threatened their flocks. The Hebrew word פסח (Pesach) actually means "to protect" or "to guard," and not "to pass over."

◆ Explain in your own words how the word פסח means "guarding." Who or what was originally in need of guarding?

When the Israelites adopted this shepherd's holiday, God became the protector who פסח over Israelite houses when the tenth plague killed each firstborn Egyptian. (See Exodus 12:42, which describes פסח as God's night of watching vigilantly over the Israelites.)

Chag HaMatzot, on the other hand, was an agriculturally based holiday. It was linked to the new spring crops. Farmers, before the new harvest, would clean out their old leavening and would even refrain from eating bread for a period of time in the hope that their fast might convince their gods that they deserved to reap a really good harvest.

When the Israelites settled in the land of Canaan and adopted these two local shepherd and farmer holidays, they also tied the holidays to their own story of being rescued from Egypt by God. The two holidays, Pesach and *Chag HaMatzot*, were eventually joined into one holiday since both were observed at the same time in the spring.

◆ Teach and discuss this lesson at your next family *Seder*.

◆ Discuss at your *Seder* times in your lives when you have needed special protection.

10 In Insights from the Tradition #D, p. 499, there is discussion about what the prince should do if he doesn't have enough money to buy all the items necessary for sacrifice. The Mishnah (*Pesachim* 10:1) teaches us that everyone must have the proper provisions for the Passover *Seder*. See Talmud *Pesachim* 99b, which states that on the eve of Passover . . . one must not eat until nightfall. Even the poorest person in Israel must not eat until he/she reclines. And he/she should be given not less than four cups of wine even if he/she receives relief from the charity plate.

◆ Why do you think it is especially important that every Jew be given the opportunity to enjoy the food and wine of the Passover *Seder*?

A story is told in *The Passover Anthology* by Philip Goodman, p. 390, of a man too poor to buy wine for his *Seder*.

A local Jew came to Rabbi Akiba Eger of Posen on the first night of Passover to ask a question. "Rabbi, is it permissible to use four cups of milk at the *Seder* instead of four cups of wine?" The Rabbi was baffled. Thinking the man might be ill, the Rabbi asked why he wanted to substitute milk for wine. The man replied that he was not ill, but could not afford to buy wine.

The sympathetic Rabbi expressed regret over the ruling, but told the man that it is forbidden to use a substitute for wine. Then the Rabbi reached into

his pocket, handed the man 20 rubles, and said, "Use these rubles to buy wine."

Afterward, the Rabbi's wife asked her husband. "Why did you give him 20 rubles for wine when two or three would have been enough?"

The Rabbi replied, "This poor man was prepared to drink milk at the *Seder*. To me, that is evidence that he also didn't have money to buy meat, and perhaps not even fish and *matzot*. The 20 rubles will enable him to observe the *Seder* properly."

◆ How did the Rabbi figure out that the man didn't have money for meat?

◆ How did the Rabbi help the poor man without embarrassing him?

◆ Run a Passover food drive for the needy in your community. Collect wine, *matzah*, and other kosher for Passover food to be delivered to those in need or for the homebound.

Extending the Text

11 The prince will be required to offer sacrifices on the New Moon, Rosh Chodesh. Each Jewish month is based on a full cycle of the moon (about 29 1/2 days).

◆ Observe the moon for a full month, from its thinnest sliver of a crescent, through the full moon, and on to its waning crescent and eventual absence from the sky. Each night or day, draw what you see and at what time of night or day it is visible. You may want to consult a Jewish calendar or a moon-phase calendar on cloudy nights.

◆ During your Passover *Seder*, go outside and observe the full moon.

12 The prince is instructed to enter and leave the Temple through the same door. In the Middle Ages, Rambam outlined many rules for entering and exiting synagogues (*Mishneh Torah, Hilchot Tefilah* chapter 11:8-10). Consider these guidelines:

- If a synagogue or a house of study has two entrances, one should not use it for a shortcut, i.e., to enter through one entrance and leave through the other to reduce the distance one travels, because it is forbidden to enter these buildings except for a *mitzvah*.

- A person who has to enter a synagogue to call a child or his friend should enter and read a portion of the Torah or relate a teaching of the Oral Law and then call his friend, so that he will not have entered a synagogue for his personal reasons alone. If he does not know how to study, he should ask one of the children to tell him the verse he is studying or, at the very least, wait a while in the synagogue and then leave, since spending time in the synagogue is one of the aspects of the *mitzvah* . . .

- A person who enters a synagogue to pray or to study is permitted to leave by the opposite door to shorten his way.

◆ Discuss these rules. Explain what you think Rambam's rationale was for each rule.

◆ Regarding the first rule cited above, can you list five *mitzvot* that can be performed in a synagogue building?

◆ Rambam teaches that spending time in the synagogue is a *mitzvah* in and of itself. What, if anything, do you think we gain by simply spending time in our synagogue building?

◆ Does this *mitzvah* provide a good reason for why many synagogues have youth groups, social activities, concerts, and carnivals, in addition to services and study?

13 Insights from the Tradition #C, p. 498, discusses the person who is unwitting and the one who is ignorant. The Pesach *Seder* features four children: one who is wise, one who is wicked, one who is simple, and one who doesn't understand enough to ask.

◆ Read about the four children in the *Haggadah*, and prepare a skit about them for your class.

14 Our most famous *nasi* was Rabbi Judah HaNasi, who codified Jewish Oral Law in the Mishnah around 200 C.E. As it says in the Passover *Seder* song, *"Echad Mi Yodeah,"* the Mishnah has six orders containing 63 tractates of Jewish law and lore:

> *Zera'im* (agriculture)
> *Mo'ed* (holidays)
> *Nashim* (women)
> *Nezikin* (property damages)
> *Kodashim* (sacrifices and ritual slaughter)
> *Taharot* (purity)

◆ Make a poster of the six orders of the Mishnah, illustrating each order with pictures that describe its contents. (For more information on the contents of each order, see *Jewish Literacy* by Joseph Telushkin, p. 151, or *Encyclopaedia Judaica*, vol. 12, pp. 93-108.)

◆ Ask your Cantor to teach your class to sing *"Echad Mi Yodeah,"* or listen to the recording *Songs of the Haggadah* by Binyamin Glickman.

15 The Rabbis tell a story about a *mezuzah* (see Connecting the Text To the Special Shabbat #8, pp. 500-501, for more on *mezuzot*) in *Genesis Rabbah* 35:3:

Ardavan sent a magnificent pearl to master Rav and asked that something equally valuable be sent in return." Rav sent him a *mezuzah*. Ardavan was furious and replied to Rav, "I sent you something priceless, and you sent me back something of hardly any value."

Rav replied, "Nothing you or I own can match the value of the *mezuzah*. Besides, you sent me something that I have to guard, whereas I sent you something that guards you while you sleep, as it says in Proverbs, 'When you walk, it shall lead you, and when you lie down, it shall guard you.'"

◆ Why was the *mezuzah* so precious to Rav?

◆ Do you feel that a *mezuzah* has magical protective powers? If not, why put it on your doorposts?

16 No prophet pays more attention to detail than Ezekiel. As Plaut writes in *The Haftarah Commentary*, p. 573, "No detail is too small, no procedure too unimportant, if it helps to assure its sanctity."

◆ There is a saying that "life is in the details." What do you think this saying means?

◆ Are you detail oriented?

◆ Review the details of the *mitzvot* of eating *matzah* and *maror* at the Passover *Seder*, including the Hillel sandwich.

◆ The Maftir reading in Exodus 12:8 instructs us to "eat the flesh [of the Pesach sacrifice] on the same night; they shall eat it roasted over the fire, with unleavened bread and with bitter herbs." Learn more about this ritual from any *Haggadah*.

Personalizing the Text

17 *Shabbat HaChodesh* signals that it's time to finish your preparations for Pesach.

◆ Practice the four questions.

◆ Learn to sing a new song at the *Seder*, such as *"Chad Gadya"* (One Kid), *"Avadim Hayinu"* (We Were Slaves), or *"Echad Mi Yode'a"* (Who Knows One?). Ask the Cantor for help. You can also write these songs out in transliteration to enable those at your *Seder* who don't read Hebrew to sing along. These songs are available on the recording *Songs of the Haggadah* by Binyamin Glickman.

◆ Your class can also volunteer to help an elderly member of your congregation prepare for Pesach.

18 Ezekiel mentions in verse 45:19 putting blood on the doorposts of the Sanctuary. Today, we affix *mezuzot* on our doorposts that contain the words of the *"Shema."*

◆ Create a *mezuzah* case out of clay that can be glazed and fired in a kiln. If you do not have access to a kiln, you and your classmates can instead each draw designs for a *mezuzah* case.

19 We learned about the four Jewish new years in Connecting the Text To the Special Shabbat #6, p. 500.

◆ Make a Jewish calendar, featuring all the holidays, and especially the four new years. Illustrate your calendar with pictures of holidays, Jewish symbols, etc.

20 Ezekiel seems concerned that the future leaders of Israel do not abuse their power (see Analyzing the Text #5, p. 500).

◆ Make a list of ten things a democratic ruler should never be allowed to do.

◆ How does the system of checks and balances prevent the abuse of power?

21 Being Jewish can be expensive, but there are lots of Jewish values that don't have to cost much.

◆ As a class, discover your own Jewish priorities by holding a Jewish Values Auction. Make signs, each with one Jewish value on it. The teacher presents all the values up for auction, and the students discuss each. Each student is given $1000 in play money with which to bid, and time to decide their own priorities and bidding strategies. Then the auction begins. Each student should end up with at least one Jewish value. Suggested Jewish values include: Shabbat, *tzedakah*, hospitality, visiting the sick, honoring our parents, Bar/Bat Mitzvah, Jewish education, synagogue affiliation, Federation contributions, Hebrew language, Jewish culture, Jewish food, Jewish marriage, holidays, *kashrut*, and Israel. Be creative!

Other Resources

22 For an excellent Passover resource book, see *A Different Night* by Noam Zion and David Dishon.

23 Passover is a detail-oriented holiday. For guidance, consult *The Passover Seder* by Ron Wolfson.

24 Play the game "Passover Past, Passover Present" in *Jewish Identity Games* by Richard Israel, p. 45.

25 Explore "Leadership Issues in Groups" in *Jewish Identity Games* by Richard Israel, p. 75.

26 For a guide to how to plan and run a Seder, see www.learn.jtsa.edu/passover/pesahguide.shtml.

27 Read the chapter on Ezekiel in *Messengers of God: A Jewish Prophets Who's Who* by Ronald H. Isaacs, pp. 121-133.

28 Discuss the portrayal of this Haftarah in *The Illustrated Torah* by Michal Meron, p. 228.

29 For more information on how to affix a *mezuzah*, see one or all of the following books: *Teaching Mitzvot* by Barbara Binder Kadden and Bruce Kadden, pp. 53-56; *The How-To Handbook for Jewish Living* by Kerry M. Olitzky and Ronald H. Isaacs, pp. 104-105; *The First Jewish Catalog* by Richard Siegel, Michael Strassfeld, and Sharon Strassfeld, pp. 12-16.

Involving the Family

30 Review how much you (as a family) spend on being Jewish every year (See Insights from the Tradition #D, p. 499). Consider selecting one aspect of Judaism to which you are willing to dedicate more money (planning a trip to Israel, buying kosher food, decorating with Jewish art and ritual objects, purchasing Jewish books, saving for *tzedakah* donations, etc.).

31 Consider purchasing beautiful *mezuzot* as Bar and Bat Mitzvah gifts for your friends and classmates.

Bar/Bat Mitzvah Project

32 Choose a meaningful *mezuzah* case for your bedroom doorpost. If you already have a *mezuzah* there, take it down and buy a new one to mark your coming of age as a Jewish adult.

OVERVIEW

The last 12 prophets are commonly known as The Minor Prophets, because their literary works are relatively short in length. They are also called "The Twelve" prophets because all 12 were written together on one scroll (whereas the other prophets — Isaiah, Jeremiah, and Ezekiel — were each written on separate scrolls). In addition, it seems that an editor (probably in the fourth century B.C.E.) combined these 12 individual prophets together in order to make them into one book. The editor took words and ideas from some of the 12 and from other sources and added them to the other of the 12 books in order to make them fit together more cohesively. As a group, these prophets cover about 300 years, from the early eighth century B.C.E. until approximately the middle of the fifth century B.C.E. They predicted and witnessed the fall of Israel and Judah, the Babylonian exile, the return of the exiles to Jerusalem, the revival of the nation, and the rebuilding of the Holy Temple.

The Twelve Prophets employed vivid imagery and metaphors, prose, and poetry to communicate God's word. Some of the themes discussed by them include: belief in a Universal God of all peoples who desires justice and mercy from everyone, God's justice and mercy, fidelity and infidelity to God, the merciful and loving acceptance of the penitent, insistence that ritual be accompanied

by justice and righteousness, a promise of future redemption, and the rebuilding of Jerusalem. While none of these themes is unique to the Twelve Prophets, there is one more theme that is uniquely highlighted by them. All but two of The Twelve describe an awesome Day of *Adonai* when God will act in a military manner and all the wicked will be punished. The idea of such a day is found only infrequently in Isaiah, Jeremiah, and Ezekiel, and seems to unite the 12 prophets as one book.

The Twelve Prophets are not compiled in chronological order. Hosea, Amos, and Micah lived and preached in the eighth century B.C.E. The Book of Hosea is the first of the group, and in it the prophet develops the metaphor of God as the husband of an unfaithful wife (Israel). The Book of Amos is the third of the 12, although it is generally believed to be the oldest of the group. Like his younger contemporary Hosea, Amos preached in the Northern Kingdom (although he was from the South). Amos preached against injustices to the poor. He also taught that religious ritual is not an end in itself, but actually a means to justice, honesty, kindness, and mercy.

The Book of Micah is the sixth of the Twelve Minor Prophets. A younger contemporary of Hosea (and Isaiah), Micah spoke out against the greed and excessive competitiveness that were destroying the social fabric of Israel and Judah. He castigated the people for the social injustice and religious abominations that ran rampant in both kingdoms. He urgently reminded the Israelites that ethics and kindness matter most.

Perhaps the best known of the Minor Prophets, Jonah, comes fifth in the group. The Book of Jonah is unique among the prophets because it is almost entirely narrative, with only one verse recording Jonah's prophetic words. Although there was a prophet named Jonah who lived in the eighth century (II Kings 14:25), it is unclear that this book was written about him; the book includes no personal information about Jonah, his call to prophecy, or his era. Scholars cannot, therefore, decide to which time period the book belongs. Several other prophets also reveal nothing of their own background in their books: Joel, Obadiah, Nahum, Zephaniah, and Habakkuk.

The last three books seem to have been written during the sixth and fifth centuries B.C.E., after the return of the exiles to Jerusalem from Babylonia. Haggai, Zechariah, and Malachi were contemporaries who prophesied shortly after the return to Judah during the period that Persia controlled Judah. According to Jewish tradition, they were the last three prophets to prophesy. Haggai and Zechariah preached concerning the rebuilding of the Temple at the end of the sixth century B.C.E. The last of the Twelve Prophets is Malachi. It is understood from his prophecies that the Second Temple's construction had already been completed, which dates him to the period after 516 B.C.E.

HOSEA 2:1-22
BAMIDBAR במדבר

This Haftarah has been paired with *Parashat Bamidbar*, Numbers 1:1-4:20. See "Connecting the Text To the Sedra," pp. 511-514, for an exploration of the many ways the two texts shed light on each other.

SYNOPSIS

The Haftarah begins with a vision of Israel's glorious future. Hosea sees that the people in both the Northern Kingdom of Israel and the Southern Kingdom of Judah will be as numerous as the sands in the sea, as they live peacefully and obediently under the guidance of God.

Yet the tone quickly turns sour as the text continues. Hosea uses a metaphor in which Israel is represented as God's unfaithful wife. Expressing God's utter disgust with the wayward wife, Hosea preaches that Israel will be severely punished for chasing after idols and rejecting her true husband.

The Haftarah then jarringly turns again to a more hopeful outlook in verse 2:16. Hosea explains how God will tenderly lead Israel out of the wilderness of sin. On that day, Israel will repent of her infidelities and enjoy a loving and mutually respectful marriage with God, instead of punishment and disgrace. Israel will be blessed with peace and prosperity, righteousness and justice, goodness and mercy, and devotion to *Adonai*.

Hosea lived in the Northern Kingdom of Israel in the first half of the eighth century B.C.E., a time when Israel was feeling insecure. Internal leadership was rocky as the throne changed hands at least six times in fewer than 20 years, often when the reigning king was assassinated. Insecurity also stemmed from external factors. Two superpowers, Assyria in the north and Egypt in the south, had been quiet, but now both were poised to expand their territories and control. Israel sat anxiously in between.

Hosea believes that Israel's troubles are punishment from God, Who is angered by Israel's practice of idolatry. The prophet pleads with his people to abandon idolatry and return to *Adonai* before it is too late.

INSIGHTS FROM THE TRADITION

A Hirsch explains that being "Children of a Living God" in verse 2:1 means having pure morals, practicing love of other people, and being dedicated to justice and fairness. When the Israelites do these things, they will be recognized as "Children of a Living God."

◆ List five things you can do every day to be a "Child of a Living God."

◆ Explain how each of these acts helps to keep God alive in the world.

B According to Rashi, the phrase "rebuke your mother" in verse 2:4 means that the Israelites should protest the actions of their nation. Rashi suggests that a nation, like a mother, produces future generations of people.

◆ In the 1960s, Americans protested the war in Vietnam and racial prejudice at home. Do you think it is our obligation to protest when we think our nation is doing the wrong thing?

◆ What do you think are some issues Americans should be concerned about today?

◆ What is your attitude toward those, such as Quakers and Mennonites, who protested the bombing of Afghanistan based on their pacifistic religious beliefs?

◆ Debate this statement: It is unpatriotic to protest against your nation when you believe it is acting wrongly. Which side of the debate do you think Hosea would take?

C Hosea says in verse 2:4, " . . . let her put away her harlotry from her face." Radak explains that it was the custom of harlots to wear makeup on their faces to appear more attractive.

◆ Do you think wearing lots of makeup is an acceptable way for women to make themselves look more attractive?

◆ Do you think politicians appearing on television should wear makeup to make themselves look more appealing? Explain your answer.

◆ Do you approve of the use of makeup? Why or why not?

D Hosea reminds Israel in verse 2:10 that the gold, silver, grain, wine, and oil it was squandering on idolatry came from God. *Berachot* 32a quotes this verse when presenting the following scenario:

A person had a child whom he bathed, dressed nicely, gave plenty to eat and drink, provided with lots of money, and then left unsupervised in a sleazy part of town. The Talmud asks: How could the child help but get into trouble?

◆ Explain how this scenario indicates that if God (or any parent) gives Israel (or any child) the resources with which to get into trouble, and then does not provide adequate supervision, one cannot blame Israel (or the child).

◆ Do you agree that having more than enough to meet one's needs and inadequate supervision leads one to get into trouble?

◆ If parents give their child too much money, and the child uses it to buy drugs, does the parent share responsibility? Why or why not?

E Radak explains regarding verse 2:16 that just as God will tenderly coax Israel to abandon evil and seek good, so we have the power to convince our friends to change their minds and follow a path of righteousness.

◆ In what ways can you be a good influence on your friends?

◆ In what ways have your friends been good influences on you?

◆ Have you ever had to coax a friend toward better behavior? How did you do it?

F Hosea says in verse 2:19 that God will help Israel repent by removing the names of the idols (*Baalim*) from Israel's mouth. If the Israelites stop talking about idols, perhaps they will stop worshiping them as well. Radak teaches that this is an indication that God aids a person's repentance according to the Talmudic teaching in *Shabbat* 104a: If a person comes to purify himself, he is afforded assistance.

◆ How will not talking about idols help Israel stop their idolatrous behavior?

◆ How might you make it easier or harder for someone to say to you that they are sorry?

◆ Do you think we have an obligation to make it easier for someone to say they're sorry, or should we make it harder for them? Consider repentance in a variety of situations: a friend who breaks a promise, a felon in jail for theft, a murderer.

G Concerning verse 2:21, Rashi teaches that when one practices righteousness and justice, one will receive loving-kindness and mercy in return.

◆ Explain Rashi's lesson in your own words.

◆ Do you agree with Rashi's lesson?

◆ Can you describe a role model who has practiced righteousness and justice and been rewarded with loving-kindness and mercy?

H Hirsch learns from verse 2:21 that our relationships with God can be made lasting and permanent only when we show concern for our fellow people — which will happen only when we are able to control our selfishness.

◆ List five selfish acts, then explore how each act could potentially hurt one's relationship with another person.

I Malbim teaches that מֹשׁפָּט *(mishpat)* in verse 2:21 means strict legal justice, while צדק *(tzedek)* — righteousness — means going beyond one's legal obligations. Similarly, רחמים *(rachamim)* — mercy — means a measured response to someone's needs, but חסד *(chesed)* means a desire to go above and beyond in providing the precise needs of a person.

◆ Can you give an example of someone meeting a moral obligation to another without going beyond it?

◆ Can you give an example of someone going above and beyond his or her strict obligation to offer more to someone in need?

◆ Describe a time when you were the recipient of true *chesed*.

STRATEGIES
Analyzing the Text

1 To understand the metaphor of the unfaithful wife, it is useful to have some information that is given in the first chapter of Hosea. There, God requests that Hosea marry a prostitute. Her marital unfaithfulness parallels Israel's infidelities with other gods and idols.

You might wonder how God could tell anyone to marry someone who was bound to be unfaithful to them, much less a prostitute. *Pesachim* 87a-b suggests that once when God complained to Hosea about Israel being unfaithful, Hosea responded that God should just get rid of them. God wanted to teach Hosea compassion, and so had him marry an unfaithful wife.

◆ Why might it be difficult to understand someone's situation if it is very different from your own?

◆ In contrast, Hertz suggests that because Hosea already had a difficult marriage, he could understand God's troubled relationship with Israel. In this scenario, did God really tell Hosea to marry a prostitute?

◆ On the other hand, Gerson Cohen writes that "because his Israelite mind had been taught from childhood to think of the relationship between God and Israel in terms of marital fidelity, in terms of love," Hosea chose this religious allegory. In other words, Hosea's marriage did not really happen, but was purely allegorical.

◆ Which explanation of Hosea's marriage to a prostitute do you prefer?

◆ What questions or difficulties does the metaphor of Israel as the unfaithful wife of God raise for you?

2 In chapter 1, Hosea gives his own children symbolic names: Jezreel, which means "I will punish the house of Jehu"; Lo-ruhama, which means "God will no longer have compassion for Israel or pardon them"; and Lo-ammi, which means "they are not my people."

◆ Explain the symbolism behind these names.

◆ In verse 2:1, Hosea changes the name "Not My People" to "Children of the Living God." He also calls them "My People" and "Lovingly Accepted" in verse 2:3. These are obviously very meaningful names that describe the relationship between Israel and God. Explain their significance or draw pictures illustrating their symbolism.

3 Hosea prophesies that the people in both the Northern Kingdom of Israel and the Southern Kingdom of Judah will be as numerous as the sands in the sea, and that they will live peacefully reunified under one leader (verse 2:2).

This prophecy was not fulfilled; after the North was destroyed, the ten tribes were taken into captivity and were never reunited with the people of the South. (For more on the historical fate of the ten tribes of the Northern Kingdom of Israel, see the Overview for Isaiah, pp. 218-219.)

◆ What do you think is the value of prophecy if it does not always come true? See the discussion on this topic in the Haftarah for *Va'etchanan*, Insight #A, p. 253.

4 Verse 2:7 can be understood in two different ways: Either Hosea charges his wife with infidelity *or* God accuses Israel of playing the harlot and chasing after other lovers.

Radak believed that the other lovers are the powerful nations of Assyria and Egypt to which Israel turned to make treaties and seek protection. Israel

expected Egypt and Assyria to fill her political and material needs.

◆ Explain how Israel's turning to other nations instead of trusting God is considered infidelity.

◆ Rabbi Joseph Kimchi, on the other hand, believed that the lovers were the sun, moon, and stars, which Israel worshiped as gods. Israel expected idols and false gods to fill her spiritual needs. Explain how Israel's involvement with idolatry is like infidelity.

◆ Reread the Haftarah. Which explanation do you think is best supported by the text?

5 In verse 2:18 God says that Israel will no longer call her husband by the name "*Baali*," which means "my master" and strongly resembles the name of a foreign god, *Baal*. Instead, Israel will call God by the name "*Ishi*," which means "my man."

◆ Explain how this change in names removes the name of an idol, *Baal*, from Israel's mouth every time Israel refers to God as her husband (see Insights from the Tradition #F, p. 509).

◆ Which name, "my master" or "my man," indicates a marriage of mutual partnership?

6 Hosea's name means "God has saved."

◆ What connection might there be between Hosea's name and this prophecy?

Connecting the Text To the Sedra

7 The Sedra is the first one of the Book of Numbers. *Bamidbar* means "in the wilderness." The book covers the 40 years of Israel's wanderings in the wilderness. The Haftarah mentions the wilderness three times:

- In verse 2:5 God wants to punish Israel by sending her with nothing into the wilderness;

- In verse 2:16 God plans to speak tenderly to Israel in the wilderness;

- And in verse 2:17, God longs for the "good ol' days" in the wilderness when Israel had just come out of Egypt.

◆ What comes to your mind when you think of the wilderness (e.g., barrenness, heat, dryness, desolation, beauty, scariness, awe)? Which of your associations are positive and which are negative?

◆ What comes to your mind when you think of the relationship between Israel and God in the wilderness (e.g., lack of food and water, manna, dependence, survival, Israel's honeymoon with God, rebellion, growing up from slavery to freedom, receiving Torah)?

◆ Create a mural depicting all the contrasting aspects of the wilderness as experienced by the Israelites.

8 This Haftarah involves Israel's rebellion against God's ways and rejection of God. It also reveals God's desire to punish Israel. The Haftarah may serve as an introduction to the various rebellions of Israel against God, several of which are recounted in the Book of Numbers.

◆ Review two of these incidents: Numbers 11:1-9 and Numbers 20:2-13.

Jacob Milgrom points out in *The JPS Torah Commentary: Numbers*, p. *xvi*, that some of the acts of rebellion described in Numbers were also described in Exodus (compare Exodus 17:1-7, 16:1-15 to Numbers 11:1-35 and 20:1-13). However, there was one difference between the way the stories were told in the two books. The Exodus version of these stories does not include a punishment, but the Numbers stories do. According to Milgrom, the reason that the Exodus

stories do not include a punishment is that they were told before the Torah was received at Sinai, but the Numbers stories are told after Torah was received at Sinai. In other words, these are different versions of the same, single event, but told with different consequences depending on whether the teller assumed a Covenant existed or not.

◆ Do you agree that punishment cannot be imposed until laws have been laid down and consequences made clear?

◆ Since God and Israel do have a Covenant by the time of the Haftarah, then why do we find the punishments of this Haftarah objectionable?

◆ It seems that until God and Israel had an official covenantal relationship, God could not punish them. Who has a relationship with you that allows them to punish you, and who does not? What marks the divide between these two individuals or groups?

9 In the Haftarah (verse 2:4), the children of Hosea (representing all Israelites) are told by their father (representing God) to rebuke their mother (representing The Nation of Israel). The goal of the rebuke is to warn her away from impure acts.

In the Sedra the camp is set up with the holy Tabernacle in the middle, the Levites around it, and then the rest of the children of Israel by tribe around the perimeter (see a diagram in the *Hertz Chumash*, p. 572, or in *The JPS Torah Commentary: Numbers* by Milgrom p. 340). According to Milgrom, p. *xl*, the function of the Levites encircling the Tabernacle is to guard the sanctuary against encroachers; they are to prevent people from polluting the holy area with their sins. In addition, the Sedra says several times that if a common person does what a priest is supposed to do, that person will die (see Numbers 3:10, 38, 4:15).

◆ Discuss this parallel between the Haftarah and the Sedra: the Nation and the Tabernacle were both to be protected from impurity.

◆ Discuss this difference between the Haftarah and Torah readings: in the Haftarah all Israelites are responsible for preventing impurity, but in the Sedra it is solely the responsibility of the Levites.

◆ Who is responsible today for guarding and keeping our Jewish laws and traditions: only the clergy or all the members of a community?

10 The names of Hosea's children are evidently all symbolic. Each of their names describes the relationship of God and Israel. In the Sedra the names of the heads of the tribes of Israel are given. These names, however, do not appear to be symbolic. Milgrom points out (*The JPS Torah Commentary: Numbers*, p. 6) that the names of the leaders of the tribes appear to be ancient names.

◆ Explain how the contrast between documented, ancient names versus purely symbolic names makes the story of Hosea, his wife, and children appear to be an allegory for God and Israel more than a story about real people.

◆ Review a book of fiction you read recently. List all the names of the characters and consider why the author chose those names.

11 It is thought that the reason the census appears in the Book of Numbers is for the purpose of military conscription. In the Book of Numbers, the children of Israel are about to leave Sinai and need to be prepared for military engagements.

In contrast, God promises in the Haftarah that in the future, after Israel has repented and returned

to God, God will "banish bow, sword, and war from the land," and they will dwell in safety, even with the animals.

In Rabbinic descriptions of the ideal future, all of God's laws and commandments are observed and all people live in harmony and without war.

◆ List as many causes for war as you can.

◆ Determine which causes would be prevented if all people followed the Ten Commandments that were received at Sinai (or other laws of the Torah).

◆ Rabbi Stephen S. Wise wrote, "War never ends war." What do you think he meant? What does end war? Consider the case of the War on Terrorism.

12 The Haftarah indicates that Hosea's children are children of harlotry, in which case it is not clear who the father is (see verses 2:6-7). However, in the future, they will know their father; they will be called "Children of the Living God."

In the Sedra a census is taken of Israel and presented by tribe, conveying a sense of legitimacy and identity.

◆ How does knowing your ancestry and/or your religious identity help guide you in life?

◆ Design a family tree for yourself that goes back at least three generations.

13 In the Sedra the Israelites are numbered in a census. Hosea says in verse 2:1 of the Haftarah that Israel will one day be as numerous as the sands of the sea. In ancient times, a large population was regarded as a sign of blessing. It was important for defense and to guarantee continuity of the community. A large population was also essential in places with an agrarian economy.

TEACHING HAFTARAH

◆ Today there are approximately 15 million Jews in the world, comprising about one-fifth of one percent of the world's population (that's two out of every 1,000 human beings). For more information on the Jewish population of the world (by country or largest cities), see http://us-israel.org/jsource/Judaism/jewpop.html.

◆ In your opinion, are Jews today as numerous as the sands of the sea?

◆ Contact your local Jewish Federation to find out the Jewish population of the area in which you live. Do you feel you have a large or small Jewish community? Would you prefer to live in a community with more or fewer Jews, and why?

Extending the Text

14 Why is Hosea critical of the harlot's use of makeup in verse 2:4? It is not makeup *per se* to which Hosea objects, but rather to its use when committing infidelity. Makeup can, however, be used to perform a *mitzvah*.

Consider makeup artist Kim Foley, who decided to teach the art of using makeup to children with disfiguring scars, burns, and birth defects. Her first patient was the victim of burns all over his body. He had his entire face rebuilt with skin grafts. With makeup, he looked in the mirror and said he "looked normal for the first time." (Source: *Megatrends for Women* by Patricia Aburdene and John Naisbitt, pp. 267-268.)

Makeup is also used by Mitzvah Clowns who paint their faces, dress as clowns and amuse, with clown antics, kids who are in the hospital.

◆ See the web site of Mitzvah Clowns Sweetpea and Buttercup (Sue and Mike Turk) at www.mitzvahclowns.com.

◆ Explain how these uses of makeup would be considered godly, whereas Hosea was objecting to uses of makeup in un-godly deeds.

◆ Learn how to put on clown makeup.

15 Hosea uses the word ונתיבותיה *(u'netivotechah)*, which means "her paths," in verse 2:8. This same word is found two other times in the Bible:

• Proverbs 3:17: "Her ways are ways of pleasantness and all her paths are peace."

• Proverbs 7:25: "Let not your mind wander down her ways; Do not stray onto her paths."

◆ Proverbs 3:17 is discussing wisdom, but Proverbs 7:25 is discussing a harlot. Explain the difference in usage of this word in both verses and compare the message and mood of Hosea 2:8 with the message in both verses.

◆ Rabbinic tradition has equated Torah with Wisdom. We see this in our Torah Service, in which Proverbs 3:17 is used as the Torah is returned to the Ark (*"Etz Chayim,"* a Tree of Life). Listen to Safam's rendition of *"Etz Chayim"* on the recording *Safam on Track*.

16 Two places are mentioned by name in verse 2:17. The Valley of Achor (also known as the Valley of Trouble) gets its name from Joshua 7:25-26. In that text a man who sinned against God by stealing property forbidden to him by God was executed along with his family.

This location, according to the prophecy, will be turned into Petach Tikvah, or Door of Hope. A place of crime and execution will become a place of hope.

A couple of lessons can be drawn from this name change: (1) When you eradicate sin, there can be renewal; and (2) judgment and punishment are not the end, because life can turn around.

514   HOSEA 2:1-22

◆ Explain how these themes are seen in the changes in outlook of the Haftarah.

◆ Plaut explains in *The Haftarah Commentary*, p. 331, that Petach Tikvah was the name given in the 1870s by Jewish pioneers to the first Jewish agricultural settlement in Ottoman Palestine. The village was moved in 1883 to its present site, where it later became a suburb of Tel Aviv. Find out more about Petach Tikvah by going to: http://jajz-cd.org.il/a00/places/pt.html.

◆ Using the *Encyclopaedia Judaica*, research the historical, theological, or geographical significance of the names of other cities in Israel. For example, look up Ein-Gedi, Herzliyah, and Rishon LeZion.

17 Hosea says that God will lead Israel tenderly out of sin. While friends and family should certainly help each other learn good ways to behave, Jewish law forbids us from ever embarrassing someone with criticism.

◆ Do you think Hosea's rebuke in verses 2:4-15 is in accordance with or a violation of this Jewish law?

◆ For information and exercises on this topic, see the Haftarah for *Shemot*, Ashkenazim, Extending the Text #19, p. 249.

18 Hosea writes of the love between Israel and God and God's jealousy when Israel strays.

◆ Reread the Ten Commandments and discuss how the metaphor of God's love and jealousy appears there, too.

19 Verses 2:21-22 are often said at Jewish weddings:

And I will espouse you forever
I will espouse you with righteousness
and justice,
And with goodness and mercy,
And I will espouse you with faithfulness,
Then you shall be devoted to *Adonai*.

Note: Espousal refers to the engagement period before a wedding (see Deuteronomy 20:7, 28:30).

◆ Ask your parents or other adults if they recited these verses at their wedding.

◆ Righteousness, justice, goodness, mercy, and faithfulness are some of God's most important qualities. In the forthcoming marriage, Israel will benefit from these qualities of God, but God will also expect them from Israel. Explain how these qualities are not onetime dowry or engagement gifts, but must be ongoing, daily attributes (in the marriage between God and Israel or in human marriages).

◆ Explain how these qualities must work both ways in a healthy relationship.

◆ According to some commentators, by starting over with a new engagement to be followed by a new marriage, Israel is given a completely fresh start at her relationship with God. However, according to other commentators, these verses do not promise a new relationship, but a repair and a restoration to an original one. Review the Haftarah for evidence that might support either viewpoint.

20 Verses 2:21-22 are recited when putting on *tefillin*. Ask your Rabbi, Cantor, or a class parent to teach your class how to put on *tefillin* and to explain when these verses are to be said.

◆ When a Jew wraps *tefillin* around her/his finger and says these verses, he/she is invoking a marriage metaphor. The metaphor, however, does not mean the literal marriage of Israel and God, but the exclusive devotion to God and God's ways.

◆ According to a *midrash*, God wears *tefillin*, and inside God's *tefillin* is a scroll that says, "Who is like my people Israel?" What does it mean to you that God is pictured acting in the same way we do (i.e., putting on *tefillin*)?

◆ What does it mean to you that God's *tefillin* expresses the uniqueness of Israel to God?

◆ What does our *tefillin* say? Our *tefillin* quotes these verses: Deuteronomy 6:4-9, 11:13-21, and Exodus 13:1-10, 11-16. Compare these verses to the wording of God's *tefillin* in the *midrash*.

◆ For more on the *mitzvah* of *tefillin*, see *Teaching Mitzvot* by Barbara Binder Kadden and Bruce Kadden, pp. 57-60.

21 Every Jewish wedding ceremony contains two parts: the espousal/betrothal and the marriage. The espousal/betrothal portion consists of thrcc parts:

a. Welcoming everyone to the *chupah*.

b. Blessings over wine, which are:

Blessed are You, *Adonai* our God, Sovereign of the universe, Who created the fruit of the vine.

Blessed are You, *Adonai* our God, Sovereign of the universe, Who has sanctified us with Your commandments, and has commanded us concerning forbidden relationships, but has allowed to us those lawfully married to us through *chupah* and betrothal. Blessed are You, *Adonai*, Who sanctifies Your people Israel through *chupah* and betrothal.

c. Bride and groom drink the wine.

◆ Explain how this portion of the wedding ceremony expresses the exclusive nature of the marriage relationship.

◆ For more on the wedding ceremony, see *Teaching Jewish Life Cycle* by Barbara Binder Kadden and Bruce Kadden, pp. 68-81.

22 Many Israeli women have chosen to use the word *"Ishi"* (my man), for husband, as opposed to *"Baali"* (my master).

◆ Why do you think these women have made this choice? Which wording do you prefer, and why?

◆ For more on this subject, read the essay by Plaut in *The Haftarah Commentary*, pp. 333-334.

Personalizing the Text

23 God taught Hosea to understand God's relationship with Israel by putting Hosea into a similar relationship with Gomer, his unfaithful wife. Sometimes we can't understand someone's position until we are in the same one.

◆ View and discuss the film *White Man's Burden*, starring John Travolta (1995, rated R for language and some violence, 89 minutes), which explores issues of racism by switching the stereotypical roles of white people and African-Americans.

◆ How does this film contribute to your understanding of the situation of the underprivileged in America?

24 God accuses Israel of playing the harlot and chasing after other lovers.

◆ Can you think of any people or things that tempt you to do something you know you should not?

◆ How do you resist such temptation?

25 Rashi teaches in Insights from the Tradition #B, pp. 508-509, that we must protest when we believe our government is behaving wrongly.

◆ Find out the names, addresses, and e-mail addresses of all of your local, state, and national government officials (mayor, state legislators, members of Congress, senators, etc.). Distribute the list to congregants.

◆ What is your local government's policy on recycling or environmental protection? (Feel free to choose another issue that interests you.) If it is not to your satisfaction, engage in a letter writing campaign or draft a petition demanding change.

26 Hosea 2:21-22 is often recited at Jewish weddings.

◆ Design engagement greeting cards featuring these verses. Your class can sell these to raise money for *tzedakah,* and people can use them to announce or acknowledge an engagement.

27 We have learned in Insights from the Tradition #F, p. 509, that God wanted to make it easier for Israel to repent. Perhaps we, too, should make it easier for people to apologize after wrongdoings.

◆ Write a letter to Dear Abby about a real or fictional time when a friend hurt you. Then write Abby's advice back to you. Will she advise you to help your friend apologize?

28 Hosea explores what it is like to have a bad marriage.

◆ Write ten rules for a good marriage.

29 Verses 2:21-22 are recited when a Jew puts on *tefillin* for morning services.

◆ Make a poster that can be set up in your synagogue's sanctuary during weekday morning services. The sign could include verses 2:21-

22 in Hebrew and English, along with instructions for wrapping *tefillin* around one's hand, and an artistic interpretation of the verses.

◆ Also consider including a *kavanah* (a reading to help the worshiper focus attention). *Siddur Mikor Hayyim* uses the following *kavanah:*

"May I be bound to the universe, doing the right thing, kindness, caring, faith, and the experience of God."

◆ For more on *kavanot* in prayer, see *Siddur Mikor Hayyim: The Source of Life,* written by Henry M. Shreibman for Brandeis Hillel Day School of San Francisco and San Rafael.

Other Resources

30 Read and discuss the classic book *The Scarlet Letter* by Nathaniel Hawthorne, which portrays how an accused adulteress is treated in Puritan America.

31 Elvis Presley performed a song called "Walk a Mile in My Shoes," which is what God seems to ask of Hosea. Read the lyrics of the song and discuss its message in class. The song may be found on the recording *Live in Las Vegas* by Elvis Presley. The lyrics may be found online at www.members.tripod.com/supermpx/ elvis_presley/w541.htm.

32 In this Haftarah Hosea rebukes Israel for its infidelity toward God. For more information and exercises pertaining to the Jewish view of rebuking, see *Teaching Jewish Virtues* by Susan Freeman, pp. 318-331.

33 Hirsch teaches in Insights from the Tradition #H, p. 510, that our relationships with God can be made lasting and permanent only when we show concern for our fellow people and control our own selfishness. Read and discuss the story, "The Princess Who Wanted to See God" in *Who Knows Ten?: Children's Tales of the Ten Commandments* by Molly Cone, pp. 14-20.

34 Read and discuss portions of *Tefillin* by Aryeh Kaplan, which explores the many significances and mysteries of *tefillin*. The book includes an illustrated explanation of how to wear *tefillin*.

35 Read and discuss the chapter on Hosea in *Messengers of God: A Jewish Prophets Who's Who* by Ronald H. Isaacs, pp. 135-140.

36 Discuss the illustration of this Haftarah in *The Illustrated Torah* by Michal Meron, p. 146. How does the artist depict the idea that God will banish bow, sword, and war?

37 For a commentary, discussion questions, and project, see the UAHC Family Shabbat Table Talk web site at www.uahc.org/shabbat/stt/3bamidbar.shtml.

38 For a *D'var Torah* on this Haftarah, see the web site for the Fuchsberg Center for Conservative Judaism in Jerusalem at www.uscj.org.il/haftarah/bemidbar5761.html.

Involving the Family

39 May all your family's marriages be good ones. Create a family *chupah* from a *tallit* or any fabric to be used at future family weddings. You can use embroidery, fabric paints, silk-screening, quilting, or other fabric techniques to create a special family heirloom. Consider featuring family wedding dates and adding new ones as they occur.

Bar/Bat Mitzvah Projects

40 Women are often the victims of violence by men who suspect them of wrongdoing. Collect clothes and toiletries to donate to a local battered women's shelter.

41 Learn to use makeup for a *mitzvah* (see Extending the Text #14, p. 514).

HOSEA 11:7-12:12
VAYISHLACH וישלח Some Ashkenazim
VAYAYTZAY ויצא Sephardim

This Haftarah has been paired with *Parashat Vayishlach*, Genesis 32:4-36:43 or *Parashat Vayaytzay*, Genesis 28:10-32:3. See "Connecting the Text To the Sedra," pp. 521-523, for an exploration of the many ways the texts shed light on each other.

previous Haftarah). The prophet who wrote this Haftarah is thought to have lived during the second half of the eighth century B.C.E., but before 725 B.C.E., when it became clear that Assyria, not Egypt, was the more serious threat to Israel's survival.

SYNOPSIS

As the Haftarah begins, Hosea explains that despite Israel's persistent rebellion against God, God remains tenderhearted toward Israel. It is not God's wish to destroy Israel, although it may happen. However, one day, Israel will learn to follow God's path. On that day, all Israelites, who may have been scattered into exile, will be gathered from abroad and resettled in their homes in the Land of Israel.

Hosea continues by discussing the sinfulness of Ephraim (which is another name for the Northern Kingdom of Israel). They are faulted for making alliances with Assyria and Egypt. They have also cheated to gain wealth. Hosea recalls that our forefather Jacob (who is equated with the Southern Kingdom of Judah) cheated his brother and wrestled with an angel until the angel had to cry for mercy.

The Haftarah concludes in verse 12:12 with the warning that the idolaters in Gilead and Gilgal will be punished.

Many scholars believe that the prophet who wrote chapters 4-14 of the Book of Hosea (including this Haftarah) lived later than the prophet who wrote the first three chapters of the book (i.e., the

INSIGHTS FROM THE TRADITION

A Regarding verse 11:9, Radak says that God is the opposite of people: people cannot control their anger and have little patience, but God is slow to anger and has much patience. Furthermore, unlike people, God never goes back on a promise, even if we sin and do not deserve fulfillment of God's promise.

- When is it most difficult for you to control your anger?

- How might you teach someone to control his or her anger?

- When is it most difficult for you to be patient?

- Who is the most patient person you know? Is this person a role model for you?

- Discuss reasons why it might not be possible for people always to keep their promises.

B Concerning verse 12:4, Hirsch explains that because the people worshiped their possessions and wealth, they forgot their role as descendants of Jacob. Jacob had received everything from God for the purpose of living morally, spiritually, and observing God's laws.

◆ Wealth, it seems, can be a means for good or for bad.

◆ In what ways do you think wealth leads to sinful behavior?

◆ In what ways do you think wealth enables morally positive actions?

◆ Identify one famous, rich person who used his or her money in admirable ways. Identify one famous, rich person whose money led them into trouble.

C Hosea says in verse 12:11 that God speaks in parables through the prophets. Rashi explains that this means that God appears in different forms or likenesses at different times. Rashi's explanation is based on the *midrash* from *Pesikta Rabbati*, which offers examples: at the Sea of Reeds, God appeared as a mighty warrior, but on Mount Sinai God appeared as an elder teaching Torah.

◆ Why might God appear differently to different people and at different times?

◆ Do you ever want to appear a certain way in one setting and another way in a different setting? If so, why?

◆ How do you picture God? Is your image of God always the same?

◆ Use disposable cameras to photograph what you see as different images of God in your world. Mount the photos in a display for your class or school.

D In verse 12:12 Hosea says the Israelites worshiped false gods on altars that were like "stone heaps upon a plowed field." *Lamentations Rabbah* (Proem 22) teaches that at first the Israelites worshiped idols in secret. When no one stopped them, they began worshiping idols in the open, although behind closed doors. Since they were still not prevented from worshiping idols, they began worshiping them on their rooftops.

Since they were not stopped, they began worshiping idols in their gardens, and then on mountaintops, and then even in the fields that they plowed for their crops — every furrow had an image on it.

◆ How does behavior such as lying, stealing, and cheating become easier each time you do it?

◆ How might you help to stop a friend who is in the habit of lying, stealing, or cheating?

STRATEGIES
Analyzing the Text

1 Throughout the Haftarah Hosea refers to the Northern Kingdom of Israel as Ephraim. This is because the tribe of Ephraim was the dominant tribe of the kingdom.

◆ Look at the tribal map on p. 624. List the ten tribes that comprised the Northern Kingdom.

◆ Make a jigsaw puzzle out of cardboard based on this map.

2 In verse 11:8 God is apparently ambivalent about how to act.

◆ Explain how this verse expresses God's uncertainty or indecision about how to act.

The cities of Admah and Zeboiim, mentioned by Hosea in 11:8, seem to be associated with Sodom and Gomorrah, which were destroyed by God (see Genesis 19) for their sinfulness.

◆ According to verse 11:8, God is ambivalent about inflicting the fate of Sodom and Gomorrah on Israel. Discuss the following explanations and any others you can add. Which do you think best explains God's ambivalence? Explain your choice(s).

• God's desire for executing strict justice seems to be fighting with God's desire to be merciful.

- God has strong, personal, and emotional connections to Israel as a parent and to Ephraim as a guide (verses 11:1-2, before the Haftarah begins).

- God feels great sorrow.

- God feels pity and compassion for those who would suffer as a result of the violence caused by God's anger.

- God is disappointed with Israel, but hopeful for the future.

- God doesn't want to hurt the innocent along with the guilty.

3 In verses 11:10-11 *Adonai* is portrayed as a lion with a thundering roar, while the Israelites are described as fluttering sparrows and doves.

- What does the image of a fluttering, trembling bird convey to you? (Examples might be timid, fearful of angering God again, subdued.)

- There is a sharp contrast in power and control. Explain the meaning of this contrast in the description of Israel returning home from exile.

- Write a poem or draw a picture employing these images.

4 In verse 12:2 Ephraim is said to shepherd (tend) a flock in the gale (literally, in the east wind which brings the Land of Israel its worst weather).

Ephraim is also accused of lying (illusion) and bringing calamity.

- What does the metaphor of a shepherd taking his flock out in bad weather mean to you?

- Explain how this metaphor might connect to leaders who lie and cause destruction.

5 In verse 12:1 God claims that Ephraim surrounded God with deceit, but it is unclear exactly what Ephraim did.

- Read verses 12:8-9 and describe the types of deceptions in which Ephraim seems to have engaged.

- In how many ways do the people of Ephraim deceive themselves?

- Debate which is worse: lying to others or lying to oneself?

Connecting the Text To the Sedra

6 This Haftarah is read by some Ashkenazim for *Parashat Vayishlach*. Other Ashkenazim recite Obadiah 1:1-21. Sephardim also use Obadiah 1:1-21 as the Haftarah for this Sedra.

- Read Obadiah 1:1-21 (see p. 560), and compare its content and message with that of Hosea 11:7-12:12. Which Haftarah reading do you prefer to complement *Parashat Vayishlach*, and why?

7 According to Hosea, God will call the exiled Israelites from exile to return to their Land (verses 11:10-11). (Note that Hosea, who prophesied before the exile, is assuming that exile will occur either in Egypt or Assyria. See also Hosea 11:5.)

In *Parashat Vayishlach*, Jacob returns to the Land of Israel from Haran where he had lived with Laban after running away from his offended brother (Genesis 32:10). Jacob is returning because God told him to return.

Sephardim read this Haftarah for *Parashat Vayaytzay*. Before Jacob leaves the Land, God promises in Genesis 28:15 to bring him back to the Land, which God does in Genesis 31:3.

- How is exile or banishment a punishment?

- When a child is punished by being sent to his/her room, from what is the child being banished?

- Why must the person banished wait for permission to return?

- Play the game *Mother May I,* in which participants must get permission before taking each step.

8 Hosea says in verse 12:3 that Jacob was punished according to his deeds.

In much of Jacob's story (of which *Parashat Vayishlach* is part), he is paid back measure for measure for his own deeds. For example, Jacob lies to his father by putting goats skins on to imitate his brother Esau; later Jacob's own sons lie to him about Joseph, using goat blood on Joseph's coat. Jacob cheats his brother out of his birthright; later Laban cheats Jacob out of the wife he wants.

- Does measure for measure punishment make sense to you? Is it an indication of a just world? Does it serve as a more potent reminder of the misbehavior?

- Explain how in the Haftarah being destroyed and taken into exile to Assyria and Egypt (see verse 11:11) are measure for measure punishments for making a covenant with Assyria and Egypt against God's wishes.

- Can you find other examples of measure for measure punishment in the Haftarah?

- Determine an appropriate punishment for such "crimes" as talking out of turn, cheating on a test, shoplifting, or not returning overdue library books. Try to choose punishments that fit the crime.

- How might your punishments prevent someone from committing the same crimes again?

9 In *Parashat Vayishlach* Jacob struggles with an angel, triumphs, and is renamed Israel.

- The Parashah portrays this event in a positive light. Read Genesis 35:11-12, which describes the blessing bestowed on Jacob/Israel immediately after the wrestling and his name change. According to the Sedra, Jacob/Israel seems to be destined for blessing and greatness as God's people.

- In the Haftarah, however, Hosea cites this scene as evidence of God's dissatisfaction with Jacob and his punishment of him. Explain how in verses 12:3-5 Hosea seems to view Jacob's struggle with the angel in a negative way.

- Write an article covering this dramatic event of Jacob wrestling with the angel. Choose to write a positive portrayal for the *Genesis Gazette* or a negative story for the *Hosea Times.*

10 In Genesis 32:11 Jacob says he is not worthy of God's kindness and loyalty. This same idea is in the Haftarah — Israel continues to be unworthy of God's abounding mercy (see verse 11:9, which indicates that God has been provoked, but controls God's temper).

God's abundant mercy is the subject of much discussion in the Jewish tradition. On Pesach, Shavuot, Sukkot, Rosh HaShanah, and Yom Kippur, we recite God's Thirteen Attributes during the morning service as follows:

"Adonai, Adonai, God, Compassionate and Gracious. Slow to anger and Abundant in kindness and truth. Preserver of kindness for thousands of generations, Forgiver of iniquity, willful sin, and error, and One Who Cleanses."

- This prayer is taken from Exodus 34:6-7. Explain in your own words the attributes of God listed in this prayer. Compare these attributes to Hosea 11:9. Are there other verses you think state similar ideas?

◆ Why is it important that God have these attributes?

◆ Do you share any of these attributes?

◆ Ask your Cantor to teach your class to sing these attributes of mercy as they are sung in the Torah Service of our Festivals.

11 Beth El, meaning the House of God, is mentioned in *Parashat Vayishlach* in Genesis 35:1, 3, and is also mentioned in Hosea 12:5. It is mentioned, too, in *Parashat Vayaytzay* (for which Sephardim read this Haftarah) in Genesis 28:19 and 31:13.

◆ What does the name Beth El symbolize in the Haftarah and in the Sedra?

◆ Beth El happens to be a popular name for synagogues. What does the name symbolize when used for a congregation?

◆ Design a logo for a synagogue named Beth El (or for your synagogue) that represents the meaning of its name.

12 Jacob kisses Rachel and weeps in Genesis 29:11 *(Parashat Vayaytzay)*. Jacob hugs his brother and they both weep in Genesis 33:4 *(Parashat Vayishlach)*.

In the Haftarah it is recalled that Jacob fought with the angel and wept (Hosea 12:3-5). However, in verse 12:5 in the Hebrew, it is unclear as to who is doing the weeping. Hertz says it was Jacob. Rashi says it was the angel.

◆ With which interpretation does the JPS translation seem to agree?

◆ Do you agree with the JPS interpretation? Why or why not?

◆ Why do you think that Jacob or the angel was crying? (For example, do they cry in anger, pain, grief, or for forgiveness?)

13 Genesis 33:18-20 mentions that Jacob spread his tent.

◆ Reread these verses.

◆ Describe Jacob's act of pitching his tent. (Did he buy the land he used or was he trespassing, did he have family there or was he a stranger, did he come with aggressive intent or in peace?)

◆ The Haftarah indicates in verse 12:10 that the Israelites will again live in tents. Do you think that Hosea's prediction of living in tents promises a reward or punishment?

◆ Organize a class overnight camping trip to learn first-hand what it is like to live in a tent.

◆ What do you like best and least about living in a tent?

Extending the Text

14 The name of Israel's national airline can be found in this Haftarah.

◆ Race with your classmates to see who can find it first. (*"El Al"* appears in verse 11:7).

◆ What does the name El Al mean?

◆ Review these key events in the history of El Al:

• El Al's inaugural flight brought the country's first president, Chaim Weizman, home from Geneva in September 1948.

• In June 1961, El Al made its first non-stop New York/Tel Aviv flight on a Boeing 707. This flight set the world record for the longest non-stop commercial flight, covering 5,760 statute miles in 9 hours, 33 minutes.

- In March 1984, El Al recorded the first international Boeing 767 flight — Montreal/Tel Aviv.

- In May 1988, El Al operated its longest non-stop flight in history: Los Angeles/ Tel Aviv: 7,000 statute miles in 13 hours, 41 minutes.

- On May 24, 1991, an El Al Boeing 747 airlifted a record-breaking 1,087 passengers — Ethiopian Jews, flying from Addis Ababa to Israel as part of Operation Solomon.

◆ For a video clip or more information about Israel's airline, go to their web site at www.elal.co.il.

15 We learned above in Insights from the Tradition #C, p. 520, that God assumes different appearances in visions to the prophets.

◆ Match the following apparitions with the prophets who perceived them:

1. God sitting on a high throne (b)
2. Man of war (f)
3. A forgiving husband (d)
4. Burning bush (a)
5. A smelter (e)
6. Radiance (c)

a. Moses (Exodus 3:2)
b. Isaiah (Isaiah 6:1)
c. Ezekiel (Ezekiel 1:28)
d. Hosea (Hosea 2:16-22)
e. Jeremiah (Jeremiah 9:6)
f. Miriam (Exodus 15:3)

◆ Choose one of these prophetic apparitions to illustrate with an abstract painting.

16 Hosea condemns traders who deal dishonestly by using false scales to deceive other people (verse 12:8).

Deuteronomy 25:13-16 states, "You shall not have in your pouch alternate weights, larger and smaller. You shall not have in your house alternate measures, a larger and a smaller. You must have completely honest weights and completely honest measures, if you are to endure long on the soil that *Adonai* your God is giving you. For everyone who does those things, everyone who deals dishonestly, is abhorrent to *Adonai* your God."

◆ What is wrong with having alternate (i.e., inconsistent) weights?

◆ According to Hirsch, people who use alternate weights have lost all sense of right and wrong. Why do you think Hirsch teaches this?

◆ Explain how having different weights erodes trust between people and primarily hurts the weaker members of society.

◆ Interview your parents to see if they have ever been the victims of deceptive business practices. Ask them in what ways they were hurt by this deception, and what, if anything, they did about it.

17 In verse 11:11 Hosea says that all Israelites will one day return like birds to their home in Israel.

In the tenth blessing of the weekday *"Amidah,"* we pray for the ingathering of all Jewish exiles to the Land of Israel: "Sound the great *shofar* for our freedom, raise the banner to gather our exiles and gather us together from the four corners of the earth. Blessed are You, *Adonai*, Who gathers in the dispersed of Your people Israel."

◆ Explain in your own words what this prayer means. What does it mean to you as a Jew living in a free country?

◆ How does the prayer express the Jewish longing to live in Israel?

◆ Does the role of the *shofar* in this parallel the roar of the lion in the Haftarah? Explain your answer.

◆ Design an illustration to accompany this prayer in a *Siddur*.

18 Hosea says that God speaks in parables to the prophets. Parables are often effective ways to get a message across to the audience.

◆ Read the following folktale and parable (two versions of it can be found in *Chosen Tales*, edited by Peninnah Schram):

A flock of eagles, flying high over the land, were able to look down at the forests, mountains, river, and lakes. Suddenly one eagle was injured and realized he would have to land quickly. He landed in a chicken coop.

He was stunned by what he saw. As an eagle, he thought all birds soared through the sky and hunted prey. But the chickens did not fly. They just flapped their wings and hopped. And they did not hunt for food, but pecked in the dirt for food. The lonely eagle stayed by himself in a corner and waited to recover so he could rejoin the other eagles.

But soon the eagle began to talk with the chickens in the coop. He began to imitate his neighbors. He grew comfortable and remained with the chickens, even after his wing had healed. A whole year passed, and the original flock of eagles with which the injured eagle flew was again flying over that same area of the land. One of the flying eagles looked down into the chicken coop and, recognizing his fellow eagle who had been injured the previous year, descended and landed next to him in the coop. But the eagle in the coop — though he looked like an eagle — acted just like a chicken, flapping his wings and hopping and pecking in the ground for his food.

The visiting eagle reminded the once injured bird that he was an eagle who belonged high in the sky with the other eagles. But the first eagle had forgotten about his past and said that he belonged right where he was — in the chicken coop.

The second eagle began to teach the first eagle about what it was like to be an eagle. After many days, the once injured eagle remembered who he really was. The two eagles soared off together high into the sky, where eagles belong.

◆ What do you think is the meaning of this parable?

◆ Do you think the parable is effective in teaching a lesson about Jewish identity, assimilation, and community?

◆ In the Haftarah (verse 12:11), God speaks in parables through the prophets. Explain why a parable might communicate a lesson better than just stating the lesson.

◆ Make puppets, then prepare a puppet show of this story to present to the younger students in your school. Facilitate a discussion after the show.

Personalizing the Text

19 God does not want to destroy Israel as Sodom and Gomorrah had been destroyed (verse 11:8). Abraham argued with God against the destruction of Sodom and Gomorrah.

◆ Imagine you are Hosea and list five reasons to convince God that Israel should be spared.

20 In Genesis 32:23-33 Jacob wrestles with the angel.

◆ Reread this story, then draw or paint your interpretation of the scene. Does your artwork reflect a positive or negative view of Jacob? Explain.

21 We have already learned that God spoke to the prophets in ways that could be understood by them (see Insights from the Tradition #C, p. 520). *Exodus Rabbah* 3:1 tells the story of how God decided how to speak to Moses. "If I reveal Myself to Moses in loud tones, I shall alarm him, but if I reveal Myself with a subdued voice, he will not take his prophecy seriously." So God decided to address Moses in his father Amram's voice. Moses was overjoyed to hear his father speak, for it gave him the assurance that his father was still alive.

◆ Explain God's reasoning.

◆ If God were to speak to you, whose voice do you think you would hear, and why?

◆ Act out a scene in which God speaks to you in a familiar and comforting voice.

22 Hosea decries the use of false scales to deceive people (verse 12:8).

◆ Interview a grocer, butcher, jeweler, or other businessperson who is affected by the rule of honest weights. Find out their view of the importance of this rule in business.

23 Hosea's name means "salvation."

◆ Why do you think this is an appropriate name for Hosea?

◆ Make your name into an acrostic, using each letter to begin a one-word description of yourself. If your name is Andy, for example, your acrostic might include A for affectionate, N for nice, D for daring, and Y for youthful.

24 Living in the Land of Israel is clearly an important theme in the Bible and Jewish history (see, for example, Hosea 11:10-11). It is considered to be the greatest of all *mitzvot*.

◆ Hold a class debate on whether or not it should be a goal of all Jews throughout the world to live in Israel.

◆ Alternatively, invite someone who has lived in Israel, or lives there now, to speak to your class about what life is like there.

Other Resources

25 God appears in different ways to different prophets. View and discuss the various presentations of God in the *Oh, God!* film trilogy: *Oh God!* (1977, rated PG, 98 minutes); *Oh, God! Book 2* (1980, rated PG, 94 minutes); and *Oh, God! You Devil* (1984, rated PG, 96 minutes).

26 Read and discuss the chapter on Hosea in *Messengers of God: A Jewish Prophets Who's Who* by Ronald H. Isaacs, pp. 135-140.

27 Discuss the illustration of this Haftarah in *The Illustrated Torah* by Michal Meron, pp. 40 and 44.

28 See the book *Welcome To Israel!* by Lilly Rivlin with Gila Gevirtz for a nice introduction to the history, geography, and everyday life in Israel.

29 See *Encyclopaedia Judaica*, vol. 8, pp. 1010-1024, for an article about Hosea. What did you learn from the article that was new to you? Report on this article to the class.

30 For a commentary, discussion questions, and project, see the UAHC Family Shabbat Table Talk web site at www.uahc.org/shabbat/stt/3vayishlach.shtml.

Involving the Family

31 Institute a system of keeping track of times when family members exercise patience and understanding with one another. For example, make a chart. Each week at Shabbat dinner, award a prize to the person who has shown the most patience that week.

Bar/Bat Mitzvah Project

32 We all slip and utter little lies now and then. We learned in Insights from the Tradition #D, p. 520, that the more often lying goes undetected, the easier it becomes to lie and the more we are likely to do it. Keep a log of all the times you utter even the smallest lie. See if keeping a log helps you detect your lies and reduce their frequency.

HOSEA 12:13-14:10
VAYAYTZAY וייצא Ashkenazim

This Haftarah has been paired with *Parashat Vayaytzay*, Genesis 28:10-32:3. See "Connecting the Text To the Sedra," pp. 530-533, for an exploration of the many ways the two texts shed light on each other.

SYNOPSIS

Preaching in eighth century Northern Israel, Hosea tirelessly urges the people to change their evil ways and avert disastrous punishment from God.

The Haftarah begins with a little history. Hosea recalls how God helped Jacob to prosper in Aram and how God helped Moses to lead the Israelites out of slavery in Egypt. He suggests by this recollection that God can help Israel, too.

Yet the Northern Kingdom of Israel (called Ephraim by Hosea) is in grave danger of losing God's support because it continues to sin and worship idols.

Hosea reminds the people in verses 13:4-13 that only *Adonai* has ever been their true God, Who freed them from Egypt and protected them in the wilderness. However, once the people were settled and grew prosperous in their Land — which God gave them — they became arrogant and forgot about God.

Now Israel faces trouble from its enemy to the east (Assyria), but God will not save them. Instead, God will allow them to be severely punished for their betrayal.

In the end, however, Hosea reminds the people that repentance and renewed loyalty to *Adonai* will still spare them from their terrible fate. If Israel returns to *Adonai*, they will be rewarded with peace and prosperity.

INSIGHTS FROM THE TRADITION

A Hosea refers to Jacob's stay in Aram in verse 12:13. Radak explains that even though Jacob was compelled to work for Laban to marry his daughters, God remained with him and blessed him with great prosperity.

◆ Sometimes it may be difficult to see that our hard work can ultimately pay off in great reward. Imagine how Jacob, who had to work 14 long years for his father-in-law so as to marry Rachel, might have felt.

◆ Can you think of something you have had to work very hard to achieve?

◆ What kept you going when you doubted if you would ever succeed?

B Hosea says in verse 13:2 that the Israelites have a tendency to kiss calves. Ibn Ezra explains that this is a proverbial expression. Righteous people kiss humans and slaughter calves, but these wicked people slaughter humans and kiss calves!

◆ What is Ibn Ezra trying to demonstrate with this expression? Do you think he meant it literally?

◆ In your own words, how would you describe people who valued property above human beings?

C Regarding verse 13:15, Abrabanel says that Israel flourished when he was with his brothers, but suffered when he was separated from his brothers.

◆ Do you think it is easier to live a Jewish life when you are part of a Jewish community?

◆ What do you think would be most difficult about being Jewish if you lived apart from any Jewish community?

D The fragrance of Lebanon mentioned in verse 14:7 is due to the fact that Lebanon is blessed with many aromatic trees and herbs. Just as their fragrance travels, explains Radak, so will the reputation of Israel travel far and wide among the nations of the world.

◆ Why do reputations "travel"? Is this a good thing, a bad thing, or both?

◆ Describe what you think is the reputation of Israel and the Jewish people in the world today. Is the reputation primarily positive or negative, and why?

E Hosea says in verse 14:8 that Israel shall blossom like the vine. Radak points out that unlike annual plants that dry up after a harvest, vines continue to produce fruit year after year. Just as vines flourish incessantly, so, too, will Israel prosper and flourish indefinitely.

◆ What do you think enables the Jewish people to survive, like a vine, year after year?

STRATEGIES
Analyzing the Text

1 Hosea says in verse 12:14 that when God brought Israel from Egypt, it was through a prophet (Moses). Hosea continues by saying that through (another) prophet, they were guarded. Commentators disagree about who this other

prophet might have been. Some argue it was Samuel and others say it was Elijah.

◆ To which prophet do you think Hosea is referring?

◆ Review Jeremiah 15:1, Hosea 13:10-11, and material on Samuel and Elijah either in the *Encyclopaedia Judaica* or in *Messengers of God: A Jewish Prophets Who's Who* by Ronald H. Isaacs. Discuss whether, in your opinion, the other prophet was Samuel or Elijah.

2 Verse 13:1 refers to the time Ephraim incurred guilt through *Baal*. This is a reference is to the events of Baal-peor, recorded in Numbers 25:1-9.

◆ Read and discuss those disturbing events.

3 Idols and false gods are described by Hosea in verse 13:3 as morning clouds, early morning dew, chaff on the threshing floor, and smoke.

◆ What message do all of these images convey about the permanence of idols?

◆ Using pastels or watercolors, create an abstract picture that also conveys this idea of transience and impermanence.

4 God is described in verse 13:7-8 as a devouring lion, a lurking leopard, and a vengeful bear.

◆ What do these images suggest?

◆ Why, according to verse 13:6, has God changed from Israel's protector to Israel's attacker?

◆ In which of these ways (protector or attacker) do you generally think of God, and why?

5 Mentioned in verse 14:1, Samaria was the capital of the Northern Kingdom of Israel.

◆ Locate Samaria on a map of ancient Israel.

◆ What is the capital of the State of Israel today?

◆ Learn the cities of modern Israel. Then, hold a class geography bee.

6 Israel is compared in verses 14:6-8 to a lily, a cedar tree, an olive tree, and a vine. A lily symbolizes beauty and fragrance, a cedar represents majesty and strength, olive trees symbolize longevity and endurance, and vines represent fertility.

◆ Which comparison do you like best, and why?

◆ Find out what your state tree or flower is, and why it was chosen.

Connecting the Text To the Sedra

7 Hosea (verse 12:13) refers to Jacob's need to flee from his home and sojourn in Aram where he earned his wives by guarding (the Hebrew root שמר) sheep.

The Haftarah (verse 12:14) continues by saying that God assigned prophets to guard (the same Hebrew root שמר) Israel when they came up from Egypt and when they lived in Israel.

In Genesis 27 we learn that Jacob had to flee his home because his brother wanted to kill him for having stolen his blessing. As the Sedra opens, Jacob asks God to provide for his needs, be with him, guard him (the Hebrew root שמר) and help him come back in peace (Genesis 28:15, 20, also 31:29).

◆ Consider this difference between the Haftarah and the Sedra: in the Sedra, God guarded Jacob, but in the Haftarah prophets guarded Israel. Why was an intermediary doing the guarding in the Haftarah?

◆ Some scholars see a pattern starting in Genesis and continuing through the entire Bible: God's involvement in the lives of humans becomes more remote and less direct. What does this pattern mean to you?

◆ Do you consider God to be remote, or directly involved in history and/or in your life?

◆ Can you find other evidence in the Bible of this pattern?

8 Jacob found God a support and guide in hard times (Genesis 28:15). Israel was freed and guarded by God after their slavery in Egypt. Similarly, Hosea implores the Israelites to consider God their only source of help (verses 12:14 and 13:4, 9).

◆ Review the Haftarah for evidence that Israel had vainly tried relying on: false gods such as *Baal* and molten images, mortal kings and chieftains, and foreign nations.

◆ In what false hopes do modern day people put their trust?

◆ On whom can you always rely?

9 Idols are condemned by Hosea in verses 13:1-2. However, in Genesis 31:30ff. household gods appear in the story without outright condemnation. Laban, father of Rachel and Leah, owns idols. Rachel steals those idols to take with her when she leaves her father's house to move to Canaan. Her theft seems to be condemned by Jacob and Laban, but the ownership of those household idols itself does not seem to be condemned.

◆ Some scholars suggest that perhaps the name given to these idols (*terafim* in Hebrew) by the biblical author may have derogatory connotations. The name *terafim* may mean "inert thing" or it may mean "to decay and become foul" (Genesis 31:19). Explain how this is derogatory.

◆ When Laban refers to the idols, he calls them "gods" (Genesis 31:30), and when Jacob denies having them, he also calls them "gods." However, Jacob here is quoting Laban (Genesis 31:32). But when the biblical narrator again refers to them (Genesis 31:34, 35), they are called *terafim*. How can you explain the difference between Laban calling them "gods" and the narrator calling them "inert, foul and decaying things"?

◆ *Genesis Rabbah* 74:5 also seeks to condemn these household gods. This *midrash* says that the only reason Rachel stole the idols from her father was to prevent him from using them. Explain how this *midrash* both condemns Laban for owning idols and praises Rachel for taking them.

◆ It is unclear how household idols were used. They may have been considered personal protectors who would intercede with the gods on behalf of the owner. For more information on ancient household gods and to see some examples, go to the web site of the Biblical Archaelogy Society: http://bib-arch.org/barso00/idol.html, or see the related article in *Biblical Archaeology Review*, September 2000.

10 In the Sedra Jacob served seven years for Rachel (Genesis 29:20), but was given Leah instead. He then served seven more years for Rachel. Leah, Rachel, and their handmaids were the mothers of all Jacob's children, the ancestors of the entire people, the children of Israel.

The Haftarah begins by stating that Jacob served for one wife, and for another wife, he guarded. The Haftarah goes on to say that with one prophet God brought Israel out of Egypt, and another prophet guarded them (see Analyzing the Text #1, p. 529).

Prophets and wives seem to be described in parallel fashion. But the Haftarah seems to be comparing apples and oranges: how Jacob took wives, but not what the wives did for him is compared to what prophets did for God, but not how God acquired them. Let's compare what both the wives and prophets did:

Wives gave birth to the people. Moses the prophet helped "deliver" the children of Israel from slavery in Egypt and the other prophet "mothered" them until they developed into a nation.

◆ Explain how both wives and prophets were essential to the founding of the people (one as a birth mother and the other as an "adoptive mother").

◆ How does your image of a prophet change when you consider them through the metaphors of wives to God and mothers to Israel?

11 Following up on Connecting the Text To the Sedra #10, above, let's now compare how both the wives and prophets were acquired. Jacob immediately loved Rachel and was willing to serve her father to earn the right to marry her. Jacob acquired Rachel through servitude. In contrast, the prophets were called by God to serve God. Moses is often referred to as "the servant of God."

◆ Review the Sedra to see in what way Jacob "served" Rachel's father.

◆ Do you think there is a difference between serving out of love and serving because one was called?

◆ Jacob clearly had a reward for his service. What reward, if any, did the prophets receive for their service?

12 We learn in the Haftarah (verse 14:5) that if the prophet could convince Israel to stop sinning and repent, God would love Israel generously (נדבה — *nedavah*).

◆ What does the expression "love generously" mean to you?

◆ In the Sedra Jacob really loved Rachel, but poor Leah was not loved (Genesis 29:31). God, seeing that Leah was not loved, aided Leah in having children and prevented Rachel from having children. What do you think of God's intervention to help Leah be loved by Jacob?

◆ Why do you think God sympathized so strongly with Leah? Did God feel loved by Israel?

◆ When Leah had her first child, she gave him a name that meant "Behold a son." To Leah, this meant that her husband would see a son and then love her (Genesis 29:32). Is there evidence that Jacob loved Leah generously after receiving the child he wanted?

◆ Similarly, review verse 13:6 of the Haftarah to see how Israel responded after receiving from God everything they wanted.

◆ Why do you think people are not always satisfied or grateful when they receive what they want?

13 The Haftarah (verse 14:5) says that God will love Israel generously (*nedavah*). In the Sedra Laban objects to Jacob having left on the sly, and protests that if only Jacob had told him his plans, "I would have sent you off *b'simchah*." *B'simchah* is usually translated as "with joy." However, Bible scholar Yohanan Muffs has studied the use of *b'simchah* in ancient literature, Bible, and Rabbinic texts, and found that it means "with willingness, alacrity, enthusiasm, and generosity."

◆ The Haftarah's term *"nedavah"* (generously) and the Sedra's term *"b'simchah"* have very similar meanings. Does this new understanding of the word *b'simchah* change your opinion of Laban in the Sedra?

◆ Read the verse that appears in the morning prayers immediately before *"Mi Chamocha"*:

Moses and the children of Israel sang to you with great *simchah*: Who is like You, *Adonai*, among the mighty? Who is like You, glorious in holiness, revered in praises, doing wonders?

In this prayer, *"b'simchah"* is usually translated as "with joy." Substitute the other possible meanings for *b'simchah*. How does it change the meaning of the prayer?

◆ Act out the scene of the verse using different translations.

14 The word disgrace, חרפה (*chayrpah*), appears in the Sedra and in the Haftarah. In the Sedra Rachel has been childless and suffered shame for many years because of it. In Genesis 30:22-23 she finally has a child and says, "God has taken away my disgrace."

In the Haftarah, since Ephraim has brought disgrace upon God through Ephraim's sins, God will pay Ephraim back for the disgrace (note that JPS translates this word as "mockery" in 12:15 instead of disgrace).

◆ Why do you think it was disgraceful in biblical times for a woman not to be able to bear children?

◆ Do you think it is still disgraceful today when people cannot or choose not to have children?

◆ What does bring disgrace upon us today?

15 The word שובה (*shuvah*), meaning "return," appears in both the Haftarah and Sedra (see Hosea 14:2 and Genesis 28:15 and 21, 29:3, and 31:3 and 13).

The word שובה also forms the basis for the Hebrew word for "repentance." To repent, then, is to return. Interestingly, this implies that we who have sinned were once in the right place, but have since strayed.

◆ Do you think all people are created basically good?

◆ How do you think Judaism helps to guide us back to the right relationship with God?

16 Aram (mentioned in verse 12:13) was a group of states north of Israel during the eleventh to eighth centuries B.C.E. These states were frequently at war with Israel. Although the Aramean states disappeared, their language, Aramaic, became the popular language of the region from about the eighth century B.C.E. on. Eventually, many Jewish communities spoke primarily Aramaic, and no longer knew Hebrew well enough to understand their synagogue Torah reading. As a result Aramaic translations of the Torah readings, called *targumim*, developed. Aramaic was used in some of the later books of the Bible, such as Daniel and Ezra. Aramaic is also the language of the Talmud, Jewish legal documents (such as a *ketubah,* a marriage contract, and a *get*, a bill of divorce), and several parts of our liturgy (including the *"Kaddish"* and *"Chad Gad Ya"* in the Passover *Haggadah*).

Aramaic does not appear in the Torah (though it is used in other parts of the Bible), except in this Sedra. Read Genesis 31:47. Laban and Jacob both name a place; Jacob gives it a Hebrew name (גלעד, *Gal-ayd*), but Laban gives it an Aramaic name (יגר שהדותא — *Y'gar Sahaduta*).

◆ For a map and more information on Aram, see the *Encyclopaedia Judaica*, vol. 3, pp. 252-256.

◆ Learn to read and recite an Aramaic prayer, such as the "Reader's *Kaddish*" or *"Bay Anah Rachaytz"* in the Torah service.

Extending the Text

17 Hosea instructs the people in verse 14:3 to take their words and return to *Adonai*. According to Radak, this means that it is sincere words, not sacrifices, that are necessary for true repentance.

In the fifth blessing of the weekday *"Amidah,"* we pray that God will help us to repent and return to the ways of Torah:

"Bring us back to Your Torah, and bring us near, our Sovereign, to Your service, and influence us to return in perfect repentance before You. Blessed are You, *Adonai*, Who desires repentance."

In the next blessing, we strike our chest as we ask God to forgive us and pardon us:

"Forgive us, for we have erred; pardon us, our Sovereign, for we have willfully sinned; for You pardon and forgive. Blessed are You, *Adonai*, the gracious One, Who pardons abundantly."

◆ Explain why logically one would pray for help in repenting before one prays for forgiveness.

◆ Check the fourth prayer of the *"Amidah,"* in which we ask for knowledge and understanding. Why might we recite this blessing before the one asking for help in repenting?

◆ Learn to recite these blessings in Hebrew and English.

18 In verses 14:6-8 Israel is compared to a variety of trees and plants. Jewish tradition teaches us to recognize the gift of fragrant shrubs, trees, flowers, herbs, grasses, fruit, nuts, and spices.

◆ Learn the following blessings over fragrances (for the Hebrew, see *The Complete ArtScroll Siddur*, p. 225), and collect items over which to make them:

Upon smelling fragrances of unknown or non-vegetable origin, or of a blend of spices, say:

> Blessed are You, *Adonai* our God, Sovereign of the universe, Who creates species of fragrance.

Upon smelling fragrant shrubs and trees, or their flowers, say:

> Blessed are You, *Adonai* our God, Sovereign of the universe, Who creates fragrant trees.

Upon smelling fragrant herbs, grasses, or flowers, say:

> Blessed are You, *Adonai* our God, Sovereign of the universe, Who creates fragrant herbage.

Upon smelling fragrant edible fruit or nuts, say:

> Blessed are You, *Adonai* our God, Sovereign of the universe, Who places a good aroma into fruits.

◆ Plan a party in which you will have to say some or all of these blessings. For example, make a centerpiece of flowers or herbs or edible fruit, or hold your party outdoors under a fragrant tree. Also serve food at your party so you will have to say the blessings over a variety of foods. Check a *Siddur* for the appropriate blessings for the foods you will be serving.

19 Flowers mentioned in the Bible are described in the *Encyclopaedia Judaica*, vol. 6, pp. 1364-1368. The flora of the Land of Israel is described in vol. 9, pp. 220-225.

◆ Read both of these articles.

◆ Make a poster with illustrations of the flowers and trees you have learned about.

◆ Alternatively, make an illustrated poster of verse 14:8, and review the lesson found in Insights from the Tradition #E, p. 529.

20 The word *"shoshanah,"* which means "rose" or "lily," is mentioned in verse 14:6. Shoshanah is a popular Hebrew name.

◆ List other flowers that are used as first names in English or in Hebrew.

◆ Learn the Israeli song, *"Erev Shel Shoshanim"* (Evening of Roses), which may be found in *B'Kol Echad*, edited by Jeffrey Shiovitz, p. 106, and on the accompanying audiocassettes *Shirei B'Kol Echad*. Both can be ordered from the United Synagogue for Conservative Judaism at www.uscj.org/booksvc.

21 Hosea accuses the people of kissing calves. Then, as today, kissing was an act of homage.

◆ Which Jewish objects is it our custom to kiss? What do we demonstrate by kissing, for example, *tzitzit*, *mezuzah*, a *Sefer Torah*, or a *Siddur*?

◆ For more information, see *A Guide To Jewish Religious Practice* by Isaac Klein, pp. 5 and 29, or *The Jewish Book of Why* by Alfred Kolatch, p. 116.

Personalizing the Text

22 Israel is compared in verses 14:6-8 to a lily, a cedar tree, an olive tree, and a vine. Today, Israelis call themselves *sabras*, after a fruit that is prickly on the outside and sweet on the inside.

◆ Bring to class a fruit that best represents who you are, and discuss the reasons why it does. Then, make fruit salad and enjoy eating it!

23 According to Connecting the Text To the Sedra #12 and #13, p. 532, God is a role model for behavior that is done "generously" or with "willingness" and "enthusiasm."

◆ List three activities that you do generously and with willingness and enthusiasm that might not be easy things to do.

24 Hosea had a very difficult job. He raced against the clock to get his people to repent before it was too late.

◆ Play *Prophets Beat-the-Clock*. The teacher arranges stations around the classroom, each with an activity to be performed, such as tying your shoe, writing "Repent" on a poster, reciting a few verses from this Haftarah, putting on your coat, and so on. Take turns running the course and completing the activities, while the teacher records your time. The student who completes the course in the shortest amount of time wins a prize. Activities should call to mind a rushing prophet!

25 Hosea, like most prophets had a thankless job.

◆ Thank these prophets now. Have a "Most Popular Prophet" contest. Each student chooses a prophet to research. On a particular day, each comes to class dressed as his/her prophet. Each "campaigns" to be the most popular prophet for the students in another class, who can vote for their favorite.

For a list of non-literary prophets, see the *Encyclopaedia Judaica*, vol. 13, p. 1176.

Also see *Messengers of God: A Jewish Prophets Who's Who* by Ronald H. Isaacs.

26 The final verse of the Haftarah says, "For the paths of *Adonai* are smooth; The righteous can walk on them, While sinners stumble on them."

◆ Pantomime or choreograph this verse.

Other Resources

27 Read and discuss the chapter on Hosea in *Messengers of God: A Jewish Prophets Who's Who* by Ronald H. Isaacs, pp. 135-140.

28 Discuss the illustration of this Haftarah in *The Illustrated Torah* by Michal Meron, p. 40.

29 Hosea portrays a renewed Israel as a shady and fragrant cedar tree and olive tree. Trees are powerful symbols. Read and discuss *The Giving Tree* by Shel Silverstein.

30 See the section on Hosea in *The Gift of Wisdom: The Books of Prophets and Writings* by Steven F. Steinbock, pp. 124-127.

31 For a commentary, discussion questions, and project, see the UAHC Family Shabbat Table Talk web site at www.uahc.org/shabbat/stt/3vayetze.html.

32 For a *D'var Torah* on this Haftarah, see the web site of the Fuchsberg Center for Conservative Judaism in Jerusalem, www.uscj.org.il/haftarah/vayatze5762.html.

Involving the Family

33 This Haftarah makes reference to Israeli flowers and plants. Each week, place fresh flowers on your Shabbat table and try to serve some fruit or vegetable that has been grown in Israel (available in most supermarkets).

34 Have a family discussion based on Insights from the Tradition #C, pp. 528-529. What were the main reasons you/your parents decided to live in your area? Was the type of Jewish community part of your decision? Are you satisfied with your community's Jewish life? Would you be more involved Jewishly if you lived somewhere else?

Bar/Bat Mitzvah Projects

35 Donate the floral arrangements you have at your Bar or Bat Mitzvah to a local hospital or nursing home. Alternatively, we learned in Insights from the Tradition #E, p. 529, that Israel would flourish year after year, like a perennial vine. Plant perennial flowers or bulbs in a garden at a local nursing home.

36 Act with *simchah* concerning your upcoming *simchah* (see Connecting the Text To the Sedra #13, p. 532). For the year leading up to your Bar/Bat Mitzvah, approach all aspects of your studies and synagogue participation with willingness, alacrity, and enthusiasm.

HOSEA 14:2-10 and
MICAH 7:18-20 and/or
JOEL 2:15-27
SHABBAT SHUVAH

 This Haftarah has been paired with *Shabbat Shuvah*, on which we read either Deuteronomy 31 or 32. See "Connecting the Text To the Special Shabbat," pp. 539-541, for an exploration of the many ways the texts and special Shabbat shed light on each other.

SYNOPSIS

The Haftarah for *Shabbat Shuvah* comprises the last part of the previous Haftarah and additional verses from Joel and/or Micah. Customs vary as to whether one reads all three prophets or just Hosea plus one of the other two.

Hosea preached in Northern Israel in the years before the destruction of that Kingdom by its enemy to the north, Assyria (i.e., eighth century B.C.E.). As this Haftarah opens, Hosea pleads with Israel to return to *Adonai* and ask for forgiveness for their sins. He begs them to recognize that salvation will not come from neighboring nations, but only from *Adonai*. *Adonai* will be like dew that will cause Israel to bloom. Israel, in turn, will cast aside its idols and look to God for sustenance.

Micah, who lived around the same time as Hosea, tells the Israelites that God is ready to forgive iniquity and receive the people in love, honoring the promise God made to Jacob and Abraham.

Joel adds a message of hope and compassion. It is unclear when Joel lived; he may have been a con-

temporary of Hosea and Micah, but some scholars suggest that Joel preached after the people had returned to Judea from exile in Babylonia (sixth century B.C.E.). In any case, Joel instructs the people to sound the *shofar*, assemble for a fast day, and ask God for pity. Apparently, the people responded to his request, for Joel reports that when the people returned to *Adonai*, *Adonai* blessed the people with new grain, wine, and oil in abundance. Joel also promises that *Adonai* will save the Israelites from the northerner and from swarms of locusts that have devastated them. (The swarms of locusts from the north are usually interpreted to be Assyria or Babylonia.) Finally, Joel promises that God will spare Israel from future humiliation.

Note: See the previous Haftarah for additional items from Insights from the Tradition, Analyzing the Text, Extending the Text, and Personalizing the Text topics that also apply to this Haftarah.

INSIGHTS FROM THE TRADITION

A "Take words with you," says Hosea in verse 14:3. Radak explains that God does not require gifts of sacrifices, but rather sincere confession and penitent words.

◆ What words do you "take with you" when you apologize to someone? When you apologize, do you bring a gift as well?

◆ How does Hosea's advice help to prepare us for the High Holy Days?

B In Joel 2:17 the prophet asks God not to let Israel become a mockery. Radak explains that if there were a famine in Israel, Israelites would search for food in other nations, where they would be subjugated and subject to derision and mockery.

Ibn Ezra adds that if the Israelites had no food, they would be in a weakened state and susceptible to attack and defeat by other nations, who would make a mockery of the defenseless Israelites.

◆ Explain how being hungry and not having money to buy food would be humiliating.

◆ At the web site www.actsofkindness.org, suggestions are made for acts of kindness that one person can do for another. One suggestion is to give money to someone at school who is hungry and forgot his/her lunch or lunch money. But that's not all; also make light of it to ease the tension and lessen the humiliation. What other ways might you go about easing the tension and reducing the embarrassment?

C The word "northerner," the enemy, in Joel 2:20 has been explained in a variety of different ways. For example, the Hebrew word for northerner can also mean "hidden." *Sukkah* 52a associates this word with our own hidden, evil inclinations.

◆ How do our secret thoughts sometimes get us into trouble?

STRATEGIES
Analyzing the Text

1 In Micah 7:18 the question is asked, "Who is a God like You, forgiving iniquity?" According to some commentators, the speaker is the prophet praising God.

However, Ibn Ezra believes the speaker may be the other nations of the world watching as Israel is returned from exile. He also suggests that the speaker may be the grateful exiles themselves praising God.

◆ Based on your understanding of Micah 7:18-20, which explanation do you prefer, and why?

◆ Which explanation do you prefer when you read Hosea 14:2-10 and Micah 7:18-20 together? Explain your choice.

◆ For further study, you may wish to find the other places in the Bible where similar questions are asked about God's uniqueness: Exodus 15:11; Psalms 35:10, 71:19, 77:14, 89:9, 113:5; and Job 36:22.

2 Different types of sins are mentioned in Micah 7:18-19. Iniquity, עָוֹן *(avone),* in verse 7:18 is considered to be an intentional sin. Transgression, פֶּשַׁע *(pesha),* in verse 7:18 is also intentional, but implies rebelliousness in the sinful act. The word חֵטְא *(chayt)* in verse 7:19 means "unintentional sin."

◆ Give examples of the three different kinds of sins.

◆ Rate the sins in order of severity.

◆ Can you think of any other category of sin that is not included in this list?

3 According to Joel 2:16, everyone is to be included in the assembly and fast day, including the old and young and the bride and groom (who are usually excused from all kinds of responsibilities during their honeymoon). According to Beth Glazier-McDonald in *Women's Bible Commentary*, p. 217, this all-inclusive call "is a measure of the danger facing the community."

◆ Explain in your own words how the all-inclusive call reflects the danger the community faced.

◆ It seems from the text that the people responded to Joel's call. It is difficult to get everyone's attention, much less participation, for a cause or issue. Has there been a recent issue that mobilized all the members of your school or community?

◆ Can you imagine a cause that would attract great interest in your school or community?

◆ How did your community rally together after September 11, 2001?

4 The passage from Joel is rich in agricultural imagery (verses 2:19, 21-24, 25-26).

◆ Choose one of these images to represent in a drawing or painting.

◆ Why do you imagine that agricultural images were so meaningful to the ancient Israelites?

◆ What images might you use today to demonstrate promise of future prosperity?

Connecting the Text To the Special Shabbat

5 *Shabbat Shuvah* is the special name given to the Shabbat between Rosh HaShanah and Yom Kippur. On Rosh HaShanah, the *shofar* is sounded to urge us to turn toward God and proclaim God's dominion over the universe. Likewise, the *shofar* is sounded in Joel 2:15.

◆ Learn to sound the *shofar* and to recognize the differences between the *tekiah, shevarim,* and *teruah* calls.

◆ For more on the reasons we sound a *shofar*, see *Teaching Mitzvot* by Barbara Binder Kadden and Bruce Kadden, pp.7-10.

6 The word שובה (*shuvah* — return) appears in Hosea 14:2.

This word also forms the basis for the Hebrew word for "repentance." During the High Holy Days, we remember that sincere repentance is what God wants from us. Repentance — return to God — is also a major theme of the prophetic books.

◆ Consider the following quotations on the subject of repentance. Then, discuss what the concept of "returning" represents in each of them.

• "Let the wicked forsake his ways, and the unrighteous his thoughts; let him return to *Adonai* that God may have mercy!" (Isaiah 55:7)

• "Amend your ways and your actions!" (Jeremiah 7:3)

• "Rend your hearts and not your garments, return to *Adonai*, for God is gracious and merciful!" (Joel 2:13)

• "It has been told, O man, what is good, and what *Adonai* requires of you: only to do justly, love mercy, and to walk humbly with your God." (Micah 6:8)

• "And the people of Nineveh believed God; and they proclaimed a fast, and put on sackcloth, from the greatest of them even to the least of them." (Jonah 3:5)

• "Let justice well up as waters, and righteousness as a mighty stream." (Amos 5:24)

• "And I will sprinkle clean water upon you, and you shall be clean; from all your uncleannesses and from all your idols, will I cleanse you." (Ezekiel 36:25)

◆ Choose one (or more) of these quotations to feature in a design for a Rosh HaShanah card that your class can print up and send to family and friends.

7 The commentators wondered what oath God promised to our ancestors in Micah 7:20, and when that oath was made.

Rashi explains that God promised at the binding of Isaac (Genesis 22:16) that because Abraham and Isaac were willing to carry out the sacrifice (although God did stop them), their merit would be remembered and counted on behalf of their descendants. Remember that the story of the binding of Isaac is the Torah reading read on the second day of Rosh HaShanah in traditional synagoges and on the first day in most Reform synagogues.

In addition, Rabbinic tradition teaches that the reason we sound a ram's horn on Rosh HaShanah is to remind God of the binding of Isaac.

◆ Reread the story of Genesis 22 to find out what role a ram plays in the story.

◆ Why do you think we want to remind God of the binding of Isaac in so many ways (the Rosh HaShanah Torah reading, our ram's horn *shofar*, and the *Shabbat Shuvah* Haftarah, which mentions an oath made by God)?

◆ According to Jewish tradition, we rely on the merits of our ancestors to ensure that God will look favorably upon us. No matter how undeserving we may be, God will forgive us because of their good deeds. (For more on this subject, see Extending the Text #17 in the Haftarah for *Vayechi*, p. 115.)

◆ Design a prayer book cover for a High Holy Day *Machzor* that features more reminders to God for why God should forgive our sins.

8 Sometimes Shabbat Shuvah falls on the Shabbat when we read the Sedra *Vayaylech*, and sometimes it falls on the Shabbat when we read the Sedra *Ha'azinu*.

In *Vayaylech*, God says, "then My anger shall be kindled" (Deuteronomy 31:17). The Haftarah includes a selection from Micah (7:18) that says, "God does not stay angry forever."

◆ Does Micah's message appear to contradict the words of the Sedra? How can you explain the contradiction?

◆ If Micah's message softens the words of the Sedra, how is this a reassuring High Holy Day message?

◆ How is this a reminder to us not to stay angry with other people?

9 In *Ha'azinu* Moses says, "May my discourse come down as the rain . . . " (Deuteronomy 32:2). The Haftarah concludes with a selection from Joel (2:23) that says, "God has made it rain for you."

◆ Moses' discourse was, of course, the teaching of Torah. In what ways can you compare Torah with rain? (For example, both are nourishing, both are necessary for life, both are gifts from God.)

◆ *Song of Songs Rabbah* 1:19 teaches, "Just as rain water comes down in drops and forms rivers, so with the Torah; a person learns two laws today and two tomorrow, until he or she becomes like a flowing stream. Just as water has no taste unless one is thirsty, so the Torah has no taste unless one labors at it. Just as water leaves a high place and flows to a low one, so the Torah leaves one whose spirit is proud and cleaves to one whose spirit is lowly. Just as water does not keep well in a vessel of silver or gold but does in the commonest of vessels, so the Torah resides only in one who makes himself/herself like a vessel of earthenware. Just as with water a great person is not ashamed to say to a lowly person 'Give me a drink of water,' so with the words of the Torah, a great scholar must not be ashamed to say to a lesser one, 'Teach me one chapter, or one statement, or one verse, or even one letter.'"

◆ Explain the analogies drawn by this *midrash*.

◆ What High Holy Day messages might this *midrash* teach us?

◆ Design a new High Holy Day Torah cover that incorporates the image(s) in the *midrash*. Hold a contest, and let congregants vote on the design they like best. Remember, High Holy Day covers are generally white.

10 Malbim teaches concerning Micah 7:19 that God will forgive the unintentional sins (see Analyzing the Text #2, p. 538) and throw them out to sea (metaphorically), where they will never be thought of again.

On Rosh HaShanah, we free ourselves of our sins by symbolically throwing them into the water in a ceremony called *Tashlich* (casting away). On Rosh HaShanah afternoon, it is traditional for Jews to walk to the edge of a river, stream, or ocean and throw bread crumbs into the moving water. The bread crumbs represent our sins, and the moving water carries them away forever.

We hope that on Rosh HaShanah our sins will be overlooked by God. By symbolically throwing them out to sea, we hope that they will disappear from God's view. We hope also that they will never return to us again. Explain the symbolic power of this act.

◆ Take a field trip to a river or beach. Bring bread and a copy of Micah 7:18-20. Hold a pre-Rosh HaShanah trial run of *Tashlich*. Recite the verses as you cast your bread. Write a diary entry describing how you feel.

Did the act of *Tashlich* help you unburden yourself of sins?

11 In Joel 2:16 the prophet says to proclaim a fast. In the next verse he calls for the assembly of all the people, including children and infants.

According to Radak, the children and infants must fast on this occasion proclaimed by Joel. When they cry from hunger, the adults will be moved to tears and will finally repent. Moreover, God will hear the weeping of the babies and have mercy on them.

In contrast to Joel's fast day, according to Jewish law, children are not to fast on Yom Kippur until they are near the age of puberty, and then they are to be trained gradually in fasting. This is typically understood to mean that for a few years before their Bar/Bat Mitzvah, children are to fast part of the day, a little longer each year.

◆ When did you first fast on Yom Kippur?

◆ What would be your advice to novice fasters for a successful fast on Yom Kippur?

◆ Do you agree with the Rabbis that children (and the infirm) should not fast on Yom Kippur? Why or why not?

12 God responds with mercy in Joel 2:19. According to Ibn Ezra, God responds mercifully because of the crying priests (verse 2:17). This reminds us of the High Holy Day teaching that "Even if the gates of prayer are shut, the gates of tears are open" *(Berachot 32b)*.

◆ What do you think this teaching means?

◆ Does your synagogue set out boxes of tissues during High Holy Day services for people who are crying tears of repentance? Speak to your Rabbi or synagogue president about the need for tissues.

TEACHING HAFTARAH

Extending the Text

13 This Haftarah contains verses from Hosea that are also found in the (Ashkenazim) Haftarah for *Vayaytzay*. For additional Extending the Text entries on Hosea 14:2-10, see pp. 533-534.

14 Hosea says in verse 14:16 that God "will be to Israel like dew."

Dew has always been an important source of water for Israel's agriculture, especially during the dry summer months when rain is highly unlikely. It is a practice among the Sephardim to insert a prayer for dew *(tal)* into the *"Amidah"* prayer between Pesach and Sukkot. During the rainy months (between Sukkot and Pesach), Sephardim and Ashkenazim both add a prayer for rain *(geshem)* into the *"Amidah."*

◆ Sephardim and Ashkenazim recite a lengthy prayer for dew on the first day of Pesach. Write your own prayer for the nourishing blessing of dew in Israel.

15 This Haftarah contains an unusual combination of the words of three different prophets. Michael Fishbane teaches in *Etz Hayim Chumash*, p. 1234, that "combinations of nonconsecutive passages occur several times in the annual Haftarah cycle." The Sages called this "skipping." However, all the selections must be taken from the same scroll. In this case, all 12 Minor Prophets were originally written on a single scroll. They come together, according to Fishbane, because "Hosea expresses confession of sins and commitment to God; Joel refers to a ritual of contrition and purification; and Micah celebrates divine forgiveness of sin."

◆ Identify one verse from each section of the Haftarah that exemplifies its author's message. Then, try a "skipping" exercise of your own: combine parts of the three verses (even rearranging single words) into one cohesive and comprehensible sentence. Compare results with other students in the class.

16 There were originally several different customs regarding the text selections for the *Shabbat Shuvah* Haftarah, according to Isaac Klein in *A Guide To Jewish Religious Practice*, p. 206. Although some congregations read only the selection from Hosea, there were at least two problems with this custom: Haftarot are supposed to include a minimum of 21 verses (which the selection from Hosea does not), and Haftarot are supposed to end on a positive note (which Hosea 14:10 does not).

◆ Read Hosea 14:10 to see for yourself how this selection ends. To solve the problem of length, the 13 verses from Joel were added. To conclude the Haftarah on a positive note, the three verses from Micah were added. Today, some Ashkenazim add the verses from Micah if the Sedra read on *Shabbat Shuvah* is *Vayaylech*. If the Sedra on *Shabbat Shuvah* is *Ha'azinu*, then the verses from Joel are added. However, Michael Fishbane reports in the *Etz Hayim Chumash*, p. 1234, that some congregations recite the verses from Hosea and Joel every year, and others recite all three selections annually. Sephardim add only the verses from Micah in either case.

Personalizing the Text

17 This Haftarah contains verses from Hosea that are also found in the (Ashkenazim) Haftarah for *Vayaytzay*. For additional Personalizing the Text items on Hosea 14:2-10, see pp. 534-535.

18 The book of Joel consists of just four short chapters.

◆ Summarize this Haftarah in four sentences. Can you do it in four words?

19 Joel orders the people to fast in verse 2:15.

◆ Organize a class Break the Fast meal for after Yom Kippur.

20 Joel talks about how good life will be in the future when God shows compassion to the Israelite nation (verses 2:18-27).

◆ Describe your own hopes for how good life will be in the new year.

21 Micah reminds the Israelites that God will keep the promise made to Abraham.

◆ Think of any promises you made during this past year that you might have failed to keep. Try to make good on them before Yom Kippur.

22 It was an old custom of the Jews of Germany to prepare candles for Yom Kippur the week before Yom Kippur (usually on the eighth day). They made wicks by measuring thread at the grave of an ancestor; the thread should be as long as the grave. Then they dipped the thread in wax, making very large, heavy candles that would burn for the 24 hours of Yom Kippur. While making the candles, they recited prayers and mentioned the fine qualities of their ancestors. This was done to help their own cause on Yom Kippur. (Source: *Days of Awe* by S.Y. Agnon, pp. 142-143.)

23 Some people used to have the custom of reading the entire Tanach during the Days of Awe (*Days of Awe* by S.Y. Agnon, p. 146).

◆ Organize a project to divide up the Tanach among the classes and read the whole text through as a group effort.

Other Resources

24 Complete p. 24 on the Twelve Minor Prophets in *Prophets Copy Pak™* by Marji Gold-Vukson.

25 For more information, read the chapter on Hosea in *Messengers of God: A Jewish Prophets Who's Who* by Ronald H. Isaacs, pp. 135-140, the chapter on Joel, pp. 141-145, and the chapter on Micah, pp. 164-169.

26 Read about *teshuvah* in *Rosh Hashanah Yom Kippur Survival Kit* by Shimon Apisdorf, pp. 75-82.

27 See a *D'var Torah* on the web site of the Fuchsberg Center for Conservative Judaism in Jerusalem at www.uscj.org.il/haftarah/vayelech5761.html.

28 See how the drawings in *The Illustrated Torah* by Michal Meron, pp. 237-238, relate to the Haftarah and to *Shabbat Shuvah*.

29 *The Jewish Spirit: A Celebration in Stories and Art* by Ellen Frankel, pp. 236-237, features a story called "Begin with Yourself," about someone who tried to change the world and eventually learned that he needed to begin with himself. Read and discuss this story as it applies to *Shabbat Shuvah*.

30 For more information on the liturgy and customs of *Shabbat Shuvah*, as well as stories, see *Days of Awe* by S.Y. Agnon, pp. 109-147.

31 For more on the Days of Awe, visiting graves, and the custom of *kapparot* (transferring sins to a chicken), see *Prayer and Penitence* by Jeffrey M. Cohen, pp. 119-129.

32 For traditional sources on *teshuvah* (repentance), see a compilation of texts in *The Journey of the Soul* by Leonard S. Kravitz and Kerry M. Olitzky.

Involving the Family

33 *Shabbat Shuvah* is the intermediate Shabbat between Rosh HaShanah and Yom Kippur. It falls during the Ten Days of Repentance, during which we ask forgiveness for our sins from those whom we might have wronged. In *Rosh Hashanah Yom Kippur Survival Kit* (p. 72), Shimon Apisdorf teaches about a little prayer called *"Tefillah Zakkah."* It says, " . . . since I know that there is no righteous person in the world who does not sin against his fellow [person], either monetarily or physically, in deed or in speech, therefore my heart aches within me . . . May no person be punished on my account. And just like I forgive everyone, so may You grant me favor in every person's eyes that they may also grant me full forgiveness." As a family, recite this prayer during the Ten Days of Repentance and ask one another for forgiveness for any wrongs each of you may have done. Then, forgive one another.

Bar/Bat Mitzvah Project

34 Famine, hunger, and social justice are prevalent themes in this Haftarah. Learn about world hunger (24,000 people die each day of hunger) and how to do something about it by visiting www.thehungersite.com. Choose a hunger related *mitzvah* project to do in connection with your Bar or Bat Mitzvah.

AMOS 2:6-3:8
VAYAYSHEV וישב

This Haftarah has been paired with *Parashat Vayayshev*, Genesis 37:1-40:23. See "Connecting the Text To the Sedra," pp. 547-549, for an exploration of the many ways the two texts shed light on each other.

SYNOPSIS

Amos was born in Tekoa near Jerusalem in the Southern Kingdom of Judah in the eighth century B.C.E. He was a shepherd by trade, but moved to the North and began to preach in the cities of the Northern Kingdom of Israel. Amos found it necessary to preach against idolatry, immorality, corruption, and terrible social injustice. Both Northern and Southern Kingdoms were enjoying great prosperity, yet social injustice and immorality unfortunately accompanied the prosperity.

In this Haftarah Amos condemns the wealthy Israelites for bribery, slavery, and exploitation of the poor. He also rails against their sexual and religious immorality.

Amos recalls that *Adonai* saved the Israelites from their enemies and enabled them to inhabit the Promised Land, where *Adonai* gave them Nazirites and prophets to guide them. But Israel only corrupted or disregarded its religious leaders. As a consequence, *Adonai* will exact upon Israel harsh punishment from which no one will escape.

As the Haftarah concludes, Amos warns the people that any misfortune that comes to them will be sent by *Adonai*. He pleads with them to listen to his prophecy. Strikingly, the imagery he uses often reflects his life as a shepherd: the sound of lions roaring over their prey, birds falling into a trap,

and the peasant burdened with debts and sold into slavery or who is without his garments that have been given as a pledge.

INSIGHTS FROM THE TRADITION

A According to Radak verse 2:6 indicates that although the Israelites were guilty of all types of terrible sins, they were not punished or destroyed until they began taking bribes from the wealthy to pervert justice against the poor — effectively selling the poor into slavery to the rich.

◆ How might the wealthy use their money and influence to tip the scales of justice toward themselves and away from the poor?

◆ Interview a lawyer to find out if the wealthy can still use money to influence our justice system.

◆ Why do you think this particular crime was the "straw that broke the camel's back" and turned God's wrath against Israel?

B *Targum Jonathan* translates Nazirites in verse 2:11 as "teachers." Rashi explains that just as Nazirites kept their distance from alcohol, so teachers of Torah must keep themselves away from the customs of the local country.

◆ What is assimilation?

◆ The Nazirites showed their dedication to God's service by keeping away from distractions like alcohol that would interfere with their duties. How might being assimilated interfere with a Torah teacher's duties?

◆ Debate: You can be both assimilated and dedicated to Judaism.

STRATEGIES
Analyzing the Text

1 Verse 2:6 is part of a refrain that Amos repeats in verses 1:3, 1:6, 1:9, 1:11, 1:13, 2:1; 2:4, and 2:6.

◆ Which nations are mentioned in each occurrence of the refrain, and what are the sins of each?

◆ What purpose do you think a refrain (or chorus of a song) serves in terms of getting a message across to the listener?

◆ Israel is mentioned last, after all the other nations. One might expect the nations to be listed in the order in which they were punished by attacks from Assyria. However, Israel was not the last to be attacked. According to Rabbi Eliezer of Beaugency, Israel is mentioned last of all the nations because the prophet wanted to discuss Israel's situation in more detail and Israel's prophecy was of prime importance to the prophet. Do you agree with this suggestion?

◆ When you summarize your day, do you sometimes abandon chronological order to tell the most important event first or last?

2 Amos criticizes the wealthy Israelites in verse 2:8 for taking clothing as a pledge. This unethical practice of acquiring the garments of the poor is in contradiction to the law stated in Exodus 22:25: "If you take your neighbor's garment in pledge, you must return it to him before the sun sets."

◆ Why is it sometimes necessary to give collateral?

◆ Why do you think the law would require someone to return a garment taken as a pledge before nightfall? (Hint: Consider that the poor had few garments, and desert nights can be quite cold.)

◆ Have you ever given something to someone or taken something from someone as a guarantee of a promise?

3 In verses 2:11-12 Amos condemns the Israelites for corrupting the Nazirites among them. According to Numbers 6:1-7, Nazirites were individuals who took special vows to live a pure life devoted to God. Nazirites were not permitted to drink wine or cut their hair.

The self-control expected of the Nazirites stood in direct opposition to the self-indulgence of the people in the time of Amos.

◆ Find three examples in the Haftarah of the Israelites' lack of self-control that would ultimately lead to their destruction.

4 Amos accuses the Israelites of ordering the prophets not to prophesy in verse 2:12. This actually happened to Amos when the priest Amaziah ordered him to stop preaching and leave.

◆ Why do you think people would want to stop a prophet from preaching?

◆ Read Amos 7:10-17 to see what transpired between Amos and Amaziah. Then, role-play this dramatic scene.

5 Amos describes in verse 2:13 a wagon slowed by its heavy burden. With this image, Amos sends a threatening message to the Israelites: the things you enjoy will be the things that ultimately destroy you.

◆ If the Israelites are the wagon, which of the following do you think is their burden that slows them: wealth, faithlessness, sin, drunkenness, greed? Argue for each of those suggestions, and make some suggestions of your own.

◆ What are the things that we, as a society, enjoy today that may threaten us in the future?

6 The translation "run away unarmed" in verse 2:16 is based on an interpretation by Rashi, who believed that the warriors would have to run away without their weapons. Radak prefers the literal translation, "run away naked," because it means that without his clothing, the warrior will weigh less and run faster.

◆ Reread verse 2:16. Which interpretation makes the most sense to you, and why?

◆ Compare this verse to the famous story in Isaiah 20:1-6.

7 Verses 3:3-3:6 contain metaphors describing God's relationship with the prophets.

◆ Explain each metaphor and how it describes the relationship between God and prophet.

◆ Each of the metaphors describes a cause and effect relationship. What is the cause and effect relationship between God and the prophets?

◆ Amos himself explains in verses 3:7-8 that *Adonai* does nothing without revealing the Divine purpose to the prophets. He says that the prophets simply say what they know to be true from God. Is Amos saying, "Don't blame me; I'm just the messenger"? Or is Amos saying more than this?

◆ Design a business card or logo for an imaginary society of Israelite peoples that incorporates one of the images in verse 3:3-6.

Connecting the Text To the Sedra

8 In the Sedra Joseph tells his dreams (prophecies) to his brothers who don't want to hear them. In the Haftarah Amos has a message from God that the people don't want to hear.

◆ Why were the messages in each story distasteful to the listeners?

◆ Sometimes we all have to hear messages we would rather ignore. Who are today's prophets, and what are their messages that we would rather not hear?

◆ Design your own print advertisement that gives people a message for their own good that they probably would rather not hear (don't smoke, exercise more, eat your vegetables, do your homework, and so on).

9 Clothing is an important symbol in both texts. In the Sedra Joseph is given and then stripped of his coat of many colors. This famous coat represented the fact that Joseph was chosen by his father and by God to be the ruler of his family. It inspired great jealousy among his brothers. In the Haftarah Amos says that even the mighty will be stripped naked of the garments that give them might.

◆ In both texts, clothes symbolize power. Can you identify any types of clothing that represent status or power in your community or school?

◆ Do you think people are treated differently depending on what they wear? Explain your answer.

10 Both texts provide shocking examples of hardhearted behavior. In the Sedra (Genesis 37:24-25), Joseph's brothers sat down to eat after they threw him in a pit. According to *midrash*, they moved away from the pit so as not to hear Joseph's calls for help (*Legends of the*

Jews by Louis Ginzberg, vol. 2, p. 14). In the Haftarah the Israelites callously exploit the poor and profit from that exploitation.

◆ Identify ways in which school can be a hard-hearted place. (For example, cliques and bullying in school both involve hardheartedness.)

◆ Write and deliver a speech urging people to change their hardhearted ways and embrace kindness.

11 The issue of personal responsibility is central in both Sedra and Haftarah. Reuben understands in Genesis 37:30 that as the oldest in the family, he should have protected his youngest brother. He realizes that he will be held responsible for Joseph's fate by their father.

In verses 38:1-11 of the Sedra, Judah neglects his responsibility toward Tamar, his daughter-in-law. Tamar, on the other hand, goes to great lengths in order to fulfill her responsibility to continue the family line at great risk to her life (Genesis 38:12-30).

In the Haftarah the Israelites neglect their responsibility to protect the poor.

On the other hand, Amos bears his responsibility to publicize God's words, even if the others do not want to hear the message.

◆ Have you ever had to choose responsibility to your community over your own personal interest? Why can that be so hard to do?

◆ Review the texts listed above. Choose students to act as Tamar, Reuben, and Amos on a panel. Interview the three figures about the importance and the challenges of responsibility to one's community.

12 Amos says in verse 3:2 that God will call Israel to account for all its iniquities. The Sedra is replete with examples of people

being punished measure for measure for the sins of their past. Consider these examples:

• Jacob's parents played favorites with their sons, ultimately hurting them both. Jacob plays favorites among his sons, ultimately hurting them all.

• Jacob lied to his father. Jacob's sons lie to him.

• A goat's blood is used to fool Jacob into thinking that Joseph was dead. Jacob had used a goatskin to fool his own father into thinking that he was his brother, Esau.

• A striped tunic is used to fool Jacob into thinking that Joseph was dead. Joseph's brother, Judah, is later fooled by Tamar's garments.

• Joseph's brothers show his bloodied tunic to Jacob, asking if he can "recognize this." Tamar later sends Judah's staff back to Judah, saying, "Recognize this."

◆ Choose one of the pairs of examples above and act out both scenes, emphasizing how the sins are requited measure for measure.

13 Both the Sedra and the Haftarah offer examples of how you cannot keep a good person down, no matter how you try. In the Sedra Joseph was a *tzadik* turned into a slave by his brothers. Also in the Sedra, Tamar was a *tzadikah* who had to debase herself to fulfill her mission. In the Haftarah prophets and Nazirites are *tzadikim* who are robbed of their power and, in effect, enslaved by the Israelites. The prophets emerge victorious because, after all, we still read their works and are greatly influenced by their ideas today.

◆ How did Joseph and Tamar emerge victorious in the end of their stories?

◆ Do you agree that you cannot keep a good person down?

14 The self-control of the Nazirites in the Haftarah (see Analyzing the Text #3, p. 546, for more information) stands in opposition to the self-indulgent behavior of Judah, one of Joseph's brothers.

◆ Read Genesis 38 and explain different ways in which Judah behaved in a self-indulgent fashion.

◆ In our lives there are times when we should indulge ourselves and other times when we ought to exercise self-control. Can you think of three examples of each?

◆ Why might it be good to indulge oneself once in a while?

◆ List your favorite indulgences.

Extending the Text

15 We learned about the importance of meeting our obligations to our community in Connecting the Text To the Sedra #11, p. 548. Rabbi Leo Baeck, a Rabbi in Germany who lived from 1873-1956, provides a model of such behavior.

According to Howard M. Sachar in *The Course of Modern Jewish History*, p. 495:

"So imposing was Baeck's reputation, in fact, that even the Nazis at first dealt cautiously with him; as late as 1938 they offered him the opportunity to leave Germany. He rejected the offer and chose instead to remain with his captive people. It was then, and during the five years of his imprisonment in the Theresienstadt concentration camp, that Baeck became a living incarnation of the affirmative faith he preached . . . Ministering to the ill and despondent, conducting clandestine religious services at the risk of his life, Baeck infused thousands of his fellow inmates with his own unshakable conviction that survival was a moral obligation, even in the depths of the Nazi hell."

◆ Do you agree that Rabbi Baeck's decision indicated that he valued his community's needs more than his own?

◆ Can you draw parallels between Rabbi Baeck and the people discussed in Connecting the Text To the Sedra #11, p. 548?

◆ Can you imagine making the same choice that Rabbi Baeck made?

◆ Why would Rabbi Baeck have risked his own life to conduct religious services in a concentration camp?

◆ In what ways is Rabbi Baeck a role model for all of us?

◆ For more on Rabbi Leo Baeck, see the *Encyclopaedia Judaica*, vol. 4, pp. 77-78.

16 Amos is recognized as the prophet of social justice, or righteousness. As Shalom Spiegel points out in *Amos vs. Amaziah* (p. 54), Amos's legacy is Judaism's continued emphasis on social justice. Spiegel notes (p. 43) that Amos taught us that worship and ritual are means to the ends of justice and righteousness. "God is justice, and [God's] holiness is exalted in righteousness."

◆ Explain in your own words Spiegel's comments.

◆ Do the following in order to further your understanding: Choose a prayer that mentions God. (For example, the ninth blessing of the *"Amidah"* says, "Bless for us, *Adonai* our God, this year and all types of crops for the best, and give dew and rain for a blessing on the earth, and satisfy us from Your bounty, and bless our year like the best years. Blessed are You, *Adonai*, Who blesses the years.") Explain what you think this prayer means.

◆ Now explain what you think the prayer means if God is Justice. (For example, in the ninth blessing of the *"Amidah,"* if God is Justice, then we pray for income so that we have resources to feed the hungry, share with others, and improve the world.)

◆ Rewrite the prayer you selected so that it expresses the expanded meaning you have given it. (For example, Bless for us, *Adonai,* our Inspiration for Justice, this year and all crops and sources of income that we may help satisfy others with Your bounty, and may we share our wealth as You share Your rain with the earth, and bless our year and our efforts to make this a more just world. Blessed are You, *Adonai,* who blesses the years.)

17 In Numbers 6 we learn about the laws governing Nazirites.

◆ Read about the Bible's two most famous Nazirites, Samson and Samuel. Samson's story is in the Haftarah for *Naso,* p. 39, and Samuel's story is the Haftarah for the first day of Rosh HaShanah, p. 48.

18 Nazirites were required to have great self-control, as we learned in Analyzing the Text #3, p. 546.

◆ Consider these words of wisdom on self-control from *Pirke Avot* 4:1:

"Who is a mighty hero? One who conquers his/her inclination or will, as it is said: 'The one who is slow to anger is better than the mighty, and the one who rules his/her spirit than the one that takes a city.'" (Proverbs 16:32)

◆ When is it most difficult for you to control your anger?

◆ What other times does one need to exert self-control?

◆ Do you agree with this teaching that one who exerts self-control is a hero?

19 The Rabbis had a lot to say about the significance of clothing (see Connecting the Text To the Sedra #9, p. 547). Discuss each quotation and state whether or not you agree with it.

• "The glory of people is the clothes they wear." *(Derech Eretz Zuta)*

• "A scholar should always wear modest clothing — not too costly or ornate, so that people should not stare at him, and not too shabby lest he be mocked." *(Menorat Hamaor)*

• "A person's clothes are the index of his or her character." (Nachman of Bratzlav)

• "A wise person should dress neatly, and should not wear dirty clothes. A person shouldn't dress flashily to attract attention. Garments should be modest and appropriate." (Maimonides)

◆ Would any of these quotations have helped Jacob, Joseph, Judah, Tamar, or the Mighty Warrior of the Haftarah (who had to shed his clothes) deal with issues involving clothing?

◆ Describe your own motto or attitude about clothes.

◆ Make a collage from magazine photos of clothing styles that best represent the lesson of one of the preceding quotations about clothes.

Personalizing the Text

20 Amos was the prophet of justice. In *Amos vs. Amaziah,* Shalom Spiegel writes (pp. 33-34), "Justice is strength . . . [W]hat soundness is to construction, or health to the body, justice is to society."

◆ Keep a journal of good deeds you do (try to do one a week). Describe how these deeds make your community a stronger place to live.

◆ For more projects related to random acts of kindness, check the web site www. actsofkindness.org.

21 In verse 2:16 the defeated warrior flees naked.

◆ Organize a clothing drive or coat drive for the poor (see Analyzing the Text #2 and #6, pp. 546 and 547).

22 The people tried to make Amos stop prophesying because they did not want to hear his message.

◆ Interview your parents or other family members about the best piece of advice they received, but that they did not want to hear (see Analyzing the Text #4 p. 546).

23 Because the Israelites have forgotten everything that *Adonai* had done for them and given them when they were a young nation, *Adonai* will punish them.

◆ Do you think you owe your parents anything for all they have done for you in your life?

◆ Write a thank-you card to your parents for everything they have done for you since you were born. Include a partial list of specific things for which you are thanking them, such as giving you food, driving you wherever you have to go, or taking care of you when you had chicken pox, and so on.

Other Resources

24 For a light but meaningful story about the importance we (mis)place on clothes,

read the children's book *The Paper Bag Princess* by Robert Munsch and Michael Martchenko.

25 Discuss the illustration of this Haftarah in *The Illustrated Torah* by Michal Meron, p. 49. Which part of the Haftarah does the illustration comment upon, and what is its message?

26 Prophets and Nazirites were devoted to one special thing. View and discuss the film *Rudy* (1993, rated PG, 112 minutes), which follows the story of a young man whose whole life had one single purpose.

27 Read and discuss the story "The Car that Ran from Mitzvahs" by Hanna Bandes in *Chosen Tales*, edited by Peninnah Schram, pp. 11-19. In this story a woman has to be told something she does not want to hear in order to change her life.

28 Read the chapter on Amos in *Messengers of God: A Jewish Prophets Who's Who* by Ronald H. Isaacs, pp. 146-153.

29 The word "justice" in Hebrew is *tzedek*, which is a form of the word we use to mean "charity." For a discussion of the topic, see the Haftarah for *Devarim*, Extending the Text #13, p. 225.

30 For a *D'var Torah* on this Haftarah, see the web site for the Fuchsberg Center for Conservative Judaism in Jerusalem, www.uscj. org.il/haftarah/vayeshev5762.html.

Involving the Family

31 Amos preached against the exploitation of the poor. Today, the poor and the young are exploited in unfair labor practices.

American labor unions protect against such exploitation. Buy only union-made clothing or visit the AFL-CIO web site at www.uniteunion.org to learn more. You can also learn more about what you can do to combat child labor at the web site for the International Labour Organization at www.us.ilo.org/ilokidsnew/kids.html.

Bar/Bat Mitzvah Projects

32 Consider the needs of the community above your own: donate the money you would have spent on centerpieces or flowers at your Bar or Bat Mitzvah reception to your favorite *tzedakah* project. In place of flowers or centerpieces, print cards that say, "Instead of flowers (or centerpieces), we have made a generous contribution to such-and-such." Since Amos was the Prophet of Justice, you might want to make your donation to the Jewish Fund for Justice, Inc., 260 Fifth Ave., Suite 701, New York, NY 10001, www.JFJustice.org.

33 Learn this week's lesson. Resolve to make school a not so hardhearted place by refusing to stand idly by when someone is being bullied or tormented (see Connecting the Text To the Sedra #10, pp. 547-548).

AMOS 9:7-15
KEDOSHIM קדשים Ashkenazim

This Haftarah has been paired with *Parashat Kedoshim*, Leviticus 19:1-20:27. See "Connecting the Text To the Sedra," pp. 555-556, for an exploration of the many ways the two texts shed light on each other.

SYNOPSIS

Born in the Southern Kingdom of Judah and trained as a shepherd, Amos lived and preached in the cities of the Northern Kingdom of Israel in the eighth century B.C.E. However, this Haftarah, which concludes the Book of Amos, includes information that could not have been known until after Amos's era (the fall of the house of David and the defeat of the house of Jacob, i.e., the defeat of Jerusalem). It is the opinion of many scholars, therefore, that most of this Haftarah was composed by another prophet after the fall of Jerusalem in the sixth century.

The Haftarah begins with the declaration that all nations are equal in God's eyes, and none are above divine retribution. Regrettably, God's eye has now been cast on the destruction of the children of Israel!

Israel will be shaken, and its sinners destroyed. However, a remnant of the House of Jacob will be saved. The righteous remnant will survive and be restored to glory. The hills will, one day, bear grain, and the vineyards will grow fruit. The ruined cities will be rebuilt. And never again will Israel be uprooted from the soil given to them by *Adonai*.

INSIGHTS FROM THE TRADITION

A According to Hertz, the first verse of the Haftarah (verse 9:7) indicates that all races and nationalities are equally dear to God.

Plaut further explains that there is no racial prejudice in the Bible. He writes in *The Haftarah Commentary*, p. 296, "The prophecy of Amos proclaims that God is the God of all humanity and that, as humans, the Children of Israel are no different from the inhabitants of Africa (Ethiopians), or Asia (Arameans), or Europe (Philistines)."

◆ What does your school or community do to combat racial prejudice and promote equality?

◆ What do you do?

B Amos says in verse 9:12 that Israel will come to possess the remnant of Edom, an enemy nation that harmed Israel. Why will Israel possess only a remnant, and not the entire territory, of Edom? According to Radak, part of Edom will lie in perpetual ruin to show future generations what happens to nations who harm Israel.

Applying Radak's rationale to Nazi concentration camps, perhaps the camps would serve as more effective memorials if they remained as they were at the end of World War II, rather than being restored, preserved, or otherwise changed.

◆ What is your opinion about what should be done with former concentration camps?

STRATEGIES
Analyzing the Text

1 Various peoples are mentioned in verse 9:7 as having been brought by God to their present location:

- Israel's Exodus from Egypt to Canaan is typically dated to the thirteenth century B.C.E.

- The Philistine settlement of Canaan is dated to the twelfth century B.C.E., according to Egyptian records. Some historians think the Philistines settled on the coast of Canaan just before the Israelites did.

- The Arameans are mentioned in twelfth century inscriptions, especially in the area of modern day Syria. Although it is unclear when they were organized into kingdoms, some historians think they were settled in Canaan by the eleventh century B.C.E.

◆ The ancient Israelites had a sense that God was active in all aspects of life, shaping history according to God's will. Do you also believe that God places nations and even individuals in certain locations and situations in order to serve a grand divine purpose?

2 The metaphor in verse 9:9 compares the Israelites to sand shaken through a sieve. Only the finest sand (the righteous remnant) will fall through, while the pebbles (the sinning multitude) will be caught.

◆ Demonstrate how a sieve works for your class. Discuss whether or not they think this is an effective image of the upheaval of an earthquake or other catastrophe.

◆ Explain how the sieve may answer the theological question: what happens to the righteous when God wants to destroy the wicked? Do you agree with the answer?

◆ Do you even agree with the metaphor? This Haftarah is always read in the springtime, near Yom HaShoah. Does this metaphor help you understand the Holocaust or conflict with your understanding of the Holocaust? Explain your answer.

3 The Book of Amos begins with the statement that Amos prophesied two years before the earthquake (verse 1:1).

◆ Identify images in the Haftarah that are reminiscent of an earthquake (see especially verses 9, 11, and 15).

◆ According to Zechariah 14:5, an earthquake rocked the Kingdom of Judah in the days of King Uzziah. Why do you think earthquake images would be especially powerful to those listening to Amos?

◆ The ancient prophets tended to view catastrophic acts of nature as chastisements from God. Do you feel the same way? Why or why not? Why do you think the prophets tended to learn moral lessons from natural phenomena?

◆ For more information on the occurrence of earthquakes in the Land of Israel, see the *Encyclopaedia Judaica*, vol. 6, pp. 340-341.

4 In verse 9:10 the Israelites boasted, "Never shall the evil overtake us or come near us."

◆ What do you think this boast means?

◆ It appears that the Israelites arrogantly believed that they were eternally safe from harm. Were these people: unwilling to listen to warnings, oblivious to what must have been obvious, blinded by their greediness, or callous?

◆ Have you ever known anyone who was arrogant or unwilling to listen to warnings? In what ways were they hurt by their outlook?

5 There is a debate as to the meaning of David's fallen booth (*sukkah*) in verse 9:11. Some possible meanings are: the righteous remnant of Israel, the dynasty (house) of the family of David, the kingdom of Judah, Jerusalem.

◆ Explain why each of these meanings makes sense.

◆ In addition, what does the metaphor of the *sukkah* convey? Is a *sukkah* strong, weak, solid, or shaky?

◆ Based on what you know from the Synopsis (p. 553) and the Overview (pp. 506-507), why do you think Israel in Amos's time is compared to a *sukkah*?

◆ Compare the use of "booth" in verse 9:11 to that of "house" in verse 9:9. How is the house made weak as a *sukkah*?

◆ Draw your understanding of the house and the *sukkah*. Compare your drawing with the illustration of this Haftarah in *The Illustrated Torah* by Michal Meron, p. 130. What emotions are represented in that illustration?

6 The hopeful note of verses 9:11-15 (the last in the Book of Amos) has led many scholars to believe that they were added by a later editor.

◆ How does the optimism in these verses compare with the tone of the beginning of the Haftarah?

◆ Does there seem to be a transition from the gloom of verse 9:10 to the optimism in verse 9:11?

Connecting the Text To the Sedra

7 The Sedra sets out rules by which Israel is to live. Contained in the Sedra is the restatement of the Ten Commandments, as well as many other laws. The point of all the laws is spelled out at the very end of the Sedra (Leviticus 20:26): "You shall be holy to Me, for I *Adonai* am holy, and I have set you apart from other peoples to be Mine."

◆ What makes one person different from another person, or one nation set apart from another nation?

◆ Juxtaposed liturgically to the end of the Sedra is the opening of the Haftarah, which states that Israelites are no different from all the other nations of the world (verse 9:7). Does the opening message of the Haftarah contradict or support the lesson from the Sedra that only the way we act distinguishes us from other people?

◆ In the *Etz Hayim Chumash*, p. 706, Michael Fishbane writes, "Kept separate, *Kedoshim* and this Haftarah's lessons cancel each other's truth concerning election; brought together, they revise one another reciprocally and suggest a more inwards and humble theology of chosenness." Design a new curriculum for your school. List the subjects that you think students need to learn between Kindergarten and Bar/Bat Mitzvah that will prepare them to act set apart as members of a holy nation.

8 Both Sedra (Leviticus 20:22) and Haftarah (verses 9:14-15) warn that a sinful Israelite nation will be ousted from its land. Since the Holocaust, modern thinkers have had difficulty seeing historical events as divine reward and punishment.

◆ Why do you think the Holocaust challenged the biblical view of historical and natural events as divine reward and punishment?

◆ Debate: The Jewish State in the Land of Israel today is a divine reward that can be taken away by God if we no longer deserve it.

9 The Land of Israel is described in the Sedra as a land flowing with milk and honey (Leviticus 20:24). In verse 9:13 of the Haftarah, Amos envisions a land waving with grain and dripping with wine.

◆ What message do you think Amos is trying to convey about the future?

◆ Make a collage of a fertile land overflowing with agricultural crops and prosperity.

◆ Compare these images of the Land of Israel with those in the song "America the Beautiful." List the similarities.

10 Verse 19:18 of the Sedra features an important rule of just behavior, "Love your neighbor as yourself."

◆ How does this rule help us to behave in a just manner?

◆ See *Teaching Torah* by Sorel Goldberg Loeb and Barbara Binder Kadden, Strategy #14, pp. 204-205, for an exercise on this subject.

◆ Amos is called the Prophet of Justice. What is justice? In his book *Amos vs. Amaziah* (p. 56), Shalom Spiegel explains, "Justice is midway between morality and reason, virtue and intelligence, love and logic. We speak rightly of scales of justice, the image suggesting a precision instrument of intact and incorruptible weights, pondering carefully contending claims." Explain Spiegel's definition in your own words.

◆ How does the rule above help us behave in a just manner according to Spiegel's definition?

◆ Design a crossword puzzle that contains various ways to "love your neighbor as yourself."

11 Amos 9:7-15 is the Haftarah for *Kedoshim*, according to Ashkenazi practice. The Sephardim read Ezekiel 20:2-20.

◆ Read both Haftarot and decide which you think best complements the Sedra.

Extending the Text

12 The Haftarah speaks of all people being equal under God (verse 9:7). Yet Jews are often called God's chosen people.

◆ How do you reconcile the seemingly contradictory ideas of all peoples being the children of God, and Jews as God's chosen people?

◆ Plaut writes in *The Haftarah Commentary*, p. 296, "Israel's special relationship with the Divine stems . . . from its historic commitment to know and do God's will. The reverse of this commitment is God's extra attention to Israel's sins, as well as a special concern for its moral future. In Amos, as in all prophets, this is both the burden and the joy of belonging to the House of Jacob."

◆ In your own words, what is the burden and the joy of being Jewish, according to Plaut? What questions does Plaut's statement raise for you?

◆ Read an article on "chosenness." See, for example, *Contemporary Jewish Religious Thought* by Arthur A. Cohen and Paul Mendes-Flohr, pp. 55-59; or the *Encyclopaedia Judaica*, vol. 5, pp. 498-502; or *Biblical Literacy* by Joseph Telushkin, pp. 319-320.

◆ Prepare questions about chosenness for a panel of Rabbis to answer. Then invite Rabbis from different movements within Judaism to answer your questions.

13 Amos declares that God's eyes are upon the sinful kingdom in verse 9:8. Consider this *midrash* about God's eyes:

Song of Songs Rabbah 8:19 teaches, "Just as a deer sleeps with one eye open and one eye closed, so when Israel acts according to the desire of the Holy One, God looks upon them with both eyes, as it is written, 'The eyes of *Adonai* are toward the righteous' (Psalm 34:16). But when they do not act according to God's desire, God looks upon them with one eye, as it says, 'Behold, the eye of *Adonai* is toward them that fear Him'" (Psalm 33:18).

◆ What do you think this *midrash* teaches about God's eyes? Why does God sometimes use one eye and at other times two eyes?

◆ Draw a picture depicting the lesson of the *midrash*. Draw another picture depicting God's eyes in the Haftarah and the implication of both of them being open.

14 Amos teaches that all nations are equal in God's eyes.

◆ Invite a speaker from the Anti-Defamation League to speak about the Jewish response for social equality and against racism.

◆ Research and present a report to your class on one topic in race relations. For historical topics, see the web site www.newhorizons.org/announce_pbsrace.html. Or, for current issues in race relations, see www.pbs.org/newsletter/bb/race_relations/race_relations.html.

15 According to the Rabbis in *Leviticus Rabbah* 10:2, Amos was nicknamed "the stutterer," based on one interpretation of the meaning of his name: עמוס means "heavy" or "laden of tongue."

◆ What other famous prophet was a stutterer? Did stuttering stop either one?

In contrast, another commentator says that Amos's words are plain and fierce and "ring with the crystal tones of a bell." (Source: Carroll Stuhlmueller in the *Collegeville Bible Commentary, Old Testament,* vol. 15, p. 7.)

◆ Based on this Haftarah, with which characterization of Amos do you agree, and why? Can you find evidence in the text for the other description?

◆ Alternatively, the Hebrew root עמס may also mean "to carry a load." How might this be an appropriate name for a prophet? What burden is Amos carrying (the world on his shoulders, the responsibility to save his people, or God's message, for example)?

◆ Draw a caricature of Amos carrying his heavy burden.

Personalizing the Text

16 The Haftarah relates how various nations were brought by God to their present location to serve a divine purpose.

◆ When did your own family settle in the United States, and from where did they come?

◆ Interview a parent or grandparent for a story about how your family came to the United States. You may wish to videotape the interviews. Share the stories with the class.

◆ Consider why your family may have been brought here. Does your family see God's hand in the move?

17 The Israelites are to be shaken through a metaphorical sieve in verse 9:9. A lesson in *Pirke Avot* 5:15 also uses a sieve as part of its metaphor:

There are four kinds of students. A sponge absorbs everything; a funnel lets in at one end and lets out at the other; a strainer lets out the wine and retains the dregs; and a sieve lets out the course flour and retains the fine.

◆ Make a poster illustrating the four kinds of students. Which kind are you?

18 Amos envisions a land waving with grain and dripping with wine. The Land of Israel is also described in the Bible as a land flowing with milk and honey.

◆ Find pictures of Israel that match either description by searching the Internet or by browsing through Jewish magazines. Mount a photo display of Israel to exhibit at your school

19 Amos was a shepherd before he was a prophet. Moses was a shepherd, too, as was King David.

◆ How might shepherding be good training for a future prophet or leader?

◆ Imagine you are a shepherd looking for a new job as a prophet. Write a résumé, featuring those job responsibilities that have prepared you most for your new career.

20 Amos was a Southerner who preached against the Northern Kingdom of Israel. According to *Midrash*, he may have been killed by Israelite King Uzziah (*Legends of the Jews* by Louis Ginzberg, vol. 4, p. 262).

◆ Read information about Amos's life in the *Encyclopaedia Judaica*, vol. 2, pp. 879-889.

◆ Using information from this Haftarah and the one preceding it, and also from the Overview on pp. 506-507, write an obituary for the deceased prophet, as it might have appeared in an Israelite newspaper. Write another version as it might have appeared in a paper in the Southern Kingdom of Judah (Amos's home).

21 Amos says in verse 9:8 that *Adonai's* eye is upon the sinful kingdom. God's eye is often depicted on the popular Jewish amulet known as the *chamsa*.

A *chamsa* (from the word "five") is a five-fingered hand used to ward off evil spirits. Frequently, God's one, watchful eye is also pictured in the middle of the hand.

◆ Do you or a family member have a *chamsa* charm or plaque at home? If so, bring it in to show the class.

◆ Design a *chamsa* drop for a necklace that features God's eye.

Other Resources

22 Amos was a shepherd. Read and discuss the story, "The Shepherd's Prayer" by Susan Danoff in *Chosen Tales*, edited by Peninnah Schram, pp. 76-80.

23 Read the chapter on Amos in *Messengers of God: A Jewish Prophets Who's Who* by Ronald H. Isaacs, pp. 146-153.

24 For a *D'var Torah* on this Haftarah, see the web site for the Fuchsberg Center for Conservative Judaism in Jerusalem, www.uscj. org.il/haftarah/ Ahare5761.html.

25 Amos preached justice for all. View and discuss the film *And Justice for All* (1979, rated R, 120 min.), in which a Maryland lawyer fights against a flawed judicial system.

26 Amos says in verse 9:8 that God's eye is upon the sinful kingdom. We often think that we can get away with wrongdoing if no one sees us do it. Read the story in the Haftarah for *Terumah*, Extending the Text #20, p. 134. Discuss how the red light mentioned by former hockey goalie Jacques Plante is like the eyes of God in this Haftarah.

27 For more discussion of the meaning of eyes in Jewish symbolism, see the Haftarah for *Kedoshim* in the Book of Ezekiel (20:2-20), Extending the Text #13, pp. 439-440.

28 For a commentary, discussion questions, and project related to this Haftarah, see the UAHC Family Shabbat Table Talk web site at www.uahc.org/shabbat/stt/3ak.shtml.

Involving the Family

29 Israel is portrayed in verse 9:15 as a tree planted on its land, never to be uprooted. *Kedoshim* is read just around planting time in the spring. Plant a tree in your yard to commemorate your Bar or Bat Mitzvah. Consider starting a family tradition of planting trees for family milestones and occasions. Place a marker near each tree identifying its significance (special markers for this purpose can be found in garden shops).

Bar/Bat Mitzvah Projects

30 Amos preached justice for all. The Jewish Organizing Initiative offers fellowships to train young Jewish adults in the Jewish tradition of pursuing social and economic justice. Donate part of your Bar or Bat Mitzvah gifts to this worthy cause. See the web site at www.jewishorganizing.org.

31 The Israelites of Amos's time suffered the devastation of an earthquake. In recent years, there have been serious earthquakes in the Middle East. The Israeli Defense Force always sends rescue teams to the locations of serious earthquakes to help the local rescue teams save lives and stabilize the situation. They send a field hospital that often stays at the location for months after the quake. They bring some survivors to Israel for medical care. (For more information, access www.jdc.org/news/turkey.cfm to learn about the long-term help Israel provided to Turkey after the disastrous earthquakes of 1999.)

Jews in America are asked to help finance the cost of these efforts. Contact the American Jewish Joint Distribution Committee, 711 Third Ave., N.Y., N.Y. 10017 to find out if they are currently collecting funds to aid earthquake relief and the procedure for donating a percentage of your Bar/Bat Mitzvah gifts to the cause.

OBADIAH 1:1-21 Sephardim and Some Ashkenazim
VAYISHLACH וישלך

This Haftarah has been paired with *Parashat Vayishlach*, Genesis 32:4-36:43. See "Connecting the Text To the Sedra," pp. 562-564, for an exploration of the many ways the two texts shed light on each other.

SYNOPSIS

Because Obadiah provides no historical or autobiographical information, it is difficult to pinpoint the setting of this Haftarah. Many scholars believe, however, that Obadiah wrote his short book following the destruction of Jerusalem by the Babylonians in 586 B.C.E. The target of Obadiah's condemnation is the nation of Edom, which assisted the Babylonians in the devastation of the Israelite nation. The Edomites were descendants of Jacob's brother, Esau, making this enemy nation actually a blood relative of Israel.

Obadiah preaches against Edom's arrogant perception that they are beyond God's reach. He predicts Edom's imminent downfall, which will be brought about by Edom's supposed allies. No one, says Obadiah, will survive the slaughter. Edom will completely vanish from the face of the earth as a result of divine retribution for its treachery against its brother, Israel.

Obadiah goes on to predict that all of Israel's enemies will be destroyed on the day of *Adonai*, and will be as if they never were. But on that day, Israel's surviving remnant will possess all the lands of its enemies. Liberators will march up Mount Zion to proclaim judgment on Mount Esau, and *Adonai* will reign supreme.

INSIGHTS FROM THE TRADITION

A *Metsudat David* explains that verse 1:5 refers to people who rob only at night, for fear of being caught by day.

◆ What do you think is the difference between a person who steals at night and one who steals in the light of day?

◆ Do you think that it is easier to do something wrong if you think you will not get caught?

◆ For more discussion on the subject of being caught, see the Haftarah for *Terumah*, Personalizing the Text #20, p. 134.

B Regarding verse 1:10, Plaut teaches that Edom's violent behavior against Israel was doubly hurtful because Edom and Israel were brothers. The nation of Edom is descended from Esau, and the nation of Israel is descended from his twin brother, Jacob.

◆ What kinds of things do siblings do that may hurt each other?

◆ When your sibling(s) tease you, how is it different from when a schoolmate or friend teases you?

◆ Ask your parents what their expectations and hopes are for the relationship between you and your sibling(s).

C Obadiah criticizes Edom in verse 1:14 for standing at the passes.

Rabbi Akiva understood "the passes" to refer to a gap in our prayers (specifically between the paragraphs of the "*Shema*"). He taught that we should not interrupt our prayers with any extraneous talking.

◆ What do you think was Rabbi Akiba's reason for this teaching?

◆ What does it say about the importance of a particular conversation when you can interrupt it with another conversation or activity?

◆ How do you feel when your parents interrupt you when you are on the phone or concentrating on your homework?

D In verse 1:15 Obadiah declares that actions are always requited. *Metsudat David* explains that just as Israel's enemies treated Israel, so will they be treated in the day of *Adonai*.

◆ Do you agree that what goes around comes around? Why or why not?

◆ Describe an example from your own life where this was the case.

STRATEGIES
Analyzing the Text

1 Obadiah's oracle contains many similarities to Jeremiah's, leading some scholars to believe that one might have even quoted the other. Compare verses 1:1-4 and 1:5-6 of the Haftarah with Jeremiah 49:14-16 and 49:9-10.

◆ In your own words, what is Obadiah saying in verses 1:1-6?

2 The terrain of Edom is described in verse 1:3. Edom was located in what is now Jordan. Its capital city, Petra, is today located between Amman and Aqaba in Jordan. In his poem, "Petra," Dean Burgen wrote, "Match me such a marvel, save in Eastern clime, A rose-red city, half as old as time."

◆ Today Petra is a popular tourist destination. Find pictures of the Rose Red City at www.panoramaproductions.net/petra.htm or access www.raingod.com and do a search for Petra.

3 A metaphor comparing Edomites to eagles nesting high among the stars is contained in verse 1:4.

◆ What do you think this metaphor is saying? (For example, is it conveying the ideas of pride, humility, obedience, or stubbornness?)

◆ The verse concludes by announcing that God will pull the Edomites down from their lofty heights. Explain how pride and arrogance might lead people to defy God's will. What other attributes might lead people to defy God?

4 Verse 1:5 demonstrates that even robbers leave something behind, as do gatherers of grapes in the vineyards. But those who will destroy Edom will leave no trace at all.

The Arabs began to expel the Edomites from their territory in the sixth century B.C.E. The Edomites were forced to settle in the Negev Desert. There, many were forcibly converted to Judaism by John Hyrcanus in the first century C.E. The remaining Edomites were annihilated by the Romans only a few years later.

◆ Design a tombstone for the nation of Edom. For the epitaph, use one of the predictions from Obadiah (verses 8-10) or from the following other texts: Jeremiah 49:14-20, Amos 1:11-12, and Lamentations 4:21.

5 Edom did not simply stand by while the Babylonians destroyed Jerusalem.

◆ Explain how Edom actively betrayed Israel, according to verses 1:11-14.

TEACHING HAFTARAH

- Compare the information provided by Obadiah in verses 1:11-14 with the account in Psalm 137:7. Both accounts refer to the Edomites' collaboration with the Babylonians in the destruction of the Temple in 586 B.C.E.

6 Obadiah 1:16 reads: "That same cup that you drank on My Holy Mount shall all nations drink evermore . . . ."

- How would you interpret this verse? Consider the following interpretations and decide which you prefer, and why.

  - Edom drank with joy at the destruction of Jerusalem, so shall all nations rejoice at the devastation of Edom.

  - Or, just as Israel drank the cup of bitterness at the destruction of Jerusalem, so shall Israel's enemies drink bitterness at the time of their own demise.

- Draw a representation of your own interpretation of this verse or of the interpretation that you prefer.

7 Obadiah envisions in verses 1:19-20 a united Kingdom of Israel that would possess more territory than it historically had before. Find the following locations on a map of the region (see Appendix C, p. 625).

(Note: "Sepharad" is often understood as Spain, but it is more likely that the word in verse 1:20 should be understood as referring to Babylonia or Asia Minor, which was called Saparda in Persian cuneiform inscriptions.)

- "Zarephath" was a town in southern Phoenicia. (verse 20)

- "The Negeb" refers to the south of Israel.

- "Shephelah" means the coastal lowlands.

- "Gilead" is the land northeast of the Jordan River.

- "Ephraimite country" is a tribal region of which Samaria was the capital.

- How do you think the besieged Israelites might have felt to hear a prediction that one day their territory would be bigger and better than ever?

- Make a word scramble with the names of these foreign nations. Give yours to another student to unscramble.

8 Obadiah's name means "servant of God." The Hebrew ending, *"Yah,"* is one of God's many names in biblical tradition.

- Why do you think "servant of *Yah*" is an appropriate name for a prophet?

- Play a word game. Write on the board "Obadiah the Servant of God." Then make as many words as you can from the letters of this phrase (e.g., toes or rose). Use a letter only once in each word (you can't make "roses" because there is only one "s"), but use letters again in subsequent words. Base the score on the length of words found, and give double credit if a student finds a word that is in the Haftarah or that he/she can argue fits the job description of a prophet.

Connecting the Text To the Sedra

9 Obadiah 1:1-21 is the Haftarah for *Vayishlach* according to the Sephardic ritual and also for many Ashkenazim. However, some Ashkenazim read Hosea 11:7-12:12 as the Haftarah for *Vayishlach*.

- Compare the two Haftarot and decide which you prefer to go with the Sedra, and why.

10 In the Sedra Jacob and Edom (Esau) enjoy a peaceful reconciliation. Unfortunately, as the Haftarah demonstrates, the relationship between the descendants of the two brothers is anything but peaceful and reconciled.

◆ To learn more about the troubled relationship between Israel and Edom, read Genesis 36:1-19, Numbers 20:14-21, I Samuel 14:47, I Kings 11:15-16, II Kings 14:7, II Chronicles 20:22, II Chronicles 25:11-12, and Psalm 137:7. Make a mural of the events described in these verses.

◆ Imagine Jacob and Esau could know the fate of their descendants' relationship. Write a letter from one brother to the other (your choice) describing his sadness and regret about the troubled state of affairs.

11 In the Haftarah Obadiah says that Edom will get its just punishment for its treachery toward Israel.

In the Sedra Dinah's brothers kill all the men in the town of Shechem in retaliation for the rape of Dinah by one man. There is great discussion among the commentators whether or not this punishment went beyond the principle of measure for measure punishment.

◆ Do you believe that the story in the Sedra involved a measure for measure response? Can you find evidence of other measure for measure responses in the Sedra?

◆ Belief in measure for measure consequences is repeated throughout the Bible and later Jewish tradition. Discuss the following statements, then choose one of the quotations to illustrate in a comic strip.

• "As I have done, so God has requited me." (Judges 1:7)

• "Those who honor me I will honor, and who despise me shall be lightly esteemed." (I Samuel 2:30)

• "They shall eat the fruit of their deeds." (Isaiah 3:10)

• "You render to every man according to his work." (Psalms 62:13)

• "Who digs a pit shall fall into it." (Proverbs 26:27)

• "The reward for virtue is virtue, and sin's reward is sin." (*Pirke Avot* 4:2)

• "God waits a long time, but then pays with interest in the end." (Yiddish proverb)

12 In the Haftarah and indeed in Jewish tradition in general, Edom is seen as a villain. Contrast his reputation with Esau's actions in the Sedra.

For example, in Genesis 33, Esau (Edom) greets his estranged brother with hugs and kisses, wants to journey with him, and even offers him some of his soldiers for protection.

In Genesis 35, Esau helps Jacob to bury Isaac, their deceased father.

In Genesis 36, Esau voluntarily moves to another land so that he and Jacob won't get in each other's way.

◆ How would you characterize Esau based on this Sedra?

◆ Why, then, does Esau have such a terrible reputation in Jewish tradition? (Note that over the years Edom came to be associated through various *midrashim* and Rabbinic traditions with Rome, one of Israel's greatest enemies. Some say that the Rabbis referred to Rome in code as Edom because they could not come right out and criticize the Romans under whose rule they lived.)

◆ Release the historical Esau from his dastardly reputation by having a testimonial dinner for him. Deliver complimentary speeches by Jacob, Isaac, Esau's children, and others.

13 There are opportunists in both Haftarah and Sedra. In the Haftarah Edom seems to have taken advantage of a situation they did not create by attacking the defeated and fleeing Israelites (verses 1:11-14).

In the Sedra the Shechemites plan to benefit economically from a situation created when Shechem raped Dinah (Genesis 34:23). Furthermore, Jacob's sons wait for the men of Shechem to be in pain from their circumcisions, and then take advantage of the situation to destroy the city.

♦ Do you agree that these are all examples of opportunistic behavior? Explain your rationale. Are there other examples of opportunistic behavior in these two texts?

♦ When is it good to act in an opportunistic fashion, and when not?

♦ Do you know anyone who has been hurt by an opportunist? Do you know anyone who has been successful acting in an opportunistic fashion?

Extending the Text

14 The Book of Obadiah is the shortest book in the Bible, containing only one chapter consisting of 21 verses.

♦ Learn the following facts about the Bible and answer the question that follows each.

• The Book of Psalms has the most chapters. How many does it have?

• There are 39 books in the Bible. List them in order.

• Traditionally, however, there are considered to be 24 books in the Bible, not 39. The smaller number is due to the fact that several books are counted as one. For example, Ezra and Nehemiah are counted

as one. Can you figure out what other books were paired together to get the number 24?

• There are five books that are called *Megillot*: Song of Songs, Ruth, Lamentations, Ecclesiastes, and Esther. Why do you think the *Megillot* are incorporated into the Bible in this order? (Hint: Passover is in the month of Nisan, which is the first month of the biblical Hebrew calendar.) Each of the *Megillot* is read in synagogue on a Jewish holiday. Match each one to the holiday on which it is read (i.e., Passover, Shavuot, Tishah B'Av, Sukkot, Purim). For more information, see the *Encyclopaedia Judaica*, vol. 4, pp. 814-830.

15 It is unclear exactly who Obadiah was. According to one theory, he was an Edomite proselyte. Of him it is written in *Sanhedrin* 39b: "From the very forest itself comes the handle of the axe that fells the forest."

♦ If, in fact, Obadiah was a descendant of Edom, how was he the best man for the job of condemning Edom?

♦ Make a business card for Obadiah that reflects the quotation from *Sanhedrin*.

16 Edom was guilty of aiding the Babylonians in the destruction of Jerusalem and the devastation of the Israelites. The Edomites were actively involved in the crime against the Israelites. During the Holocaust, many nations stood idly by as the Nazis massacred the Jewish population of Europe. Their refusal to help contributed to Hitler's crime against the Jews.

One striking example of this refusal to help came to be known as "the voyage of the damned." In June 1939, the American Government refused to provide a refuge for the 907 German Jews who were fleeing their homeland's Nazi terror aboard a ship called the St. Louis. The ocean liner, which had already been turned away from Cuba, was forced to return to Europe, where the passengers were dispersed to Belgium, France, the Netherlands, and Britain. Many of them were sent to concentration camps and killed by the Nazis.

◆ You can learn more about the St. Louis and the people who sailed on it at www.nytimes.com/learning/students/ask_reporters/articles/berger-article2.html.

◆ What other nations made the Holocaust worse? See a speech given by former Secretary of State Madeleine Albright concerning Swiss financial activities that may have prolonged the war at www.secretary.state.gov/www/statements/971115a.html.

◆ In contrast, see a Declaration by the U.S. Secretary of the Treasury on Gold Policy dated February 22, 1944 at www.yale.edu/lawweb/avalon/wwii/gold.htm. How was this Declaration a condemnation of those who stand by while crimes are committed?

◆ What do you think is the difference between the crime of refusing to help and the crime of actively hurting someone? Is one crime worse than the other? Does one crime lead to the other?

17 In Analyzing the Text #7, p. 562, we learned that Obadiah stoked the flames of Israelite hope by promising that one day Israel would be bigger and better than in the past. Today, Arab propagandists promote the myth called "Greater Israel," which accuses Israel of always trying to expand its territories to the borders predicted by the prophets (like Obadiah).

An organization called FLAME (Facts and Logic About the Middle East) seeks to debunk the myth of Greater Israel. An advertisement they placed in the *Jerusalem Post* on April 26, 2001 read:

"One of the persistent myths about the Israel-Arab conflict is that Israel is an "expansionist power" and that it is determined to aggrandize its territory so as to eventually reach from the Nile to the Euphrates. This is the concept of 'Greater Israel.' This ridiculous concept is the creation of Arab propaganda. It has been eagerly picked up by those who are not fond of the Jewish State.

Israel (including the West Bank, Gaza, and Golan taken by Israel during wars of aggression by Arabs against Israel) is just over 10,000 square miles. California is 15 times that size. The Arab countries in contrast are huge, occupying twice the area of the United States.

It seems that the size of Israel, whether 'greater' or 'lesser,' is not at all the concern of Israel's implacable Arab enemies. The very existence of Israel, of a Jewish state in their midst of whatever size, is unacceptable to the Arabs."

◆ Critique this advertisement; identify its strengths and its weaknesses.

18 The Book of Genesis is filled with stories of siblings who don't get along.

◆ Form groups, each of which reads, discusses, and then acts out for the class one of the following accounts: Cain and Abel (Genesis 4), Isaac and Ishmael (Genesis 21), Jacob and Esau (Genesis 25:19-34 and 27:1-46), Rachel and Leah (Genesis 29-30), Joseph and his brothers (Genesis 37). You may want to read and/or act out the related skits in *Parashah Plays* by Richard J. Allen.

◆ What lessons do these stories seek to teach us?

19 Rabbi Akiva taught in Insights from the Tradition #C, pp. 560-561, that we should not interrupt our prayers with extraneous talking.

Mishnah *Berachot* 2:1 identifies several points in our prayers where we may take a break and talk if we need. The points fall between the call to worship *("Barchu")* and the end of the main prayer (the *"Amidah"*).

The first break is at the end of the first blessing before the *"Shema"* (Blessed is God Who creates light).

The next break is at the end of the second blessing (Blessed is God Who has chosen Israel with love) and the *"Shema"* itself.

The third break falls after the *"Shema,"* which includes the *V'ahavta* paragraph, "And you shall love *Adonai* your God" (Deuteronomy 6), and before the next paragraph beginning, "And it shall come to pass" (Deuteronomy 11:13-21).

The next break comes between the paragraph beginning, "And it shall come to pass," and the paragraph beginning, "And *Adonai* said" (Numbers 15:37-41).

The last break falls between the paragraph beginning, "And *Adonai* said," and the paragraph beginning "True and firm."

◆ Using a *Siddur*, identify the breaks as outlined above.

◆ The Mishnah also describes what kinds of interruptions are allowed: "In the breaks, one may give greeting out of respect and return greeting. In the middle of a section, one may give greeting out of fear and return it. So says Rabbi Meir. Rabbi Judah says, 'In the middle, one may give greeting out of fear and return it out of respect; in the breaks, one may give greeting out of respect and return greeting to anyone.'" Make a chart that diagrams the differences between the opinions of Rabbi Meir and Rabbi Judah.

◆ Whom might you greet out of respect, and whom out of fear?

◆ With whose opinion do you agree, and why?

◆ The Mishnah assumes that one way to honor someone you respect is to greet him/her quickly when you meet. How might greeting someone first be a sign of respect?

20 We learned above in Insights from the Tradition #D, p. 561, that our actions are always requited.

◆ Read and discuss the following folktale about Joseph, who loved Shabbat (adapted from "Merit of the Sabbath" in *Because God Loves Stories*, edited by Steve Zeitlin, pp. 38-42):

Joseph earned his living as a jeweler. He was talented and honest and good. He observed Shabbat each week. The leather merchant whose store was next to Joseph's was not a religiously observant man, and was not a nice man either. He devised an evil plan to challenge Joseph's faith and good nature.

One Thursday morning, the leather merchant gave Joseph a beautiful diamond ring to fix. Joseph put the ring safely in his drawer and went to have lunch. While he was gone, the leather merchant secretly stole back the ring and threw it into the nearby river.

When Joseph discovered the ring was gone, he searched everywhere, but could not find it. Friday morning, the leather merchant demanded his ring. Calmly, Joseph responded that he had not fixed it yet and that he was closing his shop for Shabbat. He promised that the ring would be ready by Sunday morning. Joseph returned home to prepare for Shabbat, stopping along the way to buy some fish for their meal. He resolved to enjoy Shabbat and keep his faith that everything would turn out all right.

On Sunday morning, the leather merchant stormed into Joseph's shop, demanding his ring. Joseph opened his drawer and handed the merchant his repaired diamond ring. "This is impossible," said the leather merchant. "I heard the ring was stolen and thrown into the river." Joseph knew it had been the leather merchant who had stolen his own ring, so he explained what happened. When Joseph's wife was cleaning the fish for Shabbat, she slit the fish in half with her knife and found inside the fish a beautiful diamond ring — safe and sound.

The astonished leather merchant responded, "Joseph, there really must be something to your faith and to Shabbat. Please teach me." And Joseph became the leather merchant's teacher. The two men became good friends who spent many, many afternoons talking together in the marketplace.

◆ What lesson do you think the leather merchant learned from this experience?

◆ Does this story teach that one's actions are requited? Why, and why not?

Personalizing the Text

21 Obadiah is also associated with the Obadiah in the Haftarah for *Ki Tisa*, pp. 164-172, who was the servant of the evil King Ahab and his wife Jezebel.

The passage in *Sanhedrin* 39b says that God chose Obadiah to prophesy against Edom because he lived with two wicked people (Ahab and Jezebel), and yet did not learn to behave according to their deeds and examples. Edom (Esau), on the other hand, lived with two righteous people (Isaac and Rebecca), and did not learn from their good deeds and examples.

◆ Can you identify two people in your life who serve as good role models for you? Make a

presentation to the class on your favorite role model.

◆ Name some people in your life whose bad examples you must resist.

◆ Is it easier for you to emulate good examples or to resist bad ones? If the latter, how can you go about changing this?

22 Israel and Edom were brothers and eternal enemies.

◆ Learn the song *"Hinay Mah Tov,"* based on Psalm 133:1, which says, "Behold how good and how pleasant it is for brothers to dwell together." The song may be found in *B'Kol Echad*, edited by Jeffrey Shiovitz, p. 85, and on the accompanying audiocassettes *Shirei B'Kol Echad*. These may be ordered from the United Synagogue for Conservative Judaism at www.uscj.org/booksvc.

23 The troubled relationship between Esau and Jacob ends up in bitter betrayal between their descendants. In contrast, Proverbs 17:17 teaches, "A brother is born to aid in adversity."

◆ Interview your family and friends about times when their sibling(s) helped them out of a jam.

◆ Write a poem in praise of your own sibling(s).

24 The entire Book of Obadiah is included in this Haftarah.

◆ Choose a verse of the Haftarah to draw or paint as a cover for the short Book of Obadiah. Compare your rendition with the illustration of this Haftarah in *The Illustrated Torah* by Michal Meron, p. 44.

25 Write a book review of the Book of Obadiah.

TEACHING HAFTARAH

Other Resources

26 Read and discuss the essay, "Vengeance or Retribution?" by Plaut in *The Haftarah Commentary*, p. 89.

27 View and discuss the film *The Straight Story* (1999, rated G, 112 minutes), about one man who travels across the country on a lawn mower to make peace with his ailing brother.

28 View and discuss the film *Marvin's Room* (1996, rated PG-13, 98 minutes), about a long estranged sister who reunites with (and may have the power to save) her sister, who has been diagnosed with leukemia.

29 View and discuss the film about brothers, race, and reconciliation called *A Family Thing* (1996, rated PG-13, 109 minutes).

30 Read *The Hesed Boomerang* by Jack Doueck, which discusses how good actions beget more good actions.

31 In Abraham J. Twerski's book *I Didn't Ask to Be in This Family: Sibling Relationships and How They Shape Adult Behavior and Dependencies*, he explores the complexities of sibling relationships, as portrayed in the "Peanuts" comic strip by Charles M. Schulz. Use strips from the book for class exploration and discussion.

32 Read and discuss the chapter on Obadiah in *Messengers of God: A Jewish Prophets Who's Who* by Ronald H. Isaacs, pp. 154-156.

33 For a *D'var Torah* on this Haftarah, see the web site of the Fuchsberg Center for Conservative Judaism in Jerusalem, www.uscj.org.il/haftarah/vayishlach5762.html.

Involving the Family

34 Based on Insights from the Tradition #C, pp. 560-561, show how much you value your family time together. For one month, enjoy uninterrupted family meals by letting your answering machine get your phone calls. Remember to turn down the volume so you won't be tempted to pick up the phone.

Bar/Bat Mitzvah Project

35 Because of the troubled relationship between brothers, Israel and Edom ended up being enemy nations. Big Brothers/Big Sisters of America is America's oldest and largest youth mentoring organization, dedicated to helping young people build a great future with the help of strong and supportive relationships. Donate a portion of your Bar/Bat Mitzvah gifts to this worthy cause. Contact them at http://bbbsa.org.

JONAH 1:1-4:11 and MICAH 7:18-20
YOM KIPPUR AFTERNOON

 This Haftarah has been paired with the holiday of Yom Kippur, when we read it in the afternoon with Leviticus 18 or 19. See "Connecting the Text To the Holiday," pp. 572-573, for an exploration of the many ways the two texts and the holiday shed light on each other.

SYNOPSIS

The Book of Jonah stands apart from all the other books of the Minor Prophets because it is almost entirely a story about a prophet rather than prophetic utterances. Only one verse of the book's four chapters contains a prophecy by Jonah (verse 3:4). There is profound uncertainty about the origins of this book. Some theories date it to the eighth century B.C.E., while other theories date it to the fourth century B.C.E. (See *Encyclopaedia Judaica*, vol.10, pp. 172-3, for more details about the origins of the book.)

As the book begins, *Adonai* tells Jonah son of Amittai to go to Nineveh (the capital of Assyria, Israel's enemy) and proclaim judgment on it for its wickedness. Instead of doing as he is told, Jonah attempts to run away from serving God by boarding a boat to Tarshish (in the opposite direction).

The boat is overwhelmed by a great storm at sea. Each of the sailors prays to his own god for deliverance, and they throw cargo overboard to make the boat lighter. Through it all, Jonah is sound asleep in the ship's hold. The captain wakes Jonah and implores him to pray for help. The sailors decide to cast lots to see on whose account the storm has risen. The lot falls on Jonah, who admits that he is a Hebrew who has run away

from God's service. He instructs the sailors to throw him overboard, but the men are reluctant to comply with his strange request. Finally, they agree, and beg *Adonai* for forgiveness for their actions. After they cast Jonah overboard and the storm abates, the sailors offer a sacrifice to *Adonai*.

Adonai provides a huge fish to swallow Jonah, who remains in the belly of the fish for three days and three nights. From the fish's belly, Jonah offers a prayer of thanksgiving for being saved from the waves that would have drowned him. *Adonai* then commands the fish to spew out Jonah onto dry land.

Adonai again instructs Jonah to speak to the people of Nineveh, and this time Jonah goes at once. In Nineveh Jonah proclaims, "Forty days more, and Nineveh shall be overthrown!" The people of Nineveh believe Jonah, proclaim a fast, and put on sackcloth. Even the king of Nineveh sits in ashes, urging his people to repent of their evil ways and turn toward God to appease God's wrath. God sees that the Ninevites are sincerely repenting and renounces their punishment.

Jonah is greatly disturbed that God renounced punishment against Nineveh. He complains that he wasted his time because he knew that God is compassionate and would forgive Nineveh. Jonah is so distraught he even asks to die. We are then told that Jonah witnesses the fate of Nineveh from a place east of the city. He makes a little *sukkah* and sits under its shade. God provides a plant that grows up over Jonah to provide shade for the prophet, and Jonah is very happy to have that plant to protect him from the sun. But then God sends a worm to attack the plant so it withers.

That day, as the sun beats down on Jonah's head, Jonah grows faint and begs again for death. God asks him if he is so grieved about the loss of his plant, and Jonah says yes.

Adonai points out that if Jonah cares so much about the plant, which he did not grow himself, then doesn't it make sense that God would care about Nineveh, whose 120,000 people (and animals, too) God created?

The Haftarah concludes with three verses from the Book of Micah. These verses remind us that God forgives iniquity and remains devoted and faithful to the descendants of Abraham and Jacob.

INSIGHTS FROM THE TRADITION

A God gave Jonah a prophetic message to proclaim, but Jonah fled, suppressing God's message (verses 1:1-3). According to *Sanhedrin* 89a, one who suppresses a prophecy given to him is liable for the death penalty at the hands of God (not by a human court).

◆ Why do you think someone who suppresses a prophecy would be subject to the death penalty?

◆ If someone knows something today that would be important for others to know and yet refuses to share the information, is he/she guilty of wrongdoing? (For example, if a tobacco company employee knew about the dangers of smoking and nicotine and neglected to share that information with the public, should they be punished for their silence?)

◆ Can you think of any examples of dangerous silence (e.g., nuclear waste, terrorist activity, drug dealing)?

B In spite of having tried to suppress a prophecy, Jonah was not killed. Some argue that Jonah was spared the death penalty because his motive was to save Israel from harm. Rashi suggests one way Jonah tried to save Israel: Jonah feared that if he rebuked the Ninevites and they repented, it would make Israel look really bad. After all, the Israelites are constantly warned by prophets to heed God's word, but they don't (Rashi on 1:3). Nineveh's compliance would incline God to punish Israel for its noncompliance.

◆ What is the difference between judging behavior on its own merits and comparatively? According to Rashi, which method of judging Israel was God going to use? Which method do you think is better?

◆ When a teacher grades on a curve, which method is used? In your view, should a teacher grade on a curve? Why or why not?

C As a storm took over the ship, the sailors each began to pray to their own god (verse 1:5). *Kiddushin* 82a says that sailors are generally pious people.

◆ Why do you think the Talmud considers sailors to be pious people?

◆ There is a saying that there are no atheists in a foxhole. This means that when people are in danger (like sailors on a ship or soldiers in a foxhole), they tend to become religious and turn to God for help. Do you agree that people tend to turn to God when they are in danger or trouble? Why do you think this is so?

◆ Ask your parents or grandparents if they ever knew anyone who became more religious upon becoming ill.

D In verse 4:1 Jonah was angry that Nineveh repented and God decided not to destroy the city. According to Rashi, Jonah thought that scoffers would say Nineveh's repentance had nothing to do with their salvation. Instead, they would think that Nineveh was saved because Jonah was wrong about his original prophecy.

◆ Explain why this *midrash* suggests that Jonah was worried about what people would say about his prophetic abilities.

◆ Do you worry about what people will think?

◆ How do your worries affect your ability to do what you really think is right or what you really want to do?

STRATEGIES
Analyzing the Text

1 Jonah was told to go to Nineveh, the capital of Israel's enemy, Assyria. One possible reason Jonah tried to shirk his responsibility is given in Insights from the Tradition #B, p. 570. But perhaps there is another reason. Jonah was instructed to warn the Ninevites that they would be destroyed if they did not repent.

◆ Do you think it was possible that Jonah did not want to save his nation's enemy?

◆ Why do you think God wanted to save Israel's enemy from utter destruction by offering them the opportunity to repent?

◆ Compare Jonah's sense of morality to that of God in this story.

2 As the sailors in verse 1:5 throw their wares out of the cargo holds of the ship to help it float higher, Jonah goes down to a cargo hold to sleep.

◆ What is ironic about Jonah sleeping in a cargo hold while the sailors attempt to empty cargo to save the ship?

◆ Can you identify other ironies in the book of Jonah?

3 There is a sharp contrast between the sailors praying and Jonah sleeping in verse 1:5.

◆ Why was Jonah not praying to God?

4 When the lot fell on Jonah in verse 1:7, the sailors wanted to know who he was and why he was the cause of the storm, but they asked him very strange questions. Only after he answers these questions do the sailors ask Jonah (in verse 1:10), "What have you done?" Here are the questions from verse 1:8 that the sailors asked Jonah:

• What is your business?

• Where have you come from?

• What is your country?

• Of what people are you?

◆ Why do you think the sailors asked these particular questions in this particular order?

◆ What questions would you have asked, and in what order?

5 Jonah calls himself a "Hebrew" in verse 1:9. *"Ivri"* is a term used in the Bible to identify an Israelite in contrast to non-Israelites.

◆ Study some of the other times the term *"Ivri"* is used: Genesis 14:13, Genesis 40:15, and Exodus 3:18.

◆ Why do you think Jonah identified himself as a Hebrew to the non-Israelite sailors?

6 In verse 1:11 the sailors ask what they must do to Jonah to end the storm. Jonah tells them to throw him into the sea.

◆ What other possible answers might Jonah have offered (e.g., take me to Nineveh)?

◆ Why did Jonah not just jump into the sea himself?

◆ What does it say about the sailors that they were reluctant to throw Jonah into the sea?

What does it say about Jonah that he put them in that position?

7 Jonah sets up a *sukkah* outside Nineveh and sits under it to wait and see what would occur in the city (4:5).

◆ What do you think of Jonah based on this behavior?

◆ Based on Jonah's reaction to Nineveh's salvation in verses 4:1-3, what do you think Jonah was waiting to see?

◆ Based on what Jonah hoped to see, what is your opinion of Jonah?

8 The parable of Jonah's plant is given in verses 4:5-11.

◆ Reread this selection. Explain its significance and lesson in your own words.

◆ Make a comic strip of Jonah in his *sukkah*, enjoying the plant, then losing the plant, then listening to God's lesson.

Connecting the Text To the Holiday

9 Rabbi Sidney Greenberg teaches that Jonah ran, as we all do, from God's instructions. On Yom Kippur, we repent, stop running, and turn back to God.

◆ What does it mean that we all run from what we are required to do?

◆ List at least three times in the Book of Jonah when God exerts moral influence on characters. (For example, God steers Jonah in the right direction with the storm at sea, God instructs the Ninevites to repent, and God uses a physical parable to teach Jonah the value of mercy.)

◆ How does Judaism steer us in the right path, instruct us about what is right, and give us examples of how to behave morally?

◆ Design a cover for a *Machzor* that features Rabbi Greenberg's lesson.

10 The Ninevites repent, wear sackcloth, fast, sit in ashes, and pray to God. We observe similar rituals on Yom Kippur, our own Day of Atonement, on which we hope for the same forgiveness that God granted Nineveh.

Although we do not wear sackcloth and sit in ashes, we are enjoined to refrain from wearing leather shoes (considered a luxury) and washing ourselves.

◆ How do you think such practices as not wearing leather shoes and not washing ourselves on Yom Kippur help us to concentrate on repentance and return to God?

◆ Like the Ninevites, we spend most of Yom Kippur in prayer. The prayer services for Yom Kippur are the longest of the year. Why do you think prayer is an appropriate activity for the Day of Atonement?

While great and small observed the fast in Nineveh, according to Jewish law, children are not to fast on Yom Kippur until they are near the age of puberty, at which time they should be gradually trained in fasting. This is typically understood to mean that for a few years before their Bar/Bat Mitzvah, children should fast part of the day, then fast a little longer each year. The infirm are also exempt from the fast because one is not allowed to fast if it will endanger one's health.

◆ Plan a fasting schedule for a child from age ten on.

11 We are taught that true repentance means being in the same situation twice and not making the same mistake. When the word of God first came to Jonah, he fled. When the word of God came to Jonah a second time (verse 3:1), he went "at once" to Nineveh to deliver God's message. He did not make the same mistake a second time.

- Why do you think the measure of real repentance is to avoid making the same mistake twice?

- Do you think this is a fair measure of real repentance?

12 The Ninevites pray in verse 3:9 that God will control God's anger and avert the evil decree against them.

Throughout the Yom Kippur liturgy, we remind God that, "You are slow to anger, ready to forgive. You do not wish that the sinner die; You would have the sinner repent and live."

- Read the three verses from Micah (7:18-20) that are used to conclude the Haftarah for Yom Kippur afternoon. How do these three verses reinforce the Yom Kippur liturgy?

- We pray that God will employ both the Divine attributes of justice and compassion when determining our fate for the upcoming year. How might we learn from Yom Kippur and the Book of Jonah that we, too, ought to temper our judgment and anger with compassion toward others?

13 When Nineveh repents in verse 3:10, God renounces the calamity that was going to befall them because of their wickedness. According to *Rosh HaShanah* 16b, four (or five) things change an evil decree: charity, supplication,

change of name, change of conduct, and some say, change of place.

- Which actions did Nineveh do?

- On Yom Kippur, in the *"Unetaneh Tokef"* prayer, we review all the ways God is passing judgment on us. At the same time, we remember that repentance, prayer, and deeds of kindness can remove the severity of the decree of judgment against us. Which actions did Nineveh do to remove the severity of their decree?

- Compare *Rosh HaShanah* 16b with the *"Unetaneh Tokef."* Prayer is a type of supplication. Deeds of kindness fit into the category of charity. How is repentance a way for us to change our name, conduct, and place?

14 Jonah builds a *sukkah* immediately after he delivered his prophecy to Nineveh (verse 4:5). Similarly, we build a *sukkah* for the celebration of Sukkot immediately after Yom Kippur; some even hammer one nail in before they break their fast.

- Why do you suppose we rush, like Jonah, to build the *sukkah* immediately after fulfilling our previous responsibility (observing Yom Kippur)?

- Since Sukkot is known as the "Time of Our Joy," what do you think it means that as soon as Yom Kippur is over, we rush to begin our observance of Sukkot?

- Does the fact that Sukkot immediately follows the days of judgment reflect a positive outlook on the year to come?

MICAH 5:6-6:8
BALAK בלק

This Haftarah has been paired with *Parashat Balak*, Numbers 22:2-25:9. See "Connecting the Text To the Sedra," pp. 577-579, for an exploration of the many ways the two texts shed light on each other.

SYNOPSIS

Micah lived roughly between 740 B.C.E. and 690 B.C.E. in the town of Moreshet in the Southern Kingdom. He probably lived in a small town in the foothills between Jerusalem and Gaza near Philistine cities; country life is often evident in his images of farmers and shepherds. Micah would have been near enough to Jerusalem to be able to go and hear Isaiah prophesy. He also could have been influenced by the contemporaneous teachings of Amos who originated in a Southern town, Tekoa, not far from Micah's hometown (although Amos left home to prophesy in the North). Micah, like Amos, pleads for justice.

Micah focuses on many of the ills of his society. His main concern is people who accumulate wealth at the cost of causing misery to the destitute masses. He implores his people to stop pursuing wealth, end corrupt leadership, and live by God's demands of justice, mercy, and modesty. He warns that as the Northern Kingdom was destroyed during his lifetime (721 B.C.E.), so will the Southern Kingdom be destroyed.

In general, the Book of Micah is divided into three units: chapters 1-3 are condemnations, 4-5 are consolations, and 6-7 are a mixture. This Haftarah includes the end of the condemnations and the beginning of the consolations.

At the beginning of the Haftarah, Micah imagines a time in the future when Israel's enemies will be destroyed. A remnant of Israel will remain and will either be a blessing (like dew) or a curse (like lions) to the surrounding nations. Micah then predicts God's destruction of all the devices (chariots, divination, idols) the Israelites use in vain to strengthen themselves. Instead, they need to learn to rely only on God and God's word. Next, God argues that throughout Israel's history God has never caused them hardship, but has only helped them. God cites the Exodus from slavery and the help of the prophets, Moses, Aaron, and Miriam. God also points out that God prevented the enemy Balak from having the prophet Balaam curse Israel.

The Israelites respond by admitting their need to repent, but question whether they could ever find a sacrificial offering that would be big enough or significant enough to warrant God's forgiveness. The people misunderstand what God wants from them; Micah explains that all God really wants is for them to act justly, mercifully, and modestly.

INSIGHTS FROM THE TRADITION

In verse 5:10 Micah says that God will destroy Israel's cities. According to *Ketubot* 110b, it is better to live in a town anyway: in a city with walls, life is harder.

◆ In what ways might city life be harder than rural life?

◆ Cities, today as well as in Talmudic times, suffered from air pollution. Is air pollution a problem where you live? What is being done about it?

B In verse 6:3 God asks, "What hardship have I caused you?"

According to *Numbers Rabbah* 20:5, God always made the commandments easy to follow so as not to weary Israel. For example, God requests sacrificial animals, but says to Israel, "I did not put you to any trouble and I did not bid you weary yourselves among the mountains in order to bring a sacrifice unto Me from those that run wild, but I asked only for domesticated animals for sacrifice, from those which you find in your own yard."

◆ Explain how God made sure that the *mitzvah* of sacrifice would not be a hardship for Israel.

◆ Today, is it easy or difficult to be a Jew?

◆ Give examples of things that are easy or difficult about being Jewish. Alternatively, survey Jewish adults about what is difficult or easy for them.

C Not only does God ask, "What hardship have I caused you?" In verse 6:4 God also points out that Moses, Aaron, and Miriam were sent to Israel. *Leviticus Rabbah* 27:6 tells a parable: A king sent his messengers to a certain province, and the people of the province stood before them and served them food and drink with fear and trepidation. Similarly, God said to Israel: "I sent you three messengers, Moses, Aaron, and Miriam. Did they, perchance, eat of what was yours, or did they drink of what was yours, or did they cause you any hardship? Is it not for their sake that you were maintained, the manna being for the sake of Moses, the well for the sake of Miriam, and the clouds of glory for the sake of Aaron?"

◆ Explain how this *midrash* teaches that ordinary people have to work for a king and his

staff, but God sends prophets who work for the ordinary people.

◆ Today, do we serve our leaders or do our leaders serve us? Consider examples from youth groups, school councils, or national leaders.

D In verse 6:8 Israel is told that one of the only things they have to do in order to please God is to do justice. According to Radak, doing justice means keeping all the laws and commandments involving relationships between one person and another person.

Since this teaching concludes that the main thing required by God is that one fulfill commandments involving other people, it suggests that the prime concern of religion is how people get along.

◆ Explain Radak's teaching in your own words.

◆ How does the idea that a prime concern of religion is how people get along square with your definition of religion?

◆ Design a logo for a synagogue that reflects this religious mission. Alternatively, create a name for a synagogue that reflects this sentiment.

E Verse 6:8 also says that instead of offering sacrifices, we should please God by walking modestly with God. According to Radak, the phrase "walking modestly with God" teaches that a person's relationship with God (one's beliefs about God, and one's love for God) is private and unknown to anyone else.

◆ Do you agree that beliefs about God are, or should be, a private matter?

◆ Before we offer people an *aliyah* in synagogue, we don't ask them to confirm that they believe certain things about God. Why don't we do so? Should we do so? Why or why not?

F *Sukkah* 49b says that walking modestly with God means performing ("walking") *mitzvot* quietly, modestly, and without fanfare.

◆ Does this teaching mean that we should observe religious commandments and traditions without fanfare? What is your view of this?

◆ Consider this scenario: A teacher arrives in class every day with a cup of coffee. He sets it down, removes the lid, and, aloud, in front of a room full of students, recites the proper blessing over the coffee before drinking it. Explain what *mitzvah* (or *mitzvot*) the teacher is performing. Do you think he was performing the *mitzvah* of reciting the blessing over the coffee modestly?

◆ What good reasons might the teacher have for performing the *mitzvah* publicly?

STRATEGIES
Analyzing the Text

1 Verse 5:6 contains a metaphor that compares Israel to dew on the grass of the other nations.

◆ How does dew help grass?

◆ How will Israel or Israel's moral teachings be refreshing and give life to the nations as dew does to grass?

◆ For advanced study, see Deuteronomy 32:2, in which Moses uses similar images.

◆ Wake up early one morning to see the dew on the grass.

2 Verse 5:7 offers another metaphor describing Israel's relationship with the nations: Israel will be like a lion among the beasts.

◆ What does this image convey to you about Israel?

◆ How can it be that Israel could be both a blessing (dew) and a curse (lion) to other nations?

◆ Depict either the metaphor of the lion among the beasts or the metaphor of dew on grass in a painting or collage.

3 Verses 5:9-13 list all the devices Israel used to protect and strengthen themselves, and that they will no longer need because God will destroy the enemy.

◆ Identify each device and how it might have helped Israel feel stronger. Was it real strength or false hope? What is the difference?

4 In verse 6:3 God says to Israel, "My people! What wrong have I done you?"

◆ The Hebrew text does not contain an exclamation point (or any punctuation, for that matter). What do you think the translator wanted to indicate about the mood and emotions of the speaker by adding an exclamation point?

◆ Other translators write, "O My people, what wrong have I done you?" How is this translation different from the first?

◆ In Hebrew, "my people" is one word *(ami)*. One commentator wrote about this word, "This one tender word, repeated in verse 6:5, contains a whole volume of reproof and gives deep emotion to the argument." Explain what you think he meant.

◆ Act out the scene in verse 6:3 with different moods in mind (e.g., tenderness, frustration, anger, etc.). Convey the mood with body language and tone of voice. See if others in your class can guess which mood you were trying to convey.

5 The people respond to God's cause in verses 6:6-7. They ask what they can do to atone.

◆ What is the implied answer to all their exaggerated suggestions?

◆ Explain how the people's response indicates their understanding that they have sinned and need to atone.

Connecting the Text To the Sedra

6 In the Sedra Israel is compared to a lion eating torn prey (Numbers 23:24 and 24:9). In addition, in Numbers 22:4, Balak fears Israel will rob him of all his food and resources when he says that Israel is like an ox who licks up all the grass of the field.

◆ Explain Balak's fear of Israel. Does he see them only as a curse in his life? Does he change his mind when he hears Balaam's parables?

◆ In the Haftarah the remnant of Jacob among the nations is compared to a lion tearing its prey (verse 5:7). Compare the metaphor in each of the two texts. Are the metaphors virtually identical?

◆ The Haftarah also contains a second metaphor that says the remnant of Jacob could also be as beneficial as dew to the nations. How can both metaphors, positive and negative, be true?

Perhaps the Haftarah, with both its positive and negative views of Israel, has been matched up with this Sedra in order to teach us that we have a choice as to whether people and things in our lives serve as blessings or curses for us. In the Sedra Balak could see only danger and trouble from Israel. He could not see any potential good from them. The Haftarah may teach that if Balak could have looked at Israel with an open mind,

perhaps he could have learned from Balaam's blessings that Israel might also be good for him.

◆ Explain how Balak's outlook and expectations determined the role Israel would play in his life and the life of his nation.

◆ How might the situation between any two people or any two groups be different if they could see the benefit each might offer the other? (For example, consider siblings, in-laws, Israel and Arab countries.)

7 Both the Sedra and the Haftarah use the literary device of exaggeration or hyperbole to make a point.

◆ In Numbers 22:18, Balaam says that even if Balak gave him a house full of gold and silver, he could not say anything contrary to God's wishes. What is the point of Balaam's exaggerated statement? Does he not want to defy God or is he incapable of defying God? How does exaggeration help make the point?

◆ In verse 6:7 of the Haftarah, the Israelites make the point that not even thousands of sacrifices or rivers of oil would atone for their sins against God. In the next verse, they are told that they do not need enormous sacrifices to buy atonement. Atonement will be made through justice, goodness, and humility. What is the point of exaggeration in the Haftarah? Do the Israelites not want to atone or are they incapable? How does exaggeration help make the point?

◆ Compare the stories in the Sedra and the Haftarah. Explain how both seem to suggest that enormous material wealth cannot always buy what one wants. Why not?

◆ Compare this lesson to parents who try to buy their children's approval or love. Does it work? How can parents truly earn the respect and admiration of children?

♦ Do kids ever try to "buy" their friends' approval? If so, how? What is required to really earn a friend's trust?

8 In the Haftarah (verse 6:3), God asks Israel, "What have I done to you and what hardship have I caused you?"

♦ Based on this statement, what do you think God is feeling?

♦ In very similar language, in Numbers 22:28, Balaam's donkey asks, "What have I done to you that you hit me three times?" Review the scene and consider why the donkey asked this question. When the donkey spoke like a human being, she expressed human emotions. What was she feeling?

♦ Do a series of skits that use the phrase "What did I ever do to you?" Consider these possible characters: parent and kid, cow and butcher, lion and lion tamer, Tom and Jerry, etc.

9 Balak offers an elaborate sacrifice with seven altars, seven bulls, and seven rams in order to have the curse pronounced over Israel (Numbers 23:1-5 and again in 23:14 and 23:29).

♦ Do Balak's offerings work?

In the Haftarah the Israelites say that they would never be able to make enough offerings to God to atone for all their sins. Micah reminds them that God doesn't want fancy sacrifices, but for them to do justly and walk modestly with God.

♦ Imagine you are an advice columnist. Balak has written a letter asking why his sacrifices are not getting him what he wants (a curse against Israel). Write a response to him, based on Micah's words to the Israelites. Teach him about the importance of justice, goodness, and modesty.

10 Balaam, the prophet, appears in both the Sedra and the Haftarah. In the Sedra it is hard to understand if Balaam is a good guy or a bad guy.

♦ Examine the Sedra for evidence of both points of view. Consider these facts, and try to find more:

• Balaam refuses to say anything without God's approval.

• Balaam doesn't go to Balak until God tells him to go.

• Balaam beats his donkey and is unable to see what the animal clearly sees.

♦ Balaam also appears in a number of other biblical texts, but only in Micah is he portrayed in a positive light. Do you think this Haftarah might have been chosen for this Sedra in order to encourage us to understand Balaam as a good guy in the Sedra?

♦ For more information on the positive and negative portrayals of Balaam, see *The JPS Torah Commentary: Numbers* by Jacob Milgrom, pp. 469-471.

11 In both the Haftarah and Sedra, things happen in threes. In the Sedra the donkey sees an angel and stops three times, and three times Balaam hits the donkey. The angel chastises Balaam for acting this way and points out that it happened three times. Three times Balak builds seven altars and offers sacrifices. Balaam blesses Israel three times when Balak wants curses.

Milgrom suggests that Balaam may have repeated things three times hoping that the repetitions would offer God opportunities to decide differently.

♦ Explain how this outlook considers God to be capricious and subject to wavering and change (see *The JPS Torah Commentary: Numbers*, p. 189, verse 19). What is wrong with a capricious, fickle God? Why is it important for us to know that God is not capricious and fickle?

Things also occur in threes in the Haftarah. God reminds Israel of three prophets (Moses, Aaron, and Miriam) sent to lead Israel out of Egypt. It seems that by sending three prophets, God demonstrates to Israel an unwavering attitude toward freeing them from slavery.

But whereas the Sedra seems to teach us that God's mind can never be changed (see Numbers 23:19), the Haftarah, on the other hand, appears to teach that there is one exception to the statement in the Sedra: God's mind can be changed when it comes to forgiving sin and rescinding punishment.

◆ Why is it important that God's mind can change about sin and punishment?

◆ When is it important for people to be steadfast? When is it important for them to change?

12 In the Haftarah (verse 6:8), we find the phrase *"mah tov,"* meaning "what is good."

In the Sedra (Numbers 24:5), we find the expression *"mah tovu,"* meaning "how good."

◆ Who said this last phrase, and why?

◆ *"Mah Tovu"* has been included in our *Siddur* as the very first prayer of the morning service. What do you think it means that we begin our prayer services with the complimentary words of someone who was sent to curse us?

◆ Learn to sing *"Mah Tovu"* in a round. The song may be found in *B'Kol Echad,* edited by Jeffrey Shiovitz, p. 90, and on the accompanying audiocassettes *Shirei B'Kol Echad.* Both of these may be ordered from the United Synagogue for Conservative Judaism at www.uscj.org/booksvc.

Extending the Text

13 We wonder if there is any evidence that the leaders of Micah's time listened to his message.

Read Jeremiah 26, in which Jeremiah so angers the priests and false prophets with his prophecy that they want King Zedekiah to put Jeremiah to death. Other officials come to Jeremiah's defense and quote Micah, who had years earlier made a prophecy similar to that of Jeremiah (see Jeremiah 26:16-19). The officials make it clear that the king in Micah's era, King Hezekiah, had heard Micah's message, believed Micah, and responded with fear. The officials conclude that Hezekiah never considered executing Micah and neither should Zedekiah execute Jeremiah.

◆ Explain how this story about Jeremiah suggests that Micah was listened to and taken very seriously.

In addition, King Hezekiah is famous for having instituted religious reforms that attempted to put an end to idolatry and to bring the people to observe God's laws. We cannot know with certainty, but can only imagine, that Micah played a part in facilitating those reforms.

◆ Imagine that you are King Hezekiah. Write an entry in your diary after hearing Micah speak the prophecies contained in this Haftarah. What lesson or image from the Haftarah affected you the most?

◆ For more information on Hezekiah and his reforms, see *Encyclopaedia Judaica,* vol. 8, pp. 450-455.

14 *Ketubot* 110b teaches that one may not coerce one's spouse to move from a city to a town or from a town to a city (see Insights from the Tradition #A, p. 574). The text explains that one cannot be compelled to move from a city to a town because everything one needs is available in a city, but may not be obtainable in a town.

◆ Why might a person used to city life be unhappy moving from a city to a town?

◆ Can you think of things that are available in large cities that you cannot find in small towns?

◆ The Talmudic Sages then ask why one cannot compel one's spouse to move from a town to a city. They explain that life is hard in a city. Why might a person used to life in a small town be upset about moving to a city?

◆ Where do you imagine that you will prefer living when you are grown — city or town? Why?

15 According to *Numbers Rabbah* 20:5, God did not make hardships for the people by making onerous commandments. Rather, God tried to make the commandments as easy for Israel to fulfill as possible (see Insights from the Tradition #B, p. 575). The *midrash* gives several examples, including a parable: A human king demands that his edicts be read standing, after removing one's hat, and with great pomp. However, God tells us to recite the *"Shema"* any way we want — sitting at home, walking outside, lying down, rising up.

◆ Explain how the parable teaches that God made the commandments less difficult than a human king might have.

◆ Read the *"Shema"* to see why the parable suggests we can recite the *"Shema"* any way we want.

◆ There is a famous debate between Hillel and Shammai concerning whether one may say the *"Shema"* sitting or standing. Mishnah *Berachot* 1:3 says:

The House of Shammai says that in the evening every person should recline and say the *"Shema,"* and in the morning everyone should stand, as the verse says, "When you lie down and when you rise up."

However, the House of Hillel says that every person should recite the *"Shema"* in his/her own way, as the verse says, "When you walk by the way." Moreover, Hillel explains that the *"Shema"* says, "When you lie down and when you rise up" in order to teach the proper time of day to say the *"Shema,"* and not the proper position in which it must be said.

◆ Have a class debate, with one side arguing for Hillel's position and the other for Shammai's.

◆ How is the *"Shema"* recited in your congregation (standing or sitting)? If your own congregation recites it sitting and you visit another congregation that recites it standing, what would you do? Which custom should you follow?

◆ Interview some or all the Rabbis and/or Cantors in your city to find out what their congregation's practice is regarding the *"Shema."*

16 *Mitzvot* are typically divided into two categories: *bayn adam l'chavero* — those between one person and another person, and *bayn adam l'makom* — those between one person and God. (See Insights from the Tradition #D, p. 575.)

◆ Choose one *mitzvah* to research and to explain. Clarify whether it is a *mitzvah bayn adam l'chavero* or *bayn adam l'makom*. For information on *mitzvot*, see *Teaching Mitzvot* by Barbara Binder Kadden and Bruce Kadden, *The How-To Handbook for Jewish Living* by Kerry M. Olitzky and Ronald H. Isaacs, and/or *A Guide To Jewish Religious Practice* by Isaac Klein.

◆ Alternatively, study the Ten Commandments and determine which are *bayn adam l'chavero* and which are *bayn adam l'makom*.

◆ Discuss why we make a blessing before we perform a *mitzvah bayn adam l'makom*, but do not when we perform a *mitzvah bayn adam l'chavero*. Here are some situations that explain this practice. See if you can think of other examples.

  • If we were to make a blessing for visiting the sick (a *mitzvah bayn adam l'chavero*), and then found out we could not visit the person that day because he/she was asleep or feeling too unwell to receive visitors, our blessing would have used God's name in vain.

  • If we offer *tzedakah* to someone and they refuse it.

17 Different terms are used in the Haftarah for magic. The terms *k'shafim* (sorcery) and *m'onnim* (soothsayers) are in verse 5:11. Sorcery is understood to be attempts to change the future with magic. It is banned by Deuteronomy 18:10.

In contrast to sorcery, divination (soothsaying) is the attempt to use magic to predict, but not to change, the future. For the most part and with few exceptions, the Bible seems to allow divination. Divination was probably tolerated in Israel because it was not an attempt to change the future and God's will; rather, it could be viewed as simply an attempt to determine God's plans. The future is predicted in the Bible by interpreting dreams and omens and by consulting prophets.

It is unclear whether verse 5:11 of this Haftarah means that divination is illegal or just that God will get rid of it because it will no longer be needed (just as fortresses will no longer be needed in a time of peace in verse 5:10).

◆ Why might someone want to use magic to change the future? What might be this person's attitude toward God? Why do you think the Torah is so opposed to sorcery that it decrees a death penalty for engaging in the practice?

◆ What is so compelling to people about knowing the future that so many consult horoscopes monthly, weekly, or even daily?

Personalizing the Text

18 Israel had all types of protective devices.

◆ Interview family and friends to find out what sources of strength they have relied on in their lives (see Analyzing the Text #3, p. 576). Have the sources of strength changed as they have aged? Were some true sources of strength, but others false ones?

19 We discussed in Insights from the Tradition #C, p. 575, that our leaders serve us.

◆ Write a letter to a local official expressing your concern about a particular issue affecting your community. Request a response and see if you get one. Share your letters and responses with your classmates. Decide on an action the class can take to address each concern.

20 According to the last verse of the Haftarah, God wants us to do justice, love goodness, and act humbly.

◆ List as many ways as possible to act justly, mercifully, and humbly. See if, as a class, you can do each one during the course of the school year. Keep a class chart that records everyone's actions.

21 In Connecting the Text To the Sedra #6, p. 577, we considered the idea that people or things can be either blessings or curses in our lives, depending on how we choose to view them.

◆ Consider this famous expression: "Beauty is in the eyes of the beholder." Explain how we have choices about how we "behold" things and people.

◆ Write a *D'var Torah* about this lesson, giving examples of people or things that you (or your family) have chosen to see as blessings, not curses.

22 Exaggeration is a literary device that may be used to make a point.

◆ Write a short story with millions of exaggerations in it.

23 We read the Torah all the way through every year. We read each Haftarah again each year. Every time we read our liturgical texts, we find something new, or something seems more important to us that year than it did the year before.

◆ Choose one verse from the Haftarah that, to you, is the most important verse of the Haftarah this year. Be prepared to explain why. Depict this verse in drawing, painting, collage, or other art form.

◆ Compare your artistic rendition to the illustration of this Haftarah in *The Illustrated Torah* by Michal Meron, p. 170.

24 God is certainly not capricious, but is capable of changing plans (see Connecting the Text To the Sedra #11, p. 578). Ralph Waldo Emerson (American philosopher, 1803-1882) once wrote, "A foolish consistency is the hobgoblin of small minds" (*Self-Reliance: The*

Wisdom of Ralph Waldo Emerson As Inspiration for Daily Living, edited by Richard Whelan).

◆ What do you think Emerson meant?

◆ When is it foolish to be stubbornly consistent?

◆ Does consistency impede creativity?

The following quotation is also often attributed to Emerson (though it was actually written by Bessie Stanley in 1905):

"To laugh often and much, to win the respect of intelligent people and the affection of children, to earn the appreciation of honest critics and endure the betrayal of false friends, to appreciate beauty, to find the best in others, to leave the world a bit better, whether by a healthy child, a garden patch, or a redeemed social condition; to know even one life has breathed easier because you have lived. This is to have succeeded!"

◆ How would you compare Emerson's outlook on life to that of Micah?

25 Micah was a very influential prophet, and his example may even have saved Jeremiah from death.

◆ Hold a "Prophet for President Convention." Model it on the party conventions during which candidates for president and vice president are nominated. Form groups, each of which chooses a prophet to research and advocate for. At the convention, someone from each group makes a brief nomination speech, followed by a brief seconding speech by another group member. Groups can design posters, buttons, ribbons, balloons, etc. Students in other classes can watch the proceedings and vote for their choice as president.

◆ For a list of non-literary prophets, see the *Encyclopaedia Judaica*, vol. 13, p 1176. For information on all prophets, see *Messengers of God: A Jewish Prophets Who's Who* by Ronald H. Isaacs. Micah is discussed on pp. 164-169 of that book.

Other Resources

26 See an essay on Micah and the essence of religion in *The Haftarah Commentary* by W. Gunther Plaut, p. 393.

27 For more information on Micah, see *Encyclopaedia Judaica*, vol. 11, p. 1480-1483.

28 For a *D'var Torah* on this Haftarah, see the web site for the Fuchsberg Center for Conservative Judaism in Jerusalem, www.uscj.org.il/haftarah/balak5761.html.

29 For more on interpreting Balaam as either a good guy or a bad guy, see *The JPS Torah Commentary: Numbers*, pp. 469-471.

30 For commentary, discussion questions, and project, see the UAHC Family Shabbat Table Talk web site at www.uahc.org/shabbat/stt/3chukatbalak.shtml.

Involving the Family

31 Have a family discussion. Is your family capricious in making decisions and in discipline (see Connecting the Text To the Sedra #12, p. 579)? Why is important to be deliberate and consistent in decisions and discipline? Have a family meeting to set up guidelines for "crime and punishment" and decision making processes (who has input, who has final say, etc.).

Bar/Bat Mitzvah Project

32 Micah preached that one should walk with God. Walk with God by organizing a walkathon for your congregation to raise money for a just, good, or humble cause. Consider donating the money to help poor people buy housing, in accordance with Micah's complaint of economic exploitation, which makes life difficult for the underprivileged. The Shefa Fund works for economic justice by offering funding to low income communities. Get information at www.shefafund.org.

HABAKKUK 3:1-19 Ashkenazim
HABAKKUK 2:20-3:19 Sephardim
SECOND DAY SHAVUOT

 This Haftarah has been paired with the second day of Shavuot, on which we read Deuteronomy 14:22-16:17. See "Connecting the Text To the Holiday," p. 586, for an exploration of the many ways the two texts and the holiday shed light on each other.

SYNOPSIS

Little is known of the prophet named Habakkuk. Based on one reference in his book to Chaldeans rising to power (verse 1:6), however, it has been suggested that he lived in the Southern Kingdom of Judah at the end of the seventh century, during or just after the threat from Assyria (the regional superpower, which was overthrown by Chaldeans/ Babylonians). Furthermore, speculation about the time period of the prophet Habakkuk becomes more complicated because, according to some scholars, chapter 3 of Habakkuk (this Haftarah) was not originally part of the book. If, therefore, this chapter *was* originally part of the book, then it was uttered by a prophet who lived at the end of the seventh century or beginning of the sixth century B.C.E. But if this chapter, our Haftarah, *was not* originally part of the book, it may date from a much later time.

There has also been much speculation about the meaning of the prophet's name. The Rabbis connect his name in *midrash* to the Shunammite woman (see the Haftarah for *Vayera*, p. 183); they suggested that Habakkuk comes from the verb "to embrace," and the Shunammite woman was promised that she would have a child to embrace. The most commonly accepted interpretation, however, is that Habakkuk stems from the name of a fragrant herb.

This Haftarah differs from many other Haftarot as it is more of a psalm or prayer than a prophecy. Habakkuk begins by reminding God of the awesome deeds God has done in the past, and expresses confidence that God will again act compassionately. Such confidence is typical of a psalm. Then, Habakkuk describes his vision of God's appearance. God comes from the South (where the Revelation at Sinai occurred), and is accompanied by a great light revealing God's splendor and glory. God is also accompanied by pestilence, plague, and an earthquake, which reveal God's tremendous might. God is ready to fight with bow and arrow, water, lightning and thunder. God tramples the earth in order to rescue God's people, Israel.

The prophet shakes with fear at the sound of God's presence. Though there is no prosperity or even enough food at the present, Habakkuk is confident about the future and rejoices in the hope of a brighter day.

INSIGHTS FROM THE TRADITION

A God stands in verse 3:6. Rashi says the words "God stands" means that God waits to consider thoroughly all the evidence, judge the case carefully, and then mete out the proper punishment.

◆ According to Rashi, what does God's behavior teach us?

◆ Can you think of a situation in which quick decisions are in order?

◆ Can you think of a situation in which well reasoned decisions are in order?

◆ When a football team gathers for a long huddle, do you think it means that they are carefully deliberating a plan or that they have no idea what to do?

◆ When someone takes his or her time to make decisions, do you tend to think that person is wise or indecisive?

STRATEGIES
Analyzing the Text

1 Scholars generally classify this third chapter of Habukkuk as a psalm or prayer for the following reasons:

• It contains a petition by the author to reveal God's power in the world and defeat the enemy.

• It mentions the wonderful things God has done in the past and the hope for God to act similarly now.

• It contains a revelation of God's presence in the world.

• It describes God's victory.

• It contains the word *"selah."*

• It concludes with thanksgiving and rejoicing.

• Finally, it provides instructions for musical accompaniment.

◆ Identify each of the above items in the Haftarah.

◆ Discuss why some or all of these items are appropriate for a psalm or song of praise. You may want to compare this to Psalm 7 or 77.

◆ Follow the guidelines outlined above and write your own psalm.

2 Habakkuk uses images of light (splendor, light, rays, glory) to describe God's approach and presence (verses 3:3 and 4).

◆ What do these images of light tell you about God's presence?

◆ For more discussion and activities on the symbolism of light, see the Haftarah for *Beresheet*, Extending the Text #23, p. 282.

3 Pestilence and plague, earthquake and shattered mountains are employed as metaphors to describe God's power (verses 3:5-14). God is described as using a bludgeon to crack the skull of Israel's enemies (verse 3:14).

◆ Explain how Habakkuk is describing God as a warrior on behalf of Israel.

◆ Explain how nature responds to God's presence.

◆ Are you comfortable with these images of God? Why or why not?

4 The *"Neharim"* in verse 3:8 refer to rivers or floods. *"Yam"* is the sea.

In many psalms about God's might, God either fights monsters of the rivers and seas or uses the waters to fight battles. The waters are either the enemy or the weapons used against the enemy (in ancient mythology God had to defeat mythic gods and monsters of the sea).

◆ What do you think of water — is it powerful, evil, life sustaining, good, dangerous, or other? Explain your answer.

◆ Find news stories or pictures that portray water in each of these roles.

5 The prophet doesn't just describe God's appearance; he also describes his own personal reactions to theophany — the image of God.

◆ How does Habakkuk describe his reaction to the theophany in verse 3:16?

◆ How does Habakkuk describe the current state of affairs in Israel in verse 3:17?

◆ How does Habakkuk express his hope for future redemption in verses 3:18-19?

◆ Illustrate some of the images used in verses 3:17-19.

Connecting the Text To the Holiday

6 Teman (in verse 3:3) is to the south of Israel and may refer to modern day Yemen. Paran is associated with Seir, also south of Israel. Both of these locations are often associated with theophanies. (See Deuteronomy 33:2, in which Moses refers to Seir and Paran as the sight of his Divine revelation.)

Shavuot commemorates the giving of the Torah at Sinai. Compare Habakkuk's theophany with the one at Mount Sinai in Exodus 19-20.

◆ Illustrate one image from verses 3:3-6 of the Haftarah. Compare your illustration to that of Michal Meron in *The Illustrated Torah*, p. 245.

7 In verse 3:3 God is coming from Teman and from Paran.

◆ Why did God go to Teman and Paran? *Avodah Zarah* 2b explains that God first went to all the nations (including Teman and Paran) and offered them the Torah, but no one wanted to accept it. Finally, God offered the Torah to Israel. In order to be sure that Israel would accept the Torah, God held a mountain over Israel. Israel, therefore, agreed to take and keep the Torah. What does this story say about Torah, Israel, and God?

◆ How does this story lend an ironic twist to the holiday of Shavuot, on which we celebrate the receiving of the Torah at Sinai?

◆ Create a comic strip of the story above.

8 In verse 3:4 "a brilliant light" gave off rays on every side, enveloping God's glory. According to Kara, the brightness on the day of the giving of the Torah was as great as the light of the seven days of Creation.

◆ In what way does the giving of the Torah echo the beginning of the world for the Jewish people?

9 Kara explains that the plague that came forth from God's heels in verse 3:5 represents the angels that went ahead of God and were prepared to destroy the whole world if Israel failed to accept the Torah.

◆ How did Israel save the world, according to Kara?

◆ In what ways do you think Torah saves the world every day?

ZECHARIAH 2:14-4:7
BEHA'ALOTECHA בהעלתך
SHABBAT CHANUKAH

This Haftarah has been paired with *Parashat Beha'alotecha*, Numbers 8:1-12:16. See "Connecting the Text To the Sedra," pp. 590-593, for an exploration of the many ways the texts shed light on each other. In addition, it is also read during Chanukah. On the first Shabbat of Chanukah, we read this Haftarah and a special Maftir Torah reading from Numbers 7. See pp. 592-593 for ways these texts and Chanukah shed light on each other.

SYNOPSIS

Zechariah is identified as the grandson of Iddo, a leading priest who returned from exile in Babylonia in the year 538 B.C.E. (50 years after the destruction of the Temple by Nebuchadnezzar). Zechariah was a contemporary of another minor prophet, Haggai. Both prophets were primarily concerned with the rebuilding of the Temple after the exiles returned to Jerusalem from Babylonia.

Just before the Haftarah begins, God promises that the Temple will be rebuilt. The prophet uses this promise to encourage the remaining exiles in Babylonia to return to Jerusalem. As the Haftarah begins, God promises to dwell in the midst of the people. Zechariah prophesies that other nations will want to become God's people when they see God dwelling in the midst of Israel. But only Judah is proclaimed to be God's portion.

Zechariah next describes his vision of Joshua the High Priest being accused by the Accuser. We never actually hear the accusations, because God interrupts the Accuser, chastising him to have pity for Joshua, who has survived the ordeal of exile.

An angel of God sees to it that Joshua's filthy clothes are exchanged for clean clothes, symbolizing God's forgiveness of any of Joshua's wrongdoings. The angel then warns Joshua to walk in God's ways and otherwise fulfill God's will in order to have the privilege of communicating directly with God (like the angels). Next, Joshua is shown a stone with seven eyes, but the meaning of the stone is not explained. This section of the Haftarah ends with a vision of the ideal days of peace yet to come.

Zechariah immediately has another vision, this time of a gold candlestick with seven lamps. Zechariah asks the angel the meaning of the candlestick, but the angel does not tell him. Instead the word of *Adonai* comes to Zechariah, delivering this famous statement, "Not by might, nor by power, but by My spirit." Finally, the angel proclaims that any mountain or obstacle standing in the way of Israel's leader, Prince Zerubbabel, will be made flat so that he can set the final top stone on the completed Temple building.

INSIGHTS FROM THE TRADITION

A In verse 3:8, God says: "I will bring My servant the Branch." What does "the Branch" mean? Hirsch explains that the word "Branch" is used to represent the leader who will rebuild the Temple. He suggests that just as plants grow slowly and almost unnoticeably, so, too, the Temple will be built and the people will have their own leader — the Branch — but it will all happen in small increments.

Even major milestones that look as if they were accomplished in one big step actually involve lots of little steps. For example, consider a child who rides a bicycle for the first time. It seems like a milestone giant step, but it really is owed to many little steps: learning to pedal, riding a tricycle, using training wheels, raising the training wheels, removing the training wheels for riding on grass, and so on.

◆ Give another example of an accomplishment that may look like a major change, but really represents many little "plant-like" steps of progress.

B In chapter 4 there is a *menorah* (lamp) burning olive oil and two olive trees providing the olives for the *menorah*. After seeing the *menorah* and olive trees, Zechariah is told, "Not by might nor power, but by My spirit."

Rashi explains this strange scene in his comment to verse 4:6. The olives on the trees pick and press themselves so they are ready to be used as oil in the *menorah* without anyone having to do anything. This is meant as a sign, because just as the olives do this work themselves, so will the people not have to build the Temple with their own power or strength. It will be guided by God's spirit.

◆ Explain how the vision of the olive trees and the *menorah* teach that the building of the Temple will be accomplished with the help of God.

◆ It is a common Jewish practice that when we anticipate doing something in the future, we do not simply say, "I will do it," but rather, "with God's help, I will do it." The preface of "with God's help" reminds us that we don't accomplish things alone, but only with God's help. Do you typically see the world this way?

◆ Try saying this expression as part of your everyday conversations. Report back to your class after one week on how it felt and how others reacted to it.

C In verse 4:7 the prophet proclaims that anything blocking Zerubbabel's path as he sets out to build the Temple should get out of his way. According to Hirsch, the mountain, representing material and physical impediments, did not stand in the way of completing the building.

◆ In any kind of construction project, there are bound to be many types of physical challenges: lack of adequate building supplies, debris from the previous building in the way, work that is dangerous or physically challenging. Explain how each of these might impede a construction project.

◆ How might each of the following physical challenges affect an athlete: lack of equipment for training, overcrowded gym, routine that is just too physically difficult?

◆ Can you think of any other task that might be impeded by physical challenges?

D According to Hirsch, there was another impediment to Joshua's work — the Accuser (see verse 3:1). Hirsch suggests the Accuser represents every individual's own evil inclination.

◆ Imagine what the evil inclination might have whispered in the people's ears: they don't need to build it, they are unable to do it, they can always do it later. Can you suggest other obstacles that the evil inclination might have placed before the Israelites?

◆ The evil inclination, says Hirsch, caused the people to do other activities instead of rebuilding the Temple, and so hindered their progress with the construction. Ask your parents about a time that distractions or self-doubt hindered their progress on a project.

STRATEGIES
Analyzing the Text

1 Zechariah says that many nations will attach themselves to God and become God's people, equal with Israel (verse 2:15). This statement of universalism proclaims that God is God of all peoples.

In verse 2:17, all flesh is told to be silent. "All flesh" also indicates that everyone will universally worship God.

◆ What do you think about universalism (the concept that people of all religions worship the same God in their own way)?

◆ Create a mural that shows that all people worship One God in their own way.

◆ Being silent is a way to show respect and reverence for God's presence. How does silence show respect?

2 The expression "the Holy Land" appears in verse 2:16 and nowhere else in the Bible. A somewhat similar expression appears in Exodus 3:5, though, when God speaks with Moses at the burning bush and tells Moses that he is standing on holy ground. It would seem that God's presence transfers holiness to the ground on which it appears.

◆ Based on this information, why do you think the Land of Israel is called the Holy Land?

◆ Make a collage of photographs of radiant and beautiful Israel that conveys a bit of its holy quality.

3 Joshua is said to be "a brand plucked out of the fire" (verse 3:2). A branding iron is a long piece of metal with a stamp on one end that is heated in a fire and used to stamp an identification mark on animals or objects. Fire is often another way to express trouble. Joshua's grandfather Seraiah was killed by Nebuchadnezzar (II Kings 25:18-21), and his father was exiled, yet Joshua managed to survive exile and return to Jerusalem to become a priest. Therefore, the image of being plucked out of the fire indicates that Joshua was rescued from disaster.

The name Joshua comes from the Hebrew verb meaning "to save" and is understood to mean "God is salvation."

◆ Explain in your own words the different ways in which verse 3:2 describes Joshua as one who has been saved.

◆ Do you think that if Joshua was saved and able to return to serve in the Temple, it was not an accident, but a sign that God was watching over him?

◆ Write a journal entry for Joshua, exploring his feelings about being saved, and the responsibilities that come with his salvation.

4 The Accuser, like a prosecuting attorney, was ready to make a case against Joshua, claiming that Joshua was unfit to be the High Priest (verse 3:1). Many suggestions have been made about why Joshua might have been unfit. One explanation is that with the destruction of the Temple, God had permanently rejected Jerusalem and the priests of the Temple.

◆ Read verse 3:2. Has God permanently rejected Jerusalem, her priests, and the Temple?

◆ Read verses 1:17 and 2:16 and describe God's relationship to Jerusalem.

5 The filthy clothes that Joshua was wearing (verse 3:4) may symbolize either his sins and the guilt he carries on behalf of his people or his previous involvement in the secular world (of exile).

◆ Based on these two interpretations, what do you think the clean clothes represent?

6 Many commentators suggest that "My servant" probably means Prince Zerubbabel, the governor of Judah (verse 3:8).

Zerubbabel's name may mean that "he was begotten in Babylonia" during the exile. His grandfather had been Jehoiakim, King of Judah before the destruction of Jerusalem (I Chronicles 3:16-19). Zerubbabel was the leader of the first group of returning exiles, according to Ezra 2:2.

◆ How does Zerubbabel's name suit his background?

7 Zechariah sees a stone with seven pairs of eyes (verse 3:9). The stone may be part of the priest's head covering. (See Exodus 28:36-38 for another part of the priest's head covering that is engraved and removes guilt.) Alternatively, it may be a foundation stone, typically set in place by the king at a ceremony marking the beginning of the construction of a new Temple.

According to some scholars, the text is vague in order to represent both.

◆ What is the significance of each interpretation? Reread the beginning of chapter 3 to determine which interpretation you like best.

◆ Find the foundation cornerstone at your synagogue or school. Make a rubbing of it. To do so, hold or tape a piece of construction paper on top of the engraving. Gently rub over the paper with pastels, crayons, or pencils. Peel the paper off, and you will have an impression of the words or images that are engraved on the cornerstone.

8 The eyes in the stone (verse 3:9) may mean that God is watching and approving of the construction. See I Kings 8:29, in which Solomon builds the First Temple and asks God to have eyes open over it.

◆ Draw the stone that has seven eyes.

9 Zechariah's name includes God's name, *Yah*. It also includes the root זכר, which means "remember." In other words, his name means "God has remembered."

◆ What do you think God has remembered?

Connecting the Text To the Sedra

10 The Sedra begins with a description of a seven-branched *menorah* used in the Tabernacle (Numbers 8:2). In the Haftarah Zechariah sees in his vision a *menorah* with seven lamps.

We often interpret God as being the source of light, warmth, understanding, and enlightenment in the world. The *menorot*, therefore, give off God's light that illuminates our world.

◆ Draw a seven-branched *menorah*. On each branch write one way that God lights up your life.

◆ Alternatively, seven students can pose as a seven-branched *menorah*. Each pose should demonstrate a way in which God lights up your life.

11 In the Sedra Moses is told to prepare the Levites by cleansing them, shaving them, and changing their clothes (Numbers 8:6-7).

Similarly, in the Haftarah (verses 3:3-4), Joshua was wearing filthy clothes, and the angel arranged for him to change into clean clothes.

◆ How important do you think it is to be neat and tidy in personal appearance? Does your answer change if you are preparing to do something privately or publicly?

◆ Ibn Ezra explains that Joshua's filthy clothes indicate that the returning Israelite exiles did not have the proper accoutrements for their religious service. They had no Temple, no altar, and no priestly finery. How do you think the Israelites felt about the possibility of reinstituting the Temple practice without priestly garments, utensils, or any of the necessary accoutrements?

◆ Do you feel better prepared to perform a task when you have all the right equipment, books, supplies, and clothes for the job? Give examples.

12 In the Sedra God's presence is manifested in the midst of the children of Israel by a cloud that covered the Tabernacle. When the cloud moved, the children of Israel understood it to be a command from God for them to journey on (Numbers 9:15-23).

◆ As the Haftarah begins (verse 2:14), God promises to dwell in the midst of Israel again. What does it mean to you that God dwelt with the Israelites?

◆ Are there times when you sense that God is dwelling within your community?

◆ Interview your Rabbi, Cantor, and congregational leaders for examples from them of times when they most sensed God's presence in your community.

13 The Haftarah involves a prophet whose name means "God remembered." The Haftarah begins by telling Israel to shout loudly and Israel will be saved from exile among its enemies.

The Sedra in Numbers 10:9 says that when going to war one should sound a trumpet. Then God will remember and save you from your enemies. According to Hertz, sounding a trumpet or making a loud noise infuses courage and cheerfulness into those hearing the loud sound. This infusion is a means of obtaining God's help in overcoming danger and being saved.

◆ Make your own loud noise by writing a cheer to give the Israelites courage. Consider including a role in your cheer for classmates who can play instruments, especially loud ones!

14 The Haftarah begins by proclaiming "Shout for joy/gladness."

The Sedra in Numbers 10:10 reminds us that on the days of our gladness/joy, we should sound a trumpet.

◆ How would you define days of joy or gladness?

◆ How do you think we should mark days of joy or gladness? Compile a list of ways to observe such days. Would making a loud shout, song, or trumpet blast be part of your observance?

◆ Learn to sound a *shofar*.

◆ Ask a student who plays the trumpet to do a demonstration for the class.

15 The Haftarah begins with verse 2:14, in which God promises to dwell amid the Israelites who have returned to Jerusalem. Earlier in this same chapter (verses 2:11-13), Zechariah urges the Israelites to leave their exile in Babylon and return to Jerusalem.

◆ Many exiles in Babylonia did not return to Jerusalem. What reasons do you think they might have given for not going with Zerubbabel to Judea?

In the Sedra (Numbers 10:29-30), Moses informs his father-in-law, Hobab the Midianite, that the Israelites will be leaving and journeying to the Promised Land. Moses urges Hobab to come with them, but Hobab refuses and insists on returning to his homeland.

◆ What do you think the dilemma was for Hobab?

◆ There is no certainty in Rabbinic *midrashim* as to whether Moses' discussion with Hobab took place before the giving of the Torah at Mount Sinai or after. What do you think? How would witnessing the revelation at Mount Sinai have affected Hobab?

◆ Also, see Numbers 11 for reasons why the Israelites themselves wanted to return to Egypt.

◆ In what parts of the world was your family living when the State of Israel was formed in 1948? What reasons do you think they had for not moving to Israel then?

◆ Design a brochure that Zechariah could have used to encourage the people to return to Israel.

16 In the Sedra Numbers 10:31, Moses pleads with his Midianite father-in-law not to leave. He urges him to stay and be "eyes" for them.

◆ What do you think it means to be eyes for someone?

◆ The Israelites were setting out to journey along territory bordering Midian. How might Moses' Midianite father-in-law have been able to guide them (i.e., be eyes for them in the desert)?

◆ In the Haftarah a stone is placed before Joshua that has seven eyes on it (see Analyzing the Text #7, p. 590). What do the eyes (in verse 3:9) mean to you?

◆ How might the High Priest or God guide the people?

◆ Who are your eyes? Explain your answer.

17 In the Haftarah Zechariah has two visions, one of Joshua the High Priest and one of the candlesticks. These visions contain messages from God.

◆ Review the message of each vision of Zechariah. Can each vision have more than one interpretation?

◆ In the Sedra God explains to Aaron and Miriam how Moses is different from all other prophets. God communicates with other prophets through visions and dreams. But only to Moses does God speak directly (see Numbers 12:6-8). How does this statement by God indicate that Moses was the greatest of all prophets?

◆ Design business cards for Moses and Zechariah that reflect the way in which God communicates with each of them.

18 This Haftarah is also read on the first Shabbat of Chanukah. The connection to the *menorah* is obvious.

There is also a connection between the last verse of the Haftarah and the victory of the Maccabees. Zerubbabel will not build the Temple with his own might and power, but by virtue of the spirit of God. Similarly, the Maccabees did not win their battles due to their own might and power, but because God fought their battles for them.

We are reminded of this lesson in the *"Amidah,"* which contains a special insertion for Chanukah:

"For the miracles, the salvation, the mighty deeds, the victories, and for the battles which You performed for our ancestors in those days, at this time.

In the days of Mattityahu the son of Yochanan the High Priest, the Hasmonean and his sons — when the wicked Greek kingdom rose up against Your people Israel to make them forget Your Torah and force them to stray from Your laws — You in great mercy stood up for them in their time of trouble. You fought their fight, judged their claim, and avenged the wrong done them. You delivered the strong into the hands of the weak, the many into the hands of the few, the impure into the hands of the pure, the wicked into the hands of the righteous . . . Then your children came to the Holy of Holies and cleansed the Temple, purified the site of Your holiness, and kindled lights in the courtyards of Your sanctuary; and they established these eight days of Chanukah to express thanks and praise to Your great name."

◆ How does this prayer teach that Israel did not fight alone, just as Zerubbabel did not build the Second Temple alone?

◆ Ask your Cantor to teach the class the song *"Al Hanissim"* (For the Miracles), which comes from this prayer. The song can be found on the recording *The Chanukah Story* by The Western Wind.

19 In the Haftarah Joshua was a priest on trial. The Accuser wanted to charge Joshua with being unfit for priestly duty in the new Temple.

Similarly, there was a question about the fitness of the Maccabees/Hasmoneans to rule Israel as High Priests. They were from the priestly line of Jehoiarib priests, and thus they were themselves priests. But throughout the period of the First Temple (except when foreign worship was forced into the Temple), the position of High Priest had been filled exclusively by members of the Zadokite priestly family. In addition, during all of the period of the Second Temple, there had been only Zadokite priests until the Hasmonean revolt took the position away from the Zadokites. In spite of the fact that they were not entitled to serve as High Priest due to familial requirements, Jonathan (Judah Maccabee's younger brother) was appointed in 152 B.C.E. to the position of High Priest by the Syrians, who controlled Judea.

◆ Explain why Jonathan may not have been fit to serve as High Priest.

◆ When the Rabbis chose this Haftarah for Chanukah, what might they have been saying about whether or not the Hasmoneans were fit to be High Priests?

◆ Make political posters that ancient Israelites might have made both in favor of and against Hasmonean priests. For more information on Chanukah, the Hasmoneans, and the Rabbis, see *A Guide To Jewish Religious Practice* by Isaac Klein, pp. 226-228.

20 In the Haftarah the olives miraculously pressed themselves and refilled the *menorah* automatically (see Insights from the Tradition #B, p. 588). Similarly, there is a legend associated with the Maccabees involving olives and miracles. This legend says that when the Maccabees cleaned the Temple, they found only enough consecrated oil to last one day. Miraculously, the oil lasted eight days until they were able to get olives and make more oil.

In memory of this legend, we have a tradition of lighting candles on each of the eight days of Chanukah.

There was, however, a dispute between two Sages concerning the procedure for candle lighting (*Shabbat* 21b). Hillel said that we should light one candle on the first night and increase it by one every night until the eighth night, on which we would light eight candles. Shammai believed that we should light eight candles the first night and decrease by one every night until the eighth night, on which we would light only one candle.

◆ Do we follow the opinion of Hillel or Shammai today?

◆ Debate: Which system — that of Hillel or that of Shammai — seems better to emphasize the miracle of the oil lasting unexpectedly?

Extending the Text

21 "The Accuser" in verses 3:1-2 is a rough translation of the Hebrew, השטן (the Satan). The Satan is not an evil power rivaling God or a fallen angel of some kind. The Satan in the Bible is simply an accuser, adversary, or prosecutor who brings evidence to God that a human being is not deserving of the good fortune he is receiving.

◆ Reread verses 3:1-2 and find evidence that the Satan is not a rival or equal power to God. (See, for example, how God interrupts the Satan and tells him to leave Joshua alone.)

◆ Compare the Accuser here to the Accuser in Job chapters 1 and 2 or I Chronicles 21:1.

22 There is a difference between a *menorah* and a *chanukiyah*: a *menorah* is the seven-branched lamp used in the Temple and Tabernacle, and a *chanukiyah* has nine branches for the eight candles of Chanukah, plus the *shamash*.

When we light a *chanukiyah*, the candles are inserted from right to left (that is, the first night's candle is positioned to the far right). The candles are lit from left to right (that is, the newest candle is lit first, then the next, and all the way to the farthest right candle). After lighting, the *shamash* is returned to its special place.

Note that on Chanukah, unlike on Shabbat, the blessings are said before lighting the candles.

◆ Memorize the blessings recited upon lighting the Chanukah candles.

23 In verse 3:8 the word צמח (*tzemach* — Branch) is often interpreted as referring to the Messiah. That is, God will send a servant, the Messiah, in the future. According to *gematria* (a method of assigning values to each letter of the Hebrew *alef-bet* and then calculating the value of a word), this word totals 138.

Sanhedrin 98b says that the Messiah will be named "Menachem," a Hebrew name that means "one who comforts." The *gematria* value of Menachem is also 138. This suggests to students of *gematria* that Messiah/Branch and Menachem/Comforter are the same.

◆ Explain why you think the Messiah might be named "One who comforts."

◆ Calculate the gematria for both מנחם and צמח to verify that they both total 138.

◆ Figure out how to spell and count the *gematria* value of your own Hebrew name. Then figure out which words are equivalent in *gematria* to your name. Can you draw interesting conclusions about yourself based on the *gematria* of your name?

◆ For information on how to count a word's *gematria* value, see *The First Jewish Catalog* by Richard Siegel, Michael Strassfeld, and Sharon Strassfeld, p. 210.

24 Joshua is shown a stone (verse 3:9) with seven eyes. Radak suggests that the seven eyes represent the seven people who helped return life to Judaism after the Babylonian exile: High Priest Joshua; Prince Zerubbabel; Ezra, the scribe; Nehemiah, the governor of Judah; Haggai, the prophet; Zechariah, the prophet; and Malachi, the last prophet.

◆ Prepare and present a report on one of these leaders.

◆ Hold a party for these leaders celebrating the revival of post-Exile Judaism. Dress in costume as the character of your choice.

25 God's eyes in verse 4:2-10 may indicate that God is omniscient and omnipresent.

Traditionally, Jews have believed that God is all-knowing, all-powerful, and all-good. Such a belief has been difficult to maintain since the Holocaust.

◆ Why would the Holocaust make it difficult to believe all three things about God?

◆ Which of these descriptions of God do you accept, and why?

26 The Book of Ezra also deals with the subject of building the Second Temple. According to Ezra 6:4, the costs of building the Temple were paid by King Darius of Persia.

In addition, King Darius ordered Tattenai, the governor of the area, and other officials to stay away from the Temple site and let the rebuilding of the Temple proceed without interruptions.

Persia conquered Babylonia, which had conquered Jerusalem in the first place.

◆ Design a plaque for the entrance to the new Temple that acknowledges Darius's invaluable assistance in the rebuilding of the Temple.

Personalizing the Text

27 Zechariah witnessed the rebuilding of the Temple.

◆ Read Ezra 3:10-13 for Ezra's account of the laying of the foundation of the Temple. How did the people feel about the event?

◆ Write an editorial column for a newspaper of Zechariah's time that reflects the people's feelings regarding the new Temple.

◆ Write another editorial for our era, stating your position on a current controversial proposal to build a new Temple.

28 Biblical names often presage events in the life of the person.

◆ Write a *D'var Torah* explaining how all the names of people in the Haftarah (Zechariah, Joshua, Zerubbabel, the Accuser, the Branch) provide insight into the characters of these people. Then explain how your name provides insight into your own character. Include information about the people for whom you were named and how your shared name tells similar or even different things about each of you.

29 Learn the song: "Not by Might, Not by Power" by Debbie Friedman, which quotes the last verse of this Haftarah. The song may be found on the cassette *"Not by Might, Not by Power."*

30 The Holy Land Hotel is located in the heart of Jerusalem. It offers views of the Old City of Jerusalem, the Mount of Olives, Jerusalem's city center, and the surrounding mountains. It also houses a replica of the Second Temple.

◆ Visit the Holy Land Hotel and tour its replica either by going to Jerusalem or by going to www.holylandhotel.com.

31 According to *midrash* (*Numbers Rabbah* 14:3), the Second Temple actually rebuilt itself.

◆ Write your own story about the Temple that built itself or depict it in a painting.

32 The song *"Yibaneh Hamikdash,"* proclaims, "The Temple will be rebuilt, The city of Zion will be filled. And there we will sing a new song and be uplifted with rejoicing."

Learn and sing *"Yibaneh Hamikdash,"* which may be found in *B'Kol Echad*, edited by Jeffrey Shiovitz, p. 99, and on the accompanying audiocassettes *Shirei B'Kol Echad*. Both may be ordered from United Synagogue of Conservative Judaism at www.uscj.org/booksvc.

33 Zechariah lived in an exciting time of hope and renewal when the people returned from exile in Babylon to rebuild Judah.

♦ Write a diary entry by Zechariah.

♦ According to Maimonides (Introduction to the *Mishneh Torah*), Zechariah learned about prophecy and Israelite tradition from Baruch, the scribe of Jeremiah (who lived during the destruction of Jerusalem and the exile in 586 B.C.E.). Write about the hope Zechariah has for national revival and religious reform, and have him thank Baruch for everything he has learned.

Other Resources

34 For a representation of Zechariah by Michelangelo go to: www.kfki.hu/~arthp/welcome.html.

♦ Send a postcard of Zechariah to a favorite friend or teacher.

35 For more on the prophet Zechariah, including history, themes, and notable quotations, read *Messengers of God: A Jewish Prophets Who's Who* by Ronald H. Isaacs, pp. 188-196.

36 Discuss the illustration of this Haftarah in *The Illustrated Torah* by Michal Meron, p. 154. Why do you think Zechariah is portrayed as tiny compared to the *menorah*?

37 For more information on Chanukah observances and history, see *The Jewish Holidays: A Guide and Commentary* by Michael Strassfeld, p. 161-177, or *A Different Light: The*

Big Book of Hanukkah by Noam Zion and Barbara Spectre.

38 For more on the *menorah*, its shape and symbolism, see *The Encyclopedia of Jewish Symbols* by Ellen Frankel and Betsy Platkin Teustch, pp. 105-107. (See also pp. 107-109 in that book for information on the Messiah.)

39 For a wide variety of designs of *chanukiyot,* see *Encyclopaedia Judaica*, vol. 7, pp. 1293-1314.

40 For a commentary, discussion questions, and project, see the UAHC Family Shabbat Table Talk web site at www.uahc.org/shabbat/stt/3beha.shtml.

41 For a *D'var Torah* on the Haftarah, see the web site of the Fuchsberg Center for Conservative Judaism in Jerusalem, www.uscj.org.il/haftarah/behalot5761.html.

Involving the Family

42 Sometimes our evil inclinations tell us we cannot accomplish a difficult endeavor (see Insights from the Tradition #D, p. 588). Be a constant source of encouragement for each other. Discuss ways in which you can provide productive and valued encouragements.

For example, we learned in Insights from the Tradition #A, pp. 587-588, that even major accomplishments are made up of many little steps. Begin a family tradition of marking little steps of progress. Devise a system that will work for your family and encourage perseverance.

Bar/Bat Mitzvah Project

43 Run a clothing drive to collect suits, dresses, and other business clothing so that people, like Joshua, who are in need of suitable work clothes will be able to obtain them. Dress for Success is a nonprofit organization that provides interview suits, confidence boosts, and career development to more than 30,000 women in over 70 cities each year. Access their web site at www.dressforsuccess.org to find out more about this worthwhile organization. If there is a local chapter in your city, call to see how you can help. Alternatively, collect gently used sports equipment to donate to a local youth organization, school, or YMCA.

ZECHARIAH 14:1-21
FIRST DAY SUKKOT

 This Haftarah has been paired with the first day of Sukkot, on which we read Leviticus 22:26-23:44. See "Connecting the Text To the Holiday," pp. 600-601, for an exploration of the many ways the two texts and the holiday shed light on each other.

SYNOPSIS

The Book of Zechariah may have been written by at least two authors. The earlier chapters (1-8) seem to have been written during the construction of the Second Temple. The remaining six chapters, however, have an unclear setting and are eschatological in nature (concerned with the end of time, the Messiah, deliverance, final victory, and God's reign of peace). This Haftarah was apparently written by a later prophet after the Second Temple was already completed.

The Haftarah begins by describing a day on which God will unite all peoples in a universal acknowledgment of *Adonai* as the one and only God. On that day, God will first lure all nations to Jerusalem for battle. Any nation who fights against Jerusalem will be defeated by God (through such means as earthquakes and plagues). The remaining nations will recognize God as the only God and Jerusalem as the only place at which to worship God. Moreover, all peoples will come to Jerusalem annually to worship and thank God at the time of the pilgrimage holiday, Sukkot (The Feast of Booths). Anyone who does not come to Jerusalem for Sukkot will be punished by drought.

On that day, everything will be holy to God — from the bells around the necks of horses to ordinary metal pots. Business transactions will cease to take place on Temple grounds, and all activities in the Temple will be holy.

INSIGHTS FROM THE TRADITION

A Verse 14:9 promises that God's name will be one. *Pesachim* 50a explains that we are not currently allowed to say God's name. When we see God's four-lettered name — the Tetragrammaton — we do not pronounce it, but read it instead as *Adonai*. But, in the future world promised by God, we will pronounce God's name just as it is written.

◆ What will it mean to be on a first name basis with God?

◆ Why do you think we call some people (and God) by respectful names instead of proper names? For example, we call our parents "mom" and "dad," and we call judges, "your honor." How is this similar to calling God by the name "*Adonai*," which means "my Lord"?

B Verses 14:6-7 promises that "in that day" (when *Adonai* makes war against the nations), there will not be darkness, but continuous light. According to *Pesachim* 50a, this means that everything in the world will be topsy-turvy. It is described as a "clear world," in which people get what they merit. For example, people who are treated with respect in this world (without really deserving it) will be lightly esteemed in the next world.

◆ What other kinds of switches do you imagine might happen when the world becomes "a clear world" and people get what they merit?

◆ What do you think makes our world so "unclear" that people get what they don't really deserve?

C In verse 14:10, the prophecy indicates that the whole land will become like the *Aravah*, the flat, arid, sterile low lands. Rashi explains that this means that the whole world will become flat, and only Jerusalem will remain as a mountain that can be seen high above everything else.

◆ What does it mean to stand out as an example for everyone to see?

◆ Find out the location of the tallest building in the world. Do you think it was purposely built very high so that everyone could see it?

D God will punish any nation that does not come to worship in Jerusalem on Sukkot by withholding rain from it, according to verse 14:17. Hertz points out that the punishment of withholding rain is appropriate, as the rainy season is supposed to begin immediately after Sukkot. The punishment, therefore, will be felt immediately.

◆ Why might it be particularly effective to feel the sting of punishment immediately after doing wrong?

◆ Do you think parents should discipline their children with immediate consequences or with delayed action? Explain your answer.

◆ Find out the average length of wait in your state courts before a criminal is tried. Find out what could be done to hold these trials more speedily without eroding civil rights.

STRATEGIES
Analyzing the Text

1 When verse 14:1 says that the day of *Adonai* is coming, it means that destruction is coming to Israel's enemies. According to verse 14:2, God will bring all the nations to attack Jerusalem. As they are plundering Jerusalem, God will appear to do battle with them.

◆ Why do you think God might round up all of Israel's enemies before punishing them?

◆ Why do you think God would choose to punish Israel's enemies right in the capital of the nation?

2 When God battles the other nations, there will be neither sunlight nor moonlight, but just continuous day. This suggests that there is an end of time. Eschatology is a philosophy concerned with the distant future when history and time as we know them will come to an end.

◆ Explain how the continuous daylight might indicate that time has ended.

◆ In the creation story (see Genesis 1:1-19), light exists before the sun does. Where do you think this light came from? How might the end of time be like the beginning of time?

3 Verse 14:8 promises that water will flow to the Eastern Sea and the Western Sea. The Eastern Sea is thought to be the Dead Sea, and the Western Sea is thought to be the Mediterranean Sea.

◆ Examine a map of Israel to confirm or refute this interpretation.

◆ Draw your own geographical and topographical map of *Eretz Yisrael*.

4 According to verse 14:9, God will be King over all the earth.

◆ Read the verse in Hebrew and English.

◆ The phrase "*Adonai* is One" seems to be a quotation from the "*Shema.*" This verse is also the last verse of the "*Alaynu*" prayer (see any Traditional prayer book). Explain how this statement emphasizes the universal nature of God's reign.

5 Verse 14:12 provides a graphic description of what will happen to those people who fought against Jerusalem.

◆ View and discuss the film *Raiders of the Lost Ark* (1981, rated PG, 115 minutes). Toward the end of the film, the Nazis are destroyed in a scene very similar to the one in verse 14:12. Compare the two scenes.

Connecting the Text To the Holiday

6 God promises (verse 14:11) that there shall never again be destruction, and Jerusalem will dwell securely.

During Sukkot, we dwell in a frail *sukkah*, which is always subject to destruction and affords us very little security.

◆ What might be the symbolic message of dwelling in a *sukkah* once a year? What does dwelling in a *sukkah* help us to remember and/or appreciate?

◆ In your opinion, is the future of the Jewish people secure or fragile?

7 The Haftarah says that all survivors of this great event will make a pilgrimage to Jerusalem for the Festival of Booths (Sukkot).

Sukkot is considered the preeminent holiday. In the Bible it is called הֶחָג (*HehChag* — The Festival), as if there were no need to explain which one (see I Kings 8:1-2 and II Chronicles 5:3).

◆ Which holiday do *you* consider to be "the festival," and why?

◆ Debate which Jewish holiday is the most important for Jews to celebrate today.

8 God threatens that anyone who fails to come to Jerusalem for the Sukkot Festival will not get rain.

Mishnah *Rosh HaShanah* 1:2 teaches that on Sukkot we are judged concerning rainfall, meaning that only if we are found to be deserving will we get adequate rain. From the end of Sukkot until Passover, we include a prayer for rain at the beginning of the *"Amidah"*: "God makes the wind blow and the rain fall." Sukkot marks the beginning of the rainy season in Israel. A good rainy season is crucial for a good year of crops.

A story is told in *Ta'anit* 19a and 23a about a village that was suffering from drought. The villagers asked Honi the Circle Maker to help them. With his stick, Honi drew a circle in the dirt and stood inside it. He declared that he would not leave the circle until God sent rain. God sent a faint drizzle, but Honi said that was not what he meant. God sent a torrential deluge, but Honi said that was not what he meant either. Honi said he wanted a good, nourishing rain of blessing to fall. And it did. Honi and the people thanked God.

◆ How can rain be both a source of prosperity and of destruction?

◆ Make a mural of Honi to decorate your *sukkah*.

9 A main theme of both Sukkot and the Haftarah is Oneness. The Oneness of God is communicated in the Haftarah in verse 14:9. The oneness of humanity is expressed in the Haftarah through the idea that all humanity will be united in their worship of God (verses 14:9, 16, 17). The day on which God will come will be one unique day (verse 14:7). Also in the Haftarah we find the centrality and uniqueness of Jerusalem as the one and only place chosen by God for our worship.

Similarly, the uniqueness of the holiday of Sukkot is expressed when it is called *HehChag*, The Festival, as if there is no other.

◆ What does it mean to be unique?

◆ In what way is every human being unique?

◆ In what ways are the Jewish people unique?

◆ What makes you unique?

MALACHI 1:1-2:7
TOLEDOT תולדות

This Haftarah has been paired with *Parashat Toledot*, Genesis 25:19-28:9. See "Connecting the Text To the Sedra," pp. 605-607, for an exploration of the many ways the two texts shed light on each other.

SYNOPSIS

It is unclear exactly when Malachi lived or who he was. It is understood from his prophecies that he lived after the return to Judah from exile in Babylonia in 538 B.C.E. He also refers in the Haftarah to the destruction of Edom; the transjordanian kingdom of Edom was destroyed by Arabs near the end of the sixth century B.C.E. In addition, since part of his prophecy condemns the priests for engaging in corrupt practices in their work in the Temple, some time may have elapsed since the rebuilding of the Temple in 515 B.C.E. These references would date Malachi toward the end of the sixth century B.C.E. However, it has also been proposed that Malachi prophesied before the middle of the fifth century B.C.E. (the time of the religious reforms of Ezra and Nehemiah), as he calls for reforms that they later institute. Therefore, many scholars date him to about 500-480 B.C.E.

Malachi's prophecies also seem to reflect post-exilic life in Judah and the discontent and disillusionment that filled the people. After returning from exile with great expectations of prosperity, the people found an impoverished life. They lived in Judah under the continued domination and military control of the Persians. They probably had to pay taxes to Persia, making their difficult financial situation even worse.

The Haftarah is composed of two main sections. In the first section, God affirms love for Israel. Having gone through exile, return, poverty, and uncertainty, Israel does not see evidence of God's love, and so questions God. God assures Israel that if they would look around, they would see evidence (such as the permanent ruin of Edom) that would assure them of God's love.

In the second section, the unfaithful priests of Israel are rebuked. They are accused of corruption, disrespect, scorn for the Temple and the sacrificial system, and lack of loyalty to God and God's teachings. They are warned to resume their role as guardians and teachers of God's laws and Covenant.

INSIGHTS FROM THE TRADITION

A Verse 1:1 says that this is the word of *Adonai* declared "through Malachi." Literally, it says the word of God was "in the hand of Malachi."

According to *Exodus Rabbah* 28:6, all the prophecies of all the prophets were given to the souls of the prophets at the time of the giving of the Torah on Mount Sinai. The prophets were not allowed to reveal the prophecies told to them until they were given permission at the appropriate time.

◆ Although the prophets were born knowing the secrets, they had to keep it private until the right time. Are you good at keeping secrets?

◆ Have you ever let "the cat out of the bag" (given away a secret)? If so, describe the situation and the consequences.

◆ Design a special box for keeping secrets hidden.

B In verse 1:10, God bemoans the disrespectful sacrificial services taking place in the Second Temple and wishes the Israelites would lock the doors to the Temple so the sacrifices would stop.

Rashi explains that God wishes that there would be even one good person to rise up among the priests and close the doors of God's sanctuary, and so put an end to these abominable sacrifices.

◆ Describe the role of the one good person in Rashi's explanation.

◆ Is it difficult to be in the role of the one who stands up and stops an abomination? Why or why not?

◆ How is this the same or different from a corporate "whistle blower" (e.g., Jeffrey Wigand, who blew the whistle on his tobacco company employer)?

◆ View and discuss the film *The Insider* (1999, rated R, 157 minutes), which is the story of Wigand's action.

C God accuses the priests of Israel of profaning God's name. They have ridiculed the altar of God, claiming it is defiled and may be treated with scorn (verse 1:12).

◆ Radak explains that "profane" means that they have spread slander about God's altar. How do you think slander defiled the Temple?

◆ How might slander or gossip defile your synagogue or school?

D Hertz suggests that the priests do not literally "say" (in verse 1:12) that God's table is polluted. Rather their actions convey that they think so.

◆ Explain the expression: "Actions speak louder than words."

◆ Do you agree with this expression? Are there times when it is true, and other times when it is not true?

E Radak on verse 2:6 says that proper teachings or rulings must be not only on one's lips, but also in one's heart; they must be taught with sincerity.

◆ Explain the expression: "Do what I say and not what I do."

◆ Can parents who smoke teach their children not to smoke? Why or why not?

◆ Can parents teach their kids to exercise regularly if they themselves never exercise? Why or why not?

◆ Can you give other examples of the lesson in verse 2:6?

F Levi is praised in verse 2:6 because he served God with complete loyalty. To Radak this means that Levi performed acts of loving-kindness, justice, and charity.

◆ How do our actions toward other people show loyalty to God? Choose from the following answers and defend your choice.

• We are fulfilling *mitzvot*.

• We are treating all people as children of God.

• We are bringing justice and peace into the world.

• Since God acts with kindness, justice, and charity, we are setting God as our role model.

STRATEGIES
Analyzing the Text

1 The name of the prophet according to verse 1:1 is Malachi. This name means "my messenger" or "my angel." There is a long-standing debate about whether his name is really Malachi or whether verse 1:1 simply means that the (unnamed) prophet is God's messenger.

◆ Can you suggest any evidence from verse 1:1 that might support either side of the debate? (Consider, for example that "my messenger" would seem to indicate that God was speaking, yet verse 1:1 is not said by God.)

◆ Notice also that verse 2:7 contains a play on words with Malachi's name when it states that a good priest is God's messenger.

◆ Design a business card or logo for Malachi, God's messenger.

2 How has God shown Israel love? In verses 1:2-3 God explains that Jacob has been accepted and Esau rejected. Esau is Jacob's twin brother. Esau's descendants were known as Edom. Edom (Esau) has been destroyed, and in verse 1:4 God insists that even if the Edomites (Esau's descendants) should try to rebuild their country, they will be stopped by God.

◆ Explain the contrast between the fate of the two brothers: one brother's descendants were destroyed permanently, and the other brother's descendants suffered temporary defeat and exile, but are now restored to their land which they are rebuilding.

◆ Explain how the contrast between Edom's permanent destruction and Israel's survival should be evidence to Israel that they are loved by God.

3 Verse 1:6 refers to God as parent.

◆ Explore some of the implications of viewing God as a parent (as parent, is God a role model, disciplinarian, source of life, etc.?).

◆ Complete this sentence: As God's child, I _____.

4 God scolds the priests for showing disrespect by bringing sick or injured sacrificial animals to God's altar when only healthy, unblemished animals are fit to be sacrificed to God (verse 1:8). God tells the priests to try making the same animals a gift to their human governor.

◆ What do you think might happen to the priests if they took a sick and lame animal as a gift to their human governor?

◆ What emotions do you think God is expressing in this statement?

◆ Do you think this is a sarcastic statement from God? Explain why or why not.

◆ Draw a political cartoon depicting this scene or a modern day version of someone trying to buy favors by giving an inferior gift.

5 In verse 1:11 God says, "My name is honored among the nations." God seems to be saying that all people universally worship *Adonai*.

◆ Compare verse 1:11 to verse 1:6, in which God asks why the priests are not giving honor to God. Does it seem ironic that other nations honor God, but the priests in God's Temple do not?

6 God claims that the altar has been degraded.

◆ Discuss the different ways in which the altar of God is defiled (verses 1:12-13): by slander, by acting as if it is a bother to bring an offering, by bringing stolen offerings, by bringing sick or injured offerings.

◆ Design a poster or ad campaign that Malachi might have used to inspire the people to treat God's altar with proper respect.

7 The Rabbis tried to end each Haftarah on a positive note. This one ends with verse 2:7.

◆ Read what comes next to see why the Rabbis concluded here.

Connecting the Text To the Sedra

8 The Sedra involves competition between Jacob and Esau for their father's blessing. The family is torn apart by the competition and the need to compare the children and to choose just one as Isaac's heir.

The Haftarah begins with a comparison between Edom's (Esau's) destruction, from which they will never recover, and Israel's (Jacob's) continued existence. Despite its survival, Israel feels insecure about God's love and needs reassurance.

◆ Do you think competition between family members is good or bad? Why or why not?

◆ Children often feel pressure to perform and be better than someone else in order to deserve love. Discuss the following Hasidic story (see *Tales of the Hasidim* by Martin Buber):

Before his death, Rabbi Zusya said, "In the World To Come, they will not ask me, "Why were you not like Moses?" They will ask me, "Why were you not like Zusya?"

◆ How would a person feel, even a remarkably exceptional person, if he/she had to measure up to Moses?

◆ How does this story teach that we each have our own special value and that we should not compare ourselves to others?

◆ Make a list of your own best traits, the ones that are an expression of the real you. Decide how you can accentuate these traits over other, less desirable ones.

9 In verse 1:14 God proclaims a curse on the cheat (priest or ordinary Israelite) who swaps a good quality sacrificial animal for an inferior one. The Hebrew word translated as "cheat" can also be translated as "to act cleverly, cunningly, deceitfully, or connivingly."

◆ In the Sedra Jacob's name means "a conniving person" or "a heel." Jacob convinces Esau to swap his birthright for a bowl of soup. Explain how our forefather Jacob's behavior is less than exemplary.

◆ In our tradition, we recognize that our leaders are human and, therefore, imperfect. Match these biblical people who did great deeds with their failings:

1. David (d.)
2. Moses (f.)
3. Miriam (a.)
4. Abraham (b.)
5. Samson (c.)
6. Joseph (g.)
7. Rachel (e.)

a. Gossip (Numbers 12:2)
b. Lie (Genesis 12:10-16)
c. Behave crassly (Judges 15:15)
d. Adultery (II Samuel 11)
e. Thievery (Genesis 31:19)
f. Manslaughter (Exodus 2:12)
g. Tattletale (Genesis 37:2)

10 In the Sedra two parents each have their favorite child: Isaac prefers Esau, and Rebecca prefers Jacob (Genesis 25:28).

In the Haftarah God prefers Israel (Jacob) to Edom (Esau).

Problems arise in families when parents play favorites. The Rabbis taught on this subject: "Play no favorites: when Joseph got a many colored coat, his brothers came to hate him." (*Genesis Rabbah* 84:8)

◆ What do you think of favoritism by God and by parents? Is it okay if each child is at least favored by one parent?

◆ Interview teachers, Rabbis, relatives, and friends to find out how they deal with favoritism when raising their children.

◆ Determine whether showing no favoritism is the same as treating each child exactly the same.

◆ Write a short parenting guide, instructing parents on how to treat their children fairly and avoid favoritism.

11 Genesis 25:34 says that Esau despised (ויבז — *va'yivaz*) his birthright.

The same word is used in the Haftarah to say that the priests of Israel despised the table of *Adonai* (verses 1:6-7 and 1:12).

◆ Explain how the prophet seems to be alluding to Esau's bad behavior and to be saying that the nation of Israel is behaving like Esau instead of taking after Jacob.

◆ Explain how this connection between the Haftarah and the Sedra reinforces the idea that all people are basically alike: they have the same faults and strengths.

◆ What are those faults and strengths that most of us have in common?

12 In the last verse of the Haftarah, the priests are reminded that their role is to guard and teach God's teachings.

According to Genesis 26:5, God promised many blessings to Abraham and Isaac because Abraham guarded God's commandments, laws, and teachings.

◆ What do you think it means to be responsible for guarding and teaching commandments?

◆ Who in your community is responsible for guarding God's commandments? Who is responsible for teaching them?

◆ It is difficult to be responsible for keeping and teaching all God's commandments, so start with just one. Choose one new *mitzvah* or law that you could keep. Research it and teach it to your class. For research, consult *Teaching Mitzvot* by Barbara Binder Kadden and Bruce Kadden and/or *A Guide To Jewish Religious Practice* by Isaac Klein.

13 In the Haftarah God complains that God is like a father to Israel, but does not receive the honor that is due to a father (verse 1:6).

In the Sedra Esau decides to wait until after his father dies before he will kill Jacob in order to spare his father the pain (Genesis 27:41). *Midrash* comments on Esau's decision to wait:

"Esau acted with deliberation, saying, 'Why should I grieve my father? Rather, let the days of mourning for my father be at hand (may he die) and then I will kill Jacob.'" (*Genesis Rabbah* 67:8)

◆ Debate: Esau honored his father by deciding to wait to kill his brother.

14 In the Sedra Rebecca tells Jacob to lie to his father and to obtain Esau's blessing from him. Jacob worries that he will be found out and will be cursed. Rebecca responds that the curse will be on her (Genesis 27:13).

In the Haftarah the priests (who are responsible for teaching God's laws) lie and cheat by exchanging the people's good quality sacrifices for bad ones. God curses the priests (1:14).

◆ Stage mock trials: one in which Rebecca is being charged with causing the delinquency of a minor, and the other charging the priests with cheating God out of decent sacrifices. On what basis will you defend the accused?

Extending the Text

15 Two metaphors are used about God: verse 1:6 suggests God is a parent, and verse 1:14 indicates God is King. Both metaphors also appear in the Yom Kippur prayer *"Avinu Malkaynu"* (Our Father, Our King).

◆ Read the *"Avinu Malkaynu"* prayer. Why do you think we address God as "Our Father" in this prayer? For example, is the relationship between father and child: warm, distant, informal, formal, tense, open, secure, volatile, other?

◆ Why do you think we address God as "Our King"? For example, is the relationship between King and subject: formal, informal, close, distant, open, hidden, other?

◆ Explain how the two different images for God might serve different functions in our lives.

◆ For a contrast, see the Haftarah for Rosh Chodesh, p. 355, in which God is portrayed as a mother. Compare the images of God as mother and father.

16 Malachi teaches that one may not bring a stolen sacrifice. There is a general rule in Judaism that when one performs a religious ritual,

one may not use stolen ritual objects. For example, one may not use a stolen *tallit* for praying, a stolen *lulav* or *etrog* on Sukkot, nor may one sit in a *sukkah* built from stolen materials.

The guiding principle is that a sin may not serve as the medium with which a *mitzvah* is performed.

◆ Do you agree with this principle?

◆ Can you argue that the ends justify the means?

◆ Should charitable organizations confirm that the monies donated are acquired by ethical means? How could they go about such an investigation?

17 The priests speak slanderously about God's altar (see Insights from the Tradition, #C, p. 603). Our tradition teaches that slander is harmful to the whole world. Jonah ben Abraham Gerondi (*Shaarey Tshuva* 3) said the following:

"Know that a person who agrees with a slanderous statement when he hears it is as bad as the one who says it, for everyone will say, 'That person who listened to what has been said agreed with it, and that shows it must be true.' Even if the hearer only turns to listen to the gossip and gives the impression of believing it, he helps spread the evil, brings disgrace on his neighbor, and encourages slanderers to carry their evil reports to all people."

◆ Explain the meaning of this quotation.

◆ Explain how those Israelites who heard the slander and did not speak out in protest to stop it were sinning, too (see also Insights from the Tradition #B, p. 603, for the one who is good enough to stop evil from taking place).

◆ Come up with some strategies to avoid listening to gossip and slander.

◆ Test your strategies in role-playing scenarios.

TEACHING HAFTARAH

Personalizing the Text

18 "Whistle blowers," as discussed in Insights from the Tradition #B, p. 603, are in a tough position. If they keep quiet, they remain loyal to their corporation. If they blow the whistle, they may be disloyal, but they may also be helping the greater population. This is often a dilemma faced by police officers and military personnel. In your own lives, you may have experienced a similar conflict of loyalty.

◆ Debate this statement: In one's job, loyalty is the most important thing.

19 In Extending the Text #15, p. 607, we considered the relationship between father and child.

◆ Discuss with each parent separately, his/her ideal way of relating to you.

◆ Describe how you imagine your relationship with your parents will be when you are an adult.

◆ How do these discussions help you understand the relationship between human beings and God as implied by *"Avinu Malkaynu"*?

◆ Learn to sing the famous last line of the *"Avinu Malkaynu"* prayer. Ask your Cantor for help or listen to it on a recording, such as *The Birthday of the World Part II: Yom Kippur* by The Western Wind.

20 All Haftarot, including this one, contain many words of wisdom.

◆ Select one verse that you think is the most important verse of the Haftarah. Be prepared to explain your choice.

◆ Artistically depict your verse (i.e., drawing, painting, collage, mobile, mural).

◆ Compare your artistic representation of the Haftarah with the illustration of this Haftarah in *The Illustrated Torah* by Michal Meron, p. 34.

21 The Haftarah refers to God as parent and King, but our tradition recognizes many different ways for us to imagine and relate to God.

◆ Compile a list of different possible names for God from the prayer book (or see a list compiled in *Higher and Higher: Making Jewish Prayer Part of Us* by Steven M. Brown, pp. 62-64).

◆ Choose your favorite image or name for God. Be prepared to explain how it is different from parent and King, and why it suits you better.

22 Malachi condemns the priests' hypocritical actions. Actions speak louder than words. Play a game of *Prophet Charades*. Choose a prophet and a message to convey to your class in charades. Use this book as a reference. (If desired, the teacher can do the choosing ahead of time and prepare information cards to give to students.)

Other Resources

23 For more on gossip, see Torah Aura's Instant Lesson *Wounding with Words* by Steven Bayar.

24 Read and discuss the story "Feathers" by Heather Forest, which is about the dangers of gossip, in *Chosen Tales*, edited by Peninnah Schram, pp. 93-96.

25 To learn about a national campaign to eliminate verbal violence and promote healing, visit www.wordscanheal.org.

26 For more on the prophet Malachi, including history, themes, and notable quotations, read *Messengers of God: A Jewish Prophets Who's Who* by Ronald H. Isaacs, pp. 197-201.

27 For more on the prophet Malachi, see also *Encyclopaedia Judaica*, vol. 11, pp. 812-816.

28 See *Raising Your Child to Be a Mensch* by Neil Kurshan for information on various parenting issues.

29 For a commentary, discussion questions, and project, see the UAHC Fmaily Shabbat Table Talk web site at www.uahc.org/shabbat/stt/3toledot.html.

30 For a *D'var Torah* on this Haftarah, see the web site for the Fuchsberg Center for Conservative Judaism in Jerusalem, www.uscj.org.il/haftarah/toldot5762.html.

Involving the Family

31 God uses sarcasm to make a point, but sometimes sarcasm can be excessively sharp and hurtful (see Analyzing the Text #4, p. 604). Be on the lookout for sarcasm in family conversations and protect each other from the sting. Every time someone is sarcastic, he or she must contribute a sum of money to *tzedakah*.

32 Have a family discussion about parents and favoritism among children. Bring the subject out in the open to make sure there are no misunderstandings or hurt feelings. Help each family member feel comfortable discussing his/her feelings.

Bar/Bat Mitzvah Projects

33 Be a guardian of God's law and serve God with complete loyalty. Perform acts of justice, mercy, and loving-kindness the entire month of your Bar/Bat Mitzvah. Write about how being good to others made you feel loyal to God.

34 As a family, view and discuss the film *Pay It Forward* (2000, rated PG-13, 123 minutes). The film is about Trevor, a junior high student, who is assigned a social studies project to think of an idea to make the world a better place, then put it into action. Trevor comes up with the idea of doing a good deed for someone. That person is then supposed to do a favor for someone else as a way to "pay the favor forward." Decide on some acts of justice, mercy, and loving-kindness you and your family can do during your Bar/Bat Mitzvah year to start a cycle of paying such favors forward.

MALACHI 3:4-24
SHABBAT HAGADOL

 This Haftarah has been paired with *Shabbat HaGadol*. See "Connecting the Text To the Special Shabbat," pp. 612-613, for an exploration of the many ways the text and the special Shabbat shed light on each other.

SYNOPSIS

Malachi was a post-exilic prophet who, according to most scholars, prophesied after the Second Temple was built, but before the arrival of Ezra the scribe and Nehemiah the governor in Israel. He probably preached around 500-480 B.C.E.

As the Haftarah begins, God longs for Israel to return to righteous behavior. Only then will their sacrifices be pleasing to God, as in the good old days. God reminds Israel of its sins: sorcery, adultery, perjury, and oppression of the weak. Still, God insists that God's dedication to Israel is unchanging, as evidenced by the fact that Israel has not been destroyed in exile. God pleads with unreliable Israel to turn back, but the people deny knowing what they did wrong. God reminds them they have not properly contributed their tithes to the Temple and promises they will prosper if they do so.

God continues to accuse Israel of having spoken negatively about God. Again, they deny knowing what God is talking about. God reminds them that they have claimed there is no point to being righteous since the righteous get no reward and the wicked are not punished.

God responds that there is a written record about the righteous, and in the future the righteous will be rewarded. The wicked, however, will be destroyed on a future, cataclysmic day.

The Haftarah closes with Malachi reminding Israel to remember the teachings of Moses from Mount Sinai, and to expect Elijah to come to announce the cataclysmic day of *Adonai*.

The books of prophets conclude with this last chapter of Malachi, the final prophet of Israel.

INSIGHTS FROM THE TRADITION

A The sins listed in verse 3:5 are all committed by people who think they can't be caught. According to *Metusdat David*, these sinners obviously do not fear God and do not fear that God knows what they are doing. They believed that their sins were secret even from God.

◆ How secret is secret?

◆ Debate whether any secret can ever really be kept completely hidden.

B Verse 3:16 mentions those who esteem God's name and have been talking to each other. *Berachot* 6a explains that there are people who discuss and plan to perform *mitzvot*, but are stopped due to unforeseen circumstances. They nonetheless get credit for having performed the *mitzvah*.

◆ Do you agree that you should get credit for doing a good deed even if you only plan to do it, but aren't able to follow through on your plans due to unforeseen circumstances?

◆ List possible unforeseen circumstances that might prevent the performance of a *mitzvah*.

C Radak explains that verse 3:22 means that the teachings of Torah do not have a time limit or expiration date. Torah applied to Moses' time, and it applies to our time as well.

◆ Does your obligation to study Torah ever expire?

◆ What are your plans for Jewish study after you become Bar/Bat Mitzvah?

◆ In what way do your parents continue their Jewish studies?

D Elijah's role in verse 3:24, according to Rashi, will be to ask the children to speak to their parents about adopting the ways of God.

◆ Everyone knows that parents influence their children. How do children influence their parents?

◆ What is the most important way you ever influenced your parents?

STRATEGIES
Analyzing the Text

1 The English word "turn" appears in verse 3:7 with two different meanings. First, it indicates that Israel turned away from God, rebelled, and willfully refused to follow God's laws.

The second time, the word "turn" means to "turn" back to God, repent for having sinned, and resume keeping God's laws.

◆ How can the same word mean two different things depending on the context?

2 The Israelites are told to return or repent. According to the JPS translation, they respond in verse 3:7 with, "How shall we turn

back?" Other translations say, "Concerning what should we repent?"

◆ What is the difference in meaning between these translations?

◆ Why might the Israelites pretend not to know what they did wrong?

◆ Why might the Israelites say they do not know how to repent?

3 God responds in verse 3:8 that the Israelites defrauded God by not making the proper tithes and contributions.

◆ How would you explain to someone today that by not making charitable contributions, they are stealing from God?

4 God tells the people to perform a test. In the test people would bring the proper tithes and contributions to the Temple. Then God would provide plenty of rain and food for a prosperous life. The people protest the idea of this test, asserting that there is no purpose in doing what God wants since they have seen that the good do not benefit and the wicked are not punished.

◆ Explain in your own words why the people refuse to test God.

◆ What in their experience would make the people so cynical?

5 In verse 3:16 God promises to record in a scroll of remembrance the names and deeds of all those who revere God.

◆ Read and compare Esther 6:1, wherein the king kept a record book of good deeds performed by his citizens, with Malachi 3:16.

◆ Listen to the Gilbert and Sullivan song, "As Someday It May Happen," from the operetta *The Mikado*, which is about the Lord High Executioner's list. Explain how the little list in the song is a list of bad people, but God's list in the Haftarah is of good people. (*The Mikado* is available on cassette or CD.)

◆ Make a little list of people who are good role models in our world today.

Connecting the Text To the Special Shabbat

6 This special Shabbat is called *Shabbat HaGadol* (The Great Shabbat). Consider the following theories as to why it is called *Shabbat HaGadol*:

• In the Haftarah for this Shabbat, Malachi mentions "The Great Day of *Adonai*" (*Yom Adonai HaGadol)* in verse 3:23.

• On this Shabbat immediately before Passover, it was the custom for Rabbis to review with their congregations the details about how to observe the holiday. The Shabbat may have been called "Great" because of the importance of the coming holiday. (Some scholars think that there used to be a similar Shabbat before every festival, on which Rabbis would review how to observe that festival. Since Passover's laws and traditions are so much more complex than that of other holidays, only this special pre-festival Shabbat remains.)

• According to Rabbinic tradition, when the Israelites were still in Egypt, they had to select and tie up a lamb that would be the Paschal lamb on the night of the Exodus. It is suggested that the day on which they tied up the lamb was the Shabbat before the Exodus. It is called Great Shabbat, in part, because it took great courage to tie up a lamb in Egypt, as the Egyptians considered lambs to be sacred. It may also be a Great Shabbat because the Egyptians did not attack the Israelites for tying up a sacred animal.

◆ Make a cartoon for each of these interpretations with the heading, "You know it is a Great Shabbat when . . . "

7 One of Israel's sins, according to God in verse 3:5 of the Haftarah, is treating the stranger badly. One of the main lessons we are to learn from our experience in Egypt is not to oppress the stranger because we were strangers in Egypt.

◆ In our society a stranger is someone who doesn't know anyone and has nowhere to go. Ask your Rabbi to compile a list of people in your community who have nowhere to go for *Seder*. Help pair up those "strangers" with families who will invite them for *Seder*.

8 Passover requires a rebellious attitude. The Israelites in Egypt learned from Moses to have a rebellious attitude toward Egypt and Pharaoh. In other times in our history, Jews have rebelled against tyrants during the Passover season. For example, the rebellion against the tyranny of Rome at Masada took place on the eve of Passover. Similarly, the Warsaw Ghetto uprising against Nazi tyrants took place at Passover.

However, in the Haftarah, God says it is time to stop rebelling and follow God's laws (verse 3:7).

◆ When is rebellion right and when is it destructive?

◆ Act out skits to portray a variety of situations that require rebellion, as well as some in which rebellion is inappropriate.

9 God insists in verse 3:10 that the Israelites should bring the proper tithes and test God to see if God will keep the promise to provide them with plenty. God insists they will prosper to the point of complete satiety.

◆ A favorite song at Passover *Seder* is *"Dayenu"* (It Would Have Been Enough).

The song expresses our gratitude for all God's blessings. As a challenge, learn to sing the entire song in Hebrew.

◆ Write your own creative version of *"Dayenu,"* expressing thanks for all the blessings in your own life. For an example of a creative rewriting of *"Dayenu,"* see the *The Journey Continues: Ma'yan Passover Haggadah,* published by the Ma'yan: The Jewish Women's Project. (You may obtain this *Haggadah* from Ma'yan, 15 West 65th St., New York, NY 10023, 212-580-0099, www.mayan.org.)

10 Elijah is mentioned in the conclusion to the Haftarah as the prophet who will come to proclaim the future day of *Adonai.*

We hope Elijah will visit our homes during the *Seder* to make his announcement. We place a *Kiddush* cup on the table for him.

◆ Paint a wine glass with a special design for your family to use as a Cup of Elijah.

◆ Learn the song *"Eliyahu HaNavi"* (Elijah the Prophet). One version is available in *B'Kol Echad,* edited by Jeffrey Shiovitz, p. 13, and on the accompanying audiocassettes, available from United Synagogue for Conservative Judaism, www.uscj.org/booksvc. For an alternative melody, listen to the recording *Neshama Shel Shlomo* by Shlomo Carlebach and Neshama Carlebach.

◆ At your next *Seder,* arrange to dress in costume as Elijah. When your family opens the front door to greet Elijah, be outside ready to enter and answer their questions.

Extending the Text

11 According to the custom of the Reconstructionist Movement, verse 3:24 is quoted in the blessings following the reading of the Haftarah. See Appendix B, p. 622, for the translation of the Reconstructionist version of the blessing.

◆ Compare the Reconstructionist movement's blessings to the traditional version of the blessings following the Haftarah (see Appendix B, p. 622). What phrase has verse 3:24 replaced?

◆ Why might Malachi's description of the peaceful reconciliation of parent and child be an appropriate description of a messianic, ideal future?

12 In verse 3:20 Malachi pictures God as a "sun of victory [that] shall rise to bring healing."

This verse provides the basis for a sermon delivered by Rabbi Milton Steinberg (reprinted in *A Treasury of Comfort* by Rabbi Sidney Greenberg, pp. 272-277):

"After a long illness, I was permitted for the first time to step out of doors. And, as I crossed the threshold, sunlight greeted me. This is my experience — all there is to it. And yet, so long as I live, I shall never forget that moment . . . It touched me, too, with friendship, with warmth, with blessing. And as I basked in its glory, there ran through my mind those wonder words of the prophet about the sun which some day shall rise with healing on its wings.

In that instant I looked about me to see whether anyone else showed on his face the joy, almost the beatitude, I felt. But no, there they walked — men and women and children, in the glory of a golden flood, and so far as I could detect, there was none to give it heed. And then I remembered how often I, too, had been indifferent to sunlight, how often, preoccupied with petty and sometimes mean concerns, I had disregarded it. And I said to myself — how precious is the sunlight, but, alas, how careless of it are [we]."

◆ In your own words, describe Rabbi Steinberg's experience. How can we compare God to the sun's rays in the story?

◆ Write an original blessing that Rabbi Steinberg might have said upon walking into the sunlight.

◆ Go out and bask/play in the sun, and be thankful for your health and all your blessings.

13 Ezra and Nehemiah are mentioned in the Synopsis, p. 610. According to the Bible, Nehemiah was an exile who lived in Babylonia during the reign of Artaxerxes I (mid 400s B.C.E.) and served the King. His mission was a delicate one. He was to return from exile in Babylonia and serve as governor of Judah. His main tasks were to rebuild the walls of the city of Jerusalem and reorganize the community. He was dedicated to his community and concerned about Shabbat observances and the sanctity of the Temple. A book of the Bible is named after him.

According to the Bible, Ezra was a priest and scribe who lived in Babylonia and returned from exile to Jerusalem some time after Nehemiah. Ezra is portrayed as a religious leader who was involved with the teaching of the Law of Moses and the enforcement of those laws. It is the unproven theory of some that Ezra compiled the Law of Moses (The Torah) and brought it to Jerusalem from Babylonia. A book of the Bible is named after him.

According to *Bava Kamma* 82a, Ezra was zealous about spreading the word of Torah. He proclaimed that it be read three times per week, in addition to Shabbat mornings.

◆ Find out what those three times are, and ask your Rabbi whether or not your synagogue follows that practice.

14 Kara understands that the statement "be mindful of the Teaching of Moses"

in verse 3:22 indicates that Malachi was the last prophet and that after him prophecy would cease.

Deuteronomy 34:10 says, "Never again did there arise in Israel a prophet like Moses."

Explain in your own words how both Deuteronomy 34:10 and Malachi 3:22 indicate that Moses was the greatest prophet and that his teachings must be remembered.

In *Sacred Enigmas*, p. 111, Stephen A. Geller writes that the Bible "bespeaks a contempt for future prophets masked by an extreme deference to a dead one, Moses. Past seers, who have become [part of] sacred text, are canonical; future ones are to be viewed with such caution as to preclude any respect for them."

◆ Why do you think the Bible would tell us that Moses was the greatest prophet?

◆ Explain in your own words the argument that if a prophet had come along and contradicted the canon, there would have been a conflict. So to prevent the conflict, the Bible teaches that prophecy has ended once and for all.

15 *Shabbat HaGadol* is the Shabbat before Pesach. Here is information about the different Pesachs in our tradition:

The first Pesach was in Egypt. On the 14th day of the first month (Nisan) the Israelites were to kill the Paschal lamb at dusk and put its blood on their doorposts and eat the lamb with *matzah* and *maror*. Later that night, God took them out of Egypt (see Exodus 12).

The first anniversary of Pesach was in the desert. The children of Israel kept the Passover as it had been proclaimed to Moses (see Numbers 9:1-5).

Pesach *Shayni* was one month later. One requirement of celebrating Passover is that every participant must be ritually pure. If anyone is ritually impure (for example, they came into contact with a dead body), they may not partake of the paschal offering. Therefore, God proclaimed that there would be a second chance for anyone who missed the first one. The second chance would be on the 14th day of the second month (see Numbers 9:9-12).

Pesach of Joshua was in the Land of Canaan. When the children of Israel arrived in the Promised Land, it was spring and almost time for Pesach. In order to participate in the Pesach offering, all males must be circumcised. Since the Israelites did not practice circumcision in the desert (perhaps because the hardship of traveling made the surgery too dangerous), none were circumcised when they arrived in Canaan. Therefore, they all underwent circumcision. They then observed their first Pesach in the Promised Land (see Joshua 5:2-11).

Pesach of Josiah was unique. In the time of King Josiah, a scroll was found that explained the laws of Pesach, as well as many other laws. It seems these laws were new to the Israelites, and the king immediately instituted religious reforms and then observed Pesach. It is said that there was no Pesach ever like the one observed by King Josiah (II Chronicles 35:1-2, 16-19).

◆ Make a mural depicting the history of the observance of Pesach, including your own.

Personalizing the Text

16 In the first verse of the Haftarah, Malachi says that the offerings will one day be pleasing to God as they were in the years of old.

◆ Why do the "old days" always seem so good?

◆ Find out about what Passover was like "in the good ol' days" by interviewing your grandparents and — if possible — your great grandparents. Were the old days really good?

17 Like many prophets, Malachi uses beautiful imagery and metaphor.

◆ Choose one verse of the Haftarah to draw or paint. Be prepared to explain why you chose that verse and what it means to you. Compare your portrayal of your verse to the picture of this Haftarah in *The Illustrated Torah* by Michal Meron, p. 228.

18 The Haftarah reads like a dialogue between Israel and God.

◆ Write and perform a skit based on the text.

19 In verses 3:20 Malachi compares God to a rising sun.

◆ Watch a sunrise (see verse 3:20) and compare it to God.

20 According to Rashi (on verse 3:24), Elijah will make peace in the world.

◆ Learn a song about peace, such as *"Shalom al Yisrael"* (Peace for Israel) or *"Tein Shabbat V'Tein Shalom."* The former may be found in *B'Kol Echad*, edited by Jeffrey Shiovitz, p. 109, and on the accompanying audiocassettes *Shirei B'Kol Echad*. The latter may be found on p. 93 of *B'Kol Echad*. Both songbook and cassettes are available from United Synagogue of Conservative Judaism at www.uscj.org/booksvc.

◆ Choreograph a dance to one of the above songs.

21 Malachi was the last prophet.

◆ Write a eulogy for the prophet and for the great institution of prophecy in Israel.

Other Resources

22 For more on the prophet Malachi, including history, themes, and notable quotations, read *Messengers of God: A Jewish Prophets Who's Who* by Ronald H. Isaacs, pp. 197-201.

23 For more on the prophet Malachi, see *Encyclopaedia Judaica*, vol. 11, pp. 812-816.

24 For an excellent Passover resource book, see *The Passover Anthology* by Philip Goodman, which features historical information, stories, recipes, and more.

25 Passover is a detail-oriented holiday. For guidance, consult *The Passover Seder* by Dr. Ron Wolfson.

26 We discussed secrets in Insights from the Tradition #A, p. 610. Play the game "What is Your Jewish Secret" in *Jewish Identity Games* by Richard J. Israel, p. 29.

27 Play the game "Passover Past, Passover Present" in *Jewish Identity Games* by Richard J. Israel, p. 5.

28 For commentary, discussion questions, and project, see the UAHC Family Shabbat Table web page at www.uahc.org/shabbat/stt/hagadol.html.

29 For more information on the Warsaw Ghetto Uprising, which began on the eve of Passover 1943 (see Connecting To the Special Shabbat #8, p. 612), go to the web site of the U.S. Holocaust Memorial Museum web site at http://www.ushmm.org/outreach/wgupris.htm.

Involving the Family

30 Verse 3:22 implores us to be mindful of the Teaching of Moses (the Torah) and verse 3:24 promises a reconciliation of parents and children. Have your family embark on a parents and children Jewish education program together. Study Torah together as a family by attending a Shabbat retreat held by your synagogue, your local Hadassah, the National Havurah Committee, or organize your own. For information on regional Shabbat retreats held by The National Havurah Committee, see www.havurah.org.

Bar/Bat Mitzvah Project

31 According to the Haftarah (verse 3:8), by not making proper contributions, people steal from and defraud God. Work on fund-raisers for charitable organizations to help them raise money for their causes and to help people give appropriate levels to charity. Make sure the organizations you choose to support give the vast majority of monies collected to their actual cause and not to administrative costs.

APPENDIX A
Commentators/Commentaries

Abrabanel, Isaac ben Judah (1437-1508):
Finance Minister to the kings of Portugal, Spain, and Naples, who settled in Venice after the expulsion in 1492. He wrote important commentaries to the Bible, the *Haggadah*, and to Rambam's *Guide of the Perplexed*.

Alshich, Moses ben Chaim (1508-1593): Born in Adrianopolis, Alshich spent most of his life in Safed where he was a student of Joseph Karo (author of the Shulchan Aruch). He was a prominent *halachic* authority, whose Shabbat sermons became the basis of a well-known commentary to the Torah, *Torat Moshe*.

Baal Shem Tov (1699-1760): Born Israel ben Eliezer, this Ukrainian Rabbi was a great mystic, scholar, teacher, and the founder of Hasidism. He gave new religious strength to the disheartened Jews of Eastern Europe. His ideas and stories have greatly influenced modern religious thought.

Cohen, Gerson (1923-1991): Outstanding historian of ancient and medieval Judaism, who served as the chancellor of the Jewish Theological Seminary of America in New York.

Daath Soferim: Biblical commentary written by a modern historian, exegete, and educator, living in Jerusalem, named Rabbi Chaim Rabinowitz.

Dead Sea Scrolls: A collection of texts that were found in caves near the Dead Sea beginning in 1947. These scrolls included portions of biblical manuscripts, fragments of the *Septuagint*, *midrashic* works, and other documents that reflect the sect of Jews who lived in that region between the second century B.C.E. and the first century C.E.

Doroth HaRishonim: A history of Talmudic-Rabbinic tradition from biblical times to the Middle Ages, written by Rabbi Isaac Halevy.

Eliezer of Beaugency: Twelfth century Bible commentator who lived in France. Though it is believed that he wrote commentaries on most of the books of the Bible, only his commentaries to Isaiah, Ezekiel, and Minor Prophets have been preserved.

Exodus Rabbah: An early medieval *midrashic* work on the Book of Exodus.

Frankel, Ellen (1951-): Editor-in-Chief of the Jewish Publication Society, who has also been described as a folklorist, writer, and scholar. She is the author of many books, including *The Five Books of Miriam: A Woman's Commentary on the Torah*.

Genesis Rabbah: One of the earliest of the *midrashic* writings, this collection on the Book of Genesis is believed to date to the fourth or fifth century C.E.

Ginzberg, Louis (1873-1953): A professor at the Jewish Theological Seminary of America in New York, Ginzberg played a crucial role in the formation of the Conservative movement. His most important work was the seven-volume *The Legends of the Jews*, a retelling of hundreds of *midrashim* about the people and events of the Bible.

Greenberg, Sidney (1917-): Congregational Rabbi, author, and editor of several books, each of which was designed to help people live more meaningful lives.

Halevy, Rabbi Isaac (1847-1914): A Polish scholar whose major work was *Doroth Ha-Rishonim*, which is a history of Talmudic-Rabbinic traditions from biblical times to the Middle Ages.

Hertz, Joseph Herman (1872-1946): The first graduate of the Jewish Theological Seminary of America in New York (1894). He went on to become the Chief Rabbi of the United Hebrew Congregations of the British Commonwealth. His commentary on the Pentateuch is one of the standard texts used in synagogues today.

Hirsch, Mendel (1833-1900): The son of Rabbi Samson Raphael Hirsch, this Rabbi, educator, and writer wrote a commentary on the Haftarot based, in part, on his father's interpretations.

Honor, Leo (1894-1956): Rabbi and professor of education who wrote a commentary to the Book of First Kings. Born in Russia, Honor began his American career as an instructor at the Teachers' Institute of the Jewish Theological Seminary of America in New York. He was the founder and first president of the National Council for Jewish Education.

Ibn Ezra, Abraham (1089-1164): A scholar of Spanish origin who traveled throughout Europe and North Africa and was famous for his poems and scholarship. Ibn Ezra is best known for his commentary on the Bible, which makes extensive use of grammatical and etymological interpretation.

Ibn Nachmiash, Joseph (fourteenth century): Biblical commentator from Spain who wrote a commentary on the Book of Jeremiah.

Jacobs, Louis: (1920-): English Rabbi and theologian.

Josephus, Flavius (c. 38 C.E.- after 100 C.E.): Commander of the Galilee in the first Jewish revolt against the Romans (66-70C.E.). He eventually surrendered to the Romans, and was taken in chains to Rome where he gained the favor of the emperor Vespasian. He wrote *The Jewish War*, the main source detailing the history of the Jews in the first centuries B.C.E. and C.E. and the origin of the war between the Jews and Rome.

Kara, Joseph (born circa 1060-70): French Rabbi and commentator on Bible and liturgy.

Kimchi, Rabbi Joseph (c. 1105-c. 1170): Grammarian, exegete, and translator who lived in Spain and France. He was the father of David, the Radak.

K'li Y'kar: A commentary written on Former Prophets by Rabbi Sh'muel Laniado, who lived in Venice during the sixteenth and seventeenth centuries.

Kushner, Lawrence (1943-): contemporary Reform Rabbi, storyteller, teacher, and writer.

Lamentations Rabbah: A collection of *midrashim* on the Book of Lamentations, which was compiled in the fifth century in Palestine.

Malbim (an acronym for Meir Leibush ben Yehiel Michel, 1809-1879): A Rabbi of Russian origin who was a staunch opponent of the early Reform Movement. He wrote a commentary to the Bible that was motivated to a large extent by his desire to defend Orthodox positions and interpretations.

Metsudat David: A Commentary on the Bible written by David Altschuler and his son Yechiel Hillel in the eighteenth century.

Midrash: The word is derived from the Hebrew root "*drash*," meaning "to expound" or "to interpret." *Midrashim* (plural) are explanations and interpretations of biblical texts.

Midrash HaGadol: A collection of *midrashim* on the Torah compiled by the Yemenite scholar David ben Amram Adini in the thirteenth century. The work is important because it contains the only known record of many teachings of the Tannaim (Sages of the first and second centuries C.E.).

Midrash Proverbs: A collection of *midrashim* on the Book of Proverbs, possibly dating back to the days just after the editing of the Babylonian Talmud. This collection, which contains passages explaining the text according to its literal meaning, is incomplete in its present state.

Midrash Tanhuma: A collection of *midrashim* on the Pentateuch that dates to the early Middle Ages.

Midrash Yalkut Shimoni: A comprehensive *midrashic* anthology covering the whole Bible. The compiler, working during the Middle Ages, collected Rabbinical sayings following the order of the verses of the Bible. The compilation contains more than 10,000 statements from more than 50 different *midrashic* works.

Mishnah: The core of the oral law, this collection of legal material is presented in six "orders" (divisions). The editing of the Mishnah is attributed to Rabbi Judah HaNasi; it is thought to have been completed early in the third century C.E. in Palestine. Mishnah, together with Gemara, forms the Talmud. The word comes from the Hebrew root "*shanah*," meaning "to repeat," and refers to the learning of the oral law.

Numbers Rabbah: A collection of *midrashim* on the Book of Numbers, part of which is believed to be the work of Moses ha'Darshan of Narbonne (eleventh century). Scholars believe that *Numbers Rabbah* comprises two different collections, one from the ninth century and the other from the eleventh century. The two collections were probably joined together by a scribe in the twelfth or thirteenth century.

Pesikta Rabbati: A collection of medieval homiletic *midrashim* on the festivals of the year.

Pirke Avot: The ninth tractate of the fourth order of the Mishnah (*Nezikin*), *Pirke Avot* (Ethics of the Fathers), is one of Jewish tradition's most oft quoted texts. It is filled with wisdom, parables, and ethical lessons.

Plaut, W. Gunther (1912-): A prominent Reform Rabbi and scholar, a past president of the Central Conference of American Rabbis, Plaut is the main author and editor of *The Haftarah Commentary* as well as of *The Torah: A Modern Commentary* (both published by UAHC Press).

Psalms Rabbah: A collection of *midrashim* on the Book of Psalms. Most probably composed over the course of some centuries, it includes *midrashim* from as early as the third century C.E. and as late as the thirteenth century C.E.

Rabbi Meir: Second century student of Rabbi Akiva. *Halachist* who is often quoted in the Mishnah.

Radak (an acronym for Rabbi David Kimchi, 1160-1235): Grammarian, exegete, teacher, and public figure who lived in Spain and France. He wrote biblical commentaries on all the books of Prophets. His commentaries are known for focusing on the contextual meaning of the Bible (instead of *midrashic* meanings), focusing on grammatical issues, and being clear and readable.

Ralbag (an acronym for Rabbi Levi Ben Gershom, 1288-1344): French mathematician, astronomer, philosopher, Talmudist, and Bible commentator.

Rema (an acronym for Rabbi Moses Isserles, 1525-1572): Polish Rabbi and legal commentator who was also interested in philosophy, *Kabbalah*, homiletics, and the natural sciences.

Rambam (an acronym for Rabbi Moses ben Maimon, also known as Maimonides, 1135-1204): Rambam was one of the most important Jewish authorities of the post-Talmudic period. A physician and Jewish scholar, he wrote the *Siraj*, a widely accepted commentary on the Mishnah; *Guide of the Perplexed*, a philosophical work; and the *Mishneh Torah*, a 14-volume code of Jewish law. He also authored several important *Responsa*.

Ramban (an acronym for Rabbi Moses ben Nachman, also known as Nachmanides, 1194-1270): One of the leading scholars of the Middle Ages, Ramban is known for his participation in the disputation at Barcelona in 1263 against the apostate Pablo Christiani. He was a prolific writer whose work was influenced by Rashi, Ibn Ezra, and Rambam. His most important works are a commentary on the Torah and his writings on *halachah*. Ramban emigrated to Palestine in 1267.

Rashbam (an acronym for Rabbi Samuel ben Meir, 1080-1174): The grandson of Rashi, Rashbam lived in France. He was a commentator on both Talmud and Bible who focused strongly on the contextual meaning (the *peshat*) of the Bible, as opposed to *midrashic* interpretations.

Rashi (an acronym for Rabbi Shlomo Yitzhaki, in English, Solomon ben Isaac, 1040-1105): A very prominent French commentator. Rashi's explanations, which are noted for their clarity, cover the entire Bible and the Talmud.

Salanter, Rabbi Israel Lipkin (1810-1883): A Lithuanian Rabbi who founded the revolutionary Musar movement, which sought to encourage ethical living based on the study of traditional ethical literature.

Septuagint: The Greek translation of the Hebrew Bible, which was written between the third century B.C.E. and the first century C.E. This translation sometimes differs from the Hebrew Bible, probably because the translator was working from a version of the Hebrew Bible different from the one we have now. The name *Septuagint* means "70," because of a legend that 70 Jewish scholars, each working separately, wrote an exact Greek

translation. For more on this legend, see the article "Aristeas, Letter of" in the *Encyclopaedia Judaica*, vol. 3, pp. 439-440.

Shulchan Aruch (Prepared Table): A code of Jewish law written in 1565 by the Sephardic Rabbi Joseph Karo. The *Shulchan Aruch* came to be accepted as the definitive code of Jewish law.

Sifra: A collection of *halachic midrashim* on the Book of Leviticus that dates to the third century C.E.

Sifre: A work comprising two distinct collections of *halachic midrashim*, one of the Book of Numbers, the other of Deuteronomy. The *Sifre* was probably compiled in Palestine in the third century C.E.

Spiegel, Shalom (1899-1984): A professor of Hebrew Literature who was born in Romania and lived in Haifa before moving to the United States. His commentaries are marked by an elegant prose and a wide knowledge of Jewish texts, legends, history, and traditions.

Talmud: A body of law and lore developed in the academies of Babylonia (the Babylonian Talmud, second to sixth centuries C.E.) and Tiberias (the Jerusalem/Yerushalmi Talmud, second to fifth centuries C.E.). The Talmud consists of Mishnah and Gemara. The Rabbis whose teachings are contained in the Mishnah are known as Tannaim, while those in the Gemara are known as Amoraim. The titles of the tractates of the Talmud are taken from those orders of the Mishnah on which they are based.

Tanach: The Hebrew word for Bible, Tanach is actually an acronym of the first letters of the words Torah, Nevi'im (Prophets), and Ketuvim (Writings).

Targum: A translation of the Hebrew Bible into Aramaic. There are a number of *Targumim* (plural) that still exist today, covering different portions of the Bible.

Targum Onkelos: An Aramaic translation of the Bible dated from the first or second century C.E.

Targum Jonathan: An Aramaic translation of the Books of Prophets attributed to Jonathan ben Uzziel. This *Targum* originated in the first or second century C.E., underwent revisions, and probably reached its final form in the seventh century C.E.

Telushkin, Joseph (1948-): Rabbi and author of influential and informative contemporary books on Judaism. He is an associate of CLAL, the National Jewish Center for Learning and Leadership.

Torah: A Hebrew word used in the Bible for law or teaching. Torah has come to designate the Pentateuch (first five books of the Bible) or, sometimes, the Bible as a whole, or even the whole corpus of Rabbinic texts from the Bible through Mishnah, Talmud, and *Midrash*. It is also used as the term for Jewish study in general.

Vilna Gaon (Elijah ben Solomon Zalman, HaGRA, 1720-1797): Jewish leader and *halachic* authority who, as head of the Mitnagdim in Vilna, was an important opponent of Hasidism.

Yalkut Me'am Loez: A popular Sephardic commentary on the Bible written in Ladino and dating from the eighteenth century. The work was begun by Yaakov Culi in 1730 with the intention of giving people who didn't know Hebrew access to traditional material. Culi died in 1732, and the work was completed by a number of other writers.

APPENDIX B

Haftarah Blessings

TRADITIONAL BLESSINGS BEFORE AND AFTER THE HAFTARAH ON SHABBAT

Before the Haftarah:

Blessed are You, *Adonai* our God, Ruler of the universe, who has chosen good prophets and was pleased with their words of truth. Blessed are You, *Adonai*, who chooses Torah, Moses God's servant, Israel God's people, and the prophets of truth and righteousness.

After the Haftarah:

Blessed are You, *Adonai* our God, Ruler of the universe, Rock of all ages, Righteous in all generations, the trustworthy God, Who says and does, Who speaks and fulfills, Whose every word is truth and righteousness. Trustworthy are You, *Adonai*, our God, and trustworthy are Your words, not one of which will remain unfulfilled, for You are a trustworthy and merciful God and Ruler. Blessed are You, *Adonai*, God, trustworthy in all your words.

Show mercy for Zion, the house of life to us; and to the humbled spirit, bring salvation soon, in our days. Blessed are You, *Adonai*, Who brings joy to Zion through her children.

Bring us joy, *Adonai* our God, through Elijah the prophet, Your servant, and through the kingdom of the House of David Your anointed. Soon may he come to gladden our hearts. May no stranger sit on David's throne and may no other inherit his

honor. For by Your holy name You promised that his light shall never be extinguished. Blessed are You, *Adonai*, Shield of David.

For the Torah, for worship, for the prophets, and for this Shabbat day that You, O *Adonai* our God, have given us for holiness and rest, for honor and splendor, for all this, *Adonai* our God, we thank You and bless You. May Your name be blessed forever by every living being. Blessed are You, *Adonai*, who sanctifies Shabbat.

REFORM BLESSINGS BEFORE AND AFTER THE HAFTARAH ON SHABBAT (SHORTENED VERSION)

Before the Haftarah:

Blessed are You, *Adonai*, our God, Ruler of the universe, Who has chosen good prophets and was pleased with their words of truth. Blessed are You, *Adonai*, Who chooses Torah, Moses God's servant, Israel God's people, and the prophets of truth and righteousness.

After the Haftarah:

Blessed are You, *Adonai* our God, Ruler of the universe, Rock of all ages, Righteous in all generations, the trustworthy God, Who says and does, Who speaks and fulfills, Whose every word is truth and righteousness.

For the Torah, for worship, for the prophets, and for this Shabbat day that You, O *Adonai* our God, have given us for holiness and rest, for honor and splendor, for all this, *Adonai* our God, we thank You and bless You. May Your name be blessed forever by every living being. Blessed are You, *Adonai*, who sanctifies Shabbat.

RECONSTRUCTIONIST BLESSINGS BEFORE AND AFTER THE HAFTARAH ON SHABBAT

Before the Haftarah:

Blessed are You, *Adonai* our God, Ruler of the universe, Who has chosen good prophets and was pleased with their words of truth. Blessed are You, *Adonai*, Who chooses Torah, Moses God's servant, and the prophets of truth and righteousness.

After the Haftarah:

Blessed are You, *Adonai* our God, Ruler of the universe, Rock of all ages, Righteous in all generations, the trustworthy God, Who says and does, Who speaks and fulfills, Whose every word is truth and righteousness. Trustworthy are You *Adonai*, our God, and trustworthy are Your words, not one of which will remain unfulfilled, for You are a trustworthy and merciful God and Ruler. Blessed are You, *Adonai*, God, trustworthy in all your words.

Show mercy for Zion, the house of life to us; and to Your people Israel, be a savior soon and in our days. Blessed are You, *Adonai*, Who brings joy to Zion through her children.

Bring us joy, *Adonai* our God, through Elijah the prophet, Your servant. Soon may Elijah come to gladden our hearts. May he turn the hearts of the parents to their children, and the hearts of the children to their parents. And may Your house be called a house of prayer for all peoples. Blessed are You, *Adonai*, Who brings an everlasting peace.

For the Torah, for worship, for the prophets, and for this Shabbat day that You, O *Adonai* our God, have given us for holiness and rest, for honor and splendor, for all this *Adonai* our God, we thank You and bless You. May Your name be blessed forever by every living being. Blessed are You, *Adonai*, Who sanctifies Shabbat.

APPENDIX C

Maps

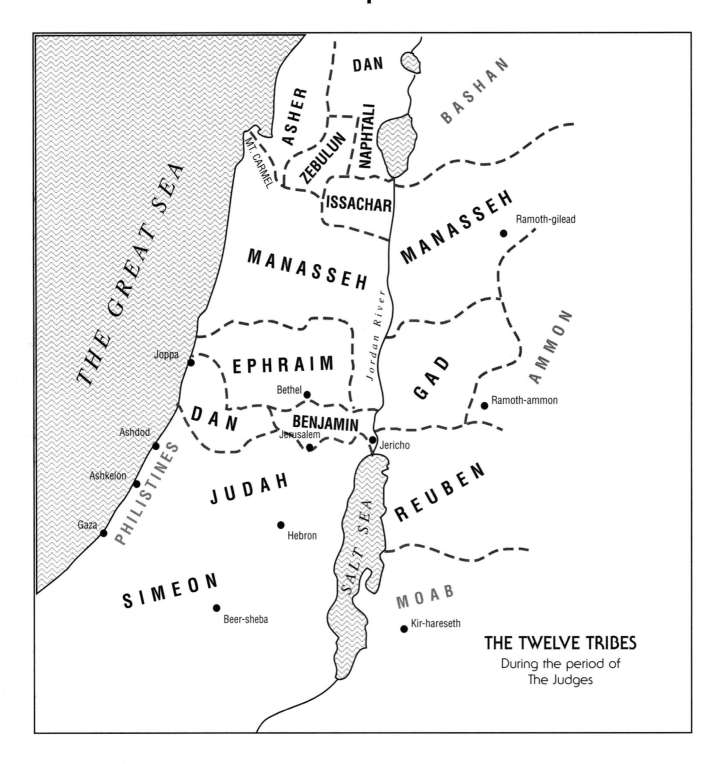

THE GREAT SEA

DAN

ASHER

BASHAN

MT. CARMEL

ZEBULUN

NAPHTALI

ISSACHAR

MANASSEH

Ramoth-gilead

MANASSEH

Joppa

EPHRAIM

AMMON

Bethel

GAD

DAN

BENJAMIN

Ramoth-ammon

Ashdod

Jerusalem

Jericho

Jordan River

Ashkelon

PHILISTINES

JUDAH

REUBEN

Gaza

Hebron

SALT SEA

SIMEON

MOAB

Beer-sheba

Kir-hareseth

THE TWELVE TRIBES
During the period of
The Judges

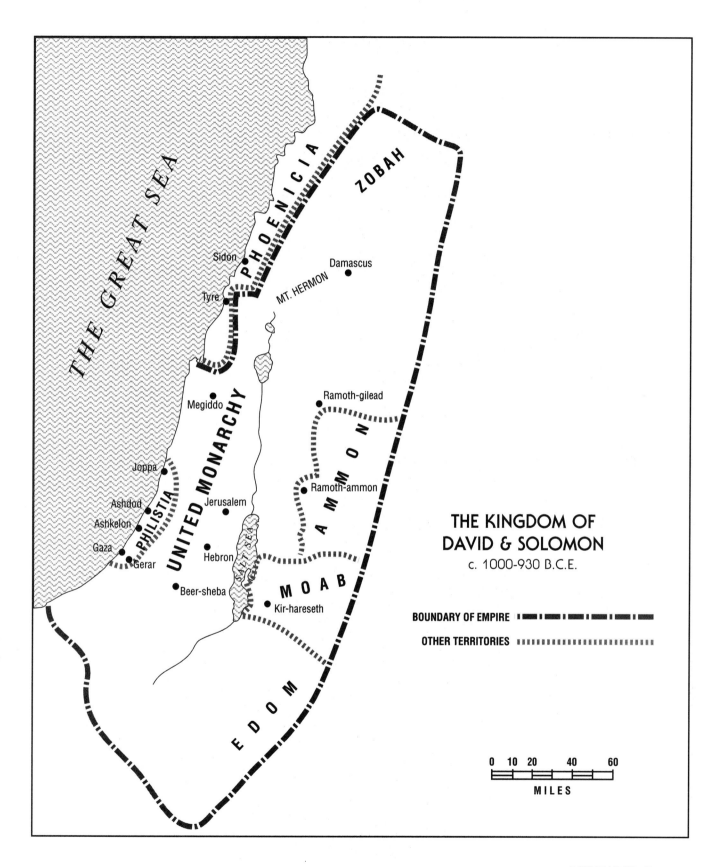

THE GREAT SEA

PHOENICIA

ZOBAH

Sidon

Damascus

Tyre

MT. HERMON

Megiddo

Ramoth-gilead

UNITED MONARCHY

Joppa

PHILISTIA

Ashdod

Jerusalem

AMMON

Ramoth-ammon

Ashkelon

Gaza

Hebron

SALT SEA

Gerar

Beer-sheba

MOAB

Kir-hareseth

EDOM

THE KINGDOM OF
DAVID & SOLOMON
c. 1000-930 B.C.E.

BOUNDARY OF EMPIRE ▬▬▬▬▬

OTHER TERRITORIES ░░░░░░░░░

0 10 20   40   60

MILES

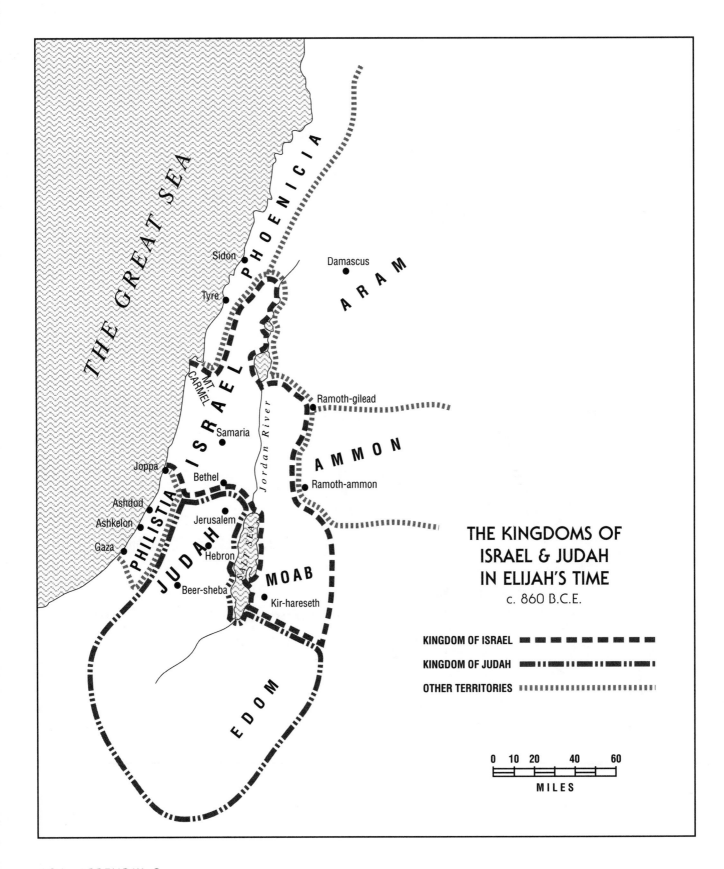

THE GREAT SEA

PHOENICIA

Sidon

Tyre

Damascus

ARAM

MT. CARMEL

ISRAEL

Ramoth-gilead

Samaria

Jordan River

AMMON

Joppa

Bethel

Ramoth-ammon

Ashdod

Jerusalem

Ashkelon

PHILISTIA

JUDAH

SALT SEA

Gaza

Hebron

MOAB

Beer-sheba

Kir-hareseth

EDOM

THE KINGDOMS OF ISRAEL & JUDAH IN ELIJAH'S TIME
c. 860 B.C.E.

KINGDOM OF ISRAEL ▬ ▬ ▬ ▬ ▬ ▬

KINGDOM OF JUDAH ▬▪▬▪▬▪▬▪▬

OTHER TERRITORIES ▪▪▪▪▪▪▪▪▪▪▪▪▪

0 10 20 40 60

MILES

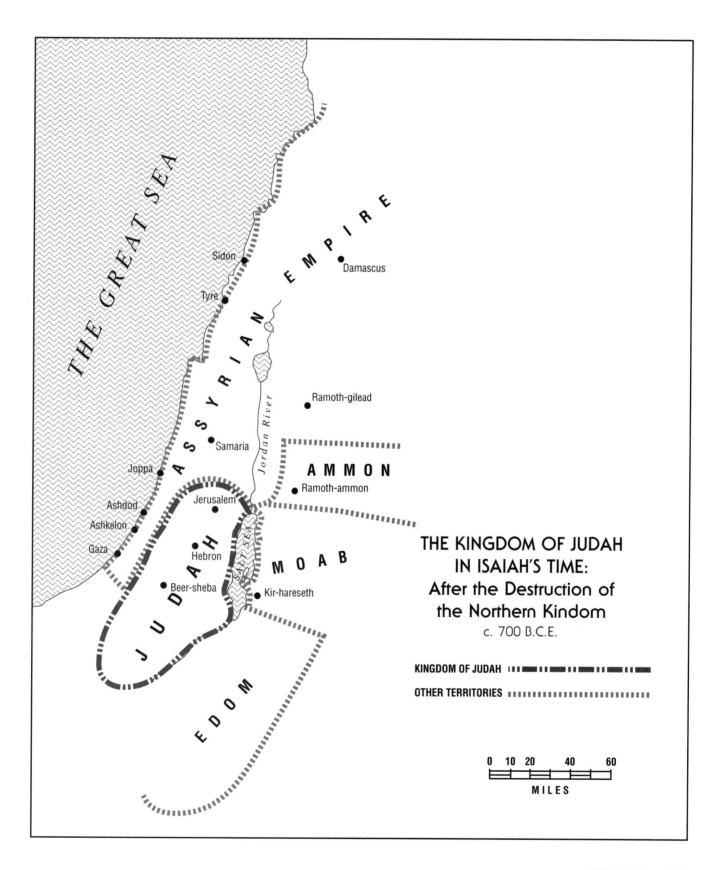

THE GREAT SEA

Sidon

Damascus

Tyre

ASSYRIAN EMPIRE

Ramoth-gilead

Jordan River

Samaria

Joppa

AMMON

Ashdod

Jerusalem

Ramoth-ammon

Ashkelon

JUDAH

SALT SEA

MOAB

Gaza

Hebron

Beer-sheba

Kir-hareseth

EDOM

THE KINGDOM OF JUDAH IN ISAIAH'S TIME:
After the Destruction of the Northern Kindom
c. 700 B.C.E.

KINGDOM OF JUDAH

OTHER TERRITORIES

0 10 20   40   60

MILES

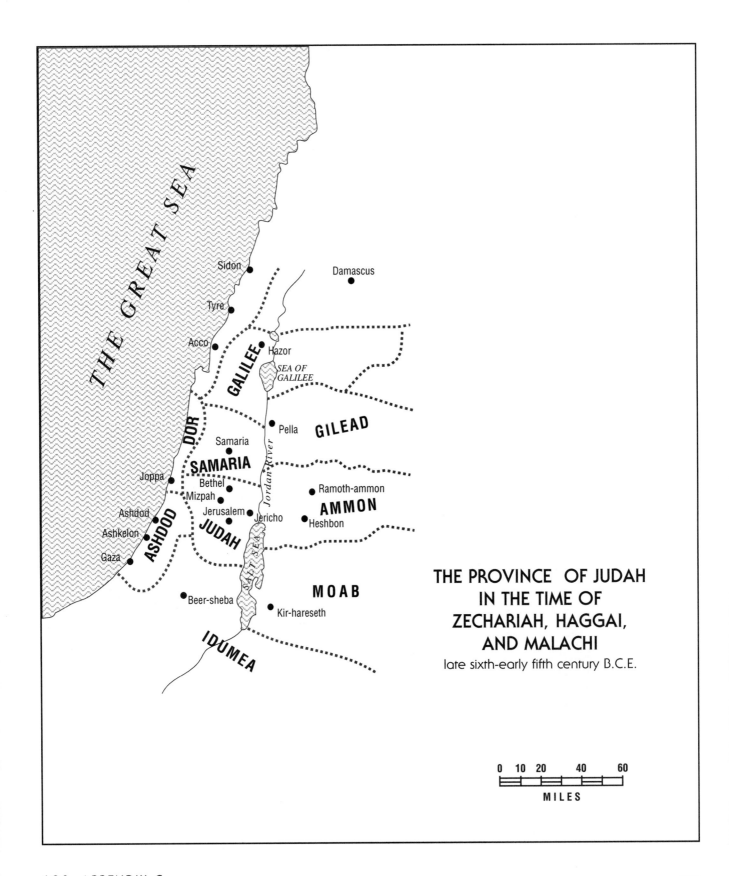

THE GREAT SEA

Sidon

Damascus

Tyre

Acco

GALILEE

Hazor

SEA OF
GALILEE

DOR

Pella

GILEAD

Samaria

SAMARIA

Joppa

Bethel

Mizpah

Jordan River

Ramoth-ammon

Jerusalem

Jericho

AMMON

Ashdod

Heshbon

Ashkelon

ASHDOD

JUDAH

SALT SEA

Gaza

MOAB

Beer-sheba

Kir-hareseth

IDUMEA

THE PROVINCE OF JUDAH
IN THE TIME OF
ZECHARIAH, HAGGAI,
AND MALACHI
late sixth-early fifth century B.C.E.

0 10 20   40   60

MILES

BIBLIOGRAPHY

Agnon, S.Y. *Days of Awe: A Treasury of Jewish Wisdom for Reflection, Repentance, and Renewal on the High Holidays.* New York: Schocken Books, 1995.

> Outstanding resource for stories, laws, customs, and inspiration related to the High Holy Days.

Alcalay, Reuben. *A Basic Encyclopedia of Jewish Proverbs, Quotations, and Folk Wisdom.* New York: Hartmore House, 1973.

> More than 5,000 sayings, arranged alphabetically by subject.

Alter, Robert. *The David Story: A Translation with Commentary of 1 and 2 Samuel.* New York: Norton, 1999.

> Elegant English translation and a line by line commentary.

Apisdorf, Shimon. *Rosh Hashanah Yom Kippur Survival Kit.* Columbus, OH: Leviathan Press, 1992.

> Easy to use guide to the High Holy Day services and customs.

Beiner, Stan J. *Bible Scenes: Joshua To Solomon.* Denver, CO: A.R.E. Publishing, Inc., 1988.

> Short skits on various subjects from the Former Prophets. Entertaining and informative teaching tool. Useful maps.

Bialik, Hayim Nahman, and Yehoshua Hana Ravnitzky, eds. *The Book of Legends: Legends from the Talmud and Midrash.* Trans. by William G. Braude. New York: Schocken Books, 1992.

> Thematic arrangement of *aggadot* and *midrashim.* Useful index.

Biers-Ariel, Matt; Deborah Newbrun; and Michal Fox Smart. *Spirit in Nature: Teaching Judaism and Ecology on the Trail.* West Orange, NJ: Behrman House, Inc., 2000.

> Building on Jewish sources, this guide fosters awareness of and respect for the environment.

Birnbaum, Philip, trans. *Daily Prayer Book: Ha-Siddur Ha-Shalem.* New York: Hebrew Publishing Company, 1949.

> A complete *Siddur* that also incorporates Rabbinic teachings, songs, and words of wisdom.

Blackman, Philip. *Ethics of the Fathers.* New York: The Judaica Press, Ltd., 1979.

> Hebrew text and translation, with commentary and biographies of the makers of the Mishnah.

Blenkinsopp, Joseph. *A History of Prophecy in Israel.* Louisville, KY: Westminster John Knox Press, 1996.

> Social-historical perspective on the phenomenon of prophecy in Israel. Excellent bibliographies.

Block, Gay, and Malka Drucker. *Rescuers: Portraits of Moral Courage in the Holocaust.* New York: Holmes and Meier, 1992.

> A remarkable book about brave people with marvelous text and photographs.

Bright, John. *A History of Israel*. Philadelphia, PA: Westminster Press, 1981.

> A scholarly and readable work that chronicles the history of the Israelite people and nation from 2000 B.C.E. to the end of the biblical period. Useful maps are provided.

Brown, Steven M. *Higher and Higher: Making Jewish Prayers Part of Us*. New York: United Synagogue of America, 1988.

> A valuable teaching tool that covers the who, what, when, how, and why of prayer.

Cardin, Nina Beth, ed. and trans. *Out of the Depths I Call To You*. Northvale, NJ: Jason Aronson Inc., 1992.

> A book of prayers for the married Jewish woman, as presented in 1786 by Giuseppe Coen to his bride. Topics include childbirth and lighting candles for Shabbat.

Cohen, A., general ed. *Soncino Books of the Bible*. New York: The Soncino Press Limited, 1985.

> Contains Hebrew text with English translation facing it, making for easy comparison of the original text and the translation.

Cone, Molly. *Who Knows Ten? Children's Tales of the Ten Commandments*. rev. ed. New York: UAHC Press, 1999.

> Presents each of the Ten Commandments with stories illustrating their meanings.

Dishon, David, and Noam Zion. *A Different Night: The Family Participation Haggadah*. Jerusalem: Shalom Hartman Institute, 1997.

> An immensely informative *Haggadah* that offers imaginative ways to engage family members of all ages in serious discussion during the *Seder*.

Encyclopaedia Judaica. Jerusalem: Keter Publishing House Jerusalem, Ltd., 1972.

> A most reliable reference for virtually every topic.

Encyclopaedia Judaica, CD-Rom Edition. Jerusalem: Judaica Multimedia (Israel) Ltd., 1997.

> An updated version of the printed encyclopedia, with media, a time line, and a search capacity.

Doueck, Jack. *The Hesed Boomerang*. Deal, NJ: Yagdiyl Torah, 1998.

> How acts of kindness can enrich our lives.

Frankel, Ellen. *The Five Books of Miriam: A Women's Commentary on the Torah*. New York: Putnam Books, 1996.

> Weaves traditional interpretation together with a woman's point of view and offers a rich variety of material for study and discussion.

————. *The Jewish Spirit: A Celebration in Stories and Art*. New York: Stewart, Tabori and Chang, 1997.

> Gorgeous book of Jewish art and enchantingly told stories.

Frankel, Ellen, and Betsy Platkin Teutsch. *The Encylopedia of Jewish Symbols*. Northvale, NJ: Jason Aronson Inc., 1992.

> Useful reference work providing history, traditional citations, and contemporary reference on all types of Jewish symbols.

Freedman, David Noel, ed. *Anchor Bible Dictionary*. 5 vols. New York: Doubleday, 1992.

> Excellent reference for information on the individual prophets, biblical locations, and technical terms.

Freeman, Susan. *Teaching Jewish Virtues: Sacred Sources and Arts Activities*. Denver, CO: A.R.E. Publishing, Inc., 1999.

Mastering *middot* and becoming a *mensch* through text study and imaginative activities.

Gevirtz, Gila. *Living as Partners with God*. West Orange, NJ: Behrman House, Inc., 1997.

Explores Judaism's mission of competing the world under the Sovereignty of God. Includes a section on the prophets.

Ginzberg, Louis. *The Legends of the Jews*. Philadelphia, PA: The Jewish Publication Society, 1992.

Comprehensive seven-volume collection of *midrashim* on subjects from Creation to Esther. The seventh volume is a complete and useful index.

Goodman, Philip. *The Passover Anthology*. Philadelphia, PA: The Jewish Publication Society of America, 1993.

All the sources and resources a family needs to understand and celebrate Passover.

————. *The Rosh Hashanah Anthology*. Philadelphia, PA: The Jewish Publication Society of America, 1992.

All the sources and resources a family needs to understand and celebrate Rosh HaShanah.

————. *The Sukkot-Simhat Torah Anthology*. Philadelphia, PA: The Jewish Publication Society of America, 1992.

All the sources and resources a family needs to understand and celebrate Sukkot and Simchat Torah.

————. *The Yom Kippur Anthology*. Philadelphia, PA: The Jewish Publication Society of America, 1992.

All the sources and resources a family needs to understand and celebrate Yom Kippur.

Goodman, Robert. *Teaching Jewish Holidays: History, Values, and Activities*. rev. ed. Denver, CO: A.R.E. Publishing, Inc., 1997.

The consummate encyclopedia of holiday activities.

Hertz, Joseph H., ed. *The Pentateuch and Haftorahs*. London: Soncino Press, 1960.

This book of weekly Torah portions, Haftarot, and holiday readings is in standard use in many synagogues around the world.

Hoenig, Sidney, general ed. *Judaica Books of the Prophets: Joshua — The Twelve Prophets*. New York: The Judaica Press Inc., 1996.

Offers Hebrew text and English translation of traditional commentaries to the books of prophets.

Isaacs, Ronald H. *The Jewish Bible Almanac*. Northvale, NJ: Jason Aronson Inc., 1997.

An excellent resource of accessible information for beginners in biblical studies.

————. *Messengers of God: A Jewish Prophets Who's Who*. Northvale, NJ: Jason Aronson Inc., 1998.

Provides biographical information, historical context, Rabbinic interpretation, popular quotations, and literary content of Jewish prophets.

————. *Understanding the Hebrew Prophets.* Hoboken, NJ: Ktav Publishing, 2001.

Introduces students to the world of the prophets and the ideas of prophecy.

Topics include: what is a prophet, what is prophecy, literary and pre-literary prophets, false prophets, women prophets, values of the prophets, prophecy in liturgy.

Israel, Richard J. *Jewish Identity Games: A How-To-Do-It Book.* Los Angeles, CA: Torah Aura Productions, 1993.

Games and activities for fifth graders through adult.

Jacobs, Louis. *The Jewish Religion: A Companion.* Oxford: Oxford University, 1995.

The book, a repository of information arranged alphabetically by topic, makes complex issues in Judaism readable and clear.

Jaffe, Nina, and Steve Zeitlin. *While Standing on One Foot: Puzzle Stories and Wisdom Tales from the Jewish Tradition.* New York: Henry Holt Inc., 1996.

Wonderful stories to read, ponder, try to solve, and read again.

Kadden, Barbara Binder, and Bruce Kadden. *Teaching Jewish Life Cycle: Traditions and Activities.* Denver, CO: A.R.E Publishing, Inc., 1997.

Celebrate Jewish life, with hundreds of creative activities for all ages.

————. *Teaching Mitzvot: Concepts, Values, and Activities.* rev. ed. Denver, CO: A.R.E. Publishing, Inc., 1988.

An exceptional guide to learning and teaching about *mitzvot*.

Kadden, Bruce, and Barbara Binder Kadden. *Teaching Tefilah: Insights and Activities on Prayer.* Denver, CO: A.R.E. Publishing, Inc., 1994.

The who, what, when, where, why, and how of Jewish worship.

Klagsbrun, Francine. *Voices of Wisdom: Jewish Ideals and Ethics for Everyday Living.* Middle Village, NY: Jonathan David, 1980.

Readable passages from Jewish literature throughout the ages that cover themes of vital importance to our modern age. A very useful anthology.

Klein, Rabbi Isaac. *A Time to Be Born, A Time to Die.* New York: United Synagogue of America Department of Youth Activities, 1976.

A short, informative guide to Jewish customs and practices regarding death and mourning.

————. *A Guide To Jewish Religious Practice.* New York: Jewish Theological Seminary of America, 1992.

Detailed and comprehensive guide to Jewish practice for home and synagogue, from the perspective of the Conservative Movement.

Kolatch, Alfred J. *The Jewish Book of Why.* Middle Village, NY: Jonathan David Publishers, Inc., 1981.

Answers fundamental questions about all aspects of Judaism. Detailed index.

————. *The Second Jewish Book of Why.* Middle Village, NY: Jonathan David Publishers, Inc., 1985.

Answers fundamental questions about all aspects of Judaism. Contains a detailed index to both volumes.

Kozodoy, Ruth Lurie. *The Book of Jewish Holidays*. West Orange, NJ: Behrman House, 1997.

Introduces students to the celebrations and customs that define the Jewish year. Innovative activities, recipes, and family projects.

Kravitz, Leonard, and Kerry M. Olitzky. *Pirke Avot: A Modern Commentary on Jewish Ethics*. New York: UAHC Press, 1998.

English and Hebrew texts with word by word commentary.

Lieber, David L. *Etz Hayim: A Torah Commentary*. New York: Jewish Publication Society, 2001.

Includes the Hebrew text, a modern translation, and commentaries covering the basic meaning of the text, *midrash* on the Torah text, as well as a commentary on the weekly Haftarot.

Loeb, Sorel Goldberg, and Barbara Binder Kadden. *Teaching Torah: A Treasury of Insights and Activities*. rev. ed. Denver, CO: A.R.E. Publishing, Inc., 1997.

A teacher's "bible" for teaching the Five Books of Moses.

Mandel, Scott. *Wired into Teaching Torah: An Internet Companion*. Denver, CO: A.R.E. Publishing, Inc., 2000.

Bringing the Jewish classroom into the cyberage. Parallels the book *Teaching Torah*, but may be used to supplement any Torah curriculum.

Meron, Michal, illustrator, and Alon Baker, ed. *The Illustrated Torah*. Jerusalem: Gefen Publishing House, 2000.

Structured like a synagogue *Chumash*, with weekly Torah readings separated by the Haftarot, this is a family friendly text that involves a delightful collaboration between artist and text.

Milgrom, Jo. *Handmade Midrash*. Philadelphia: Jewish Publication Society, 1992.

Midrash, artwork, and psychological insights into the Book of Genesis.

Newsom, Carol, and Sharon H. Ringe, eds. *The Women's Bible Commentary*. Louisville, KY: Westminster John Knox, 1998.

Introduction and summary of each book of the Bible, with a focus on female characters, symbols, and issues.

Plaut, W. Gunther. *The Haftarah Commentary*. Trans. by Chaim Stern. New York: UAHC Press, 1996.

Useful information about the prophets, their times, and their works. Hebrew text, translations, commentaries, essays, additional readings.

Reisman, Bernard. *The Jewish Experiential Book: The Quest for Jewish Identity*. Hoboken, NJ: KTAV Publishing House, Inc., 1979.

Games, icebreakers, projects, parties, and family activities — all of which explore issues of Jewish identity, history, leadership, values and education. A new edition of this book is scheduled for publication.

Rosenberg, Stephen Gabriel. *The Haphtara Cycle: A Handbook To the Haphtaroth of the Jewish Year*. Northvale, NJ: Jason Aronson Inc., 2000.

Invaluable reference on the Haftarot, their historical background, relationship to their Sedra, exegesis, and helpful maps.

Salkin, Jeffrey K. *Being God's Partner: How to Find the Hidden Link between Spirituality and Your Work*. Woodstock, VT: Jewish Lights Publishing, 1994.

> Offers new insights as to how to view our occupations, as well as how to choose a career path.

————. *Putting God on the Guest List: How to Reclaim the Spiritual Meaning of Your Child's Bar or Bat Mitzvah*. Woodstock, VT: Jewish Lights Publishing, 1993.

> Offers core spiritual values, explanations, instruction, and inspiration about becoming Bar or Bat Mitzvah.

Samuels, Ruth, et al. *Prophets, Writings and You: A Value Clarification Text*. New York: Ktav Publishing House, Inc., 1989.

> Elementary level book containing stories about prophets, as well as exercises, review questions, and activities for students.

Schram, Peninnah, ed. *Chosen Tales: Stories Told by Jewish Storytellers*. Northvale, NJ: Jason Aronson Inc., 1997.

> Masterful analogy of traditional and modern Jewish stories, as told by their storytellers.

Schwartz, Richard. *Judaism and Vegetarianism*. New York, NY: Lantern Books, 2001.

> The whys of vegetarianism and Judaism.

Schreibman, Henry M. *Siddur Mikor Hayyim: The Source of Life*. San Francisco, CA: 1996.

> Siddur designed for the Brandeis-Hillel School of San Francisco and San Rafael. Includes modern translations, interpretations, and inspirational kavanot.

Shapiro, Mark Dov. *Gates of Shabbat: A Guide for Observing Shabbat*. New York: CCAR Press, 1991.

> Includes basic ceremonies for home observances and background material for the origins and purposes of the rituals.

Siegel, Danny. *Gym Shoes and Irises: Personalized Tzedakah*. Spring Valley, NY: Town House Press, 1988.

> Inspirational stories of *mitzvah* heroes and practical suggestions for personal *tzedakah*.

Siegel, Richard; Michael Strassfeld; and Strassfeld, Sharon, eds. *The First Jewish Catalog*. Philadelphia, PA: The Jewish Publication Society, 1973.

> (For annotation, see Strassfeld, Sharon, and Michael Strassfeld, eds., *The Third Jewish Catalog*, below.)

Stern, Chaim. Pirke Avot: *Wisdom of the Jewish Sages*. Hoboken, NJ: KTAV, 1997.

> English and Hebrew texts with word by word commentary.

Strassfeld, Michael. *The Jewish Holidays: A Guide and Commentary*. New York: Harper & Row, 1985.

> Comprehensive, authoritative, and provocative guide to the practice and meaning of the annual holiday cycle.

Strassfeld, Sharon, and Michael Strassfeld, eds. *The Second Jewish Catalog*. Philadelphia, PA: The Jewish Publication Society, 1976.

———. *The Third Jewish Catalog*. Philadelphia, PA: The Jewish Publication Society, 1980.

> This volume and the other two in the series are logically arranged, and provide lively, innovative, thoughtful, and provocative information on various topics on the Jewish experience.

Stuhlmueller, Carroll. *Collegeville Bible Commentary, Old Testament: Volume 15: Amos, Hosea, Micah, Nahum, Zephaniah, Habbakuk*. Collegeville, MN: The Liturgical Press, 1986.

> Short pamphlet, with maps, historical information, commentary.

TANAKH: The Holy Scriptures: The New JPS Translation According to the Traditional Hebrew Text. Philadelphia, PA: The Jewish Publication Society, 1985.

> Standard translation on which the citations in this book are based.

Telushkin, Joseph. *Biblical Literacy*. New York: William Morrow and Co., Inc., 1997.

> Contains a vast amount of information on biblical stories and laws compressed into short, easy to read chapters. Also features insightful questions comparing biblical issues with those of contemporary society.

———. *Jewish Literacy*. New York: William Morrow and Co., Inc., 1991.

> The most important things to know about Jewish religion, people, and history. Useful index.

———. *Jewish Wisdom*. New York: William Morrow and Co., Inc., 1994.

> Ninety-one brief chapters cover a variety of ethical, spiritual, and historical lessons through quotations of great thinkers and works.

———. *Words that Hurt, Words that Heal*. New York: William Morrow and Co., Inc., 1996.

> Explores the tremendous power words have to shape relationships. Sensitizes the reader to the subtleties of speech.

Twerski, Abraham J. *I Didn't Ask to Be in This Family: Sibling Relationships and How They Shape Adult Behavior and Dependencies*. New York: Topper Books, 1992.

> Using the gentle humor and insight of the "Peanuts" comic strip by Charles M. Schulz, Rabbi Twerski explores how our brothers and sisters shape our adult behavior.

Wolfson, Ron. *The Shabbat Seder*. Woodstock, VT: Jewish Lights Publishing, 1996.

> Complete information on how to make Shabbat at home.

Zeitlin, Steve. *Because God Loves Stories: An Anthology of Jewish Storytelling*. New York: Touchstone, 1997.

> Treasury of Jewish stories from ancient tales to contemporary parables, humor, and stories.

Zion, Noam, and David Dishon. *A Different Night: The Family Participation Haggadah*. Jerusalem: The Shalom Hartman Institute, 1997.

> A Haggadah for all Jewish denominations, all ages, and all levels of Jewish knowledge that

features stories, discussions, explanations, readings, songs, activities, and games. A useful Leader's Guide is available.

Zion, Noam, and Barbara Spector. *A Different Light: The Hanukkah Book of Celebration.* New York: Devora Publishing, 2000.

Offers stimulating information and a host of projects related to all aspects of Chanukah, including history, poetry, ethics, politics, literature, and more.